ISLAM AND NAZI GERMANY'S WAR

ISLAM AND NAZI GERMANY'S WAR

DAVID MOTADEL

The Belknap Press of Harvard University Press
CAMBRIDGE, MASSACHUSETTS
LONDON, ENGLAND
2014

Library of Congress Cataloging-in-Publication Data

Motadel, David.
Islam and Nazi Germany's war / David Motadel.—
First printing.
pages   cm.
Includes bibliographical references and index.
ISBN 978-0-674-72460-0 (alk. paper)
1. World War, 1939–1945—Participation, Muslim.
2. National socialism and Islam.   3. Arab countries—
Foreign relations—Germany.   4. Germany—Foreign
relations—Arab countries.   I. Title.
D810.M8M68   2014
940.530917'67—dc23   2014021587

Book design by Dean Bornstein

CONTENTS

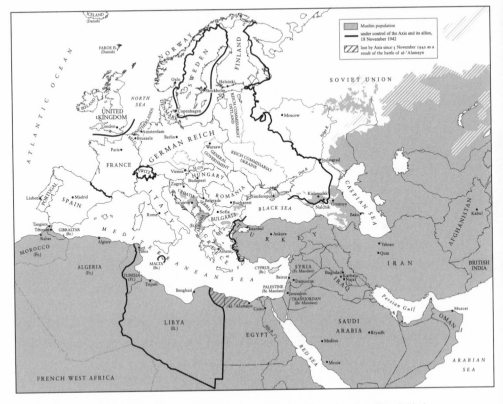

Nazi Germany and the Islamic World (Department of Geography, University of Cambridge).

ISLAM AND NAZI GERMANY'S WAR

Introduction

The Second World War involved significant parts of the Islamic world. Around 150 million Muslims between North Africa and Southeast Asia lived under British and French rule, and more than 20 million were governed by Moscow. At the height of the war, when Japan advanced into Muslim lands in Southeast Asia and German troops entered Muslim territories in the Balkans, North Africa, the Crimea, and the Caucasus and approached the Middle East and Central Asia, all major Axis and Allied powers began to see Islam as politically and strategically important.

It was at this time, in 1941–1942, that Berlin began to promote an alliance with the Muslim world against their alleged common enemies, most notably the British Empire, the Soviet Union, and the Jews. In the Muslim war zones, in North Africa and the Middle East, the Crimea, the Caucasus, and the Balkans, the Germans presented themselves as the friends of Muslims and defenders of their faith. At the same time, they began recruiting tens of thousands of Muslims into the Wehrmacht and the SS. Most of them came from the Soviet Union, though many were also enlisted in the Balkans and, albeit in fewer numbers, from the Middle East. German authorities founded several Muslim institutions, such as the Berlin Islamic Central Institute (*Islamisches Zentralinstitut*), inaugurated in 1942, and employed numerous religious leaders from across the Muslim world to support their efforts. Among the most prominent were the Lithuanian mufti Jakub Szynkiewicz of Vilnius, who propagated Hitler's New Order as the foundation of an Islamic consolidation and revival in the Muslim territories of eastern Europe and Central Asia; the Bosnian Islamic dignitary Muhamed Pandža, a leading member of the Sarajevo 'ulama and ally of the Germans in the Balkans; and the legendary mufti of Jerusalem, Amin al-Husayni, who called on the faithful between Morocco and the Malay peninsula to wage holy war against the Allies. Stretching across three continents, this effort represented a major attempt to politicize Islam and to involve Muslims in the war on the German side.

For Berlin, Muslims became relevant in two contexts, both connected to a general shift in the course of the Second World War that took place in 1941–1942. Geographically, as the European war turned increasingly into a world war, Muslim areas became war zones. In 1942, German soldiers had occupied a vast territory from the Channel Islands in the West to the Caucasus mountains in the East; they stood in Scandinavia and in the Sahara desert. At once, German troops were encountering large Muslim populations in the Caucasus and the Crimea, in the Maghrib and the Balkans. Countless minarets now stood on Hitler's invaded territories. Germany controlled Muslim metropolises like Tunis, Sarajevo, and Bakchisarai. Almost all of the few non-European territories occupied by the Germans were populated by Muslims, and even within Europe, in the Balkans, Berlin increasingly tightened its hold over Muslim areas. Of perhaps equal importance, the German regime anticipated that many more would come under its control once the Islamic belt between the Asian and European theaters was conquered. The prospect of winning Muslim support in these areas became all the more important as this belt seemed, for a short period, to emerge as the decisive battleground of the war.

Strategically, Germany's attempts to mobilize Muslims against their enemies were not the result of long-term planning but developed over the course of the war as the tide turned against the Axis. In this respect, these efforts can be seen as part of a general shift toward strategic pragmatism and the logic of total mobilization.[1] Late into 1941, officials in Berlin still thought victory was imminent. German policy was directed toward the long-term future, expressed most explicitly in the "General Plan East." This outlook began to change after the defeat at Moscow and America's entry into the war in late 1941, when the Germans began to realize that their blitzkrieg strategy had failed and that the war would continue. By the end of the following year, the debacles at Stalingrad and al-'Alamayn and escalating partisan insurgency across the occupied territories led to a change in German strategy. Berlin's policy tilted increasingly toward short-term ends and the immediate necessities of the war itself. Various factions in Berlin sought to build bigger war coalitions, displaying a remarkable degree of pragmatism. Ideological barriers became less decisive. Racial guidelines were suddenly relaxed. As war losses mounted and massive shortages in manpower became apparent, both the Wehrmacht and the SS began to recruit volunteers from all parts of the occupied territories. Berlin started to promote a European alliance against Bolshevism.[2] Even in countries that had suffered the most, such as Poland or the Soviet Union, German officials tried to win support for the idea of a pan-European struggle against Bolshevism. Another facet of this pragmatic shift was Berlin's anti-imperial campaign. Nazi Germany sponsored various anticolonial nationalist leaders and groups—among them Indian, Iraqi, and Palestinian—and made attempts to support anti-imperial uprisings around the world.[3] All of these developments were dictated by the exigencies of the war rather than by ideological considerations. Berlin's efforts to rally the Islamic world can be seen as an important facet of this shift toward strategic pragmatism and total mobilization.

Germany's courtship of Muslims was not only an attempt to control and stabilize Muslim areas behind the front. It was also, and perhaps more importantly, an effort to stir up unrest behind enemy lines, most notably on the unstable Muslim fringes of the Soviet Union, as well as in British (and later Free French) colonial domains in Africa, the Middle East, and Asia. Eventually it also aimed to mobilize Muslims into the German armies.

In order to win Muslims over, German authorities made extensive attempts to employ Islam. Religious policies and propaganda were used to enhance social and political control in the occupied territories and war zones, to recruit Muslims into the Wehrmacht and the SS, and to rally the faithful in enemy territories and armies. Germany's policies involved Islamic institutions and religious authorities. Its propaganda drew on politicized religious imperatives and rhetoric, sacred texts and Islamic iconography to give the involvement of Muslims in the war religious legitimacy. Although these policies, as with so many other German policies during the war, were characterized by improvisation and ad hoc measures, they were overall remarkably coherent.

Berlin's policies toward Muslims were the expression of a specific set of assumptions, ideas, and conceptions about Islam that informed German officials. They frequently reduced Muslims to their religious affiliation, no matter how pious they were or how different their notion of Islam. Indeed, the terms "Islam" (*Islam* or *Mohammedanertum*) and "Muslim" (*Muslim, Moslem, Mohammedaner,* or *Muselmane*) became primary bureaucratic categories in official documents. Although German authorities often recognized the diversity and complexity of the Muslim world in principle, in practice they frequently fell back on essentialist ideas about Islam as an entity with distinct characteristics. Most significant were the notion of Islam as a political force and the idea of global Islamic unity: German officials commonly assumed that in the "Muslim world" religion and politics were tightly intertwined. Islam was seen as an inherently political and even militant force. More importantly, Berlin's efforts were based on the assumption that Islam could be employed and instrumentalized for Germany's own political and military aims. Islam was perceived to offer a comprehensible and coherent religious code that could be utilized. Islamic imperatives, which Muslims seemed to follow, appeared to provide an ideal ground to legitimize power and authority. The employment of religion in propaganda and policies aimed at Muslims therefore seemed to be an ideal way to both control and mobilize them. Furthermore, officials in Berlin tended to imagine the Muslim world (*Muslimische Welt*, *Moslemische Welt*, *Mohammedanische Welt*, or *Weltmuselmanentum*) as an undifferentiated territorial and political entity, a conception that directly affected the geographical scope of their policy measures. This became most obvious in the notion of "world Islam" (*Weltislam*, *Weltmuselmanentum*, or *All-Islam*), to which German officials regularly referred. Unsurprisingly these assumptions and conceptions repeatedly clashed with the realities on the ground.[4]

This book examines the ways in which German authorities—most notably in the Wehrmacht and the SS but also in the Foreign Office (*Auswärtiges Amt*), the Propaganda Ministry (*Reichsministerium für Volksaufklärung und Propaganda*), and the Ministry for the Occupied Eastern Territories (*Reichsministerium für die besetzten Ostgebiete*)—engaged with Islam in an attempt to build an alliance with Muslims in Germany's occupied territories and in the wider world. It asks how Islam was employed in practice in the war zones, as well as in military recruitment and mobilization. Simultaneously, it addresses the underlying political conceptions about Islam that informed decision makers and officers in the German capital and in the field.

Adopting a transregional view, the book looks at the lands of the Muslim belt, stretching from the Sahara desert to the Balkan peninsula to the borderlands of the Soviet Union and beyond. It takes into account the different religious and political conditions in these areas.[5] In fact, German officials encountered various forms of Islam, ranging from Sufi movements in the Maghrib to the more orthodox forms of Islam of the urban 'ulama in the Balkans, to more heterodox strains of Islam in the southern fringes of the Soviet Union. On the ground, Germany's engagement with Islam could be complex, also involving questions about policies toward Muslim Roma and Jewish converts to Islam. To be sure, this book focuses on German policies and is neither a social history of Muslim life in the war zones of the Second World War nor an account of Muslim responses to Nazi Germany. Yet it looks at Muslims who got directly involved in German policies toward Islam and who usually pursued their own agendas.

A comprehensive study of Germany's policy toward Islam during the Second World War has not yet been written. Generally, when analyzing Nazi Germany's relationship with the Muslim world historians have focused on geographical, national, and ethnic rather than religious categories. Numerous studies have addressed German policies in North Africa, the Middle East, the Balkans, the Crimea, and the Caucasus.[6] Research on Germany's policies toward the Middle East, moreover, includes biographical studies of the mufti of Jerusalem.[7] Some of these regional and biographical works have alluded to the role of Islam.[8] In particular, studies on the Arab world and on al-Husayni have pointed to religious policies and propaganda. This book draws on these regional and biographic studies. Its focus is on the specific role of religion in Berlin's policies toward the Muslim world. Its geographical scope ranges from North Africa to the Middle East and from the Balkans to the Soviet borderlands. It draws, for the first time, a comprehensive picture of Nazi Germany's policy toward Islam in its full breadth, a picture that could not be depicted by any regional or national study (for example, of Nazi Germany's policies in the Middle East, the Soviet Union, or the Balkans) or by any biography (for instance, of the mufti of Jerusalem). The book is an attempt to put Islam on the political and strategic map of the Second World War.

It thereby also contributes to the more general history of Berlin's religious policies in the Second World War. While many studies have addressed German wartime engagement with Christian groups—Catholics, Protestants, or Eastern Orthodox populations—and countless have examined the murderous policies toward Jews, Muslims, one of the most prevalent religious groups in some of the war zones, have been surprisingly neglected.[9]

Nazi Germany was not the only power that sought to employ Islam to mobilize support in the Muslim world. In fact, both of its Axis partners, Japan and Italy, made similar efforts, and by the middle of the war they faced competition not only from the British but also from the Americans and Soviets, all promising to defend Islam and to protect the faithful, a phenomenon that may be called the Muslim moment of the war. As early as 1937, Il Duce arranged to be presented with a bejeweled "Sword of Islam" (which had actually been produced in Italy) at a public ceremony in Tripoli, thereby symbolically promoting himself as the patron of the Muslim world.[10] Italy, Il Duce declared, would respect the "laws of the Prophet." "Mussolini is traveling through Africa and thereby is paying homage to Islam. Very clever and cunning. Paris and London are immediately suspicious," Goebbels commented in his diary.[11] Italy's employment of Islam reached its height during the war, with Italian propagandists throughout the Muslim world glorifying Mussolini as a "protector of Islam." An even more comprehensive and better organized attempt to instrumentalize Islam was made by Japan, aimed at mobilizing Muslims across Asia against Britain, the Netherlands, China, and the Soviets.[12] Although, as in Italy, the origins of this policy could be traced back to the late 1930s—the "Greater Japan Islamic League" (*Dai Nippon Kaikyo Kyokai*) and the Tokyo Mosque were both founded in 1938—Japan intensified its political and propagandistic engagement with Islam during the invasion of the Dutch Indies in spring 1942. Paid Muslim emissaries organized local Islamic leaders and communities to aid the incursion of Japanese troops. In a drive to give an Islamic character to the occupying regime, military authorities tried to co-opt the local 'ulama, who had felt suppressed under the Dutch. Japanese officials began thrusting prepared texts on imams to be included in their Friday sermons and encouraged the faithful to say prayers for the emperor and for the success of the war. They also forced numerous groups into a common representative body, the "Council of Indonesian Muslims" (*Majlis Sjuro Muslimin Indonesia*, or *Masjumi*). In early April 1943, the 'ulama and Islamic dignitaries from Sumatra and Malaya were summoned to a conference in Singapore, at which the Japanese announced to the Muslims of Southeast Asia that Tokyo was the true protector of their faith. The 'ulama departed the meeting, giving formal expression of their satisfaction with Japan's commitment to protect Islam, and declared Muslim support for the war effort. A second conference of religious leaders was convened in December 1944 in Kuala Kangsar on the Malay peninsula. From the Japanese capital, the Tatar imam Abdurreshid Ibrahim ('Abd al-Rashid Ibrahim), the "patriarch of the Tokyo Mosque" and "respected patriarch of the Muslim world," preached a warlike interpretation of jihad. "Japan's cause in the

Greater East Asia War is a sacred one and in its austerity, is comparable to the war carried out against the infidels by the Prophet Muhammad in the past," he proclaimed in the summer of 1942.[13]

For the Allies, Islam appeared both as a potential threat and as a powerful instrument of political warfare. Winston Churchill, who had experienced the political significance of Islam first as a young officer during the late nineteenth-century wars at the Northwest Frontier and in the Sudanese Mahdi rebellion, took Islamic anti-imperialism quite seriously.[14] In early 1942 he stressed that Britain "must not on any account break with the Moslems," who represented a strong force in the empire and formed a significant element of Britain's own military personnel, most notably in the British Indian Army.[15] The prime minister's opinion was widely shared by British officials.[16] After the outbreak of the war, London had established an intensive program to strengthen the ties between the empire and the world of Islam. In 1941 British authorities opened the East London Mosque, and the Churchill War Cabinet decided to build the London Central Mosque in Regent's Park to demonstrate London's respect for Islam.[17] Washington, too, was becoming aware of the significance of Islam. As early as November 1940 a major national daily anxiously raised the question: "Whom will the Muslims support during the European War?"[18] Once US troops arrived in Muslim territories, policies and propaganda frequently took Islam into consideration. In 1943, the US military distributed religious pamphlets that called for jihad against Rommel's troops in North Africa.[19] The US War Department trained its soldiers in how to interact correctly with Muslims and prepared manuals designed to instruct them in the basics of Islam. Even the Kremlin, which had ruthlessly suppressed Islam in the interwar years, changed its policy in 1942, establishing four Soviet Muslim councils, or "spiritual directorates."[20] New mosques were built, Muslim congresses were organized, and Moscow started openly supporting Islamic religious practices, permitting even the hajj pilgrimage, which had been banned before the war. Speaking from the "Central Muslim Spiritual Directorate," headquartered in Ufa, Abdurrahman Rasulaev, Stalin's "red mufti," launched a series of propaganda appeals, calling on the Muslims of the Soviet Union to rise up against the Nazi aggressor and to pray for the victory of the Red Army. This was a direct response to Germany's campaign for Islamic mobilization on the southern fringes of the Soviet Union. Overall, the Allies' religious policies propaganda not only sought to counterbalance Axis attempts to provoke unrest in their Muslim territories and indeed the wider Islamic world but also aimed at mobilizing their Muslim subjects for the war effort.

This history of the politics of Islam during the Second World War may be seen as part of a much wider story of attempts by non-Muslim powers to instrumentalize the Muslim faith for political and military purposes. In the imperial age, European empires regularly employed religious policies and propaganda to stir up the Muslim subjects of rival colonial powers. During the Crimean War, the British, French, and Ottomans tried to incite the Muslims on the Crimean Peninsula and in the Caucasus.[21] One of the most significant attempts to employ Islam in political and military strategy was the Central Powers' efforts to revolutionize pious Muslims in the First World War.[22] In autumn 1914, the German and Ottoman governments commissioned a proclamation of pan-Islamic jihad from the shaykh al-Islam, the highest religious authority of the caliphate in Constantinople. Distributed across the Muslim world in Ottoman Turkish, Arabic, Persian, Urdu, and Tatar, the decree called Muslims to holy war against the Entente powers. Over the course of the war, Berlin and Constantinople made extensive efforts to incite, as Wilhelm II put it, "the whole Mohammedan world to wild revolt" against the British, Russian, and French empires.[23] German and Ottoman authorities utilized pan-Islamic slogans and networks in North Africa, the Middle East, Russia, and India. The British, French, and Russians responded with their own religious policies and propaganda.[24] Islam was perceived to be a powerful political force that could have an impact on the war. "It would appear, indeed, that Pan-Islamism has always had either behind it or paralleling it the imperialistic policy of some European power whose aims and interests at the moment seemed to coincide with those of Islam or of some Moslem potentate," wrote the American scholar Dwight E. Lee in 1942.[25] The attempts by both Axis and Allies to engage with Islam in the Second World War were finally followed by Western support of Islamic anti-Communist movements in the Cold War—an episode that ended with the backing of the *mujahidin* in Afghanistan, where Washington distributed not only stinger missiles but also Qur'ans.[26]

Scholars have expressed some interest in the history of great power engagement with Islam. The by far most comprehensively researched part of the story is the German-Ottoman campaign for Islamic mobilization during the Great War.[27] This campaign is not only generally recognized as significant by historians of the First World War.[28] It is also considered a crucial event in the modern political history of Islam by scholars of Islamic history.[29] The Second World War has, by comparison, received less attention.[30] Those historians of modern Islam who have paid attention to it at all have tended to play down or even deny its significance. "In World War II, Islam as such was not involved, though Muslim individuals and groups fought on both sides," Jacob M. Landau wrote in his influential work on the politics of pan-Islam.[31] The following chapters demonstrate that in 1941–1945, Berlin's engagement with Islam was at least as extensive as in 1914–1918. Indeed, in contrast to the First World War, the Germans from late 1941 onward recruited thousands of Muslims into their ranks. In fact, Muslim mobilization during both world wars forms an essential part of the political history of the Islamic world in the first half of the twentieth century.

On a more general level, this study addresses the relationship between religion and power, specifically, the role of religion as an instrument in world politics and military conflict. It contributes to our understanding of the ways by which governments actively sought to use religion to expand their political influence and to wage wars. Attempts to mobilize religious groups were part of great power politics throughout the nineteenth and twentieth centuries. Religious groups—populations defined along religious lines—were regularly considered powerful political forces that could be utilized. Statesmen and officials of major powers frequently presented themselves as protectors of specific religious groups to exert political influence and potentially provoke unrest, division, and insurrection in territories ruled by rival or enemy powers, and also to conquer and pacify occupied territories in military conflicts. Tsarist Russia claimed to be the patron of Orthodox Christendom in Europe and the Middle East, Imperial France claimed to be the protector of Christianity in the Middle East, the Ottomans claimed to be the defender of global Islam, and major European powers routinely insisted that they sought to protect Christian groups, Jewish minorities, and Islamic populations beyond their own territories. In order to win the allegiance of religious groups and rally them to a political cause, various religious policies and propaganda designed to appeal to religious passions were adopted. These policies were based on a series of assumptions: Religion was usually seen as a source of authority that could legitimize involvement in a conflict and even justify violence. Populations were reduced to their religious affiliation. It was assumed that they were pious and driven by religious doctrine. Overall, religious groups were seen as objects that could be geopolitically exploited. In effect, religious policies became policies of international affairs and conflict.

Scholars have generally paid less attention to this phenomenon than one might imagine. As the field of international history has experienced a rising interest in nonstate actors, they have shown more and more interest in population politics in conflict and war, in policies targeted at entire populations.[32] Historians have thereby mostly concentrated on the politics of population groups defined by ethnicity or nationality during conflicts and wars.[33] They have shown that entire ethnic groups—particularly those, of course, whose loyalties to their rulers seemed unstable—were seen as politically and strategically significant, inquired into the ways great powers tried to exploit them, and examined how these policies created ethnic divisions and frictions. Less studied is the use of religious population groups in great power rivalry and conflict, with the exception of Islamic mobilization during the First World War.[34] Our knowledge of the actual employment of religious policies and propaganda is sparse. The history of the Islamic mobilization campaigns during the Second World War, particularly Nazi Germany's policy toward Islam, is ideal for studying the politics of religion in conflict and war and may contribute to our understanding of religion as an instrument in world politics and military conflict more generally.

The following chapters examine the ways in which German authorities conceptualized and instrumentalized religion for political and strategic ends. The book looks at the employment of religious policies, examining the engagement with religious institutions, religious authorities, and religious customs, as well as at religious propaganda, addressing the use of religious doctrine, rhetoric, and iconography. The question of the role of Islam in German policies and propaganda is discussed in three parts: general strategic and ideological debates that took place in Berlin (Part I); German policies and propaganda in Muslim areas, specifically the Eastern Front, the Balkans, Northern Africa, and the Middle East (Part II); and military mobilization of Muslims from the occupied territories (Part III).

Part I establishes the general framework of Germany's engagement with Islam during the Second World War. It inquires into continuities between the Third Reich's engagement with Islam and Imperial Germany's policy toward Islam in the colonies before 1914 and its campaign for

Islamic mobilization during the First World War. It shows how Islam remained on the agenda of German foreign policy experts in the interwar period and how it increasingly became an issue after the outbreak of the war in 1939. The section examines policy papers and memoranda on the strategic role of Islam as well as discussions on Islam within the Foreign Office, the Wehrmacht, the SS, and the East Ministry. Usually these strategic debates were inseparable from ideological discourse about Islam and Nazism carried out by a number of Nazi ideologues and by members of the Nazi elite, including Hitler and Himmler.

Part II examines the role of Islam in German policies toward Muslims in the war zones, both in its occupied areas and behind the front lines, specifically in the Eastern territories, the Balkans, North Africa, and the Middle East. In the war zones, German authorities frequently viewed Islam to be of political importance. German soldiers were instructed to respect religious customs and conventions when dealing with Muslims. On the Eastern Front, army officials even ordered the reestablishment of mosques, madrasas, and pious endowments (waqf) and the reestablishment of religious rituals, holidays, and celebrations, with the intention of undermining Soviet rule. German military authorities also made extensive use of members of the 'ulama in the Eastern territories, the Balkans, and North Africa. This second part also explores how German officials employed Islam in their propaganda directed toward the Muslim war zones, both in the occupied front areas and, more importantly, behind the front lines.

Part III addresses the role of Islam in German policies toward Muslims in the German army. From 1941 onward, the Wehrmacht and the SS recruited thousands of Muslim soldiers. They were organized in formations such as the Wehrmacht's Muslim Eastern Legions, the Arab contingent of the Wehrmacht, the Eastern Muslim SS Division, and Islamic SS units in the Balkans. The section examines the role that religion played in the recruitment, spiritual care, and propagandistic indoctrination of these soldiers. It shows that German army officials granted Muslim recruits a wide range of religious concessions, taking into account the religious calendar and religious laws such as ritual slaughter. Both the Wehrmacht and the SS also launched special ideological education programs for Muslim soldiers. Military propaganda was spread in the form of pamphlets, booklets, and, most importantly, journals. A prominent role in the units was played by military imams, who were responsible not only for spiritual care but also for political indoctrination.

The book draws on German, English, French, Bosnian (Serbo-Croatian), Albanian, Arabic, Persian, and Tatar sources from more than thirty different local and national archives in fourteen countries, including collections in Berlin, Freiburg, Koblenz, Frankfurt, Munich, Stuttgart, Cologne, Bonn, Leipzig, Vienna, Washington, London, Paris, Moscow, Warsaw, Prague, Riga, Simferopol, Zagreb, Sarajevo, Tirana, and Tehran. The work of reconstructing the story of Germany's engagement with Islam was often arduous. This is not only because documents on the subject are scattered throughout different archives and libraries. In the various consulted archival collections, files on "Islam" usually do not exist. Consequently, a substantial amount of time was spent going through countless general files that promised to contain information on Islam. Often hints in individual sources stored in these files seemed to be random and cannot be understood without the knowledge that their content related to a general policy. Step by step, a general image unfolded, showing that Berlin made a substantial and often remarkably coordinated attempt to employ Islam in its war efforts.

�֎ PART I ֎

FOUNDATIONS

CHAPTER ONE

Origins

On 25 July 1940, just after the fall of France and at the outset of the Battle of Britain, the retired diplomat Max von Oppenheim sent the German Foreign Office a seven-page memorandum on the incitement of rebellion in the enemy's Islamic territories.[1] It was time, he explained, for a comprehensive strategy to mobilize the Islamic world against the British Empire. In cooperation with influential religious figures like the pan-Islamic leader Shakib Arslan and the mufti of Jerusalem, Amin al-Husayni, German officers were to provoke unrest in the entire Muslim corridor from Egypt to India. Aged eighty, Oppenheim knew what he was speaking about. Few had shaped Germany's policy toward Islam in the late Kaiserreich as much as he had.

Trained as a lawyer and fluent in several Middle Eastern languages, Oppenheim had long traveled through Africa and the Middle East.[2] In 1896 he was recruited by the Foreign Office and worked for twelve years in Cairo, where he monitored political developments in the Muslim world. During the Mahdi rebellion in Sudan, he had first encountered Islam as a political force. He had discussed questions of politics and Islam with the young Shakib Arslan and prominent Islamic reformers like Muhammad 'Abduh. With the Ottoman Sultan Abdülhamid II he had exchanged thoughts about pan-Islamism, which the Sublime Porte propagated to rally support both within and outside of its empire. Wilhelm II personally read Oppenheim's political reports about the Muslim world.

The Imperial Politics of Islam

German diplomats, politicians, and colonial officials had increasingly engaged with Islam since the late nineteenth century. Imperial Germany ruled over substantial Muslim populations in its colonies—in Togo and, more importantly, Cameroon and German East Africa. In these possessions, German authorities from the outset sought to employ religion as a

1.1 Muslim policemen wearing the fez in the German colony of Cameroon, 1891 (BPK).

tool of rule.[3] Local Islamic structures were left intact as long as Muslim leaders accepted the colonial presence. Shariʻa courts were recognized, waqf endowments left untouched, madrasas kept open, and religious holidays acknowledged. German officials ruled through Muslim intermediaries and Islamic dignitaries, who, in return, gave the colonial state legitimacy. In the eyes of German colonial officials, often isolated and anxious to secure order and prevent uprisings, this policy of indirect rule proved highly effective. Only after the turn of the century did they occasionally tighten control in the Islamic areas and confront religious leaders unwilling to cooperate. German troops fought Mahdist revolts in northern Cameroon (1907) and were mobilized when the so-called Mecca letters had provoked unrest in Togo (1906) and German East Africa (1908).[4] Yet, overall, these frictions did not change German policies, which continued to use Islam to enhance colonial control (Figure 1.1).

With the German involvement in the Muslim world, state officials and experts discussed Islam increasingly as a political category.[5] Schemes for a policy toward Islam, or *Islampolitik*, were widely debated in colonial and government circles. At colonial congresses, Islam and colonial policy toward Muslims were regularly at the top of the agenda. An important part in these debates was played by experts in Islamic studies. Previously preoccupied with research on classical Islam, they now began to engage in research on the contemporary Muslim world and to discuss the practices of imperial policies toward Islam. Scholars like Carl Heinrich Becker, who taught at the newly established Colonial Institute (*Deutsches Kolonialinstitut*) in Hamburg, and Martin Hartmann and Diedrich Westermann, both of whom taught in Berlin, placed their knowledge in the service of empire. After the turn of the century, the Colonial Office (*Reichskolonialamt*) supported their investigations of Islam in the colonies. They were to accumulate knowledge on its spread, impact, and potential threat to German rule and on the Muslims' connections to the wider Islamic world. The three largest surveys were launched by Becker in 1908,[6] Hartmann in 1911,[7] and Westermann in 1913,[8] although only Westermann published his results. An important forum for specialist debates about Islam and colonial policies became the German Society for the Study of Islam (*Deutsche Gesellschaft für Islamkunde*), with its periodical, *Die Welt des Islams* (*The World of Islam*), both established in 1912. Two years earlier, the journal *Der Islam* (*Islam*) had been founded at the Colonial Institute in Hamburg, providing another medium for discussions of contemporary Islam and politics.

Most experts supported the employment of religious structures in the colonies. In contrast to indigenous animist religions, regularly dismissed as savage, Islam was seen as a civilized faith governed by a specific set of rules, norms, and dogmas that could be studied and used. The best-known proponent of an active employment of Islam in colonial policies was Becker.[9] Islam was not, he claimed, a threat to colonial government but could and should be used to bolster imperial rule and guarantee peace, stability, and order. Becker believed that the "danger of Islam" would fade once the right colonial policy was adopted. Muslim institutions, itinerant preachers, and pilgrims should be kept under strict surveillance, while Islamic law, madrasas, and pious endowments should be formally recognized. Becker was highly influential on policy making in Berlin. His views were supported by other scholars, including Diedrich Westermann.[10] Only a small minority of experts, most notably Martin Hartmann, opposed any accommodation of Islam in the colonies.[11] Hartmann perceived the Muslim religion as a threat that had to be controlled. Pointing to the alleged militant spirit of

Islam, religious fanaticism, Mahdism, and the danger of holy war, he warned colonial officials not to rely on Muslim authorities and institutions. Overall, however, criticism of German colonial policies toward Islam was limited to Christian missionary circles, which saw in Islam a threat to their work and to the colonial state and regularly accused German administrators of enabling the expansion of Islam in the colonies by favoring Muslims.[12] In practice, their activism had little effect.

In contrast to their British, French, Dutch, and Russian colleagues, German colonial officers did not see Islamic anti-imperialism and pan-Islamism as a threat.[13] In Berlin, Islam was mainly considered an opportunity, not just in the colonies but also in the context of Wilhelm II's *Weltpolitik*. This became most obvious during the kaiser's Middle Eastern tour in the autumn of 1898 and in his spectacular speech, given after visiting the tomb of Saladin in Damascus, in which he declared himself a "friend" of the world's "300 million Mohammedans."[14] One inspiration behind this effort was, in fact, Oppenheim, who by then had become one of the most tireless promoters of the political potential of pan-Islam. German officials were well aware that the specter of Islamic revolt and pan-Islamic mobilization haunted government corridors in London, Paris, and St. Petersburg.[15] Indeed, in many anticolonial struggles in the Muslim world Islam played a major role in legitimizing, unifying, and organizing resistance to imperial intrusion.[16] German courtship of Islam finally culminated in Berlin's efforts to mobilize Muslims during the First World War.

Muslim Mobilization during the First World War

On 11 November 1914, the Ottoman shaykh al-Islam, Ürgüplü Hayri, issued five fatwas (legal opinions) calling on Muslims around the world to wage holy war against the Entente powers and promising them the status of martyr if they fell in battle.[17] Three days later, in the name of the sultan-caliph, Mehmed V, the "commander of the faithful" (*amir al-mu'minin*), the decree was publicly read out to a large crowd outside the great Fatih Mosque in Constantinople. Afterward, in an officially organized rally, masses with flags and banners moved through the streets of the Ottoman capital, cheering for jihad. The texts of the fatwas were composed in the usual fashion, each including a doctrinal and hypothetical question to the shaykh al-Islam and his answer. Addressing not only Ottoman subjects but also Muslims living in the Entente empires, the proclamation was translated into Arabic, Persian, Urdu, and Tatar. In the following months, local 'ulama, including the powerful Shi'a *mujtahid*s of Najaf and Karbala, reacted with decrees supporting the call for holy war.[18] Across the Ottoman Empire, imams carried the message of jihad to believers in their Friday sermons.

The fatwas of the shaykh al-Islam drew on an unusual concept of "jihad." Throughout history, the meaning of "jihad" had always been highly fluid, ranging from intellectual reflection to military struggle against infidels.[19] A particularly influential interpretation distinguished between "lesser jihad" (*al-jihad al-asghar*), which is the armed fight against unbelievers, and "greater jihad" (*al-jihad al-akbar*), which is the personal inner struggle of every individual for moral self-improvement. Interestingly, the fatwas of the shaykh al-Islam did not follow this interpretation, declaring the war against the sultan's enemies an *al-jihad al-akbar*. Moreover, compared to earlier proclamations of jihad, the decree was theologically unorthodox (though not unprecedented) as it called for a selective armed jihad directed only against the British, French, Montenegrins, Serbs, and Russians but not against the Ottomans' Christian allies, Germany and Austria-Hungary. Thus, the war was not a religious war in the classic sense, waged between "believers" and "infidels." As only Britain, France, Russia, Serbia, and Montenegro had turned hostile to the Islamic caliphate, only they could be considered enemies of Islam. The fatwas pronounced that it was the duty of all Muslims governed by these powers to fight a jihad against their rulers, while proclaiming it a great sin for Muslims to fight the caliphate's allies.

Although the declaration of holy war can be seen as part of the Ottoman politics of pan-Islamism, pursued by the Porte since the reign of Abdülhamid II to sustain unity within its heterogeneous empire and to win support abroad, German officers and Islam experts were intimately involved in the jihad plan.[20] In fact, it was the Germans who had pushed for the proclamation of jihad at the beginning of the war.[21] In Berlin, the scheme had been under discussion for quite some time. At the height of the July Crisis, Wilhelm II had already made his famous comment about the inflammation of the Islamic world. Helmuth von Moltke, chief of the general staff, formally confirmed the idea in a memorandum the following month, ordering to "awaken the fanaticism of Islam" in the Muslim populated possessions of Germany's adversaries (Figure 1.2). In October 1914, before

1.2 Wilhelm II meets the shaykh al-Islam in Constantinople, 1917 (*Ullstein*).

the Ottomans had entered the war, Max von Oppenheim had worked out a 136-page policy paper titled "Memorandum on the Revolutionizing of the Islamic Territories of Our Enemies" (*Denkschrift betreffend die Revolutionierung der islamischen Gebiete unserer Feinde*). After a German-Ottoman military alliance had been secured, religious violence was to be incited in the Muslim areas in the enemies' colonies and imperial peripheries.[22] The Islamic hinterland of the rival empires was to be destabilized to keep troops away from the fronts of Europe. A "call for holy war" was to be proclaimed "as soon as Turkey attacks," he urged, describing "Islam" as "one of our most important weapons," one that could be "decisive for the success of the war." Oppenheim made a number of concrete suggestions. Religious revolt had to be provoked in India, supported by smuggled German weapons; the Caucasus was to become a hotbed of Islamic upheaval; Egypt was to be conquered; Muslim prisoners of war from the colonial troops of the Entente had to be courted and mobilized against their former imperial masters. The time for a "revolt of Islam" was ripe, he asserted.

Just as they had before the war, German scholars and experts played a significant role in promoting the instrumentalization of Islam. Ernst Jäckh, a young German political scientist with an interest in Islam who in 1948 would become one of the founders of the Middle East Institute of Columbia University, had as early as August 1914 outlined a scenario in which an Ottoman declaration of jihad would mobilize the forces of "pan-Islam" with "destructive hatred" against British and French rule "from India to Morocco."[23] Hartmann wrote comparable texts during the war, now advocating the exploitation of Islam for strategic ends.[24] In autumn 1914, after the outbreak of the conflict but before the Ottoman Empire had entered the war, Carl Heinrich Becker, then a professor in Bonn, published a brochure titled *Deutschland und der Islam* (*Germany and Islam*).[25] Islam was the Achilles' heel of Russia, Britain, and France, he explained. Berlin had for decades seen "Islam as an international factor."[26] Due to its prewar efforts, Imperial Germany was known to be the friend of Islam, a status Berlin must now exploit. An alliance with Constantinople would involve Islam, which could become "a factor of the utmost significance" in the war.[27] Although the political employment of religious sentiment would not decide the outcome of the war, it would contribute significantly to the war effort. Furious, the Dutch Islam expert Christiaan Snouck Hurgronje, one of the world's leading authorities on contemporary Islam, accused his German colleagues, most notably Becker and Hartmann, of spreading religious hatred.[28] In an article published in early 1915 he argued that it was the Germans who had pushed forward the idea of religiously charging the war. Hurgronje referred to countless statements made by German scholars about the political significance of Islam, criticizing them for dishonoring their profession. Becker was not impressed. Religion was a legitimate instrument in world politics, he responded in an article.[29] In the first years of the war, a full-blown Islam mania spread across the Reich. The German press was bursting with articles on the holy war; Islam experts gave public lectures on the alliance with the Muslim world; numerous booklets and brochures on the jihad appeared.[30]

The center of Germany's Islam campaign was the Intelligence Office for the Orient (*Nachrichtenstelle für den Orient*) of the Foreign Office and High Command, led by Max von Oppenheim (and later, when Oppenheim went to work from Constantinople, by Consul Karl Schabinger von Schowingen and after him by the scholar Eugen Mittwoch).[31] It employed a vast staff of academic experts, diplomats, military officials, and Muslim collaborators, among them the famous Tunisian cleric Salih al-Sharif al-Tunisi, the Egyptian preacher 'Abd al-'Aziz Shawish, and the prominent Tatar pan-Islamist Abdurreshid Ibrahim. They organized and coordinated propaganda for Muslim lands, stretching from North Africa to British India. Drawing on the language of holy war and martyrdom, the core element of this propaganda was religion. Some of the texts were also translated into German, most notably al-Tunisi's *Haqiqat al-Jihad* (*The Truth about the Jihad*), a tract that was published in German translation by the German Society for the Study of Islam, with Martin Hartmann contributing a foreword and Karl Schabinger von Schowingen the afterword.[32] The Intelligence Office for the Orient was also responsible for Muslim prisoners of war who were to be recruited to fight on the side of the Central Powers.

In the winter of 1914–1915, the German military founded special camps in Wünsdorf and Zossen, south of Berlin, for Muslim prisoners of war.[33] They held several thousand soldiers from Africa, India, and the tsarist empire who had fought in the British, French, and Russian armies. From the outset, the Germans were at pains to win the prisoners over. To demonstrate their respect for Islam, they granted the Muslims various concessions and special religious rights (Figures 1.3 and 1.4). Muslims were allowed to perform their daily prayers, celebrate religious holidays, carry out ritual slaughter, and bury their dead according to Islamic rites. In the Wünsdorf camp the Germans even constructed a mosque, designed after the Dome of the Rock in Jerusalem—it was the first functional Islamic house of worship ever built in Germany. Much attention was paid to propaganda and political indoctrination. The *Nachrichtenstelle für den Orient* distributed several propaganda papers among the prisoners, most importantly *al-Jihad*, which was published in Arabic, Russian, and Tatar and was to be read out by the literate to their comrades.[34] Also imams were employed in the camps to provide religious care and to spread political propaganda. The most notable of them was the Volga Tatar Alimjan Idris (also Idrisi).[35] In his late twenties, Idris had studied theology and philosophy in Bukhara, Istanbul, Lausanne, and Liège and had been employed by the Ottoman War Ministry before entering the service of the Germans in early 1916. In Wünsdorf and Zossen he soon became famous for his impassioned speeches and sermons. As late as autumn 1918, on the occasion of the highest Is-

1.3 Mosque of the Muslim prisoner of war camp in Wünsdorf, near Berlin, 1916 (*Ullstein*).

1.4 Prisoners of war, praying in the Muslim camp in Wünsdorf, near Berlin, n.d. (1914–1918) (*Ullstein*).

lamic holiday, the feast of sacrifice (*'Id al-Adha* or *Qurban Bairam*), which is celebrated at the end of the hajj, he addressed the prisoners, decrying that the "holiest" parts of the Islamic world suffered "under the yoke of the English and French" and calling the war a "loud signal for the awakening" of the faithful.[36] Several hundred Muslims were recruited in Wünsdorf and Zossen and sent to Constantinople to join the Ottoman army during the war, though, overall, far fewer volunteered than German authorities had hoped.

Across the world, German embassies and consulates circulated pan-Islamic propaganda. Paid propagandists spread the message of holy war in mosques and market squares. Berlin also organized various missions to incite rebellions in the Muslim hinterlands of the Entente empires.[37] In the first months of the war, a number of German expeditions were sent to the Arabian peninsula to win the support of the Bedouins and to conduct propaganda among pilgrims. There were also attempts to spread propaganda against Anglo-Egyptian rule in Sudan.[38] In the Levant, the diplomat Curt Prüfer, who, before the war, had served at the German consulate in Cairo, where he had become Oppenheim's protégé, was to organize propaganda and insurrection in British Egypt.[39] In Cyrenaica, German emissaries tried to convince the warriors of the Islamic Sanusi order to attack Egypt.[40] The Sanusi had organized powerful resistance against imperial intrusion in the previous decade, calling for jihad against French troops in the southern Sahara and fighting the Italians following the invasion of Tripolitania in 1911. After lengthy negotiations with Shaykh Ahmad al-Sharif al-Sanusi and considerable payments, the Sanusi finally took arms, attacking the western frontier of Egypt, but were after some initial victories stopped by the British army. Attempts to arm and incite Muslim resistance movements in French North Africa and British and French West Africa had some success but overall posed no serious threat.[41] In early 1915, a mission under Major Friedrich Klein set out for southern Iraq to meet the Shi'a *mujtahids* of the holy cities of Karbala and Najaf.[42] Although the leading Shi'a scholars had already issued decrees in support of the Ottoman fatwas in late 1914, the Germans convinced five 'ulama, after extensive talks and significant bribes, to write up another proclamation of holy war. Some Shi'a dignitaries in Iran followed.[43] Groups of German agents were also operating in Iran, the most famous led by consul Wilhelm Wassmuss, to orchestrate local insurrection against the Russian and British military presence.[44] The most important German missions in the Islamic world, however, were aimed at spreading revolt from Afghanistan into the Muslim border region of British India—the notorious Northwest Frontier—led by Oskar Ritter von Niedermayer, a Bavarian artillery officer who had studied geography and Oriental studies and had traveled in Iran and India before the war, and Werner Otto von Hentig, a diplomat who had previously served in Beijing, Constantinople, and Tehran.[45] Although Niedermayer and Hentig headed rival expeditions, they united in Tehran, moving on to Afghanistan to incite Afghans and Indians against the Raj. Toward the end of the war, when the Reichswehr moved into the southern fringes of the shattered tsarist empire, German officials and propagandists also engaged with Muslims in the Caucasus and the Crimea.[46] It was the endpoint of a costly campaign to promote Imperial Germany as the patron of Islam.[47]

Overall, German-Ottoman attempts to employ Islam for the war effort failed. Nevertheless, in London, Paris, and St. Petersburg, officials were alarmed, maintaining military reserves in their Muslim colonies, troops that could have otherwise fought in the trenches of Europe. The efforts to incite Muslims throughout the colonial world "caused no end of trouble to the Entente Powers," as a French army report stated in 1916.[48] And yet Berlin and Constantinople did not ultimately succeed in inciting larger uprisings. The idea that "Islam" could be used to provoke an organized revolt was a misconception. The influence of pan-Islam was overestimated. The Muslim world was far too heterogeneous. More importantly, the campaign lacked credibility. It was all too clear that Muslims were being employed for the strategic purposes of the Central Powers, not for a truly religious cause. The Young Turks had no religious credentials. The power of the caliphate was limited. The sultan lacked religious legitimacy and was less universally accepted as caliph than officials in Berlin had hoped.

Finally, the Entente powers organized an efficient religious countercampaign. The French circulated decrees of loyal 'ulama denying the authority of the Ottoman sultan to issue a call for jihad and declaring support of the Triple Alliance a divine duty.[49] At the same time, Paris produced various Islamic pamphlets, tracts, and journals promoting France as a *puissance musulmane*, or "Muslim power." Religious leaders were actively involved in mobilizing Muslims to fight on the battlefields of Europe. The British responded to Constantinople's call for jihad with their own religious propaganda.[50] Islamic dignitaries across the British Empire exhorted Muslims to support the Entente. Influential pan-Islamist figures like Rashid Rida condemned the jihad as an unscrupulous and self-seeking venture, accusing the Young Turks of apostasy. Encouraged by the colonial government, some 'ulama in British India even issued fatwas against the sultan's proclamation of holy war.[51] Even the Mahdist leader 'Abd al-Rahman al-Mahdi of Sudan, son of the legendary messianic rebel of the 1880s, worked with the British and called for war against Constantinople.[52] Tsarist authorities, too, employed religious dignitaries to denounce the German-Ottoman jihad campaign.[53] Shortly after the proclamation of the Ottoman fatwas, one of the highest Islamic authorities of the Romanov Empire, the mufti of Orenburg, called the faithful to arms against their empire's enemies. And when touring his imperial realm after the outbreak of war in 1914, the tsar made sure to visit a number of mosques, promoting himself as the true protector of Islam. In the end, many Muslims proved loyal to the Entente governments. Hundreds of thousands fought in their colonial armies. With the Arab Revolt, Britain, in contrast to the Central Powers, even succeeded in spreading rebellion in the volatile imperial hinterlands of its adversaries, not only using propaganda but also making concrete promises of independence.[54] When the sharif of Mecca, Husayn Ibn Ali, and his sons Faisal and Abdallah switched sides in mid-1916, overrunning garrisons and port cities, it became clear that German-Ottoman propaganda had failed. In fact, the defection of the custodians of the Ka'ba damaged the legitimacy of the Ottoman caliphate considerably. The Arab Revolt had, especially at the beginning, a strong religious character. Sharifian propaganda, as famously reflected in the pages of Husayn's British-sponsored newspaper, al-Qibla, justified the revolt against Constantinople in religious terms, accusing the Ottomans of corrupting the purity of Islam and betraying the community of believers. The Young Turks were perceived by the rebels as "godless transgressors of their creed and their human duty" and "traitors to the spirit of the time, and to the highest interests of Islam," as T. E. Lawrence later put it.[55] The British even promoted the idea of a Mecca-based Arab caliphate—in contrast to the Ottoman caliph, Sharif Husayn could claim direct descent from the Prophet's tribe, the Quraysh. Islamic propaganda, it became clear, could also be used against the Central Powers.

After the war, some observers believed Islam to be politically insignificant. Pan-Islamic mobilization had failed. In 1924 the caliphate was abolished. In some countries, most notably Kemalist Turkey, Pahlavi Iran, and Zogist Albania, new political elites tried to enforce secular visions of modernity. Yet, these developments must not be overestimated. In fact, the interwar years may very well be seen as a period of global Islamic resurgence. The end of the caliphate was followed by political unrest across the globe. The Khilafat movement shook British India.[56] In the Arabian peninsula, the London-backed Husayn of Mecca was overrun by Ibn Saud's Wahhabis when proclaiming himself caliph in 1924.[57] Secular rulers, be they in Ankara, Tehran, or Tirana, faced fierce resistance from the pious parts of their populations.[58] In Afghanistan, King Amanullah's modernizing government was embroiled in a continuous struggle with Islamic opposition in the 1920s that eventually cost him the throne.[59] In many parts of the Muslim world, Islam stood at the center of emerging political mass organizations. In Egypt, the Muslim Brotherhood (*Ikhwan al-Muslimin*), founded by the schoolteacher Hasan al-Banna in 1928, within a few years became a mass movement, inspiring political groups from West Africa to Southeast Asia.[60] Pan-Islamic congresses were organized in Mecca and Cairo (both in 1926), Jerusalem (1931), and Geneva (1935), forming an Islamic international of scholars, intellectuals, and political leaders.[61] As it became clear that the great powers were not willing to grant Muslims in the Middle East, Africa, and Asia the right of self-determination, Islamic anti-imperialism revived, alongside secular anticolonial movements.[62] Throughout the 1920s and 1930s, British, French, Dutch, Italian, and Soviet authorities were confronted by local resistance groups in their Muslim possessions, calling for jihad against foreign intrusion.[63] The specter of Islamic insurgency on India's notorious Northwest Frontier was even reflected in a number of famous Hollywood movies, such as the *Lives of a Bengal Lancer* (1937), with its impressive scenes of praying and fighting Muslim masses; it was apparently Hitler's favorite film, which he and his entourage watched repeatedly in his private cinema at the Berghof.[64]

Interwar Debates and the Geopolitics of Islam

Throughout the interwar period, Islam continued to be on the agenda of German government officials.[65] At the same time, German policy experts published a wide range of articles and books on the role of Islam in world affairs, particularly during the 1930s, creating a discourse that would run into the war years of 1939–1945. Perhaps the most important center of these debates became Karl Ernst Haushofer's *Institut für Geopolitik* in Munich, where scholars debated the future role of Islam in world politics.[66] Its publication, the *Zeitschrift für Geopolitik*, frequently printed articles on the caliphate question, European imperial policies toward Islam, and the revival of pan-Islamism. Indeed, the experts at the institute took religion as a power in world affairs quite seriously, speaking about the "geopolitics of religion" (*Religions-Geopolitik*).[67] Haushofer himself had a keen interest in the Muslim world and a general weakness for "pan" ideas, be they pan-Asia, pan-Europe—or pan-Islam.[68]

A recurring subject in these debates about Islam was the lack of a political and religious center after the abolition of the caliphate. In November 1938 a writer in the *Zeitschrift für Geopolitik*, Hans Rabl, discussed the institution of the caliphate in geopolitical terms.[69] As the First World War had proven that the power of the caliphate had been overestimated, its abolition would have little impact on the political significance of Islam.[70] Even without a center, though, the "vigors of Islam," as the author put it, would remain a strong political force. The Qur'an and the shari'a represented absolute institutions, and imams and 'ulama would continue to exercise their influence across the world.[71] Discussing the consequences this had for the European powers, Rabl assured his readers of a political antagonism between Islam and the French and British empires, while praising Mussolini's "extraordinarily intelligent and sympathetic attitude" toward the Muslim faith and explaining that Il Duce was "in wide Islamic circles" viewed as the "patron of Islam."[72]

Two months after the outbreak of the Second World War, the political scientist Hans Lindemann gave a comprehensive overview of the geopolitics of Islam.[73] In his article "Islam in Rising and Attack," he argued that Islam formed a strong bond across continents and had to be considered an eminent political power in world affairs.[74] Images of Islam as politically passive, lethargic, and dependent were incorrect and mostly propagated by Christian missionaries. Lindemann examined Islamic movements around the world and their implications for the European powers.[75] He too referred to Japan's and Italy's policies of friendship with Islam, which he interpreted as efficient instruments for undermining the French and British empires.[76] Two years later, in 1941, Lindemann elaborated on these ideas in his book *Der Islam im Aufbruch, in Abwehr und Angriff (Islam in Rising, Defense and*

Attack).[77] Islam, he affirmed, was the Achilles' heel of the Allied powers. Germany and Italy, in contrast, had nothing to fear from Islam. Yet, even for them it was of "great importance" to adopt the right policies toward Muslims and "not to offend their religious sentiment."[78] Such arguments were widely accepted among his colleagues.

In March and April 1942, when German tanks rolled toward Cairo and approached the southern fringes of the Soviet Union, the journal published an article in two parts, titled "The British Policy towards Islam," which discussed British policies toward Muslims in India, the Middle East, and, though only marginally, Africa.[79] The author drew on the notion of pan-Islamic solidarity and presented Islam as a political power.[80] "Literature and newspapers brought the Indian Mohammedans in close and constant touch with the Muslim World [*Weltislam*]," he explained, which, he stressed, had last been demonstrated by the Indian Khilafat movement.[81] Muslim mobilization during the First World War had failed only because the Ottoman leadership had long renounced Islam.[82] The Muslim world, he insisted, was opposed to the British Empire as London's policy toward Muslims, particularly in Palestine, had strengthened "anti-English sentiment in Islam."[83] The involvement of the British Empire with Islam in different regions of the world was discussed in a number of wartime articles. Some contributions addressed British divide-and-rule policies toward Hindus and Muslims in India.[84] Others inquired into anti-British Islamic insurgency on the Northwest Frontier.[85] In 1940 the geopolitical expert Walter Leifer examined British involvement in the Arab world, identifying Islam as a strong political force.[86] The Ottoman religious mobilization of Muslims during the First World War had failed only because of the historical political rivalry between Turks and Arabs about the "leadership of Islam."[87] In the following issue of the *Zeitschrift für Geopolitik*, a special on "Rupture Lines of the Empire," an article about Egypt claimed that the British Empire was not only fighting its "traditional fight against Arabism" but also "against Islamic nationalism and the religion of Islam."[88] London's policies were both an "assault on an Arabic country" and an "assault on Islam!"[89]

Before the war, articles in the *Zeitschrift für Geopolitik* concerned with the involvement of the great powers in different parts of the Muslim world had already emphasized the political significance of Islam, pan-Islamic movements, and an alleged antagonism between Islam and the European empires. A piece on French engagement with Islam concluded: "One of the most important problems, if not the most important problem, of French colonial policy is the relationship between France and Islam."[90] Similarly, in the following year, an analysis of imperialism in the Dutch East Indies claimed that the "relationship between Holland and Islam" was "among the most important problems of Dutch colonial policy."[91] Also Britain's alleged policies to archive a "division between Hindus and Mohammedans" in India were discussed.[92] In 1936 Heinrich Eck, an expert in eastern European studies, described in an article on Soviet Central Asia the "religious problem" as the "key to understanding" the relationship between the Central Asian peoples and the Kremlin.[93] "With the awareness that an open fight with Islam would bring about heavy resistance in the Asiatic man, the Soviet government uses discreet means," he claimed, though making clear that Moscow's attempts to control Islam had failed: "Nonetheless, the Movement of the Godless has bred an intense bitterness among the Central Asian peoples, among whom religious fanaticism and the millennia [*sic*] old traditions are firmly anchored in their nature."[94] Identifying pan-Islamism as the strongest force of resistance, he finally connected Central Asia to the wider Muslim world: "A decisive factor, which will determine fates not only in Central Asia but also in the entire Orient, is pan-Islamism."[95]

The articles published in *Geopolitik* were part of a wider debate on Islam and world politics. Among the two most remarkable books in this respect, which Hans Lindemann particularly recommended in *Der Islam im Aufbruch, in Abwehr und Angriff*, were Paul Schmitz's *All-Islam! Weltmacht von morgen?* (*All-Islam! World Power of Tomorrow?*) of 1937 and Thomas Reichardt's *Der Islam vor den Toren* (*Islam at the Gates*) of 1939.[96] Published just a few months before the beginning of the Second World War, Reichardt's book argued that Islam had become again a strong political force, one with a global reach.[97] "Differences in Islam exist, but they are not substantial," he explained.[98] If not a "world power," Islam was at least "a world factor of the first rate."[99] Rejecting the popular belief that nationalism would eventually replace religion, he wrote: "Religion as a private affair—this is a decadent idea of the West, which the East will never comprehend and even less accede to!"[100] The call for holy war during the First World War had failed only because it was launched by the Young Turks, whose atheist views were well known.[101] Reichardt examined the political approaches of the great powers toward Islam and Islamic anti-imperialism in depth.[102] He discussed Dutch policies in Indonesia, US policies in the Philippines, and French policies in Africa. Britain, he asserted, had launched a policy of suppression of the Muslim faith.[103] "In this way, English attitudes towards Islam in the end add up to the same as the French attitude: to hatred, strife and revolt."[104] The religious policies of the liberal empires had antagonized Muslims: "When Islam looks at the West, it sees in democracy, in parliamentarianism, capitalism, individualism, in unrestrained mechanization and in the blind belief in progress all things which it opposes."[105] Reichardt also examined Soviet suppression of religious institutions, the destruction of mosques, and the persecution of religious figures, concluding that "Islam sees Bolshevism as its main enemy."[106] In contrast, Japan and Italy had wisely included Islam in their policies.[107] Like all "authoritarian and total states," Germany, too, had "nothing to fear from the rise of Islam."[108] The relationship between Germany and Islam was elaborated upon in detail in a final chapter, contributed by the Egyptian physician and pan-Islamic activist Zaki Ali.[109] Ali referred to Imperial Germany's policies toward Islam, Wilhelm II's Damascus speech, and Germany's attitude toward Islam in its colonies.[110] "Respect for Islam, its religious culture, institutions and religious buildings was the guideline," he claimed before discussing alleged ideological affinities between Nazism and Islam.[111]

Like Reichardt, Schmitz underlined the worldwide political significance of Islam in his book *All-Islam*.[112] Using the language of *Geopolitik*, Schmitz described his vision of a bloc of Muslim nations rather than a pan-Islamic state.[113] Connected by religion, this coalition would become the "world power of tomorrow."[114] Islamic solidarity was strengthened through a transnational Islamic public and the pilgrimage to Mecca, which, in Schmitz's eyes, generated a "politically highly significant consciousness that something such as an Islamic community exists."[115] Unsurprisingly, Schmitz also examined the policies of the great powers toward Islam, describing Italy's and Japan's courtship of the Muslim faith and Muslim resistance to the French, British, and Soviets. He left no doubt about the religious nature of this resistance and the usage of the Qur'an by anti-imperial leaders for the "religious fanatization of the masses."[116] Although Schmitz was not an academic expert but a reporter who had lived in various Muslim countries and was now working as the official correspondent of the NSDAP party organ, *Völkischer Beobachter*, in Egypt, *All-Islam* was well received in academic circles. It was not only geopolitical experts who referred to him but also scholars in Islamic studies. In 1942, as Germany had begun to engage with Islam in the war zones, *Der Islam* published a positive review of the book.[117] Given the "undeniable significance" of Islamic countries and the "unmistakably increasing interest" in Islam shown by "further circles in Germany," the book was highly relevant, the reviewer, Richard Hartmann, wrote.[118] In fact, Hartmann, a professor of Islamic studies in Berlin who toward the end of the war acted as a consultant to the SS, himself also contributed to the debate about the politics of Islam during the war and supported Schmitz's idea of the coexistence of Islam and nationalism, particularly in his 1944 monograph *Die Religion des Islam* (*The Religion of Islam*).[119]

Throughout the 1930s and early 1940s, German policy experts well beyond the circles of the *Institut für Geopolitik* showed a good deal of interest in Islam. The renowned *Zeitschrift für Politik*, edited by the *Deutsche Hochschule für Politik* in Berlin, too, provided an important forum for debates on the issue.[120] Although some of its contributors, among them war veteran Curt Prüfer, were skeptical about the political significance of religion in the Muslim world, many still considered Islam a major geopolitical force.[121] In early 1938, six months before the *Zeitschrift für Geopolitik* explored the issue, the *Zeitschrift für Politik* had broached the question of a political center in Islam, detecting the new "pole of Islam" in Mecca under Ibn Saud.[122] After the First World War, Islam had grown into a "remarkable political and religious power," it was asserted.[123] Throughout the interwar period the *Zeitschrift für Politik* also dealt with the problem of Islamic anticolonialism in the European empires, publishing contributions ranging from Muslim resistance in the French Empire to pan-Islamism in the Dutch East Indies to Islamic insurgency on the Northwest Frontier.[124] Moreover, some articles examined the jihad of the First World War, reassessing not only German attempts to stir up Islamic revolt but also the countermeasures adopted by the Triple Entente.[125] In 1941, after the German involvement in the Maghrib, the *Zeitschrift für Politik* provided a detailed discussion of the 1914 jihad, going so far as to argue that it had not been a complete failure and may very well have succeeded.[126] During the war years the journal also published a number of pieces that dealt with Germany's Muslim collaborators, most importantly the mufti of Jerusalem, in connection with more general questions about the geopolitics of Islam.[127] Overall there was a considerable overlap in the debates about Islam in the *Zeitschrift für Geopolitik* and the *Zeitschrift für Politik* in the 1930s and 1940s. And finally, after the beginning of the war, military journals, too, showed interest in Islamic issues. In 1942, for instance, the *Militärwissenschaftliche Rundschau* assured its readers that Islam was "extraordinarily vital" and "in the ascendancy" rather than "ossified or even close to decay" and formed, through a "sentiment of solidarity," a strong, global, political bond.[128]

An important facet of the debate was the role of Islam in the Muslim parts of the Soviet Union. The major advocate of the idea that Islam was the strongest bulwark against the Soviet regime was the young Turkologist and Islam expert Johannes Benzing, who would become one of the most important Orientalists in postwar Germany. He made this claim first in 1937 in an article published in the journal *Osteuropa*.[129] Benzing gave a detailed account of the Kremlin's suppression of religious structures in its Muslim regions and its attacks on the 'ulama, mosques, customs, and rituals.[130] He claimed that the Soviets' fight against Islam was fiercer than its suppression of Orthodox Christianity, as Islam was "far more dangerous" for them.[131] Muslim defiance of Moscow was religiously charged, and the "main carrier of this resistance" was the "clergy (mullahs)."[132] Benzing promoted his thesis well into the war and would eventually advise the SS on Islam in the Soviet Union.[133] His views were widely shared by his prominent senior colleague and rival, Gerhard von Mende, a Riga-born Turkologist who taught in Berlin and later joined the East Ministry during the war. In his book *Der nationale Kampf der Russlandtürken* (*The National Struggle of the Turkic Peoples of Russia*), published in 1936, Mende discussed the rise of nationalism among Russia's Turkic population, referred to as Eastern Turks (*Osttürken*), since the late nineteenth century, considering in depth the role of Islam in their resistance to the central state.[134] Although he believed that Islam had been weakened politically after the turn of the century, he argued that religion was an integral part of the emerging national consciousness of the Eastern Turks and had recently proven to be a strong force against the Soviet regime. The eminent Islam expert Gotthardt Jäschke, who reviewed Mende's book in *Die Welt des Islams*, was thrilled, emphasizing "the great significance of Islam in the fight for völkisch survival."[135] Islam, he summarized, offered the Turkic peoples a strong bulwark against the "Bolshevist policy of disintegration."[136] It would be "interesting," he wrote, to determine "how many mosques have been closed so far."[137] Two years later, Jäschke, a professor at Berlin who had briefly worked for the *Nachrichtenstelle für den*

Orient during the First World War and later as a German diplomat in Turkey and the Caucasus, published his own thoughts about Communism and Islam in *Die Welt des Islams*.[138] "Anyone who is familiar, even if only superficially, with the religion of the Prophet Muhammad and the teachings of the Jew Karl Marx and its ghastly expression by Lenin and Stalin knows what an abyss separates them," he proclaimed, adding: "Just as a pious Muslim already, intuitively, emotionally rejects Marxist socialism, so must a true Bolshevist perceive Islam to be, like other religion, an 'opiate of the people' and fight against it with the same remorselessness as against nationalism."[139]

Again it was Paul Schmitz who contributed most to the wider dissemination of these ideas. His *Moskau und die islamische Welt* (*Moscow and the Islamic World*), published in 1938 in the notorious *Bolschewismus* (*Bolshevism*) book series of the NSDAP central publishing house Franz Eher, examined the Kremlin's policies toward Muslims.[140] It gave a detailed account of the Soviet suppression of Islam, denouncing Moscow's "political and religious rape" of its Muslim population.[141] Claiming that Soviet oppression had been "ineffective," he asserted that the "Islamic religion" remained not only the "life fundament" of most Muslims but also the strongest vehicle of anti-Soviet resistance.[142] In the final part of the book, Schmitz discussed the political implications of this situation for Germany: "Under the leadership of Adolf Hitler, we Germans have understood the role of Bolshevism and debunked it in front of the world, and we also know about the significance of the Islamic world in the fight against the Comintern. From this result the ties of friendship that bind us to the Islamic peoples."[143] Johannes Benzing, who reviewed the book in *Die Welt des Islams*, recommended it as "a good introduction."[144] The debate ran on into the war years. Just after the invasion of the Soviet Union in the summer of 1941, for instance, Karl Krüger, a professor in Berlin and an expert on Eastern questions, published an article on the Muslims of the Soviet Union in the *Organ des deutschen Orient Vereins*, asserting that Islam in Central Asia could become a significant factor in the war and even making concrete suggestions for propaganda slogans.[145]

It is finally worth noting that experts in southeastern Europe would also to some extent engage in debates about the politics of Islam once German troops got involved in the Muslim territories of the Balkans. Most notable among them was Franz Ronneberger, head of the Foreign Office's intelligence and research branch for southeastern Europe in Vienna, the so-called *Dienststelle Dr. Ronneberger*, and one of the regime's rising experts on the Balkans. In the autumn of 1942 Ronneberger published a lengthy article on the significance of Islam in southeastern Europe on the front page of the *Völkischer Beobachter*.[146] Compared to the millions of Muslims outside Europe, the Muslims of the Balkans, who numbered no more than 2 million, seemed to be insignificant. "It would be to miss the point, however, to infer from the numerical proportion alone to the actual significance of the European Muslims in the Islamic world," Ronneberger wrote. "Everything" happening to the Muslims of the Balkans, he claimed, "is thoroughly registered and observed in the rest of the Muslim world [*Mohammedanertum*], just as, conversely, the European Mohammedans take the strongest interest in the fate of their brothers in faith, especially in the Near East and in Northern Africa." Ronneberger went on to argue that Germany's approach to Islam in the Balkans had to be with consideration of its relations with the Muslim world. It was not only the Muslims of the Soviet Union, who had been fighting their "grim defense against Bolshevism," but "the entire Muslim world" that was ready to stand up and fight on the side of the Axis powers, readers were told. In the summer of 1943, the southeastern European studies journal *Volkstum im Südosten*, edited by Ronneberger and others, published an article titled "On the Mohammedan Problem in Bosnia and Herzegovina," which dealt with the politics of Islam in southeastern Europe in more depth, again considering the Muslim population an ally of Nazi Germany.[147]

Although complex and fluid, the discourse on Islam and politics was characterized by some recurring narrative lines, ideas, and assumptions. It drew on an essentialist notion of "Islam" as an ontological entity. This entity was commonly considered to be intrinsically political. Moreover, the debates reflected a territorial notion of "Islam," merging conceptions of religion and geography and understanding "Islam," or more precisely the "Islamic world," as a geographical unit spanning from North Africa to East Asia. On the eve of the Second World War, German experts agreed, for the most part, about both the political significance of Islam and its global reach, often referred to as "world Islam" (*Weltislam*) or "pan-Islam" (*All-Islam* or *Pan-Islam*), although their assessment of the strength of pan-Islamism as a political force varied. One of the more widely debated themes was the failed Muslim mobilization campaign of the First World War. Remarkably, almost no author saw the event as proof of the political insignificance of Islam. Rather, scholars referred to the lack of authenticity of the (secularist) Young Turks and the obvious nonreligious causes of the call for holy war. Experts also showed a remarkable interest in the abolition of the caliphate and the problem of the lack of a center of Islam, discussing questions of global religious authority and political influence. Some looked to new centers (Cairo or Mecca); others believed that a caliphate was irrelevant to the political strength of Islam. Another recurring subject was an alleged dichotomy between religion and nation, though most authors balked at the idea that they were irreconcilable.[148] Finally, all authors examined the policies of the great powers toward Islam, agreeing that Muslim religious sentiment was antagonized by the policies of the British, French, Dutch, and Soviet empires, while recognizing Italy's and Japan's approaches as sensible. Wherever political statements were made in regard to Germany, Islam was generally presented as a political opportunity. Only a few experts regarded Islam as politically lethargic, and even fewer saw in it a political threat.[149]

Foreign observers were convinced of the practical impact of the experts on German policy making in the Muslim world. Analyzing Germany's war efforts and propaganda in North Africa and the Middle East, the British foreign policy specialist Robert L. Baker detected the influence of "General Doktor Karl Rudolf von Haushofer," noting that his "geopoliticians have tried very hard to apply the formulas of their science to the Middle East."[150] Baker would even discuss in detail particular articles on Islam published in the *Zeitschrift für Geopolitik*, including Rabl's piece "On the Caliphate," Lindemann's text "Islam on the March," and a special monthly feature on "India and the Near East," which Haushofer himself had written for many years, to his Anglo-American readers.[151] They had embarked on an "obvious search for a racial or religious movement that can be used to destroy Britain's power in the Middle East."[152] Islam, Baker asserted, played a central role in this endeavor:

> The war brought a change in the geopolitical attitude toward pan-Islam. Here again the requirements of Nazi propaganda were probably responsible, because of the hope of rousing the Moslem world to declare a Jihad, or Holy War, against Britain and France. For many years before the war pan-Islam was regarded by the geopoliticians as nothing more than an interesting dream, but one that could

not be realized because of differences in race, language and doctrine, and also because the movement was politically lethargic and lacked a State-center.[153]

Their writings, Baker believed, were directly related to German policy efforts: "Both they and the German radio propaganda in Arabic encouraged Islam to challenge British 'tyranny.' . . . The geopoliticians have dug up material suitable for use in wooing the Arabs and Moslems by Dr. Goebbels' efficient radio propaganda in Arabic and other tongues."[154] Yet, Baker also hinted at the problem of a lack of concrete concessions: "All three of the Axis partners have taken a strong interest in pan-Islam as a weapon against the British, but so far as is known they have kept their promises to the fanatics vague."[155] In a way, this criticism of German Islam experts recalled Snouck Hurgronje's accusations during the First World War.

The influence of *Geopolitik*, particularly its theories of *Lebensraum* in the East, on Nazi policy makers, strategists and, indeed, Hitler personally, is well known.[156] Many of the studies on Islam were read in Berlin's ministries and departments responsible for the Muslim world during the war.[157] Whether their writings on Islam had any impact, as Baker claimed, is speculation. Yet, notions expressed in these academic debates were to a remarkable extent reflected in discussions among and decisions made by the regime's authorities in Berlin after the Muslim world came into their focus.

CHAPTER TWO

Berlin's Muslim Moment

Max von Oppenheim's memorandum of 1940, in many respects an adapted version of his plan of 1914, created few ripples at the Foreign Office.[1] In his response, Under State Secretary Theodor August Habicht informed Oppenheim that the "questions raised are already being considered in detail at the Foreign Office."[2] In reality, until then, German officials had shown little interest in the Middle East and even less in the wider Muslim world. Neither Hitler's foreign policy schemes, which he had developed before 1933, nor any strategy of the 1930s, had made such a policy necessary.[3] Hitler's plans were focused on eastern Europe. In the non-European world, including its Muslim territories, Berlin acknowledged the imperial interests of Italy, Spain, and Britain, which Hitler sought as allies.

With the outbreak of the war and, more importantly, following Italy's military failures in North Africa and the Balkans in early 1941, this outlook changed. When the Germans encountered Muslim contingents of the French army in 1940, Wehrmacht and Foreign Office officials had made some first attempts to use Islam in their propaganda, but these efforts were relatively unsystematic and ad hoc. It was only in 1941, when German troops became involved in North Africa, advancing toward the Middle East, that policy makers in Berlin began to consider the strategic role of Islam more systematically. Officials in the Orient section of the political department of the Foreign Office were the first to consider Islam in their policies toward Muslim regions.

The Foreign Office and the Making of Germany's Policy toward Islam

In the summer and autumn of 1941, German officials in the Foreign Office discussed the political significance of the Muslim world and the employment of Islam for the German war effort. A systematic instrumentalization of Islam was first proposed by the diplomat Eberhard von Stohrer in a memorandum of 18 November 1941.[4] Asserting that in the future course of the war, the Muslim world would soon become more important, he suggested that there should be "an extensive Islam program," which should include a statement about the "general attitude of the Third Reich toward Islam." Stohrer recommended the creation of a committee of Islam experts to work out such a program. Convinced that National Socialist ideology was aligned with "many Islamic principles," he wrote: "In Islam, the Führer already holds a pre-eminent position because of his fight against Judaism." After all, Islam was "similar to National Socialism" in that it rejected the idea of a "clergy;" the imams had "the role of teachers and judges, but not of clerics," he explained. Stohrer was well aware that his proposed program could draw on the tradition of the "policy of friendship toward Islam pursued before and during the [First] World War." Consequently, he put forward the name of Werner Otto von Hentig, who had not only been involved in Muslim mobilization during the First World War but had also directed the Orient section before 1939, to organize the proposed committee of experts. The time was ripe, Stohrer urged. After the defeat of France, Germany had gained an "outstanding position" in the "northern African Islam area" and won much sympathy "in the eyes of the Muslims" by fighting Britain, "the suppressor of wide-reaching Islamic areas."[5]

Stohrer, who had long served in Cairo and was now ambassador to Madrid, wrote the memorandum while on holiday in Berlin, where he had discussed these issues with some friends—among them Pierre Schrumpf-Pierron, an officer in the *Abwehr*, the Wehrmacht intelligence, who had previously been employed as an agent in Cairo.[6] A few months earlier Schrumpf-Pierron had also sent a memorandum to the Foreign Office about the use of religion in North Africa and the Middle East.[7] Berlin had to be prepared to reorder the region and convince the Muslim population that it would not leave it to the despised Italians. To win the support of Muslims, the memorandum suggested that German policy and propaganda should draw on the Islamic faith. Such a policy would be particularly promising in Arab areas, as "the Arab Muslim" was a "de facto fanatic." Schrumpf-Pierron also alluded to an alleged affinity between Nazism and Islam on which an alliance could supposedly be based. "The structure of Islam, incidentally, has much in common with National Socialism: above authority, below 'democracy,'" he claimed, adding that Hitler was admired throughout the Muslim world. "He has defeated France and is already by now indirectly compelled ultimately to pursue a pro-Islamic and anti-Jewish policy in North Africa," Schrumpf-Pierron wrote. The rest of the Middle East had to be approached in the same way, he insisted.

Initially, officials at the Wilhelmstraße disagreed about whether religion or the various ethnic (i.e., Arab, Turanian, Turkish, Berber, or Iranian) nationalisms would provide the best basis for a strategic alliance with the Muslim world. After all, diplomats still remembered the failure to instrumentalize Islam during the First World War. Just as in the academic debate, discussions among diplomats often revolved around an alleged dichotomy between "nation" and "religion." As early as March 1941, Ernst Woermann, head of the Foreign Office's political department, had noted in a memorandum on the Arab world that the "Islamic idea ('holy war')" was in the current situation "not usable."[8] "Arabism and Islam do not overlap," he explained. The Arabs of North Africa and the Middle East, who were to be won for the Axis cause, would fight "not for religious, but for political aims." Even Woermann, however, could not completely dismiss the role of religion. "The questions of Islam require tactful handling," he urged. Although the dispute was never fully resolved, over the following months Woermann increasingly gave up his opposition to Islamic propaganda.

In early 1942, officials in the political department sat together to systematically discuss whether, "apart from national (for instance Arabic, Indian propaganda)," also "general Islamic" propaganda should be made in Muslim-populated areas of the world.[9] Although the guidelines worked out during these debates stated that "general Islamic propaganda on religious grounds" and "slogans like 'holy war'" should be avoided, they stressed that religion should not remain unexploited: "A measured exploitation of the Islamic idea in the propaganda announcements for the Arab countries and for the Mohammedans of the Soviet Union is desired."[10] As discussions on the issue continued over the following months, lingering reservations were gradually set aside, and in spring 1942, Woermann would report to his superior, State Secretary Ernst von Weizsäcker, that the "Islamic question" was now "dealt with thoroughly" in the political department, "both from the political and the propagandistic side": "The religious fundamentals of Islam are thereby utilized, especially in the propaganda for the Mohammedans of the Soviet Union and of the Arab countries."[11] Only in India "Islamic propaganda" was not "at the moment" considered "useful" as German officials tried to avoid taking sides in the conflict between Muslims and Hindus.[12] Indeed, in practice, officials in the Foreign Office increasingly drew on Islam in their policies toward the Muslim world. The Wilhelm-straße organized a major pamphlet and broadcast propaganda campaign in North Africa and the Middle East and eventually even in India, which employed not only nationalist but also strong religious rhetoric, preaching a Muslim-German alliance (see Part II).

These efforts were mainly coordinated by the Orient section of the political department.[13] Responsible for North Africa, the Middle East, and India, it was directed by the career diplomat Wilhelm Melchers, who had formerly held posts in Addis Ababa, Tehran, and Haifa. One of the most notable figures of the Orient section was Fritz Grobba, an Orientalist who during the Islamic mobilization campaign of the First World War had first led a battalion of Muslim volunteers, recruited in the camps of Wünsdorf and Zossen, to the Ottoman Empire and later served in Palestine. The "shrewd and highly polished Dr. Grobba," as *Foreign Affairs* once put it, had been German ambassador in Iraq in the interwar period and was now in charge of Arab affairs.[14] Also concerned with German policies and propaganda in North Africa and the Middle East was the aged Curt Prüfer, another veteran who had been involved in German policies in the Muslim world during the First World War.[15] Between the summer of 1941 and the end of 1942, the Foreign Office set up an Islam program, which included the employment of religious figures and the establishment of the Islamic Central Institute in Berlin.

The most prominent religious leader employed by the Foreign Office was Amin al-Husayni, the peacock-like mufti of Jerusalem. Born at the turn of the century into the patrician al-Husayni family, he had briefly studied at al-Azhar and at the seminary of Rashid Rida before serving as an officer in the Ottoman army in the First World War.[16] In mandate Palestine, al-Husayni had quickly risen to power, though he had many enemies, most importantly the followers of the influential al-Nashashibi clan, which had long rivaled the al-Husaynis. In 1921 the British authorities appointed him mufti of Jerusalem—giving him the newly invented title "grand mufti" (*al-mufti al-akbar*)—and, a year later, president of the Supreme Muslim Council and chairman of the General Waqf Committee in Palestine, not anticipating that al-Husayni, an ardent Jew-hater, would soon become a major proponent of the opposition to British rule and Jewish migration to Palestine.[17] In autumn 1937 the mufti was finally forced to flee to Lebanon, moving from there to Iraq, and, after the failure of the Iraqi pro-Axis coup, to Tehran. In autumn 1941, when Iran was invaded by the Allies, he escaped via Turkey to Italy. On 6 November 1941 a German plane brought him to Berlin.[18]

On 28 November 1941, in the presence of Ribbentrop, Grobba, and two German interpreters, al-Husayni was received by Hitler in the New Reich Chancellery (Figure 2.1).[19] In his memoirs the mufti, eager to present himself as a great statesman, described in detail the splendor of the reception:

> I did not expect that my reception at the famous chancellery would be an official one, but a private meeting with the Führer. I had just arrived at the wide square in front of the chancellery and stepped out of the car in front of the entrance of the great building, when I was startled by the sound of a military band and guard of honor composed of around two hundred German soldiers who had gathered in the square. My escorts from the Foreign Office invited me to inspect the guard, which I did. Then we entered the chancellery, and passed through its long colonnades and impressive portals until we reached the large reception hall. There, the head of state protocols greeted me, and after a short while led me to the Führer's special room. Hitler greeted me warmly with a cheerful face, expressive eyes, and clear joy.[20]

Their conversation was limited to an exchange of empty courtesies and the affirmation that they were fighting against common enemies—the British, Jews, and Bolshevism.[21] When al-Husayni asked Hitler for a written guarantee of Arab, and especially Palestinian, independence, the dictator evaded the issue. After al-Husayni's repeated request, Hitler told him that in the current state of the war it was too early for these kinds of questions but asserted his "uncompromising fight against the Jews," which also included the Jews of the Arab lands. Another request for a meeting with Hitler in 1943 was unsuccessful.[22]

The mufti settled in Berlin and, in the following years, tried to influence German policies toward the Muslim world. He soon became notorious for his intrigues against rivals, most importantly the former Iraqi prime minister Rashid 'Ali al-Kilani, who had also come to Berlin after his defeat in Iraq.[23] Grobba, who was responsible for Arab collaborators, supported al-Kilani. To end the conflict, the diplomat and *SS-Brigadeführer*

2.1 Amin al-Husayni and Hitler in the New Reich Chancellery, Berlin, 28 November 1941 (BAK, *Image 146-1987-004-09A, Hoffmann*).

Erwin Ettel, former ambassador to Tehran, was finally assigned to supervise al-Husayni.[24] In the following months, Ettel and the mufti, with the support of Prüfer, successfully plotted against Grobba and al-Kilani. In late 1942, Grobba was pushed out of the Foreign Office; al-Kilani lost his influence.

Al-Husayni's activities in Berlin have been examined by a vast body of literature, most importantly in the biographies by Joseph Schechtman, Klaus Gensicke, and Jennie Lebel.[25] Yet, biographical research on the mufti tends to overestimate his influence in Berlin. In the end, his impact was strictly limited. His plan to gain concrete concessions and to secure guarantees for Arab and Palestinian independence—his main concern—failed.[26] His proposals were successful only insofar as they coincided with German interests. The most dramatic example was his intervention to hinder the emigration of Jews from Germany's southeastern European satellite states to Palestine.[27] Instead of putting the mufti at the center of the narrative, it seems more reasonable to see him as part of a more general German policy directed toward the Islamic world. German officials used him as a propaganda figure when circumstances necessitated. After all, he was paid well for his services. He received a monthly salary of no less than 90,000 reichsmarks and was provided with several residences for himself and his entourage.[28]

The Foreign Office used the mufti mainly to fuel its propaganda toward the Arab and Muslim world. Although al-Husayni had presented himself initially as an Arab nationalist rather than a pan-Islamic leader, Berlin was more and more interested in his a role as a religious figure.[29] In October 1942, just before his dismissal, Grobba noted that the mufti had "so far enjoyed the special trust of the German political and military offices because of the clerical vestment he wore."[30] At the same time, Ettel assured Ribbentrop that the mufti could be employed not only for German propaganda in North Africa and the Middle East "but beyond, among all Islamic peoples from North Africa to the Indonesian Archipelago."[31] This was of course a vast overestimation of al-Husayni's actual religious and political influence.

Among the lesser-known, though no less interesting, Muslim figures who worked for the Foreign Office was imam Alimjan Idris (Figure 2.2).[32] After his employment in the Muslim prison camps in Wünsdorf and Zossen during the First World War, the Prussian War Ministry had kept him in charge of the former Muslim prisoners until 1921. A year later Idris was sent to the Soviet Union to encourage Muslim students from Central Asia to study in Germany but was arrested by suspicious Soviet authorities. After a few months in prison he was released, with the help of the Germans, and returned to Berlin. In 1933 Idris was hired by the Orient section of the political department of the Foreign Office as an advisor. He seemed to have few ideological scruples about working for the new regime. In 1933 Rashid Rida's pan-Islamic organ, *al-Manar*, published a letter by Idris in which he defamed Jews as corrupt, despicable, and repulsive and asked for Rida's opinion on contradictory Qur'anic passages about Jews.[33] Following the outbreak of war in 1939, he was employed in the Orient section of the Foreign Propaganda Broadcast, which was run jointly by the Foreign Office and Goebbels's Propaganda Ministry. Involved initially in the Arabic program and later in Turkish broadcasts, Idris would work for the propaganda section until the end of the war, although both the Wehrmacht and

2.2 Alimjan Idris (1887–1959) (*Ilyas Gabid Abdulla, Islam in West Deutschland, Munich, n.d.*).

the SS later became interested in his services. Idris spoke various Turkic languages, including Turkish, Usbek, and Kirgizian, as well as Russian, Persian, Arabic, French, and German. The Foreign Office had even commissioned him to write a Persian translation of *Mein Kampf.* To fuel its propaganda efforts, the Wilhelmstraße employed various other Muslim helpers. Among them were the Arabs 'Abd al-Halim al-Naggar and Muhammad Safty, who also directed the Foreign Office's new Islamic institution—the Islamic Central Institute—which became a hub of German Islam propaganda.

The Islamic Central Institute was inaugurated at half past four on the afternoon of 18 December 1942, in a ceremonial building of the Luftwaffe (*Haus der Flieger*), 5 Prinz-Albrecht-Straße, in the heart of Berlin.[34] The day was chosen according to the religious calendar. The Muslim world celebrated the pilgrimage feast of *'Id al-Adha*. Two hundred guests had been invited.[35] Exploiting the religious context, the German authorities used the grand opening to advance their political propaganda and promote German friendship with Islam. The inaugural speech was given by al-Husayni, who cloaked his political message in the mantle of religious rhetoric: "In the name of God, I open this Islamic institute," he began, and continued with a theological, though highly politicized, reflection on the meaning of the *'Id al-Adha*, the Feast of Sacrifice.[36] The day, he asserted, "unmistakably alludes to the duty of self-sacrifice and the highest commitment." He went on to urge Muslims to recognize the need to make sacrifices for the war effort and then reflected on the meaning of the war for Muslims. Their "tremendous number" and "their willingness to sacrifice," he proclaimed, would put the Muslims in a good position to pursue their own aims in the war. "This war, which has been unleashed by world Judaism, offers Muslims the best opportunity to free themselves from persecution and oppression, if they capitalize on this opportunity properly," he declared, adding: "Such an opportunity will not arise again for a very long time." Most of the speech contained religiously charged torrents of hatred against the alleged common enemies of Germany and Islam:

> Among the most bitter enemies of the Muslims, who from ancient times have shown them enmity and met them everywhere constantly with perfidy and cunning, are the Jews and their accomplices. . . . The holy Qur'an and the life story of the Prophet are full of evidence of Jewish lack of character and their malicious, mendacious and treacherous behavior, which completely suffices to warn Muslims of their ever-constant, severe threat and enmity until the end of all days. And as the Jews were in the lifetime of the great Prophet, so they have remained throughout all ages; conniving and full of

hatred toward the Muslim, wherever an opportunity offered itself to them.

The Americans and the British had invaded Muslim lands in North Africa, he fulminated. England in particular would not "content itself with usurping the Muslims of India" and, by "suppressing Egypt, Palestine and other countries," it had "further extended the persecution of the Muslims and driven the fury of war into many Muslim countries," for instance, by occupying Iraq, Iran, and Syria. In the Balkans, the British had given money and weapons to the Communists so that they could "savage Muslim men, women and children in Bosnia." Al-Husayni also commented on Islam in the Soviet Union: "In addition to Jews, Americans and English are the Bolshevists with their irreconcilable enmity toward Islam. They have suppressed and persecuted 40 million Muslims in their empire. They have destroyed their religious and national institutions, trampled on their freedom and rights, and abolished their institutes and charity organizations by force." Finally, he called for global Muslim resistance in the form of a religious imperative: "The Muslim who fears somebody else besides God or yields to his enemies and places his fate voluntarily in their hands is not a Muslim anymore." Only the readiness to make sacrifice would bring victory, he concluded. "There is no god but Allah!"[37]

The event was closely controlled by the Foreign Office.[38] The speech had been approved by Ribbentrop personally. It was broadcast across North Africa and the Middle East. In Germany, too, the event received considerable attention. The party organ, *Völkischer Beobachter*, ran an article headed "This War Could Bring Freedom to Islam!" and printed a full-page report about the *'Id al-Adha* celebration, the Islamic ideal of self-sacrifice, the speech, and the opening of the institute.[39] Similarly, the *Deutsche Allgemeine Zeitung* reported on the "Liberation Battle of Islam."[40] A local Berlin paper ran an article titled "The Spokesman of 400 Million Accuses," and another one printed photographs of al-Husayni giving his "accusatory speech against the oppressors of Islam."[41]

In fact, the institute had already been founded, under the name Islam Institute (*Islam-Institut*), in 1927 by activists of the Muslim community in Berlin.[42] The Muslim minority of the capital had grown throughout the interwar period, centered on the mosque in Berlin-Wilmersdorf, which had opened in 1928, and various other organizations such as the Islam

Institute.[43] After years of inaction, members of the community, under the leadership of the al-Azhar-educated Sudanese journalist Kamal al-Din Galal, had made an attempt to reopen the institute in September 1941 and found support at the Foreign Office. The institute was reestablished in the summer of 1942. Although officially run by members of the Muslim community in Berlin, the institute was controlled by the regime. The inauguration ceremony, organized under the auspices of the Foreign Office, was a purely political event and gave a clear image of the extent to which the Nazi state was involved. The driving forces in the Foreign Office were Wilhelm Melchers and Curt Prüfer.[44] And the Wilhemstraße also dealt with the institute's finances.[45] The Muslims who officially ran the institute were closely linked to the Foreign Office. Apart from General Secretary Galal, both the chairman, 'Abd al-Halim al-Naggar (later replaced by Hasan Abu al-Suud), and the director, Muhammad Safty, worked for the broadcast propaganda service of the Foreign Office. To underline its pan-Islamic character, the Foreign Office also made sure to include Syrians, Palestinians, Turks, and Afghans on the board of the institute.[46] It was based in an apartment on the Klopstockstraße in the well-to-do Zehlendorf neighborhood, provided by the SS.[47] Indeed, by the time of the inauguration of the Islamic Central Institute, the SS and other parts of the regime had also become interested in Islam.

Other Offices and the Expansion of Germany's Policy toward Islam

As the war progressed, German troops moved into Muslim areas in the Balkans and in the Soviet Union, in the Crimea and the Caucasus, where other branches of the regime would follow up on these policies and make use of the then-established structures.

The Foreign Office, which had been increasingly sidelined since the beginning of the war, had little influence in the Muslim regions of the Eastern territories and the Balkans but remained the leading institution in charge of North Africa and the Middle East and would continue its policies and propaganda in these regions until the end of the war. Through its early engagement with Islam, the Wilhelmstraße set the tone and established a policy structure that included the employment of Muslim religious and political figures such as al-Husayni or Idris.

In the Eastern territories, attempts by the Foreign Office to maintain some influence failed. Friedrich-Werner Graf von der Schulenburg's "Russia committee" at the Wilhelmstraße was largely irrelevant.[48] The man on the committee responsible for the Muslim areas of the Soviet Union was Werner Otto von Hentig, assisted by Alimjan Idris.[49] After dealing with various issues concerning Middle Eastern affairs in the first years of the war, Hentig found himself in charge of the Muslim Turkic population of the Soviet Union and, between autumn 1941 and summer 1942, also served as the Foreign Office's representative in the Crimea. Hentig advocated the formation of a Muslim bloc against Moscow. In late 1941, he produced a detailed plan for the political mobilization of the Muslims in the Soviet Union, suggesting the spread of propaganda through broadcasts, pamphlets, and emissaries.[50] Convinced of the power of pan-Islamic solidarity, Hentig frequently stressed the "proliferating effect" that policies toward Muslims in the Eastern territories would have on the wider Islamic world and connected discussions about the Muslims of the Soviet Union to Germany's more general policies toward Islam.[51] "Their treatment cannot be detached from the treatment of all other Mohammedan peoples," for which Germany had established clear "slogans," he wrote in a memorandum in early 1942.[52] On the whole, however, Hentig and his colleagues at the Wilhelmstraße had only little influence on policies on the Eastern Front. Irrelevant were also the more general political schemes for the future New Order in the East produced in the Foreign Office. Some circles around Schulenburg advocated Crimean independence. In the Caucasus, a cluster of puppet states was to be formed, with which the Foreign Office would maintain relations. Schulenburg even organized an expensive conference of some forty Caucasian exile politicians at the Hotel Adlon to discuss the postwar administration of these areas. In Alfred Rosenberg's Ministry for the Occupied Eastern Territories, officers observed the Foreign Office's involvement in these affairs with suspicion. Eventually, in the summer of 1942, Rosenberg convinced Hitler to formally rule that the Wilhelmstraße had no competence in occupied Soviet territory.[53]

Yet, Rosenberg's ministry had little influence itself in the Muslim parts of the Eastern war zones, in the Crimea and the Caucasus.[54] Within the East Ministry, several factions competed with different visions of the role of these areas in the future New Order. Initial plans foresaw the

Germanization of the entire Crimea and the establishment of a Reich Commissariat in the Caucasus. As the war situation worsened, another group sought the support of non-Russian ethnic minorities in order to break up the Soviet Union. These included the Crimean Tatars and the Caucasian peoples, although Rosenberg favored a Georgian-led Caucasian bloc over Muslim domination. To this end, the East Ministry gathered some non-Russian émigrés from the Soviet Union and founded national committees. The driving force behind this policy was Gerhard von Mende, who, in the summer of 1941, had left academic life to work in the political department of Rosenberg's ministry, where his main area of responsibility was the Caucasus. Mende worried that ideas that referred to wider political units, most importantly pan-Turan and pan-Islam, counteracted the strategy to dismantle the Soviet Union into small controllable pieces. Islamic solidarity needed to be checked, he warned. "The Islamic world is a whole. German action toward the Moslems in the East must be such as not to prejudice Germany's standing among all Islamic peoples," Mende explained to a historian after the war.[55] Other factions in the ministry were more conciliatory toward an instrumentalization of Islam. A memorandum from the political department in autumn 1941 stressed the importance of Islam in the war and affirmed that the positioning of the Third Reich as a "protector of Islam" would promise "great political successes."[56] Ultimately, the East Ministry pursued no special policy toward Islam; Islam was a concern only as part of the ministry's general religious policy schemes, which treated religion as an aspect of national culture and supported it only as part of the national splintering policy. As with the plans of the Foreign Office, these schemes remained largely irrelevant in the Muslim areas of the Eastern territories, with the exception of the Baltic region, the Reich Commissariat Ostland, with its Tatar minority (see Part II). The Crimea and the Caucasus were placed under military administration as long as they were under occupation.

It was the Wehrmacht that directed German policies in the Eastern Muslim war zones in the Crimea and the Caucasus.[57] The army engaged in substantial religious policies toward Muslims in these areas. Five months after the invasion of the Soviet Union, in November 1941, a Wehrmacht report titled "The Spread of Islam among Prisoners of War" assessed the degree of piety among Muslim prisoners of war who had fought in the Red Army in order to draw conclusions about the role of Islam in the Soviet

Union in general.[58] Although noting that Moscow's policies had alienated some Muslims from their faith, the report asserted that strong religious sentiment could be expected in rural Muslim areas, referring to the "generally existing fanaticism of Mohammedans." Islam, it was made clear, was the Soviets' weak flank. "The task of the Reich is, therefore, to support all efforts for the strengthening of Islam." Such a policy would make Germany appear as a "Protector of Islam."[59] Overall, a "revitalization of Islam" would have positive political results. A similar assessment was given a few months later, in May 1942, by the military intelligence office of the Wehrmacht in a memorandum titled "The USSR and Islam."[60] It asserted that "Communist propaganda had not been able to weaken Islam in Soviet Russia." Muslim religious sentiment (and closely linked tribal nationalism) had to be "exploited." The paper presented a detailed assessment of Soviet policies toward Islam since the October Revolution, both in the USSR's own Muslim territories and in the outside world. Muslims had proven to be a bulwark against Communism because "the Mohammedan religion is utterly opposed to the philosophical view of Bolshevism," with its atheist dogma.[61] In the course of 1942, as the army struggled to fortify its rule over the Crimea and German troops marched into the Caucasus, the idea of employing Islam against Moscow became more popular among Wehrmacht officers. Indeed, in the Muslim war zones, both in the Caucasus and the Crimea, military authorities engaged in a substantial policy of religious concessions and religious propaganda to win over local collaborators and to pacify these areas. Across the Muslim borderlands of the southern Soviet Union, German military authorities began to promote the Third Reich as the liberator of the faithful from the Bolshevist yoke (see Part II).

Moreover, the Wehrmacht began recruiting thousands of Muslim prisoners of war into its so-called Eastern Legions (*Ostlegionen*). Endorsed by Hitler, these units were formed under the auspices of the Saxon war veteran Ralph von Heygendorff and Oskar Ritter von Niedermayer, Hentig's old rival from the times of the jihad during the First World War.[62] In the interwar period, Niedermayer had first been military attaché at the German embassy in Moscow, later taught as a professor of war studies in Berlin, becoming a high-profile policy expert on the Soviet Union, Islam, and geopolitics, and finally, in 1941, entered the Wehrmacht again. Given his experience, he seemed particularly well suited to deal with Muslim recruits from the Soviet Union.[63] Idris, who remained in the service of the Foreign

Office, was now also regularly employed by the Wehrmacht, while army officials showed less interest in the mufti.[64] In some cases, particularly for the recruitment of prisoners of war and propaganda in the units, the army command cooperated with the East Ministry. Religious care was provided, and a religious propaganda campaign launched to politically influence the Muslim recruits. The Wehrmacht also established a further Islamic institution in Germany, imam courses at the University of Göttingen, to educate military mullahs (see Part III).

Finally, from early 1943 the SS became interested in Muslim affairs. Its engagement in Islamic policies first began in the Balkans, where the Germans became more involved from early 1943 onward, and soon expanded toward Muslims from the Soviet Union. In the end it was the SS, more than any other institution of the regime, that tried to exploit Islam for the war effort. Following their conception of the militant nature of Islam, leading officials in the SS—most importantly Heinrich Himmler; Ernst Kaltenbrunner, in charge of the Reich Security Head Office (*Reichssicherheitshauptamt*); his foreign intelligence chief, Walter Schellenberg; and Gottlob Berger, the pompous Swabian SS general who directed the SS Head Office (*SS-Hauptamt*), which was responsible for the recruitment and organization of the Waffen-SS—were convinced of the advantages to be gained from the exploitation of the Muslim faith.[65] The involvement of the SS inevitably resulted in various frictions with other institutions, like the Foreign Office in the Balkans or the East Ministry and the Wehrmacht in the Eastern territories.

In the Balkans, the SS pursued a radical pro-Muslim policy and launched an Islamic propaganda campaign that met with resistance from the Foreign Office (see Part II).[66] At the same time, Berger's SS Head Office began to form Muslim SS units with recruits from Bosnia, Herzegovina, and Albania, which had a distinct religious character (see Part III).

From late 1943 onward, the SS began to extend this policy to the Muslims of the Soviet Union.[67] The SS Head Office now sought to employ Islam and pan-Turanian ideology to revolutionize Stalin's Muslim subjects against Moscow. The cornerstone of this campaign was the new Eastern Muslim SS formation. In charge of its implementation was *SS-Hauptsturmführer* Reiner Olzscha of the SS Head Office's general "Volunteer Section," which was led by *SS-Standartenführer* Erich Spaarmann.[68] A careerist in his early thirties, Olzscha was one of the regime's rising experts on Central Asia, also leading the SS research group *Arbeitsgemeinschaft Turkestan*.[69] The most comprehensive outline of this scheme for the mobilization of the Muslims of the Soviet Union was given by Olzscha in a memorandum of 24 April 1944.[70] The lack of professionalism and the inefficiency of the East Ministry and Foreign Office in exploiting Moscow's non-Russian minorities made it necessary for the SS to step in, he wrote. Instead of splitting the Turkic groups, as the Wehrmacht had done in its Eastern Legions, the Muslims, the "strongest non-Slavic and non-Christian minority" of the Soviet Union, were to be formed into a solid bloc that could be directed against Moscow. Islam, with its "Russian- and Christian-hostile nature," as Olzscha put it, was the best force to undermine Stalin's state. Although Soviet suppression had weakened religious sentiment, Islam had to play a significant role in German political strategies on the Eastern Front. In fact, Olzscha called for the "strengthening of Islam" among the Muslims of the Eastern territories in order to "create an additional detonator for the disintegration of the Soviet enemy." Since, however, the "all-Islamic idea" was not as vital as in the Arab world, it had to be cautiously "reawakened." Olzscha underlined these ideas a month later in another report, again urging for the exploitation of the "almost 30 million Mohammedan Turks" of the Soviet Union.[71] In the Eastern Muslim SS formation, the "common faith" of the soldiers had to be strongly supported. The reawakening of Islam meant the strengthening of anti-Bolshevik forces, he declared.[72] In practice, the SS began to employ Eastern Muslim formations and provided its soldiers with special religious care and religiously charged political indoctrination and in 1944 also opened a mullah school in Dresden for the education of field imams—Idris was employed by the SS to direct the school (see Part III). To support this policy, the SS also employed experts on Islam in the Soviet Union, most notably Johannes Benzing. Olzscha was of course well aware that this program for Islamic mobilization had its precedents in the policies of Imperial Germany, reminding his interrogators after the war that in the First World War special provisions and a mosque had already been provided for Muslim prisoners of war and that during the Second World War the issue had occurred again.[73]

Eventually, toward the end of the war, the SS tried to expand the mobilization of Balkan and Eastern Muslims into a pan-Islamic mobilization campaign, targeting Muslims from all over the world. In his Nuremberg interrogation, Melchers remembered that the SS policy went more and more "in the direction of a mobilization and arming of every available Mohammedan."[74] "It is a matter of fact that the SS Head Office at the time strongly played with the pan-Islamic idea," Olzscha later explained.[75] The SS Head Office recruited Muslims in the Baltic, established plans for an Arab formation and a Muslim Indian army, considered recruiting Muslims from Bulgaria, and even began screening Muslim East African prisoners of war. Memoranda from the SS Head Office now had titles such as "Mobilization of Islam."[76] Within the SS Head Office, all of these formations, and more generally all political affairs regarding Muslim areas from North Africa to Turkestan and India, were to be organized in a section under Olzscha.[77] Though the section was reordered several times during 1944 and never became fully operational, it included an "Islam Office," which was to ensure a coherent policy toward all Muslim groups (see Part III).[78]

The increasing takeover of Muslim affairs by the SS can be illustrated in the case of the mufti, who was used more and more by the SS, while the Foreign Office considered him less and less important. In early 1943, supervision of the mufti was transferred from Ettel to Prüfer and Melchers and later to Hentig, who were less enthusiastic about him. In his Nuremberg interrogation, Melchers emphasized his poor relationship with the mufti.[79] Ribbentrop, Melchers explained, had gradually lost interest in his Arab collaborator. The mufti, now increasingly preoccupied with the SS, no longer even informed the Foreign Office of his activities. To the SS, which was more concerned about the Balkans and the Soviet Union, the mufti presented himself as a pan-Islamic leader.

Overall, German involvement with Islam during the Second World War had not been planned. It developed over the course of the war and gradually involved more and more war zones and parts of the regime. To a certain extent, this policy drew upon the political and strategic traditions of Germany's previous involvement with Islam, most notably during the First World War. Indeed, a closer look reveals significant continuities in both personnel and ideas. A remarkable number of officers who had engaged in Germany's policy of Muslim mobilization during the First World War became involved again. The most significant example is the elderly Oppenheim. In the Foreign Office, veterans like Fritz Grobba, Curt Prüfer, and Werner Otto von Hentig worked on Islamic affairs again, and some of them, most notably Hentig and Prüfer, kept in close contact with their former mentor, Oppenheim.[80] In a postwar testimony, Oppenheim even wrote that the Orient section of the Foreign Office had repeatedly turned to him for advice, asserting that he had kept the "best relations" with his old protégés and even with Melchers.[81] The Wehrmacht employed Oskar Ritter von Niedermayer. Alimjan Idris, who had rallied the faithful at the Wünsdorf and Zossen camps during the First World War, worked for the Foreign Office and later the Wehrmacht and the SS.

It is naturally more complicated to show that Nazi officials drew upon a reservoir of ideas about Islam and politics that had been established since the imperial period.[82] Nonetheless, some general observations can be made. German officials and experts had conceptualized Islam as a political instrument since the imperial era. They established an idea of Islam as something that could be used not only for social and political control in the colonies but also for active mobilization, a conception that had informed German policies during the First World War. The idea of Islam as a political force did not disappear after 1918. In the interwar period, especially during the 1930s, many experts discussed the politics of Islam, noting that Islam, despite the failed Muslim mobilization in 1914, remained a strong power in world affairs and a weak flank of the British, French, and Soviet empires. An important role in this respect was played not only by Haushofer's geopolitical thinkers but also by regional studies experts like Gerhard von Mende and Johannes Benzing.

An advantage of using Islam rather than ethnic and national slogans was that Berlin could avoid encouraging declarations of national independence. Anxious not to interfere in Italian, Spanish, and, later, Vichy interests in North Africa and the Middle East, and Croatian sovereignty in Bosnia and Herzegovinas, and eager to avoid promises about the future political status of the national minorities of the Soviet Union, German authorities sought to evade questions of national independence. Moreover, religion seemed to be a useful policy and propaganda tool to address ethnically, linguistically, and socially heterogeneous populations. Coherent policy and propaganda was much easier to organize for "Muslims" rather than for individual ethnic and national groups, such as distinct campaigns for Berbers and Arabs in North Africa, for individual non-Russian minorities in the Caucasus, the Crimea, and Central Asia, for the peoples of Bosnia, Herzegovina, and Albania in the Balkans, and so on. Finally, in the context of the delicate relationship between Nazi race theory and non-European peoples, the use of religious slogans ultimately enabled the Germans to avoid ethnic categories.

The Problem of Ideology

The promotion of an alliance with the Islamic world was first and foremost motivated by material interests and strategic concerns, not by ideology. However, it was the willingness to deal pragmatically with questions about race, as well as the lack of anti-Islamic attitudes among the regime's leadership, that made the promotion of such an alliance possible. After all, the Third Reich was an ideological state and the Second World War an ideological war, a *Weltanschauungskrieg*. Ideology mattered.

The most obvious obstacle to the regime's policy toward the Muslim world was its racism. Hitler had already postulated the racial inferiority of non-European peoples, particularly Arabs and Indians, in *Mein Kampf*. Praising the idea of European imperial hegemony, he had ridiculed anti-imperial movements as a "coalition of cripples" (*Koalition von Krüppeln*), which because of "racial inferiority" could never be an ally of the German people.[83] Hitler's chief ideologue, Alfred Rosenberg, in his *Der Mythus des 20. Jahrhunderts* (*The Myth of the 20th Century*), had explicitly welcomed the subjugation of the Islamic world under European imperial rule.[84] Soon after the seizure of power, however, German officials showed themselves to be more pragmatic.

For diplomatic reasons, Berlin had from early on tried to avoid any explicit racial discrimination against non-Jewish peoples from the Middle East. In fact, Turks, Iranians, and Arabs had been explicitly excluded from Nazi racial restrictions after the introduction of the Nuremberg laws—the Law for the Defense of German Blood and Honor and the Reich Citizenship Law—in 1935 had sparked international tensions with Turkey, Iran, and Egypt.[85] Following requests from the Turkish embassy, which was concerned about the legal discrimination against Turks and German citizens with Turkish background, the Wilhelmstraße in early 1936 urged that a definite decision be made about the racial classification of Turks.[86] Anxious not to damage relations with Turkey, the Foreign Office, Interior Ministry, Propaganda Ministry, and NSDAP Office of Racial Politics (*Rassenpolitisches Amt der NSDAP*) all agreed to send a clear signal to Ankara.[87] Although the Nuremberg laws referred to "Jews" and persons of

"German or kindred blood," these categories were in practice refined to "persons of German and kindred blood" and "Jews and other aliens," with the official commentary on the laws defining that the peoples of Europe and descendents of Europeans in the non-European world who had remained racially pure could be considered "kindred." In an internal decree, German authorities now clarified that Turkey was part of Europe, at the same time adding that other Middle Eastern countries like Egypt or Iran could not claim to be European. This statement was soon leaked to the foreign press and caused an international diplomatic storm. On 14 June 1936, *Le Temps* reported that Berlin had decided to exempt Turks from the Nuremberg laws, while Iranians, Egyptians, and Iraqis were considered "non-Aryan."[88] A day later, similar articles appeared in *La Bourse égyptienne* and in the Turkish newspaper *République*, causing an uproar among Iranian and Egyptian officials.[89] At once, the Foreign Office issued a press release, stating that these reports were unfounded and that this should have been immediately obvious given the fact that the Nuremberg laws do not refer to the term "Aryan" at all.[90] The Egyptian and Iranian ambassadors in Berlin, who insisted that their peoples were "kindred" with the Germans, were assured that the press reports were baseless and that the Nuremberg laws targeted only Jews.[91] Yet, the delicate question of whether Arabs and Iranians were considered "kindred" with Germans remained open, and whereas the Egyptian ambassador in Berlin merely demanded clarification that Egyptians were not targeted by German racial laws, Tehran's ambassador insisted on a definite statement that Iranians were considered racially related to the Germans.[92] After all, Riza Shah had, a year earlier, ordered that his country be called "Iran" instead of "Persia" in international affairs; the name "Iran" is a cognate of "Aryan" and refers to the "Land of the Aryans," and Iranian officials had internally made no secret that they believed this term useful given that "some countries pride themselves on being Aryan."[93] To discuss the issue, representatives of all major ministries assembled at the Foreign Office on 1 July 1936.[94] Walter Groß, head of the NSDAP Office of Racial Politics, made it clear that any formal declaration on racial relations was out of the question. Yet, it was agreed to inform the ambassadors that the racial laws did not target (non-Jewish) foreign citizens and that Iranian and Egyptian citizens were thus treated in the same way as other European (and indeed non-European) foreign nationals: marriage between (non-Jewish) non-German men and (non-Jewish) German women were accepted, while marriages between (non-Jewish) non-German women and (non-Jewish) German men were, after a racial examination of the woman, also possible. The question of German citizens with an Arab or Iranian background was studiously avoided. The Egyptians were conciliated.[95] Tehran, too, seemed satisfied after Groß had assured the Iranian ambassador in a meeting in Berlin that Germany's racial laws would not apply to Iranians even though Groß had evaded any definitive statements about the question of racial kinship.[96] A year later Groß confirmed in an internal note that, although he was not willing to restrict the racial legislation to Jews only, German authorities should act pragmatically when foreign policy interests were involved.[97] In short, the regime proved willing to be pragmatic when it came to the question of racial policies and relations with Turks, Arabs, and Iranians.

While the exclusion from racial discrimination could be backed by some race theory with regard to Persians and Turks, the case of the Arabs was more problematic, as they were seen by most racial ideologues as "Semites."[98] Regime officials were well aware that the term was problematic, as it targeted groups they did not wish to offend. As early as 1935, the Propaganda Ministry therefore instructed the press to avoid the terms "anti-Semitic" and "anti-Semitism" and to use words like "anti-Jewish" instead, as the fight was only against Jews and not Semites in general.[99] When the Arab world became part of Berlin's strategic planning during the war and German officials became even more concerned about not offending Arab sensibilities, efforts to prohibit the use of these terms were intensified. In early 1942, the office "Anti-Semitic Action" (*Antisemitische Aktion*) within the Propaganda Ministry was renamed "Anti-Jewish Action" (*Antjüdische Aktion*).[100] Later that year, Goebbels reiterated his instructions to the press to avoid the terms "Semitism" and "anti-Semitism" in their propaganda.[101] During the war, the Foreign Office, the *Amt Rosenberg*, and the SS would issue directives bolstering these decrees.[102] Ultimately, even the NSDAP Office of Racial Politics would support the abolition of the terms. In an open letter to Rashid 'Ali al-Kilani, which was published in the Nazi organ *Weltkampf* in late 1944, Walter Groß insisted that Jews had to be "strictly distinguished" from the peoples of the Middle East.[103] Therefore, the term "anti-Semitism" was wrong and had to be changed to "anti-Judaism." The text concluded: "National Socialist race theory in fact recognizes Arabs as members of a high-grade race, which looks back on a glorious and heroic history."[104] On trial in Jerusalem, Adolf Eichmann after the war reiterated this point, explaining that the term "anti-Semitism" was "incorrect" and should be replaced by "anti-Judaism," as the category "Semites" also included Arabs.[105]

As the deteriorating military situation made the recruitment of Muslims from the Balkans and the Soviet Union necessary, here, too, racial guidelines were relaxed. In 1943, when the Germans moved into Bosnia and Herzegovina, the SS declared the Muslims of the Balkans part of the "racially valuable peoples of Europe."[106] In fact, they were the first non-Germanic peoples allowed to enter the ranks of the Waffen-SS (see Part III). General Edmund Glaise von Horstenau, the Wehrmacht's plenipotentiary general in Croatia, jokingly called the new allies "Musligermanics" (*Muselgermanen*).[107]

Berlin took a similar approach to the Muslim Turkic peoples from the Soviet Union, targeted by German recruiters.[108] Although the non-Slavic minorities of the Eastern territories were generally considered racially superior to Slavs, these distinctions had initially played no role in practice. Ironically, it was these Soviet "Asiatics"—Caucasians and Central Asians—who played the central role in the regime's notorious *Untermensch* campaign, more central, in fact, than Russians or Ukrainians. In National Socialist propaganda, the term "Tatar," originally a collective name for the Eastern Turks, had a most derogatory meaning. Again, the Germans modified their language. In March 1942 the East Ministry issued an instruction about the term "Tatar" (*Tatare*), which was from then on to be avoided.[109] Instead, expressions like "Idel-Ural peoples" (*Idel-Uraler*) for the population of the Volga-Ural area, "Crimean Turks" (*Krimtürken*), and "Azerbaijanis" (*Aserbeidschaner*) had to be used. A few months later, the Propaganda Ministry ordered the press to refrain from polemics against these groups.[110] In an article in the *Zeitschrift für Politik*, von Hentig even argued that the term "Tatar" was not derogatory but honorable.[111] German propaganda toward Muslim Eastern Turks fighting in Hitler's armies was at pains to demonstrate respect. One article, published in field journals distributed among volunteers from the North Caucasus, explained that all tribes of the North Caucasus formed a *völkisch* unity and belonged to the Indo-Germanic race.[112] Quoting Groß, another article asserted that "German race theory" was "not directed against other peoples," with the exception of Jews.[113] However, racial mixing between Germans and Eastern Turks had to be avoided for the benefit of both peoples. German officers were instructed to explain to the "Turkic peoples" that they were "racially valuable" but that their "bloodstream" was different from the Germans' and therefore mixing would have negative consequences for both sides.[114] In 1944, when more and more Eastern Turkic volunteers were being deployed in the Reich, an instruction sheet ordered German soldiers to make sure that "the volunteer shows our German women respect and the necessary reservation," in the name of the "purity of the blood."[115] Unwilling to give up racial doctrine, German authorities had to strike a balance between ideology and military necessity. In practice, however, Muslims, not just from the Eastern territories but also from North Africa, the Middle East, and the Balkans, were frequently victims of racial discrimination (see Parts II and III).

While race posed an obstacle to German policies toward Muslims, the situation was different with religion. Islam had often been described in traditional European racial theories as a religion of (Arab) Semites or even as an inferior "Semitic religion," a view first promoted by the eminent French Oriental scholar and race theorist Ernest Renan in his infamous lecture "Islam and Science," given at the Sorbonne in 1883.[116] Yet, the notion of Islam as a "Semitic religion"—thus, a racist view of religion—did not play a major role in the thinking of Nazi officials and ideologues about Islam. In fact, many of them, including Hitler, distinguished between race and religion when speaking about Islam.

A number of members of the Nazi elite expressed their sympathy for Islam. The man who was perhaps most fascinated with the Muslim faith and enthusiastic about what he believed to be an affinity between National Socialism and Islam, was Himmler.[117] After discussing the Muslim SS division in the Balkans with Himmler and Hitler in Berlin in February 1943, Edmund Glaise von Horstenau noted that Himmler had expressed his disdain for Christianity, while explaining that he found Islam "very admirable."[118] Hitler had made a similar remark. A few months later, according to Horstenau, Himmler brought up the subject again: "We also spoke about the Muslim question. He came again to speak about the heroic character of the Mohammedan religion, while expressing his disdain for Christianity, and especially Catholicism."[119] The most intimate insights into Himmler's attitude toward Islam are given by his doctor, Felix Kersten, in his notorious memoirs.[120] Kersten wrote an entire chapter on Himmler's "Enthusiasm for Islam," a chapter that for some reason was excluded from the English translation.[121] Himmler, convinced that Muhammad was one of the greatest men in history, had apparently collected various books on Islam and biographies of the Prophet.[122] On 2 December 1942, he told Kersten that he wanted to visit the Islamic countries to continue his studies once the war was over.[123] According to the physician, Himmler saw Islam as a masculine, soldierly religion, telling him in late 1942:

> Mohammed knew that most people are terribly cowardly and stupid. That is why he promised every warrior who fights courageously and falls in battle two [sic] beautiful women. . . . This is the kind of language a soldier understands. When he believes that he will be welcomed in this manner in the afterlife, he will be willing to give his life; he will be enthusiastic about going to battle and not fear death. You may call this primitive and laugh about it . . . but it is based on deeper wisdom. A religion must speak a man's language.[124]

Himmler, who had left the Catholic Church in 1936, would regularly contrast his idea of Islam with Christianity, particularly Catholicism. Christianity made no promises to soldiers who died in battle, he lamented. There was no reward for bravery: "And now compare this, Herr Kersten, according to these points of view, to the religion of the Mohammedans, a religion of people's soldiers."[125] Islam he considered a practical faith that provided believers with guidance for everyday life: "Look, how intelligent this religion is."[126] The *Reichsführer* would also come to share his interpretation of Islamic history with Kersten. He regretted that the Turkish Muslim armies had failed to conquer Europe in the seventeenth century:

> Let us assume that the Turks in whose ranks Europeans were fighting as well, even in high positions, had conquered Vienna and Europe in 1683 instead of having been forced to retreat. If the Mohammedans had gained the victory at the time and Islam had then swept victoriously over Europe, the Christian churches would have been completely depoliticized. . . . For the Turks were religiously tolerant, they allowed each religion to continue to exist, provided it was no longer involved in politics—otherwise it was finished.[127]

Kersten later asserted that he "had learned something" from Himmler's remarks "about Mohammedanism."[128] Toward the end of the war, in the autumn of 1944, he was summoned to Hochwald, Himmler's field quarters in Eastern Prussia. Finland had just declared war on Germany, and Himmler was bedridden with stomach cramps. Entering Himmler's bedroom, Kersten noticed: "He was still in bed and in great pain. The Koran lay on his bedside table."[129] According to Kersten, Himmler had become acquainted with the Qur'an through Rudolf Heß.[130]

Unsurprisingly, Himmler was particularly eager to share his ideas on Islam with the grand mufti.[131] In his memoirs, al-Husayni remarked that most of his discussions with Himmler had revolved around the Islamic and Arab world. Al-Husayni had been particularly fascinated by Himmler's ideas about the European confessional wars:

> Among Himmler's unique statements which we heard on one of our visits was his remark relating to his study of German history. He stated that the past religious wars between Catholics and Protestants faced by the German people of the Dark Ages, such as the Hundred Years War and other wars, had reduced the population of Germany from 35 million to five million. The brave and warrior-like people of Germany were the people who had lost the most from these wars. Then he said, "There were two opportunities for us then, and for Europe as a whole, to be saved from this bloodbath, but we missed these opportunities. The first appeared when the Arabs invaded from the West (from Andalusia) and the second was when the Ottomans invaded from the East. Unfortunately, the German people played a big role in routing these two invasions, and depriving Europe of the flourishing spiritual light and civilization of Islam."[132]

Recounting this historical speculation, al-Husayni after the war made no secret of the fact that he had been much impressed by Himmler's "intelligence, cunning, and breadth of knowledge."[133]

Himmler's views on Islam and history were shared by his right-hand man in the Waffen-SS, Gottlob Berger, who also believed in a strong affinity between Germanic and Islamic culture. One SS officer, Erich von dem Bach-Zelewski, spoke to his US interrogators in Nuremberg about Berger's ideas on Islam, which he had expressed during the war at a meeting with Himmler and al-Husayni:

> Berger developed a new historical theory by saying Germany would be better off and the old Germanic Kultur would not have perished if

at that time in Vienna God wouldn't have helped the Europeans, that is the Germans, but rather would have helped the Moslems or Mohammedans, because if they had been victorious in Vienna, then Jewish Christianity wouldn't have been able to spread all over Europe and we would really have a Germanic culture and not a Jewish one.[134]

It is unknown whether Berger had picked up these ideas about 1683 from Himmler, or the other way around, or if the situation was in fact the same as that recalled by al-Husayni. In any case, Berger's positive attitude toward Islam repeatedly made itself clear in his directives when organizing Muslim SS units (see Part III).

Hitler showed himself equally fascinated with Islam. In *Mein Kampf* he had recognized the rapid "advance" of the "Mohammedan faith" in Africa and Asia, compared to which Christian missionaries there "can show only very modest successes."[135] Yet, at the same time he had dismissively noted that a "holy war" in Egypt would soon end in British machine gun fire.[136]

After the war, Eva Braun's sister, Ilse, remembered that Hitler had often discussed the Islamic religion with her and Eva.[137] In his table talks, Hitler repeatedly compared Islam with Christianity in order to devalue the latter, especially Catholicism. In contrast to Islam, which he portrayed as a strong and practical faith, he described Christianity as a soft, artificial, weak religion of suffering.[138] Whereas Islam was a religion of the here and now, Hitler told his entourage, Christianity was a religion of the kingdom to come—a kingdom that was, compared to the paradise promised by Islam, deeply unattractive.

For Hitler, religion was a means of supporting human life on earth practically and not an end in itself. "The precepts ordering people to wash, to avoid certain drinks, to fast at appointed dates, to take exercise, to rise with the sun, to climb to the top of the minaret—all these were obligations invented by intelligent people," he remarked in October 1941 in the presence of Himmler.[139] "The exhortation to fight courageously is also self-explanatory. Observe, by the way, that, as a corollary, the Mussulman [*sic*] was promised a paradise peopled with houris, where wine flowed in streams—a real earthly paradise," he enthused. Christianity, in contrast, promised nothing comparable: "The Christians, on the other hand, declare themselves satisfied if after their death they are allowed to sing Hallelujahs!"[140] Two months later he commented in a similar vein: "I can imagine people being enthusiastic about the paradise of Mahomet [*sic*], but as for the insipid paradise of the Christians!"[141] Hitler would also compare Islam with other Asian religions that he admired. "Just as in Islam, there is no kind of terrorism in the Japanese State religion, but, on the contrary, a promise of happiness," he declared on 4 April 1942.[142] In contrast, Christianity had "universalized" the "terrorism of religion," which in his eyes was a result of "Jewish dogma." A few months later, when engaging in his usual agitation against the Catholic Church, which was, he told his audience, foisted on the Germans by "Jewish filth and priestly twaddle," he expressed his anger that the Germans had been haunted by Christianity, "while in other parts of the globe religious teaching like that of Confucius, Buddha and Mohammed offers an undeniably broad basis for the religious-minded."[143] Fulminating against the Christian Church's adherence to "proven untruth," he came again to speak of Islam:[144] "It adds little to our knowledge of the Creator when some person presents to us an indifferent copy of a man as his conception of the Deity. In this respect, at least, the Mohammedan is more enlightened, when he says: to form a conception of Allah is not vouchsafed to man." Expanding on this topic, he reflected on Islamic history. The Islamic period of the Iberian peninsula he described as the "most cultured, the most intellectual and in every way best and happiest epoch in Spanish history," one that was "followed by the period of the persecutions with its unceasing atrocities."[145]

Hitler had expressed this view before. After the war Albert Speer remembered that Hitler had been much impressed by a historical interpretation he had learned from some distinguished Muslims. To quote Speer:

> When the Mohammedans attempted to penetrate beyond France into Central Europe during the eighth century, his visitors had told him [Hitler], they had been driven back at the Battle of Tours. Had the Arabs won this battle, the world would be Mohammedan today. For theirs was a religion that believed in spreading the faith by the sword and subjugating all nations to that faith. The Germanic peoples would have become heirs to that religion. Such a creed was perfectly suited to the Germanic temperament. Hitler said that the conquering Arabs, because of their racial inferiority, would in the long run have been unable to contend with the harsher climate and conditions of the country. They could not have kept down the more

vigorous native, so that ultimately not Arabs but Islamized Germans could have stood at the head of this Mohammedan Empire.[146]

Here Hitler distinguished between Islam and the "race" of its followers. Whereas he perceived Islam to be a superior religion, he described its Arab adherents as an inferior race. However, Hitler did not perceive Islam as a "Semitic" religion as such, separating religion from race. Despite his fascination with Islam as a religion, for Hitler the race of its followers remained a silent but persistent problem. He concluded this historical speculation about the Islamic conquest of Europe by remarking: "You see, it's been our misfortune to have the wrong religion. . . . The Mohammedan religion . . . would have been much more compatible with us than Christianity. Why did it have to be Christianity with its meekness and flabbiness?"[147]

Hitler's adjutant, Nicolaus von Below, also remembered in his memoirs that Hitler had been impressed by the thought that Charles Martel's victory in 732 had contributed to the disintegration of Europe and that it was, in fact, the Eton-educated Aga Khan III, at that time president of the League of Nations, who had, when visiting the Obersalzberg in October 1937, captivated Hitler with the idea that "Islam could have kept the unity of Europe."[148] Below remarked: "Hitler found his own view of the course of history affirmed by the Aga Khan. He would often evince his sympathy for Islam." Two years later, in the summer of 1939, Hitler discussed the same issue with the Saudi envoy Khalid al-Hud al-Qargani at a reception at the Berghof. Werner Otto von Hentig, who attended the meeting, reported: "The thought, thrown into the conversation by Khalid al-Hud, of what would have become of Europe if Charles Martel had not defeated the Saracens, but instead had instilled in them the Germanic spirit, and so, carried by Germanic dynamism, had transformed Islam in their own way, was discussed," adding: "The Führer described this line of thought as very remarkable."[149] Whether it was al-Hud who came up with the idea (as Hentig claimed) or Hitler had picked it up two years earlier from the Aga Khan (as Below recounted) and then brought it up again with the Arab envoy must remain an open question. In any case, Hitler was thoroughly fascinated by this historical speculation. Hermann Neubacher, special representative of the Foreign Office for the Balkans, also noted in his autobiography that "Hitler showed great sympathy for Islam" and that he was convinced that "if the Germans had become Muslims, they would have achieved more in history."[150] According to Neubacher, Hitler had further described Islam, in a conversation, as a "religion of men" (*Männerreligion*). Gendered notions of Islam—the idea that the religion was a strong, masculine, martial faith— were indeed expressed repeatedly by both Himmler and Hitler. Henry Picker, an official in the Führer Headquarters who took notes of Hitler's table talks, remembered that Hitler had often praised the "attitude" of the "soldiers of Islam."[151]

To be sure, our knowledge of the ideas about Islam that circulated within the Nazi elite mostly comes from memoirs and postwar testimonies, which, of course, must be read with caution. Nonetheless, these accounts draw a remarkably coherent picture of the ideological notions of Islam prevalent among the higher echelons of the regime. And admiration for Islam was by no means limited to the Nazi elite. In fact, similar attitudes appear in a number of ideological books and articles that were published in Germany during the 1930s and 1940s.

A major figure promoting an ideological interpretation of Islam in Germany was the Nazi propagandist Johann von Leers, who advanced the idea of a historical hostility between Islam and Judaism. The Qur'an, he claimed in an article in the propaganda journal *Die Judenfrage* in late 1942, described the Jews as satanic.[152] The Islamic world had kept the Jews suppressed, whereas in Europe they had been allowed to emancipate. It was Islam, Leers argued, that had prevented the Arabs from being dominated by Judaism. The Islamic struggle with the "Jewish problem" had already begun in the times of the Prophet.[153] "Unquestionably, one result of Mohammed's hostility toward the Jews," he declared, was that "oriental Jewry was completely paralyzed by Islam," adding: "If the rest of the world had adopted a similar approach, we would not have a Jewish question today."[154] Infuriated by their treatment in Muslim lands, Jews had become the fiercest conspirators against Islam, even orchestrating Christian polemics against Muslims, Leers continued. "It may thereby be noted that the Crusades were, to a not inconsiderable extent, also unleashed by Jewish agitation." Finally, he praised "the immortal contribution of the religion of Islam" to the defense against Judaism. "Islam," Leers concluded, "opened for many peoples the path to a higher culture and gave its adherents an education and human form that still today makes a Muslim who is serious about his faith one of the most dignified phenomena in this chaotic world."[155] In another article, Johann von Leers again warned against "Christian polemics" about Islam: "For the pious Muslim, to be sure, the Jew is an enemy, not merely an unbeliever who may convert or who might be, albeit not a follower of Islam, a respectable man—the Jew is in fact the predestined enemy, who already wanted to bring down the work of the Prophet."[156] After the war Leers settled in Egypt, where he converted to Islam and took the name "Omar Amin von Leers." Another propagandist of the regime who spread similar ideas was Else Marquardsen-Kamphövener, a publicist who had grown up in Istanbul and who would continue to write on Islam in postwar Germany. At the height of the war, Marquardsen-Kamphövener published an article on "Islam and Its Founder" in the journal *Wir und die Welt*, offering an anti-Jewish interpretation of the Prophet's life.[157] In the times of Muhammad, the Jews had, for the first time, encountered a hostility "which still exists today and will last as long as there are Mohammedans," she explained.[158]

In the war years, the German papers printed various articles that carried similar messages.[159] The Propaganda Ministry, in fact, repeatedly instructed the press to promote a positive image of Islam. Even before the war, Goebbels had warned the editorial offices of newspapers and magazines that any criticism of Islam was "undesirable." [160] Urging journalists to give credit to the "Islamic world as a cultural factor," the Propaganda Ministry in autumn 1942 instructed magazines to discard negative images of Islam, which had been spread by church polemicists for centuries, and instead to promote an alliance with the Islamic world, which was described as both sharply anti-Bolshevik and anti-Jewish.[161] References to similarities between Jews and Muslims, as manifested in the ban of pork and the ritual circumcision, were to be avoided. A few months later, the ministry added that magazines should report about the "USA as the enemies of Islam."[162] In early 1943 it similarly decreed that they should stress America's and Britain's hostility toward the Muslim religion.[163] That spring, the ministry instructed German journalists to report on the "persecution of the Mohammedans by the Soviets."[164] Cases of violent suppression of the Muslims and their faith in the Soviet borderlands and occupied territories were to be used as leverage to discuss the Soviet Union as an enemy of Islam in more general terms. The reason for the hostility of "Soviet Jews" toward Islam was that the Muslims, compared to other minorities in the Soviet Union, had put up the strongest resistance to Bolshevism. Yet, these instructions were not always effective. Not all propagandists and party ideologues conformed to the official discourse on Islam. When, for instance, the prominent Nazi journalist Helmut Sündermann published an article in the *Völkischer Beobachter* in late 1944, comparing Islam with Bolshevism, SS officials were alarmed, complaining that it had offended Muslim readers and requesting stricter censorship.[165]

Ideological interpretations of Islamic history echoing those of the regime's elite, ideologues, and propagandists can also be found, though often in more subtle form, in academic writings after 1933, most importantly those of German Orientalists.[166] In a public lecture on Islamic art delivered in 1934 in Berlin, the respected Oriental scholar Ernst Kühnel constructed a theory of the affinity between Nordic culture and Islam.[167] Because of their cultural similarities, Kühnel told his audience, the Normans had developed great sympathy for Islamic art and culture after conquering Sicily. Islam conformed much more to the conquerors' "Nordic nature" (*nordisches Menschentum*) than did the culture of the "Frankish world," which they had always perceived as something foreign.[168] Kühnel was by no means the only expert in Oriental studies to construct such links to Islam. In his "Remarks on Modern Islam," the eminent Orientalist Hans Heinrich Schaeder also suggested that a closeness existed between the Germanic peoples and Muslims.[169] Schaeder also stressed the Prophet's hostility toward the Jews, as did his colleague Franz Taeschner of the University of Münster.[170] Johann Fück, professor of Oriental studies at the University of Frankfurt, portrayed Muhammad as a "natural Führer" and Islam as a *völkisch* bulwark against "foreign infiltration" (*Überfremdung*).[171] Similar interpretations can also be found in the writings of the race theorist Ferdinand Clauß. A close companion and competitor of Hans F. K. Günther, Clauß was one of the regime's major race ideologues, whose book *Race and Soul* (*Rasse und Seele*) became one of the most influential works in the field. In his writings, he postulated that a considerable affinity existed between the "Nordic race" and Islam.[172] Toward the end of the war, Clauß also wrote reports for the SS Head Office about "points of contact" between the "liberation struggle of Islam" and Germany's war, suggesting the propagation of the "commonalities in the worldview between National Socialism and the Qur'an."[173] Under the title "Preparation of an Operation for Winning Over the Islamic Peoples," he reflected on the age-old friendship between Germans and Islam and pointed to the "ideological proximity" of "National

Socialism" to the "beliefs of Islam."[174] His attempts to become involved in German policies toward Islam were unsuccessful. Clauß remained a great admirer of Islam after the war and converted to it.

Finally, all of the major geopolitical writers on Islam, most notably Schmitz, Lindemann, and Reichardt, referred to alleged ideological affinities between Nazism and Islam. Schmitz explicitly mentioned anti-Jewish passages of the Qur'an.[175] Lindemann claimed that "Islam and National Socialism exhibit manifold parallels and analogies." He referred to the Nazi leadership principle (*Führerprinzip*), which was, in his eyes, similar to the idea of the caliphate—in his language, the "Führer of the believers"—as well as to the strict commitment to their respective causes and struggles and to the ideal of discipline.[176] To substantiate his claims, he drew on examples from the Qur'an and the life of the Prophet.[177] Thomas Reichardt, for his part, characterized Islam as an "authoritarian and total" political power.[178] Islam was described as the "arch enemy" of the "democratic powers" and "Bolshevism."[179] Confronting negative misconceptions, which he believed were spread by the church, Reichardt characterized Islam as inherently modern and revolutionary.[180] In the last chapter of Reichardt's book, the pan-Islamic activist Zaki Ali elaborated on these ideas.[181] Islam, he affirmed, went through a process of renewal after the First World War, just like Germany under Hitler. Nazism and Islam shared a hatred of Bolshevism, and the idea of the caliphate was nothing less than the "Führer of the believers" (he used this expression before Lindemann).[182] "In accordance with National Socialism, Islam sees the ideal state expressed in the *Führerprinzip*, as Islam knows no dynasty," he proclaimed.

Other Muslim writers in Germany promoted similar views. Remarkable in this respect is the book *Islam, Judentum, Bolschewismus* (*Islam, Judaism, Bolshevism*), published in 1938, by Mohamed Sabry.[183] For Sabry, the Qur'an and the Muslim faith formed the best bulwark against Bolshevism: "The deep bond between Muslims and their religion is the best guarantee that Bolshevism can never gain a foothold in the Islamic countries."[184] Moreover, he stressed that Judaism had been the arch enemy of Islam since ancient times.[185] Drawing on the Nazi belief in a connection between Judaism and Bolshevism, he explained: "The Jewish mentality created Bolshevism and Bolshevism is the carrier of the Jewish mentality. Made by Jews, led by Jews—therewith Bolshevism is the natural enemy of Islam."[186] He tried to substantiate his ideas with quotations from the Qur'an, other religious texts, and with references to the life of Muhammad. The book was published by the *Deutsche Hochschule für Politik* in its series *Ideen und Gestalt des Nationalsozialismus*, which was dedicated to the ideological education of Germans.[187] Written along the same lines was a booklet on Islam and National Socialism published by a Muslim writer in German-occupied Paris.[188] In 1940, German censors considered the publication of a manuscript titled "The Prophet Mohammed and the Jews" (*Der Prophet Mohamed und die Juden*) by the Syrian writer Zeki Kiram, who had served in the Ottoman army and had come to Berlin in the First World War.[189] A well-known Islamic publicist and disciple of Rashid Rida, Kiram had briefly worked as a translator for the Foreign Office. His text was eventually rejected due to "factual flaws and mistakes."[190] In 1942, he made another attempt and submitted a manuscript titled "Nordic Belief in God, Islam, and the Zeitgeist" (*Nordischer Gottglaube, Islam und Geist der Zeit*) to the publishing house of the *SS Ahnenerbe*.[191] This project, too, failed. The SS agreed with Kiram's view on Islam and his fierce attacks on the Roman Church but was offended by his idea that the Christian faith was connected to the Nordic racial nature of the German people.[192] A German biography of the mufti, written by the Arab publicist Mansur al-Din Ahmad, met with greater approval from the German authorities. In late 1942, the Foreign Office sent the manuscript of his book to the Propaganda Ministry, declaring that publication would not be problematic.[193] The Propaganda Ministry was willing to publish 10,000 copies, twice as large a print run as was usual during that period of the war. Although it was approved, it seems that the book never came out. In 1943, however, Berlin did print a biography of the mufti, authored by Kurt Fischer-Weth.[194] It contained the usual praise of the Muslim faith and proclaimed the "rebirth of the Islamic force."[195]

In September 1943, the NSDAP explicitly stated that it accepted members who were "followers of Islam."[196] The circular, signed by Martin Bormann personally, emphasized that, as the party accepted Christians as members, there was no reason to exclude Muslims. This decision gave legal expression to the lack of genuine ideological reservations about Islam.

❧ PART II ❧

MUSLIMS IN THE WAR ZONES

CHAPTER THREE

Islam and the War in North Africa and the Middle East

On the morning of 11 February 1941, German troops landed on the shores of Tripoli in Italian-ruled Libya and in the following months advanced toward Cairo and the Middle East. At the same time, Berlin launched a major, religiously charged propaganda campaign directed at the region, promoting Germany as the defender of the faithful.

The population in most parts of North Africa and the Middle East at the time had been subjugated to direct or indirect imperial rule. In the nineteenth century, as the Ottoman Empire crumbled, the European powers had taken control of North Africa and, following the Ottoman collapse, had come to dominate major parts of the Middle East. On the eve of the Second World War, Fascist Italy ran an oppressive colonial regime in Libya. France ruled Algeria and the protectorates of Tunisia and Morocco, with the exception of the northern coastal strip of Spanish Morocco, and governed the Levantine mandates in Syria and Lebanon. Great Britain controlled the territories of Egypt, Palestine, Transjordan, Iraq, and beyond, having established a vast, though undeclared, empire in the Middle East.[1] At the same time, Zionist mass migration to mandate Palestine was widely seen as a European attempt to colonize the country, leading to a growing number of riots, most notably the revolt of 1936–1939.

From the outset, European imperial authorities had been confronted with various forms of resistance. Anticolonial nationalism (both religious and secular) was on the rise, especially among urban elites. One of the most persistent and socially widespread forces of anti-imperial mobilization was religion. Anticolonialism and Islam were in fact often closely intertwined, with religious authorities leading anti-imperial movements and employing Islamic rhetoric to unite Muslims—a phenomenon that could be observed particularly well in North Africa, where almost every major anticolonial revolt since the nineteenth century had been coupled with the call for armed jihad.[2] The British Empire had frequently fought Islamic uprisings, most famously the legendary Mahdi revolt in Sudan. The French conquests in North Africa had been followed by a number of similar rebellions, among them the revolts of 'Abd al-Qadir and the Qadiri order. After the turn of the century, the French became embroiled in a colonial war against the warriors of Muhammad Ali al-Sanusi and his Islamic order in the southern Sahara. The Sanusi movement would later also wage jihad against Italy's conquest of Cyrenaica. The Italians suppressed the rebels with great brutality, marking the crushing of the resistance in 1931 with the public hanging of the elderly Sanusi commander, 'Umar al-Mukhtar.[3]

Hitler had not planned to move into North Africa or to get involved in the Middle East, having always considered the territories as being justly under European imperial rule. Throughout the 1930s, Berlin cared little about an alliance with the region's Muslim population. A prominent example of this lack of interest in Arab matters is the Haavara-Transfer Agreement, which Berlin had signed with the Jewish Agency in the summer of 1933, supporting Jewish passage from Germany to Palestine; the contract caused much suspicion among Muslims in Palestine and beyond.[4] In general, Berlin considered the region as part of the Italian, Spanish, French, and British spheres of interest. After the fall of France, Hitler even allowed Vichy to keep the French possessions in the Maghrib and Mashriq, along with the rest of its colonial empire. Berlin's famous "Arab proclamation" (*Arabienerklärung*) of 1940 spoke only vaguely about Germany's "feelings of friendship for the Arabs."[5]

It was the military situation that led to a German involvement in the region.[6] In late 1940, Italian troops under the command of General Rodolfo Graziani were forced more and more on the defensive in their war against the British in North Africa. To prevent a military disaster, Hitler finally agreed to send support, deploying Rommel's Africa Corps in early 1941. For the following two years, German troops fought in Tunisia, the Libyan Desert, and on the fringes of Egypt, where they advanced until they reached the small desert train station al-'Alamayn in July 1942, just 150 miles from Cairo. After the defeat there by Bernard Montgomery's Eighth Army in early November, the Germans quickly retreated. In the same month, Anglo-American troops landed in Algeria and Morocco ("Operation Torch") to support Montgomery's battle against the remains of Rommel's tank army. Eventually, in January 1943, the Germans retreated to Tunisia. On 13 May 1943, Colonel General Hans-Jürgen von Arnim, who had succeeded Rommel a few months earlier, capitulated at Tunis.

The military involvement in the Maghrib changed German strategic thinking about the Middle East.[7] Following the invasion of the Soviet Union in the summer of 1941, the German army command drew up plans to advance from North Africa to the Middle East, uniting with German troops coming from the Caucasus. At once, Iran became subject to German military interest.[8] As early as the summer of 1941, Berlin became embroiled in the failed coup of Rashid Ali al-Kilani in Iraq and sent a special mission under General Hellmuth Felmy to Baghdad.[9] Al-Husayni, at this time still in Iraq, called for a "holy war" against Great Britain on the state broadcast.[10] Employing full military force, the British thwarted the coup. In the same months, British and Free French soldiers occupied Vichy-controlled Syria and Lebanon, while Anglo-American and Soviet troops invaded Iran.[11] They considered the region important not only because of its oil fields but also because of its geopolitical location. Seen from a wider perspective, the war in North Africa and the Middle East was, no doubt, also an imperial war.[12]

With German involvement in the region, the local populations in North Africa and behind the enemies' front lines in the Middle East were soon seen as strategically significant. In the Maghrib, where the army was dependent on long supply lines, Berlin could not afford any conflicts with the local Muslim population living along the coastal roads. More importantly, a pro-German population behind the front lines, in North Africa and the Middle East, could weaken the Allied position.

In an attempt to win over the Muslim population, Berlin launched a massive propaganda campaign in North Africa and the Middle East. Pamphlets and radio broadcasts were designed to win support among Muslims in the German rear areas in the Maghrib, foster a defeatist atmosphere, and stir populations into open revolt behind Allied front lines in Egypt and the wider Middle East. Officials in Whitehall had a "considerable fear of the Muslims, a fact that is exceptionally important for us, and which we exploit extensively in our propaganda directed at Arabia," Goebbels noted in his diary in the summer of 1942.[13] Indeed, by that time, Axis propaganda directed at North Africa and the Middle East had already intensified. This propaganda was mainly organized and directed by the Orient section of the political department of the Foreign Office in cooperation with the Propaganda Ministry and partly with the Wehrmacht.

Axis agents distributed pamphlets carrying, as *Foreign Affairs* put it, "their gospel among the pilgrims en route to and from the Holy Cities."[14] Berlin spread stories of alleged attacks by the Allies against Islam and their "misbehavior—especially towards mosques and holy places." A few months later the same journal remarked: "Thus he [Hitler] has had his agents at work for months stirring up Islamic resentment against England. He hopes to be able to capitalize among the Moslems from his position as the world's greatest Jew-baiter . . . Hitler is manifestly endeavoring to arouse all Moslems against Britain."[15]

Indeed, German propaganda in the region propagated a politicized version of Islam, promoting Germany as the friend of Islam and the Allies as its enemy. Berlin made explicit use of religious rhetoric, terminology, and imagery and sought to engage with and reinterpret religious doctrine and concepts to manipulate Muslims for political and military purposes. Sacred texts such as the Qur'an and religious imperatives such as jihad were politicized to incite religious violence against alleged common enemies, most notably the British Empire, the United States, Bolshevism, and Judaism. Besides references to mutual foes, recurring topoi in German propaganda included references to values that Nazism and Islam supposedly shared, such as the ideals of order, leadership, and strength.

Islam, Anticolonialism, and the Battle of France

Among the first Muslims ever targeted by German propaganda during the Second World War were colonial soldiers fighting in the French army during the Battle of France.[16] Using pamphlets and loudspeakers, the Germans urged these Muslim troops to change sides. Most of this propaganda drew heavily on religious rhetoric, slogans, and iconography. In early 1940, for instance, army propagandists dropped pamphlets behind the French lines, printed in green, the color of the Prophet, and written in both French and Arabic, addressing France's North African "Muslims."[17] To reach ordinary colonial soldiers, the Arabic texts of the leaflets were not in standard Arabic but in Maghribi dialect, or *Darija*. One of the flyers, shaped like a flag and adorned with a silver saber, warned the pious not to defend "the enemies of Islam" and called on them to desert: "Come over to the Germans, who have never done any harm to Muslims" (Figure 3.1a and b). Another one, with the same message, proclaimed: "The true Muslim never

3.1a and b German propaganda pamphlet, 1940 (both sides)
(BA–MA).

fights for the enemies of Islam, who have taken your mosques and turned them into churches, and who today send you to die to save the lives of Christians" (Figure 3.2a and b). Both leaflets invoked the recent past of anticolonial resistance in North Africa, referring to 'Abd al-Karim's jihad in the Moroccan Rif, the Algerian resistance leader Khalid ibn Hashim (Amir Khalid)—'Abd al-Qadir's grandson—and the anticolonial movement in Tunisia. In Wehrmacht circles and at the Foreign Office, sporadic discussions about propaganda for Muslim soldiers in the French forces and promoting the Third Reich as a "friend of the Mohammedans" had begun in late 1939.[18] One of the first suggestions was to produce small amulets shaped in the form of the "hand of Fatima" (hamsa).[19]

Captured Muslim soldiers—their number rose to nearly 90,000 during the Battle of France—were treated cautiously by the authorities.[20] Following the military engagement in North Africa in 1941, they were increasingly considered politically significant. Just as in the First World War, German officials were eager to demonstrate their respect for Islam, granting Muslims various privileges. On 12 May 1941, the Wehrmacht ordered that the prisoners' religious customs were to be tolerated.[21] Directives about the burial of French prisoners of early 1942 instructed that deceased Muslims were to have a wooden plate with the symbol of a fez instead of a cross on their graves.[22] Referring to "reasons of Islamic politics" (islampolitische Gründe), the army command eventually also ordered respect for Islamic dietary requirements, with beef or mutton to be substituted for pork.[23] In a prisoner of war camp near Berlin, a mosque constructed in Maghribi style, was built.[24] Smaller mosques and prayer rooms were also established in other camps. Imams, usually ordinary prisoners who could read the Qur'an, were employed to provide religious care and to act as propagandists, giving collaboration religious legitimacy.[25] To indoctrinate the prisoners, the Germans also distributed camp papers and pamphlets.[26] The intent behind these policies was not only to potentially recruit inmates as guides, informers, and propagandists in the Maghrib but also, more generally, to create positive images of Germany that the soldiers would spread when sent back to their home countries. Indeed, after the Germans engaged militarily in North Africa, many of these prisoners were released. Overall, however, inmates seem to have been less receptive to German advances than officials in Berlin had hoped. In practice, many Muslim captives faced ill treatment by their German guards.[27] Muslims from sub-

3.2a and b German propaganda pamphlet, 1940 (both sides) (BA–MA).

Saharan Africa suffered particularly brutal abuse; hundreds were shot in the early period of the war.[28]

A great interest in the fate of North African prisoners of war was expressed by the religious dignitaries of the *Grande Mosquée de Paris*. Situated on the Left Bank, in the fifth arrondissement, the mosque had been built by the French government after the First World War to express its gratitude for the Muslims' war efforts and was directed by the charismatic Algerian religious scholar Si Kaddour Benghabrit, who had supported the French politically and propagandistically between 1914 and 1918.[29] After the fall of France, Benghabrit soon began to engage with the Germans (Figure 3.3). Concerned about the well-being of Muslims in the prisoner of war camps, he consulted with officials of the German embassy in Paris in early 1941, asking for special provisions.[30] Benghabrit even proposed to send a number of North African imams, assuring the authorities that he would personally take responsibility for their loyalty. He also offered his own services, proposing to supervise the religious affairs of the prisoners and indicating that he was prepared to speak on Germany's Arabic broadcast propaganda service. The Germans were naturally not interested in opening their camps to unknown Maghribian imams.[31] Yet they were still eager to establish good relations with the mosque. One of the most important centers of Islam in Nazi-occupied Western Europe, it was not only the heart of the Muslim community in France, which had grown to more than 100,000 during the war, but also had close ties to the Maghrib. German officials in Paris supported Si Kaddour Benghabrit and made some attempts to use the mosque for their propaganda.[32] Benghabrit, for his part, tried to improve conditions for his community by cultivating cordial relations with the authorities. Still, German officials kept a close eye on the mosque, suspecting that it provided Jews with certificates attesting that they were Muslims.[33] After the war, claims were made that the mosque had organized help for hundreds of Jews, but so far no archival evidence has been found to substantiate these stories.

During the war against France, Berlin also made some first attempts to influence Muslims in the French colonial world, using both broadcast and print propaganda. A pamphlet produced by the Foreign Office and distributed in French North Africa in the spring of 1940 called on Muslims to turn against their imperial masters, interweaving anticolonial and religious rhetoric.[34] It portrayed the war as a sacred opportunity to rise against

3.3 Si Kaddour Benghabrit, rector of the Grande Mosquée de Paris, greets Wehrmacht officials (*Archive of the Mémorial de la Shoah, Paris*).

imperial oppression—"God has given you this opportunity, which you must not pass up!"—and, in fact, went even further, declaring that anticolonial resistance was a "duty to your religion" and predicting "God's punishment" for those refraining from it.[35] The pamphlet was full of references to the (alleged) oppression of Islam under French rule, accusing France of suppressing the shari'a, banning Qur'anic education in schools, attacking mosques, and pursuing missionary aims. The struggle against the colonial regime was therefore a divine duty supported by Allah: "God will send you help if you are faithful to your fight," the leaflet said, promising those who joined the war against France the status of martyr: "The gates of paradise will be opened for you, and they are fortunate who can achieve this." The Foreign Office produced 10,000 copies of the pamphlet, which were sent via the German embassy in Madrid to Morocco.[36] It gives a good insight into the sort of propaganda that was to follow in the coming years. Yet, as Germany's general political line toward the Islamic world was not yet clear, these early efforts to deal with France's Muslims remained ad hoc and tentative. A more organized campaign for Islamic mobilization

3.4 Africa Corps in the city of Tripoli, Libya, 1941 (*Ullstein*).

only began with the military engagement in North Africa in the spring of 1941 (Figure 3.4).

Islam and Print Propaganda in the North African War Zone

The advances of the *Panzerarmee Afrika* in the Magrib were accompanied by a major propaganda campaign. German planes dropped tons of pamphlets, postcards, and leaflets over the war zones and behind the lines of the British army, addressing the local Muslim population. This propaganda was organized by the Foreign Office in cooperation with the Wehrmacht. On the ground it was directed by the German diplomat Konstantin Alexander von Neurath—son of the Reich protector of Bohemia and Moravia and former German foreign minister Konstantin von Neurath—who from May 1941 was the Foreign Office's liaison officer at Rommel's army.[37] Neurath was particularly interested in geopolitics and Islam, as is reflected in a list of books and journals he ordered from Berlin.[38]

Although the pamphlets drew on a variety of themes, ranging from praise of the regime's technological, economic, and military superiority to anticolonial nationalism, a remarkable number had a religious tinge. One of them, produced in the autumn of 1941, when German forces had advanced to the Egyptian border, prepared the civil population behind the front line for the offensive, explaining that "German racial thought" recognized every race as "God given" apart from the "corrupt, parasite Jewish one" and assuring readers that the German people "will support your fight against the English and the Jews with warm sympathy and—God willing—soon with more."[39] Another, created at the same time, began with quotations from sura 8 (*al-Anfal*): "O believers, when you encounter the unbelievers marching to battle, turn not your backs to them" (8:15) and: "Whoso turns his back that day to them, unless withdrawing to fight again or removing to join another host, he is laden with the burden of God's anger, and his refuge is Gehenna—an evil homecoming!" (8:16).[40] The text that followed put these passages into the political context of the war, portraying the Soviets as unbelievers and the British as their willing executioners. Containing a detailed account of the suppression of "millions of people" under Stalin's "satanic yoke," it warned of Moscow's schemes for the wider Muslim world. "Only Germany can save the world, and she will also save you and your religion from subjugation under the threatening red flag." Drawing on the authority of the Qur'an once again, the pamphlet ended with a quotation from the "victory" (*al-Fath*) sura: "He knew what you knew not, and appointed ere that a nigh victory" (end of 48:27). The British counteroffensive in late 1941 thwarted Rommel's plans for a final offensive into Egyptian territory.[41] Pushed back to the western border of Cyrenaica, it would take him until the following year to start his next offensive eastward.

The second advance through Cyrenaica in spring 1942 was accompanied by an even more intensive pamphlet campaign. As German troops were marching on Cairo, the Foreign Office and Wehrmacht began preparing pamphlets for the Egyptian population. On 8 April 1942, the command of the Africa Corps formally requested a propaganda campaign in Egypt, seconded by Neurath a month later; and on 25 June 1942, after German troops had crossed the Libyan-Egyptian border, Neurath again reported to Berlin that Rommel had asked for propaganda to Egypt.[42] The Foreign Office informed Neurath that 1.1 million new pamphlets had been printed, including 100,000 copies of "Green Is the Color of the Muslims."[43] Three days later the first dispatch of 450,000 pamphlets was flown to Cyrenaica for distribution in Egypt.[44] The rest were dispatched over the following days. Another 1 million pamphlets were in print, and more in preparation.[45] On 30 June 1942, four planes brought no fewer than 1.3 million pamphlets to North Africa, including 6,000 postcards with the *hamsa* and 1,000 postcards celebrating the reception of the Palestinian mufti in Berlin.[46] On 2 July 1942, another 2 million leaflets were dispatched, including 100,000 "Green Is the Flag of the Muslims," and 6,000 *hamsa* postcards.[47] On 12 July 1942, a further 760,000 propaganda flyers followed, among them 200,000 copies of the newly created "Call of the Grand Mufti."[48] The float continued all summer. Among the Arabic propaganda material distributed were also 300,000 copies of the pamphlet "O Egypt."[49] Promising Egyptians liberation from imperial oppression, it assured the pious of Allah's support: "God will bring justice to Egypt and destroy British injustice and its empire, the unjust, violent criminal."[50] By the end of August, the Foreign Office had produced 10 million Arabic propaganda pamphlets, of which more than 8 million had been distributed.[51] In Berlin, plans had already been drawn up to turn Cairo into a new center of German propaganda in the Islamic world and to co-opt the religious leaders of al-Azhar, but the defeat at al-'Alamayn and the British counteroffensive ultimately thwarted these plans.[52]

After Operation Torch, pamphlets increasingly attacked the United States as well. In January 1943, for instance, the Foreign Office produced the Arabic brochure "Islam and the Democracies," condemning both London and Washington.[53] A pamphlet proclaimed: "The English, Americans, Jews, and their allies are the greatest enemies of Arabism and of Islam!"[54] Another leaflet, featuring a picture of the Hand of Fatima, began with an anti-Jewish verse from the Qur'an—"Thou wilt surely find the most hostile of men to the believers are the Jews and the idolaters" (5:82 [85])—and continued within a religious frame of reference: "The Jews and usurers, they take from the believers what they own, and therefore they should be punished. The American and English, invading the Maghrib, are the friends of the Jews; Roosevelt and Churchill eat out of the Jews' hand. Anyone who is against the Jews must also be against the Americans and the English."[55] Remarkably, the basis of the pamphlet was again Islamic scripture, from which the syllogistic logic then followed: Jews are the enemies of Islam; the Americans and the English are the friends of the Jews; ergo the Allies are the enemies of Islam. The anti-Jewish content of sura 5 (*al-Ma'idah*), used here, had actually been discussed in German publications since the late 1930s, notably in Paul Schmitz's *All-Islam* and Mohamed Sabry's *Islam, Judaism, Bolshevism*.[56]

When Rommel's army, pushed out of the Libyan and Egyptian desert, finally retreated to Tunisia, German propagandists continued their work there. On the ground, the propaganda was coordinated by Rudolf Rahn, German consul in Tunis and thus the highest civil representative of the Reich in North Africa. The propaganda guidelines for Tunisia clearly instructed that promises of national independence had to be avoided but that religious references were to be used to promote the Axis powers as "friends of the Mohammedans" and denounce "Anglo-American oppressors," "godless Bolshevism," which not only "persecuted the believers and destroyed mosques" in the Soviet Union but also suppressed Muslims in "other Mohammedan countries," and "Judaism," which "expelled the Mohammedans from Palestine and the holy sites."[57] These guidelines were adopted in practice. Among the propaganda material distributed in Tunisia was the small brochure *Germany and Islam* (*Almaniya wa-l-Islam*), a tract with rich illustrations and little text, promoting German friendship with Islam.[58] In the end, no fewer than 6 million pamphlets were distributed in Tunisia.[59]

The major hub for the spread of German pamphlets in the western parts of North Africa became neutral Spanish Morocco. The Foreign Office and the Wehrmacht intelligence operated two propaganda offices in the country, one in the capital, Tétouan, and one in the port city of Tangier. The Tangier zone, an area of fewer than 100,000 inhabitants, which had been under international mandate before being occupied by Spain in the summer of 1940, became the front line of the propaganda war between Axis and Allies in the Maghrib.[60] In the summer of 1942, an official of the Tangier bureau, located in the German general consulate, reported on the success of the German publications that had been distributed among local authorities.[61] Among the principal slogans of this propaganda were "England is the enemy of Islam!" and "Germany will win the war—God willing!" On the occasion of the 1942 'Id al-Adha, the Tangier office distributed 10,000 copies of a pamphlet that proclaimed:

O Muslim Friends! For the Festival of Sacrifice we send you wishes for God's protection and blessing! You know that in your entire history you have always had one great friend: Germany! You know that your enemies, the Jews, English and Americans, are also Germany's enemies, and that your hope for a better future for the Arabic peoples is also the hope and aim of Germany! Heil to you and the mercy of God![62]

Another pamphlet distributed in Morocco around the same time called on the faithful to rise against the Anglo-American invaders, who were the "allies of the Jews and the Bolsheviks," to defend the "religion of the Prophet."[63] Moreover, the consulate produced leaflets exhorting pious Moroccans to "act" against "infidels and Jews," the "British," "Americans," and "French traitors," and their allies, the "Bolsheviks," who were raging "against Islam."[64] In spring 1943, the Germans, now under serious military pressure, spread a proclamation in Morocco urgently calling for jihad, while drawing parallels between the current conflict and the wars of the Prophet.[65] Beginning with a reference to the great battles of Uhud and Badr, it declared that the warriors of Muhammad had not lost their courage and had overcome the test set to them by Allah. The current war, "for the first time in centuries," was a "new test": "Beware, o brothers, of being among those who only wait and who don't want to see the right path, just as those who scorned God's Prophet—God's glory and mercy be upon him—in the days of hardship." Now everybody had to choose between the "ways of God and tradition" and the "ignominy of Bolshevism"—between "faith" and "enslavement by the Jews." The pamphlet was interspersed with three long quotations from the Qur'an—among them verses from sura 3 (al-'Imran), which refers to the battles of Uhud and Badr. Even after German troops had withdrawn from North Africa, the US Office of War Information reported that German agents were continuing to spread among Muslims in Morocco the rumor that they would be forced to convert to Christianity if the Axis lost the war.[66] The Allies put great pressure on the Spanish authorities to close the German general consulate in Tangier, to which Franco finally succumbed in the summer of 1944.

Some propaganda pamphlets produced in Berlin were distributed more widely in different parts of North Africa. The Foreign Office sent thousands of copies of the pamphlet "Struggle of the Mohammedans" both to Spanish Morocco and to Tunisia.[67] Photographs of the mufti of Jerusalem printed on posters and postcards, his poems written on amulets, and pamphlets with his propaganda speech given at the opening of the Islamic

Central Institute were also sent for distribution not only to Tunis but also to Tangier—and occasionally at the same time in other places, including Ankara, Athens, Sofia, Bucharest, and Zagreb.[68]

Eventually, the Wilhelmstraße even prepared material propaganda for the North African war zone. Sugar cubes were distributed, every lump wrapped in paper on which a pious political phrase was written in Arabic: "With God's help Germany's victory is certain."[69] Officials in Berlin also discussed the production of small tea bags to be attached to amulets or pamphlets, although it is unclear whether the plan ever materialized.[70] Propagandistic amulets—described in an internal document as "talismans with the swastika and a devotional saying or an imprecation"—as well as perfumed papers with a Qur'anic proverb and a proclamation of friendship, were also spread.[71] Appealing to the senses of taste, smell, and vision, these objects combined material culture, religion, and political propaganda.

Finally, German pamphlets also targeted areas in the Middle East—Syria, Lebanon, Palestine, and beyond. The *New York Times* had early on reported about Nazi propagandists in the Middle East who portrayed Hitler as the "protector of Islam."[72] In August 1942, for instance, German planes dropped 296,000 copies of a leaflet over Syria warning of a greater Jewish state encompassing large parts of the Middle East, which would be founded after an Anglo-American victory, and expressing the hope that "with God's help" the Allies would be defeated.[73] Berlin also produced 50,000 copies of a propaganda brochure, showing photographs of al-Husayni's meetings with Muslim SS soldiers for distribution in the Eastern Mediterranean.[74] Apparently Nazi propagandists in the Levant had also spread a song, with the lines: "No more Monsieur, no more Mister./Go away, get out of here./We want Allah in heaven, and Hitler on earth."[75] In the heartlands of Islam, meanwhile, Japanese agents distributed pamphlets among pilgrims in Mecca, calling all Muslims to unite, summoning them to a holy war, and presenting Hitler as a model statesman with the courage to stand up to the British.[76]

German print propaganda for the Arab world additionally took the form of tracts, booklets, or journals, most notably the journal *Barid al-Sharq* (*Eastern Post*), edited by Kamal al-Din Galal of the Islamic Central Institute in Berlin and financed by the Propaganda Ministry.[77] During the war, fifty-five issues of the paper were published and distributed, in particular among the population in the North African war zone and among

Muslim prisoners of war. Although its circulation rose steadily, no issue ever ran to more than 5,000 copies. Articles in *Barid al-Sharq*, dominated by the usual anti-British, anti-Communist, and anti-Jewish agitation, also drew on religious themes.[78] They dealt with the suppression of religion in the Soviet Union and the Anglo-American exploitation of the Islamic world, and, on the other side, with German friendship with Islam and the activities of the Islamic Central Institute in Berlin. The journal also published several speeches by members of the Nazi elite, by al-Husayni (including his calls for jihad), and, on the occasion of the hajj in 1944, by the head of al-Azhar, the elderly Muhammad Mustafa al-Maraghi, even though he was known for his pro-British leanings. Contributors included the Lebanese pan-Islamist Shakib Arslan and Abdurreshid Ibrahim, who, after his service for Germany during the First World War, had now become imam of the Tokyo Mosque, giving the paper a further pan-Islamic tinge. Johann von Leers wrote on issues such as the suffering of the Muslims in India and the antagonism between Communism and Islam. The editors of *Barid al-Sharq* also published an Arabic-language brochure with the title *Islam and the Jews* (*al-Islam wa-l-Yahud*), based on a series of articles that the journal had run earlier under the same title. Numerous copies were distributed in Tunis.[79] In spring 1942, the German consulate in Tangier reported the "confiscation" of several boxes of the brochure by Spanish officials.[80] Files stored in the archives of the Foreign Office in Berlin indicate that the distribution of *Barid al-Sharq* in the Tangier zone repeatedly caused friction between German officials and the local Spanish administration during the North African campaign.[81]

The SS played only a small role in Germany's propaganda efforts targeting the Middle East and North Africa. Perhaps the most significant example was the attempt by SS officers to portray Hitler as a religious figure. Stohrer had already mentioned in his memorandum that the Qur'an contained "a number of suras which can be interpreted easily by every Islam expert as prophetic words indicating the emergence of a Führer."[82] On 14 May 1943, two months after the defeat of the German army in North Africa, Himmler gave orders to the Reich Security Head Office "to find out which passages of the Qur'an provide Muslims with the basis for the opinion that the Führer has already been forecast in the Qur'an and that he has been authorized to complete the work of the Prophet."[83] After almost four months, the head of the *Reichssicherheitshauptamt*, Ernst Kaltenbrunner, reported that there were no passages in the Qur'an that could be used but that Muslims in some parts of the world held messianic beliefs that alluded to the "return of the 'light of the Prophet,'" allowing "for a connection to the Führer."[84] In a second letter, Kaltenbrunner pointed to the idea of the "Mahdi," which was, he explained, central to "Islamic eschatology": "The Mahdi is supposed to appear at the end of times to defend the faith and to lead justice to victory."[85] Indeed, messianic beliefs had been common in both the Shi'a and the Sunni world for centuries. After all, Mahdi uprisings had frequently troubled the imperial powers.[86] Kaltenbrunner's experts were most likely aware of this. On the side, the head of Himmler's personal staff, Rudolf Brandt, also involved Gottlob Berger's SS Head Office, as well as the SS Ahnenerbe to support this research, though neither organization was able to offer much help.[87] Before long, Berger reported that his Islam experts had found nothing useful.[88] The head of the SS Ahnenerbe, Wolfram Sievers, turned for help to the famous Indologist Walther Wüst, rector of the University of Munich, who submitted a rather useless report.[89] Meanwhile, however, officials at the Reich Security Head Office had made some progress. On 6 December 1943, Kaltenbrunner sent another report to Himmler with some practical results: experts of the research section "Orient" (Forschungsstelle "Orient") of the Reich Security Head Office had found out that the "Führer" could be portrayed "neither as the Prophet nor as the Mahdi" but that he could suitably be promoted "as the returned 'Isa (Jesus), who is forecast in the Qur'an and who, similar to the figure of Knight George, defeats the giant and Jew-King Dajjal at the end of the world."[90] The Reich Security Head Office accordingly produced a propaganda pamphlet in Arabic. Portraying the Dajjal as the Jewish enemy, it read as follows:

We have been taught that the Dajjal will appear at the end of days; a monster that will deceive and betray the people. This will be a time of great oppression for the believers. The famous Arab [sic] historian Abu Ja'far Muhammad ibn Jarir al-Tabari said that the Dajjal was a giant and a Jewish king who will rule the whole world. Muhammad ibn Ismail Abu 'Abd Allah al-Ja'fai al-Bukhari said that the Dajjal was fat with curly hair. / O Arabs, do you see that the time of the Dajjal has come? Do you recognize him, the fat, curly-haired Jew who deceives and rules the whole world and who steals the land of the Arabs? Truly, he is a monster, and his allies are devils! We have been taught that the rule of the Dajjal will not last. 'Abd Allah ibn 'Umar al-Baidawi said that God will send his servant, who will kill the Dajjal with his lance and destroy his palaces. / O Arabs, do you know the servant of God? He has already appeared in the world and already turned his lance against the Dajjal and his allies, and has wounded them deeply. He will kill the Dajjal, as it is written, destroy his palaces and cast his allies into hell.[91]

Although the Mahdi, the Dajjal, and 'Isa are all prominent figures in Islamic eschatology, the way they were presented here was novel. Himmler immediately approved the text and ordered the pamphlet to be printed.[92] The Propaganda Ministry produced 1 million copies.[93] The idea behind this pamphlet may seem absurd today, yet, as mentioned, Mahdist revolt had proven to be a major disruptive force for the European empires in previous decades, and messianism had always been particularly potent in times of war.

The idea of promoting Hitler and his ideas as Islamic was not new. As early as 1938, Werner Otto von Hentig had insisted on asking a scholar of the Qur'an to help translate *Mein Kampf* into Arabic.[94] The translation was to be compatible with Islam and written in the "solemn tone" of the Qur'an, which was "understood and appreciated" throughout the "entire Islamic world." Hitler's political message was to be given religious connotations. "If this should be successful, then the Arabic translation of the book of the Führer will find fertile ground and resonance from Morocco to India," Hentig wrote, suggesting that German emissaries in Mecca should present the first copies of the translation to Muslim leaders during the hajj. The pro-British journal *L'Orient*, published in Beirut, reported on these plans: "German Orientalists prepare a falsification of the Qur'an with political intentions. They present, in the form of Qur'anic verses, a selection of passages from *Mein Kampf* so that Muslims will believe that Hitler is the messenger of God and that his book is of divine inspiration."[95] European newspapers printed similar articles.[96] The Wilhelmstraße made several attempts to translate *Mein Kampf* into Arabic, and by the 1930s a number of Arabic extracts were circulating in North Africa and the Middle East, but the whole text was never fully translated before the end of the war.[97] The most prominent figure officially commissioned to translate the book in the 1930s was Shakib Arslan, but he never delivered.[98]

In the last phase of the war, long after the Germans had left the Maghrib, propaganda pamphlets again specifically targeted Muslim soldiers in the ranks of the Allies' armies. Employing a heavily religious rhetoric, they exhorted North African soldiers fighting in Europe to "wake up" from their "deep sleep," to change sides to join their "German friends," and to use their weapons against their enemies in order to free their countries and "win the blessing of God."[99] Another flyer reminded the "brave warriors of North Africa" of "what the despotic oppressors" had done to them—they had given their countries to the Jews and Bolshevists, the "greatest enemies of Islam." It concluded: "It is a mortal sin to fight on the side of your enemies and at the same time betray your country and savage your religious commandments and teachings. Why do you fight against your brothers the Germans, with whom you are connected purely by friendship and love?"[100] Another pamphlet proclaimed that an Allied victory would prolong the bondage of Arab countries and further weaken "the whole of Islam," claiming, in typical elevated rhetoric: "It is your duty to defend your fatherland and your religion. Preserve your blood for this holy purpose!"[101] It was signed by al-Husayni, just like another appeal, which rang with calls for sacrifice:

> Today you go on the way to death! If you want to sacrifice your life, then you are only allowed to sacrifice it in the holy name of Allah and for the fortune of your fatherland; this would be the death of the martyr, who lives eternally in the Kingdom of God. However, if you sacrifice yourself for your enemies, the Allies, these protectors of the Jews, these enemies of Islam and the Prophet—peace upon his soul—then you would die the death of traitors, who are scorned in this world, and in the other world go to meet the most severe punishment.[102]

Overall, German pamphlets distributed among the peoples of North Africa and the Middle East dealt with a variety of subjects, ranging from praise of German military superiority to attacks against their enemies. Remarkable, though, was the centrality of references to Islam in these leaflets. Drawing on religious texts, like Qur'anic verses, and couched in a language of piety, they sought to utilize the full authority of Islam to endorse their violent political messages. A major obstacle, though, remained widespread illiteracy in North Africa and the Middle East, which severely restricted their impact, even if it is taken into account that the literate would often read the leaflets to others and spread their message by word of mouth. The materiality of the pamphlet could partly compensate: design—color, shape, and illustrations—most prominently the color green and the shape of the *hamsa*, and in some cases, scent and taste, were employed—all means that could appeal to an illiterate audience. Finally, another way to avoid the problem of illiteracy was to use a new medium—the radio.

Islam and Broadcast Propaganda in North Africa and the Middle East

More important than pamphlets and journals for spreading Germany's message of religious revolt was Berlin's broadcast propaganda to North Africa and the Middle East. Fascist Italy had launched an Arabic service from Radio Bari as early as 1934.[103] In 1939, just months before the outbreak of the war, Berlin finally also began to broadcast short programs to the Maghrib and the Middle East. These efforts were stepped up drastically after Hitler sent troops to North Africa, and German stations ultimately aired daily propaganda reaching as far as Mecca and Medina. "Axis Radio Blankets Islam," ran a *New York Times* headline during the war in the Maghrib, warning of the attempts "to fertilize the traditional seeds of discontent which have been sprouting in the Islamic world."[104]

The major transmitter of German propaganda to North Africa and the Middle East stood in Zeesen (Radio Berlin), a small town south of Berlin.[105] Since the Berlin Olympics in 1936, the city had housed one of the most powerful shortwave transmitters in the world, which, during the war, became a center of Nazi propaganda. From 1939 onward, Zeesen broadcast in standard Arabic every day, soon adding programs in Maghribi Arabic, and broadcasts intended for Turks, Iranians, and Indians. In fact, the Orient office of the radio station, directed by the journalist Gustav Bofinger, had absolute priority over all the other foreign broadcast offices in Zeesen.[106] It employed around eighty staff members, including typists, translators, and announcers.[107] As the war evolved, Germans also used stations in occupied Europe, broadcasting in Maghribi Arabic and in Berber, or *Amazigh*, from Paris (Radio Paris-Mondial), and, later, in standard Arabic from Athens (Radio Athens). Radio Berlin continued transmitting throughout the war until it was eventually shut down in April 1945.

The program was coordinated by the Propaganda Ministry, specifically its broadcast department, with its Middle East expert Leopold Itz von Mildenstein; the Foreign Office; and the propaganda department of the High Command of the Wehrmacht. The chief responsibility for the content of the propaganda to North Africa and the Middle East lay with the Foreign Office, particularly the broadcast department, directed by Nazi veteran Gerd Rühle and his young deputy, Kurt Georg Kiesinger, later chancellor of the Federal Republic; its Orient section was under Kurt Munzel.[108] Also involved was the Orient section of Ernst Woermann's political department. The general themes of the program were worked out in the weekly meetings of the so-called country committees of experts from different parts of the Foreign Office—Fritz Grobba, for instance, long ran the "Arab committee." Among the Muslim employees was Alimjan Idris, who worked for the Arabic as well as the Turkish broadcasts.[109]

The Germans hired some powerful personalities. Head announcer of Radio Berlin's standard Arabic service was the Iraqi journalist Yunus Bahri.[110] In his late thirties, Bahri arrived in the German capital in early 1939, beginning his work for Zeesen immediately. "Berlin could never have been able to find a better-suited man to be its propaganda instrument through the Radio," a British intelligence report remarked: "He is a man famous for nothing more than his dirty tongue, intrigues and a first-class inventor of lies and mischief maker and above all ready to be hired by anyone who pays a good price."[111] An ardent anticolonial activist, Bahri had traveled widely in the Islamic world, having worked as a political publicist in the Dutch East Indies, and later settled in Iraq, where he had published a newspaper and worked as an announcer for the state broadcast station. With his sharp voice, aggressive speeches, and marked ability to raise his voice, his broadcasts quickly became the earmark of Germany's Arabic service. The elderly Max von Oppenheim, who was introduced to Bahri in wartime Berlin, later noted: "He was a half-wild man, quite bright, with a good radio voice, who, even more than the other Arabs in Berlin, loved to surround himself with young German girls; hot-tempered and rowdyish, he repeatedly bullied his workmates at the radio station with slaps to the face."[112]

While Bahri was Berlin's most prominent Arab announcer, the Germans employed various other speakers from almost all parts of the Arab world.[113] Notable among them was a religious figure—the Moroccan cleric, pan-Islamic thinker, and anticolonial activist Taqi al-Din al-Hilali, who after the war attained world fame as a translator of the Qu'ran into English.[114] A disciple of Rashid Rida, al-Hilali had taken up his studies in interwar Germany before joining Radio Berlin on the recommendation of Richard Hartmann and other Orientalists. He, too, soon became one of Zeesen's most prominent Arab agitators over the airwaves.

Although the Germans decided on the content of the program, the speakers had some leeway to manipulate it. Shortly after the first airings, a Middle East expert in the Foreign Office complained that some of the Muslim speakers, "above all the Iraqi announcer Yunus Bahri," gave the program "a personal tinge" that was "not always in our interests."[115] Although the Germans supplied the propaganda texts and had established a thorough system to control both the interpreters who translated them and the announcers who recorded them, Bahri frequently managed to introduce his own messages. "It is an open secret that the speaker Yunus Bahri repeatedly slightly changed the text that was given to him," the official protested. As these modifications usually seemed minor, Alimjan Idris, who checked the recorded material before it was sent out, often did not intervene. Moreover, the modulation phase—the period before the beginning of the official program when the wavelength was adjusted—provided the announcers with another opportunity for manipulation: although speakers were meant to answer letters from listeners during this period, Yunus Bahri often used the time to air his own opinions.[116] In his memoirs, Bahri gave the impression that he had run the station almost by himself, referring to himself as "the leading head of German foreign broadcasting," while for instance downplaying the role of Idris, "the Muslim Turkestani mujahid," as an "impromptu translator" of his office.[117]

Reaching listeners not only in the Middle East but also in many parts of the Maghrib, the service in standard Arabic was considered particularly important by the Germans. The scripts of the program provide a rich source of information about the content of Nazi propaganda aimed at North Africa and the Middle East.[118] As a general overview of the program is already available, the following paragraphs concentrate only on selected cases to highlight the role that religious slogans, terminology, and rhetoric played in these broadcasts.[119]

Usually delivered in a strident and sensationalist tone, Berlin's standard Arabic program was quite distinct from the other stations broadcasting in the region. The program always began with readings of Qur'anic verses, an idea initially put forward by Alimjan Idris.[120] Propagandists at the Foreign Office were particularly eager to obtain recitations from countries of the Islamic world, believing that they had more authenticity than those produced in the Reich. After the occupation of Tunis, for instance, they wasted no time in acquiring Qur'an recordings from local Tunisian imams.[121]

As in pamphlet propaganda, religion was used in these programs to portray the British Empire, the United States, Bolshevism, and Judaism as the enemies of Islam. Perhaps most frequent were Berlin's calls to oppose British rule. On 29 July 1942, when Rommel marched on Cairo, German broadcasts commanded: "It is the duty of Moslems, whenever the British exaggerate in their evil doings and oppressions, to invoke the name of Allah to fight them."[122] Berlin's Arabic service certainly made sure that no Muslim forgot these "evil doings," repeatedly reporting on (alleged) British oppression of Muslims around the world. It lamented the execution of a "martyr" from Palestine—a "hero who, in his fight for freedom, reminds us of the companions of the Prophet."[123] It used stories about (alleged) British repressions of Muslims in India to declare that "the latest enemies of Islam are the British."[124] It reported British suppression of Islamic religious movements in Egypt, claiming that the British "spread immorality" in Muslim lands and were responsible for "criminal actions against Islam."[125] Among the central religious themes was British disrespect for mosques and sacred places. "Both Italian and German propaganda continually emphasize the destruction of holy places by British planes," noted an officer of the US Office of War Information in October 1941.[126] In the summer of the following year, Berlin's Arabic service repeatedly claimed that London used Egyptian towns as ammunition depots and camps for its troops and thereby exposed historic monuments and mosques to potential damage.[127] The broadcasts blamed London for the abolition of the caliphate and the banning of religious celebrations in Cairo.[128] In the winter of 1942, Berlin reported that the British, because of their fear of a major Muslim gathering, hindered hajj pilgrims in Egypt and India from traveling.[129] Berlin also confronted "allegations announced by enemy broadcasts" that had reported that German submarines were ready to attack pilgrimage ships.[130] German forces, the broadcast assured listeners, would not attack any vessel carrying pilgrims under whatever flag they sailed as long as they were informed of the schedule in advance. Some time later, when recounting the safe arrival of Egyptian pilgrims on the Arabian peninsula, Berlin boasted: "It is therefore obvious that the Pilgrim ships crossing the Red Sea have only arrived safely in Jidda because the Axis powers wished them to do so."[131] Whitehall, on the other hand, had done everything to spoil the pilgrimage, Berlin claimed. On the occasion of the next hajj season, in September 1943, Zeesen accused Britain of preventing Palestinian and Indian pilgrims from leaving their countries.[132] A month earlier, the station had announced: "The de Gaullists, those charlatans to whom the British have given power in Syria, have adopted a decision to forbid the pilgrimage either by land or sea routes."[133] The Free French were thus just like the British in their "hatred not only of the Moslems but also of the Islamic religion." London was well aware "that if the Moslems are united there is no power on earth that could defeat or intimidate them." Sometime later, Radio Berlin became more explicit. Listing statistical data, the announcer claimed that 400 million Muslims would form a force much greater than the strength of the Allies and declared: "This Moslem force will oppose Britain if it does not submit to the wishes and aspirations of the Moslems."[134]

The principal supporters and beneficiaries of British attacks on Islam—and indeed European imperialism in general—were, according to Radio Berlin, the Jews. Indeed, the closer Rommel's troops came to Cairo, the more passionate the anti-Jewish agitation became. In early July 1942, when Rommel had crossed the Egyptian border, the Arabic speaker in Zeesen claimed that the Jews were fleeing the country: "Once more we thank God that Egypt will be cleaned from these poisonous reptiles."[135] And in the same month, when the Italian-German tank army was approaching Egypt's heartland, Berlin announced: "The Jews are planning to violate your women, to kill your children and to destroy you. According to the Moslem religion, the defense of your life is a duty which can only be fulfilled by annihilating the Jews."[136] The speaker in fact explicitly called for violence: "Kill the Jews before they kill you." In spring 1943, after German troops had left the African continent, Radio Berlin assured its listeners of the solidarity of Muslims in China, Japan, India, and the rest of the world, who stood united against common enemies and, most importantly, the Jews.[137] Toward the end of that year, it claimed that the Qur'an cursed Jews "for their evils" and that "Mohammed also hated them because they wanted to kill him."[138] With reference to the holy book, one of the Arabic demagogues at Radio Berlin announced a month later: "The Jews are the worst enemies of Islam, and always have been."[139] Zeesen continued airing this sort of anti-Jewish tirade until the end. Perhaps the most significant was al-Husayni's notorious hate speech of 1 March 1944, in which he raged: "Kill Jews wherever you find them, for the love of God, history and religion."[140] It is remarkable to note that Radio Berlin not only tried to fuel concerns about the Jewish colonization of Palestine but also went far beyond this, employing the conventional Nazi narratives, stereotypes, and conspiracy theories about Jews and eventually calling for their murder. Indeed, German propaganda combined Islam with anti-Jewish agitation to an extent that had not hitherto been known in the modern Muslim world.

Anti-American propaganda was overall less religiously charged. Only occasionally would the speakers in Germany employ references to Islam, usually in order to portray Americans as culturally inferior. On 5 September 1942, for instance, Berlin fulminated:

> We were not surprised when Radio Boston, a few days ago, broadcast a talk which caused great laughter. The programme was started with eccentric dance music and then in a loud voice, the announcer cried: "Allah Akbar." These people do not know whether they are praying to God or the devil. They are a nation of strange people with strange habits. These Americans, who always trample upon the feelings of the Moslems with their irreligious manners and ways, now dare to say that the Germans have no respect for religion.[141]

In the following year, Berlin's Arabic service blamed Americans for being "slaves of the money bag," of economic exploitation, and of having low moral standards, asserting that "American efforts will be broken on a solid rock—the rock of Islam."[142]

Finally, Radio Zeesen's Arabic service utilized Islam in its anti-Soviet agitation. On the eve of the battle of al-'Alamayn, when German tanks were rolling into the northern Caucasus, the speaker in Berlin declared: "We must fight Bolshevism just as we have fought the Jews and the Imperialists."[143] And following the retreat of the Wehrmacht from the Caucasus mountains a few months later, Berlin reported horrific stories of Soviet persecution of Muslims in the region: "In places sacred to the Moslems, such as Mosques and Moslem schools, where the Imams performed their duties, those Imams were hanged on gallows, or shot before the eyes of their followers and relatives." Reports about Stalin's repression of Muslims and the destruction of Islam in the Soviet Union were broadcast every few weeks. Listeners were usually reminded of the closure of mosques and the ban on religious rituals: "Russia was, and still is, the most hostile country to the Moslems."[144] In spring 1943, a talk was aired on "Communism and Islam," full of stories about massacres and the closing of mosques: "Communism is based on the following of Satan."[145] A few months later, the Arabic announcer in Berlin read aloud a letter allegedly written by two Caucasian resistance fighters, addressed to al-Maraghi in Cairo, listing atrocities committed by the Bolshevists against Islam.[146] In late 1943, when warning about the Soviet penetration of North Africa and the Middle East, Zeesen assured listeners that Stalin had realized that Islam was "a strong obstacle" to his plans, as Bolshevist and Islamic principles were "diametrically opposed."[147] As late as August 1944, Berlin announced that Moscow had "destroyed the Mosques," "burned the Koran," and "prohibited the Moslems from practicing their religion"—"Bolshevism is contrary to Islam."[148]

In contrast, Berlin's Arabic broadcast propaganda characterized the Germans as the most trustworthy defenders of the Muslim faith. The "Arab proclamation" of 5 December 1940 had soon been followed by a more detailed broadcast declaration of German friendship with the Arab world and, indeed, Islam, emphasizing the tradition of Germany's scholarship on the Qur'an, and Islamic history, as well as its admiration of Muslims: "The studies of German scholars have shown a special interest in the figure of the Prophet and his life," the speaker boasted.[149] The German program also referred to principles allegedly held in common by Islam and Nazism. On 22 May 1943, a talk on "Islam and National Socialism" highlighted the ideal of order, which was supposedly inherent in both the Qur'an and National Socialist doctrine, along with an allegedly shared unconditional "love of strength."[150] Increasingly prominent were reports about Muslim life under German occupation in other parts of the world, notably the Balkans and the Eastern territories. Berlin declared on 5 August 1942, that German and Italian authorities in Albania were repairing damaged mosques.[151]

In countless airings, Germany claimed it was protecting Muslims in south-eastern Europe against atrocities committed by Serbian Četniks and Communist partisans backed by London and Washington.[152] In early 1944, a broadcast detailed a brutal raid on a Muslim village by partisans who had allegedly looted the local mosque and then forced all of the Muslim women into the house of worship with the intention of raping them there—only the German soldiers' speedy arrival had saved them.[153] A few months later, a report affirmed that "Greater Germany" was ready to defend the rights of the Muslims of the Balkans.[154] And after the attempt on Hitler's life on 20 July 1944, the speaker in Zeesen announced: "Balkan Moslems rejoiced at the news of the Fuehrer's safety after the recent incident."[155] "Thanksgiving prayers were said in Mosques all over the Balkans last Friday" because, it was explained, Hitler was seen by the Muslims as their "saviour from the criminal Bolsheviks."[156] Berlin also boasted of its religious policies in the Eastern Muslim areas, though less frequently. On 13 October 1943, for instance, listeners were told: "The Bolshevists have executed tens of thousands of priests and also many Moslem Ulemas; they have destroyed mosques, confiscated their property and burned their homes. When the German armies conquered the Crimea, they gave the Moslems back their rights and reopened their mosques."[157] The issue of Muslim volunteers in the German armies was, however, more delicate. The dilemma became most obvious on 22 May 1944, when the Arabic program first reported that the Allies were using Muslim soldiers from North Africa on the Italian front as "cannon-fodder," while a few hours later it praised Muslims fighting under German command in the Balkans.[158]

Germany's employment of Islam in its broadcast propaganda for the Arab world went beyond contrasting the friends and the enemies of Islam. Radio Berlin also broadcast a purely religious program, the so-called religious weekly talk (religiöser Wochentalk), which carried political messages only between the lines, if at all. Gerd Rühle explained in an internal note that these airings were first and foremost intended to stimulate interest in the German programs more generally, though he added that the talks also drew on religion to stress the necessity of resistance against foreign rule.[159] The "religious weekly talks" usually began by addressing listeners with the exhortation "O Mohammedans!" or "O, servants of God!"—rallying cries that were repeated during each show. The talks were meant to impart moral advice to Muslims, teaching them about ethical questions and religious values. Full of references to the Qur'an, the life of the Prophet, and early Islamic history, they were cast in the rhetorical form of a sermon. Talks on "Piety," "Truthfulness," "The Proper Treatment of Servants, Slaves, and Animals," "Truthfulness and the Strength of Faith," or "Pilgrimage" advised Muslim listeners to be pious, to return to the traditions of the Prophet, and to follow the idea of the community of the faithful.[160] Many of these commentaries implied that Muslims had become weak because they had strayed from the path of Islam. Only religion would help them to become powerful again and to defend themselves against their enemies. In a talk on "munificence" in December 1940, for instance, the speaker claimed that religious values had once made the Islamic empire great but that straying from Islam had led to the "rage of God and his Prophet" and to consequent decline.[161] A month later, the announcer of a talk on "Selfishness" expressed the wish for an Islamic revival: "May God help the Mohammedans to act according to the commandments of their religion; may he make them again mighty after the decline, so that they can defeat their enemies."[162] The following month, the presenter exhorted listeners to "wake up!" blaming them for being in a deep sleep, which had led to weakness, the decline of the Islamic empire, and the disintegration of the global *umma*.[163] Another recurring narrative was that the enemies of Islam had deliberately kept Muslims uneducated and superstitious. A talk on "Scholarship and Education" lamented the fact that many Muslims were allegedly not familiar enough with their faith and blamed those who would consciously keep them uneducated in order to suppress and rule them.[164] Similarly, a talk on "Renewal and Superstition in Islam" called for a return to the foundations of Islam and the tradition of the Prophet. Modernism and superstition had been spread only by the enemies of Islam. "These have been primarily the Jews," it was claimed, adding the usual reference to sura 5: "Thou wilt surely find the most hostile of men to the believers are the Jews and the idolaters."[165] Only a few of the scripts of these religious talks have survived the war and are stored today in the German archives—most of the US monitoring scripts do not contain these programs. Yet, officials in Washington were well aware of them: "As usual, one of Berlin's shows in Arabic was dripping in religious chants, passages from the Qur'an, and sweet, oily language," an intelligence officer of the Office of War Information sneered in spring 1942.[166]

Finally, Berlin made extensive use of the events of the religious calendar. Messages broadcast on Islamic holidays merged reflections about religious celebrations with the rhetoric of war. As early as January 1941, the transmitter aired its *'Id al-Adha* wishes with a meditation on the ideal of "sacrifice" in the fight against one's enemies, a homage to "manliness and heroism," and the strength of religion as a weapon against foes: "Truly, God is with the faithful."[167] Two days later, the Arabic announcer in Berlin connected his wishes for the *'Id al-Adha* with a speech about his life in the Reich, confronting the "lying reports" of Allied propaganda about the situation in Germany.[168] Similarly, the following Islamic New Year (the migration, or *hijra*, of the Prophet from Mecca to Medina), Berlin's Arabic service broadcast not only its celebratory wishes but also its hope for victory against the imperial suppressors, invoking a quotation from sura 8: "Help comes only from God" (8:10).[169] Two days later it added a sermon-like speech in which it urged believers to be pious and invoked the lessons taught by Muhammad: "Be like your Prophet, namely be men of deed and not of word and take an example in the past so that you are prepared for the future."[170] From the time al-Husayni took up residence in Berlin, these kinds of programs also included his speeches. Thus, on the occasion of the *'Id al-Adha* in December 1942 the Berlin service broadcast not just the usual holiday wishes connected with a call for sacrifice in the battle against Islam's enemies, but also al-Husayni's speech on the inauguration of the Islamic Central Institute.[171] On 19 March 1943, his lecture at the Islamic Central Institute for the *Mawlid al-Nabi* celebrations (birthday of the Prophet) was aired—"no Islamic country from the Atlantic to the Far East" had been spared from the "hostile oppressors," al-Husayni agitated, asserting that "God alone is merciful, and far too just to grant them victory."[172] At the end of Ramadan (*'Id al-Fitr* or *Uraza Bairam*) on 1 October 1943, his address to his "Mohammedan brothers in all parts of the world" was aired. Interspersed with various quotations from the Qur'an, his speech admonished the audience to remain steadfast in their faith and to fight against imperial oppression: "Follow your faith, because it leads to victory!"[173] As late as September 1944, the Arabic service of Berlin, in its New Year message, called on believers to pray for the defeat of the Jews and British imperialism.[174] One of the more remarkable events in this context was the *Mawlid* in March 1944, which included a report about the Berlin mosque and was described by a US broadcast monitoring officer as follows:

> The announcer said that the celebration this year was different from that of any previous year as it was marked by sadness and regret, as the Mosque has been destroyed by barbaric Allied raids. The Allies care little for the sanctity of religious monuments—they are merely brutes. The Mosque was struck on the 13th February. The announcer then said that a short play would be relayed depicting the events of that memorable day. After a short silence, the Sheikh of the Mosque was heard reciting verses of the Qoran in deep but calm tones. The verses were appeals to God and to Allah to safeguard the lives of Moslems and the prosperity of Islam. In the dim distance planes roared and now and then the sound of a falling bomb and explosion were heard, but throughout the raid the reader went on reciting the verses from the Qoran in the same calm tones. The announcer then appeared on the scene and said that on the day following the raid the Sheikh of the Mosque was standing in the open in the bitter cold. Nevertheless, he was still reciting the Qoran. Again the voice of the Sheikh was heard reciting: 'God is great, Allah is great!' and repeating once again more verses from the Qoran in a calm tone. The announcer again came on the scene and said that the Sheikh's voice is [sic] the voice of truth, telling the Islamic world that the enemies of Islam will [sic] not desist in their endeavours until Islam has crumbled away. The announcer said that amidst such destruction the "Mouled El Nabi" was celebrated. Moslems gathered to wish each other the greetings of the season and then voices from the gathering were heard.[175]

Overall, Germany's Islamic broadcast propaganda aimed at North Africa and the Middle East may be divided into two categories (although in practice they were often intertwined in a single propaganda piece): reports on the enemies of Islam and reports on its friends. As in print propaganda, Islam provided a language, metaphors, and imperatives that were used by German propagandists for their political cause. Nazi propaganda employed a heavily religious language, as well as religious concepts and references to sacred texts. Anti-British, anti-Bolshevik, and anti-Jewish agitation was frequently interspersed with quotations from the Qur'an. Occasionally, even nonreligious terms were translated into a religious language, as in the case of the German word for "dive bomber," "Stuka" (*Sturzkampfflugzeug*), which was translated into Arabic as an "aircraft that like the eagle of the Prophet flies down from heaven and destroys the enemy on the ground."[76] Moreover, Berlin's broadcast propaganda in standard Arabic regularly employed pan-Islamic references, for instance, reporting about Islam in the Soviet Union, India, or Germany. At the same time, it suggested the idea of a global Islamic battle waged alongside the Axis.

The content of Radio Berlin's program in Maghribi Arabic was quite similar to that in standard Arabic, following the same religious-political themes, though having a regional focus on North Africa. The same holds true for the Arabic programs of Radio Athens and Radio Paris-Mondial. Paris-Mondial also reported on Muslims in Axis France. In early 1943, for instance, it sent a documentary, made by its head announcer, the Rif Moroccan Muhammad Bouzid, about Muslim workers on the Atlantic coasts voicing their praise for Hitler.[77] Although the German authorities considered the programs in Arabic of first importance in their propaganda in North Africa and the Middle East, they also increased the number of those in Turkish, Persian, and Urdu.

In the Turkish broadcasts, though, only very few attempts were made to exploit Islam.[78] When Berlin employed some modestly religiously charged propaganda in the early phase of the war, the Turkish press instantly responded with biting criticism and ridicule, stressing that religion should never be a theme in political propaganda, mocking these attempts as a sign of German indecency, and reminding readers of Wilhelm II's unsuccessful attempts to exploit Islam a few decades earlier.[79] Hitler's ambassador to Ankara, Franz von Papen, warned that "an appeal to the religious sentiment" was attractive only, "if at all," to the "lower classes," though even they would hardly accept religious propaganda from a "cultural center of the Occident."[80] A year later, German officials would nevertheless contemplate the establishment of a pirate station that would attack laicism and the suppression of Islam in Turkey.[81] Overall, however, as in debates by German experts before the war, Laicist Turkey remained a special case.

By contrast, Germany's Persian service—staffed with notorious propagandists such as head announcer Shah-Bahran Shahrukh, political dissident Nezameddin Akhavi, and Davud Monshizadeh, who after the war would found Iran's Fascist Sumka Party—increasingly drew on religious themes. After the occupation of Iran in the summer of 1941, German propaganda would routinely accuse the Allies of violating religious sites and sentiments in the country. Among the standard propaganda slogans was the claim that "Anglo-Soviet troops" had "defiled mosques in Iran."[182] As the Germans advanced into the southern regions of the Soviet Union in the summer of 1942, nearing the Iranian border, new guidelines were given out, which, in addition to the usual slogans, explicitly instructed propagandists to denounce the British and Soviet "policy of oppression" in "other Mohammedan countries."[183] Radio Berlin accused Washington of pursuing "missionary activity" in Iran, London of not only meddling in "political" but also "religious" matters of the country, and Moscow for its general "hostility toward religion."[184]

A particularly popular trope of German propaganda in Iran was Shi'a messianism. As early as February 1941, Erwin Ettel, then envoy in Tehran, made specific suggestions in this respect. From the Iranian capital he reported that numerous Shi'a "clergymen" had spoken to the people "from old divinations and dreams, and interpreted them as saying that the Twelfth Imam was sent to the world by Allah in the form of Adolf Hitler."[185] Ettel suggested supporting these developments and trying to "clearly emphasize the fight of Muhammad against the Jews in history and that of the Führer in modern times. Connected by an equation between the British and the Jews, an extremely effective anti-English propaganda would be carried to the Shi'a Iranian people." Ettel proposed using the famous Qur'anic verse 5:82 (85) alongside a quotation from *Mein Kampf* ("Hence today I believe that I am acting in accordance with the will of the Almighty Creator: by defending myself against the Jew, I am fighting for the work of the Lord") to prove that Muslims and Nazis shared the "same objectives in the fight." The propaganda officer of the German embassy in Tehran had already collected material about the issue. German propagandists were to take it up in their broadcasts and, in the case of positive feedback, supplement it with pamphlet propaganda. Yet he urged caution, as "crude propaganda" could offend the "deep feelings of the faithful." Local channels seemed best suited to convey propagandistic messages, and Ettel emphasized in particular the political significance of the clergy in Iran, with its efficient information and propaganda network with hubs in Mashhad and Qum, which German propagandists should try to exploit.[186] These views were shared by his colleagues. Assessing German propaganda in Iran, Hans Alexander Winkler, who had been cultural attaché at the German embassy in Tehran before the Allied occupation, wrote in early 1942 that the most promising propaganda themes for Iran were those drawing on the religious beliefs and aspirations of Iranians, particularly the return of the Twelfth Imam.[187] Winkler asserted that among both the rural population and the urban intelligentsia, beliefs were expressed connecting the rise of Adolf Hitler to the return of the Mahdi. Even the Shi'a clergy, according to the diplomat, cultivated these ideas. Given the "disposition of the Iranian towards religious fanaticism," Winkler saw in such beliefs "strong forces" that German propaganda could employ, ideally connected to anti-Jewish resentment. Apparently German propaganda did indeed present Hitler as a God-sent savior.[188] Soon, even the newly installed shah, Muhammad Riza Pahlavi, publicly expressed concern about Axis broadcasts portraying the German dictator as a religious figure and defender of Islam.[189]

Propaganda targeting the Muslims of British India—an area also covered by the "Orient Office" of Radio Zeesen—was particularly sensitive. Berlin aired three different daily programs to India, including *Azad Muslim (Free Muslims)* in Urdu. Yet, in 1943, it was broadcasting only fifteen minutes a day. Instead of addressing individual religious groups, the regime's India propaganda usually blamed England for cultivating religious hatred.[190] With Subhas Chandra Bose, Berlin's main Indian collaborator, officially pursuing a policy of unity among India's different religious groups, it was almost impossible for Zeesen to preach holy war in its radio programs on the subcontinent. As the war progressed, however, even in the Indian case German propaganda drew increasingly on Islam. One of the more notable examples was a speech by the mufti in Urdu translation on Sunday, 23 August 1942, in which he addressed the Muslims, denouncing London's hostility toward Islam around the world and calling on them to resist British rule.[191] London reacted promptly in its Arabic broadcast, assuring listeners of the steadfast support of the Indian Muslims for the Allies.[192] In the following month, the Italian Indian service sent a declaration by the legendary Pashtu rebel leader Mirza Ali Khan, known as the Fakir of Ipi, who fought in Waziristan, approving al-Husayni's speech and proclaiming that the enemy of the Axis was also the enemy of Islam and India.[193] The text of Ali Khan's statement originated, in fact, not in the mountains of northern Waziristan but in an Italian propaganda office in Rome.[194]

Even so, the Germans were indeed in contact with Mirza Ali Khan and his followers on the Northwest Frontier, a hotbed of unrest in British India since the nineteenth century.[195] In the interwar period, Ali Khan had emerged as the major rebel commander of the area, and, like many of his predecessors, he was not merely a political leader but also a religious dignitary calling for jihad against imperial intrusion. To put down the guerillas and prevent attacks against the imperial infrastructure the British kept a great number of Indian Army contingents in the region. German officials had been studying the Northwest Frontier for some time. A fifty-two-page report on the region, written in 1941, stressed the strategic importance not only of the Sunni majority, "fanatic enemies of the British," but also of their "religious fanaticism."[196] Around the same time, Berlin began, in cooperation with the Italians, systematically supporting Ali Khan, supplying money, weapons, and ammunition.[197] German documents show that supplies were organized through the German mission in Kabul, directed by veteran diplomat Hans Pilger, who employed local couriers. On the British side, intelligence reports reveal imperial concerns about these contacts.[198] The reports show that Afghan provincial authorities did indeed try everything to prevent Axis transports from crossing the Durand Line.[199] Over the course of the war, the British gradually choked off the flow of the supplies until they stopped altogether in 1942. In autumn 1942, Ali Khan turned to al-Husayni and al-Kilani in a letter, carried by one of his messengers to the German mission in Kabul, affirming that he would continue his fight against the British despite a lack of arms and ammunition.[200] For the German public he was the "Freedom Hero of Waziristan."[201]

With the exception of the rebels of the Northwest Frontier, most of India's Muslim population remained calm. The Muslim League, which developed into the biggest Muslim mass organization during the war years, proved loyal to Britain. Its leader, Muhammad Jinnah shrewdly used the situation to push for partition but at all times remained loyal to the British.[202] In the Indian provinces, Muslim leaders called for war against the Axis.[203] Of course the attitudes of Islamic movements and groups in India cannot be limited to the Muslim League. Some were indeed more hostile to the British rulers, such as the members of the Jam'iyat al-'Ulama, an organization of leading Indian 'ulama, under Maulana Kifayat Ullah, the unofficial mufti of India, who was openly anti-imperialist and repeatedly arrested; German officials even toyed briefly with the idea of establishing direct contact with Kifayat Ullah.[204]

Muslim Responses to the German Courting of Islam

The reception and the effectiveness of Germany's broadcast propaganda are difficult to assess. In most parts of North Africa and the Middle East, no elaborate mechanisms to monitor public opinion were in place. Intelligence reports drew no coherent picture. While Allied authorities tended to believe that the population supported their cause, Axis officials tended to believe the opposite—a result of the specific reactions they received from trusted collaborators and of their personal interest in promoting their own propaganda work as a success. Texts from Muslim writers, on the other side, usually represented only a small segment of society. To be sure, overall German propaganda faced many obstacles.

First there were technical problems. While illiteracy posed a serious obstacle to pamphlet propaganda, the reception of broadcasts was limited for a host of reasons. Only few in North Africa and the Middle East owned broadcast receivers. According to a 1941 study by the US Office of War Information, by far the highest number of shortwave radios in the Arab world could be found in Egypt, with 55,000 receivers, while there were only twenty-six registered in Saudi Arabia.[205] Of course, many, if not most, of them were in the hands of Europeans. In the major war zone, Cyrenaica, the Muslim population owned virtually no broadcast receivers, according to a front report from Neurath.[206] Radios, however, were often available in public places—in bazaar stores, town squares, and coffeehouses—where people gathered. The Germans were well aware of the importance of the radios in these places. When still in Baghdad, Fritz Grobba tried to bribe coffeehouse owners to tune in to Zeesen.[207] Nevertheless, broadcast propaganda could never reach an audience on the scale it did in Europe. And even those few with access to radios regularly faced technological problems, most importantly a shortage of electricity and insufficient wavelength capacity. Moreover, as the ruling powers in most areas of the region, the Allies enforced strict censorship—especially in public places—and made extensive efforts to jam German broadcasts.

In terms of content, too, Nazi propaganda faced several major obstacles. First, the often aggressive tone, vulgar language, and violent content of the programs were aimed mainly at uneducated segments of society. Their appeal to the educated elites who in fact owned most of the radios—and even to the audiences in urban coffeehouses—may have been weaker.

Contemplating the "violence of the language used in the German broadcast," Miles Lampson (later Lord Killearn), British ambassador to Egypt, noted: "It is possible that this violence appeals to the more primitive type of listener but it should tend, one may hope, to defeat its purpose among the more cultivated Orientals, whose sense of propriety is strongly developed."[208] One Egyptian diplomat told an English colleague that the horror stories about British troops in Muslim lands—"stories of drunken orgies, rape, killings"—were often so obscene that his wife regularly insisted on turning off the radio as listening to the program made her feel sick.[209] Berlin's airings "provide just the stuff the extremists want to work on fanatical elements" but were "ridiculed in moderate quarters," the British representative in Syria reported.[210] His colleague from a Persian Gulf post observed that the local Muslims found "amusement in the fact that Yunis [sic] Bahri can work himself up into a pitch of excitement at will."[211] Second, German propaganda—both print and broadcast—avoided the thorny question of independence from colonial rule. Respecting the imperial interests of Italy, Vichy France, and Franco's Spain in North Africa and the Middle East, authorities in Berlin had to accept that their alliances cost them much sympathy among Muslims. Third, the blatant exploitation of religion—the strident piety promoted by German propaganda—offended many believers.[212] Fourth, German propaganda faced problems of credibility and authenticity, as even the most naïve listeners were aware that it served profane political interests. Finally, and perhaps most importantly, the Germans had no hegemony over public opinion. As the mightiest powers in the region, the Allies organized a massive campaign to counter the propaganda, which will be discussed later.

Overall, German propaganda failed. Uprisings against the Allies in North Africa and the Middle East did not take place. Moreover, desertions of Muslim soldiers from the enemies' ranks remained marginal.[213] With no weapons or practical help and under strict Allied control, even for those who were receptive to German calls for holy war, a revolt, or even major acts of sabotage seemed impracticable. Research on the reception of Nazism in different parts of North Africa and the Middle East suggests that its impact should not be overestimated.[214] On the whole, opinions expressed in the public sphere were quite diverse—reflecting the heterogeneity of the societies in the region—ranging from fascination and sympathy to concern and contempt. Yet, whatever their views, the vast majority showed no reaction to Berlin's calls for religious violence and revolt. It is, moreover, striking that the Islamic slogans of Germany's propaganda also had little resonance in religious circles and among the leading 'ulama—as a broad-sketch view quickly reveals.

Among the listeners of Radio Berlin in Iran is said to have been the young mullah Ruhollah Musavi, in the holy city of Qum.[215] Every evening, Musavi, who had a radio set built by the British manufacturer Pye, appar-ently hosted numerous mullahs and seminary students who came to his house to listen to Zeesen's Persian service. Mullah Musavi, who later be-came known to the world as Ayatollah Khomeini, seemed little impressed by the German program. In 1942 he published the tract *Kashf al-Asrar* (*The Revealing of Secrets*), his first political statement, in which he not only agitated against the antireligious polemics of the Pahlavi state and called for rule on the principles of Islam but also raged against oppressive regimes more generally, denouncing the "Hitlerite ideology" (*maram-i Hitleri*) as "the most poisonous and heinous product of the human mind."[216] Some other younger clerics had more pro-German leanings, most famously the ardent anti-imperialist Ayatollah Abu al-Qasem Kashani, whose father, the late Ayatollah Mostafa Kashani, had died fighting British troops in south-ern Iraq during the jihad of the First World War, and who, in 1943, was arrested for pro-German activities by British authorities.[217] The conserva-tive clerical establishment in Iran, however, abstained from politics, re-signed to their seminaries.[218] Prominent clerics such as Ayatollah Muham-mad Husayn Burujirdi, who shortly after the war emerged as the sole *marja'-i taqlid*, the highest religious authority in Shi'a Islam, preached po-litical quietism.[219] Outside Iran, too, Shi'a authorities remained cautious. The Shi'a 'ulama of Najaf and Karbala was not, unlike during the First World War, united behind Germany.[220] In early 1940, Amin al-Husayni, then in Baghdad, tried to persuade some of the Shi'a leaders of southern Iraq to endorse his jihad, approaching the senior clerics 'Abd al-Karim al-Jaza'iri and Muhammad Kashif al-Ghita, who had both played prominent roles in Iraqi politics during the interwar years.[221] While al-Jaza'iri gave short shrift to the Palestinian mufti, Kashif al-Ghita was more receptive, issuing a fatwa with a call for holy war against the British Empire, which was also announced by Yunus Bahri on Radio Berlin on 13 February 1940—though with little effect.[222] No major Shi'a uprising broke out during the war. The Germans had little more impressive to record than some graffiti: in early

1942 a German diplomat reported that in both Beirut and Damascus the slogan "Hitler, the successor of 'Ali" had appeared on the walls, scrawled by Shi'a rebels or possibly by German agents.[223]

In the Mashriq, German propaganda received a mixed reception. On the fringes of the Arab world, in the Persian Gulf region, Muhammad al-Qasimi, who would later become amir of Sharjah of the United Arab Emirates, recalled the propaganda war in his memoirs: "The news from the German radio station, with the sharp tongue of the Iraqi broadcaster Yunus Bahri, would infuriate the supporters of the Allies, just as the news coming from the BBC Middle East Service through the voice of the Syrian Munir Shamma angered the supporters of the Axis. From the windows overlooking the fort's front square we children watched the fighting between the two sides."[224] According to al-Qasimi, wartime propaganda divided the listeners: "Half of the people supported the Allies and half supported the Axis powers." This diversity of opinion prevailed in many parts of the region. Prominent 'ulama and religious authorities, however, in most cases remained silent, with only a few notable exceptions. After the 1941 invasion of the Vichy Levant, for instance, the powerful mufti of Lebanon, Shaykh Muhammad Tawfiq Khalid, openly sided with the Allies.[225]

Closer to the North African front line, in Egypt, the attitude of the population was similarly mixed. Anwar al-Sadat, then a young officer in wartime Cairo, later claimed that there were strong pro-German sentiments among the population: "The general feeling in Egypt was against the British and, naturally, in favor of their enemies," he recalled, adding: "They demonstrated in the streets, chanting slogans like 'Advance Rommel!' as they saw in a British defeat the only way of getting their enemy out of the country."[226] Al-Sadat was part of the revolutionary "Free Officers" group, which—in the name of the people—sought armed revolt during the war and even collaborated with German agents, an entanglement that, in the summer of 1942, eventually led to his arrest. British reports give a more nuanced assessment of the local mood, suggesting that political attitudes were not static but continuously changing during the war years. Miles Lampson cabled from Cairo that Rommel's first offensive in Cyrenaica in spring 1941 had "thoroughly frightened the Egyptian public."[227] Even German propagandists were aware of the lack of pro-German sympathies in the country at that time.[228] During the second offensive the following year, however—coinciding with the Anglo-Egyptian government crisis of

4 February 1942, and the great anti-British student protests—the situation was different. Demonstrations in the streets of Cairo were often accompanied by pro-German chants—as later recalled by al-Sadat.[229] Horrified, Lampson noted the "Long live Rommel" slogans, while the German officials excitedly reported "Heil Rommel" cries in Cairo.[230] Yet, as Rommel advanced further in the summer of 1942 and actually crossed the Egyptian border, suddenly posing a real threat, the mood changed again. Lampson now observed a "lack of hostility among [the] Egyptian population."[231] "Some elements who, out of anti-British feeling, were enthusiastic about the Germans at a distance, seem seriously alarmed now that the German menace is so much nearer," he cabled to Whitehall.[232] Once the German advance was stopped, he reiterated that the "rapid Axis advance eastward" had "given the country a throughout fright," though "the attitude of the Egyptians, particularly the Moslems," had been "remarkably good and calm."[233] Similarly, at the height of the Battle of al-'Alamayn, he summarized: "Appearance of the enemy at the doors of Egypt has caused a very general realization of the unpleasantness of an Axis occupation, even amongst elements hitherto notoriously anti-British. Result has been a considerable turn of feeling in our favour."[234] And the British advance that followed Montgomery's victory was also, according to Lampson, welcomed by the majority in Egypt: "Our occupation of Tripoli has caused general delight as definitely relieving Egypt of invasion bugbear," he cabled in early 1943.[235]

Germany's call for jihad also had, on the whole, little resonance among the country's religious groups and organizations. The Islamic establishment mainly refrained from making political statements. Shaykh 'Abd al-Majid Salim, the influential mufti of Egypt during the war years, was one of the country's main proponents of political neutrality.[236] His even more powerful rival, Muhammad Mustafa al-Maraghi, the reformist rector of al-Azhar, the heart of the traditional 'ulama, followed a similar line. A student of Muhammad 'Abduh, al-Maraghi had served as chief *qadi* of the Sudan and president of the Supreme Shari'a Court in Cairo and enjoyed close ties to the court.[237] A British report of 1941 described him as in "a class by himself among Egyptian divines."[238] Although vigorously pleading for the neutrality of the Islamic world in the war, al-Maraghi had usually been a loyal partner of the British Empire. The *Daily Telegraph* even celebrated him as one of the Crown's most trusted allies: "It is not true, as ignorance might suppose, that anti-British feeling flourishes most in conservative

Islamic circles," it explained, referring to al-Maraghi as "one of Egypt's clearest heads and most vigorous characters," who was with the British empire "on most issues."[239] The political activities of Azhari students—many of whom were more radical and pro-German in their views than their rector—were closely controlled by the authorities.

And yet, while the traditional 'ulama remained quiet, popular Islamic revivalist movements like the Muslim Brotherhood, with their fervent hostility to British imperialism, were more receptive to advances from their enemy's enemies.[240] In the 1930s, the German legation in Cairo had even supported the organization financially.[241] Now, during the war, certain factions of the Muslim Brotherhood, which had become Egypt's biggest Islamic organization, expressed some sympathy for the Axis. Egyptian police reports reveal that some of its followers even distributed subversive pro-Axis pamphlets as Rommel's troops marched on Cairo.[242] "The Ikhwan were naturally excited by the advance of the enemy to Al-'Alamein, and some pro-German speeches were made," a British military intelligence report stated.[243] Alarmed, the authorities kept the group under firm control. Its papers were temporarily banned, a number of its branches closed, its meetings placed under surveillance, and several of its provincial leaders arrested. Hasan al-Banna's house was raided by security forces looking for revolutionary pamphlets, and he and his right-hand man, Ahmad al-Sukkari, were even briefly taken into custody. In the end, al-Banna openly pledged his loyalty to the ruling authorities.[244] Fearful of Islamic unrest, the British remained cautious nonetheless. As late as 1944, long after the defeat of the Germans in North Africa, an intelligence report described the organization as "a potential danger that cannot be discounted."[245]

In the Maghrib, German calls for religious revolt were also met with reservations. On the major battlefield, the desert wastes of Cyrenaica, Konstantin von Neurath observed a mixture of attitudes among the Muslim population, ranging from friendliness to outright hostility.[246] Having suffered under ruthless Italian subjugation, most Muslims in the area were opposed to Mussolini and his German ally.[247] Religious movements were often the spearhead of this anticolonial opposition, most importantly of course the Islamic Sanusi order, the strongest religious and political force in the region. Having fought on the German side during the First World War, the Sanusis had now changed sides. Its leader, Muhammad

Idris al-Sanusi, who had succeeded his older cousin Ahmad al-Sharif al-Sanusi after the defeat in First World War, now, from Egyptian exile, called on his followers to take up arms on the side of the Allies.[248] Sanusi warriors even fought alongside the British army against the Axis, seeking a Sanusi amirate in the postwar order. Once Rommel's troops were ousted and Italian rule was crushed, the Sanusi network of *zawiya*s was reestablished in many areas of Cyrenaica, forming new religious and administrative centers. In liberated Tripolitania, too, the influential religious establishment quickly sided with the Allies. In early 1943, the mufti of Tripoli made a public statement praising Churchill and Great Britain.[249] Across the North African war zone few seem to have accepted the Germans as liberators of Islam.

Berlin's calls for religious violence against Jews also generated mixed responses from Muslims in North Africa and the Middle East. To be sure, the war years saw a rise in anti-Zionist, and indeed anti-Jewish, resentment across the region, and German propaganda nurtured it. On the local level, however, relationships between Jewish and Muslim communities were often complex—depending on specific social and political conditions—and cannot easily be generalized. There were no major anti-Jewish riots during the war. The most significant anti-Jewish outburst was the pogrom in Iraq, known as *farhud*, when, after the failed al-Kilani coup in 1941, a Muslim mob attacked Jewish houses and shops, murdering 179.[250] German troops in the North African war zone did not have enough time to systematically organize the extermination of the Jewish population. Italian and Vichy authorities did, however, adopt various anti-Jewish policies.[251] The reactions of the Muslim population to these measures were diverse, ranging from collaboration and profiteering to indifference and, in some cases, empathy. There were also some cases of Muslim solidarity with their Jewish neighbors. Troubled by the Vichy government's anti-Jewish laws, Sultan Muhammad V of Morocco famously supported his Jewish subjects.[252] He also refused to consider Jewish converts to Islam (though insignificant in number) as Jewish—confronting racial definitions of Jewishness. In Algeria, too, parts of the Islamic establishment showed open solidarity with the Jewish population.[253] The eminent Islamic dignitary Shaykh Tayyib al-'Uqbi even issued appeals banning attacks on Jews. In Tunisia, the beys showed some solidarity with their Jewish minority.[254] In Libya, Muslims did not attack their Jewish neighbors during the war.[255] In Egypt, the Muslim population also refrained from engaging in any major acts of anti-Jewish violence before 1945, although the war years did see a massive rise in anti-Zionist agitation, with at times outright anti-Jewish overtones.[256]

Overall, it is hard to reach definitive conclusions about the reception of German religious propaganda in the region. But the snapshots suggest that it was far less successful than officials in Berlin had hoped. Future research will have to refine this picture, taking different local conditions more thoroughly into account.

It is also noteworthy that, as soldiers, Muslims from North Africa, the wider Middle East, and beyond massively contributed to the Allied war effort. Many thousands of Muslims fought under British command.[257] Indeed, they constituted the largest religious group of the British Indian Army, which grew to more than 2 million men and formed the biggest volunteer force of the war. Across the Islamic world, Muslims served the empire. In Palestine, about 9,000 Muslims were recruited into units of the British army—with the help of al-Husayni's arch rival, Fakhri al-Nashashibi. Muslims also loyally served under British command in the legendary Arab Legion of Transjordan, which was employed in different parts of the Middle East. In North Africa, Libyan Sanusi fighters were mobilized into the Sanusi Arab Force (later Libyan Arab Force). At the same time, thousands of Muslims fought in the ranks of the Free French Forces (*Forces françaises libres*). From French North Africa alone no fewer than 233,000 men enlisted to fight against Nazi Germany—134,000 Algerians, 73,000 Moroccans and 26,000 Tunisians—eventually liberating Europe.[258]

Still, the Allies took Germany's propaganda very seriously. "In view of Egypt's position in the Mohammedan world there is no telling how wide might be the repercussions of any unrest starting in the Valley of the Nile," *Foreign Affairs* warned in July 1941.[259] British, American, and Free French propagandists tried to respond to German propaganda with their own Islamic programs, entering into a propaganda war about the political meaning of Islam in the conflict.

Allied Responses to the German Courting of Islam

Shortly after the landing of Rommel's troops in North Africa, the *Frankfurter Zeitung* lamented that London was trying with "great effort" to turn the Islamic world against Nazi Germany, accusing "British propaganda" of using the Qur'an to prove "an ideological affinity between Islam and democracy."[260] In fact, debates at Whitehall about the political and propagandistic role of Islam had already started, on the eve of the war.[261] Using the same methods as the Germans, British propagandists drew extensively on the authority of Islam to promote their political messages.

London ran or controlled some of the most powerful radio stations in the region.[262] The BBC Arabic shortwave service in Daventry had reacted promptly to Zeesen's Qur'an references and recitations. Stewart Perowne, an official responsible for the station's Arabic program, reported on the eve of the war: "On the evening of the opening of the Berlin broadcasts, as soon as I had heard the first programme, I took steps to increase the number of our Koran recordings."[263] Utilizing the capacities of their global empire, British officials were in a position to hire some of the world's finest reciters. They made particular use of the celebrated reciters of the London-controlled Egyptian State Broadcast.[264] Over the course of the war Qur'an recitations were stepped up and eventually also delivered at the beginning of the station's Arabic news bulletin. Islam also regularly featured prominently in the program itself.

At the same time, British propagandists flooded North Africa with pamphlets, here, too, employing Islam for political purposes.[265] Attacks on the Nazi regime regularly included an accusation of atheism. A pamphlet distributed in 1941 warned Muslims of the "Godless" Germans who sought to "destroy religion in the world," as it was "the one pillar which will stand against their tyranny."[266] "On the orders of Hitler," it claimed, "German aeroplanes will from now on bomb mosques, zawiyas, tombs of saints, and other shrines." Drawing on sacred scripture, the pamphlet also included a reference to verse 114 (108) of sura 2, concerning Allah's punishment of those who strive to destroy Islamic places of worship. Other pamphlets accused German propagandists of exploiting religion. Attacking the use of Islam in Nazi propaganda, one leaflet distributed in 1941 blamed Berlin for "profaning the Muslim religion" in order to "deceive" the pious.[267] Quoting passages from the hadith on the subject of truth, it condemned all sorts of lies spread by Nazi propaganda. A similar pamphlet was spread the following year, featuring a photograph of Goebbels.[268] Another leaflet set quotations from the Qur'an denouncing adultery next to Nazi slogans encouraging Germans to produce offspring by any possible means.[269] "This type of propaganda is always good down here where the Mohammedan religion is taken seriously," an official in London internally commented on the text.[270] Most of these pamphlets nicknamed Hitler a *khanzir*, "pig," with obvious religious connotations.

Furthermore, London produced pamphlets portraying Great Britain as the defender of Islam and religion in general. A leaflet distributed in 1941 explained that one reason that Great Britain would be victorious was that "the British believe in God and God's commands" and therefore "cannot be defeated by an enemy such as Hitler who knows no God and no religion."[271] The following year the British spread a brochure in the North African war zone that showed the *hamsa* and below it the Arabic letter "nun" (victory sign) inscribed with the words: "Britain's victory is certain."[272] Like their German counterparts, London's propagandists also made use of the religious calendar by selecting specific Islamic holidays to distribute pamphlets that mixed political messages with felicitations on the religious occasion. At the beginning of the month of Ramadan in 1941, the British circulated postcards wishing the people an "exalted, blessed and happy month of Ramadan" in the name of "the people of England and her allies."[273] A 1942 Ramadan pamphlet, richly illustrated and adorned with quotations from the Qur'an, proclaimed to the faithful: "On the occasion of the glorious month of Ramadan the champions of freedom and brotherhood amongst men in the British Nations and the Americas wish their Moslem friends a blessed peace and a fortunate Id el Fitr."[274] The most important occasion of the Islamic calendar for British propaganda, however, was the annual pilgrimage. Indeed, London made every effort to facilitate the hajj during the war years and eagerly advertised these measures propagandistically.[275] In late 1941, at the end of the hajj season, officials distributed an Arabic postcard that praised British efforts to enable Muslims of the empire to travel safely to the Hijaz and to protect them from Hitler's aggressions.[276] The following season, a pamphlet assured believers that even in times of war the empire was prepared to provide pilgrims with ships and protection for their journey to Mecca: "In view of the friendship and the support given her by the Moslem peoples throughout the world, Britain regards it as her honourable privilege to play her part in enabling the pious haji to reach the shores of their holy land."[277] Visualizing British bonds with Islam, it featured colorful images of the Woking Mosque near London, a carpet showing the Ka'ba, and a vessel carrying pilgrims. In the same year, loyal leaders from the Islamic world were presented with an elaborate hajj brochure containing glossy illustrations and Qur'anic verses.[278] Finally, some pamphlets distributed by London's emissaries in North Africa would go so far as to interpret the war in the Maghrib as part of a wider struggle of the Islamic world against the Axis. One propaganda leaflet even praised "Chinese Moslem warriors," who, under Chiang Kai-shek, were fighting the Axis in Asia.[279]

Apart from these pamphlets, London produced a number of war journals in Arabic, among them *News of the Week* (*Akhbar al-'Usbua*), *War News* (*Akhbar al-Harb*), and the *Arab Listener* (*al-Mustami al-'Arabi*), all featuring Islamic issues. The first issue of *Akhbar al-'Usbua* (1 May 1942) even proclaimed that the time was not far away when the Muslims would declare jihad against the Axis dictatorships and their allies.[280] *Al-Mustami al-'Arabi* included articles on subjects like the discrepancies between National Socialism and Islam or the alleged Nazi suppression of the Muslims of Poland.[281] The Germans monitored all of these activities with apprehension. Among the British propaganda material assessed in Berlin were the illustrated hajj pamphlet of 1942, the *hamsa* brochure, and a pamphlet on Abdullah of Jordan, who was promoted as a descendent of the Prophet—thus, as in the First World War, the British capitalized on their Hashemite allies' sacred genealogy—and featured the slogan "Britain's victory is certain—insha'Allah."[282]

Berlin's Muslim allies were usually ignored in British propaganda—particularly Amin al-Husayni. Harold MacMichael, high commissioner of Palestine, had from the beginning advised refraining from direct attacks.[283] The "only sound course is to avoid any mention of Haj Amin," he suggested, since "attacks on Haj Amin by us merely serve to enhance his reputation."[284] As all assaults on the renegade cleric were eagerly taken up by Berlin for counterattacks, their only effect would be to create the impression that he was an important authority in the world of Islam. "My feeling still is that, except possibly for an occasional disdainful reference to him in passing, it is the best to leave him alone," MacMichael wrote at the height of the North African campaign.[285] Mandate authorities had stripped al-Husayni of his worldly offices but decided not to deprive him of his title of "grand mufti," anxious to avoid the impression of British interference in matters considered religious by Muslims.[286]

London employed its own religious figures to oppose German propaganda. Most important in the North African war zone were the leaders of the Sanusi brotherhood, especially, but not exclusively, Muhammad Idris al-Sanusi himself. On 19 December 1942, the British army even organized a grand *'Id al-Adha* spectacle in the Cyrenaican port city of Benghazi to celebrate the religious holiday with Sanusi troops.[287] Present was the Sanusi commander Rida al-Mahdi al-Sanusi. In Cairo and Alexandria, the British set up a volunteer propagandist organization that consisted of religious leaders, all graduates of al-Azhar.[288] Across the empire, British authorities encouraged Islamic leaders to call the pious to support the war effort. In 1940, Lord Linlithgow even suggested a "Pan-Islamic Conference" to demonstrate that the "Axis expansion in Mohammedan regions" was "against the interests of Islam," although the plan was blocked by officials in Whitehall, fearing that such a gathering could too easily turn into "an anti-British affair."[289]

Finally, Washington made similar propaganda efforts. When Anglo-American troops landed in Algeria and Morocco to launch Operation Torch, agents of the Office of Strategic Services (OSS) dropped religious pamphlets, addressing the people in Arabic ("Praise be unto the only God. In the name of God, the Compassionate, the Merciful, O ye Moslems") and informing them that "the American Holy Warriors have arrived . . . to fight the great Jihad of Freedom."[290] The pamphlet was written by two US secret agents, Carlton Coon and Gordon H. Brown, both of the OSS and working in the Atlas Mountains of Morocco. It was created at the request of the chief of the OSS, Major General William J. Donovan. Coon later recounted that when they had written the text in English, they gave it to a local Arab who began to read it aloud in the manner of a holy man reading the Qur'an. Struck by the lyricism that crept into the text as he declaimed, they decided to use not their own version but a revision based on the Arab's rendition. It was signed "Roosevelt." US propaganda broadcasts also employed religion. During Ramadan 1943, the Voice of America in Arabic broadcast a speech by a Muslim scholar from the United States who asserted that there were several mosques in Detroit, one in Brooklyn, and also one in Chicago.[291] A month later, a report by the Office of War Information noted: "We now have religious programs on the principal Moslem holidays."[292] It also said: "We feel that having Koran readings every Friday is probably too often" as the "Germans have used the device of Koran readings so frequently that it has become something of an earmark of the

Axis type of propaganda." Yet, by 1944, Washington was broadcasting Qur'an readings several times a day.[293]

Alongside religion, Allied propagandists also found it convenient to emphasize Nazi Germany's racist ideology, its racist beliefs about the inferiority of other peoples, especially those outside Europe, and its conception of Arabs as "Semites."[294] The French had used this approach from the outset.

French authorities, who from the beginning monitored German efforts to exploit Islam, organized various countermeasures.[295] On the eve of the war, they distributed the anti-German brochure *Le racisme et l'Islam* in the Maghrib, which emphasized the incompatibility of Islam and National Socialism.[296] High-ranking French imperial officials attended religious celebrations in early 1940, promoting the Third Republic as the protector of Islam and denouncing Berlin's Islamic propaganda as doomed, just as it had been in 1914.[297] Free French authorities later continued these policies. As Vichy authorities were ousted from North Africa, Charles de Gaulle declared in a broadcast that "France is and will remain the sincere and tested friend of the Muslims."[298] Even Moscow's propaganda in North Africa and the Middle East drew on Islam, using broadcasts and pamphlets and sending trusted Islamic dignitaries to the region to promote Stalin as a friend of the faithful.[299]

The Germans tried their best to discredit this propaganda. In July 1942, Berlin's standard Arabic broadcast service denounced the opening of the London mosque at Regent's Park as cheap propaganda and a result of the "British intent to fool the Moslem people," asserting that the "Moslems [will] never forget their humiliation" by the British Empire.[300] On a religious show broadcast by the BBC, Zeesen saw blatant heresy. "The British mock your Qoran," Radio Berlin announced.[301] "Will you allow it to become a subject of their mockery?" The BBC was called "an infidel station." London had "for long years" profaned "the sanctity of the traditions of Islam," the speaker proclaimed. "The British will never deviate from their policy which they set down long ago and by which they hope to crush Islam." With some frustration, Zeesen called on its Arab listeners:

We wonder where those persons are who pretend to defend Islam. Where are the Ulemas and sheikhs? Where are those who demonstrated in the streets of Aleppo and Damascus in defence of their religion? Where, indeed are those martyrs of Cairo? Where are the brave men in Baghdad? Where are the heroes of Damascus, who all claimed to be the defenders of their religion, their traditions and their Qoran?[302]

German Soldiers and Islam in the North African War Zones

Germany's attempts to employ religion for its war efforts in North Africa were largely limited to pamphlet and broadcast propaganda. Immediate interference with the religious life of the local population, as in the Eastern territories or to some extent in the Balkans, rarely took place, as Germany never properly occupied areas of North Africa. Officially, Berlin acknowledged the primacy of Italian, Vichy, and Spanish interests in the region and regarded its own presence there as strictly military. Mussolini continued to rule Libya. Tunisia remained under a Vichy administration, namely, under the executive of the *résident général*, Jean-Pierre Estéva, and, nominally, the bey of Tunis. Only near the end of the campaign, in November 1942, when the German-Italian forces retreated to Tunisia, did the Germans take over parts of the administration in the country—simultaneously with Hitler's occupation of the rest of France—though the German command depended on the French administration.[303] Between autumn 1942 and spring 1943, roughly the period of German military rule over Muslim mountaineers in the Caucasus, around 2.5 million Tunisian Muslims lived under Nazi occupation, although the Germans were clustered in Tunis, then a city of roughly 400,000.

Despite its minimal administrative involvement with local Muslims, the Wehrmacht was in daily contact with the coastal population of North Africa between early 1941 and early 1943, in Tunisia, Libya, and, briefly, western Egypt (Figures 3.5, 3.6, and 3.7). The army command made significant efforts to avoid alienating Muslims. After all, German propaganda for North Africa and the Middle East promoted a clear image of the Third Reich as a friend of Islam, and the army was eager to preserve this image on the ground. Convinced of the strategic importance of religion, the Wehrmacht command tried to train soldiers to respect the religious sentiments of the Muslim population.

As early as 1941, the High Command of the Wehrmacht distributed the sixty-four-page military handbook *Der Islam* among troops fighting in

3.5 German officers and local leaders, Cyrenaica, September 1942 (*Ullstein*).

3.6 Soldiers of the Africa Corps, Siwa Oasis (Western Egypt), 1942 (*Ullstein*).

3.7 A young Muslim and a German, Libya, 1942 (*Ullstein*).

North Africa to train them to behave correctly toward Muslims (Figure 3.8). The booklet was intended not only to introduce soldiers to practical dos and don'ts when interacting with Muslims in the field but also to give them a concise overview of the history and traditions of Islamic culture.[304] The declared aim of the brochure was to prevent the sorts of behavior Muslims perceived as insulting or offensive. It warned that the German soldiers' lack of knowledge or their misconceptions about Islam could get them into an "unpleasant, obstructive, under certain circumstances even dangerous situation."[305] To prevent religious unrest, the brochure aimed to help Wehrmacht soldiers understand the "thinking and doing of a devout Muslim."[306] Often speaking of the "Muslim" in the singular, the brochure promised to be a tool to decode the Muslim psyche.

The main part of the booklet gave a concise overview of Islamic history and informed its readers of basic Muslim teachings and schools, rites, celebrations, and customs. "The knowledge of the religious foundations of the life of Islamic peoples," it explained, would "prevent . . . mistakes."[307] It concluded with nineteen general guidelines that soldiers were advised to follow on the ground.[308] The recurring principle was respect for Muslims:

Der Islam

VON

OBERFELDARZT

PROF. DR. ERNST RODENWALDT

1941   Heft 52

Tornisterschrift des Oberkommandos der Wehrmacht Abt. Inland

3.8 *Der Islam*, Tornisterschrift des Oberkommandos der Wehrmacht (Ernst Rodenwaldt), 1941 (BA–MA).

by showing the wrong attitude toward Muslims, the text instructed, "every possibility for communication and sympathetic cooperation is at risk from the outset, and sometimes made impossible."[309] Conversely, it was made clear that there was "no better key to the psyche of the Muslim than when he feels that one knows his faith and pays respect to it."[310] Consequently, the brochure appealed to the German soldier to show "unreserved respect" for Islam.[311]

The list of practical instructions included pragmatic advice. "If you wish to have a conversation with a Muslim about Islam, assume equality between your and his religion," soldiers were told, ignoring the realities of German supremacist propaganda.[312] The men were given concrete examples of how to employ religion to their advantage. A Mecca pilgrim was deemed to be of particular tactical value. "Approach those persons who have made the pilgrimage to Mecca, hajjis, with respect."[313] They were to be recognized through their physical attributes: "Mostly, they are distinguishable through the wearing of a turban, a beard, and a white garment."[314] There were even instructions about how to make friends with the hajjis: "Conversation with a hajji, a chat about his experiences during the pilgrimage awakens in him the proudest experience of his life and convinces him that the stranger also appreciates the distinction of his status."[315] When encountering Muslim beggars, on the other hand, soldiers were advised that they could give them money. "Give beggars small alms in small denominations with a friendly mien. Never reject them in a surly manner. If you don't have coins with you, or if you don't want to give anything, say pleasantly in the local language: 'Allah will provide.'"[316] Soldiers were advised to use religious language also on other occasions: "If you organize an appointment with a Muslim for the future, add to the arrangement the word 'Insha'Allah,' 'God willing'; for example: 'We will meet tomorrow at 2 o'clock . . . Insha'Allah!'"[317]

Particular attention was paid to sacred places—mosques, shrines, and cemeteries—that soldiers encountered across North Africa.[318] Houses of worship, the booklet advised, were to be treated with great caution, even in a combat situation. "Never enter a mosque unless you are invited to visit it, or if the guard of the sanctuary shows you his approval to let you in. At any sign of rejection, refrain. Never try, though, on Friday or during the hour of the noon prayer to enter a mosque."[319] Military necessities and religious respect could, at times, conflict: "If the visit to a mosque is tied to any preconditions, such as the laying down of arms and removal of shoes, your self-respect demands that you refrain from the visit."[320] The booklet similarly sought to balance sensitivity about religious sites with military necessity: "If at all possible, avoid constructing defense sites that might destroy a Muslim tomb. Tombs count as sacrosanct."[321]

Moreover, soldiers were trained to respect religious rituals, most importantly Muslim prayers. "Respect it if a Muslim, according to his custom, performs his prayer in public. Don't observe him curiously during what is for him a holy act. Do not disturb him. Do not try under any circumstances to take a photograph of him during prayer."[322] Soldiers were also cautioned about Islamic dietary requirements. It was explained that it was "wrong and tactless" to offer alcohol to a Muslim.[323] "Never oblige a person to eat food or drink drinks that are forbidden to him by law (pork, wine). Do not cheat him either under any circumstances regarding the nature of the food which you offer him."[324] Soldiers also learned that Muslims are, like Jews, circumcised (*khitan*). "In a Muslim country, it is considered an honor to be invited by a family to take part in the circumcision celebration of one of their children." Any such invitation would make it clear that they saw in him a "friend of Islam."[325]

Finally, soldiers were particularly cautioned about (perceived) Muslim gender roles. "In a Muslim town, no matter how many curious girls' and women's eyes look down from the grilled windows to the street, it is enormously tactless to greet them or wave up. . . . It is forbidden to address a Muslim woman or girl on the street or in a shop, even though she might lift her veil."[326] Points 13 to 15 of the instructions regulated gender interaction in detail. Even in military situations, soldiers had to adapt their practices: "If you have to gather information at a Muslim house, ring or knock, then turn your back to the door, in order that you do not see the woman who might be answering"; "Never ask a Muslim about his wife or other adult members of the family."[327]

In general, the booklet was based on the assumption that Muslims were governed by a coherent system of religious beliefs and practices that could be learned and practically used. Remarkably, its author, Ernst Rodenwaldt, was not an Islam expert but a medical specialist in malaria and the head of the tropical medicine institute at the Military Medical Academy in Berlin.[328] He was later responsible for infecting the Pontine marshes with malaria in 1943, causing, in all probability, 100,000 Italians to contract the disease and an unknown number to die of it. Rodenwaldt based his booklet on studies from the imperial age, the works of the German Orientalists Martin Hartmann (*Der Islam*, 1909) and Traugott Mann (*Der Islam einst und jetzt*, 1914), the Dutch Islam experts Christiaan Snouck Hurgronje (*Mekka*, 1888–1889) and Theodoor Willem Jan Juynboll (*Handbuch des islamischen Gesetzes*, 1910), and, finally, the (Jewish) Habsburg Orientalist Ignaz Goldziher (*Mohammedanische Studien*, 1889–1890).[329] The brochure thus drew on a tradition of Islam studies that had served to provide a resource for colonial officers. Rodenwaldt himself had had some experience with the imperial politics of Islam, having served in the Ottoman Empire during the First World War and later worked in the Dutch East Indies.

The German army distributed similar booklets about other issues to inform the troops about local conditions; one, for instance, was designed for Tunis alone.[330] Another, titled *Muhammad and Islam* (*Muhammed und der Islam*), was given out to train pilots posted in North Africa.[331] Moreover, troops were frequently instructed by leaflets and by articles published in *Die Oase*, the Wehrmacht's official field paper, and later, in *Die Karawane*, the paper for the troops in Tunisia.[332] Whether German soldiers were actually willing to carry leaflets, journals, and booklets with them through the heat of the Sahara remains open to speculation, but the efforts that army authorities made to distribute such instructions and pocket manuals show that they believed Islam to be militarily significant. A US report acknowledged German success in the Wehrmacht's training: "German soldiers were taught many of the points of Arab courtesy and were under strict orders to avoid offending the Arab population."[333]

In contrast, German propagandists were eager to make use of the apparent bewilderment of the local Muslim population at the behavior of US troops. In late 1942, Grobba's "Arab committee" suggested propagandistically exploiting the GIs' alleged misconduct.[334] Around the same time, the propaganda unit for Tunis was instructed to "especially emphasize" the "disrespect for the customs and conventions of the Mohammedans by the Americans," suggesting the slogan: "They are the allies of godless Bolshevism, which in other Mohammedan countries and in the Soviet Union persecutes the believers and pulls down mosques. The Axis powers, on the other hand, respect religion. Therefore, all Arab countries pray for their victory."[335] Evaluating a survey of attitudes among its troops, US military intelligence noted, in summer 1943, that the "American soldier definitely looks down on the Arab," cautioning: "We have definitely to respect the Moslem places of religion and the practice of Mohammedanism."[336] In fact, the US War Department had handed out an Islam manual, too, designed to instruct GIs in North Africa in the customs of Islam.[337]

As the Muslim population in Libya and western Egypt never stood under direct German administration, Wehrmacht officers only sporadically dealt directly with religious affairs. In some cases they consulted with the shaykhs of the local Sufi orders, whom they deemed politically influential in the frontline areas.[338] In Tunisia, where the Germans became more closely involved with the Muslim population (Figures 3.9 and 3.10), they tried to maintain good relations with the urban 'ulama and other religious dignitaries. Some of them were even employed as propagandists, among them religious scholars of the grand Zaytuna Mosque and University in Tunis.[339] A number of collaborating Islamic dignitaries were later evacuated along with the Wehrmacht troops. In late 1942, officials in Berlin even discussed sending the mufti of Jerusalem on a propaganda tour to Tunisia, but, due to the unstable military situation, these plans were eventually abandoned.[340]

German attempts to employ religion on the ground in Tunisia became most obvious during Islamic celebrations. The occupation of Tunis coincided with the 'Id al-Adha—or 'Id al-Kabir, as it was also called in the Maghrib—on 19 December 1942, the same day the British organized their celebration in Benghazi. Naturally, the Germans, too, did not miss the opportunity to exploit and politicize the day. In the late afternoon, Hans-Jürgen von Arnim and Rudolf Rahn paid an official visit to the bey of Tunis, Muhammad VII al-Munsif, to show their respect for Islam. Their motorcade of four large cars drove "at the solemn speed of 25 kilometers per hour," as Rahn reported, along the main road, the Avenue de Paris, before leaving Tunis in the direction of the coastal town Hamman Lif, where the Husainid ruler resided.[341] In front of the Winter Palace, hundreds of cheering people saluted the convoy. The bey's guard extended them an honorary welcome. In their conversations with the bey, the Germans promised that the next 'Id al-Adha would take place in times of peace. Arnim emphasized that he was trying to keep the war as far away from the population as possible. More important than these consultations, though,

3.9 German soldier and Muslim camel driver, Tunisia, 1943 (*Ullstein*).

3.10 Muslims performing guard service for the Germans, Tunisia, 1943 (*Ullstein*).

was the public display of German respect for Islam. Enthusiastically Rahn telegraphed Berlin to urge full propagandistic use of the "solemn reception" on the "'Id al-Kabir celebration" and the "reception by the espaliering population."[342] The propaganda paper *Signal* printed an entire series of photographs of the reception.[343] Accusing the bey of collaboration, the Allies later sent him into exile.

German concerns for respectful treatment of Islam derived primarily from tactical considerations. Yet, military priorities could also set limits to them. This became most clear in the discussion about air raids on Cairo. After Axis planes began bombing areas around the Egyptian capital in the summer of 1941, the Egyptian government protested, via a Swedish channel, to the German legation in Stockholm. Well aware of the Germans' purported friendship for Islam, the Egyptians argued that Cairo was not only an "open city without any fortifications" but also "a holy city for the Muslim world like Rome is for the Christian world."[344] At the Foreign Office, Ernst Woermann, who had always expressed reservations about German engagement with Islam, could not have cared less. In an internal note, he objected that Cairo was characterized not by its holy places but by its strategic and military significance, housing major British political and military headquarters as well as barracks of troops, warehouses, and magazines.[345] After all, he wrote, "Cairo cannot be counted among the line of holy cities to which Mecca, Medina, and Jerusalem belong." It was wrong to refer to Cairo as an open or even a holy city. Woermann's harsh response may have also been intended to quiet colleagues who were often all too eager to accept arguments related to Islam. To the Stockholm embassy he wrote on 18 September 1941, that the Egyptian government should address its protest to the British government, which was turning Egypt and its biggest city into theaters of war.[346]

The population of North Africa was, of course, constantly exposed to the violence of the war. The conflict brought massive destruction, especially to the coastal areas of Cyrenaica. Villages and towns were bombed, mosques and sacred sites destroyed (Figure 3.11). Many people in the front zones suffered from severe food and water shortages. Moreover, on the ground German attitudes toward Muslims frequently did not meet the standards laid down by training or the expectations raised by propaganda. This becomes obvious in a number of reports from the front zones complaining about the "quite clumsy" behavior of German troops toward the Muslim population and their failure to understand Muslims as part of a "religious and cultural sphere," which had to be considered a "significant factor" in the war effort.[347] Insights into the attitudes of ordinary German soldiers toward Muslims from the Maghrib are given by a memorandum of March 1942, written by Ahmed Biyoud, a North African exile in France who was working for the Germans and who tried to alert them to the problems North African prisoners of war were facing in their daily contact with Wehrmacht guards.[348] The Muslims had often learned "that the real opinions and feelings of the Germans seem to contradict the proclamations and broadcasts of German government offices." "Everywhere," Biyoud claimed, "we are termed 'colored' or even 'black'; almost every German soldier gives us clearly to understand that he counts us to be one of the most despised races of the world. Even expressions like 'Jew,' 'Nigger,' 'black scoundrels' etc. are not uncommon." Drawing on religion, Biyoud complained that "we as Mohammedans" felt little attracted by the alcohol consumption of German soldiers in prison camps. To support his cause, Biyoud even referred to Germany's general policy toward Islam: if Berlin "still wants to stick to" its "Islam-friendly manifesto" made earlier, it was important to

3.11 A destroyed mosque in North Africa, 1942 (BPK).

make sure that German officers respected Muslims in personal encounters.[349] The Wehrmacht took the memorandum quite seriously.[350] Complaints like these do not seem surprising given the fact that Muslims from North Africa—along with sub-Saharan Africans—had regularly been the subject of right-wing hate propaganda in Germany ever since the occupation of the Rhineland in 1923.[351] In his memoirs, the author Klaus Mann described this German propaganda in vivid terms, recalling the "grisly cartoons and captions" about the "coloured troops" in the Rhine and Ruhr zones: "I recollect in particular one rampant account to the effect that a single Moor had raped not only scores of virgins and children but, as a climax of depravity, a handsome mare, sole and treasured belonging of an upright Rhenish peasant tribe."[352] These kinds of negative stereotypes had also reemerged in German propaganda during the early phase of the war against France in 1940 and, though soon stopped, had an impact on ordinary German soldiers—both on the continent and in North Africa.[353]

To conclude, Islam played a significant role in German warfare in North Africa and the Middle East. Berlin launched a major religiously charged propaganda campaign not only to win Muslim support in its conquered territories in the Maghrib but also, more importantly, to stir up violence behind the front lines. At the same time, attempts were made—not always successfully—to train German soldiers to respect the Muslim native population and to engage with local religious leaders. In spring 1943, German troops withdrew from North Africa—Berlin's propaganda continued.

CHAPTER FOUR

Islam and the War on the Eastern Front

When German tanks crossed the Don River and advanced on the Cauca-sus in the summer of 1942, Soviet authorities grew worried about their Muslim southern flanks. Konstantin Umanskii, an official of the People's Commissariat of Foreign Affairs and former Soviet ambassador to Wash-ington, reminded the BBC correspondent Alexander Werth of the history of Muslims in the region:

> I must say that I am a little worried about the Caucasus . . . the Tar-tars in the Crimea are, to a large extent, disloyal. . . . they never liked us. It is well known that during the Crimean War they gladly "collaborated," as we'd now say, with the English and the French. And, above all, there are religious factors, which the Germans have not failed to exploit. Nor do I trust the mountain peoples of the Caucasus. Like the Crimean Tartars, they are Moslems, and they still remember the Russian conquest of the Caucasus which ended not so very long ago—1863.[1]

Indeed, the Muslim population of the Crimea and Caucasus was gener-ally seen as disloyal. Islam, in fact, had been a key marker of opposition and resistance to the central state ever since Muscovy's sixteenth-century ex-pansion into the Muslim areas of the Volga-Ural region, the tsarist an-nexation of the Crimea and the Caucasus in the eighteenth and nineteenth centuries, and Russia's nineteenth-century expansion into Central Asia.[2] Although the Russian government adopted a variety of measures to employ Islam to bolster its rule in the Crimea and the Caucasus, as it did in its other Muslim territories, the regions were considered potential hotbeds of Islamic insurgency. Throughout the nineteenth century, Muslim mountain communities in the North Caucasus engaged in a bitter guerrilla struggle against Russian troops.[3] Their holy war, or *ghazawat*, was led by religious leaders, the three legendary imams Ghazi Muhammad, Hamza Bek, and, most famously, Shamil, the "lion of Chechnya." The imams not only organized the anti-tsarist resistance in the mountains of Dagestan and Chechnya but also proclaimed an imamate, forcibly relocating Muslim communities who refused to follow Islamic law and join the holy war against the Russian invaders. Tens of thousands of tsarist soldiers died fighting against the rebels; the Muslim death toll rose even higher. At outposts across the southern empire, Russian officials were anxious about "Islamic fanaticism," or *musulmanskii fanatizm*.

The Bolsheviks' seizure of power worsened the situation. Following a brief period of moderate policy toward Muslims, including the toleration of mosques, madrasas and Islamic foundations, and even attempts by Muslim Bolsheviks like Mirsaid Sultan Galiev to promote a "Soviet Islam," the 1929 laws of religion aimed to suppress all religious sentiment.[4] Under Stalin, the Muslim areas suffered not only from forced economic collectivization but also from unprecedented religious persecution. Soviet authorities saw Islam as subversive to the new social and political order in their Muslim borderlands. Their propaganda portrayed Islam as a vestige of a feudal and backward society. The publication of most Islamic literature and periodicals was stopped. Waqf property was expropriated. With Islamic law banned, the religious courts lost their authority, at least formally. Moscow used every means it could to break the influence of the 'ulama on the population. Mullahs were considered pillars of traditional society and promoters of anti-Soviet resistance and often even accused of involvement in counterrevolutionary plots directed by foreign secret services.[5] Some were put on show trials, and many were executed. Soviet authorities at the same time targeted mosques and madrasas. In the 1930s, the notorious "Society of the Godless" permeated the Muslim territories with aggressive atheist propaganda, reviving old resentments against the central state. Its activists occupied mosques, painted Soviet slogans on their walls, and hoisted red flags on their minarets.[6] In some areas, officials sent marching bands into Islamic houses of worship or chased pigs through their sacred halls. By the time of the German invasion in 1941, most of the more than 20,000 mosques that had existed across the Muslim territories in 1917 had been pulled down or turned into secular schools, public libraries, social clubs, and restaurants.

Yet, all these attempts to destroy religious structures and sentiments in the Muslim areas failed. Islam continued to play a crucial role in shaping social and political life.[7] In many parts of the North Caucasus, Muslims still settled disputes through illegal shariʻa courts, often disguised as "reconciliation commissions." Religious madrasas remained important, educating children during the official school holidays in the summer months. In the state schools, Soviet teachers complained that Muslim children refused to touch textbooks that they deemed atheist. Moscow's campaign against the veil and against religious celebrations were, overall, similarly unsuccessful. In the month of Muharram, Shiʻites in Azerbaijan would continue to perform the ritualized passion plays (*taʻziya*) and to carry out the public self-flagellation with blunt daggers and iron chains during *ʻAshura* processions. When local authorities staged street celebrations with cheerful music, the processions regularly turned into violent riots with thousands involved. Antireligious provocations were regularly met with fierce resistance. When the Soviets set up a pig-breeding farm in the Muslim village of Dargo in Chechnya, within hours locals had killed the entire herd. These conflicts often had a local dimension, being fought between enthusiastic believers and Muslim party cadres. In the North Caucasus, popular revolt and guerilla war were endemic in the interwar period.[8] Many of these rebellions were led by religious leaders—particularly the shaykhs of the outlawed but influential Sufi brotherhoods—who frequently declared holy war against Moscow and combined religious slogans with the call for independence. In the eyes of many Muslims, Bolshevism was just another form of Russian imperialist domination. More than ever before in Russian history, Islam became a marker of difference and opposition to the central state.

Looking back, Konstantin Umanskii had good reason to be anxious. Now, in the summer of 1942, the Kremlin feared a wave of Islamic revolts on its southern fringes that eventually might spread to the vast regions of Central Asia. The more than 20 million Muslims of the Soviet Union, comprising around 15 percent of its total population, could become a dangerous political force. With the German occupation of the Crimea in autumn 1941, a quarter of a million Sunni Tatars had come under Nazi rule. In early August 1942, the Wehrmacht advanced into the Muslim-populated parts of the northern Caucasus mountains, most importantly the valleys of Karachai-Circassia and Kabardino-Balkaria. By October, German troops stood on the borders of the Chechen-Ingush region, though never breaking through to Grozny. Behind the front lines, particularly in Chechnya-Ingushetia and, to a lesser extent, Karachai-Circassia and Kabardino-Balkaria, anti-Soviet uprisings broke out, drawing considerable numbers of Red Army troops.[9] Among the most determined and efficient insurgent groups were those led by religious leaders, most importantly the guerrillas of Qadiri shaykh Qureish Belkhoroev, who held out in the mountains of Ingushetia and Eastern Ossetia until 1947. In both the Caucasus and the Crimea, the majority of Muslims welcomed the end of the hated Soviet rule with enthusiasm, regarding the German troops with goodwill and hope. In many areas, Wehrmacht troops were greeted with chants of "liberators." In the Crimea, Muslims sent the German command fruits and textiles for "Adolf Effendi."[10] In the Caucasus, German soldiers were astonished by the warm welcome they received.[11] An intelligence report of the SS Security Service (*Sicherheitsdienst,* or SD) on the Caucasus noted that while the Russian and Ukrainian populations were reserved, the Muslim mountaineers of the Karachai area had received the Germans enthusiastically.[12]

Umanskii's concerns about the German exploitation of Islam in these areas were not unfounded, either.[13] In Germany, the press was already alluding to the long tradition of anti-Russian opposition in the Caucasus and the jihad of Imam Shamil, whom the *Deutsche Allgemeine Zeitung* praised as a "preacher of the war of religion and extermination against the Russians."[14] On the ground, German military authorities did not miss the opportunity to present themselves as the liberators of Islam. In their attempt to stabilize and pacify the rear areas of the front, the Germans made extensive use of religious concessions and propaganda, politicized Islamic practices and celebrations, and tried to base their rule on religious institutions. In both the Caucasus and the Crimea, the religious question became a key characteristic of German occupation and propaganda policy. Like most German efforts to employ Islam, such policies were born out of the necessities of the war.

The Muslim population had played little role in Berlin's long-term plans for the Eastern territories.[15] The Crimea was to be colonized by Germans and renamed Gotenland; indeed, Hitler's plan for the Germanization of the peninsula included the deportation of the entire local population. In the Caucasus, the situation was different. The area was invaded primarily to secure the oil fields of Maikop, Grozny, and Baku and to open a flank to the Middle East. As the Caucasus lay outside the range of German settlement plans, Berlin's blueprints for the region in the future New Order remained sketchy. Nevertheless, plans for civil administration had been drawn up for both areas. In the Crimea, the General Commissariat of the Crimea, designated to be ruled by the Austrian party veteran *Gauleiter* Alfred Frauenfeld, never materialized. Frauenfeld took over only five districts in the north that the army had relinquished. Strictly speaking, these districts lay outside the Crimean peninsula, and Frauenfeld was subordinated to his archenemy Erich Koch, ruler over the Reich Commissariat of the Ukraine. In the Caucasus, Rosenberg had planned a Reich Commissariat, similar to those in Ostland and the Ukraine. As early as 16 July 1941, Hitler had approved Rosenberg's protégé Arno Schickedanz to run this future Reich Commissariat. Yet, he too never took command. The plans of Berlin's bureaucrats and experts for a civil administration were never implemented. Equally irrelevant in the realities of the occupation were the bold plans pursued by some sections of the East Ministry, around Mende, and the Foreign Office, around Schulenburg, and their émigré protégés in Berlin, to install national councils. Schulenburg had even recruited a grandson of Imam Shamil, Said Shamil. "His name already personifies the program of the liberation of the North Caucasus from Bolshevist rule," the diplomat rejoiced, adding that he was a "well-known personality in the whole Mohammedan world."[16] It didn't help. Since both the Caucasus and the Crimea continued to be frontline zones, power in both areas remained under military administration for the entire period of German occupation.

Facing a worsening military situation in 1941–1942, the Wehrmacht commanders of the Crimea and Caucasus at times adopted a more pragmatic approach than that taken in other parts of the occupied Eastern territories.[17] In the Caucasus, with its long volatile front line and mountain areas, their primary goal was to secure a stable rear for the German army. But also in the Crimea, a strategically sensitive position on the Black Sea that lay close behind the front, the military was concerned about ensuring a stable hinterland. For those in charge, the military situation made the need for collaborators more apparent.

The army command in both areas saw in the Muslim population natural allies.[18] In contrast to the Russians and Ukrainians, the Crimean Tatars and Caucasian mountaineers were seen as genuinely opposed to the Soviet central state. Moreover, in racial terms, these groups were considered of ethnically higher standing than Russian, Belarusian, or Ukrainian Slavs. Ultimately, the Muslim religion of the Crimean Tatars and of the majority of the Caucasian mountaineers played a significant role. The history of Islamic resistance in these areas was well known. Islam was considered inherently anti-Bolshevik. And, after all, the Muslim population was believed to be an integral part of the Islamic world, and German policies on the ground were regularly seen as an element of Germany's wider Islam campaign.

On a more general level, the attempts made by Wehrmacht authorities to employ Islam in their policies in these areas were part of a broader policy toward religion, which aimed to grant religious concessions to Muslims, Orthodox Christians, and Catholics alike in the hope of keeping the hinterland of the southern front calm.[19] Considering the general German policy lines in the East, the range of concessions that the army command was willing and able to grant was limited. Economic reforms and the abolishment of the *kolkhoz* system, which indeed became a prominent German propaganda slogan, were opposed by the economic agencies concerned with food supply for the troops. National independence, a claim often forwarded by the non-Russian minorities, was out of the question. As a consequence, the Germans found it easiest to make inexpensive religious concessions, which could often be granted on the spot. Nazi propaganda promoted religion as part of local tradition, suppressed by Soviet rule, while avoiding the delicate question of national independence. The military command hoped that religious and other cultural concessions would enhance work ethic and collaboration and distract from unwanted political activism. Comparing the situation to other areas under German occupation in the East, historians have noted, however, that the religious question became particularly significant in the occupation of the Crimea—and especially in its Muslim areas.[20] The situation in the Caucasus was similar. Indeed, German attempts to position itself as the liberator of Islam came most remarkably to the fore in the Muslim regions of the northern Caucasus mountains.

Religion and Warfare in the Caucasus

In the summer of 1942, the Wehrmacht marched into the Soviet-controlled Caucasus.[21] Incapable of holding the wide and unstable front, however, they were soon forced to go on the defensive. The outer valleys of the northern Caucasus were held only until mid-January 1943. During the occupation, the Caucasus stood under the military command of Army Group

A, led by General Field Marshall Wilhelm List and, from November 1942, after Hitler himself had briefly taken command, General Ewald von Kleist. On the ground, General Ernst-August Köstring, an aged army officer who had served in the Ottoman Empire during the First World War and had been German military attaché in Moscow (replacing Niedermayer in 1932), became Commissioner-General of Caucasian Affairs in the army group, with army veteran Lieutenant Hans-Heinrich Herwarth von Bittenfeld as his aide. These Wehrmacht officers all were more pragmatic than their counterparts elsewhere in the East. Although the Caucasus section of the East Ministry under Gerhard von Mende had only consultative competence, it sent Otto Bräutigam as a liaison officer to the high command of Army Group A; Bräutigam arrived at Kleist's headquarters in Stavropol in late November 1942.[22]

Army officials on the ground agreed that the full toleration of religious customs by German troops was pivotal in pacifying the Caucasian mountain region. In his widely circulated memoranda to the Wehrmacht command, Theodor Oberländer, a renowned expert on eastern Europe, officer in the military intelligence, and commander on the Caucasian front, stressed that the German troops would encounter many "devout Muslims" in the North Caucasus and that their treatment was of geopolitical significance: "The way that we treat them will be of particular importance for the future stance of Islam towards Greater Germany."[23] List and his staff generally agreed. When German soldiers entered the Caucasian mountain passes, List issued an order that demanded they treat the population as allies, tolerate religious beliefs and customs, and respect "the honor of the women of the Caucasus."[24] Some weeks later, an instruction sheet was distributed requiring the troops to respect the Islamic faith.[25] "Religion and religious customs and conventions of the Caucasians must be respected and are not to be ridiculed," the leaflet advised soldiers, "even though they may appear odd." After Kleist took over, he carried on with List's policy. As late as December 1942, according to an army report, Kleist urged his commanders to be aware of the pan-Islamic implications of their decisions in the field: "Among all of the German Army Groups, Army Group A has advanced the furthest. We stand at the gates to the Islamic world. What we do and how we behave here will radiate deep into Iraq, to India, as far as to the borders of China. We must constantly be aware of the long-range effect of our actions and inactions."[26] At a meeting with officials of the East

Ministry and the Wehrmacht, Kleist's representative, Herwarth von Bittenfeld, underlined that a pragmatic occupation policy in the Muslim valleys of the Caucasus was crucial to "obtain the required political effect with respect to the Islamic world."[27] The East Ministry followed the Wehrmacht's line.[28] Bräutigam was instructed to avoid promises of national independence and instead to emphasize the fight against Bolshevism and German respect for "the confessions, particularly Islam."[29] From the Caucasus desk of the East Ministry in Berlin, Mende stressed the importance of religious rights, dietary requirements, religious feasts, funeral rites, and, finally, conduct toward Muslim women.[30] The SS had no objections. An SD intelligence report noted that the German commanders in the field all agreed that for the pacification of the North Caucasus, the "antagonism of the population to Russia" and their "rootedness with Mohammedanism" were to be exploited.[31]

At once, mosques were reopened and became physical signs of the change of rule. A decree instructed that even those houses of worship that had been closed by the Soviets and used for profane purposes were not to be occupied by German troops but reopened for the population.[32] From Cherkessk, German officers reported that not only had the mosque been restored, but new minarets had also been erected.[33] In the religiously mixed areas of the northern fringes, too, mosques were reopened, most importantly in the former provincial capital of Maikop.[34] "Everywhere the mosques have been reactivated or rebuilt," Ehrenfried Schütte, a commander of Oberländer's unit, reported from the front, adding: "They are better and more frequently attended than the few churches that work again."[35]

The German army also endorsed the reintroduction of Islamic education into the elementary school curricula.[36] Islam was an exception in this matter, as it was not until later in the campaign that the same concession was made to non-Muslims.[37] In December 1942, a report noted that it was "mainly the Muslims" who welcomed the "introduction of religious lessons into the school curricula."[38] In the early weeks of the campaign, the East Ministry advised that "madrasas, which had been expropriated by the Soviets, should be returned."[39] Whether this was ultimately implemented is unknown, but it is not unlikely.

Toward the end of the short occupational period, Army Group A ordered that in Muslim areas of the Caucasus, Friday—instead of Sunday—

would become the day of rest, making the day of communal prayer (*jumuʿa*) a day of rest.[40]

The return of Islam was often carefully staged by Wehrmacht officers. The Balkars, for instance, were symbolically presented with a Qur'an after German soldiers occupied the area.[41] To propagate religious concessions and promote Germany as the friend of Islam, the army also distributed pamphlets.[42] Though mostly written in the East Ministry, which usually attempted to address religion in general rather than Islam in particular, a number of these propaganda leaflets concerned Islam exclusively. Promoting an "alliance with the Greater German Reich of Adolf Hitler," one of them denounced the "Bolshevist villainy" that oppressed "freedom and faith," and assured readers that, even though Germans had a different religion, the Third Reich would respect all beliefs and was ready to "secure you the freedom of faith for the future."[43] Another pamphlet drew on the idea of a Muslim community that expanded beyond the Caucasus: "The Muslims of the Crimea, who after 25 years are free to pray again in their mosques, fight in the tens of thousands in German uniform against Bolshevism and partisan gangs."[44] References to the Crimea were recurring. "Your Muslim fellow believers from the Crimea are already arrayed for battle in their thousands to wage war against Bolshevism," another pamphlet proclaimed, noting that Crimean Muslims "have already often declared their gratitude to the German leadership for their spiritual liberation."[45] A similar message had been directed toward Caucasian Red Army soldiers during the siege of Sevastopol in early 1942. A German propaganda pamphlet had informed them that Muslims from across the Soviet Union had joined the Wehrmacht in the fight "for freedom from the Bolshevist yoke."[46] "In many telegrams the Muslims have expressed their deep gratitude to the Führer of the German Reich that after twenty years of religious rape they can now pursue again their worship in their mosques," it added.[47] Sevastopol fell in June.

Across the northern Caucasus, the Germans soon saw religion as one of their most important instruments of political warfare. As an army official at the town command of Cherkessk remarked in a monthly report in November 1942, the effect of religious concessions could not be overestimated.[48] The "Mohammedan Circassians" especially would be full of gratitude, he noted, adding that the "permission for free religious worship more and more turns out to be the strongest instrument of propagandistic influence on the population."[49] "Despite the suppression of all religious faith by the Soviets," the officer was surprised to see that "the Mohammedan youth seems in parts still closely bound to Islam, and might also be more easily won over by it completely again, whereas the Russian youth is fully estranged from Orthodox Christianity." The general position report for the region similarly remarked that in "the Mohammedan areas youth participation in the practice of religion is noticeable."[50] Ehrenfried Schütte reported from the front that "the local Mohammedan population" had proven themselves the most trustworthy, having "endured Sovietization incomparably better than the other local groups."[51] At the end of 1942, an SD intelligence summarized that the Muslim mountaineers would respond "with gratitude" for the new "freedom of religion."[52]

Ultimately, it was the reintroduction of religious holidays and celebrations that became the most significant concession as the German occupation of the northern Caucasus mountain area coincided with two major religious holidays—the end of Ramadan, the *Uraza Bairam* in October, and, seventy days later, the pilgrimage feast, *Qurban Bairam*. Religious festivities were turned into spectacular liberation celebrations, symbolically marking the change of rule. They became emblematic of the short German occupation in the Muslim mountain areas, most importantly the *Uraza Bairam* celebrations in the Karachai city of Kislovodsk and the *Qurban Bairam* celebrations in Nalchik, in the Kabardian area.[53]

On Sunday, 11 October 1942, a delegation consisting of Generals Köstring, Homburg, Riecke, von Roques, and von Greifenberg, agricultural expert *Oberkriegsverwaltungsrat* Otto Schiller, Paul Körner, who was the head of Göring's Four-Year-Plan Office, and other high-ranking German officials, visited Kislovodsk, which had been occupied two months earlier.[54] Surrounded by the rock face of the Karachai mountain massif, Kislovodsk had been a popular spa town since the tsarist era and was now characterized by the modern architecture of its Soviet sanatoria. Since the early morning, the streets had been busier than usual. The entrance of the main road to the town was decorated with a swastika flag and the green flag of the Prophet with the Muslim crescent. At the town hall, an enormous garland adorned an image of Hitler. At the end of the main road a gigantic painting was erected, depicting the Karachai warriors on horseback bearing flags of liberation. In the streets, Karachais, Balkars, Kabards, and other local groups mingled. The town was preparing for the *Uraza Bairam* celebrations, the end of the sacred month of Ramadan.

Across the Karachai mountains, believers were preparing for the event. Under Soviet rule, they had not openly observed the *Uraza Bairam*. Now, for the first time in a quarter of a century, Muslims were again allowed to organize religious festivities. Desperate to pacify the hinterland and well aware of the effect this concession would have on the mood of the population, the military had ordered full toleration of the event.[55] The celebration became a key marker of difference between Soviet and German rule. In fact, the Wehrmacht command did not miss the opportunity to portray Germany as the liberator of the Muslim mountain peoples. Hence, the celebration was not just a symbol of religion, of Islam, but also of politics, of liberation from Soviet rule.

This became most obvious in Kislovodsk (Figures 4.1, 4.2, and 4.3). From the outset, the Germans manipulated the meaning of the feast for their strategic interests. The *Uraza Bairam* became a political event. Political change was staged as a religious celebration—"liberation Bairam," as Otto Schiller put it. The agricultural expert, who had served with the embassy in Moscow and was now assigned to organize the future agrarian order in the Caucasus, wrote a detailed six-page report about the celebration for the East Ministry.[56]

The public decoration of Kislovodsk reflected not only Islamic but also Nazi iconography. Behind the honorary tribune for Muslim leaders, religious dignitaries, and Wehrmacht representatives, an oversized, open papier-mâché Qu'ran was arranged, showing in Arabic script two pious quotations. On the right page was the *shahada*, the statement of faith: "There is no god but Allah/Muhammad is his Prophet" (*La ilaha illa Allah/Muhammadan rasul Allah*). On the left was the popular and often quoted Qur'anic verse 13 from sura 61 (*al-Saff*): "Help [comes] from Allah/and a nigh victory" (*Nasr min Allah/Wa fath qarib*).[57] While the first slogan demonstrated the new freedom of religion, the second, in the context of war, signaled, in the form of a religious imperative, the Karachais' willingness to fight alongside the German army against the Soviet enemy. Nailed above the Qur'an was an enormous wooden Reich eagle with a swastika. Flags framed the tribune on either side—the green flags of Islam with a small crescent and swastika flags.

4.1 The end of Ramadan (*Uraza Bairam*) in Kislovodsk, Caucasus, 11 October 1942, parade (*Ullstein*).

4.2 The end of Ramadan (*Uraza Bairam*) in Kislovodsk, Caucasus, 11 October 1942, parade (*Ullstein*).

4.3 The end of Ramadan (*Uraza Bairam*) in Kislovodsk, Caucasus, 11 October 1942, prayer (*Ullstein*).

The public display of the Arabic script was in itself remarkable. The Arabic alphabet, the holy letters of the Qur'an, had formed one of the few bonds among Moscow's Muslims before the Soviets had forcefully replaced it with Latin, and later Cyrillic, letters and accused anyone opposing this reform of religious fanaticism.[58] In some parts of the Islamic Soviet Union, Soviet propagandists publicly burned books printed in Arabic. The abolition of the Arabic script caused much resentment among Muslims. In the 1920s, the remaining mullahs in the Caucasus and Crimea had even called for hunger strikes to protest against the policy. The letters on the papier-mâché Qur'an were thus in themselves a marker of the end of Soviet rule.

The first part of the celebration, the actual ceremony, took place on a hill outside the city. Central to the ceremonies were the prayer and commemoration rituals. "They perform devotional prayers on a hillside outside the city, bowing South towards Mecca," reported a German war correspondent.[59] "The qadi leads their prayers and they, collectively, repeat his words." In fact, imam Ramazan, one of the highest religious authorities among the Karachais, led the prayer, although *qadi* Ibrahim, the Islamic jurist of the area, was present as well.[60] The Karachais kneeled on their prayer rugs in long rows, directed toward Mecca, listening to the Arabic words. The second part of the ritual was distinctly political. Led by Ramazan, the Muslims repeated praise and thanks to Allah for the liberation by Hitler, "the great leader of the German people," and the German Wehrmacht. In an emotional speech, Ramazan commemorated the sufferings of the Muslim mountaineers and the Karachai Muslims who had died in their struggle against Bolshevism. God had sent Hitler and his army as liberators, and every Karachai, declared Ramazan, "in the mosque or in the family" would be full of gratitude and would embrace "the Führer, the German people, and the brave soldiers" in their daily prayers.

The German officers played an integral part in the course of the celebrations. Köstring was lifted onto the arms of the people, who carried him in triumph and tossed him into the air as a token of acclaim and honor. Eager to exploit the opportunity of the religious feast, he gave a propaganda speech in Russian, praising liberation from the Soviet yoke, thanking the Karachais for their trust, and celebrating their common bonds. Köstring announced the abolition of the *kolkhoz* system (which never took place) and the mobilization of a Karachai volunteer squadron to fight alongside the Wehrmacht. His speech also drew on the historical narrative of Muslim resistance in the Caucasus. Köstring was quite pleased with his performance. Remembering the "impressive celebration" after the war, he wrote: "The success was astonishing, the rejoicing indescribable."[61] His aide, Herwarth von Bittenfeld, later remarked that Köstring was celebrated like a "prince."[62]

The festivities reached their peak with the solemn oath of the Muslims, who vowed their determination to fight on the front together with the German Wehrmacht. The military alliance was subsequently affirmed by a parade of Karachai horsemen carrying a swastika flag and the green flag of Islam. Again Nazi and religious symbolism merged. Before the official part of the celebration was completed, a similar parade was organized in front of the "cemetery of heroes" in the city center to commemorate those who had died in revolt against Moscow. A dinner in the city hall followed with dances, among them the "prayer of Shaykh Shamil," which again drew on the regional history of jihad.

The celebrations became part of the Wehrmacht's political warfare. A look at the members of the German delegation gives an idea of the importance military officials attached to the religious event. And they were not alone in doing so. Well aware of the politics of the religious celebration, the Red Army tried to prevent the *Ramadan Bairam*. The day before, Soviet planes had airdropped flyers warning the population not to attend the feast and promising to end it in a hail of bombs. In the end, however, only one bomb was dropped, far away from the center of the city, and failed to spread panic.

A number of similar religious celebrations, staged as liberation spectacles, took place in the Caucasus. The second largest of these events was the *Qurban Bairam* held on 18 December 1942, by the Sunni Balkars and Kabards in Nalchik, capital of the Kabardino-Balkar area, which had been occupied less than two months earlier.[63] As the highest Islamic holiday, celebrated at the height of the hajj, the event was seen by Wehrmacht officials, eager to repeat the success of the Kislovodsk ceremonies, as an ideal opportunity to demonstrate the bonds between the Wehrmacht and the local population, Germany, and Islam. Muslim representatives in Nalchik, under mayor Selim Zedov, a former civil servant who resumed power after the Soviet retreat and who was swiftly approved by the Wehrmacht, had prepared for the celebration with the Germans days in advance.[64] On 17 December 1942, a convoy containing General-Major Wilhelm Stubenrauch, commander of the rear area of Tank Army I, Otto Bräutigam, Theodor Oberländer, and a group of other high-ranking officials, including two other generals and several officers of the Wehrmacht's propaganda division, drove up the icy roads of the misty Karachai mountain passes to Nalchik. The following morning, the group gathered in Nalchik's great cinema hall for the Islamic pilgrimage celebrations. The religious ceremony formed the core of the event. The prayer, led by the local *qadi*, Khaniukov, a Kabard, took place on the cinema stage. The Germans sat in the front rows. "Kneeling with the body bent forward, around 50 leading figures of the Kabards performed their prayers. The movements of the clerics were solemn and controlled, and the religious ceremonies took place in dignified seriousness," Bräutigam later recalled in his memoirs.[65] "We were very impressed." Oberländer, too, revealed, in a letter to his wife: "This Mohammedan service has made a great impression on me."[66] During the celebrations, General-Major Stubenrauch, representing Kleist, and Otto Bräutigam stepped forward to publicly praise the alliance. According to Bräutigam's official report for the East Ministry, the approximately 400 Muslims reacted with enthusiasm and applause. Muslim representatives thanked the Germans for their "liberation from Bolshevism" and for giving them an opportunity to celebrate the *Qurban Bairam* again, vowing steadfast loyalty to Adolf Hitler. They also presented the Germans with gifts, including carpets, clothing, and horses for Hitler, Keitel, and Kleist. Wehrmacht officials distributed not only captured weapons, lighters, and watches but also small Qur'ans, affirming German respect for Islam. The celebrations continued late into the evening. As *Qurban Bairam* celebrations last for four days, the German delegation did not miss the opportunity to visit another town in the area. The next day, the convoy drove to the small mountain village of Gundelen, the center of the Balkars on the hillside of the Elbrus Mountain. Public speeches were made, and consultations with local dignitaries took place.[67]

The celebrations at Nalchik and Kislovodsk became the outward characteristic of German rule in the Caucasus. On both occasions the German press printed detailed reports. A newspaper announced that "those who witnessed these hours derived a lasting impression of the love of freedom and the respectability of these men, who offer their lives for their ideals."[68] Excited about the lavish display of Islamic and Nazi iconography, another war correspondent wrote: "Next to the flag of the Reich waves the green banner with crescent and star, under which once Muhammad prevailed over the Jews." Both would stand for the "never ebbing strength" of people who fight "for a better world order."[69] "Uraza Bairam 1942," it claimed, was "more than an avowal of a small, but tough mountain people to its faith." It was a "demonstration of joy to a world political development" and would be remembered by future generations as the "beginning of a new epoch." German papers also published photos of the event in Kislovodsk.[70] "One still spoke often of this celebration," Bräutigam remembered after the war.[71]

Plans to establish Muslim organizations and a religious administration, a bureaucratization of Islam, as pursued in the Crimea, never materialized due to the short period of occupation. The German troops in the Caucasus were soon isolated. The battle of Stalingrad strained supplies. At the same time, Soviet troops in the south, commanded by the military genius General Ivan Vladimirovich Tiulenev, were restored to combat readiness and began to advance. In late December 1942, Hitler endorsed the retreat from the Caucasus mountains to avoid utter annihilation. A fortnight after the *Qurban Bairam* celebrations, on 4 January 1943, Nalchik was reconquered by the Red Army. A few days later, the last German tanks rolled out of Kabardino-Balkaria. Although Germany's occupation of the Caucasus was short, it was perhaps Berlin's strongest attempt to position itself as the defender of Islam on the Eastern Front. The longest and most coordinated policy toward Islam in the East, by comparison, was launched in the Crimea.

Religion and Rule in the Crimea

In the autumn of 1941, German and Romanian troops led by General Erich von Manstein invaded the Crimea.[72] In September, they reached the Perekop area and soon conquered the entire peninsula, with the exceptions of Kerch, which fell after heavy fighting in May 1942, and Sevastopol, one of the strongest fortresses in the world, which was stormed after a lengthy siege in July 1942. The Wehrmacht, assisted by the SS, particularly by *Einsatzgruppe D*, led by Otto Ohlendorf, and, from July 1942, Walther Bierkamp, held the Crimea under brutal and exploitative rule for almost two and a half years until early May 1944, when the last German position on the peninsula surrendered to the Red Army. The roughly 250,000 Sunni Tatars, whom the Germans hoped to win over as collaborators, constituted almost 25 percent of the peninsula's population, with strongholds in the mountains as well as in bigger cities like Bakchisarai, Yalta, and Simferopol, known as Aqmescit (*Aq Masjid*)—the "White Mosque"—until the eighteenth century.[73]

In their attempt to win over the Muslims, German army officials soon began granting a wide range of religious rights and concessions. Immediately after the invasion, Manstein ordered his soldiers to respect Islam. In his infamous order of 20 November 1941, which demanded that the "Jewish-Bolshevist system" be "exterminated once and for all" and became one of the key documents used by his prosecution at Nuremberg after the war, Manstein urged his troops to treat the Muslim population well to win them as collaborators: "Respect for religious customs, particularly those of the Mohammedan Tartars, must be demanded."[74] The terms "Muslim Tatars" and "Mohammedan Tartars" were not unusual as the Germans often identified Tatars not only ethnically but also according to their religion. Two months later, a military instruction sheet explained to the troops that the Tatars were devout Muslims and that Islam had to be respected."[75] In his pro-Tatar line Manstein was supported by Werner Otto von Hentig, now liaison officer of the Foreign Office at his 11th Army.[76] Hentig became a relentless promoter of an accommodating policy toward the Muslim Tatars and Islam. In a field post letter to his old mentor, Max von Oppenheim, of late 1941, he boasted that the army in the Crimea was dedicating "the greatest attention" to the "Muslim problem."[77] In spring 1942, he even warned that Germany's policy toward the Crimean Muslims had a pan-Islamic impact on Germany's position in the Caucasus, Turkey, the Arab world, Iran, and even India.[78] Manstein was convinced that the strict respect of religious practice was key to winning the collaboration of the Tatars, explaining in an interview given in August 1942 to a correspondent of the *National-Zeitung:* "Today, the Tatars welcome liberation from Moscow simply because the blasting of the chains has returned to them the free religious practice of Islam."[79]

Indeed, the military administration of the Crimea observed that religious life was developing particularly actively among the Muslim population.[80] Even the younger generation, which under Soviet rule had in part become religiously indifferent, would maintain general customs and honor rules, a German army official remarked in March 1942: "The Tatars are Mohammedans and generally take their religion seriously, without therefore being fanatics."[81] One year later, a report noted that "in contrast to the

Orthodox Christians, among Tatars the participation of the youth in religious life is rising, especially in the villages."[82]

Shortly after occupying the Crimea, the Germans reintroduced religious celebrations of both the weekly and the yearly cycle. Initially, the official day of rest on the entire peninsula was Sunday. In some areas, though, Muslims tried to convince the German authorities to grant a day of rest on Friday instead.[83] Soon rumors spread that the local commands in some areas had agreed to the arrangement. On 30 March 1943, the High Command of the Crimea finally gave the order that Fridays were to be designated as a general day of rest for Muslims.[84] In addition, major religious holidays were reintroduced. On 14 August 1943, the army ordered that the Muslim population was to be granted a day of rest on all major Islamic holidays. Across the peninsula, *Mawlid* festivities took place on 19 March, the end of Ramadan was celebrated on 1 October, the *Qurban Bairam* on 8 December, and the Islamic New Year on 28 December 1943.[85] In Simferopol, the Germans organized a greater Ramadan celebration that year as Muslim volunteers who were fighting in the German army also took part. "It was further proof of the friendship and good cooperation, and a day of freedom," a Wehrmacht propaganda journal for Muslim soldiers announced.[86] Religious rituals and feasts regularly became politicized. In fact, their mere reintroduction was political. German reports give evidence of prayers of thanks and invocations to Allah for the Wehrmacht and Hitler.[87] On one occasion a celebration was organized that included not only prayers and public declarations of loyalty to the occupation authorities but also a mass circumcision ceremony: "The circumcision of 50 children, which for reasons of political convenience was explicitly tolerated by the SD, must thereby be emphasised," a Wehrmacht commander reported.[88] In some areas, Muslim leaders even began to collect money for the German dictator.[89]

Perhaps the most significant change in Muslim religious life was reflected in the restoration and reopening of mosques and prayer halls closed by the Soviets.[90] "From the minarets of the Tatar villages the mullahs again called the faithful to prayer," Herwarth von Bittenfeld romanticized after the war.[91] In Berlin, Goebbels, on 30 January 1942, rejoiced in his diary that, "after they had been allowed to call out their religious chants from their minarets again," the Tatars had lost all initial reservations toward the Wehrmacht: "It is interesting to note how significant the clever exploitation of the religious question has been here."[92] By March 1943, fifty mosques had reopened on the peninsula.[93] Some sources speak of even higher numbers, indicating that in the year 1943 alone, 150 mosques were restored, along with 100 provisional prayer houses, run by a total of 400 Muslim clerics.[94] By tolerating or even supporting the rebuilding of mosques, German officials explicitly politicized the buildings' meaning. At once, minarets and mosques with their claims of religious representation were employed for German political aims.

As in the Caucasus, the military administration also introduced religious education into the curriculum of secular Tatar schools.[95] At the same time, plans to reopen madrasas were made. A major restoration project concerned the grand madrasa of Bakchisarai, which had been almost completely destroyed under Bolshevik rule.[96] In Eupatoria, the city's 600-year-old madrasa, which had been used as a storage depot by the Soviets, was cleaned and restored. As long as it was organized and monitored sufficiently, religious education was not seen as a risk by the German authorities but considered a cheap concession and a convenient bulwark against Bolshevist propaganda.

The reestablishment of a religious infrastructure and the restoration of mosques and madrasas were monitored and controlled by the Germans through a complex administration, the religious sections of so-called Muslim committees (*mohammedanisches Komitee*), which were founded in the bigger cities of the Crimea.[97] The Wehrmacht played up these *Müsülman Komiteleri*, as the Tatars called them, as the descendants of the "Muslim committees" from the time of the civil war and German occupation in 1918.[98] As the Wehrmacht strictly prohibited political activism, the committees were concerned primarily with religious affairs. In the end it was the religious board, the dominant part of every Muslim committee, which became a central pillar of German rule and political warfare.

The Germans soon centralized the work of the committees under a Muslim central committee, founded in Simferopol (also known as the Tatar committee of Simferopol) on 3 January 1942.[99] During the tsarist period, Simferopol had been the center of Islam in the Crimea and the seat of the Crimean mufti. It was headed by Jamil Abdurashidov, who was only temporarily replaced between late 1942 and early 1943 by Eredzhep Qursaidov.[100] Its most important section was the religious board (*Religionsdezernat* or *Krimreligionsdezernat*), which became the central religious authority of

Crimean Muslims under German rule. Run by the Islamic dignitary Alimseit Jamilov, the board controlled, directed, and coordinated the local committees and Muslim life across the peninsula.

The religious board of the Simferopol committee oversaw all plans for mosque building and renovation, the foundation of new madrasas, and the reintroduction of religious instruction in secular schools.[101] Moreover, it was designed to control the inner life of these institutions. Although imams and religious teachers were elected by the local Muslim population, the religious board of the central committee was to check their suitability and had the last word on appointments. It was also authorized to train imams and provide them with guidelines for their work. Finally, it was to provide uniform curricula for religious courses and Islamic madrasas.

In late 1942, the Germans tightened the system even more, merging the local Muslim committees into a more regulated institutional framework.[102] Local mosque councils (*Moscheen-Rat*) were founded to serve as institutional centers in the provinces. Their creation ensured that the mosque communities were strictly organized and controlled. The mosque councils received their statutes from Simferopol and had to produce regular reports on their work. Members of every local mosque community were to elect the mosque council of ten to fifteen persons. The establishment of these councils went swiftly. In February 1943, the SS reported that a number of local Muslim committees, among them those in Feodosiia, Yalta, and Bakchisarai, had already adopted the new statutes of the Simferopol central committee and were about to organize the local councils accordingly.[103]

The institutionalization of Islam through ecclesiastical structures was not new in the Crimea but had its precedent in the tsarist empire, which Robert Crews pointedly characterized as a "church for Islam."[104] Similar structures were now not only presented by Nazi propaganda as religious liberation but also employed by German authorities for their own administrative and military interests. The statutes of the Simferopol committee stated clearly that its purpose was both to represent Muslims and "to actively support the interests of the German Wehrmacht, the German civil administration, and the German police."[105] Hentig noted that the Simferopol committee was completely at the disposal of the occupation authorities.[106] The Germans used the system mainly for two purposes—as a tool of rule and control and as an instrument of propaganda and military mobilization.

As a tool of rule and control, the councils and their centralized institutional framework were employed to monitor and regulate Muslim life. The Simferopol central committee was placed under the authority of the SS Security Police (*Sicherheitspolizei*, or Sipo) and SD.[107] It also had to compile reports about its work.[108] In practice, the SS followed a quite interventionist policy, even deposing religious figures and imams considered unreliable. The Germans were particularly anxious to make sure that the councils were not taken over by Tatar separatists. Indeed, followers of the Tatar nationalist organization *Milli Firka* (*National Party*), which sought an independent Muslim state in the Crimea, tried to use the Muslim committees as a cover. In late 1942, a number of Muslim committees organized an assembly to discuss the foundation of a Tatar governmental body.[109] The main architect of these efforts was Ahmed Ozenbashli, a physician who, after the German invasion, had begun to play a leading role in the Simferopol committee. The Germans, however, were in control, stopped the activities, and from then on restricted the functions and influence of the Simferopol committee.

As an instrument of propaganda and mobilization, the committees, and most importantly their religious boards, were extensively used by the military administration. Their very existence bestowed religious authority on collaboration with the Germans. According to its statutes, the Simferopol committee was to exploit "all matters of cultural life" propagandistically.[110] It was instructed to launch propaganda among the Muslim population and mobilize it in the battle against partisans (Figure 4.4). During the inaugural ceremony of the Muslim committee of Simferopol, the presiding imam had explained that Islam demanded that Muslims align themselves with the Germans.[111] In the following months, the central committee engaged in a vast Islamic propaganda and mobilization campaign.[112] The Muslim committees organized sermons for Muslim volunteers in the Wehrmacht and SS. "Religious anti-Bolshevist propaganda," as they put it, was carried into Muslim towns and villages across the Crimea.[113] In the countryside, some recruited imams spread German propaganda in their sermons.

A main propaganda instrument of the Simferopol central committee was its newspaper, *Azat Kirim* (*Free Crimea*).[114] Founded in early 1942, it was edited by the Muslim intellectual Mustafa Kurtiev, who led a small staff of writers based at 14 Pushkinskaia Street in Simferopol. *Azat Kirim* was published twice a week and widely circulated among Crimean Muslims. In

4.4 Crimean Tatars in German uniform in front of the Big Khan Mosque in Bakchisarai, Crimea, 1943 (BPK).

1943, each issue ran to 10,000 copies, although the demand was estimated to be at least four times greater. Its content was controlled and censored by the propaganda section of the German military command in Simferopol. According to the Simferopol Muslim committee, the paper was intended to enhance the Tatars' loyalty to the Germans and the Wehrmacht, to mobilize Muslims into the German forces, and to support the fight against Jews, Freemasons, and Communists.[115] It claimed to support the reintroduction of the "rights of the Mohammedans of the Crimea," which had been suppressed by "Bolshevist-Jewish-Russian rule." The editors were also well aware that their propaganda efforts could be seen as part of a wider German campaign of pan-Islamic mobilization and even asked to be regularly informed by Berlin about German publications in Turkish, Arabian, Persian, and other "Oriental" languages in order to align their propaganda with the wider campaigns. In early 1943, Kurtiev even suggested the foundation of a central Muslim organ to be distributed, if not across the entire Muslim world, then at least among all Muslims of the Eastern territories.[116] "World events and the historically unprecedented war, which has gripped a significant part of the Muslim world, require extensive propaganda in the field of German-Mohammedan friendship," he claimed. Kurtiev's office was also involved in other forms of print propaganda. In early January 1943, it requested copies of *Mein Kampf*, remarking that "the Mohammedans of the Crimea are strongly interested in the classic work of the Führer."[117]

The issues of *Azat Kirim*, which today can be found in the Crimean State Archives in Simferopol, reveal that its propaganda, along with endless rants against Communists and Jews, included numerous articles on the religious question. Rejoicing at the liberation of Islam from "Bolshevik-Jewish oppression," one article reported the German involvement in the repair of mosques, particularly the reestablishment of the seventeenth-century Mufti Jami Mosque of Feodosiia, which had been turned into a church during the tsarist period.[118] Other articles attacked Soviet atheism. One piece, for instance, declared that only savages had no religion: "God, Prophet, religion, and faith belong to the people of high civilization."[119] Bolshevist attempts to "exterminate" the civilization of the Crimean Muslims had failed: "The great God did not allow this to happen," the paper insisted: "With the command of God, Adolf Hitler saved us from the hold of these oppressors." Most of the texts on Islam were on religious celebrations. For example, during the *Qurban Bairam* in 1942, *Azat Kirim* printed not only general reflections on the purpose of the sacrifice.[120] It also reported on celebrations that took place across the peninsula.[121] Most articles interwove the subject with political statements: "The great German nation, as well as its allies, the great Italian and Japanese people, respected this most important religious festival of the Muslims and helped them to celebrate it," one writer proclaimed.[122] Even the mufti's inauguration of the Islamic Central Institute in Berlin, on the 1942 *Qurban Bairam*, was a subject.[123] The paper repeatedly praised the "glorious mufti of Jerusalem," who had "raised the flag of jihad against Anglo-Saxon states."[124]

Some of the most revealing articles on religion, however, dealt with practical religious matters. One piece raised the sensitive issue that many Muslims in the Crimea simply were financially unable to perform a sacrifice on *Qurban Bairam*.[125] Another piece addressed disputes over wine production—declared forbidden (*haram*) by some Crimean mullahs even though it was important for the economy of some Tatar villages—arguing, with reference to sacred texts, that it was only the consumption, not the production and sale, of wine that was prohibited by Islam.[126] Finally, numerous contributions dealt with the new religious administration. These articles went well beyond the mere announcements of new statutes and regulations of the Muslim committees.[127] They included detailed accounts of the activities of the Simferopol central committee, reporting on the reopening of mosques, the reintroduction of religious holidays, the reestablishment of religious education, and the opening of soup kitchens.[128] The most controversial issue here was the appointment of new mullahs. Writers often not only offered their opinions on the role and responsibilities of religious dignitaries but indeed also criticized the appointment of religious personnel deemed unsuitable.[129] Overall, the articles in *Azat Kirim* give insights not only into the role and function of religion in occupation propaganda in the Crimea but also into the limits of German attempts to revive Islam on the peninsula. In addition to the paper, the Muslim central committee eventually also engaged in broadcast propaganda aimed at Crimean Muslims.[130] Although generally aired only in the Russian language, German radios broadcast a Tatar program on Fridays, the day of congregational prayer.

Though organized by the committees, religious propaganda in the Crimea was, of course, fully aligned with the general German directives.

The first temporary guidelines for propaganda aimed at the Tatars, circulated by the East Ministry in late 1941, emphasized the role of religion: "The most important thing for them is the free practice of religion," it explained, suggesting the slogan: "The German Reich has an amicable and benevolent attitude to all Mohammedans. Therefore, do not believe the Bolshevik propaganda, which alleges that you as Mohammedans are to be suppressed and shot."[31] The Germans also sporadically engaged in their own propaganda efforts, for instance, by distributing miniature versions of the Qur'an, which came with special magnifying glasses.[32] These sets were common souvenirs that Muslims would bring home from Mecca during the 1930s and 1940s. An SS report remarked that these kinds of religious gifts were also made to honor individual imams.[33]

Throughout the occupation period, Muslim leaders sent reports to the German authorities. Often written in the form of petitions, they give an idea of the practical limits of Germany's attempts to revive Islam in the Crimea. In fact, the reports submitted by the Simferopol central committee reveal that life for Muslims was often different from what German propaganda tried to portray. German officials on the ground did not always cooperate with Muslim representatives.[34] In 1942, for instance, the local committee in Eupatoria founded a madrasa with 130 students, which was closed by the local German command after only two weeks. The Muslims of Eupatoria then complained via the Simferopol committee, stressing the "need to give the children a religious education and to battle the godlessness which has remained from Bolshevist rule."[35] These kinds of conflicts were particularly common in areas where the Germans had installed Russian collaborators in the local administration. In Simferopol, Russian personnel refused Muslim requests for money from the city fund for the restoration of a mosque.[36] In other places, Russian authorities closed Muslim schools.[37] Apart from friction between Muslims and local authorities, the Crimea faced a general shortfall of Muslim dignitaries for mosques and schools.[38] At one point, the central committee asked for clerics to be sent, especially from Romania, to the Crimea and at the same time suggested that young Crimean imams be educated in madrasas in Romania and Bosnia.[39] Furthermore, there was a severe lack of religious books.[40] In 1943, German authorities agreed to import Qur'ans and other religious publications for the Crimean madrasas from abroad.[41] Overall, the petitions show that Muslim representatives frequently tried to employ the German occupational regime to their advantage. Their main requests—the restoration of the two major traditional Muslim institutions, the waqf and the muftiate—however, were contested by the Germans.

The religious system—mosques, madrasas, Muslim committees, and their personnel—endorsed by the German administration, was costly. Initially, renovations of religious places and employment of Muslim clerics were financed mainly by donations from the populace.[142] Traditionally, these costs were covered by religious endowments, the waqf, which administered the common property of the religious community, including buildings, wastelands, and grazing lands.[143] The institution of the waqf was based on the shari'a and had formed an important part of Muslim communities across the world for centuries. The income from donations and economic activities was used to pay the Muslim clergy, religious teachers, and theology students, as well as to finance the upkeep of mosques, religious property, and charity projects. Officially acknowledged in tsarist Russia, the Crimean waqf complex possessed legendary wealth and land across the peninsula. The tsarist government had declared the waqf indefeasible, most importantly through an imperial decree of 1829, which put it under the tutelage of the Crimean muftiate, and, two years later, through a decree confirming that it was the main financial resource for mosques, madrasas, and mullahs. The Soviets had abolished the waqf and confiscated all of its property.

Under German occupation, the issue was soon raised. On 13 December 1942, Alimseit Jamilov's religious board of the Simferopol Muslim committee sent a memorandum about the waqf question to the German command.[144] Thanking "the glorious German Wehrmacht" for having "liberated" the Crimean Muslims and for restoring religious life, it elaborated on the "great and difficult task" of reviving Islamic institutions in the Crimea, which came with huge expenses. As the reinstitutionalization of Islam could not be achieved without substantial financial resources, the restitution—at least in part—of former waqf property, including buildings that were unattended and dilapidated, was urgently needed. The central committee in Simferopol itself wanted to move its religious board into one of the former waqf houses on Kaitarnaia Street; the building had once housed the Crimean mufti before being turned into a residential house by Soviet officials.[145]

The formal reestablishment of the waqf did not take place. Yet, the German authorities seemed prepared to deal with the question on a local level. With the reopening of mosques and religious schools, former waqf property was de facto returned to the Muslim communities in many parts of the peninsula. Also, the temporary statutes for the local Muslim communities, which were adopted by a number of communities in the winter of 1942–1943, explicitly listed waqf property as a source of income.[146] According to the statutes, the local mosque councils were to administer all waqf land, mosques, office buildings, and residential houses of clergy and staff. They were also allowed to collect funds from charitable donations (*zakat*) and to use them to finance mosques and imams, religious education, and charity projects. The central religious board of the Muslim central committee in Simferopol was financed by waqf funds, deriving income from restaurants and other businesses, which, according to an SS report from spring 1943, generated a monthly income of 10,000 rubles and an unknown sum of charitable donations.[147] It remains unclear, however, whether the term "waqf" related to newly donated funds or traditional waqf properties. More generally, German economic and agricultural agencies were prepared to favor the peninsula's Muslim population in the distribution of agricultural land.[148]

The waqf issue was closely connected with the question of the reintroduction of a mufti, who had traditionally administered religious life in the Crimea. In Imperial Russia, the Crimean muftiate had been of considerable importance to Muslims even beyond the peninsula. The tsarist empire had employed a mufti in Ufa and one in Simferopol and later, for the Muslims of the Caucasus, a Sunni mufti and a Shi'a shaykh al-Islam in Tiflis. The Crimean muftiate in Simferopol, which comprised the mufti, his deputy, the *qadi al-'askar*, and six *qadis*, was responsible for sermons and prayers, marriages and divorces, inheritances, the administration of mosques and madrasas, and, most importantly, the waqf. The spiritual board of Simferopol, endorsed by the Wehrmacht, functioned in many respects like the muftiate, although it was symbolically less significant and restricted in its influence. Soon, the Simferopol committee suggested to the Germans the restoration of the Crimean muftiate. In his memorandum of 13 December 1942, Jamilov had connected the issue of the reestablishment of the waqf to the question of the muftiate.[149] The Simferopol Muslim committee, at the same time, promised that the introduction of a mufti would have a propagandistic impact not only on the "Muslims in Russia" but also on the "entire Muslim world."[150] On another occasion, Muslim leaders promoted the foundation of a muftiate by claiming that the moral revival of the Tatars was possible only through religion.[151]

The Germans were well aware that the reintroduction of a Crimean mufti would create a powerful new political figure. Nervous about Tatar political activism, army authorities saw the appointment of a supreme religious dignitary as a profound risk. Pleas for the reestablishment of a muftiate initially fell on deaf ears in Berlin. Increasing (and increasingly reciprocal) attempts by both Axis and Allied powers to present themselves as the friends of Islam finally changed German attitudes. In October 1943, when the Soviet government, as part of its relaxation of antireligious activities, created a muftiate in Tashkent, the East Ministry finally advanced a proposal for the establishment of a Crimean muftiate.[152] In November, Richard Kornelsen, an official in the East Ministry's political department, now led by Gottlob Berger, wrote a memorandum about the issue:

> In order to effectively counteract Bolshevism which, as the most recent events demonstrate, now also seeks to win influence in the Islamic world, it is imperative that from our side we generously employ all means at our disposal to fight it. The most immediate step is to have the election of the mufti in Tashkent declared invalid and to expose Stalin on the grounds that antireligious Jewish Bolshevism has no moral right, given the treatment of the Mohammedan population of the Soviet Union, to appear as the friend or patron of Islam, that the Mufti of Tashkent is nothing but a puppet in the hands of Moscow, and that the current Stalinist policy toward Islam is only a continuation of the theater that began in 1917.[153]

Kornelsen's proposal for a muftiate went well beyond the Crimea, discussing Crimean politics within a broader framework of Islam in the Soviet Union. The rationale was not the local pacification of the Crimea but the instrumentalization of Islam in the war more generally. The most effective countermove, he suggested, would be a congress of Muslim dignitaries representing the Crimea, the Caucasus, Turkestan, and the Volga Ural region. At this congress, he recommended that the German state give solemn recognition to a Crimean Tatar mufti, who would be elected in advance. The congress was to take place in Berlin and to be exploited propagandistically to the utmost. Muslim representatives from areas outside the Soviet Union were to participate as guests. Berger reacted to the proposal with one of his notorious notes in the margins: "Agreed."[154] The approval of Berger, who had also remained chief of the SS Head Office, could be interpreted as an endorsement by the SS.

Quickly, a plan for the establishment of a Crimean muftiate was put to the Wehrmacht. In this memorandum, the East Ministry first claimed that the institution would strengthen Germany's position on the peninsula, naturally the main concern of the army command in the Crimea, stressing that it was "in the German interest" to have "a trustworthy personality as mufti" who could be used "to influence the Tatar population."[155] Moreover, the mufti was to counteract Stalin's propaganda: "The election of a Crimean Tatar mufti can, later on, be used by us as a basis for propaganda against the Stalinist policy towards Islam." Ultimately, the proposal referred to the idea of wider pan-Islamic mobilization, explaining that "the election of a mufti would be of the greatest political and propagandistic significance in its effects both within the Soviet Union and in the Near East." Working toward Hitler's well-known sympathies for Muslim mobilization, the memorandum also referred to the "wish of the Führer to make advances toward the Mohammedan peoples." The memorandum left little room for objections. In its final part, it included some practical suggestions. To keep the process simple, the waqf question was not to be connected to the establishment of the muftiate. Only the heads of the Muslim committees, the heads of the religious boards, and all members of the religious board of the Simferopol committee were to be eligible to vote. The process was to be overseen by the Wehrmacht. The East Ministry had even chosen a suitable candidate for the post: Ahmed Ozenbashli.

Ozenbashli was an unlikely nominee.[156] A ruthless careerist, he had played a leading role during the upheavals of the revolution and in the civil war years and had later been employed as an official in the Soviet administration in the Crimea. There, however, he had fallen out with his superiors and had spent some time in a prison and in a labor camp. When the Germans invaded the Soviet Union, he was working as a physician in a practice near Kharkov. Eager to make a career in the post-Soviet Crimea, he had moved to Simferopol and become quite influential within the central Muslim committee. His plans were more ambitious, though. Despite his lack of religious education, Ozenbashli had early claimed the position of mufti and was now vigorously promoting his plan. The military authorities in the Crimea, however, had observed his activities with increasing suspicion. In the end, his efforts to extend the work of the Muslim committees to political issues had offended the SD. Fearing arrest, Ozenbashli had fled the peninsula in early October 1943 and headed to Odessa, from where, with the help of the Romanian secret police, he had gone to Bucharest. Although his escape did not stop the bureaucrats in the East Ministry from putting his name forward, army officials were less enthusiastic about the candidate and, indeed, the entire plan.

Worried that a muftiate would become a breeding ground for political activism, the Wehrmacht command responded sharply to the East Ministry's plan. "The creation of a regional government on a Mohammedan basis and the formation of a grand muftiate in the Crimea are not contemplated. Nor are there any plans in this respect. They would constitute a break with the hitherto pursued policy," it responded.[157] The military command feared uncontrollable political activity, remarking that "of late the Tatars have proved extremely unreliable." Internally, the East Ministry's proposal had caused some consternation and frantic consultations in the Wehrmacht.[158] Army officers on the ground had little understanding for such schemes, especially given the "unreliability" of "Ozenbashli and comrades."[159]

The SS did not follow a consistent line in the matter. Perhaps unaware of Berger's endorsement of the muftiate, some SS representatives in the Crimea were also cautious. "The questions of the muftiate are not currently so much in the foreground," stated an SS report dated 2 February 1944, pointing to the evacuation of large numbers of the Tatar population from partisan territory around the Crimean mountains and the massive recruitment for the army.[160] Nonetheless, in some parts of the SS, the mufti question was pursued further. On 5 March 1944, *SS-Hauptsturmführer* Stoecker, responsible for the Crimean Tatar questions at the SD, along with a number of SS officers from the propaganda section, visited Walter Schumann, the Wehrmacht's commissioner of Simferopol, to discuss the idea of a Crimean muftiate.[161] Schumann expressed reservations. On the ground, Wehrmacht officials had other problems. The Red Army had returned to the peninsula, and the Germans were retreating.

SS officers continued discussing the question of the muftiate to the end of the war. After the Crimea had been reconquered, eager proponents of Islamic mobilization within the SS Head Office began contemplating a general muftiate for all Eastern Turks. The issue was now discussed solely in terms of Islamic mobilization and propaganda and with reference to the morale of Muslim volunteers in the German forces. Reiner Olzscha even consulted Richard Hartmann.[162] Hartmann warned that the establishment of one muftiate for all Sunni Muslims of the Soviet Union would concentrate immense power in the hands of one person and also pointed out that there was no qualified candidate available for the post.

In the East Ministry, too, the question of a muftiate remained on the table after the German retreat from the Crimea, and here, too, it was now discussed in more general terms, as an institution for all Eastern Muslims. In the summer of 1944, Berger ordered Gerhard von Mende to speak with al-Husayni about the issue. Again concerns about the establishment of a Soviet muftiate and, more generally, Moscow's increasing propaganda efforts across the Islamic world dominated the discussion. Mende reported: "In order to successfully counteract Bolshevist propaganda through the installation of a muftiate in Tashkent, the grand mufti would welcome it, if from the German side, experimentally, a muftiate would be established."[163] The foundation of a muftiate for the Crimean Tatars was to be connected to an appeal to all Muslims of the Soviet Union, affirming the Third Reich's pro-Islamic stance. Again the name of Ozenbashli was put forward. In fact, Mende had already contacted him and asked him to come to Berlin at once. Ozenbashli, however, showed no interest. A Tatar informant, who had been sent by the East Ministry and the Gestapo to Romania in June 1944, had reported that Ozenbashli was willing to come to Germany only if he was certain to be made mufti.[164] Disillusioned, Ozenbashli no longer believed in a German victory and now hoped that the British would soon land in Romania. After the Soviet occupation of the country, he was swiftly arrested by Red Army soldiers. Bureaucrats in the East Ministry continued to debate the issue, even drafting a decree for the establishment of an Eastern muftiate.[165] In autumn 1944, the political department of the East Ministry reported on the plans in its newsletter: "At the moment negotiations are pending about the foundation of a muftiate. This project is, in regard to its impact, of the utmost importance."[166] As late as March 1945, as the Red Army marched on Berlin, the head of the Tatar section in the ministry, Count Leon Stamati, put forward the idea of a "Crimean muftiate" that would be, "in the tradition of the past," at the same time "a supreme mufti for all Mohammedans of the Soviet Union."[167]

A few days later, Alimjan Idris, too, wrote a report on the foundation of the muftiate. He was more critical. Most of the Muslim prisoners of war he had met were indifferent to a muftiate or were more interested in national independence than religious leadership. They preferred an alliance of Muslim peoples instead of a unified Islamic empire, he explained. Yet, Idris also understood that religious concessions might be the best alternative to national sovereignty. If the Turkic peoples of the East were not to be unified or granted national independence after the war, they should be organized "under a uniform religious organization," Idris wrote, adding: "If this were the case, the leader of this organization would have to be elected from its own Islamic scholars."[168] The handling of the muftiate question can be seen as an exception to the general line of the East Ministry, which was usually less enthusiastic about the employment of Islam in the East.

Islam and the Civil Administration in the Reich Commissariat Ostland

Berlin was not always cautious when it came to the question of a muftiate. In fact, in their efforts to restore the muftiate, the Crimean Muslims had initially been encouraged by the permission granted to Tatar Muslims in Vilnius to install a mufti in Hinrich Lohse's Reich Commissariat Ostland.[169] The Tatar minorities in Poland, Lithuania, Latvia, Estonia, and Belarus had been among the first Eastern Muslims the Germans had encountered.[170] Most of them now lived in the area of the Ostland. Under the protection of the Grand Duchy of Lithuania, which comprised today's Poland, Lithuania, and Belarus, Muslim Tatars from the Crimea, the Volga region, and the Caucasus had settled in the area since the fourteenth century. Over the following centuries, they had enjoyed special rights and freedom of faith, forming a distinctive Muslim culture, as reflected, for instance, in the picturesque wooden mosques of Kruszyniany and Bohoniki. After the Soviet invasion of Poland and Lithuania in 1939, Moscow deported many Muslim Tatars, especially those of Lithuania and Belarus, to Siberia. Islam was suppressed. Mosques were destroyed, turned into warehouses, or used for other purposes, like the mosque of Kaunas, which was turned into a public library. Contemporary observers in the United

States and Britain were convinced that the suppression of Islam continued under German rule.[171] Yet, the reality was more complex. As in other parts of the Eastern territories, Nazi authorities attempted to promote Germany as the liberator of Islam.

In contrast to the Crimea and the Caucasus, Muslim life in the Ostland fell mainly under the control of the East Ministry.[172] Islam had no special status but was usually regulated by the East Ministry along with other religions. In May 1942, for instance, Rosenberg's general instructions about religion to the civil administration in the Ostland and the Ukraine emphasized that among the tolerated religious groups and organizations was "the Mohammedan population."[173] A year later, he instructed the civil administration in the occupied territories, as well as state, party, and army, on the dates of Islamic religious holidays on which Muslim workers in all occupied territories were to be exempt from duty.[174] Rosenberg specifically mentioned the celebrations of *Mawlid*, *Uraza Bairam*, and *Qurban Bairam*, which were celebrated respectively on 19 March, 1 October, and 8 December of that year. Finally, Rosenberg instructed the local command in Muslim areas to consider—"after consulting the leading local Mohammedan cleric"—turning the Islamic New Year on 28 December 1943, into a holiday. Wherever the military-economic situation made such breaks impossible, Rosenberg advised local officers to communicate restrictions to religious holidays through religious intermediaries or, as he put it, "the leading Mohammedan clerics."

In practice, these policies were welcomed by many of the Muslims of the Ostland. At least this was the impression of Werner Otto von Hentig.[175] Similarly, a prominent Crimean exile politician, Edige Mustafa Kirimal, who visited the area in early 1942, reported to the East Ministry that the Muslims were "thankful" to the Third Reich for their "liberation from the Bolshevik hell."[176] They had reopened their mosques and could enjoy full religious freedom. Both Hentig and Kirimal observed that, favored by the German administration, many Muslims were employed in the civil administration and in the local police forces.

In Riga, the local mullah, Shakir Eriss, who had run a Turkish café before being elected imam of Riga in the 1920s, assured the German authorities of his "greatest gratitude" for having been given "permission to hold common and public sermons again, which many Mohammedans have not been free to experience during the 25 years of Communist rule."[177] The Soviet era had been the "culmination" of a long history of anti-Muslim suppression by the Russian central state, he explained, adding: "Communism treated the hallowed principles of Islam with complete disrespect." Yet, Eriss claimed that Muslim culture had been preserved within families. Eriss was described by the authorities of the Reich Commissariat as "absolutely pro-German."[178] He was also made imam of the numerous Muslim prisoners of war who were concentrated in Latvia and worked in labor units in Riga, Dünaburg (Daugavpils), and Wenden (Cēsis).[179] Eriss would eventually go so far as to suggest the establishment of Muslim units within the Wehrmacht—"Mohammedan units only under German officers and with Mohammedan symbols"—obviously unaware that recruitment of Muslims had already started.[180] Though eager to collaborate wherever he could, Eriss's activities were mainly limited to the Riga region. A more significant role in Islamic affairs in the Ostland (and beyond) was played by his colleague in Vilnius.

In early 1942, the Germans, more specifically Adrian von Renteln, Rosenberg's sinister general commissioner of Lithuania, officially endorsed Jakub Szynkiewicz as the mufti of Lithuania (Figure 4.5).[181] Based in Vilnius, where most Lithuanian Tatars lived, Szynkiewicz now led the so-called Lithuanian muftiate. He would soon try to expand his influence to other parts of the Reich Commissariat and, indeed, is usually referred to in German documents as the mufti of the Ostland.[182] Szynkiewicz left no doubt about his unconditional loyalty to Hitler's Germany. "We firmly believe that God will help Germany to exterminate Bolshevism and to establish a new order in all of Russia," he wrote to his old acquaintance Alimjan Idris in Berlin, as this was the only opportunity "for our Mohammedan brothers" in the East "to free themselves from the Russian yoke."[183] In his mid-forties and stateless, Szynkiewicz had long-standing contacts with Germany and had actually been educated in Berlin.[184] Having also enjoyed the trust of the Polish government, he had served as mufti of Poland in the interwar period.[185] The Polish government, after the First World War, had founded a muftiate in Vilnius for the Tatar Muslims of the entire region, who had previously been nominally subordinate to the tsarist muftiate of the Crimea. In the interwar period, Szynkiewicz had presided over Poland's seventeen mosques and three prayer houses. He had been very active, pub-

4.5 The mufti of the Ostland: Mufti Jakub Suleyman Szynkiewicz in his office (NAC).

lishing prayer books, instructions for imams, and texts on Islamic theology in Arabic and Polish. Fluent in a number of Middle Eastern languages, he had visited the Hijaz, Palestine, Syria, Turkey, Bulgaria, and Bosnia, been received by King Fuad in Cairo, mingled with Islamic leaders like al-Husayni and Shakib Arslan, and represented his community at all pan-Islamic congresses of the 1920s and 1930s.

Jakub Szynkiewicz was the uncle of Edige Szynkiewicz, better known as Edige Kirimal, whose father was Lithuanian.[186] According to Kirimal, Szynkiewicz also enjoyed a very positive reputation among Crimean Tatars. Indeed, the Tatar minorities of the Baltic, Belarus, and Poland had traditionally maintained close links with the Muslim Tatars of the Crimea. It was therefore not surprising that the question of establishing a Crimean muftiate was revitalized in 1942 when news spread about the founding of a muftiate in the Reich Commissariat Ostland.[187] Even the head of the Wehrmacht administration of the Crimea complained that the question of a muftiate in Vilnius and in Simferopol had not been settled consistently.

Obviously, regarding the East Ministry's policies in the Ostland, the civil and the military administrations had not communicated with each other on such important political issues, he criticized.[188] Considering the links between the communities, Richard Kornelsen, for his part, ultimately even contemplated evacuating the Crimean Tatars to Lithuania: "One must also consider whether it would be advantageous to bring a part of the Crimean Tatars to the Ostland (Vilnius area)."[189]

In practice, the muftiate of the Ostland was also likely to affect the small group of Muslims, no more than 7,000, in wartime Poland, as the Polish Muslim population had always formed one community with the Muslims in Lithuania. In fact, some reports suggest that Szynkiewicz also acted as the mufti of Muslims of the General Government.[190] In Warsaw, the Germans installed a pro-German imam who had no Polish Tatar background to replace the al-Azhar-educated imam of Warsaw, Ali Woronowicz. During the German-Soviet invasion, Woronowicz was on a visit to Eastern Poland, where he was arrested by the Red Army and later deported. Although the Muslims in the General Government were few in number, the Germans were well aware of their political significance. Berlin cautiously monitored Allied propaganda in the Middle East, which portrayed Axis forces as desecrators of Polish mosques and reported that the Muslims of Poland had become the subject of particular maltreatment because German troops equated them with Jews.[191]

Realities of War and Soviet Responses

Allied propaganda reports claiming that the Germans treated Polish Muslims like Jews may not have been entirely invented. Trained in racial terms and stirred up by propaganda defaming the "Asiatic" peoples of the Soviet Union as subhuman beings, ordinary German soldiers were not prepared for dealing with Muslims in the East. In the early months of the Barbarossa campaign, in the front areas, many Muslims, specifically prisoners of war, were executed by SS squads on the assumption that the fact that they were circumcised proved that they were Jews.[192] In the summer of 1941, at a high-level conference of the High Command of the Wehrmacht, SD, and East Ministry, under the chairmanship of General Hermann Reinecke, Colonel Erwin von Lahousen, who represented the head of the military intelligence service, Admiral Wilhelm Canaris, became embroiled in a fierce argument with Gestapo chief Heinrich Müller, "Gestapo-Müller," about these executions. In particular, the selection of hundreds of Muslims, possibly Crimean Tatars, who had been "conveyed to special treatment" because they were taken for Jews, was brought up. Müller calmly acknowledged that some mistakes had been made in this respect. It was the first time, he claimed, that he had heard that Muslims, too, were circumcised. On 12 September 1941, Reinhard Heydrich sent out a directive, cautioning the SS Task Forces to be more careful. The "circumcision" and "Jewish appearance" of the Turkic Muslims did not constitute sufficient "proof of Jewish descent," he explained.[193] Muslims were not to be confused with Jews. On the eve of the summer campaign, in May 1942, the East Ministry issued a decree on the identification of "Jews" in the occupied Eastern territories clarifying that only in the Western Russian areas should circumcision be seen as a marker of Jewishness.[194] "In those regions, though, in which Mohammedans exist we will not be able to base the Jewishness of the person on the circumcision alone." In Muslim areas, other characteristics like names, origins, and ethnic appearance had to be taken into account.

On the southern fringes of the Soviet Union, however, German killing squads still had difficulty distinguishing Muslims from Jews. When the *Einsatzgruppe D* began murdering the Jewish population of the Caucasus and the Crimea, it encountered a special situation with regard to three Jewish communities that had long lived closely alongside the Muslim population: the Karaites and Krymchaks in the Crimea and the Judeo-Tats, also known as "Mountain Jews," in the northern Caucasus.[195] In the Crimea, SS officials were puzzled when they encountered the Turkic-speaking Karaites and Krymchaks. Following a meeting with Ohlendorf in Simferopol in December 1941, two Wehrmacht officers, *Oberkriegsverwaltungsrat* Fritz Donner and Major Ernst Seifert, reported that it was interesting to note that "a large part of these Jews on the Crimea is of the Mohammedan faith," while there were also "Near Eastern racial groups of a non-Semitic character, who, strangely, have adopted the Jewish faith."[196] The Germans' confusion about the classification of Karaites and Krymchaks, who were, in fact, both of Jewish faith, was striking. In the end, the Karaites were classified as ethnically Turkic and spared, whereas the Krymchaks were considered ethnically Jewish and killed. According to Walter Groß, the Karaites were spared because of their close relations with the allied Muslim Tatars.[197] A few hundred Karaites were even recruited into the Crimean

Tatar volunteer units.[198] In the Caucasus, the Judeo-Tats took their case to the Nalchik regional committee, which promptly raised the issue with the army staff. *SS-Oberführer* Walther Bierkamp, now head of the *Einsatzgruppe D*, told Bräutigam that when he had personally visited the "Mountain Jews" in the Nalchik area, they had been extremely hospitable.[199] Bierkamp found that, aside from their religion, they had nothing in common with Jews. Conversely, he recognized Islamic influence, as the Tats also practiced polygamous relationships. Bierkamp ordered that these peoples were not to be touched and that in place of "Mountain Jews" the term "Tats" was to be used.[200]

As the Germans began screening the occupied territories of the Soviet Union for the Roma population, they soon also encountered many Muslim Roma.[201] Indeed, the majority of the Roma in the Crimea was Islamic.[202] They had for centuries assimilated with the Tatars, who now showed remarkable solidarity with their Muslim coreligionists. Shortly after their foundation, the Muslim committees had apparently sent petitions to the Germans, asking for the protection of the Muslim Roma. An article about them, published in *Azat Kirim* on 27 March 1942, explained that the group distinguished itself from the ordinary "gypsies" in its "language, rituals and manners" and was ethnically related to "Iranian tribes."[203] Backed by the Tatars, many Muslim Roma pretended to be Tatars to escape deportation and death. Islam, too, was employed to this end. A remarkable example was the roundup of Roma in Simferopol in December 1941, when the captured tried to use Islamic symbols to convince the Germans that their arrest was a mistake. An eyewitness noted in his diary:

> The gypsies arrived en masse on carriages at the Talmud-Thora Building. For some reason, they raised a green flag, the symbol of Islam, high and put a mullah at the head of their procession. The gypsies tried to convince the Germans that they were not gypsies; some claimed to be Tatars, others to be Turkmens. But their protests were disregarded and they were all put into the great building.[204]

In the end, many Muslim Roma were murdered. Nevertheless, as the Germans had trouble distinguishing Muslim Roma from Muslim Tatars, some—around 30 percent—survived, and, as with the Karaites, a number of Muslim Roma were even recruited into German Tatar auxiliary units. During his interrogation at the *Einsatzgruppen* trial, when asked about the persecution of "gypsies" in the Crimea, Ohlendorf explained that the screening had been complicated by the fact that many Roma and the Crimean Tatars had shared the same religion: "That was the difficulty, because some of the gypsies—if not all of them—were Moslems, and for that reason we attached a great amount of importance [to the issue] to not getting into difficulties with the Tartars and, therefore, people were employed in this task who knew the places and the people."[205]

Among the Muslims of the Caucasus and Crimea, initial hopes for better treatment, encouraged by the Germans, were soon shattered. Many increasingly recognized that the Germans were simply conquerors using them as instruments for realizing their own plans. In spite of all German efforts to make religious concessions and stage colorful spectacles to win over the Muslims of the Caucasus and the Crimea, everyday life would often be characterized by the violent realities of the war. Romanian troops showed little respect for Islam from the outset. From the Caucasus front, German officers reported to the headquarters of Army Group A on the "unfavorable effects" of the "conduct of the Romanian allies" toward Muslims.[206] In Berlin, Quartermaster-General Eduard Wagner, in his notes for a meeting with Hitler, wrote that he had had the "worst possible experiences" with Romanian soldiers in the Caucasus, reporting on "lootings" and "abuse," which would cause the "strongest reactions" among the Muslims in particular.[207] In the Crimea, Romanian authorities regularly favored the Orthodox population over Muslims in areas under their occupation. Romanian Orthodox field priests, who came with the Romanian occupation troops, even attempted to actively influence religious life in the Crimea.[208] Concerned about their own policy line, German army officers finally stepped in to curb the activities of their ally's clerics.

Yet, as the occupation continued, the attitudes of German officials in the Crimea toward the Muslim population cooled.[209] Toward the end of the war, the Germans were increasingly concerned about the infiltration of Tatar settlements by partisans and responded with violence. Between December 1943 and January 1944, the Luftwaffe dropped firebombs on more than one hundred mountain villages in the southern and inner Crimea, according to Kirimal.[210] In early 1944, the Crimean Tatar villages Argin, Baksan, and Kazal were razed to the ground by the Germans. Looting, physical maltreatment, and discrimination spread into the Muslim areas. In the Caucasus the situation was not much better.[211] The army's supply lines were unstable, and German soldiers often did not follow orders about food acquisitions and payments. In nursing homes, hospitals, orphanages, and sanatoria, including those in Kislovodsk, sick and disabled persons were abused and killed to increase food provisions. Paranoid about partisan activities, German troops shot hundreds (thousands, according to some estimates) of civilians during the short period of the occupation.[212] The destruction in the northern Caucasus was immense. "It is unimaginable, what values were destroyed here," a German soldier wrote to his parents during the retreat from the Caucasus: "Only who saw and sees it with his own eyes, can believe it."[213]

Soviet responses to Germany's Islam campaign in the East were twofold. On the one hand, there was a shift in the Kremlin's policy toward Islam, reflected in a number of religious concessions and propaganda that appealed to the religious sentiments of Soviet Muslims.[214] After all, tens of thousands of Muslims fought in the Red Army, many of them from the Crimea and the Caucasus.[215] Just after the German invasion, Abdurrahman Rasulaev, who was appointed by the Kremlin as the mufti of Ufa, called on the Muslims of the Soviet Union "to rise up in defense of their native land, to pray in the mosques for the victory of the Red Army and to give their blessing to their sons, fighting in a just cause."[216] Hitler was out "to exterminate the Moslem faith," he warned. A few weeks later, Rasulaev declared that the "Islamic masses have arisen" to fight the German invaders.[217] "The Islamic civilization which is to be found all over the world is to-day menaced with destruction by the German Fascist bands unless the Moslems of the world stand up to it and fight," he warned. And in September 1941 he urged the Soviet Muslims "to defend our country in the name of religion."[218] "In mosques and in private prayers pray to God to help defeat the enemy of the Red Army." In his sixties, Rasulaev, son of a renowned Muslim dignitary and member of a distinguished Bashkir family, became Stalin's most important propagandist in the Muslim areas of the Soviet Union and beyond. On 15 May 1942, his authority as head of all Soviet Muslims was confirmed at a Soviet Muslim congress in Ufa. Islamic dignitaries used the occasion to give accounts of German atrocities against the Muslims in the Crimea. The Germans were accused of having "wrecked mosques," "removed holy symbols," "banned public prayers," and "outraged national and religious customs in every imaginable way."[219] Gradually Moscow set up an extensive religious administration for its Muslim subjects, centered on the so-called spiritual directorates. The first one was the central directorate headed by Rasulaev in Ufa. In October 1943, at the Muslim congress in Tashkent, a spiritual directorate for the Sunni Muslim population of Central Asia and Kazakhstan was founded under the revered eighty-two-year-old Uzbek mufti Ishan Babakhan.[220] The following year, the Kremlin created a spiritual directorate for the Sunnis of the North Caucasus, based in Buynaksk under Mufti Khizri Gebekov, and one for the Shi'ites of Azerbaijan, led by Shaykh al-Islam Akhund Agha Alizade in Baku. Shi'a dignitaries elected Alizade, who had been trained in Shi'a theology in Karbala and Najaf in the 1890s, at a congress in Baku in May 1944 and sent a message of allegiance to Stalin, addressing him as the "God-sent and wise head of the Soviet government."[221] "May Allah light the victorious path of our fighters and help them clear the Fascist filth for ever from the earth!," they proclaimed. Ironically, Rasulaev, Gebekov, Babakhan, and Alizade had all experienced imprisonment, exile, or both before Stalin decided to employ them in his war effort. Desperate for total military mobilization, Soviet propagandists appealed to the religious feelings of Muslims and called for jihad against the German invaders. Stalin was praised as the patron of Islam. The Germans were condemned as the most ruthless enemies of Muslims and their faith. Rasulaev's directorate in Ufa distributed pamphlets in Uzbek, Turkmen, Tajik, and Persian, commanding the faithful, in the words of the Qur'an, to "kill the enemy wheresoever thou findest him."[222] On 31 October 1942, when the struggle for the Caucasus reached its height, the entire second page of *Pravda* was printed in Turkic, with a Russian translation opposite, declaring: "Behold the fate of the Moslem peoples of the Crimea and the Caucasus; their peaceful villages are being burned and looted by the Germans."[223] Soviet propaganda would eventually even draw on the memories of Imam Shamil's holy war. The Muslims of Dagestan, Soviet newspapers announced, contributed 25 million rubles for a tank column named "Shamil."[224] In the reopened mosques across the Soviet Union, imams were to open their sermons with a fixed formula: "Soviet authority is given by Allah. Therefore everyone who turns against Soviet authority turns against Allah and Muhammad, his Prophet."[225]

The Kremlin's policy toward its Islamic population also had a harsher side. Stalin reacted with brutal measures to what he perceived as open collaboration of Muslims in the Crimea and the Caucasus with the enemy.

During the war, Soviet propaganda not only portrayed the Crimean Tatars as misled by traitors, offering them full amnesty if they changed sides, but also called for the fight against Muslim collaborators.[226] In the last weeks of the German occupation in the Eastern Muslim territories, panic broke out. Many Muslims in the Crimea and the Caucasus decided to escape with the Germans. A trek of North Caucasians followed the retreat of the German army. Tens of thousands, the OSS reported, left the Caucasus with the Germans.[227] Describing the "endless columns, which move westward," the *Völkischer Beobachter* compared the situation to the strategic population relocations during the nineteenth-century *ghazawat*.[228] In the Crimea, Tatar leaders tried to convince the German authorities to evacuate at least some of the most prominent Muslim collaborators.[229] They even sought help from al-Husayni in Berlin. Appealing to the Palestinian as "the religious leader of the Mohammedan world that marches alongside Germany," they warned about the looming physical annihilation of the Crimean Muslims.[230] But the toothless mufti was in no position to help. The Germans were preoccupied with pulling out their own troops. Eventually, only a small number of Muslims, among them many members of the Simferopol Muslim committee, most notably its former head, Eredzhep Qursaidov, and the leader of the religious board, Alimseit Jamilov, managed to flee the peninsula by plane or boat.[231] Those Crimean Muslims who ended up in Germany appealed, with the help of al-Husayni, to the Germans to be settled in the same region so that they could live together and raise their children in the Islamic way.[232]

After the German withdrawal from the Caucasus and the Crimea, Stalin deported those Muslims (together with Christian Volga Germans and Buddhist Kalmyks) whom he perceived as traitors.[233] On 17 and 18 May 1944, the entire Muslim Tatar population of the Crimea was forcibly transferred to Central Asia and Kazakhstan. Following the Soviet conquest of the Crimea in April, many Crimean Muslims deemed collaborators were executed by NKVD cadres. In the Muslim quarters of Simferopol, the streets were lined with bodies hanging from telephone poles and trees. In the Caucasus, Soviet authorities charged the Karachais, the Balkars, and the Chechens and Ingush with high treason. In the case of the Balkars, the *Qurban Bairam* celebration served, in fact, as evidence to support the charge of treason.[234] In November 1943 the entire Karachai population was brought to Central Asia and Kazakhstan. In early March 1944 the Balkars were deported to Kazakhstan and Kirgizia. Even though Chechnya-Ingushetia had never been fully occupied by the Germans, the scattered anti-Soviet uprisings in the region had provoked anger in the Kremlin. The Chechens and Ingush were deported in late February 1944. Bidding farewell to their homes, some whispered the words of prayer "*La ilaha illa Allah*" (There is no god but Allah).[235]

CHAPTER FIVE

Islam and the Battle for the Balkans

Advancing into the Kingdom of Yugoslavia in the spring of 1941, German troops were surprised by the enthusiastic welcome they received from large parts of the Muslim population. Anton Bossi Fedrigotti, liaison officer of the Foreign Office to Maximilian von Weichs's invading Second Army, reported that the soldiers had been utterly astonished to be jubilantly greeted by the Muslims, though he quickly explained that this reaction was "only natural" as the Muslims had always been the fiercest opponents of the Orthodox Serbs who had dominated the country.[1] In Sarajevo, Fedrigotti noted, Islamic leaders had called on their followers to decorate the streets with flags to express their joy at the German invasion.[2] The day after the occupation of the city, a Muslim crowd cheered as the Germans tore down the plaque commemorating the assassination of Archduke Franz Ferdinand. Afterward, they participated in a German military parade that took place along the banks of the Miljacka. "The entire mood of the Muslim population on this day demonstrated that here, too, far away from Germany, exists a tremendous adoration for the Führer," Fedrigotti wrote. A few days later, on the occasion of Hitler's birthday, Muslim leaders organized mass rallies and celebratory prayers in the mosques, to which the German military authorities were invited.[3] To be sure, German reports about the enthusiasm of the Muslim population need to be read with caution. The Germans could record only what they saw, and those Muslims who were opposed to Axis aggression stayed silent or expressed their concerns in private. But although the attitudes of the Muslims toward the invasion can hardly be generalized, most felt little loyalty to the collapsing kingdom (Figures 5.1, 5.2, and 5.3).

The Muslims of the region had, for most of their history, enjoyed special rights and a certain level of autonomy in their religious life and organizations, first under the Ottomans, then, from 1878, under the Habsburg monarchy, and, after 1918, in the Yugoslav kingdom. And yet, Yugoslav rule had quickly proven to be less tolerant than that of its imperial prede-

5.1 German soldiers and Muslims in Sarajevo after the fall of Yugoslavia, 1941 (*Archive of the Historical Museum of Bosnia and Herzegovina, Sarajevo*).

cessors.[4] Although Muslims under the leadership of Mehmed Spaho, head of the powerful Yugoslav Muslim Organization (*Jugoslovenska Muslimanska Organizacija*), had retained much of their religious autonomy in the interwar period, most felt repressed under Orthodox Serbian hegemony (as did many Catholic Croats) and, in 1941, welcomed the fall of Yugoslavia.

German authorities initially made few attempts to engage with the Muslim population in the Balkans.[5] In fact, Hitler did not intend to get involved in the Muslim territories when dissolving the Kingdom of Yugoslavia in the spring of 1941. While German troops occupied Serbia, the Muslim areas fell under the administration of the Italians (Montenegro, including the Sandžak of Novi Pazar), the Bulgarians (Macedonia), and, most importantly, the newly created Croatian Ustaša state (Bosnia and Herzegovina), which governed the majority of the Muslims of the former Yugoslav kingdom. It was the escalation of the war in late 1942 that would eventually lead to German political involvement with the Muslims of the region.

5.2 German soldiers on the streets of Sarajevo, 1941 (*Ullstein*).

5.3 German soldiers talking to Muslim women in Sarajevo, 1941 (*Ullstein*).

The Ustaša regime, with its fascist vision of a Catholic Croatia, soon proved to have little respect for its Muslim subjects. And yet, while murdering Jews and persecuting Orthodox Serbs, Ante Pavelić, *Poglavnik* of the Independent State of Croatia, did at least formally try to accommodate the Muslim population. He made Islam the second state religion, and Ustaša officials declared the Muslims to be "the flower of the Croatian people."[6] The regime also employed a number of Islamic leaders, most prominently perhaps Ismet Muftić, the mufti of Zagreb, who became a vigorous promoter of the Ustaša state and, officially at least, sustained shari'a (*šeriat* in Bosnian) courts, madrasas, and waqf (*vakuf* in Bosnian) properties. In the center of Zagreb, the new government even opened the colossal Poglavnik Mosque (*Poglavnikova Džamija*) (Figures 5.4 and 5.5). Before long, however, the Muslim population was caught in the crossfire of a bitter civil war.

From early 1942, the Balkans became increasingly engulfed in a severe conflict between the Croatian regime, Communist partisans, and Orthodox Serbian Četniks.[7] The partisans, led by the former Habsburg soldier and Bolshevik revolutionary Josip Broz, better known as Tito, clashed with both Ustaša troops and Četniks. The Četnik movement, which under Dragoljub "Draža" Mihailović fought for a restoration of the monarchy and a Greater Serbia, waged war not only against Ustaša troops and Catholic villages but also against Tito's partisans. The Muslim population was repeatedly attacked by all three parties. Ustaša authorities had employed Muslim army units to fight Tito's partisans and Četnik militias, and had used them to control Serbian Orthodox areas. Soon Muslim villages became the object of retaliatory attacks by both partisans and Četniks. Particularly violent were the Četnik reprisals against Muslims in East and South Bosnia and in parts of Herzegovina, where Ustaša authority had always been unstable. Mihailović burned down entire villages. His men became feared for killing Muslims by cutting their throats. Estimates of the number of Muslim victims grew into the tens of thousands. Despite Pavelić's warm words for Islam, Ustaša authorities overall did little to prevent these massacres. Even worse, in areas where Muslim leaders engaged in local cease-fire agreements with Četnik and partisan commanders, Catholic Ustaša units responded by repressing the Muslim population. German military reports pointed to the mounting discord between the Muslims and the Croatian state.[8] More and more Muslim leaders in Bosnia and Herzegovina pleaded

5.4 The Poglavnik Mosque, converted from the Ivan Meštrović Art Pavilion, in Zagreb, 1944 (*Archive of the Croatian Historical Museum, Zagreb*).

for independence. Attempts to build Muslim militias for self-defense were, on the whole, a failure. As an ultima ratio, some leading Muslim representatives turned to the Germans. In a memorandum of 1 November 1942, addressed to Hitler, they asked for Muslim autonomy under a German protectorate in Bosnia and Herzegovina.[9] Bemoaning the plight of the Muslim population, they railed against the Catholic Church, Četnik Orthodoxy, and Communist partisans while professing their "love and loyalty" for Hitler.[10] Remarkably, the Muslims tried to employ pan-Islamic references to strengthen their case, emphasizing that the Bosnian Muslims

5.5 Ali Aganović, Ante Pavelić, Ismet Muftić, and Siegfried Kasche at the opening of the Zagreb Mosque, 1944 (*Archive of the Croatian Historical Museum, Zagreb*).

were an integral part of the "300 million Muslims" in the world and that they were willing to align themselves with the Axis against "Judaism, Freemasonry, Bolshevism, and the English exploiters." They also referred to other "suppressed Islamic peoples" whose leaders had sought protection from the German regime.[11]

The Germans were in a dilemma. Berlin accepted the Ustaša state and its rule over the Muslim territories of Bosnia and Herzegovina. Hitler had sent only diplomatic and military representatives to Zagreb, most importantly the Austrian Nazi veteran General Edmund Glaise von Horstenau, accredited as the Wehrmacht's representative in Croatia, and *SA-Obergruppenführer* Siegfried Kasche, Germany's envoy in Zagreb. Kasche had little sympathy for the Muslims and would, until the end, support the Ustaša regime. Although he believed in the political significance of Islam and had, in fact, repeatedly warned of the global implications—or "resonances in the Islamic world," as he once put it—of Germany's policy toward the Muslims in southeastern Europe, he was well aware that his own political influence, as the German envoy in Croatia, was tied to the stability of the Ustaša regime.[12]

In practice, however, the situation was changing.[13] From autumn 1942, as parts of the Croatian state, particularly Bosnia and Herzegovina, seemed to be spinning out of control, German troops became increasingly involved in the Muslim territories. All operational areas were subsumed under German military command, forcing Pavelić to give up de facto sovereignty of parts of Croatia. In late 1942, Horstenau was forced to share power with General Rudolf Lüters, who became commander of the German troops in Croatia. In early 1943, a major offensive was launched against all insurgents in central Croatia, Bosnia, and Herzegovina. Soon the SS would also become involved. In late March 1943, Himmler sent *SS-Brigadeführer* Konstantin Kammerhofer to Zagreb as the official SS commissioner on the spot. Kammerhofer had limited respect for either Ustaša authorities or the German envoy, Kasche. Ignoring all complaints, he instantly put parts of North Croatia under the authority of the SS. Convinced that the SS would be more effective than the wavering Ustaša security forces, the Wehrmacht did not resist. Kasche was increasingly sidelined and isolated. By the end of 1943, the SS had further strengthened its influence. Between spring and autumn 1944, it practically ruled the Muslim areas within Sava, Drina, Spreča, and Bosna.

Less concerned than Kasche and the Foreign Office about Ustaša authority, the Wehrmacht and, more importantly, the SS saw the Muslims as useful allies. Military reports and internal papers regularly referred to the alleged pro-German attitude of the Balkan Muslims and to their impact on the wider Muslim world. It was the pan-Islamic character of the Muslims, Rudolf Lüters wrote in a report in spring 1943, that provoked the Četniks. "It is especially the apparently supranational, religiously determined behavior which angers the Serb with his overarching national pride."[4] A Wehrmacht commander who would brief German troops fighting in Bosnia emphasized not only the pro-German attitude of the Muslims but also that the "950,000 Muslims" of Bosnia and Herzegovina "know very well that they represent the some 500,000,000 Mohammedans to the Greater German Reich and the Axis."[5] German support for the Muslim population would therefore have a propagandistic effect on "other Mohammedan countries." These views were shared by officers in the SS intelligence and by other German officials on the ground.[6] It was a set of reasons—the idea of a pro-German attitude of the Muslim population as well as considerations of their alleged significance within the wider Islamic world—which prompted the Wehrmacht and the SS to seek cooperation with the Muslims when trying to pacify the region from early 1943 on.

Soon, as the German military stepped up its operations in the Balkans, the Wehrmacht and the SS extended this policy to Muslims in areas occupied by the Italians. In early 1943, German troops got involved in the Sandžak area, the Muslim mountain belt between Montenegro and Serbia, which was formally under the rule of the Italians, who had, as the civil war escalated, turned a blind eye to Četnik massacres of the Muslim population. The German army command immediately ordered the soldiers to treat only the Muslims as allies, while encouraging them to act ruthlessly toward the rest of the population.[17] In autumn 1943, when Italy changed fronts and withdrew from the Balkans, the Sandžak was formally taken over by German troops. Moreover, the Muslim majority of Albania, which included Kosovo and had been under Italian occupation since 1939, now also came under the control of the Germans, who installed a puppet regime in the country.[18] In the Epirus area of northwestern Greece, which bordered Albania and had been under Italian rule as well, German military authorities sought cooperation with the Albanian Muslim Cham minority, which provided militias to pacify the region.[19] German involvement in

these territories was overseen by Hermann Neubacher, as Hitler's plenipo-
tentiary for southeastern Europe responsible for Albania, Montenegro,
Serbia, and Greece and an ardent supporter himself of an alliance with the
Muslims of the Balkans.

As usual, Hitler fully endorsed German courtship of the Muslims. Neubacher, who regularly discussed the situation in southeastern Europe at the
Führer Headquarters, recalled after the war that Hitler had firmly supported a "positive Muslim policy" (*positive Muselmanenpolitik*) in the region.[20]
According to Neubacher, Hitler's view of the Muslims in the Balkans was
also influenced by considerations about pan-Islamic implications. Discussing "the political significance of Balkan Islam in regard to the Middle East,"
Neubacher had tried to explain the connection to Hitler in terms easy to
understand: "When you strike a Sandžak Muslim, a student in Cairo reacts!"
Such arguments resonated with Hitler, who was apparently so impressed by
the phrase that he soon used it himself. Years after the war, Neubacher
would reaffirm these views, asserting that the fate of the Muslims of the
Balkans was closely monitored by believers throughout the Islamic world.[21]

Indeed, when strategically mapping the region, the Germans defined
the Muslims primarily in terms of religion.[22] This was to a certain extent a
consequence of the situation on the ground. With ethnic and linguistic
distinctions being marginal, religion had long been a principal marker of
communal difference in the Balkans. Confessional bonds, be they Roman
Catholic, Eastern Orthodox, Jewish, or Muslim, were strong. Although of
course none of these communities was homogeneous and the lines between
them were not impermeable, they shaped the social and political landscape
across the region. Even in an age of shattering empires and rising nation-
states, most Muslims, both in the urban centers and among the rural population, continued to see themselves primarily as "Muslims." While some
had embraced national affiliations (such as "Croatian" or even "Serbian"),
and many would also emphasize their regional (such as "Bosnian" or "Her-
zegovinian") or urban identities (such as "Sarajevan" or "Zagrebian"), religious loyalties (as "Muslims") remained crucial. Furthermore, religion had
a political meaning, with religious leaders and institutions exerting significant political influence. In the conflicts of the Second World War, the
political-confessional divisions came most radically to the fore, and the
Germans eagerly fueled and instrumentalized them for their political and
military aims.

In effect, religion became crucial to Germany's policy toward Muslims in the region. In their attempts to seek Muslim support, the German army command and, more importantly, the SS made significant efforts to employ religiously charged propaganda and to engage with religious dignitaries and leaders on the ground. More generally, German officials frequently discussed these policies toward Islam in the Balkans with reference to Germany's campaigns for Islamic mobilization in other parts of the world. Focusing on Bosnia, Herzegovina, and the Sandžak, the following pages examine the ways in which German officials promoted the Third Reich as the protector of Islam in the Balkans. These efforts began in spring 1943, when the SS initiated the foundation of a Muslim SS division, which is discussed in the final part of the book, and sent the mufti of Jerusalem on an extended propaganda tour across the Balkans.

The Tour of the Mufti

In late March and early April 1943, the SS sent Amin al-Husayni, who had been increasingly preoccupied with propaganda and consultancy work for the SS, on a tour of the Muslim-populated territories of the Ustaša state.[23] Carefully staged by the SS Head Office, the spectacle marked the beginning of Germany's campaign to win Muslim support in the region and to mobilize the male population into the German army. Al-Husayni's role as an Islamic figure was to bestow religious legitimacy on the German war effort. His task was to promote support for Germany among the Muslim population and negotiate with local Muslim leaders, clerics, and warlords. Berlin thereby adhered to the conception (fostered by al-Husayni himself) that the mufti was comparable to an Islamic pope, whose words would have authority among pious Muslims around the world. The employment of the Palestinian religious leader not only reflected the idea of global Islamic solidarity but also underlined the religious character of German efforts to win Muslim support in the Balkans.

Greedy for influence, al-Husayni had boasted in a conversation with Gottlob Berger about his great influence throughout the entire Muslim world.[24] The cause of Muslims in southeastern Europe, he claimed, had long been his special interest. Indeed, when visiting Rome in 1942, the mufti had already received a delegation of Islamic dignitaries led by the mufti of Mostar, Omer Džabić, a proponent of a Muslim state in the Balkans.[25] A large deputation of Yugoslav Muslims had also participated in the Muslim congress in Jerusalem in 1931, where some had established ties with al-Husayni.[26] Among many Muslims in the Balkans, the Arab mufti enjoyed remarkable respect. As early as August 1942, *Osvit*, a major Muslim newspaper in Sarajevo, had published an interview with al-Husayni that had aroused interest both in Croatia and among German officials.[27] *Osvit* remarked that the mufti had become the spearhead and protector of millions of oppressed Muslims. Al-Husayni affirmed Hitler's and Germany's amity for Islam and claimed that the Muslim world stood entirely on the side of Germany, Japan, and their allies. The British Empire would be fought until its collapse, just like Russia, which had been an enemy of Islam for centuries— Islam was the natural enemy of the Communist doctrine, he insisted. "Recently, the Führer confirmed to me that Germany follows with great interest the fight of the Islamic world against its oppressors and does not intend to enslave or suppress any Islamic country."[28] The victory of the Axis would be the victory of the Islamic peoples. In the autumn of that year, the *Völkischer Beobachter* reported that al-Husayni donated 15,000 lira to the Muslims of the Balkans.[29]

Officers of the SS Head Office planned the tour down to the minutest detail and prepared the mufti well in advance.[30] He was, of course, limited to playing a representational role. Berger had assured the mufti that he supported him "not only for practical reasons" but "from a full heart." Yet he made no secret of his practical intentions, adding that the SS would "not believe in promises" but wanted to have "proof" on the spot. On 30 March 1943, the Junkers 52 of Kurt Max Franz Daluege, head of the Order Police (*Ordnungspolizei*, or Orpo for short), crossed the Alps.[31] On board were the mufti and a number of SS officers, most importantly *SS-Sturmbannführer* Schulte and *SS-Untersturmführer* Rempel of the SS Head Office and *SS-Hauptsturmführer* Hermann, representing the SS Reich Security Head Office. Moreover, two Gestapo officers accompanied the mufti, as well as a pistol sniper.[32] The tour took two weeks. After visiting Zagreb (1–2 April), the group flew to Banja Luka (3–4 April) and set off from there to Sarajevo (5–9 April), before returning to Zagreb (10–11 April).[33]

During his travels, the mufti met with Ustaša representatives, including Pavelić, and German and Italian officials. More significant, however, were his consultations with the local 'ulama in Zagreb, Banja Luka, and Sarajevo, which underlined the religious character of the journey.[34] In

Sarajevo he received Muslim leaders and dignitaries from all parts of Bosnia and Herzegovina, from Tuzla and Mostar, as well as delegations from the Sandžak and Albania. Al-Husayni was particularly impressed by the Friday prayer (*džuma-namaz* in Bosnian) in Sarajevo's grand Gazi Husrev Beg Mosque and his meeting with the city's religious establishment afterward, recalling years later in his memoirs the warm welcome he had received.[35] "For the Bosnian Mohammedans, the mufti was first and foremost significant as a Mohammedan," a German diplomat noted.[36] "The pious accepted him as a just Muslim; he was honored as a descendant of the Prophet; friends from his theological studies in Cairo and from the pilgrimage to Mecca welcomed him." In the name of the Axis, al-Husayni affirmed solidarity with the destiny of Muslims in the Balkans, emphasizing, as the Germans observed, "his deep repulsion" for atrocities committed against "religious facilities like mosques" by partisans, who, he claimed, were "paid by Moscow and London."[37]

Throughout the tour, the mufti made extensive use of religious rhetoric. His speeches, sermons, and appeals were delivered in Arabic, with local interpreters translating them. When visiting the Gazi Husrev Beg Mosque, he gave such an emotional speech about the torment Muslims had suffered that parts of the audience burst into tears.[38] Bemoaning the situation of the Muslims in the Balkans, he assured the faithful that only the inner refuge of Islam made life bearable. His sermon included the call to war on the side of the Axis. Mustering all his religious authority, he warned throughout his visit that doubts about an Axis victory would be a sin. The mufti employed not only religious language but also pan-Islamic rhetoric. The Germans noted with satisfaction that al-Husayni emphasized the common nature of the battle fought by the Muslims of Croatia and the Muslims from other parts of the Islamic world, in Palestine, Syria, or Egypt, who were troubled or oppressed by "anti-Muslim elements," be they "Muscovite arsonists," "English tyrants," or "American exploiters."[39] To the press, the mufti announced that the "Muslims in the Islamic world" would follow the situation in the Balkans with "the greatest concern."[40] "The outrage in the Islamic world" against the "Serbian gangs" and their allies was "significant and bitter." According to US intelligence, al-Husayni condemned the Allies for the massacres of Muslims in the Balkans. "The Muslims," al-Husayni declared, "blame England for supporting these Bolshevik hordes, whereas, at the same time she pretends to support Islam."[41] His pan-Islamic rhetoric was exactly what the Germans wanted to hear. Not surprisingly, the mufti later summed up in his report to the Germans: "Islam fights Bolshevism and the Muslims know without doubt that their destiny is linked with that of Germany and the Axis and that they are only threatened by Serbs, Communists, and the Allies."[42]

The SS reacted enthusiastically to the tour. "The visit of the grand mufti has been a success in every way; also politically it has been received exceptionally well and positively, and may contribute quite considerably to pacification in this area," Berger reported.[43] Emphasizing the tour's religious dimension, he declared: "It has proved anew that the grand mufti possesses a fully functioning intelligence apparatus and commands extraordinary prestige in the entire Mohammedan world." Sustaining misconceptions about the mufti's universal authority among Muslims and the possibility of winning large-scale support through Islam, Berger even suggested similar tours on the Eastern Front: "The grand mufti is also by all means prepared to travel to the Crimean Tatars, i.e., to the Mohammedans of the currently occupied Eastern territories and to activate them in every form for Germany."

The Wehrmacht cooperated through the entire campaign. "The German generals," Berger reported to Himmler, had done the SS "an extraordinary political and military service" when making the mufti's trip possible.[44] A month after the beginning of the campaign, in May 1943, Lüters rejoiced that "the treatment of Muslims [*Muselmanenbehandlung*] had become a propaganda weapon of the first order for Germany."[45]

Attempts by the SS and the Wehrmacht to employ Islam in the Balkans had many opponents. The SS faced heavy resistance from Italian authorities and the Ustaša regime, both well aware of the politics of the tour and anxious to maintain their respective spheres of influence. As soon as the mufti's plane had landed in Zagreb, the Italians tried to stage all kinds of plots to stop the tour. In his memoirs, al-Husayni remembered that after his arrival in the Croatian capital, a high-ranking Italian diplomat flew in from Rome to prevent his trip to Bosnia and that he had been warned that the Italians could not guarantee his safety should he choose to travel to the war-torn area.[46] After the mufti had returned to Berlin, the Italians urged the Germans "with respect for Italy's special Croatian and Islamic interests," as Ernst Woermann reported, to ensure that any future contact between the mufti and the Muslims of the Balkans be organized through Italian channels.[47] The SS could not have cared less. Equally unsuccessful was the intervention of the Ustaša regime. The Croatian government had reacted "quite dismissively" to the tour, Berger noted.[48] However, as he boasted in a letter to Himmler, the Ustaša officials very quickly "reversed" their attitude after he had directly confronted the Croatian envoy in Berlin. The Ustaša regime still tried to control al-Husayni throughout the visit. On his tour from Zagreb to Sarajevo, the mufti was escorted by two representatives of the Ustaša state.[49] Croatian government officials tried to isolate him from Muslim leaders who were not part of the regime. Nonetheless, the SS officer Karl von Krempler, a former Habsburg official who was now involved in the recruitment of Muslims in the Balkans, sidelined the Ustaša agencies and organized confidential meetings with various Islamic dignitaries and separatist leaders.[50] Officially, of course, the Germans tried to conceal this friction with the Ustaša leadership. The *Deutsche Allgemeine Zeitung* simply reported that the mufti was in Bosnia "at the invitation of the Croatian government."[51]

The SS also faced some internal resistance. Kasche and the Foreign Office were opposed to the trip. In their eyes, the courtship of the Muslims would only further undermine the Ustaša regime. When the mufti visited Kasche's office in Zagreb, the envoy did not receive him and only sent his card.[52] Furious, Kasche internally complained that the tour had sparked rumors among the Muslim population that Berlin was prepared to support the creation of a Muslim state in the region.[53] In general, the new course of the SS and the Wehrmacht toward Islam in the Balkans, reflected in the mufti's tour and the deployment of the Muslim division, was interpreted in the Foreign Office as an attempt to "fortify" Islam in southeastern Europe, as the diplomat Hans Alexander Winkler, now in Berlin, put it.[54] In the immediate aftermath of the mufti's tour, Winkler had visited Zagreb and Sarajevo and subsequently worked out an eight-page memorandum about Germany's policy toward Islam in the Balkans, expressing serious concerns about the new direction.[55] Winkler's view of Islam in the region differed from his perspective of Islam in Iran, about which he had written a year earlier—the religious situation in southeastern Europe was special, he believed. He showed an understanding of why the military found the Muslims, who in Winkler's eyes were entirely pro-German and still remembered the days of the Habsburg Empire, as ideal allies. The SS must appreciate their "racial material, the soldierly tradition and the anti-papal spirit," he remarked. Yet, he sounded a note of caution with respect to German support for Muslims in the Balkans. First, he warned that German support for an "autonomist Islam" (*autonomistisches Mohammedanertum*) in the region would undermine the Ustaša regime. The mufti's tour had given a boost to "Mohammedan self-confidence," and the deployment of the Muslim division would give rise to a "religious idea" with the "utmost disruptive" effect on the Ustaša state. Second, Winkler expressed his concerns about the "pan-Islamic, non-European orientation" of Muslim collaborators in the Balkans. Unlike the SS, he perceived pan-Islamism as a risk, not an opportunity. The tour of al-Husayni had contributed to this risk. "The mufti regards the world situation under a very widespread Mohammedan perspective, which for us is completely alien." This perspective, Winkler stated, was entirely "anti-European."[56] A classical Orientalist with a profound expertise in Egypt, Winkler had joined the Foreign Office only in 1939, served in Tehran until 1941, and afterward as a Foreign Office representative at the Africa Corps until he was wounded in the summer of 1942 and returned to the Orient section of the Foreign Office in Berlin.[57] His memorandum reflected a relatively unusual perception of Islam, expressing a classical European notion of the religion and the Occident, a view that did not really fit into the pragmatic and rationalized conceptions of SS officers like Berger or military representatives such as Lüters, who were convinced of the usefulness of Islam for their war effort. Winkler's warnings had little impact. He, Kasche, and the Foreign Office no longer had any significant influence on the German political course in the Balkans, while the SS and the Wehrmacht pursued their policy toward Islam.

On the way back to Berlin, al-Husayni stopped over for a few days in Vienna, where he met Muslim representatives and was constantly attended by *Reichsstatthalter* Baldur von Schirach and high-level SS functionaries, who showed him the local attractions and discussed world politics with him.[58] The small Muslim community of Vienna was formally recognized during the war years as the Islamic Community of Vienna (*Islamitische Gemeinschaft zu Wien*), led by a certain Salih Hadzicalić, a professor of Islamic theology from Bosnia.[59] The Muslims of Austria, most of them from Bosnia and Herzegovina and based in Vienna, found increasing support from the Nazi authorities, who considered them important in relation to German policies both in the Balkans and indeed the wider Islamic world, just like the Muslim community in the other former Habsburg region, the Protectorate of Bohemia and Moravia, where German authorities endorsed the expansion of the institutional framework of the Muslim religious community during the war years.[60]

The mufti's tour of the Balkans was framed by a wider campaign. "The German program in Croatia calls for the use of the some 850,000 Moslems residing mainly in Bosnia as the basis for anti-Bolshevik and anti-Jewish measures," Leland Harrison, the US ambassador in Bern, reported to Washington.[61] The mufti contributed funds, furnished by German sources, for war relief among the Muslim population. During the course of the visit the German authorities had announced that some 50,000 tons of potatoes and 10,000 tons of sugar were being sent to Croatia. Al-Husayni had, according to Harrison, also assisted in the foundation of a Muslim propaganda center in Zagreb, which "appealed to the Moslem population for support of the Axis."[62] The tour was followed not only by the employment of the Muslim SS division but also by a major religiously charged propaganda campaign to win over the Muslim civil population for Hitler's New Order (Figures 5.6 and 5.7).

Religious Propaganda

Considering Ustaša sensibilities, the Germans avoided employing Islam in their propaganda in the Balkans before the spring of 1943. "A propagandistic influence of the Muslim population was withheld, as such is not wanted from the Croatian side," a report of the Propaganda Squadron Southeast remarked in summer 1942.[63] "Only" 10,000 copies of a "small illustrated brochure in the Croatian language" titled *The Life of the Muslims in Germany* (*Život Muslimana u Njemačkoj*) had been printed for distribution in West Bosnia, where German units had begun fighting again. In fact, *The Life of the Muslims in Germany* was twenty-seven pages long.[64] It contained many photographs of Muslim life in the Reich, including pictures of the Wilmersdorf Mosque, and short texts about individuals from all parts of the Muslim world who worked in Germany. Its aim was to identify the Third Reich as the friend of Islam, assuming a pan-Islamic sense of identification between Muslim peasants in West Bosnia and Muslim civilians in Germany. The brochure was the first significant piece of German religious propaganda launched in the Muslim areas of the Balkans.

5.6 German soldiers and a Muslim woman in Mostar, Herzegovina, 1944 (*Ullstein*).

5.7 Distribution of cigarettes in a Muslim village, Bosnia, 1943 (*Ullstein*).

With the beginning of further German military involvement, this kind of propaganda intensified. Brochures and pamphlets were distributed in Muslim towns and villages, propaganda posters were put up on streets, town squares, and trains. The print propaganda that survived the war, most of it stored in the German Military Archives in Freiburg, has, interestingly, never been examined in any study of the Balkans during the Second World War. It paints a clear picture of the ways in which German authorities employed religion as a political instrument against their enemies. German propaganda pamphlets would usually portray the British, Americans, and Jews as the foes of Islam, who pulled the strings behind the scenes of the Balkan theater and were responsible for the miserable situation of the Muslims there. Other pamphlets, which were distributed on the spot in more specific tactical situations, characterized Tito's partisans and Četniks as the enemies of Islam. In any case, as in their propaganda efforts toward the wider Muslim world, the Germans repeatedly drew on religious sentiment.

First, German propaganda merged Islam with Jew-hatred. One of the most significant examples of this kind of religiously charged anti-Jewish propaganda dispersed among Muslims of the Balkans was the brochure *Islam and Judaism (Islam i Židovstvo)*.[65] It propagated the idea of an age-old hostility between Muslims and Jews, beginning with the conflict between the Prophet and the Jewish community of Khaybar. 10,000 copies of the publication were distributed by German propagandists on 21 February 1943. Half of the texts were circulated among Muslims by the local office of the Propaganda Squadron Croatia in Banja Luka; the remaining copies were spread by its local representative in Sarajevo.

Generally, however, it was British and Soviet imperialism that played the central role in German propaganda toward the Muslim population. A pamphlet circulated in the summer of 1943 proclaimed to "Muslims" that the culprits who brought "misery and death, blood and tears" were none other than the "agitators in London and Moscow." Only the victory of the Axis would "mean the end and the extermination of all enemies of Islam." The Muslims of the SS division were portrayed as part of a broader pan-Islamic mission, as "the first who could fight under these victorious banners, not only for the freedom of your homeland, but also for the liberation of Islam from its enemies." The pamphlet was adorned with a flag depicting the crescent and star. On 5 June, 15,000 copies were distributed by General Walter Stettner's infamous First Mountain Division. The

Luftwaffe dropped another 35,000 copies in the areas of Konjic, Blagaj, Goražde, Rogatica, Fojnica, Visoko, Travnik, and Maglaj on 7 June 1943. The pamphlet concluded with a simple message: "Islam has one enemy: England. Islam has one friend: Germany. Muslims: Your place in this battle is set."[66] Typically the leaflets would address the Allied powers jointly, speaking of the "danger of English, American, and Soviet imperialism"[67] or warning of plots against Islam made in "London and Moscow."[68] Yet, if one of these powers was mentioned most frequently, it was the Soviet Union or, more generally, Bolshevism, portrayed as the atheist enemy of Islam. A pamphlet addressing the "Muslims of Bosnia and Herzegovina" warned: "A red wave from the East threatens to swallow all peoples and religious communities in the Balkans!"[69] The pamphlet declared that their "brothers in faith" in the Soviet Union had already been "trampled down" by the Kremlin. Only if the Muslims went to arms on the German side could they prevent their "total extermination by the Soviet fury," a fury that had already caused the deaths of "hundreds of thousands of Muslims in the Soviet Union." "To arms," it called the Muslims and praised the SS division "Handžar." Even more colorful language was used in another pamphlet, which drew on the religious associations of the green flag of the Prophet. It asked rhetorically: "Must Stalin's plan become a reality? Must the green flag of the Prophet run red with the blood of the Muslims?"[70] It referred to massacres of Muslims by Tito's partisans in the area of Čapljina. "The bloodsucker Stalin will allow his entrusted Tito to spill the blood of Muslims elsewhere." The reason for the alleged Soviet hatred of Muslims was also given: "Because every Muslim protects his faith, his old customs and conventions against Communist overthrow!" The pamphlet contained an image of a mosque with a minaret and a (supposedly green) flag. In the front it showed a depiction of Stalin and below him a fictional quote: "I will take care that *this* flag also turns red. As is necessary, with the blood of the Muslims alone."

On a more tactical level, German propaganda toward Muslims campaigned against Communist partisans and Četniks. In fact, Muslim combatants in their ranks were the first the Germans encouraged to change sides. A pamphlet addressing the "fighters of the Bosnian and Muslim brigades" of the partisans, for instance, claimed that Tito had made empty promises to Muslims and was now on the retreat, facing hunger and cold.[71] The Muslims were called upon to change sides before it was too late. Another pamphlet referred to atrocities committed by the partisans, remembering "353 murdered Muslims" from the area of Vlasenica and giving a detailed two-page "report" about the cruelty of the Communist partisans and their determination to kill all Muslims. It concluded with the call: "Muslims! Do you want to continue watching your extermination quietly?"[72] These texts were often religiously charged as well. A pamphlet that called for Muslims in Tito's ranks to change sides was prefaced by the quotation: "Fire at the mosque with the cannon!"[73] These were the alleged words of Tito's commanders, when they had ordered an attack on the town of Velika Kladuša. The (remains of the) mosque of Velika Kladuša, the pamphlet explained, now stood as evidence of the attack by the "Communists." Employing religious rhetoric, the pamphlet called on those "who believe in God" to "take aim with the weapons against the Communists." A pamphlet addressing "Muslim fighters" asked why Tito ridiculed their faith and customs and insulted Muslim women.[74] The answer was immediate: "Because human and religious ideas, customs, and conventions are incompatible with Communist ideas" and "because you and the people of the right faith will always be a plague upon godless Bolshevism!" The top of the pamphlet featured a picture of a mosque with a crescent on its roof and a minaret. Similar propaganda was directed at the smaller number of Muslims who fought in Četnik ranks. A pamphlet addressing the "Muslim brothers!," for instance, counteracted Četnik propaganda toward Muslims, reminding them that Mihailović's troops had killed everything that was "Islamic or Croatian."[75] "Muslims know very well who their enemy is," the pamphlet read.

Religious images and illustrations, especially of mosques and minarets, played a remarkable role in many of these pamphlets. Visual propaganda had the advantage that it could also reach those who were illiterate. Besides illustrated pamphlets, Germans also distributed propaganda posters depicting mosques.[76] One of them showed Roosevelt dropping bombs on Mostar, represented by a skyline of roofs and minarets.

Many of the pamphlets addressed Muslims in religious terms, as "Muslims" (*Muslimani*) or "Muslim brothers" (*braćo muslimani*) rather than as, for example, "Bosniaks" (*Bošnjaci*) or "Bosnians" (*Bosanci*). Some aimed at Muslims along with other religious groups, addressing, for instance, "Muslims, Catholics, Orthodox of Bosnia" or "Croats and Serbs: Muslims, Catholics and Orthodox" or the "honest Croats, Muslims and Orthodox in the partisan ranks!," exhorting them to support the German side.[77] Another pamphlet asked "Muslims, Catholics and Orthodox" to remember that the Bolsheviks not only would spread "murder and burning" but also stood for the "extermination of faith and religion."[78]

Eventually, Islam was also considered a propaganda instrument to counter Turkish influence in the Balkans. When Ankara broke off all relations with Berlin in the summer of 1944, the Germans became concerned about the reaction of the Muslims of southeastern Europe, who traditionally had strong links with Turkey. Although claiming that the Turkish decision was unlikely to have any impact on the "Muslim population" (*Muselmanentum*) in the Balkans, Hermann Neubacher suggested propagandistically deploying Islam against Kemalist laicism and modernity.[79] It is unknown whether this suggestion found its way into actual field propaganda.

After the employment of the Handžar division, reports and pamphlets about it became a strong instrument of German propaganda directed toward Muslim civilians. Moreover, from early 1944, when the division was deployed after several months of training abroad, its propaganda section also became active in the ideological education of the civil population.[80] In spring 1944, for instance, it put up charcoal-drawn propaganda posters for the *Mawlid* (*Mavlud* in Bosnian) celebrations in the occupied Muslim areas.[81] Moreover, it employed a loudspeaker van to address local *Mawlid* celebrations.[82] The division also produced pictorial reports of the soldiers' religious celebrations, which were then posted in window displays.[83] Previously, in autumn 1943, the SS had given a photographic report about the soldiers' *Ramadan Bairam* (*Ramadan Bajram* in Bosnian) celebrations to the Croatian press for publication. Concerned about the SS campaign, Ustaša authorities had turned to Kasche, complaining that the article had been foisted upon them. The SS propaganda division of the Balkans had taken the article back and had turned to Himmler for further advice.[84]

Soon the German command would also use the division's military imams to reach out to Muslim civilians. Propagandistically trained, they were sent into the mosques to lead the Friday prayer and "carry," as an SS report put it, the "ideas of the division" to the people.[85] The report noted that the "imams continuously hold gatherings in the mosque for the civil population, which are framed by Islamic prayers." These religious gatherings were used to spread political ideas and propaganda, especially to explain the work of the division and to agitate against Tito. "Such meetings are held by the imams in all the larger towns in the area of the division's employment. The imams also conducted diverse *Mawlid* celebrations in these places and have achieved a very good propagandistic effect on the civil population as, during solemn speeches, allusions were made to the division and its aims."

The SS also employed its Muslim soldiers as propagandists. Pamphlets aimed at the civil population, which were created by the division's propaganda section, were not just airdropped from planes but also given to the soldiers to be sent, along with their field mail, to their families, neighbors, and friends.[86] Soldiers were instructed to tell their relatives to forward the pamphlets, to achieve a maximum readership. Moreover, the SS created pamphlets signed by Muslim soldiers calling for war against Tito. One such pamphlet, signed by an SS man who had previously fought for Tito, not only railed against the partisans but also carried anti-Jewish hatred: "It is the Jews and the Jews' menials. Who has had the whole capital in their hands? The Jews. Who has lived at ease? Only the Jew." Now, he claimed, the SS division would bring back "freedom, order, and justice."[87] Another pamphlet, anonymously signed by a group of Muslim SS men, denounced the "godless hordes of Tito," which had turned Bosnia into a "vale of tears:" "Our unshaken belief in the great man [Hitler], who leads the freedom-loving peoples of Europe against the adversaries of God and mankind, gives us the strength to carry out the fight and the tasks successfully." In the usual manner, religious imperatives were connected with political appeals: "Who is not for us and with us, is against us . . . Therefore it is your holy duty to follow completely this, our call! . . . Heil Hitler!"[88]

German Authorities and Religious Dignitaries and Organizations

In contrast to the Caucasus and the Crimea, German authorities found Islamic institutions and networks intact when they arrived in the Balkans. Before 1943, German interactions with the religious leaders, the 'ulama, and their institutions were rare. German Foreign Office officials dealt almost exclusively with the Muslim representatives of the Ustaša state and faced the problem that a powerful Muslim leader did not exist. The two most important Muslim factions within the Ustaša regime were led by the Muslim vice premier, Džafer Kulenović, and by Hakija Hadžić, Pavelić's supremo in Bosnia and Herzegovina.[89] A veteran politician, Kulenović had been a minister in the Kingdom of Yugoslavia and, following the death of

Mehmed Spaho in 1939, had become president of the Yugoslav Muslim Organization. According to a German diplomat, he drew first and foremost on religious slogans and only second on Croatian nationalism but was still accused by many Muslims of being an Ustaša puppet. Hakija Hadžić, who promoted Croatian nationalist slogans rather than religious ones, had only a small following, mostly among the intelligentsia.[90] Another German official of the legation in Zagreb observed in March 1943 that there was "no personality" who could be considered a generally accepted leader.[91] "The solution to the Muslim question is mainly a leadership question," he stated. Muslims of the Ustaša regime had little authority in the Muslim population. The situation seemed clearer in the case of the religious establishment, which was believed to wield more genuine power and influence over the people.

As religious structures were fully institutionalized, they could be understood and, possibly, utilized. Organized within the so-called Islamic Religious Community, the faithful were under the authority of the highest religious leader, the *ra'is al-'ulama* (head of the 'ulama), or *Reis-ul-Ulema* in Bosnian.[92] The *Reis-ul-Ulema* was assisted by the *'ulama majlis* (council of the 'ulama), or *Ulema-Medžlis* in Bosnian, the supreme council of the Islamic community, which consisted of the *Reis-ul-Ulema* and four other eminent dignitaries and oversaw the waqf endowment, madrasas, and shari'a courts as well as the work of the local imams, 'ulama, and *hojas* (*hodžas* in Bosnian). This administration had been introduced in 1882 by Habsburg bureaucrats anxious to loosen the Muslims' religious bonds with the Ottoman Empire and keen to monitor and control Islam in the Balkans, and had survived in the Yugoslav kingdom and under the Ustaša regime. Eager to present themselves as protectors of Islam, the Germans made no direct attempts to interfere with the Islamic administration. As they became more involved in the Muslim areas of the Balkans in early 1943, however, German officials increasingly engaged with religious leaders. In the end, the SS even employed an important member of the *Ulema-Medžlis* for their political and military aims (Figures 5.8, 5.9, 5.10, and 5.11).

At the time of the German invasion of Yugoslavia, the office of *Reis-ul-Ulema* was held by Fehim Spaho, former president of the High Shari'a Court in Sarajevo and brother of Mehmed Spaho. Although Spaho initially enthusiastically supported the Ustaša regime, hoping that it would allow him to realize his own aims—most importantly bans on gambling, prostitution,

5.8 Fehim Spaho (1877–1942)
(*Gazi Husrev Beg Library, Sarajevo*).

and mixed marriages, and a rigid enforcement of the veil—he soon lost faith in Pavelić.[93] Salih Safet Bašić, who informally replaced Spaho after his death in early 1942, had a rocky relationship with the Ustaša.[94] Concerned with the protection of their community, both leaders sought good relations with the Germans. In fact, Spaho had cultivated his contacts with German officials in the months leading up to the invasion of the Balkans and kept them informed of atrocities against Muslims during the war.[95] Other members of the *Ulema-Medžlis* went further. As the Muslims' situation deteriorated in 1942 and 1943, many of them embraced the idea of Muslim autonomy under Berlin's protection. Their hopes were fueled by the tour of the mufti, the establishment of the Muslim SS division, and Germany's massive religious propaganda campaign.

Both Fehim Spaho and Salih Bašić were opposed for being too progressive by more puritan members of the *Ulema-Medžlis*, most notably Mehmed Handžić. Al-Azhar-educated, Handžić was a leading Islamic revivalist with pan-Islamic leanings who taught at a madrasa in Sarajevo and served

5.9 Mehmed Handžić (1906–1944)
(*Gazi Husrev Beg Library, Sarajevo*).

as the head librarian of the grand Gazi Husrevbegova Biblioteka.[96] He was president of El-Hidaje (The Right Path), a society of revivalist 'ulama.[97] Its youth organization, the Young Muslims (*Mladi Muslimani*), attracted a considerable following, among them Alija Izetbegović, who in 1990 became the first president of Bosnia-Herzegovina. Handžić and his supporters had quickly become disillusioned with Ustaša rule and were now advocating an autonomist agenda and seeking German help. During al-Husayni's tour, he met with the mufti in Sarajevo, gave him a warm welcome address at a banquet at city hall, and afterward published an article about the visit in El-Hidaje, the official organ of his society.[98] In a consultation with German embassy officials in Sarajevo in mid-April 1943, Handžić urged

5.10 Ali Aganović (1902–1961)
(*Gazi Husrev Beg Library, Sarajevo*).

the Germans to intervene more extensively.[99] He blamed the Ustaša for the suffering and murder of Muslims. The Croatian regime had adopted the same policy toward Muslims as that pursued by the Serbs in the Yugoslav kingdom, he claimed—a policy of annihilation. The Muslims in Pavelić's government were not true representatives of the people but had been bought, he told the Germans. Although he enthusiastically welcomed the foundation of the Muslim SS division, he made it clear that this was not enough. The only solution was an independent Muslim state under Hitler's protection. Handžić even suggested a religious resettlement plan to create purified Muslim areas. The Muslim population had been deeply impressed that German soldiers had fallen in battle against the enemies of Islam. And the mufti's visit had also sent the right signals. There was no doubt, Handžić assured the Germans, that the Muslims were the natural allies of the Third Reich. He was well aware of what the Germans wanted to hear. Giving them the impression that their religiously charged propaganda had fallen on fertile soil, he pushed his own agenda, most notably the strengthening of self-defense and the establishment, de facto and, if possible, de jure, of autonomy from the Ustaša.

5.11 Muhamed Pandža (1897–1962) (*Archive of the Croatian Historical Museum, Zagreb*).

Handžić was not the only member of the 'ulama to seek a tighter alliance with the Germans. Ali Aganović, a widely respected member of the *Ulema-Medžlis*, who repeatedly consulted with German officials, followed a similar line.[100] Although publicly he paid lip service to the Ustaša regime until the end, he, too, soon had lost faith in Pavelić and begun to press the Germans for a stronger involvement in the Muslim Balkans.[101] At a meeting in the spring of 1943, Aganović assured officials from the German legation in Zagreb that Muslim religious autonomy could be achieved only through political independence.[102] Emphasizing the importance of the Muslims of the Balkans within the wider Islamic world, he also discussed pan-Islamic policies and the reestablishment of the caliphate, an office he believed should be given to the mufti of Jerusalem. The idea was not new. In late 1942 British intelligence had been alarmed when the Muslim press of Croatia discussed the idea of reestablishing the caliphate under al-Husayni.[103]

While Handžić and Aganović made their appeals for an alliance with the Third Reich behind closed doors, other members of the 'ulama stood openly in the service of the German authorities.

The most important collaborator of the *Ulema-Medžlis* was Muhamed Pandža, a leading religious dignitary and a member of El-Hidaje.[104] From a prominent Sarajevo family of religious leaders and educated at the most prestigious Islamic institutions in the country, Pandža had always kept a certain distance from the Ustaša regime and was now publicly pleading for Muslim autonomy under German protection. His strong pro-German attitude made him an ideal collaborator for the Wehrmacht and the SS. The SS employed him at once for the recruitment of Muslim volunteers, a mission that he would carry out with all his religious authority, as the final part of the book discusses. Aside from military mobilization, the Germans would also use Pandža as an intermediary to support their efforts to pacify the Muslim areas.

A significant role in this respect was played by the socio-religious organization Merhamet—also known as the Muslim Charitable Society Merhamet (*Muslimansko Dobrotvorno Društvo Merhamet*)—in Sarajevo, which was led by Pandža.[105] Merhamet became a major provider of humanitarian aid during the war years, running soup kitchens, orphanages, and refugee camps, and it also became increasingly involved politically. For the Germans, Merhamet became a valued partner, and they believed it important to retain good relations with the organization. When, for instance, Merhamet requested the return of a Muslim orphan who had been adopted by a German Catholic family, brought to Germany, and converted to Catholicism, Nazi authorities swiftly intervened, returned the child, and entrusted it to a Muslim family in Sarajevo.[106] On the ground, military officials soon regarded Merhamet as the most important representative body of the Muslims in Bosnia and Herzegovina. The organization repeatedly negotiated over food supplies with the Area Commander of the German Police in Sarajevo, *SS-Oberführer* Werner Fromm.[107] And when Berlin initiated a relief fund in early 1944 (see later discussion), Berger suggested that clothes for Muslim refugees be distributed through Merhamet.[108] Only too happy to employ the local Muslim structures, Himmler authorized Merhamet to oversee the distribution.[109]

The SS saw Merhamet as a strong partner. Yet, it was not fully controlled by the Germans and would follow its own interests. In September

1943 the second secretary of the organization, Mehmed Tokić, who had actually been hired by the SS as a covert informer, would threaten German officers with an open rebellion against the Croatian state.[110] The Muslims, Tokić made clear, despised the Ustaša regime and sought to live in a German protectorate instead, similar to Austrian-Hungarian times. Berger tried to defuse the situation, rejecting any threats levied by the "Muslim leadership" and warning that violent uprisings such as these would make things even worse for the Muslims.[111] Merhamet's leaders soon became disillusioned with the Germans. In the end, Muhamed Pandža too lost hope in the Third Reich. He went into the woods, founded the Muslim Liberation Movement (*Muslimanski Oslobodilački Pokret*), and called for armed self-defense and Muslim autonomy.[112] Addressing his "Muslim Brothers!" in a propaganda pamphlet, Pandža now declared war against Ustaša and Četniks.[113] He announced: "Everything we serve is the well-being of the Islamic community and our nation." "Muslims," he proclaimed, in his usual religious rhetoric, now had to fight "with faith in God and his help, bravely and dauntlessly" for survival. Although some SS circles in Berlin were concerned about these developments, Krempler, who had repeatedly dealt with Pandža in the field, emphasized that he was still pro-German.[114] Hitler, whose trust in the Muslims remained unbroken, excused Pandža's defection with the remark that the Muslims needed to protect themselves.[115] Pandža, who later made contact with Tito's partisans, was finally captured by German troops in eastern Bosnia and handed over to the Ustaša authorities. He was not the only Islamic leader who had become disillusioned.

Violence and Shattered Hopes

Promises made to Muslims by the Germans, eager to present themselves as the protectors of Islam, contrasted sharply with the realities of war. In practice, the Germans were simply not able to pacify the Muslim areas. The collaboration between Muslim leaders and the Germans nurtured the hatred directed against them by partisans and Četniks. Although the Germans had promised that the sole purpose of the Muslim division was the protection and pacification of the Muslim areas of Bosnia and Herzegovina, Himmler had sent it for training to France and, later, Germany. Unprotected, the Muslim population became the target of retaliatory attacks. In the autumn of 1943 Tito's partisans initiated a major offensive in

Bosnia. Thousands were killed. Tens of thousands were soon on the run (Figure 5.12). The relatives of Muslim volunteers in particular were targeted by partisans. Muslim refugees gathered in the hundreds in depots, barns, stables, and basements, an SS field report noted.[116] Many of them had no proper clothes and suffered from malnutrition. Across the Islamic world, these events were followed closely. The Egyptian press reported on the situation, and Nahas Pasha even donated 20,000 pounds for the refugees.[117] On 11 January 1944, the SS representative for Croatia, Konstantin Kammerhofer, wrote to Himmler, apparently concerned about not only the local situation but also the effects this had on the wider Muslim world:

> As a consequence of the partisan struggle in Croatia about 230,000 people, around 210,000 of them from the area of Bosnia, are currently on the run. The situation of these people is the worst possible that could be imagined. At the present time, no human being can describe the tragedies that are taking place among these masses. . . . The majority of the refugees comprises Muslim. . . . With regard to the Muslims in the 13th SS Bosnian-Herzegovinian Volunteer Mountain Division as well as to the problem of world Islam [*Weltmuselmanen-Problem*] it has to be considered anew if you, Reichsführer, should call for special support to provide relief needed by the refugees.[118]

Himmler was convinced. On the occasion of the *Bairam* celebration in autumn 1943 the SS had already collected money for the Muslim population in Bosnia, and, shortly after, Himmler had ordered a second relief fund.[119] During the second collection alone more than 120,000 reichsmarks were raised.[120] Himmler would add another 100,000 from his own funds.[121] In January 1944 Berger reported that 225,000 reichsmarks had been amassed.[122] The money was used mainly for clothing, which was then distributed.[123] Still, these projects amounted to only a drop in the bucket. The SS policies toward Muslims had compromised the Muslim population while leaving it militarily unprotected.

Finally, in late February 1944, the SS sent the Handžar division back to the Balkans. For a short period, the situation for Muslims—at least in parts of the region—eased. The Muslims responded with hope and thanks. On April 20, 1944, for instance, Krempler reported that prayers for Hitler took place in all the towns of the Sandžak.[124] A Muslim delegation from the area sent Hitler a telegram of obeisance:

5.12 Muslim women return to their ruined village in the Bosnian mountains, 1943 (*Ullstein*).

The Muslims of the Sandžak, who shoulder to shoulder with the brave German soldiers participate in the battle against the bandits, celebrate your birthday today and send fervent prayers to the almighty Allah for your personal long life and happiness, in the unshakable and deep trust in the final victory of the German people and the salvation of us Muslims.[125]

Hitler thanked the Muslims, and let them know that he had been "very delighted" by the letter.[126] Similar demonstrations of loyalty followed. In July 1944 Muslims from the Sandžak area sent a gramophone record with a prayer of thanks and praise in Arabic for Hitler.[127] In Berlin, Rudolf Brandt sent the record to the SS propaganda section to be exploited by the SS or by Goebbels's Propaganda Ministry.[128]

In spring 1944 northern and eastern Bosnia effectively came under the control of the SS and Himmler's Muslim division (Figure 5.13). The infamous SS "Guidelines for the Securing of Public Peace in Bosnia" (*Richtlinien für die Sicherung des Landfriedens in Bosnien*) give a good idea of the intended occupational regime in the area and of the utilization of religion to support it.[129] In the towns and villages, SS officers were to install reliable local leaders who would function as intermediaries between the population and the Germans. Every Friday, the day of the *džuma-namaz*, these representatives had to read out the SS's weekly propaganda slogans. Schools were to be put under the command of trusted locals—"teachers, imams, particularly suited women" but "no intelligentsia," as the SS specified. More importantly, the SS scheme envisaged a massive religious resettlement with the aim of creating homogeneous Islamic towns and villages. "It is the aim, under any circumstances, to create in the country communities a population of the same confession," it was stated. Moreover, the SS guidelines endorsed a war of extermination against partisans and other hostile groups, as well as aggressive domination of the civilian population. "The point is to annihilate the enemy," the guidelines made clear, encouraging commanders to be particularly "ruthless." Goebbels acknowledged in his diary that Himmler had "stopped the terror against the Mohammedan population."[130] In the end, the reign of the SS in the area was too short-lived and the German war bureaucracy too chaotic for these schemes to be fully implemented. The soldiers of the Muslim division nonetheless became notorious for acting particularly brutally, spreading fear and terror.

To some extent, the population relocations envisaged by the SS guidelines mirrored the demands of some Islamic autonomists. But although Himmler internally toyed with the idea of creating a future military protectorate, or "military frontier" (*Wehrgrenze*), as it had existed in the Habsburg era, for the time being the SS was in no position to realize the hopes of the Muslim autonomists in Bosnia and Herzegovina.[131] Similarly, when, in the final months of the war, Bedri Pejani, a prominent Albanian Muslim politician, sought help from the mufti of Jerusalem for the foundation of a Muslim state in the Balkans, uniting Kosovo, cleansed of Orthodox Serbs, and the Sandžak with Bosnia, Herzegovina, and Albania, the Germans quickly thwarted these ambitions.[132] Immediate Muslim independence, many Muslim leaders had to realize, was out of the question.

As the German military situation deteriorated, many Muslims lost hope in an Axis victory. In July 1944 a Wehrmacht report described the attitude of the Muslim population toward the Germans as inconsistent, a fact that now made them "in every respect unreliable."[133] In the final months of the war, many no longer counted on German help and looked for alternatives.

5.13 German tanks in a Bosnian Muslim village, 1944 (*Ullstein*).

Muslim self-defense groups, like Pandža's Muslim Liberation Movement, grew.[134] Many young Muslims, a German army report noted in June 1944, organized themselves into local paramilitary units.[135] Indeed, the militias, most importantly the Green Cadre (*Zeleni Kader*) of the pro-German warlord Nešad Topčić, attracted more and more Muslim men. Supported by religious leaders like Mehmed Handžić, they not only protected Muslim villages but also committed atrocities among the Orthodox population. Attempts by the Četniks to recruit Muslims into their ranks had, unsurprisingly, only little success.[136] Tito's partisans, on the other hand, seemed to be a viable alternative to both the Germans and the Muslim militias. As the war situation worsened in the winter of 1943–1944, increasing numbers of Muslims joined their ranks. "The Muslims in Bosnia, too, who once welcomed us with such great enthusiasm, have completely turned away from us and go in masses to the partisans," Horstenau noted.[137] "The Ustaše criminals have shoved a good part of the Muslims into a slaughterhouse for the Germans and into a bloody civil war. Draža Mihailović's Četniks have committed unheard-of crimes against the Muslim population," partisan commander and ideologue Milovan Đilas rejoiced in a speech to his comrades: "It has become clear to the Muslims that only participation in the People's Liberation Struggle can save them from total destruction."[138] A first Muslim partisan unit had been formed as early as the summer of 1941, and Marshal Tito willingly repeated Moscow's religious wartime propaganda, which portrayed Communism as the only hope for Islam. In the brochure *Muslims in the Soviet Union: Religion in the Soviet Union* (*Muslimani u Sovjetskom Savezu: Religija u Sovjetskom Savezu*), distributed by partisan propagandists in the autumn of 1944, Stalin's state was depicted as a paradise for the pious.[139]

The Germans dealt with those Muslims whom they suspected of betrayal with great brutality.[140] In a number of punitive missions against Muslim villages and settlements whose inhabitants were accused of sheltering partisans, German troops executed Muslim women and children. Mosques too were attacked. In late 1944, German forces broke into the building of El-Hidaje in Sarajevo to search for evidence against a number of members of the Young Muslims who were suspected of working with the enemy. And despite all official efforts to promote Germany as the protector of Balkan Islam, ordinary soldiers in the field often had little respect for Muslims and their religion. When the German soldier Egbert Korbacher entered the town of Niš in Serbia, for instance, he jeered: "In Niš, the Orient begins. This is not exaggerated, since its key feature, the dirt, is so convincing that it doesn't at all need the mosques and minarets." The Albanians, he wrote, were "not that stupid—the best sign is that Jews were not here."[141]

The genocide of Jews and Roma in the Balkans embroiled the Islamic community immediately. In the months after the fall of Yugoslavia, many Jews tried to escape persecution by converting to Islam.[142] In the city of Sarajevo alone, no less than 20 percent of the Jewish population is estimated to have converted to Islam or Catholicism between April and October 1941. Alarmed, Ustaša authorities soon intervened, banning these conversions in the autumn of 1941. Those who had converted were still often not safe from persecution, as it was race, not religion, that defined Jewishness in the eyes of Ustaša bureaucrats. Even *Reis-ul-Ulema* Fehim Spaho endorsed this official line, publicly declaring in late 1941 that conversion had no impact on race and that Jewish converts to Islam would still remain racially Jewish. On the other hand, Spaho made considerable efforts to help Jewish converts to Islam, urging Ustaša authorities to protect them and exhorting the 'ulama to offer them shelter. Still, a number of Jews managed to escape concealed as Muslims, some of them literally disguised in the Islamic veil.[143] The attitudes of Muslims toward the persecution of the (unconverted) Jewish population cannot be generalized, ranging, as elsewhere, from collaboration and profiteering to empathy and, in some cases, solidarity with the victims. Shortly after the fall of Sarajevo, Fedrigotti observed that "dozens of Mohammedans" dismantled the copper roof of the Great Sephardic Synagogue to sell the metal in the bazaar.[144] Merhamet took over a large textile factory that had been expropriated from its Jewish owner and soon became a major supplier for the German army.[145] Others helped. Derviš Korkut, the Muslim director of the city museum, not only hid the legendary Sarajevo Haggadah, a beautifully illustrated Sephardic scripture of the fourteenth century, from German officials who sought to confiscate it but also gave refuge to a young Jewish woman who later escaped to the partisans.[146] The Muslim businessman Mustafa Hardaga from Sarajevo hid an entire Jewish family. Albanian Muslims famously saved many of their Jewish compatriots.[147] The Germans, for their part, were nevertheless confident that their religiously charged anti-Jewish propaganda in the Muslim areas fell on fertile soil.

Finally, Muslims in the Balkans were particularly affected by the persecution of the Roma, as many Roma were of the Islamic faith. Eager to integrate Muslims into the Croatian state, Ustaša authorities excluded the largely settled Muslim Roma of Bosnia and Herzegovina, the white gypsies, from persecution and deportation.[148] The protection of the white gypsies led to a wave of conversions of Christian Roma to Islam, and these acts, too, as in the case of Jewish conversions, were eventually prohibited by the Interior Ministry in Zagreb. Throughout the war, the *Ulema-Medžlis* showed concern about the safety of Muslim Roma and repeatedly complained to the authorities in Zagreb about arrests of white gypsies. Prompted by Fehim Spaho, the Ustaša government even intervened on behalf of Muslim Roma in German-occupied Serbia, urging the German officials there not to persecute Muslim gypsies.[149] Also in Macedonia and Albania, where most of the Roma were Muslim, their religious affiliation gave them some protection, although it is worth noting that the Bulgarian occupation authorities in Macedonia showed little respect for Islam in general.[150] In contrast to Croatian and German officials, the Bulgarian military administration did not even try to court Muslims.[151] Shortly after the occupation of Skopje, Bulgarian authorities had occupied the building that housed the Islamic religious bureaucracy and a madrasa and confiscated the waqf funds, leaving the employees of the religious administration without pay. On the streets, Muslim men wearing the fez and veiled women were harassed. In the end, Fehim Spaho intervened. Skopje had been a religious administrative center in the Yugoslav kingdom and, as the *Reis-ul-Ulema* in Sarajevo had presided over two religious centers—in Sarajevo and Skopje—Spaho felt responsible for the Macedonian Muslims and asked Ustaša officials to alert the Germans to these events. The Croatian Foreign Ministry did indeed contact the German legation in Zagreb with a request to intervene in Sofia on behalf of the Muslims of Skopje—to what effect is unknown. Overall, both the persecution of Muslim Roma and Jewish converts to Islam revealed the extent and limits of the influence of the Islamic administration under Axis rule.

After the war, Muslims across the Balkans were widely stigmatized as collaborators. Nevertheless, the Communist regime in Yugoslavia did initially refrain from direct attacks on Islam.[152] Only the most notorious Islamic collaborators, such as Ismet Muftić, Pavelic's mufti of Zagreb, were executed, while others, such as Salih Bašić, remained in office. Muhamed Pandža and Ali Aganović received long prison sentences (Mehmed Handžić had died in 1944). The Poglavnik Mosque was shut down, and its minarets were blown up. After the consolidation of power, the new rulers engaged in a more rigorous crackdown on Islam, which culminated in the legendary anti-veiling campaign of Tito's Antifascist Women's Front. In the newly created People's Republic of Albania, Enver Hoxha launched an even fiercer attack on religious institutions, rivaling the Stalinist terror against religions of the interwar years.[153] Accused of treachery, the Muslim Cham Albanians of the Epirus area were targeted by the nationalist militias of Napoleon Zervas's National Republican Greek League, which massacred many, plundered and burned down villages, and expelled the survivors to Albania.[154] Overall, Axis wartime attempts to court Muslims were followed by retaliation against alleged collaborators and years of suppression of Islam across southeastern Europe.

PART III

MUSLIMS IN THE ARMY

CHAPTER SIX

Mobilizing Muslims

On 11 January 1944, Heinrich Himmler greeted a group of Muslim military commanders from Bosnia in the barracks of the *Führerheim Westlager*, on the drill grounds of Neuhammer in Silesia. "It is quite clear to me," he proclaimed: "what is there to separate the Muslims in Europe and around the world from us Germans? We have common aims. There is no more solid basis for cooperation than common aims and common ideals. For 200 years, Germany has not had the slightest conflict with Islam."[1] Germany and its leaders had been friends of Islam over the last centuries, the *Reichsführer* declared, not just for pragmatic reasons but out of conviction. God— "you say Allah, it is the same"—had sent the Führer, who would first free Europe and then the entire world of the Jews. The head of the SS then evoked alleged common enemies—"the Bolsheviks, England, America, all constantly driven by the Jew." Himmler's audience represented tens of thousands of Muslim recruits deployed in units of the Wehrmacht and the SS. Most of these Muslims came from the territories of the Soviet Union, though many were also recruited from the Balkans and some, albeit in fewer numbers, from the Middle East. These recruits were told that, in the name of Islam, they were to liberate their countries from foreign rule. It became one of the greatest mobilization campaigns of Muslims led by a non-Muslim power in history, by far surpassing similar efforts made by the Reichswehr in the First World War.

The deployment of Muslim units was part of a more general development in the Third Reich's recruitment policies.[2] Between late 1941 and the end of the war, hundreds of thousands of non-German volunteers from all parts of the occupied territories enlisted in the German armies. Their recruitment was not the result of long-term planning but a consequence of the general shift toward more pragmatic and short-term planning that began after the failure of the Barbarossa plan and Hitler's blitzkrieg strategy in late 1941 and intensified after the defeats of Stalingrad and al-'Alamayn and the rise of partisan insurgency across the continent. After Barbarossa, in the autumn of 1941, the German military command was confronted with a drastic shortage of manpower. By the end of November, the Germans had registered 743,112 men as dead, wounded, or missing in action.[3] This meant that almost a quarter of the entire eastern army had collapsed. German soldiers, it became clear, could not win the war alone.

The Wehrmacht began recruiting among prisoners of war and the civilian populations in its occupied territories in the East in late 1941.[4] Azerbaijanis, Turkestanis, Kalmyks, Ukrainians, Georgians, Armenians, and various others fought in the Wehrmacht's so-called Eastern Troops (*Osttruppen*). The mastermind behind this project was the pragmatic Claus von Stauffenberg. In late 1942 the new troops were put under the central command of General Heinz Hellmich, who was appointed General of the Eastern Troops (*General der Osttruppen*). In January 1944, the post was renamed General of the Volunteer Units (*General der Freiwilligenverbände*), and Hellmich was replaced by General Ernst-August Köstring. Köstring became involved in military mobilization in the East as an Inspector of Turkic Troops after the Caucasus had been reconquered by the Red Army in early 1943. The Eastern Troops were growing fast. In mid-1943, more than 300,000 recruits were fighting in their ranks.[5] A year later, these numbers had doubled. The vast majority of the Eastern Troops comprised non-Slavic minorities from the southern fringes of the Soviet empire (Turkestanis, Volga Tatars, North Caucasians, Azerbaijanis, Georgians, and Armenians), which, from early 1942, were organized within the six so-called Eastern Legions. Most of them were Muslims. Apart from the Eastern Legions, a Kalmyk cavalry corps and several smaller formations, among them Estonian, Lithuanian, Latvian, Finnish, Ukrainian, Belarusian, and Cossack units, fought under the command of the Eastern Troops. In late 1944 Hitler even agreed to enlist Russians into Andrei Vlasov's Russian Army of Liberation. The Wehrmacht also experimented with various smaller volunteer formations outside the Eastern territories, most prominently Arab units and Subhas Chandra Bose's Indian Wehrmacht legion "Azad Hind."

The formation of non-German SS divisions was similarly the result of the unexpected evolution of the war.[6] Initially, Himmler had founded the first three German SS divisions—*Leibstandarte Adolf Hitler, Das Reich*, and *Totenkopf*—with the intention of establishing an army independent from the Wehrmacht. The Waffen-SS, however, was originally much smaller than the Wehrmacht, and enlisting Germans became increasingly difficult. From late 1940 on, Himmler recruited West and North Europeans, beginning in Norway and the Low Countries. After Stalingrad, the mobilization effort was accelerated. The ethnic German "Prinz Eugen" Division was created to help combat partisans in the Balkans. Men from Latvia and Estonia were soon enrolled in the Waffen-SS, followed by others. Toward the end of the war, when Hitler lifted his ban on the formation of non-Germanic SS units, the Waffen-SS expanded rapidly. Among these non-Germanic volunteer formations were Crimean, Turkic, and Caucasian SS units in the East and Albanian and Bosnian divisions in the Balkans. Many of them were dominated by Muslims. Eventually nearly half a million of the soldiers of the Waffen-SS, organized in nineteen of its thirty-eight divisions, were recruited outside Germany.[7]

Most of the recruits were driven by material interests. Among prisoners of war, a significant incentive was the prospect of pay and better provisions. For captured soldiers from the Red Army in particular, fighting for the Germans seemed to be an attractive prospect compared with remaining in the appalling conditions of the camps.[8] Other recruits, from the Balkans and the Crimea, for instance, hoped to protect their families and villages from partisans and bandits. Ideology and political motives also played a role. Nationalism, religious hatred, and anti-Bolshevism drove many into the German ranks. Under the banner of the swastika, the volunteers believed that they would be supporting the fight against Bolshevism or British imperialism and for the liberation of their countries from foreign rule. The Germans, for their part, did everything they could to propagandistically play up the potential ideological motives of their foreign helpers.

Initiated primarily to save German blood and balance the drastic shortage of manpower in the German armies, the commands of the Wehrmacht and the SS also saw the propagandistic value of these non-German units, which they hoped would influence the morale in the enemy's armies and hinterland. The recruitment of Muslims, in this context, was of particular relevance as it became part of Germany's general engagement with Islam. Once these units were deployed in the field, German officials promoted the idea that they were part of a broader campaign for Islamic mobilization, just as Himmler did in his Silesia speech.

Muslims in the Wehrmacht

Hitler was generally skeptical about the recruitment of non-Germans, especially of volunteers from the Soviet Union. But while he was most uncomfortable when it came to the enlistment of Slavic Russians, Ukrainians, and Belarusians, he considered Muslims to be the only truly trustworthy soldiers and supported their recruitment unconditionally. When discussing non-Russian volunteers from the East at his military headquarters, Wolf's Lair, on 12 December 1942, Hitler urged the military command to be extremely cautious in organizing Caucasian formations in the Wehrmacht, which he considered to be a general risk: "I really don't know, I must say, the Georgians are people who are not Mohammedans. . . . For the time being, I consider the formation of battalions of these pure Caucasian peoples as very risky, while I don't see any danger in forming pure Mohammedan units. . . . Despite all explanations, either from Rosenberg or from the military side, I don't trust the Armenians either. . . . The only ones I consider to be reliable are the pure Mohammedans."[9] Hitler explicitly placed Muslims not only above the Armenians but also above the Georgians, who were Rosenberg's protégés. "I consider only the Mohammedans to be safe," Hitler declared. "All the others I consider unsafe."[10] The reasons for Hitler's unconditional trust in the Muslims were diverse. Apart from his positive ideological views of Islam, his experiences during the First World War may have influenced him. Moreover, he may also have been impressed by the collaboration of the Muslims in the northern Caucasus and the Tatars in the Crimea.

Hitler's opinion of Muslims from the East was shared by the Wehrmacht command. The recruitment of Muslims was regularly justified with reference not only to the army's shortage of men and the propagandistic value of the units but also to religion—on the assumption that Islam would enhance strong soldierly qualities. All three of these motives—the lack of manpower, the alleged militant qualities of Muslims, and the propagandistic impact of their recruitment—were expressed in countless military orders and instructions issued by the Wehrmacht. "The deployment of the armed legions is not simply meant to save German blood," the High Command of Army Group South stated in the summer of 1942, when instructing German soldiers on the Wehrmacht's Muslim helpers, "but also as a political weapon to undermine and reduce the enemy's power to resist."[11] Moreover, the recruitment was explained with reference to the "political-religious attitude of the Turkic peoples (Mohammedans)" and their "largely positive soldierly qualities," which "obliged" the German command to "exploit" them to "the greatest possible extent." A few weeks later, the head of the army general staff, Franz Halder, emphasized that the recruitment was not just for the "reinforcement of the combat strength of the German formations" and "for the propagandistic impact" on enemy troops and civilians.[12] Halder also underlined the "political and religious attitude of the Turkic peoples as well as their good soldierly qualities." On the same day, an instruction was sent to the German staff of the Muslim legions asserting that the "significance" of the Muslim battalions "lay not only in their military value, but also in their propagandistic effect on the enemy and on the population in the respective countries."[13] Similarly, Oskar von Niedermayer, who became responsible for the formation of the Wehrmacht's Muslim Turkic legions, stressed in his deployment order that Muslim units would not only "strengthen the combat power of the German formations" but also serve a "propagandistic" purpose.[14] Moreover, the "political-religious attitude" and the good "soldierly qualities" of the Muslim Turkic peoples, he made clear by repeating earlier instructions, "obliged" the army to "exploit" prisoners of war for the German cause. Niedermayer also shared Hitler's perception of Muslims. "Experiences" had shown that Christian Armenians and Georgians had to be monitored more carefully than the "actual Mohammedan Turk people," he wrote.[15] This view became dominant among the German army command. Discussing the recruitment of volunteers from the Soviet Union with Hitler in the summer of 1943, Wilhelm Keitel, head of the High Command of the Wehrmacht, reaffirmed Hitler's positive view of the Turkic volunteers, in whom he saw the "fiercest enemies of Bolshevism."[16] The positive attitude toward Muslim volunteers was reflected in the formations: Muslims eventually constituted the largest religious group of non-Russian Wehrmacht recruits from the Soviet Union.

In the Eastern territories, the Wehrmacht had already begun recruiting Muslim volunteers before the Eastern Troops were set up.[17] Facing a worsening war situation, in late 1941 army commanders on the front line began, on their own initiative, wherever necessary, to look for local collaborators and combed the prisoner of war camps for auxiliary volunteers, the so-called *Hilfswillige* (*Hiwis* for short). Plenty of Soviet deserters, prisoners of war, and volunteers from the local population signed on as sentries, ammunition carriers, translators, drivers, cooks, and servants, and some were already fighting alongside frontline troops before the winter of 1941. Among the earliest of these auxiliary combat troops were the first Muslim formations of the Third Reich. In October 1941, the Wehrmacht created a Caucasian unit under the command of Theodor Oberländer, the so-called *Sonderverband Bergmann*, and a Turkic unit commanded by the eccentric adventurer Andreas Mayer-Mader, who had traveled throughout Central Asia and served as a military advisor to Chiang Kai-shek.[18] A month later, the army leadership ordered the creation of one Turkestani and one Caucasian unit, each of one hundred men, within the 444th Protection Division. Like Mayer-Mader's unit, they were fighting partisans in southern Ukraine. Oberländer's soldiers, once trained in Silesia and Upper Bavaria, advanced alongside the Wehrmacht into the Caucasus. Berlin was satisfied with the military performance of the Muslims, and the Muslim troops maintained this early prominence when the Wehrmacht began recruiting non-Russian volunteers more systematically into its Eastern Legions.

The order for the establishment of the Eastern Legions was issued on Hitler's approval by the High Command of the Wehrmacht on 22 December 1941.[19] The first two legions, the Turkestani Legion (*Turkestanische Legion*) and the Caucasian-Mohammedan Legion (*Kaukasisch-Mohammedanische Legion*), both founded on 13 January 1942, consisted almost entirely of Muslims. The Armenian Legion (*Armenische Legion*) and the Georgian Legion (*Georgische Legion*) followed in February, the North Caucasian Legion (*Nordkaukasische Legion*) in August, and the Volga Tatar Legion (*Volga-Tatarische Legion*) in September. In the end, four of the six legions founded in the East were Islamic or dominated by a large Muslim majority: the Turkestani Legion, the Caucasian-Mohammedan Legion (later renamed Azerbaijani Legion), the North Caucasian Legion, and the Volga Tatar Legion.[20] The two non-Muslim legions, which Hitler mistrusted, were the Armenian Legion and the Georgian Legion. The commanders and the chief staff (*Rahmen- und Stammpersonal*) of the formations were German. Two operational headquarters (*Organisationsstäbe*) were created, which were responsible for the military and ideological training of the legions' field battalions. The first was the so-called *Aufstellungsstab der Ostlegionen* (later renamed the *Kommando der Ostlegionen*), which was based in the General Government at the military training area in Rembertów and, from summer 1942 on, in Radom. It was chiefly organized by Ralph von Heygendorff, who held the command between 1942 and early 1944. The *Kommando der Ostlegionen*, however, was responsible only for the recruits from the area of the Army Group North and Middle. Volunteers from the area of Army Group South were trained separately in the Ukraine and later in Silesia—their operational headquarters was the 162nd Turkestani Infantry Division (*162. Turkestanische Infanterie-Division*), which was under the command of Oskar von Niedermayer until his replacement by Ralph von Heygendorff in 1944. By 1943, no fewer than seventy-nine infantry battalions had been created by the operational headquarters and sent to the front.[21] Fifty-four of these were Muslim or dominated by Muslims. Further battalions were still being trained. Eventually, according to some estimates, around 35,000 to 40,000 Muslim Volga Tatars (Volga Tatar Legion), 110,000 to 180,000 Muslim Turkestanis (Turkestani Legion), and 110,000 Muslim and Christian recruits from the Caucasus (North Caucasian, Azerbaijani, Armenian, and Georgian Legions) fought in the German Wehrmacht.[22] Among the recruits from the Caucasus were at least 28,000 Muslims from the North Caucasus and 25,000 to 38,000 Muslims from Azerbaijan. Armed with antitank guns, grenade launchers, machine guns, and automatic weapons, they fought in the various areas of the eastern war zone. Three Muslim battalions were employed in Stalingrad, and many fought in the Caucasus mountains. In the end, Muslim field battalions of the Eastern Legions were spread over the entire European continent. They were employed in the Balkans to put down Tito's partisans and fought on the French and Italian invasion fronts. A total of six battalions took part in the defense of Berlin in 1945. In the last phase of the war, the 162nd Turkestani Infantry Division, which had been turned from a training unit into a field division comprised of some of its last trained battalions, was employed against partisans in Slovenia and in fights against US troops in northern Italy. By the end of the war, tens of thousands of Muslim recruits of the Eastern Legions had fallen in battle.[23] In addition to the combat formations, many thousands of Muslims were recruited into labor, building, and supply units, and, from 1943 on, even physically unfit Muslim prisoners of war were recruited into four labor battalions and one labor reserve battalion.[24]

Outside the Eastern Legions, some Muslim auxiliary troops were fighting as an integrated part of regular German Wehrmacht units. The largest of these was created on the Crimean peninsula, where, in early 1942, Manstein's 11th Army had begun to directly enlist Muslims.[25] After the German invasion, some Crimean Tatars had volunteered for military service. In a letter to Hitler, a leading member of the old Muslim elite had expressed "great gratitude for the liberation of us Crimean Tatars (Mohammedans)," who had suffered under the "sanguinary Jewish-Communist rule," and offered their military support: "For the speedy annihilation of the partisan groups in the Crimea, we sincerely ask you to allow us, as experts of the routes and paths of the Crimean forests . . . to establish under German command standing armed formations."[26] The following month, the 11th Army began enlisting. It was the "suggestion of leading Tatar and Mohammedan figures," Keitel noted in early 1942, which had prompted the Wehrmacht to ask Hitler for permission to start recruiting among the Crimean Muslims.[27] Throughout the war, Crimean Tatars operated in purely Islamic units within the 11th Army. In the end, up to 20,000 of them were fighting in German units on the peninsula.[28] The army command was struck by the discipline and combat power of the Tatar units. "Their value in partisan counterinsurgency cannot be estimated highly enough," assured an army report in March 1942.[29] They kept the inland routes from the coast free of partisans and secured the sensitive mountain roads. Soon they also gained a grim reputation for being especially cruel during antipartisan operations. In the Yaila Mountains, Muslim units burned down partisan bases and killed unknown numbers of civilians. Impressed with their efficiency, the German command transferred the Tatar battalions to Romania when the Crimea was evacuated in spring 1944.

Less successful were the Wehrmacht's attempts to establish Arab formations—despite the massive German propaganda campaign in North Africa and the Middle East. In July 1941 the army set up the so-called *Sonderstab Felmy*.[30] Led by First World War veteran Hellmuth Felmy, one of its main purposes was to recruit and train Arab volunteers for the Wehrmacht within its so-called German-Arab Training Detachment (*Deutsch-Arabische Lehrabteilung*, or DAL), which was established in late 1941. The unit was composed of "German troops and people from the Oriental countries, who are Mohammedans throughout," and was intended to operate in the Arab world following a German victory in the Caucasus.[31] The Muslim soldiers of the German-Arab Training Detachment were to form the basis of a future "Arab Legion," already celebrated by its recruits as the "Arab Freedom Corps" (*al-Mufraza al-Arabiyya al-Hurra*). The project turned out to be more difficult than expected. The *Sonderstab Felmy* experienced serious problems in attracting Arabs. By the end of May 1942, only 130 Arabs had been recruited, with another 50 about to enlist.[32] One obstacle to German recruitment efforts was Turkey's decision to refuse passage to Germany to Arabs who had fought for al-Kilani in Iraq.[33] Ultimately, most of the volunteers were recruited from prisoner of war camps. Some had been students in Germany. The unit was first stationed at Cape Sunion, on the southern end of the Attica peninsula, where they awaited deployment to the Middle East. There were many conflicts among the Arab recruits. In his memoirs, al-Husayni claimed that Felmy would now and then seek his advice to settle these disputes. "The general complained to us about the trouble caused by the Arab students . . . and the arguments that constantly broke out between them," the mufti recalled, acknowledging that "unfortunately" this was "a clear truth and a painful reality."[34] He failed to mention, however, that Felmy was particularly concerned about the effects of the mufti's own intrigues and struggles with al-Kilani on the soldiers.[35] In August 1942, when German troops finally began their advance on the Caucasus and a breakthrough to the Middle East seemed imminent, the *Sonderstab Felmy* and its military formation were moved to Stalino (Donetsk) in the Ukraine.[36] The Arab component had grown to 800 men, now comprising four companies. After the conquest of the Caucasus mountains it was intended that they move to support the northern invasion of the Middle East. This, of course, never happened. While the 5,200 German soldiers of the *Sonderstab Felmy* fought, with heavy losses, on the Caucasian front, the Muslims, organized in one company of Arabs from Palestine, Syria, and Iraq and three companies of Arabs from Tunisia, Algeria, and Morocco, were stationed in a camp a few hundred miles behind the front line.[37] In November 1942 the High Command decided to move the four Muslim companies of the *Sonderstab Felmy* via Italy to North Africa, where they were to fight alongside Rommel's army.[38] Upon arrival in Tunis, they joined Arab volunteers who had been recruited in the Maghribian war zone.[39] According to Rahn, by February 1943 no fewer than 2,400 Arabs stood under German command in North Africa.[40] Among them were the soldiers of the Vichy unit *Phalange Africaine*.[41] The recruits were to form three combat battalions: "Tunisia" (*Tunesien*), "Algeria" (*Algerien*), and "Morocco" (*Marokko*), though only "Algeria" became operationally ready.[42] The Arabs of the *Sondestab Felmy* formed only a reserve unit and were never employed in combat. The Arab volunteers of the "Algeria" battalion proved unreliable.[43] After a few disappointing attempts to employ them on the front and with a rise in desertions and defections, the army's High Command decided to turn the Arab formations into labor units. Compared with other Muslim recruits, the Arab volunteers proved to be exceptionally disloyal—a complete failure.

Muslims in the SS

The SS also recruited thousands of Muslims into its ranks. In fact, Himmler shared Hitler's favorable attitude toward Muslim soldiers. On 2 March 1943, after a meeting with the *Reichsführer-SS*, General Edmund Glaise von Horstenau wrote about Himmler's enthusiasm for the foundation of the Muslim SS division in Bosnia:

> Himmler certainly approved of my timidly voiced opinion that in the Bosnian Division the conventional SS cultural policy would be well complemented by the addition of field muftis. Christianity he dismissed simply on account of its softness. The hope for the paradise of Mohammed had at any cost to be fostered with the Bosnians since this guaranteed heroic performance. . . . Himmler regretted the disintegration of the Austro-Hungarian military border and again and again spoke about the grand Bosnians and their fez.[44]

In the following months Himmler would argue repeatedly in the same vein. As late as March 1945 he would praise "the dauntless Mohammedans" of the Waffen-SS.[45] Like the Wehrmacht officers, he and his subordinates in the SS Head Office also frequently considered the global propagandistic impact of Muslim soldiers in German uniform. Imagining pan-Islamic unity, Gottlob Berger once explained the employment of Muslim units in southeastern Europe as an attempt "to reach out to the Mohammedans of the whole world, since these are 350 million people who are decisive in the struggle with the British Empire."[46] Similarly, an internal SS report emphasized that the division was to show the "entire Mohammedan world" that the Third Reich was ready to confront the "common enemies of National Socialism and Islam."[47]

SS recruiters first began to target Muslims in the Balkans, where, in early 1943, the partisan war threatened to divert more and more troops from the German army, already heavily weakened by defeats in the East and in North Africa. The largest Muslim SS unit of the region was formed in Bosnia. From February 1943 on, Himmler recruited thousands of Muslims into the 13th SS Waffen Mountain Division (*13. Waffen-Gebirgs-Division der SS*), which later was renamed "Handžar" (*Handschar*).[48] The formation was enthusiastically supported by the leading Muslim autonomists, who, in their memorandum of 1 November 1942, had already suggested the establishment of a volunteer unit under German command.[49] Handžar's deployment took place under the auspices of the Croatian ethnic German SS-Division "Prinz Eugen" and its choleric commander, *SS-Gruppenführer* Artur Phleps. A considerable part of the division comprised members of the feared Muslim militia of Major Muhamed Hadžiefendić, which had been created by the Ustaša government in northeastern Bosnia in 1941.[50] In the field, the leading German recruiter of Handžar became Karl von Krempler, who had grown up in Serbia and Turkey and was fluent in Bosnian. Although the majority of the Muslim population appeared to approve of the establishment of this division, fewer of them initially volunteered than had been anticipated. In time, though, recruiters enlisted around 20,000 volunteers.[51] Praised by German propaganda in Croatia as "warriors against Bolshevism and Judaism," they were to become both a political and a military force in the region.[52]

The Ustaša regime followed these events with the utmost suspicion. Its initial attempts to control the project failed. The SS gave short shrift to Zagreb's requests to include the word "Ustaša" in the name of the division.[53] In the end, the Germans assured Pavelić that around 15 percent of Handžar would be made up of Catholics and that his regime would be involved in the recruitment process.[54] In reality, Bosnians perceived the division as a "Mohammedan issue," as Winkler put it.[55] Pavelić's representative and liaison officer, Alija Šuljak, a Muslim who was notorious for his aggressive Ustaša propaganda, was quickly sidelined by German recruitment officers around Krempler.[56] Many Muslims even deserted the Croatian army to join the new SS formation. Although Pavelić saw his hands tied, his regime missed no opportunity to hinder the establishment of the Muslim division. In April, Phleps complained to Berlin that the Croatian government "uses all possible means to obstruct or at least to delay the formation considerably."[57] The head of the SS Reich Security Head Office, Ernst Kaltenbrunner, reported similar complaints.[58] In some cases, the Croats came at night for Muslim volunteers who had already been enlisted in the ranks of the SS, forced them out of their beds, and sent them to Croatian army barracks.[59] Furious, Himmler ordered his police commissioner on the spot to clamp down on this practice and to search both Croatian barracks and the concentration camps Nova Gradiška and Jasenovac, declaring that he had "definitive and very precise reports" about young men who had been "transported to concentration camps simply because they have enlisted with us." The perpetrators, he suggested, should themselves be taken to concentration camps or be executed.

Eager to avoid further Croatian sabotage, the SS moved Handžar to southern France, where the division was trained under the command of First World War veteran *SS-Oberführer* Karl-Gustav Sauberzweig. The German officials in the Balkans, most notably Horstenau, expressed concern about the transfer at this critical point of the war. Himmler, however, coolly rebuffed any such objections. But before long the concerns of the officers on the ground proved to be well founded. In the summer of 1943, when Tito initiated a major offensive in Bosnia, the relatives of Muslim volunteers were targeted first by the partisans. In France, their sons and husbands soon got wind of the developments at home. They knew that their families were left completely vulnerable and without any viable defense. Shocked by these events, especially since the Germans had promised them employment in their own country to protect their homes, many of the Bosnian volunteers became disillusioned. Discontent rose. In the night of 16–17 September, a group of soldiers rebelled and shot an officer.[60] Although caught off guard, the Germans quickly put down the revolt, with fifteen soldiers killed. Numerous rebels were arrested and publicly executed by firing squads. Berger blamed not the Muslims but the (around 2,800) Catholics of the formation.[61] A bit later Hitler expressed the same opinion, stressing that only the Muslims of the division had been proven trustworthy.[62] Soon Handžar was moved to the Silesian training ground at Neuhammer, where Himmler visited twice and gave his motivational speech. Al-Husayni, too, was sent there. Publishing a photo series of his visit to Neuhammer, the *Wiener Illustrierte* explained to its readers that the Muslims were to fight in the SS ranks with "fanatic faith in their heart," knowing "that only on the side of Germany can they sustain their freedom of faith and freedom of life."[63] Finally, in late February 1944, the Muslims were sent back to the Balkans. "Our Führer, Adolf Hitler, has kept his promise. A new era is dawning. We are coming!," announced a propaganda leaflet distributed throughout Bosnia.[64] Another one declared, "Now we are here!" to fight "every enemy of the homeland."[65] Hitler and Himmler had personally approved these pamphlets.[66] Handžar was mostly used for anti-partisan operations in northeastern Bosnia and acquired a grim reputation for its brutality and violent excesses.[67] A British liaison officer with Tito's partisans reported on the division's atrocities: "It behaves well in Moslem territory, but in Serb populated areas massacres all civil population without mercy or regard for age or sex."[68] After the war, an officer of Handžar gave a graphic report of crimes committed by members of the division: "One woman was killed and her heart taken out, carried around and then thrown into a ditch."[69] Hermann Fegelein, Himmler's liaison officer at Hitler's headquarters, reported to Hitler on the atrocities of Handžar during a military briefing on 6 April 1944, describing how the Muslim division had spread fear across the Balkans: "They kill them with only the knife. There was a man who was wounded. He had his arm tied up and with the left hand still finished off 17 enemies. There are also cases where they cut out their enemy's heart."[70] Hitler was not interested. "I couldn't care less" (Das ist Wurst), he replied, and carried on with the meeting's agenda. A few months later, an internal Wehrmacht report noted: "Muslims have done very well, and so they must be extensively supported and strengthened by military and civil agencies."[71] Berger, too, was impressed, declaring that "fighting against Tito and the Communists thus becomes for the Moslems a holy war."[72] When Kersten asked him about Handžar's military performance, he replied: "First class, they are as tough as the best German divisions were at the beginning of the war. They regard their weapons as sacred.... The Moslems cling to their flag with the same passionate courage, the Prophet's ancient green flag with a white half-moon, stained with the blood of ancient battles, its staff splintered with bullets."[73]

Soon, however, it became clear that more local help was needed in the Balkans. Desperate for manpower, German recruiters began to target Albanian Muslims. In early 1944 Hitler endorsed the formation of a Muslim division of Albanians, the 21st SS Waffen Mountain Division

(*21. Waffen-Gebirgsdivision der SS*), called "Skanderbeg."[74] Skanderbeg, which was deployed in Kosovo, in the area between Peć, Priština, and Prizren, was to operate in northern Albania and the borderlands of Montenegro. It consisted of recruits from the local civilian population, prisoners of war, and Albanian soldiers from Handžar. Enlistment of civilians was, as documents in the Albanian Central State Archive show, organized in close cooperation with the institutions of the Albanian puppet state, most importantly the Ministry of Defense.[75] Keitel ordered the release of Albanian prisoners of war of the "Muslim faith" to swell the ranks of the unit.[76] The basis of the new division, however, was formed by the Albanian contingent of Handžar.[77] Himmler expected "great usefulness" from the unit since the Albanians who fought in Handžar had proved to be highly motivated and disciplined.[78] In practice, though, the division suffered from a shortage of equipment and armaments and a lack of German staff to train new recruits. Over the summer and autumn of 1944, only a single battalion had been readied for combat and employed to fight partisans. "Day-in, day-out and night-in, night-out, Skanderbeg units advanced into the mountains to cover the flanks of the retreating troops," observed a German soldier in Prizren.[79] "They were the horror of the partisans."[80] Ultimately, the battalion became directly involved in Nazi crimes. In July 1944 the commander of Skanderbeg, August Schmidhuber, reported that his men had taken measures to crack down on "Jews, Communists and intellectual supporters of the Communists."[81] Between 28 May and 5 July the Albanians had captured "a sum total of 510 Jews, Communists, and supporters of gangs and political suspects." Skanderbeg was also involved in retributive hangings following acts of sabotage.[82] With the numbers of deaths and desertions rising, the division was shrinking steadily. Equally problematic was the formation of a third Muslim division of the Waffen-SS in the Balkans, the Bosnian 23rd SS Waffen Mountain Division (*23. Waffen-Gebirgsdivision der SS*), known as "Kama."[83] Established in June 1944, Kama comprised both Muslim civilians and several units from Handžar. After a series of desertions, the SS was compelled to disband the unit in late October 1944, only five months after its founding.

In the East, the SS was initially cautious. The Security Police and the Security Service of the SS in the Crimea were first to recruit Muslims systematically, using them as auxiliaries. Based on an agreement with the 11th Army, in early 1942 Otto Ohlendorf employed some of the recruited

Crimean Muslims in his *Einsatzgruppe D*. Soon 1,632 Muslim volunteers were fighting in fourteen so-called Tatar self-defense units (*Tatarenselbst-schutzkompanien*) of *Einsatzgruppe D*, scattered across the Crimean penin-sula.[84] An SS report about the volunteers praised the Tatars for being "ex-plicitly opposed to Bolshevism, Jews, and Gypsies."[85] Ohlendorf's right-hand man, Willi Seibert, noted that they had "proved their supreme worth" in combat against partisans.[86] Eventually, SS officers developed the idea of founding another Muslim division in the East. Walter Schellenberg, head of the foreign intelligence of the SD, had discussed the deployment of a formation of Turkic and Tatar volunteers as early as 1941 in the Reich Security Head Office but had given up on these plans due to a lack of person-nel and resources.[87] In autumn 1943 the idea was revived and discussed by Schellenberg and Berger.[88] On 14 October 1943, Schellenberg sent Berger a memorandum on the formation of a "Mohammedan Legion of the Waffen-SS" composed of Muslims from the Soviet Union.[89] The "political-ideological basis" of this unit was to be "Islam alone," it stated. Convinced that the di-vision would have a political and military impact throughout the Islamic world, Schellenberg summarized his ultimate "aim" in one sentence: "For-mation of Mohammedan units for the increasing revolutionization and winning over of the entire Islamic world." Thrilled, Berger recommended the plan to Himmler. The deployment of an Eastern Muslim division was a "political matter of the highest significance and importance," he stressed, by which "another part of the Mohammedan world would be won" for Germany's war.[90] Its formation would demonstrate "that we are serious about friendship with the Mohammedan world."

The following month, Himmler began recruiting among Soviet Mus-lims for an Eastern Muslim SS Division (*Ostmuselmanisches SS-Division*), the name emphasizing the religious character of the formation.[91] The Wehrmacht agreed to transfer its Turkic battalions 450 and I/94 to the SS, where they were to become the basis of the new division.[92] Andreas Mayer-Mader, who was still in charge of his Muslim unit, now called Turk Battalion 450, and part of the Turkestani Legion, was recruited by the SS to become commander of the new formation.[93] He seemed particularly suit-able, as he claimed to be an expert in the Muslim faith and on the verge of converting to Islam.[94] The Eastern Muslim SS Division was never fully employed, however. Mayer-Mader's command remained limited to the di-vision's so-called 1st Eastern Muslim SS Regiment (*1. Ostmuselmanisches*

SS-Regiment), which derived from the two Wehrmacht battalions. In early 1944 it contained only 800 men.[95] In spring 1944 Fritz Sauckel, Hitler's general plenipotentiary for labor deployment, released all of those Turkic and Tatar workers from the Labor Service who were willing to fight in the new Muslim unit.[96] SS enlisters also recruited Muslims from prisoner of war camps.[97] With the help of Josef Terboven, Reich commissar for Norway, the SS even screened the prisoner of war camps across Norway for a few hundred detained Muslims.[98] The High Command of the Wehrmacht, though, was increasingly resistant to SS attempts to recruit from its Muslim legions, seeing the SS more and more as a rival in the East.[99] Mayer-Mader, who faced resistance within his unit, was soon discharged, and later killed in mysterious circumstances. He was succeeded by several officers, among them the sadistic *Hauptmann* Heinz Billig (March–April) and the Nazi careerist *SS-Hauptsturmführer* Emil Hermann (April–July).[100] The 1st Eastern Muslim SS Regiment first fought partisans in the area around Minsk before being sent to Poland to join the infamous Dirlewanger Regiment in the suppression of the Warsaw uprising—as was a regiment of the Azerbaijani Legion of the Wehrmacht.[101]

Meanwhile, the SS continued to pursue the plan of the Eastern Muslim SS Division—now called the Eastern Turkic SS Corps (*Osttürkische Waffenverband der SS*).[102] Responsibility for the recruitment of the Eastern Turkic Muslims now fell to Reiner Olzscha of the volunteer section of the SS Head Office. First, the SS needed a new commander, one who was familiar with the Muslim world. A German officer who had served in the Ottoman army during the First World War and a former colonial officer from the Dutch army were suggested.[103] In the early summer of 1944, Berger finally found a suitable man—an officer familiar with "the Eastern Turkic-Islamic world."[104] Himmler's new commander of the Eastern Turkic SS Corps was fifty-nine-year-old Wilhelm Hintersatz, better known as Harun al-Rashid Bey, an army officer from Brandenburg who had converted to Islam during the First World War and who had worked with Enver Pasha on the Ottoman general staff.[105] During that time he had also met Otto Liman von Sanders, for whom he felt a deep admiration.[106] The campaign for Islamic mobilization in the Great War had strongly influenced Hintersatz, as it had so many others. After 1918 he had become involved with the former Muslim prisoners of war from the Wünsdorf Camp and had served in Italian intelligence in Abyssinia in the 1930s, claiming in his curriculum vitae that the "trust of the native Mohammedans" had been his best "instrument" there.[107] "The Mohammedans saw in me a fellow believer, who prayed with them without timidity in their mosque," he boasted. He had "always been ready" to cut the "Achilles' heel" of Germany's "most dangerous enemy," England, which, in his view, was Islam.[108] Married with two children, the qualified engineer was not the archetypical adventurer. He had become involved with Islam and Islamic politics by chance. Playing up his "Islamic connections" and describing his "affiliation with Islam" and the trust he enjoyed among Muslims as his "essential instrument," he had impressed SS officers.[109] Before his appointment, al-Rashid had worked as a liaison officer of the Reich Security Head Office with the mufti of Jerusalem.[110] Olzscha contacted al-Rashid in May: "I wish to make you a very concrete proposition, which also first and foremost considers the position which distinguishes you as a Mohammedan and former officer."[111] Indeed, within the SS Head Office, al-Rashid's appointment was explained with reference to his "close relationships to the Islamic world" and the SS propaganda for the "Turkic-Islamic world."[112]

The Eastern Turkic SS Corps under Harun al-Rashid was to become a reservoir of all Eastern Muslim volunteers.[113] Its base became the 1st Eastern Muslim SS Regiment, although it was restructured into three, and later four, battalions (Crimea, Turkestan, Idel-Ural, and finally Azerbaijan). Al-Rashid's most prominent volunteer was Prince Mansur Daoud, a distant cousin of King Faruq of Egypt, whose recruitment strengthened the unit's pan-Islamic character.[114] Impressed by his performance, al-Rashid reported that Daoud had proven to be a "substantial political factor" and that he, "in the closest cooperation with the chief mullah," conducted "effective propaganda."[115] By December 1944 around 3,000 Muslims had been enlisted in the Eastern Turkic SS Corps; in early 1945 it had grown to 8,500.[116] Ultimately, the formation of the complete corps failed, but the SS managed to mobilize significantly more Muslims than had fought in the 1st Eastern Muslim SS Regiment. In the end, the SS began enlisting every Eastern Muslim within its reach. In the summer of 1944, for instance, 800 former soldiers of the Tatar units, which had been evacuated from the Crimea to Romania, were recruited into the Tatar SS Waffen Mountain Brigade (*Tatarische Waffen-Gebirgs-Brigade der SS*) and fought, armed only with carbines, in Hungary before being integrated into al-Rashid's corps.[117] SS recruiters would even screen the

Reich Commissariat Ostland for Muslim cannon fodder. In March 1944 the head of Vienna's Islamic community, Salih Hadzicalić, was consulted by the SS Head Office about the Muslims of Vilnius, prompting the SS to contact Mufti Szynkiewicz about Muslims there.[118] As late as November 1944, the SS command in Danzig reported to the SS Head Office on the "transfer of Muslim members of the police to the Waffen-SS," specifically two Muslim soldiers who had been recruited in the Ostland.[119] In late 1944 Himmler decided to organize some of the Eastern Muslims into two regiments of a newly founded Caucasian SS Corps (*Kaukasischer Waffenverband der SS*).[120] Varying in size between 1,000 and 2,000 men, the corps was split into four regiments, of which two were to be Muslim or dominated by Muslims: Northern Caucasian and Azerbaijani (the non-Muslim regiments were Armenian and Georgian). The Azerbaijanis of the Eastern Turkic SS Corps, however, successfully petitioned not to be mixed with Christian Armenians and Georgians in this new corps but to remain in al-Rashid's purely Islamic formation.[121] As the war was nearing its end, the recruiting process became more and more chaotic. The morale of the troops suffered. In late December 1944 some of the men of the Turkestani regiment, led by their commander, Ghulam Alimov, revolted in the Hungarian-Slovakian border area.[122] Along with 400 to 500 of his men, Alimov arrested all German officers and even executed some of them before escaping into the woods to join the Slovak partisans. In January 1945, however, many of the deserters returned, while only 250 to 300 stayed with the partisans. In the last months of the war, the corps fought in northern Italy, where it finally surrendered to the US Army.

From the beginning, officers in the SS Head Office understood the massive mobilization of Eastern Muslims as part of a general campaign that aimed to revolutionize all Muslims of the Soviet Union against Moscow. A particularly eager proponent of this policy was Emil Hermann. A veteran officer of the SS, Hermann had been responsible for the military and political organization of the Eastern Muslim SS troops before briefly taking over command of the 1st Eastern Muslim Regiment. Olzscha explained after the war that Hermann had hoped to advance his career through the Islamic question and in fact aspired to run an office for Islamic affairs, planned in the SS Head Office.[123] As early as 14 December 1943, Hermann referred to the endeavor to "set Islam in motion" (*den Islam in*

Bewegung bringen werden) in a general memorandum about the foundation of the Eastern SS formation.[124] Although the paper spoke in general terms about the "registration of the currently available Muslim peoples with the aim of employing them in the fight against the enemy powers," it was mainly concerned with the Muslims of the Soviet Union. Compared to the Arabs, their hatred of foreign rule, which was based on their religiosity, was even more powerful, Hermann wrote. Their "great love of freedom" and the "teaching of Islam" generated a "tremendous pride," which the SS had to consider in order not to make the same mistakes as the Wehrmacht. Berger reacted to the memorandum with one of his simple notes in the margins: "Yes, agreed!"[125] Five days earlier, when meeting Gerd Schulte, an officer of the SS Head Office who was assigned to oversee the establishment of the Muslim division, Mayer-Mader suggested that the SS should become the protector of the Eastern Turks. Schulte corrected him, emphasizing that one would have to speak about the "patron of all Muslims."[126] Mayer-Mader understood. In a special report, he outlined his idea for a unit that was organized strictly along Islamic lines and would accommodate Muslims from all parts of the Soviet Union.[127] He also pointed to the division's effects on the wider Islamic world and discussed its employment in terms of Germany's general policy on Islam. "Our enemies well know that the interests of Islam and Germany run parallel," he claimed, describing Muslims and Germans as "the most natural allies." Almost the entire Muslim world was colonized by the Soviets, British, and French. But even though many Muslims saw "the only hope for Islam in an alliance with Germany," more had to be done. Apart from propaganda, practical measures were needed "to show the common man that Germany sees in Islam an equal friend and ally." The most efficient measure was the formation of the division of Eastern Turkic Muslims, which would soon influence all Muslims of the Soviet Union. On 4 January 1944, Mayer-Mader, joined by Heinz Billig, who at that time still led the staff of the new division in Berlin, met Schulte again and established the future goals of the new division. The "short-term objective" was to function as a "task force against Bolshevism." The "long-term objective," the SS men decided, would be not only the "liberation of Turkestan" but also the broader "activation of the Muslims" (*Aktivierung der Moslems*) of the Soviet Union.[128] It was this misconception, the notion that Islam was a bloc that could be "activated," which dominated the views of German SS officers toward the end of the war.

This idea came even more to the fore in the summer of 1944, when the plans for the Eastern Muslim SS formation were reorganized. Reiner Olzscha wrote a whole series of reports on this matter, all roughly based on his general memorandum of 24 April 1944 about the involvement of the SS in Eastern Muslim affairs.[129] In a report dated 7 June 1944, he discussed the Eastern formation in terms of a wider aim to mobilize Eastern Muslims against the Soviet Union.[130] Stressing that the Muslims were the strongest non-Slavic and non-Christian minority of the Soviet Union, that their religion was a genuine bulwark against Moscow, and that their history of uprisings had proven their anti-Russian and anti-Bolshevist stance, Olzscha argued that the "struggle for freedom of the Mohammedan Turk people" provided an ideal basis for an alliance with Germany, an alliance that would be welcomed in wider parts of the Islamic world. Similar notes followed. In one of them, Olzscha argued that "hundreds of thousands of Turkic Muslims" would form the "strongest subversive minority of the Soviet Union" and should be "exploited" by the SS.[131] In another, he described the new Eastern Muslim SS formation as a "platform for political fanaticization of the Eastern Turks in the fight against Bolshevist Russia."[132] Berger agreed.[133] Not only the political-national motives but also the "Mohammedan worldview" of the Eastern Muslims were to be used "as an effective bulwark against Bolshevism," he wrote to Himmler.[134] In some further instructions Berger specified that Himmler's order for the formation of the "Eastern Turkic Corps" aimed to concentrate all "Turkic Mohammedan anti-Bolshevist forces" for the purpose of "the inner fragmentation of the Soviet Union."[135] Berger's plans for the Eastern Muslim Corps and the splintering of the Soviet Union, however, clashed with the realities of the war. In practice its units were not employed on Soviet territory. Nevertheless, officers at the SS Head Office were convinced by the plan. In a report to Berger, *SS-Hauptsturmführer* Ulrich, an official at the SS Head Office, urged the pursuit of the "desired ultimate goal," which, he summarized, was the "revolutionalization of the anti-Bolshevik forces in Russia through Islam, as a detonator within the state." "If this impact, through the 30 million Muslims in the Soviet Union, is to be effected, nevertheless, the deployment of the Eastern Turkic Corps cannot be relinquished."[136] The SS Head Office would follow these plans until the downfall of the Third Reich in 1945.

A vigorous promoter of Islamic mobilization in the last months of the war was the new commander of the Eastern Muslim formation, Harun al-Rashid, who, like Olzscha and Berger, described the corps as a "platform for the fanaticization" of the Muslims in the Soviet Union.[137] He had "guaranteed" Olzscha a "loyal, combat-ready and soldierly valuable Mohammedan military force" (*mohamedanische Waffenkraft*).[138] Underlining the importance of employing purely Muslim units, he also pleaded for stronger "Islamic-religious influence."[139] To guarantee this, he suggested, in June 1944, the deployment and training of the new corps in Bosnia and Herzegovina, where they could join the Muslim SS units already there.[140] In the Balkans it would be possible, he stressed, to direct "our people" into the mosques and to bring them under the influence of the Bosnian 'ulama. Al-Rashid went as far as to suggest that, in case the Germans never conquered the Soviet Union, the Eastern Muslims could settle among the "very pro-German Mohammedan population of the Balkans."

The efforts by the SS to mobilize Muslims were increasingly opposed by the Wehrmacht and the East Ministry. The Wehrmacht feared the disintegration of its Muslim legions. Indeed, Harun al-Rashid internally suggested transferring "all Mohammedan formations" to the Waffen-SS.[141] More forceful opposition to the SS policy of Islamic mobilization of the Eastern Muslims came from Mende and officers of the East Ministry. When the SS began organizing its first Eastern Muslim units in late 1943, Mende's protégé, the Turkic exile Veli Kajum, concerned about losing influence, protested that "the SS pursued 'pan-Islamic' aims."[142] The SS swiftly confronted Kajum.[143] In February 1944 Mende himself stepped in, writing a lengthy report about the new SS line for Berger, who had by then also seized control of the political department of the East Ministry.[144] Mende acknowledged the central role Islam played in the deployment of Muslim units in the Balkans: "The Western Muslim SS-Division of the Bosniaks can be successful under the unifying idea of Islam because the Bosniaks, who speak Croatian, distinguish themselves from the linguistically undifferentiated Croatian and Serbian environment only through Islam and the particular habits deriving from it. For them Islam is therefore the embodiment of their difference and the bond to the greater Islamic world."[145] However, he vehemently protested against expanding this policy to the East: "The situation among the Mohammedans in the Soviet Union is very different." The Wehrmacht had divided Muslims into the four legions according to their ethnicity. "The unification of the Mohammedans of the Soviet Union in the Eastern Muslim SS Division requires a change from the hitherto political-propagandistic treatment," Mende cautioned. Basing policy toward the Eastern Muslims on "the unifying power of Islam" would inevitably lead to a pan-Turanian movement that could not be controlled. Somewhat inconsistently, he claimed that, in any case, Islam played no decisive role in the East. Only 5 percent of Eastern Muslims were still attached to Islam, and only an additional 20 percent would possibly be receptive to a religious campaign. It was the "national question," Mende asserted, that played the "decisive role." Moreover, he warned that "the strong emphasis on unifying Islam" would make the smaller non-Muslim peoples of the Eastern territories, Georgians and Armenians, feel "subordinated," which would make them turn to Moscow. Still, even Mende acknowledged that the SS policy would have "positive effects on Turkey and probably on the entire Mohammedan world." He suggested a compromise. The volunteer formations should remain structured along ethnic lines, but this policy could be "complemented by a strong emphasis on the general principles of Islam and through the support of the fraternal bond between the greater Turkic-speaking units."[146] The SS could not have cared less. A few months later, in the summer of 1944, Mende turned again to Berger to repeat his concerns—once more without success.[147] Finally, on 13 September 1944, representatives of the SS Head Office, including Olzscha and Ulrich, met to consult with Mende.[148] Mende once more complained about the pan-policies of the SS. The SS remained firm. Mende's position conflicted not only with that of the SS Head Office but also with that of his colleague Johannes Benzing, who supported the SS line. The interwar academic debates about the impact of Islam in the Soviet Union had turned into a conflict over policy making.

The SS policy toward the Muslims of the Eastern territories had a larger dimension. In the final months of the war, Muslim mobilization in the East became part of a full-scale pan-Islamic campaign launched by the SS. "Mobilization of Islam" was, indeed, the title of a memorandum written by the ambitious Emil Hermann in late February 1944.[149] It suggested nothing less than an operation aimed at ensuring "that the whole Islamic world is set in motion" (*dass der gesamte Islam in Bewegung gerät*). Hermann outlined a gigantic pan-Islamic mobilization project targeting all countries within reach of the SS:

It is proposed to effect a Führer order via the Reichsführer-SS, which summons all capable Muslims within reach in Europe to come to a specific staging point. It must include both Mohammedan civil workers as well as O.T.-laborers [workers of the Organization Todt], prisoners of war, etc. The assemblage of the Mohammedans in Spain, France, Italy, Greece, Romania, Bulgaria, Albania, and Croatia would have to be carried out in cooperation with the Foreign Office and the foreign governments. . . . This campaign of orchestration would have to be preceded by a promotion exercise by the grand mufti via broadcast, press and pamphlet propaganda. The 13th Bosnian Waffen Mountain Division as well as the Eastern Muslim and Albanian [divisions], which are currently being deployed, would serve as a substantial propaganda instrument. . . . With regard to the Crimean Tatars, it is proposed to assemble the mullahs (Odessa or the Crimea itself) and to let the grand mufti speak to them in person. The Mohammedans of the countries of Spain, France, Italy, and Greece can be considered for the Arab Legion. There are only a few Mohammedans in Romania, so a separate formation would be unrealistic. With the Mohammedans of the Bulgarian region, a legion of Pomak Muslims could be employed. Circa 450,000 Pomak Muslims live in Bulgaria, who are suppressed by the Bulgarian government. During the deployment of new Mohammedan formations it must be considered that the officer posts are given to Mohammedans or Germans.[150]

The plan never materialized, although, in the last year of the war, the SS made considerable (and mostly unsuccessful) attempts to mobilize, or "activate" as Berger and other SS officers had put it, Muslims wherever possible—not just from the Soviet Union and the Baltic but also from Africa, South Asia, and the Middle East. In the autumn of 1943 Himmler asked Berger to assess the issue of including Indian Muslims in Handžar. Berger answered that his "in-depth investigation" had shown that their integration into the Bosnian unit was not possible, as Indian Muslims would feel first Indian, not Muslim.[151] He also advised against the employment of an Indian Muslim Formation (*Indischer Moslemverband*) on the Eastern Front, as he feared desertion to India.[152] The plan was never pursued. Shortly afterward, Berger came up with another idea. In December 1943, after having consulted the mufti, he suggested to Himmler that they recruit Muslims from eastern Africa who were imprisoned in France: "These Mohammedans would like to fight against the English and Americans in Italy."[153] Berger expressed his wish to discuss the issue with Otto Abetz, the German ambassador to Paris. This never happened, either. Ultimately, SS recruitment of Arabs was largely unsuccessful, as it had been in the Wehrmacht. In France, under the auspices of the SD, the *Brigade Nord-Africaine*, a contingent of around 180 Algerians, which operated under the infamous Parisian Gestapo officer Henri Lafont and the Algerian nationalist Muhammad al-Mahdi, known as "SS Muhammad," was created in early 1944.[154] The unit fought the French resistance in central France but, as the military situation in France deteriorated, disintegrated within months. The plan to establish an "Arab-Islamic army" (*Arabisch-Islamische Armee*) for the Waffen-SS, as suggested by al-Husayni in the summer of 1944, proved to be entirely unrealistic.[155] The SS reported that only 300 Arabs were available for the establishment of such an army, although Berger was still convinced that more Arab volunteers might be recruited in the future.[156] Once again, the idea never materialized. Even plans for a smaller Arab infantry regiment proved unfeasible.[157]

As the SS tried more and more desperately to enlist every Muslim within reach, eventually even concentration camps were screened for potential recruits.[158] In the spring of 1944 Himmler ordered Berger to contact Oswald Pohl, head of the SS Economic and Administrative Head Office (*SS-Wirtschafts- und Verwaltungshauptamt*) and in charge of the general organization of the concentration camps, to discuss the recruitment of Muslim prisoners for the Waffen-SS.[159] Himmler's personal administrative officer, Rudolf Brandt, even sent Berger a detailed list of Muslim concentration camp detainees, which had been compiled by Pohl's bureaucrats (Figure 6.1).[160] Titled "Account of the Inmates of the Islamic Faith" (*Aufstellung über die Häftlinge islamitischen Glaubens*), it listed all male and female Muslim prisoners in the camps Auschwitz (I–III), Buchenwald, Dachau, Flossenbürg, Groß-Rosen, Mauthausen, Natzweiler, Neuengamme, Ravensbrück, Sachsenhausen, Stutthof, and Bergen-Belsen. Altogether, 1,130 Muslim men and nineteen Muslim women were recorded. Most of them were

Über die Häftlinge islamitischen Glaubens.

(Männer:)

	Afrikaner (frz.Hol.)	Albaner	Bulgaren	Franzosen	Griechen	Holländer	Italiener	Kroaten	Polen	Russen	Serben (Jugoslawen)	Tartaren	Türken	Ukrainer	Staatenlose	Zusammen:
Auschwitz I										1						1
Auschwitz II		3					1	7	1	26	2					40
Auschwitz III										4	1					5
Buchenwald		5	1	30		1	55	1		182	4					279
Dachau	2	42			1					23	7					75
Flossenbürg				9						20						29
Gross-Rosen		3						8	1	75						87
Mauthausen		9		19			5			73	19			2		127
Natzweiler		3		2			4	1		21	4					35
Neuengamme		15	1	1			138			33	11					199
Ravensbrück							3			13	3	1				20
Sachsenhausen		37	1	11		1	129			24	16			1	1	222
Stutthof										11						11
Bergen-Belsen																
Insgesamt:	2	117	3	72	1	2	349		4	506	67	1		3	1	1130

(Frauen:)

	Afrikaner (frz.Hol.)	Albaner	Bulgaren	Franzosen	Griechen	Holländer	Italiener	Kroaten	Polen	Russen	Serben (Jugoslawen)	Tartaren	Türken	Ukrainer	Staatenlose	Zusammen:
Auschwitz										2	7					9
Ravensbrück										9					1	10
Insgesamt:										11	7				1	19

6.1 List of Muslim concentration camp inmates, compiled by the SS Economic and Administrative Head Office, 1944 (BAB).

from eastern and southeastern Europe and had presumably been interned as political prisoners. Still, the list was incomplete, as some groups, most notably Muslim prisoners from Arab countries, were not included.[161] The SS Head Office reacted swiftly, prompting a bureaucratic process that lasted half a year and involved the SS Reich Security Head Office, the SS Economic and Administrative Head Office, and Himmler's staff. Finally, on 16 November 1944, Olzscha reported to Berger that the SS Reich Security Head Office had, despite repeated requests, not yet determined whether some of the Muslims in the concentration camps were suitable for recruitment.[162] Berger informed Himmler of these problems and suggested calling a halt to the process.[163] A part of the Bosnian Muslims had, at the request of the Ustaša government, already been released in the meantime, and the remaining Muslims, who were interned "because of various offenses," would surely not make good soldiers, the chief of the SS Head Office wrote. Himmler did not pursue the issue further.

Overall, a closer look at the non-German formations of both the Wehrmacht and the SS reveals that Muslims played a significant role within them. While the Wehrmacht was the first to begin recruiting Muslims and mobilized far more overall than Himmler, the SS became the strongest force in the military mobilization of Muslims near the end of the war. Both Wehrmacht and SS authorities considered the soldiers' religious identity to be important when forming Muslim units. Leading German officials, most notably Hitler, Himmler, and Berger, repeatedly used religious rather than national or ethnic categories when speaking and writing about these formations. As in other cases of non-German mobilization by the Wehrmacht and SS, the recruitment of Muslims was launched primarily to balance the shortage of manpower. Yet, in the Muslims' case, considerations of general war propaganda as well as notions of the Muslims' trustworthiness and soldierly quality played an exceptional role. Consequently, the Wehrmacht and the SS recruited a vast number of Muslims and, as the following chapters show, decided to provide them with special religious care and propaganda.

CHAPTER SEVEN

Islam and Politics in the Units

On 28 January 1944, as Muslim troops in the Wehrmacht and the SS were fighting on all fronts, Himmler spoke at a conference of functionaries of the NSDAP's Office of Racial Politics, which was also attended by Goebbels.[1] Boasting about the European recruits in the Waffen-SS, he suddenly began to speak about his Bosnian division: "And here, with this Muslim-Bosniak division, the SS has for once deployed a division which is entirely religious in nature." The anticlerical party ideologues must have caught their breath, and Himmler appeared to be well aware of that. "You have understood correctly: totally religious, entirely Muslim," he affirmed. Every battalion had its imam, and he had, "with the authorization of the Führer," even reintroduced the old Habsburg rights: "The devout Muslims get the food which their religion dictates. They have the absolute freedom to exercise their religious practices, religious habits and customs." And then, after praising the religious character of the division, Himmler finally revealed his personal opinion about these religious concessions for the Muslim recruits: "I must say, I don't have anything against Islam because it educates men in this division for me and promises them paradise when they have fought and been killed in battle. A practical and attractive religion for soldiers!" He received strong, sustained applause.

Behind closed doors, among his party comrades, Himmler's opinion of Islam seemed more pragmatic and less idealistic than one might have concluded when listening to him talk to the Muslim volunteers in Silesia. The speech revealed that it was cool reasoning rather than ideological fervor that shaped his ideas about Muslim soldiers. It also showed that Himmler was conscious of the significance of Islam when he deployed the Muslim division and that he was convinced that the Muslim faith strengthened military discipline and combat morale.

This view was widely shared in the SS and the Wehrmacht. Once the Muslim units were established, it was important to keep the soldiers' morale high. Islamic sentiment, it was believed, would enhance military discipline and the willingness to fight. German officials perceived Islam as characteristically aggressive and were convinced that it would motivate soldiers for combat. Islam, it was believed, could make war just and legitimate for Muslims. In a "holy war," killing was no longer prohibited. Sacrifice in battle became an honor. Moreover, the conception of a genuine incompatibility between Islam and Bolshevism and, in some cases, the idea of an antagonism between Islam and Judaism made the Muslim faith seem an ideal pillar of the Muslim units. Finally, Islam—more specifically Islamic rituals, laws, and authorities—seemed a potential instrument to enhance discipline and order in the units. Islam also appeared to provide a strong bond that could be used to foster group cohesion in the formations. The esprit de corps in Germany's Muslim units could draw on both the regimental and the religious community.

In consequence, the Wehrmacht and the SS not only tolerated religious practices in the Muslim units but also actively supported and instrumentalized them. In the initial phases of the recruitment process, German officials tried to use religious arguments to promote the war against alleged common enemies. After the units were deployed, this policy was pursued further. Muslims were granted various religious concessions with respect to dietary, celebratory, and burial practices. In fact, Germany's policy measures often went far beyond the basic needs and expectations of the Muslim volunteers. In the units, European military structures and practices—like drill, tactics, and command hierarchies—merged with the religious customs and norms of the Muslims. This phenomenon is indeed well known from the history of the European colonial armies, most notably of the sepoy regiments in British India.[2] Overall, military effectiveness, it was believed, derived from the way military organization was connected to the particular religion of the soldiers.

To be sure, throughout the centuries religion had been an important matter in most armies.[3] Food and faith were among the most imminent concerns of soldiers on the frontlines, struggling for survival, and military commanders generally considered religious care crucial for the strengthening of discipline and fighting morale. In Hitler's armies, though, the place of religion was contested.[4] Although the military command supported some 1,000 Protestant and Catholic battlefield chaplains and the provision of pastoral care, other parts of the regime, most importantly the powerful party organizations, tried to curb Christian influence in the units. In the non-German formations, both in the Wehrmacht and the SS, Berlin generally followed a policy of noninterference in religious affairs. All denominations were free to practice and to promote their religion. The Germans' intense efforts to accommodate and encourage Islam in the units were very unusual compared to the policies adopted toward other religious groups. Whereas the use of Christian army chaplains in the Wehrmacht's Eastern Troops was, at least initially, prohibited, the Germans provided military imams for its Muslim units from the beginning.[5] And by the time Christian chaplains and even Buddhist lamas were employed in the volunteer units of the Wehrmacht and the SS, allowances for Islamic religious practices in the units had assumed a much larger scale. Indeed, the number of field imams employed for the Muslim troops proportionally exceeded the number of Christian army chaplains employed by the Third Reich in the German and non-German units. In the Muslim formations, religion played a more important role. One reason for this was a general mistrust of Christianity and especially of the Orthodox Church. Moreover, Christian volunteers in the legions, most notably Georgians and Armenians, showed far less religiosity than their Islamic counterparts, Bosnians, Turkestanis, Azerbaijanis, North Caucasians, and Crimean Tatars. The decision to support religion in the Muslim units was made on the assumption that Islam was particularly well suited to mobilize, discipline, and motivate soldiers. Moreover, the accommodation of Islam in the units seemed important given Nazi Germany's claim of friendship with the Muslim world.

Religion and Recruitment

From the outset, Islam played a central role in the recruitment of Muslim volunteers. German authorities employed religious figures, ranging from members of the 'ulama in the East and the Balkans to Berlin's Islamic dignitaries and leaders who had come to Berlin, to call upon Muslim prisoners of war and civilians to join the ranks of the German army. A number of religious figures willingly utilized their networks to aid the German recruitment efforts and translated German enlistment appeals into sacred language to lend the process religious and moral legitimacy.

An early example of the employment of the local 'ulama in German recruitment efforts was the formation of militias by Manstein's 11th Army in the Crimea. On 3 January 1942, a meeting of the Muslim committee in Simferopol marked the beginning of the recruitment of Crimean Tatars.[6] Among the German attendees were officers of *Einsatzgruppe D*, including Ohlendorf, who represented the German command. The event had a strong religious character. It included elements of religious performance and gave the local imam a prominent role. After presenting a general outline of the battle against Bolshevism, a prominent mullah from Simferopol addressed his fellow Tatars, explaining that their religion and faith commanded them to take part in this holy battle alongside the Germans and that the annihilation of Soviet rule would return to them their freedom of religion. The chairman of the committee added: "It is an honor for us to have the opportunity to fight under the Führer Adolf Hitler, the greatest man of the German people." Satisfied, Ohlendorf thanked the Tatars and assured them that he had spoken to his men, who recognized the necessity of the common struggle against the godless. Under the eyes of Ohlendorf and his entourage, the Muslims then marked the beginning of their fight with a prayer. All of the assembled Tatars rose solemnly to repeat the words of their mullah, praying for "the achievement of a speedy victory and of the common aim, as well as for the long life of the Führer, Adolf Hitler."[7] After two more prayers, one for the German people and the German army and another for the German soldiers who had died in battle, the meeting ended. A week later, the Simferopol committee extended its aims, adding: "The Crimean committee sees it as its holy obligation to participate jointly with the German army in the liberation of the Muslims of the Soviet Union."[8]

Similar ceremonies were repeated in other Muslim areas where the Wehrmacht and the SS were recruiting. The most extensive use of the 'ulama was made in Bosnia and Herzegovina. In fact, the SS endorsed local religious bodies to enlist Muslim volunteers. The official recruitment pamphlet for Handžar called Muslims to enlist at their local confessional centers, effectively sidelining the Ustaša authorities.[9] Across the region, religious leaders and imams became enthusiastic recruiters.[10] One of the most important figures who took on the role was Muhamed Pandža.[11] He was described by a field imam of Handžar, Hasan Bajraktarević, as the "true initiator, greatest propagandist, recruiter, and fighter for the foundation and replenishment of this division."[12] According to the imam, it was Pandža who had convinced the "Muslim clerical leadership" to support the deployment of Himmler's division. They then launched the "strongest propaganda" and provided imams for the recruitment. In the end, the success in enlistment was to a significant extent due to these religious institutions and, above all, to Pandža himself. "Everybody knew," Bajraktarević explained, that what Pandža recommended must be "genuinely Islamic and patriotic." In some towns, before recruits were allowed to enter the division's enlisting office they were required first to see Pandža, who prepared them mentally for their mission.[13] Unsurprisingly, Berger, never tired of stressing the importance of Islam, was a strong advocate of the involvement of Islamic dignitaries in the recruitment process. "Recruitment of the volunteers is entirely in the hands of the Moslem priests, who are far closer to realities than the Christian ones," he explained to Kersten.[14] Berger, in fact, was eager to put recruitment completely in the hands of the imams.[15] Later, Sauberzweig also employed the military imams of his division for recruitment activities. In November 1943, for instance, he sent Bajraktarević and two other imams of Handžar to Bosnia and Herzegovina to recruit volunteers.[16] "From the first day onward," the imams reported on the mobilization effort, they had been in "constant contact" with the local "Muslim clerical leadership."[17] An SS report summarized that the "Islamic clergy" had contributed "considerably" to the formation of the division.[18] The SS command in the Balkans tried to support its recruiters with religiously charged recruitment posters that depicted the green banner of the Prophet.[19]

In the East, Jakub Szynkiewicz, the newly installed mufti of the Ostland, became involved in the recruitment of Muslim prisoners and swore in new volunteers through a religious ceremony.[20] Speaking to new recruits in the Baltics in early 1944, he underlined the slogan "that the Muslims, for political and religious reasons, can never ally with Bolshevism, which is the ideology of godlessness."

Also, Islamic collaborators who worked in the German capital were regularly flown in to aid the mobilization of Muslims in the field. In early 1942 the High Command of the Wehrmacht commissioned Alimjan Idris to oversee the enlistment and swearing in of several thousand Muslim prisoners of war in a camp in the General Government.[21] Given his work with Germany's Muslim prisoners of war during the First World War, he must have seemed particularly well suited to the task. At once, Idris went to the camp, where he distributed not only cigarettes but also Islamic literature and pamphlets. His visit caused some concern among the military command and the East Ministry.[22] In accordance with his orders, Idris had spoken to Muslim recruits about religious and political issues in his position as an Islamic religious dignitary. Without the endorsement of Berlin, however, he had allegedly praised the policy of Turkey, which, he had asserted, had shown considerable interest in the situation of Muslim prisoners of war in Germany. Idris was swiftly recalled to Berlin.

In the Balkans, Himmler and Berger employed the mufti of Jerusalem to promote enrollment in the Handžar division. In fact, the aim of the mufti's tour in spring 1943 was not only to win back the trust of the Muslim civil population but also to promote the new division and to give a religious character to SS recruitment in the Balkans. Al-Husayni's efforts to promote military recruitment during his tour seemed successful. By the time he left the Balkans, thousands of Muslims had enlisted, much to the delight of SS officials. Nevertheless, Berger's plans to send the mufti also on a tour in the Eastern Front, to "activate," as he put it, the Muslims there, never materialized.[23] In fact, al-Husayni played almost no role in SS recruitment efforts in the East. He was used here, it seems only once, on 14 December 1943, when the SS sent Mayer-Mader to him with a delegation of Muslim recruits from the Eastern Muslim SS Corps. The mufti boasted that the soldiers had assured him that they would "fight shoulder to shoulder with their German comrades for the common cause until final victory" after he had told them about "the good treatment of the Muslims" in the Bosnian SS units and "the sympathy of the German leadership toward the Muslims, the freedom of their countries and their understanding of the Islamic cause."[24] Emil Hermann reported the meeting as a great success: "Only after the remarks of his Eminence did the Turkmenian officers realize the importance of the activation of the whole of Islam."[25] Berger reported to Himmler that the Turkmenian officers had reacted with enthusiasm to the call for the "fight of Islam against the enemy powers."[26]

As in the Balkans, the SS was eager to employ pan-Islamic arguments when launching its Muslim recruitment campaign in the East. A mobilization pamphlet, calling on all "Muslims" to sign up with the newly created Eastern Muslim SS Division, left no doubt that Germany and the entire Muslim world were fighting on the same side.[27] The "common enemies," the SS proclaimed, had a strong interest in "killing as many Muslims as possible" in the war in order to be able to rule, rob, and exploit "Muslim countries" even more freely, reminding readers that the majority of the world's

Islamic population, "two hundred and thirty-two million Muslims," had to suffer "under English, American, French, and Russian foreign rule." Only if Germany were victorious would Muslims have an opportunity to gain their independence: "If Germany is defeated, the last hope for you Muslims ever to become free also fades."

The employment of religious dignitaries and propaganda gave Islamic legitimacy to the recruitment campaign. Still, whether the fight for Islam and religious freedom was decisive in persuading the majority of Muslims to enter the ranks of the German army remains debatable. To be sure, some recruits were driven by religious hatred and ideological fervor and receptive to the slogans of the Islamic authorities employed by Berlin. Overall, however, Muslims often had rather profane motives for enlisting. Red Army soldiers who were recruited in prisoner of war camps primarily had material interests. Pay and army rations were obviously preferable to suffering from hunger, cold, and disease in the camps. Many simply hoped that a German uniform would help them to survive the war. In late 1942 the propaganda section of the Wehrmacht distributed questionnaires among some of the volunteers, asking them about their incentives for enlisting. Among the most common answers were the desire to escape the miserable conditions of the prisoner of war camps. Anti-Bolshevism and opposition to the Soviet state also played an important role.[28] A year later, Ralph von Heygendorff explained to the German personnel of his Eastern Legions that, although idealist motives played a "not inconsiderable" role, the "majority of soldiers interned in prisoner of war camps have without a doubt material motives for joining the German troops."[29] In areas where the Wehrmacht and the SS recruited from among the Muslim civilian population—in the Crimea and the Balkans—volunteers hoped to use German arms to protect their families. Historians have emphasized the "central role" that the newly introduced religious rights in the Crimea played in motivating these Muslims to enter the German ranks.[30] Yet, many recruits in the Crimea also saw military service as an opportunity to defend themselves against bandits and partisans and to improve the situation of their families. In the Balkans, likewise, Muslim volunteers often simply hoped to defend their villages against Četnik, partisan, and Ustaša forces. When early German mobilization efforts did not lead to the expected rise in recruitment numbers, the SS began enlisting Muslims in some areas by force. In Travnik, central Bosnia, for instance, the roundup and conscription of Muslim recruits for Handžar took place during prayer, when recruiters entered a mosque and forcibly hauled away those men who seemed fit for military service.[31] The following morning, a number of these "recruits" fled into the forests.

Religious Ritual and Military Discipline

All Muslim soldiers enlisted in the German army enjoyed special religious rights. This policy, to some extent, had a precedent in the concessions granted to Muslim prisoners of war who had fought in the French Army.[32] In 1942 the Wehrmacht was the first to give concrete orders to this effect concerning Muslim recruits. The general directives for the Eastern Legions of 24 April 1942 had already instructed German officers to attach special importance to the "mental and confessional care of the legionnaires."[33] Two months later, German personnel working with Muslims in the Turkic battalions were instructed to "meet the religious needs" of the legionnaires.[34] "Experience has demonstrated that in the interest of discipline, religious care can, especially among the Mohammedans, raise general morale," the soldiers were told. A bit later, the operational headquarters under Niedermayer (162nd Turk Division) circulated regulations for religious practices in the Muslim field battalions.[35] It introduced an organizational basis for the religious life, including daily prayers, religious holidays, burial rites, dietary requirements, the employment of field imams, and the introduction of a religious-military hierarchy. In an order, Niedermayer explained that respect for religion formed the basis of the education and training of the soldiers.[36] The second operational headquarters, under Ralph von Heygendorff, issued similar decrees. When most of the battalions were fighting in the field, in the summer of 1943 Heygendorff reminded the German personnel to "respect" the "religious customs" of the "pious Mohammedans."[37] At the same time, he instructed his German officers to stress toleration of religion in their units: "It has to be emphasized that we grant complete religious freedom, whereas Bolshevism has suppressed the church."[38] In autumn 1944 the German personnel of the legions, which were now fighting in the defense of the Reich, were told that the "morale" of the Muslim soldiers would be strengthened if what was perceived as "holy" by the volunteers was respected.[39] "Members of the volunteer formation of the Mohammedan faith are trained by the best academic experts of Islam according to the rules of their belief, in order to comply with the units' wish for religious care by mullahs," the instruction sheet explained. It added that Germany itself had some "Mohammedan mosques" and that it was "the first European country to have printed the Qur'an in the original Arabic text and also in other versions and to have provided it to the volunteers." Eventually, Niedermayer even distributed 600 copies of Rodenwaldt's booklet *Der Islam* to train his German officers.[40] When the Waffen-SS began to create its first Muslim units in the Balkans in early 1943, it adopted the same strategy. In his mobilization order for Handžar, Himmler had already instructed that the Bosniaks should be granted "the old rights, which they had in the Austrian army," namely, the "free practice of religion, wearing of the fez."[41] Later, the Muslims of the Eastern SS Corps were to enjoy the same kind of religious concessions as the Muslims of Handžar.[42] The SS, too, made efforts to teach the German officers in Muslim units about Islam. Even a short German field manual was planned.[43] The SS Head Office had first considered distributing Rodenwaldt's *Der Islam* but soon abandoned the plan as it seemed too detailed for their purpose. In the end, a shorter brochure was produced, though never distributed because some SS officers objected to its focus on the Arab world.

Both the Wehrmacht and the SS guaranteed that their Muslim soldiers could follow daily religious rituals as well as observe the celebrations of the religious calendar. In August 1942 Niedermayer issued instructions exempting Muslims from military service during times of daily prayer.[44] On Fridays, their military service ended at four o'clock in the afternoon. Heygendorff's operational headquarters advised its German personnel to be respectful "when a Muslim, according to his traditions, performs his prayer in public," "not to watch him curiously during this, what was for him, a holy act," and to "avoid any disruption."[45] "In no case" were German soldiers permitted "to take photos of him during prayer!" Religious feasts and major Islamic holidays were also respected. After the war, Heygendorff boasted that he "mounted grand spectacles for the major celebrations such as 'Ramadan,' the 'Birthday of Mohammed,' etc."[46] The observation of the holy calendar gave Nazi authorities an ideal opportunity to utilize religious performances to convey political messages, celebrate a German-Islamic alliance, and promote themselves as patrons of Islam. As early as 1942, Niedermayer had allowed his Muslim legionnaires to go off duty from the afternoon of 9 October to noon on 10 October in order to celebrate the end of Ramadan.[47] German propaganda papers for the legions draw a vivid picture of religious celebrations in Muslim Wehrmacht units. In 1943, for instance, they reported on the *Ramadan Bairam* in a military recreation camp of the legions, attended by Gerhard von Mende and Heinz Unglaube of the East Ministry.[48] Another paper reported on simultaneous celebrations in a Caucasian unit in the Reich: "Here in Germany, the North Caucasians have the opportunity to organize their celebrations. In Soviet Russia this was never possible. This reveals, once again, how strong the friendship of Germany is."[49] Similarly, the report on the Ramadan celebration in a unit of the Azerbaijani Legion stressed that "the German authorities had done everything" in order to celebrate the feast "with dignity," again reminding Muslims that "there was no possibility of celebrating churchly feasts in the Soviet Union."[50] In autumn 1944, when the war had already reached the Reich, German propaganda for the legions spread reports of Ramadan celebrations in the units now employed in Germany.[51] In late 1944, the Germans organized splendid *Qurban Bairam* celebrations for soldiers of the Idel-Ural Legion in Dresden, Dargibell, and Breslau (Wrocław).[52] At the same time, the Azerbaijanis celebrated the *Qurban Bairam* in the Bohemian spa town of Carlsbad and in Berlin.[53]

The SS made even more extensive use of the daily religious practices and celebrations of the Islamic calendar. Every unit of Handžar held daily prayers, led by military imams. On Fridays, the SS granted the soldiers of the division a break from 10:00 a.m. to 2:00 p.m. for lunch, ablutions, and the Friday prayer, the *jumu'a*.[54] The *jumu'a* included the *salat*, the congregational prayer, and the *khutba*, the sermon that preceded the prayer and included comments on current affairs. Traditionally, the *khutba* had a distinct political function in Muslim societies and could now be exploited by the German authorities.[55] The act of the *jumu'a* itself was moreover to strengthen a sense of community as well as to enhance order and discipline in the units. "The dźuma [*sic*] is to be performed in a firm and ordered fashion," the SS instructed. Indeed, a series of propaganda photographs of the ritual show a field on the drill grounds of Neuhammer with Muslims arrayed in orderly lines, kneeling in prayer, facing Mecca, and their imam (Figures 7.1 and 7.2). Similar pictures were taken during the *Ramadan Bairam* celebration in Neuhammer in autumn 1943.[56] The German command eagerly exploited this occasion. Politicizing the sacred, Sauberzweig gave a speech to the soldiers, in which he linked reflections on the religious event with a call to arms: "So today's Bairam feast shall be for us an occasion for reflection, a celebration of faith and confidence, a source of delight and strength, an exhortation for unity and, at the same time, a rallying call for battle," he proclaimed.[57] "We want to become the best soldiers of our Führer!" Afterward, the imam of the division also addressed the troops. "The speeches of the division commander as well as of the division imam surely made a deep impression on the soldiers of the division," Zvonimir Bernwald, a German interpreter who served in Handžar, later wrote in his memoirs.[58] Indeed, the Germans were confident that the religious celebrations were crucial in boosting morale. In spring 1944 Sauberzweig ordered the organization of a "dignified celebration" of the *Mawlid*, with extra rations and prayers in all of the units of Handžar that were not directly involved in combat.[59] A few weeks later, directives formally regulated major religious holidays, most importantly the *Mawlid*, the month of Ramadan, *Ramadan Bairam*, and *Qurban Bairam*.[60] These instructions even provided a detailed calendar of Islamic holidays for 1944. During the month of Ramadan (20 August to 18 September 1944), soldiers were allowed to fast and to attend the special prayers, the *tarawih*. During the celebrations of *Mawlid, Ramadan Bairam*, and *Qurban Bairam*, the soldiers were, if the military situation allowed, exempt from duty. The feast marking the end of Ramadan (18 to 20 September 1944) began with a "great service at sunrise" on the first day; the second and third days were free of military service in the afternoons. During *Qurban Bairam*, the highest Islamic holiday (26 to 29 November 1944), soldiers were exempt from duty for the full four days. On these occasions, the imams were ordered to give political and religiously charged lectures, motivating the soldiers to fight. For *Ramadan Bairam* the imam was to speak on the meaning of the celebration and about "soldiery duties," while during *Qurban Bairam* a lecture was to be given on the meaning of the celebration, with reference to the life of soldiers and soldierly duties.[61] Finally, also in the Eastern formations, the SS tried to introduce religious holidays, although, due to the war situation, these were less regulated than in the Balkans. In the autumn of 1944, for instance, the entire 1st Eastern Muslim SS Regiment was, with Berger's permission, pulled out of the front lines to celebrate the end of Ramadan.[62]

German authorities also took Islamic dietary requirements into account. In his 1942 regulations, Niedermayer guaranteed that the Wehrmacht

7.1 Prayer of Muslim recruits of the SS Handžar Division, Neuhammer training ground (Silesia), 1943 (BAK, *Image 146-1977-136-03A, Mielke*).

would respect his Muslim soldiers' Islamic dietary customs, particularly the prohibition of pork.[63] Similar orders were given out for the Arab Wehrmacht soldiers.[64] The SS made even greater efforts to satisfy Muslim dietary requirements. Himmler became personally involved in the issue. In July 1943 he ordered Berger to find out "what Islam dictates to its soldiers with regard to provisions," adding that he was willing to guarantee the observance of religious requirements.[65] A few days later, Berger informed Himmler that soldiers had to abstain from pork and alcohol.[66] The *Reichsführer* reacted promptly, ordering: "All Muslim members of the Waffen-SS and police are granted, according to their religious rules, the steadfast special right never to receive for provision pork or sausage that contains pork or drink alcohol. A comparable alternative must be guaranteed in every case."[67] The SS even established a Muslim cooking course near Graz in southern Austria.[68] The concession was intended to strengthen the Muslims' morale, but it was also propagandistically relevant, Himmler emphasized. Despite all of its efforts, the SS remained concerned about

7.2 Prayer of Muslim recruits of the SS Handžar Division, Neuhammer training ground (Silesia), 1943 (BAK, *Image 146-1977-137-20*, Falkowski).

anti-German propaganda in the Balkans, which spread rumors that the Muslims of Handžar were forced to eat pork.[69] An internal SS report described these stories as "particularly ridiculous" but, at the same time, "exceptionally effective." "Such rumors should not be underestimated; one has therefore to confront them."[70]

German concerns about Islamic dietary regulations were not always shared by the Muslim recruits themselves. Most Muslims from the Eastern territories, for example, would consume alcohol, as is reflected throughout the archival documents. Muslims from the Balkans, on the other hand, often had stricter views. "They were more afraid of an empty tin can that had contained pork than of a hand grenade," a German soldier wrote about the Muslims of Skanderbeg after the war.[71] In any case, from the German perspective, it seemed most efficient to make wide-ranging provisions for food and drink.

Eventually Berlin even lifted the ban on ritual slaughter, a practice that had been prohibited (with the exception of emergency slaughter) for anti-Semitic reasons by the Law for the Protection of Animals (*Reichstierschutzgesetz*) of

21 April 1933.[72] During the Battle of France in 1940, German propaganda had still used horrific photographs that defamed slaughtering Muslim prisoners of war as bloodthirsty and savage.[73] In 1943 Heygendorff advised the German staff of the Eastern Legions to tolerate ritual slaughtering.[74] "The Mohammedans," he explained, "have their own customs in the slaughter of cattle, which appear crude and repulsive to us." Nevertheless, the German officers were instructed "to avoid a hasty, inequitable, and harsh judgment." Finally, on 6 February 1944, the High Command of the Wehrmacht formally ordered the General of the Volunteer Units, Köstring, to fully suspend the Law for the Protection of Animals in the case of all Muslim soldiers in the German army:

> The religious care of the Mohammedans within the Wehrmacht is an important component of the anti-Bolshevist antipropaganda [sic]. The Mohammedan celebrations require the ritual slaughtering of sacrificial animals. It is important not to affront the Mohammedan units by the application of a law that was passed at a time when the deployment of Mohammedan units in the German Wehrmacht could not have been anticipated. Accordingly, Mohammedan units employed in the German Wehrmacht are to be allowed to slaughter animals according to their customs and conventions.[75]

Before issuing this order, the Wehrmacht had sought Himmler's endorsement. An official of Himmler's staff had responded: "It has so far been considered self-evident that one does not interfere in the religious customs and conventions of these Mohammedan SS units and that therefore ritual slaughtering was also readily allowed by implication."[76] Even in this highly ideological matter, the SS demonstrated pragmatism. In practice, it fully tolerated ritual slaughter—though not without causing some confusion among its lower echelons. In January 1944, for instance, the office of Wilhelm Koppe, Himmler's infamous Higher SS and Police Leader East, in Cracow, inquired at the SS Head Office about granting Muslim soldiers the right to ritual slaughter. The SS officer in Cracow acknowledged that the Muslims were granted "every religious freedom" and that ritual slaughter "constitutes a holy practice for the Mohammedans."[77] On the other hand, however, he expressed concern as "ritual slaughter, according to the National Socialist view, is not defensible."[78] Replying immediately, the SS Head Office gave unambiguous instructions: "For tactical, political, and military reasons there are no objections to ritual slaughter in the Turkic units, all the more so as there is no intention to turn the Mohammedans into National Socialists."[79] For the soldiers of Handžar, the SS eventually also endorsed the slaughter according to Islamic ritual.[80]

Finally, on 28 June 1944, the High Command of the Wehrmacht gave a further order to also grant Muslim prisoners of war the right to practice ritual slaughter.[81] Again, the step was explained with reference to total military mobilization. "In the case of this exceptional permission, it must be noted that here too the religious care of Mohammedans has to be regarded as part of anti-Bolshevist propaganda, which, by emphasizing respect for the Mohammedan religion, is to contribute to the sustenance and enhancement of the motivation of the Mohammedans to engage in Germany's struggle," an internal report clarified.[82] In the final months of the war, these new policies even reached provincial Germany. In July 1944, members of a Muslim labor unit employed in the Upper Swabian village of Laupheim applied to the district farmers' council (*Kreisbauernschaft*) for a license for ritual slaughtering.[83] The council refused, whereupon a member of the Muslim unit turned to the head of the district authority (*Landrat*) and alluded to the Wehrmacht's June order. The district authority contacted the interior minister of Württemberg, who was equally perplexed. Eventually, the Reich Interior Ministry in Berlin ordered that "war-imprisoned Mohammedans are allowed to slaughter animals according to their ritual method."[84]

As with diet, the Germans also took into account Islamic conventions for clothing (at least, as they imagined them)—uniforms and emblems. When the Wehrmacht introduced special emblems for the Eastern Legions, the insignia of several Muslim units reflected religious iconography. This was most apparent in the arm patch of the Turkestani Legion, which featured the phrase "Allah is with us" (*Biz Alla Bilen*), along with the depiction of a mosque.[85] The mosque represented the great Mosque Shah-i Zinda of Samarkand. The medieval building on the Uzbek plateau was considered to be one of the holiest sites for Muslims in Central Asia.[86] As elsewhere, the SS adopted and extended the policy of the Wehrmacht. Handžar's insignia and flag, for instance, were emblazoned with the traditional Islamic scimitar, the *handžar*, which Bosnians associated with the era of Ottoman and Austrian rule and also gave the division its name.[87] The saber was set above the swastika, combining Nazi and Islamic iconography, visually symbolizing their alliance. Later, the Handžar insignia was also sewn onto the collars of the uniforms of the Eastern Turkic SS Corps.[88] Flags and emblems of various units were colored, either fully or in part, green. This, a German commander solemnly proclaimed when introducing the green flag of the Wehrmacht's Azerbaijani Legion, was "the color of the Muslims, the color of Mohammed."[89] Green, "the color of Islam," as an internal SS memo clarified, became the defining characteristic of the Eastern Muslim SS Corps, reflected on its armbands as well as its flag, which also depicted stripes, a crescent, a star, and a swastika.[90]

In the Balkans the SS went even further, designing Islamic headgear for its Muslim recruits. The fez became a distinguishing feature of Handžar's soldiers, a gray one for the field uniform and a red one for full dress.[91] The fez, which allowed the forehead to touch the ground during prayers, had become a distinctive material symbol of Islam in the late nineteenth century.[92] Over the course of the nineteenth century it had spread across the Muslim world, and by the end of the century, even Indian Muslims had begun to wear the fez as a symbol of a pan-Islamic solidarity with the Ottoman caliphate. In the religiously heterogeneous societies of the Balkans, the hat became a clear marker of confessional boundaries. Again, Himmler put himself personally in charge, and became involved in every detail of the Muslim division's dress code. After inspecting the preliminary designs, he requested changes, complaining that the form and color of the fezzes too closely resembled those of the Moroccans.[93] Himmler ordered them to be "redyed and cut a bit shorter" since, he maintained, "these outward semblances are tremendously important for the stabilization of the division." Himmler not only expressed interest in the details of Islamic dress culture but also connected cultural symbols directly with military morale and discipline. The fezzes were adorned with the Nazi eagle and the SS skull and bones insignia, again depicting the alliance between the Third Reich and Islam.

The Germans also made efforts from the outset to accommodate Islamic funerary practices and rites within the army's military organizational framework. In his general instructions of summer 1942 Niedermayer regulated the way in which dead Muslim soldiers in the Turkic units were to be buried: face and feet were to be wrapped with white cloth and the coffins covered with a white sheet (and later with the flag of their legion) by the leading field imam.[94] Soon, Heygendorff's headquarters of the Eastern Legions gave similar instructions.[95] Graves were to be oriented

7.3 Muslim recruits of the SS Handžar Division attend an Islamic burial, 1944 (*Ullstein*).

toward Mecca. Even the grave plates and headstones were adjusted to reflect Islamic iconography. The Muslim gravestones were made in the form of a plate instead of a cross and engraved with Islamic symbols, usually crescent and star. Burial ceremonies for those who died fighting for Hitler's New Order were led by military imams, according to Islamic ritual. The Wehrmacht command had, as shown, first dealt with the issue of Islamic burial when engaging with Muslim prisoners of war from the French army and indeed soon gave out similar orders for the burial of Soviet prisoners of war.[96] The SS followed suit in its own units. In Handžar, the imams had complete authority over funeraries (Figure 7.3).[97] Fallen Muslims were covered with linen (and if linen was not available, with paper) before being buried in a coffin. In a combination of military and religious ritual, they were entombed with military honors (so long as they had not committed suicide or been executed) and according to Islamic ritual by the imam. If no imam was present to conduct the ceremony, the prayer had to be spoken by an imam at some point in the future. In practice, the majority of dead Muslim soldiers in the Balkans were buried in existing military cemeteries and usually in the presence of an imam. In the Balkans, the SS commissioned local Muslim artisans to produce Islamic gravestones.[98]

Military Imams

The most important aspect of Berlin's efforts to strengthen the Islamic faith in its Muslim units was the employment of field imams. The official function of these "mullahs," as the Germans usually called them, was to provide spiritual succor and to lead the prayers. In practice, military imams were also intended to maintain control, discipline, and order within the units, to bestow religious legitimacy on the war, and to motivate Muslim soldiers to fight.

In the Wehrmacht's legions, the position of military imam was first introduced in the summer of 1942. The command of the operational headquarters of the 162nd Turk Division soon decided to set up a full religious-clerical hierarchy corresponding to the ranks of the military units: a "division mullah" (*Divisionsmulla*), who was installed at the headquarters; "legion mullahs" (*Legionsmulla*), who oversaw religious practices in the four Muslim legions; and "battalion mullahs" (*Battalionsmulla*, also called *Regimentsmulla*), who were employed in the individual battalions.[99] The division mullah and religious advisor to the central command of the 162nd division was Chief Mullah (*Obermulla*) Jumabaev. For the Azerbaijani Legion, Imam Pashaev was appointed legion mullah, while Mullah Inoyatev held the same position in the Turkestani Legion. The legion mullahs were authorized to appoint dozens of individual battalion mullahs for the units. Both the legion mullah and the division mullah held the military rank of company commander (*Kompaniefübrer*). The various battalion mullahs were appointed as platoon leaders (*Zugfübrer*). Division and battalion mullahs were to wear turbans, displaying their religious authority.

The establishment of a formalized religious hierarchy implied a level of religious institutionalization largely unknown in the Muslim world (even among twentieth-century Shi'ites). In fact, the Wehrmacht introduced into Islam a clerical system that had more in common with Christian ecclesiastical structures than Islamic modes of religious organization. In the new system, German (or, more generally, European) military rules, hierarchies, and structures fused with Islamic religious structures to create a hybrid, militarily organized religion. The religious hierarchy directly corresponded to the levels of military organization. The different clerical ranks were related to their deployment in divisions, legions, and battalions. Equally, the military ranks bestowed upon the mullahs were chosen according to the size of the unit in which they served. The combination of religious position and military rank provided them with a mixture of religious and military authority.

In May 1943 the SS adopted a similar policy in the Balkans, introducing various positions for imams in Handžar.[100] The plan of the SS to give its imams armbands with the crescent and star to distinguish them from the troops and to bolster their authority was rejected by the Foreign Office because both symbols constituted the national emblem of Turkey.[101] Like the Wehrmacht, the SS founded a sophisticated bureaucratic system of imams and regulated their responsibilities, military status, and duties in detail. The system became more complex once the division was employed in the field in March 1944.[102] Sauberzweig issued a "Service Instruction for Imams" (*Dienstanweisung für Imame*), which replaced an earlier one from spring 1943, telling imams in detail how to organize themselves within the units and how to execute their duties, primarily the "spiritual care" and "ideological education" of soldiers.[103] Moreover, Sauberzweig gave out an order that regulated the status of the imams in relation to soldiers and German officers.[104] In the individual units (regiments or battalions), the imams were granted the status of officers of the commanding staff. Leading imams also carried a pistol and, in combat, a machine pistol.[105] All of the imams were subordinated to the so-called division imam, who was based at the division headquarters and worked directly with Sauberzweig. The post was first held by *SS-Sturmbannführer* Abdullah Muhasilović, who had served in the Yugoslav army and was the most experienced imam among Handžar's recruits.[106] His deputy was Imam Husein Džozo, a respected religious leader who had studied at al-Azhar in the 1930s and now assumed the rank of an *SS-Hauptsturmführer*.[107] Toward the end of the war Muhasilović was replaced by the young *SS-Obersturmführer* (then *SS-Hauptsturmführer*) Halim Malkoč, who had also served in the Yugoslav army and had been the battalion imam of Handžar's SS Mountain Pioneer Battalion 13 (*SS-Gebirgs-Pionier-Bataillons 13*).[108] When recruiting the first military imams for Handžar, the mufti of Jerusalem recalled in his memoirs, the SS again sought help from the religious institutions in Bosnia and Herzegovina and from Muhamed Pandža, who was put in charge of the selection of young imams, mostly graduates of the prestigious Gazi Husrev Beg Madrasa in Sarajevo and of al-Azhar.[109]

Later the SS also established a system of field imams in its Eastern Muslim units.[110] Chief imam of the 1st Eastern Muslim SS Regiment was a certain Imam Kamalov.[111] In August 1944 negotiations were held about the post of a "chief imam" of the entire Eastern Turkic SS Corps, in which both al-Husayni and Harun al-Rashid became involved. In the end, three candidates were put on the short list.[112] The first was Alimjan Idris, even though he was already occupied at the Foreign Office and the Ministry of Propaganda, organizing German propaganda for the Muslim world. The second candidate was a Crimean Tatar who had fled to Romania—his name is unknown today. Moreover, there was Mullah Abdulgani Osman, a Muslim who had for some time been in charge of Tatar prisoners of war by order of the East Ministry and had also written on religious matters for the propaganda paper of the Wehrmacht's Volga Tatar Legion.[113] Like Idris, with whom he had a problematic personal relationship, he had been in Germany since the First World War. Although al-Rashid had preferred Abdulgani Osman, apparently the Crimean Tatar was first asked to take the job.[114] Eventually the Usbek Nurredin Namangani became "chief imam" of the corps, holding the officer rank of *SS-Untersturmführer*.[115] Freed by German troops from an NKWD prison in Minsk in 1941, Namangani had first served as imam in Mayer-Mader's Wehrmacht unit before it was transferred to the SS. Abdulgani Osman continued recruiting prisoners of war, though now for the SS. In November, Olzscha issued an authorization that gave Osman access to all of the companies and factories in the Reich and the occupied territories that employed workers from the East to ensure that the Muslims among them also enjoyed spiritual care and, more importantly, could be recruited to fight within the ranks of the SS.[116] In the last months of the war it was becoming equally difficult to find qualified Muslims to fill imam posts in the units of the Eastern Turkic SS. Al-Rashid made some attempts to enlist imams from the Wehrmacht.[117] In the end, though, he recruited them primarily from among his own soldiers and had them trained in the field by his chief imam.[118]

The major task of imams in the Wehrmacht and the SS was to maintain discipline and fighting morale. They were responsible not only for the spiritual care of soldiers but also for the support of German military justice in the units and the troops' ideological indoctrination.

Both the Wehrmacht and SS made frequent use of the religious authority of their field imams when settling legal disputes or imposing disciplinary punishments. They were to give legal sentences religious authenticity and legitimacy. In his general instructions for military justice of 15 May

1943, Heygendorff recommended that "for all difficult penal law cases" in "Mohammedan units" there should be consultation with the "mullah" before any judgment was made.[119] After the war, he recalled that the punishment suggested by the imams was usually more severe than that which the German officer intended to impose.[120] In practice, field imams also acted as prosecutors and intermediaries, actively approaching the German command to ask for punishment of Muslim delinquents in their units. Well aware of their new religious rights, Muslim soldiers sometimes tried to use religious arguments to escape punishment. In May 1943, for instance, a Muslim legionnaire who had manipulated his paybook swore on the Qur'an and his flag that he was innocent.[121] When his guilt was later proven, Heygendorff noted furiously that the "legionnaire did not balk at abusing what are, for a Mohammedan, the holiest symbols just to substantiate his mendacious statements." In another case, a murderer legitimized his deed with reference to the traditions of vendetta. When the imam of his unit was consulted, the cleric dismissed the claim as a crude excuse. These cases were made public among the German staff of the Eastern Troops to urge them to consult an imam in every eventuality. Control of military justice, however, remained in the hands of the Germans, who were often reluctant to accept justice on Islamic grounds. In one case, a Muslim officer who had executed a Turkic recruit when he caught him violating statute "§175 St.G.B.," which prohibited homosexuality and bestiality (it is likely the latter was the case as only one man was shot, according to the report), claimed "that the Mohammedan faith and the traditional law" made this punishment necessary.[122] The Germans consulted the imam of the battalion, who confirmed the death penalty. Yet, the Wehrmacht's military justice administration (*Heeresfeldjustizabteilung*) did not accept this judgment since the officer had, in their eyes, acted as a vigilante. Like the Wehrmacht, the SS also made some attempts to combine Islamic and German military justice. In May 1944 Fürst ordered that Muslim soldiers of the Eastern Turkic SS Corps be judged "at least formally" by their own judges—"jurisdiction in accordance with Islam."[123] In Handžar, Sauberzweig did not go this far. He only ordered that the imams were to talk to Muslim delinquents and to "influence" them "morally and ethically."[124]

Over the months, the imams became pillars of control in the units. Imam Malkoč played a central role in the suppression of the revolt of Villefranche in autumn 1943 by convincing the Muslim recruits to turn against the rebel leaders.[125] Similarly, it was the chief imam of the Eastern Turkic SS Corps, Nurredin Namangani, who questioned the Alimov rebels for the Germans after their revolt in December 1944.[126] After the revolt, al-Rashid reported that the unit, "substantially influenced by the mullahs and especially by the chief mullah," was stabilized again.[127] The SS also attempted to use the imams for control and surveillance in the units. In Handžar, the division imam had to send frequent reports to Sauberzweig, informing him about the morale in the units, among the imams, and among the civil population.[128] In the summer of 1944, for instance, Handžar's division imam forwarded two letters that he had received from a unit imam to show the attitude of Muslim SS soldiers fighting in the Mostar region.[129] Likewise, every unit imam of Handžar, at least from spring 1944 on, was required to submit monthly reports to the German command.[130]

Arguably the most important duty of the military imams was the spread of propaganda. The "mullahs" were expected to spearhead the promotion of a German-Muslim alliance in the ranks. Heygendorff told his German officers that there was "no doubt" that the mullahs, if treated properly, would be the "best prop in the education of our legionnaires."[131] Rosenberg emphasized that "Muslim clerics" had a role to play as disseminators of anti-Bolshevik propaganda in the units.[132] In a programmatic statement by the operational headquarters of the 162nd Infantry Division to all legion and battalion mullahs in May 1943, mullah Jumabaev emphasized: "It is necessary that we accompany our youth into battle, that we cheer their efforts to defeat the enemy, that we are familiar with military training and prove to be courageous in all situations."[133]

In its attempts to turn Muslim recruits into political soldiers, the SS in particular made use of the imams as propagandists in the units. On 19 May 1943, Berger issued a general decree on the "Ideological-Spiritual Education of the Muslim SS Division," which identified Handžar's field imams as the most important transmitters of political-religious propaganda.[134] The decree made clear that the imams were to act as the major propagandists in the units and gave a detailed outline of the intended nature of their propaganda. The propaganda was to emphasize the alleged "common enemies" of Germans and Muslims, identified as "Judaism," "Anglo-Americanism," "Communism," "Freemasonry," and "Catholicism (Vatican)," together with alleged shared ideals, including militancy, the role of morality, and tradition. In the program, Berger also clarified his ideas about the relationship between Islam and National Socialism from a *völkisch* perspective: "It is not intended to find a synthesis of Islam and National Socialism or to impose National Socialism on the Muslims." Rather, Berger instructed that National Socialism was to be seen as the "genuine *völkisch* German worldview," while Islam was to be seen as "the genuine *völkisch* Arabic worldview." The Muslims of the Balkans would "*völkisch-racially*" be part of the Germanic world, while remaining ideologically part of the Arab world: "Through the deployment of a Muslim SS division there may hereby, for the first time, be established a connection between Islam and National Socialism, or rather between the Arab and the Germanic world on an open, honest basis, as this division, in terms of blood and race, is influenced by the North; in terms of ideology, in contrast, by the Orient."[135]

The propaganda work of the imams of Handžar was organized by a special office for political and ideological education. This office was under the command of the political officer of Handžar, Heinrich Gaese, a former schoolteacher, and later, after the division had returned to the Balkans, of Ekkehard Wangemann, a pastor from Mecklenburg. It was concerned with all political and cultural matters, including Islam.[136] A party veteran, Wangemann took his job particularly seriously. On 8 April he summoned all imams and commanders of the division to a school next to the great mosque of Brčko.[137] In his speech to them, Wangemann left no doubt about the central role Islam played in the unit's propaganda.[138] "It has become clear that the political interests of National Socialism and those of Islam converge to a large extent, and that, furthermore, the ideological foundations also rest, in certain points, on the same basis." The division, he made clear, was not just a military unit in the Balkans but had the "higher political purpose of building a bridge from Europe to world Islam" (*Weltislam*). Every imam had been thoroughly instructed about this higher purpose. It was absolutely necessary, Wangemann emphasized, that the imams be supported by the German officers in their endeavor "to raise the soldiers to become good Muslims." Similarly, Handžar's "Service Instruction for Imams" of 1944 taught imams that "National Socialism and Islam are close in their ideological foundations."[139] "They have, moreover, the same enemies. The educational aim is therefore the same for both: the determined and enthusiastic fighter, who is willing to risk his life for a better European order." The imam's military value lay in his contribution to the "physical and mental well-being and thereby the military effectiveness and combat strength of the troops." In short: "The imam is the custodian of Islam in the division. He must evoke and reveal the strengths of religion to support the development of the members of the division to become good SS men and soldiers." Following the Friday prayer, the imams were to indoctrinate the soldiers politically.[140] They also gave weekly political classes, usually held in the early morning, in which they would comment not only on religion but also on the current political and military situation. Moreover, they were to spread their propaganda constantly while interacting with the soldiers in the field, during halts, cantonment, and battle: "The imam therefore also must follow the troops in combat and offer, through devoted commitment of his person, a stirring incentive."[141] The Handžar command tightly controlled the imams' propaganda activities. While their spiritual work in the units was overseen by the division imam, their propaganda work among the troops was controlled by Sauberzweig and Gaese, and later by Wangemann, who continuously instructed the imams on ideological matters.[142] In practice, the imams incessantly used religious occasions to spread political messages. At the *Ramadan Bairam* celebrations on the training grounds of Neuhammer in 1943, for instance, division imam Muhasilović delivered a speech that firmly interwove politics and religion. "The Muslims of the entire world are engaged in a terrible struggle to the death," he claimed, putting the mission of the division in the context of a wider, pan-Islamic framework.[143] Repeating the usual dichotomy and referring to holy scripture, Muhasilović declared that the entire world was divided into two camps:

> One stands under the leadership of the Jews, about whom God says in the Qur'an: They are God's enemies and yours. And that is the English, Americans, and Bolsheviks, who fight against faith, against God, morality and a just order. On the other side stands National Socialist Germany with its allies, under the leadership of Adolf Hitler, who fights for God, faith, morality and a better and fairer world order, as well as for a fair distribution of all goods that God has created for all people.

The imam then reminded the soldiers of the misery their families were enduring back in the Balkans and called for the liberation of their homeland.

"Then we will celebrate our Bairam feast again in peaceful contentment because we follow the way and perform the labor that God has shown us."[144]

Well aware that their lack of religious authenticity could become an obstacle if they tried to engage directly in Islamic propaganda, the Germans were eager to use the imams as carriers of their propaganda in the units. Several Wehrmacht instructions explicitly warned Germans not to engage in religious propaganda. "Beware, however, of the mistake," a leaflet warned German officers in the summer of 1943, "of engaging in religious propaganda," emphasizing that this was the task of the imams.[145] A few months later, another instruction sheet underlined: "No religious propaganda from our side," again remarking that this was to be left to the "mullahs."[146] German officers were advised to support the imams and to enhance their respect and influence. At the same time, the Wehrmacht command stressed that the "legionnaires have to fully accept them as religious leaders." Indeed, the Germans were cautious when it came to the imams' authority. In a North Caucasian battalion, the commander asked to replace his battalion imam, explaining that, "in regard to the prominent role that religious life plays among the Islamic peoples," he was "unsuitable, as he possessed no authority among the legionnaires."[147] In Handžar, Wangemann even requested the replacement of the division imam, Muhasilović. Although he acknowledged that Muhasilović was a good speaker, he complained that he had "however completely failed as leader of the imams."[148] Nothing happened, and a few months later Muhasilović deserted and had to be replaced by Malkoč.[149]

Muhasilović was not the only imam who deserted in the final months of the war. A commander from the Eastern Legion, Hans-Günther Seraphim, reported that during the deployment of his unit (part of the 162nd Infantry Division) in Italy toward the end of the war, the only case of desertion was the escape of a mullah.[150] The battalion mullah of an infantry regiment fighting in Italy ran off, taking with him all religious charitable donations, and allegedly relocated to San Marino "to open a bar there." If the story was true and not a sarcastic invention of the Wehrmacht officer who recounted it, this would have been, of course, one of the highest forms of religious sin. In the course of the war, however, there were few critical reports about the military mullahs. Overall, they seemed to meet the demands of the Germans, who appeared persuaded of their usefulness. A few months after the employment of the imams, an army propaganda officer reported that they had proven themselves to be "especially intractable enemies of Bolshevism."[151] A year later, an instruction sheet addressed to Wehrmacht officers of the Eastern Legions emphasized that the mullahs regularly engaged in combat, even though they were not required to do so, and, with "their weapon in their hand," were a "shining example" to their units.[152]

Imam Schools

Few of the mullahs in the German units had worked as imams before the war. In particular those from the Soviet Union usually had little theological training, given Moscow's restrictions on religious life. Most of them were merely respected individuals who were roughly familiar with religious ritual and doctrine. The so-called imam courses and mullah schools were to provide military imams with some kind of religious education.[153] More important, however, was the need to ensure the highest level of ideological trustworthiness among them since they were to function as important distributors of ideas and propagandists. In all of the courses, the military imams were trained according to a specific religious interpretation colored by Berlin's political objectives and, ultimately, according to Nazi ideology. It is remarkable that this Islamic education was organized within a German institutional framework and at times even led by German teachers, endowing non-Muslims with significant authority in matters of religious knowledge, representation, and interpretation.

The idea to establish a school to educate imams—initially with the intention of employing them in prisoner of war camps to win over Muslim Red Army soldiers—had been circulating since autumn 1941.[154] In June 1944 the Wehrmacht finally institutionalized this education in the form of mullah courses (*Mullahlehrgänge*) given in some army barracks in Göttingen. These courses were organized by the young and ambitious Orientalist Bertold Spuler, a party member who had just been appointed professor at the University of Munich and who after the war became one of Germany's leading experts in Islamic studies.[155] Although Spuler had a solid understanding of the history and practice of Islam, a command of the various languages of the participants, and an ability to read the Qur'an in Arabic, the fact that a non-Muslim was acting as a religious authority and teaching

Muslims in matters of faith provoked some protest.[156] Spuler, however, consulted with the chief imam of the Turkestani Legion, Mullah Inoyatev, who held the position of an official inspector of the courses and was soon supported by the mufti of the Ostland, Jakub Szynkiewicz.[157] Szynkiewicz had fled his residence in Vilnius in early July, before it was occupied by Red Army soldiers, and arrived in Göttingen in late August. He was a recognized authority on Islamic theology. His doctoral dissertation on medieval Islamic writing became a classic in the field.[158] More importantly, Szynkiewicz had experience in the organization of religious instruction as he had set up courses for the education of imams in interwar Poland.[159]

By the end of 1944, Spuler had organized six mullah training courses in Göttingen, each of thirty to forty Muslims. The classes often lasted no longer than two weeks.[160] Spuler wrote numerous reports about his activities in Göttingen for the command of the Eastern Troops, and these draw a detailed picture of the courses. From the outset, Spuler attended to the religious demands of his students. In a general memorandum, which he sent to the army command before the first course began, he urged respect for the Muslims' religious practices.[161] Religious rituals and holidays had to be included in the course schedules. On Fridays no classes were to take place, and the *jumu'a* had to be organized. Rugs were to be provided for the prayer rituals. The German staff was not to watch the prayers, Spuler insisted. "The prayer of a human being is no spectacle!" The food was to be prepared strictly according to Islamic rules and, ideally, by a Muslim cook. Indeed, once the courses started, the Wehrmacht made sure not to deliver pork, and a Turkestani cook prepared the food in accordance with Islamic demands.[162] And when the third course conflicted with the month of Ramadan, Spuler took this into account, accepting that the fasting, combined with the summer heat, would have a negative effect on the students' ability to concentrate.[163]

The spectrum of students in Göttingen was diverse. In the second course, Spuler was very much impressed by a Muslim who had been trained in a religious madrasa as a boy and had memorized the entire Qur'an.[164] Generally, though, the students had little knowledge of theological issues and the history of Islam. The official educational aim of the courses, according to Spuler, was to teach the basic principles of theology and to acquaint future military imams with some of the principal rituals.[165] In the first part of the courses, Spuler taught the Qur'an and discussed some of its most important passages. He lectured on the life of the Prophet, general aspects of Islamic history, the history of the Turkic peoples, and, most importantly, the political role of Islam in the war. Daily readings from the Qur'an and recitations were also part of the program. Spuler believed that only a strict interpretation of Islam would be suited to military imams: "It does not require any explanation that the basis has to be the orthodox . . . conception of Islam (devoid of any modern critique)."[166] In the second part of the seminars, practical issues were taught. The students learned how to lead prayers and services, as well as how to conduct funerals and to arrange the feasts of the yearly religious cycle.[167] Spuler asked to employ a "reliable Muslim cleric" to direct this part of the course.[168] Initially, the chief imam of the Turkestani Legion, Inoyatev, was to assume the job but did not turn up in Göttingen for the first course.[169] During the third course, Szynkie- wicz finally arrived and took over the practical part. A polyglot and cosmo- politan with a good sense of German interests, he made a "very good im- pression" on Spuler.[170] Inoyatev became involved only once, delivering a guest lecture to the students of the second course on the role of the field imams in the war against Stalin and the extermination of Bolshevism.[171] Spuler's syllabus could hardly hide the fact that one of the central pillars of the courses was the ideological and political training of future imams. They were instructed to conduct theological discussions with individual soldiers, defend the legion against attacks from heretics, and encourage the soldiers to fight alongside the Germans.[172] The principal aim of the courses was to motivate the mullahs to emerge as convinced enemies of Bolshe- vism and to use their religious authority and standing to influence soldiers at the front.

After each course, the students had to take written exams, which were divided into a theological and a practical part. The questions were, from the perspective of a contemporary Islamic scholar, rather simple and give an idea of the low level of religious knowledge among the imams from the East. The theological part of the test included questions about the life of the Prophet, the *hijra*, Muhammad's wars and his death, the five pillars of Islam, the main sources of Islamic law, the exegesis of the Qur'an, and the influential medieval Islamic theologian al-Ghazali.[173] The second part of the exam included such questions as "What are we to answer the god- less?" and about "The (spiritual) weapons of the mullah."[174] Graduating mullahs, Spuler had suggested in his initial memorandum, should be given a specific badge of rank that displayed their religious authority.[175] He had proposed an emblem depicting crescent and star in gold or silver. Spuler also hoped to bestow specific decorations that would appeal to the "mentality of the Muslims."[176] Whether these badges and decorations were ever created is unknown.

The languages of instruction were Turkish and other Turkic dialects, most importantly Uzbek.[177] Occasionally lessons were also taught in Tajik and Russian. At times Spuler had to improvise. In the fifth course, for instance, lectures were translated from Russian into Avar for two Avar students.[178] Spuler also faced some difficulties with the religious literature. The Qur'an was available in Arabic but not in Russian or Turkish, not even in extract form, although Spuler repeatedly asked for translations.[179] Attempts by the Wehrmacht to acquire translated copies of the Qur'an from the Islamic Central Institute in Berlin were unsuccessful.[180] In the end, Spuler translated parts of the Qur'an from Arabic into Turkish for his students.[181] Only very few imams, mostly students from the Caucasus, had some knowledge of Arabic.

A major problem for Spuler's courses was the participation of both Sunnis and Shi'ites in the same classes. The first class, which was attended by Sunni Turkestanis and Shi'a Azerbaijanis, had, according to Spuler, already revealed friction between the two groups.[182] He observed "that the confessional division is even stronger than the national one" and that the two Sunni Azerbaijanis mingled mainly with the Sunni Turkestanis rather than with the Shi'a Azerbaijanis.[183] A second attempt to organize a joint class for Sunnis and Shi'ites during the third training session failed as well.[184] Spuler noted that the differences between the groups proved too profound. Dogmatic and religious-historical questions could not be covered without exposing significant differences. Spuler, who was skeptical about mixing the groups from the outset, ultimately advised against teaching Sunnis and Shi'ites together.[185] Alluding to "the depth of the religious sentiment and force of Shi'a confessional conviction" and the "religious fervor of the Shi'ites," he warned the Wehrmacht command not to "propagate an artificial unity, which does not exist and which is rejected by the Muslims."[186] Spuler's criticism was also directed against the SS, which had fewer reservations about promoting Islamic unity.

The SS established several of its own programs for the religious instruction of field imams. As early as summer of 1943, the SS Head Office had organized a short training course for the first imams of Handžar. Co-ordinated by the division's propaganda section, the imams were trained for three weeks in a villa in Babelsberg, near Berlin. Interpreter Zvonimir Bern-wald, who was involved in organizing the course, later remembered the initial bewilderment of the German SS officers who had been assigned to establish the curriculum.[187] As all of the participants—among them Abdul-lah Muhasilović, Husein Džozo, and Halim Malkoč—had received a solid theological education before the war, religious instruction was considered to be of lesser importance—a major difference from the courses organized for military imams from the Soviet Union.[188] The aim of the Babelsberg course was rather to teach the imams National Socialist ideology and to turn them into motivated SS officers. Once all of the participants had ar-rived in Babelsberg, the Germans sent al-Husayni to them to set out the overall agenda of the course. In his speech to the imams, the mufti pro-moted the idea of an intimate relationship between National Socialism and Islam.[189] His remarks basically echoed the points that had been made in Berger's decree on the "Ideological-Spiritual Education of the Muslim SS Division" two months earlier but went further, constituting in fact the most elaborate attempt ever made to connect National Socialist ideas with Islam. The mufti emphasized four principal areas that formed the basis of an alliance between the Third Reich and the Muslim world. First, he de-clared that, throughout history, Germany had never attacked or acted with hostility to any Islamic country. He then talked about the usual three al-leged common enemies. Germany, he argued, confronted "world Judaism," the "hereditary enemy of Islam"; England, which repressed millions of Muslims, had destroyed Muslim rule in India, and had played a major role in the abolition of the Ottoman caliphate; and finally Bolshevism, which "tyrannized 40 million Muslims" and posed a direct threat to the entire Islamic world. The mufti then referred to traits allegedly shared by Islam and Nazism. National Socialism in "many respects" overlapped with the "Islamic worldview," he proclaimed. Also, Islam and National Socialism both prized the idea of leadership. After the death of the Prophet, Muslims had followed the authority of a single person, the caliph; the Nazis fol-lowed the absolute authority of the Führer. Islam, the mufti explained, im-posed "order, obedience, and discipline" on Muslims, just like National Socialism did on Germans. One of the main duties of each Muslim was the permanent fight against the enemies of Islam; to fall in this battle was a divine honor. In principle, Muslims were prepared to sacrifice everything for their doctrine, just like National Socialists were for their ideology. Also, the mufti explained, the attitudes of Muslims and National Socialists toward the ideals of community, family, procreation, motherhood, and the education of children were very similar, as was their work ethic. From beginning to end, the speech was cast in deeply religious rhetoric interspersed with verses from the Qur'an and examples from the early history of Islam, which gave it the character of a sermon. The Qur'an called on "all Muslims" to fight against the Jews, al-Husayni explained, recalling the tale of the Jews of Khaybar, who had attempted to kill the Prophet. Qur'anic verses were also introduced to support the ideal of a single leader, to portray Islam as a great power, and, most importantly, to prove the "militant spirit of Islam." The Qur'an, the mufti argued, called for "the fight to ultimate victory." He concluded: "It is the task and duty of all Muslims to unite for the defense of this impending threat and to cooperate with their friends hand in hand. The genuine cooperation of the 400 million Muslims with their true friends, the Germans, can have a great influence on the course of the war and is, for both sides, very advantageous." The Muslim division of Bosnia was on a "holy mission" to spearhead this alliance.[190] In practice, some of the themes outlined in al-Husayni's speech were given higher priority than others in the classes, as Bernwald later recalled: While teachers engaged in anti-Jewish agitation and discussed the evils of the Anglo-Americans and godless Communism, portraying Tito's partisans as enemies of Islam, subjects like Freemasonry and Catholicism were largely ignored.[191] Finally, the imams also received some military training.

The following year, shortly after the Wehrmacht had launched the courses in Göttingen, the SS, too, institutionalized religious instruction for field imams. In 1944 the SS Head Office founded two Islamic centers for religious education. The first was opened in April, in the small town of Guben in Brandenburg. The idea had been on the table since late 1943, when Berger had suggested that Himmler open an institute for the education of imams, which would also train them "politically in an appropriate way."[192] The so-called imam institute (*Imamen-Institut*) was set up in a run-down hotel that had been taken over by the SS.[193] After the building had been hastily turned into a school, the SS organized an inauguration ceremony on 21 April 1944, which was attended by Berger, Imam Husein Džozo, and al-Husayni. In his opening address, delivered in Arabic and translated into Bosnian, the mufti expressed his delight at the founding of the institute, in which he saw proof of the "prosperity of the alliance between Muslims and the Greater German Reich."[194] This alliance, he pointed out, was firmly based on "common interests and objectives." Finally, al-Husayni exhorted the future imams: "Your obligation is not just to lead your comrades in prayer and in religious matters but also to strengthen that moral attitude within them, which Islam demands from the Muslim and which makes him a brave soldier who despises death in order to achieve a free life." Their "duty," al-Husayni concluded, was the "strengthening and deepening of the alliance between the Muslims and their ally: Greater Germany." A second speech was given by Imam Džozo, who thanked Himmler and Berger for their "sincere friendship" with "us and all Muslims."[195] Džozo emphasized the historical moment of the war that would transform the world: "In this transformation, two great ideological powers met, became acquainted, and fraternized: the force of the Islamic view of life and the National Socialist political worldview." The institute, the imam announced, was to strengthen the "friendship between the Islamic world and National Socialist Germany," declaring: "We are ready and strongly determined to take great pains for the realization of the new world and the New Order."[196] The courses were taught by Arab scholars from the clique of the mufti and some Bosnians around Džozo.[197] Combat drills and shooting instructions were also part of the curriculum. "The madrasa believed in combining spiritual training with full military training, so every imam was a trained fighter and officer," al-Husayni later remembered.[198] The mufti himself repeatedly visited the school to give lectures and meet students and teachers.[199] According to al-Husayni, fifty imams graduated in Guben in two terms of four months each. In the final months of the war, the SS would indoctrinate Bosnian imams in locations closer to their area of deployment. In late autumn 1944, when the division was already dissolving, it organized a training course for sixty imams of Handžar near Budapest.[200] The SS even organized an incognito visit by the mufti, scheduled for 7 October 1944, though it is unclear from the surviving documents whether it ever took place.

The SS set up the Guben institute primarily to train imams for the units of the Balkans. For Muslim recruits from the Eastern territories, it founded a second, much bigger institution in Dresden, which was formally connected to Olzscha's *Arbeitsgemeinschaft Turkestan*. The so-called

SS mullah school (*SS-Mulla Schule*) opened on 26 November 1944. As in Guben, the SS used the inauguration ceremony to celebrate a German-Muslim alliance. This time the opening speech was given by Walter Schellenberg, who repeated the usual rhetoric.[201] Drawing on historical associations, he emphasized Germany's traditional bonds with Islam and its long-standing support for the Muslim world, which had been constantly exploited by the imperial powers. Germany, the head of the SD foreign intelligence reminded his audience, had already favored Muslim prisoners at the Wünsdorf prisoner camp during the First World War. "The outbreak of the Second World War took place at a time," he explained, "when the völkisch powers in the Soviet Union had not yet been broken, whereas the decline of the cultural and religious traditions had advanced threateningly." Schellenberg welcomed the willingness of the non-Russian people of the Soviet Union to fight with Germany against Bolshevism and called Islam the "most important bulwark against a national, *völkisch*, and cultural uprooting of the Eastern Turks," as well as a remedy to prevent their "infection by Bolshevism." In this respect, Islam was seen as the "custodian" of the Eastern Turks' "biological substance." He called upon the Muslims to teach the younger generation "the traditions of the past, in order to be able to cope with the future," and to confront the "crutches of Bolshevik ideology" and of the "Russian, racially impure worldview." The speech demonstrated a surreal self-confidence. In fact, Schellenberg's proclamation of the liberation of Islam from Soviet suppression came at a time when most of the Eastern territories had already been reconquered by the Red Army. However, he left observers in no doubt about the propagandistic character of the school, where the transfer of religious knowledge had become a secondary goal.

The school was based in a villa at 2 Lothringer Weg in the affluent Blasewitz neighborhood of Dresden. The building had previously been owned by a Jewish family and later been used by the Nazis as a *Judenhaus* to group Jews together, and had repeatedly been mentioned by the famous Jewish diarist Victor Klemperer, who, in early November 1944, also noted the "mysterious Muslim study group" there.[202] Reiner Olzscha, who was assigned to set up the school, wrote a report after the war that draws a detailed picture of the institution.[203] The interior of the building was designed to reflect Islamic architectural styles. The main entrance hall was decorated with a mosaic patterned after those of the mosques of Central

Asia and adorned with Qur'anic verses. Another room, which was similarly ornamented and furnished with a prayer niche, or *mihrab*, and rugs, became the school's prayer hall. The SS also purchased various Islamic cultural artifacts such as vases and pictures to provide what was, in their eyes, an authentic Islamic environment. Responsible for the interior architecture of the villa was Kurt Erdmann, an expert in Islamic culture and art history in the Asian department of the Pergamon Museum in Berlin. The renovation and redecoration of the building, which Erdmann oversaw together with architects from Berlin and Dresden, took half a year. "The outer appearance was to resemble Islamic religious facilities to create the right atmosphere," explained Olzscha after the war. He also acquired various Islamic books from France, Bosnia, and the Netherlands. Among them were some rare ancient Islamic texts purchased in Sarajevo. Qur'ans could apparently be obtained free from the Propaganda Ministry.[204] Yet, as in Göttingen, translations of the Qur'an were limited. Before the opening of the school in November, the East Ministry had already announced that, for the courses in Dresden and Göttingen, the "possibilities for the acquisition of Qur'ans from different countries were exhausted."[205]

A major obstacle emerged in the search for a qualified director for the school. The SS leadership hoped to appoint Alimjan Idris. Idris, however, was still in the service of the Propaganda Ministry and the Foreign Office, where he was one of the men in charge of Germany's propaganda in the Islamic world, especially the Turkic-speaking regions. Thus, when Olzscha offered him the Dresden job in November 1944, Idris had to refuse.[206] However, he agreed to come to Dresden once or twice a week to supervise the classes and to teach until a permanent director was found. The Propaganda Ministry was displeased with the plans of the SS Head Office to recruit Idris since, as State Secretary Naumann of the ministry put it, he constituted "the soul of our Turkish broadcast program."[207] Nevertheless, in the end, the Propaganda Ministry agreed to release Idris three days a week, and so he became the unofficial director of the mullah school.[208] "He seemed to be a convinced Mohammedan . . . and was for this reason as well as his knowledge and his age especially suited for the school," Olzscha remembered later.[209] Idris brought with him his son, Ildar Idris, who worked as an interpreter and assistant to his father until he was drafted into the Eastern Muslim SS Corps.[210]

In contrast to the Wehrmacht in Göttingen, the SS was eager to employ only Muslims as teachers.[211] For the recruitment of staff, Olzscha consulted Professor Richard Hartmann. Olzscha first hired a certain Doctor Murad. Born in Mecca but of Tatar origin, Murad claimed that he had run a madrasa in Turpan in the Muslim Uyghur region of Xinjiang before he came to Germany, where he had studied medicine. He had impressed Olzscha with his knowledge of the Qur'an and his language abilities. Murad was involved in the planning of the school, but friction with Olzscha and Idris led to his departure before it opened. The recruitment of teachers proved to be difficult. In the end, two elderly mullahs from the Crimea were hired. Moreover, Shakir Eriss, the imam of Riga, who had fled with his wife from the advancing Red Army, arrived at the school. Though soon judged an unsuitable teacher by Idris, Eriss was allowed to stay at the school as a guest. The staff also included an Arab, a Bulgarian Muslim, and the eager Major Killinger, a retired German army officer and convert to Islam. Given this group, it is hardly surprising that Olzscha noted after the war that "until the end, Idris remained the only fully qualified instructor." The SS had initially hoped to recruit teachers from among the most gifted students of each class, who would then be trained in an advanced course for their tasks.[212] Until the end of the war, Olzscha and his colleagues tried in vain to appoint religiously educated Muslims, including the Syrian Rida Muhammad Stambuli and the Azerbaijani Mehmet Resulzade.[213] As late as March 1945, Idris made an attempt to recruit five writers from the SS newspaper *Türk Birligi*, but the plan derailed by the chaos of the last weeks of the war.[214]

The dormitories of the SS mullah school in Dresden could accommodate fifty students at a time, but this capacity was never fully utilized. The courses were to last from one to two years, but, due to the military situation, they were cut back to just a few weeks. Students came from the units or, in some cases, were recruited directly from prisoner of war camps, where they were screened by mullah Jumabaev.[215] Only three classes were taught in Dresden during the final months of the war. A first group of sixteen students graduated in January 1945, followed by a class of twenty-one students and another of twenty-three.[216] In early 1945 Idris also gave a number of lectures to sixty-two imams of a Turkic labor brigade of the Wehrmacht, which included Uzbeks, Tatars, Azerbaijanis, and North Caucasians, among others.[217] He advocated that the school in Dresden should train not only Muslims from Turkestan but imams from all ethnic groups.[218] The SS was receptive to such pan-Islamic ideas.

The theological program of the SS school sought to overcome the antagonism between Sunnis and Shi'ites. In his lectures in Dresden and in his speeches to soldiers of Muslim units at the front, Idris constantly preached against religious sectarianism.[219] For the Germans, this strategy came with obvious organizational advantages. Only Spuler, having separated Sunnis and Shi'ites at the Wehrmacht's school, opposed the antisectarian politics of the SS as well as Idris's overall program of instruction.[220] Idris, who argued that the schism had been artificially constructed in the history of Islam, prevailed.[221] The school's educational program was designed by him in consultation with Hartmann.[222] It included readings from the Qur'an and lessons on Qur'an exegesis, classes on Islamic history, and instruction in the Arabic language. In the last months of the war, Idris also lectured on political issues such as the "imperialist and Islam-hostile policy of the three powers, England, America and Soviet Russia, and the Islam-friendly policy of Germany, which had prevailed for at least the last 200 years," as he put it.[223] Using examples from history, he warned his students that an Anglo-American-Soviet victory meant slavery at the hands of the "international Jews."

In the final months of the war, the command of the Eastern Troops decided to make use of the new SS school and also to send the Wehrmacht imams to Dresden for instruction.[224] Spuler was assigned to survey the courses for the Wehrmacht but was only sporadically consulted by Idris.[225] Mufti Szynkiewicz, too, was now ordered from Göttingen to Dresden.[226] The idea to educate imams jointly for both the Wehrmacht and the SS had been discussed for some time. Before the opening of the school in Dresden, in a meeting with Gerhard von Mende on 27 July 1944, al-Husayni explained that he had been approached from various sides about founding a "mullah school."[227] Since he was under the impression that the Germans had no clear idea about the actual organization of such a project, he told Mende that he himself wanted to make some practical recommendations for a future mullah school. Such a school, he suggested, should be used by both the Wehrmacht and the SS. It would require a specialized teaching plan, appropriate teaching materials, and a practicable language of instruction. Most revealing in this context were the mufti's remarks about the role of religion. Aware of Mende's and the ministry's skepticism about the attempts of the SS to launch a pan-Islamic mobilization campaign in the Eastern territories, the mufti acknowledged that "today a comprehensive Islamic idea is not politically effective." The school, al-Husayni explained, should operate under the auspices of the East Ministry, which would then cooperate with both the Wehrmacht and the SS. A school run by the weak East Ministry was unthinkable. Moreover, al-Husayni's nationalist visions conflicted with the actual policy of the Wehrmacht and the SS at that point. The mufti was never offered an active role at the Dresden school.[228] The episode showed once again that al-Husayni had little influence on the decision-making process in Berlin. The Germans consulted and used him when necessary, but he had no power of his own. After the opening of the school in November, the mufti nonetheless wrote to Himmler to thank him.[229] Himmler replied swiftly: "I give expression to my conviction that our German-Islamic cooperation and bond will be awarded with the ultimate victory over our enemies."[230]

Soon the school was engulfed by the war. The villa, with its Islamic literature and artifacts, was burned to the ground during the devastating Allied bombardments of Dresden between 13 and 15 February 1945, and the remaining Muslims and staff were evacuated to the small town of Weissenfels.[231] On 23 February the SS Head Office "urgently" asked the local command of Weissenfels for provisions and accommodations for the members of the school.[232] The local military authorities were baffled and suggested closing the school since Idris was urgently needed at the Propaganda Ministry and the imams were required in their units.[233] Unimpressed, the SS simply answered that there was no order about the dissolution of the school.[234] The further fate of the staff and students is unknown.

Overall, the three Islamic seminaries established during the war were too short lived to have made much of an impact. Even before the courses at the SS mullah school in Dresden had begun, Idris had explained his concerns about timing.[235] The instruction of the mullahs, he criticized, had begun far too late. He warned that the mullahs should not be separated from their units during the critical phase of the war. Nevertheless, the history of the religious courses is another example of the extent to which Berlin tried to expand its Islam project in the final period of the war.

After the end of the Second World War, General von Heygendorff compiled a list of ten points that summarized the measures taken to support the Islamic faith in the Muslim units of the Wehrmacht.[236] Islam, he wrote, was promoted:

1. By the selection of eligible men and their instruction in the mullah schools in Göttingen and Dresden-Blausewitz;
2. By the establishment of positions for mullahs and chief mullahs in the field commands of the divisions, battalions, and companies;
3. By the decoration of mullahs with special emblem badges like the turban and crescent;
4. By the distribution of Qur'an publications among the legionnaires;
5. By the regulation of prayer times;
6. By the exemption from service on Fridays and during religious feasts;
7. By the consideration of fasting customs and dietary requirements;
8. By the acquisition of mutton and rice for the festive days;
9. By the orienting of the graves of fallen volunteers toward Mecca by means of compasses, and the marking of gravestones with crescents instead of crosses;
10. By thoughtful and tactful conduct toward the foreign religion and its rites.

Heygendorff's explanation of these efforts was rather simple: "Many of our Turkic volunteers were pious Mohammedans. Convinced adherents of Islam cannot be Bolshevists. Therefore, nothing seemed more reasonable than the promotion of Islam in our volunteer formations in every imaginable way."[237] Indeed, the Germans were convinced that pious Muslims would be particularly hostile to the Soviet Union and therefore especially reliable allies. Moreover, the granting of special religious concessions and spiritual care was primarily intended to maintain military discipline, to control the thousands of volunteers, and, most importantly, to boost the fighting morale.

CHAPTER EIGHT

Islam and Military Propaganda

Ever since Imperial Germany's campaign for Muslim mobilization in the First World War, General Oskar Ritter von Niedermayer had been convinced of the use of Islam to stir up Muslims. On 15 January 1943, as German troops retreated from the Caucasus and the military situation at Stalingrad became hopeless, Niedermayer issued general "Suggestions for Political Instruction in Turkic Units" (*Anhaltspunkte für den Politischen Unterricht in turkvölkischen Einheiten*) for his Muslim field battalions.[1] Unsurprisingly, Islam was an important part of the recommended propaganda themes. German propaganda in the Muslim units was to construct a historical tradition of friendship between Germany and the Islamic world. Propagandists were to remind Muslim soldiers of Wilhelm II's solemn declaration after visiting Saladin's tomb in Damascus in 1898. The emperor's proclamation was to be presented as the foundation of Germany's friendship with Islam, which had continued with the German-Ottoman alliance in the First World War, and Germany's strong relations with Iraq, Iran, and Afghanistan during the interwar period. A few months later the SS issued a similar set of guidelines for Handžar, Gottlob Berger's decree on the "Ideological-Spiritual Education of the Muslim SS Division."[2] Further instructions for military propaganda among the Muslim troops followed.

The guidelines issued by the Wehrmacht and the SS addressed all officers who became involved in the propaganda in the Muslim units. The ideological indoctrination of Muslim soldiers did not, in fact, lie exclusively in the hands of the field imams. The army launched a wide-ranging propaganda program, employing political officers and setting up numerous military journals and newspapers. This propaganda, too, was religiously charged and designed to legitimize the war, to radicalize Muslim soldiers, and to stir them up for battle. Above all, it sought to provide an Islamic interpretation of the war. Religious imperatives and slogans were employed to make the war a divine duty—to turn it into a "just war." Moreover, Muslim recruits had to be convinced that they were not ordinary mercenaries in an infidel army but soldiers who were fighting for their own cause. The objectives of Muslims and their religion were constructed in congruence with those of the Third Reich. The promotion of supposed shared values and of alleged common enemies, most notably Bolshevism, Anglo-American power, and Judaism, were recurring themes in the propaganda for Muslim troops.

Political Officers and Religious Propaganda

From the outset, the Wehrmacht employed German and Muslim political officers (*weltanschauliche Schulungsoffiziere*), who were to cooperate closely with the imams in the indoctrination of Muslim troops. Political officers, in fact, were introduced at the same time, in the summer of 1942, also in the regular German Wehrmacht units.[3] Ideology, the army command believed, was the most effective instrument to boost military morale. The tasks of the political officers were similar to those of the Soviet political commissars, who had impressed the German leadership, though it was anxious to avoid any comparison. Historians have argued that the Wehrmacht's political officers played a considerable role in the brutalization of German warfare. The mission of the ideological officers in the Muslim units was generally quite similar to that in the German units, although they were to found their propaganda on Islamic rhetoric and slogans. A propagandist of the Eastern Legions once summarized his work with the simple statement that he was trying to mobilize all available forces "for the holy war."[4] Legionnaires who were chosen to act as propagandists in their units were sent to Berlin for short training courses. The reports that have survived the war give a sense of the role religion played during these stays.[5] The political officers would not only tour the capital and listen to political lectures on subjects such as the "National Socialist Germany" but also attend Friday prayers at the Wilmersdorf Mosque. Excursions to the Muslim cemetery in Berlin, which had been built by the Ottoman legation, were also part of the schedule, added to stress the deep connection between Germany and Islam. The Germans carefully monitored the Muslims' behavior at these Islamic sites. The report on the sixth course recounted that only the Turkestanis were impressed by the graveyard, whereas the Caucasians were more reserved, while the account of the following course remarked: "Particularly impressive for the legionnaires this time was the visit to the mosque and the grave of their national leader."[6] It also noted that most of the soldiers had never been in a house of worship before. Once employed in the field, the propagandists remained under the strict control of the German staff of their units. A directive for German officers serving in the Turk battalions urged them to monitor the work of the propagandists carefully, emphasizing that the Muslims were to be told that they were fighting not just against Bolshevism and for national and economic factors but also for the "reopening of the houses of worship and the respect of confessions, customs, and conventions."[7] Another internal instruction sheet recommended that German commanders attend political speeches by the propagandists in the units both to underline their importance and to see how the volunteers reacted to them.[8]

In the Crimea, the 11th Army also trained Crimean Tatar propagandists in special courses. In these classes, Muslim officers learned that "National Socialism perceives the nation as a sacred institution" and that "Germany grants full religious freedom."[9] "The crucial point," the teachers would emphasize, "is the friendship of Germany as well as of Italy and Japan to the principal people of Islam, to the Arabs" and that the "entire Arab world" was "in bitter opposition to England." A Wehrmacht official, who in the spring of 1942 attended eight courses, training more than eighty Crimean Tatar propagandists, noted that the participants were "pleasantly struck" to learn "that there is also a large mosque in Berlin."[10]

The SS made similar efforts. Early on, convinced of the close connection between ideology and military discipline, Berger had introduced political officers in the German units of the Waffen-SS and soon also created these positions in the Muslim units.[11] In March 1944 Wangemann's political section organized a course for the Handžar's propagandists (*Einsatzredner*) with lectures on themes such as "Aim and Mission of the Division," "The Pious Muslim and the People of Different Faiths in Bosnia," and "Why the Muslims Are Fighting on Germany's Side"—the latter two courses were taught by the division imam, Abdullah Muhasilović.[12] Later that month Handžar organized a more in-depth course for future German and Muslim propagandists. The general directives of the course reflected Berger's synthesis of National Socialism and Islam. The future political officers attended lectures on subjects like "National Socialism and Islam," "The Life of Our Führer," and "The Meaning of This War."[13] After the course, the soldiers took written exams that consisted of twenty questions, ranging from "Why can a man who loves his people not be a Communist?" to "For which values are the states allied with Germany fighting?" to "For what reasons are National Socialism and Islam fighting together?"[14] The question about Communism was answered by one German officer as follows: "Communism is against everything national, against the faith." On the values for which he was fighting, he wrote: "For the preservation of customs, freedom, the right to live."[15] And finally, he knew too how to respond to the question about the connection between National Socialism and Islam: "Islam and National Socialism have common enemies and also overlap in belief."[16] The Muslim *SS-Rottenführer* Josip Vukelić answered the same question neatly in line with Himmler's propaganda: "They have common enemies: Bolshevism, Judaism, Anglo-Americans, Freemasons, and political Catholicism."[17] The Bosnian felt equally confident about the question on Communism: "Because it destroys all its values, religion, family, and equates everything." About shared values, he wrote: "In order to maintain religion, nationality, and custom and conventions."[18] In his report that month, Wangemann ordered that only those who had participated in these courses were eligible to be promoted to the position of *SS-Unterführer*.[19] The SS organized similar courses for its Muslim recruits from the East. In September 1944 Fürst made inquiries in Berlin about the recruitment of officers for the "political-religious education," who could teach, among other topics, "The History of Islam," "The Short History and Geography of the Islamic States," and, of course, "The Life of Shamil."[20] In addition, Idris, already informal director of the mullah school in Dresden, gave lectures on "The Significance and History of Islam for the Eastern Turks."[21] Spuler also gave some seminars.[22]

Islam, Military Journals, and Print Propaganda

Both the Wehrmacht and the SS produced and circulated numerous propaganda publications among their recruits, which frequently drew on religious slogans, concepts, and rhetoric. Berlin distributed brochures, such as the anti-Jewish booklet *Islam and Judaism*, which was spread among not only the civil population of Bosnia and Herzegovina but also the Handžar recruits (Figure 8.1).[23] The publication sought to frame anti-Jewish hatred within a religious context to motivate Muslims to fight in the German

8.1 German edition of the propaganda brochure *Islam and Judaism* being read by soldiers of the SS Division Handžar, 1943 (BAK, *Image* 101III-Mielke-036-23, Mielke).

Weltanschauungskrieg. At the same time, Berger planned a broader ideological publication for Handžar, which he envisioned as a more general "political combat organ for the entire Mohammedan world."[24] Sauberzweig, moreover, regularly wrote open propaganda letters to his Muslim soldiers that were read aloud by the imams in their units.[25] Among its Muslim recruits from the Eastern territories, the SS distributed religious propaganda as well. It included a pamphlet signed by the mufti, addressed "to my Muslim brothers!"[26] The Allied powers, he declared, "since time immemorial count among the traditional enemies of Islam; they suppress the Muslims, occupy their countries, fight their religion, and prepare the worst for their future." Now the Allied powers, "driven by world Judaism," the pamphlet claimed, stood in battle against the Axis, led by Germany, "the country that has never been an enemy of Islam and has never attacked an Islamic country." The Third Reich was fighting "our common enemies" and seeking to secure a "safe and happy future for the Islamic world." "Onward, on the side of Germany, brimming with steadfast belief that victory is without doubt near," the text urged, closing with a verse from the Qur'an and exhorting the soldiers: "Arise and fight for God, with your property and goods and with your soul."[27]

The Wehrmacht, too, had begun to circulate religiously charged propaganda. "Particularly needed are treatises about the life of the Führer as well as Qur'ans," Bräutigam noted when ordering propaganda material for the Eastern Muslim units in late 1942.[28] Religious writings, Wehrmacht officials believed, were especially important in sustaining military morale. The "Qur'an," Köstring's aide, Herwarth von Bittenfeld, later recalled, was published "in large quantities."[29] In particular, miniature Qur'ans, which were also given out in the Crimea, were widely distributed among the soldiers of the Eastern Legions, who carried them in steel capsules around the neck.[30] Amulet lockets and leather pouches containing Qur'anic verses had been carried by Muslim soldiers in battle across the world for centuries, and the Germans now eagerly exploited the practice.[31] Wehrmacht officials repeatedly ordered these Qur'anic talismans. And when organizing his courses in Göttingen, Spuler requested them for his imams.[32] In 1944, during consultations with some Azerbaijani leaders, Heygendorff was informed of an "urgent need for Qur'ans enclosed in metal cans."[33] "It is generally noted that these talismanic Qur'ans are of great significance," it was asserted. Officials even discussed the plan of ordering Turkish Qur'ans from Turkey as they could not be printed in Germany due to the worsening war situation.

The most common propaganda publications distributed among the troops were military journals and newspapers. Shortly after the deployment of Handžar in 1943, the SS began publishing the magazine *SS-Handžar* for the soldiers of the division.[34] The division's propaganda section was responsible for its content. Printed in German and Bosnian, the paper consisted of eight pages of text and a four-page illustrated supplement. *SS-Handžar* was initially published fortnightly but appeared less and less frequently as the war situation deteriorated. Many of the magazine's articles drew on memories of the Austro-Hungarian era.[35] Imagining the tradition of a historical alliance, Sauberzweig praised in an article the "heroic deeds" of the old Habsburg regiments.[36] Issues featured stand-alone quotations from Hitler, the Prophet, and the Qur'an.[37] The imams of the division were explicitly instructed by the German command to write for *SS-Handžar*.[38]

In late 1943 Imam Husein Džozo contributed a piece, "On the Tasks of the SS Man," in which he agitated against "Bolshevism, Capitalism, and Judaism."[39] A significant number of articles called to arms against the alleged enemies of the faithful. "Bestial Bolshevist hordes and criminals, on London's payroll, stain the sanctuaries of the proud Bosnia," one author fulminated.[40] Another lamented that atrocities against the Muslim population in the Balkans would continue even during the most sacred periods of the religious calendar: "It is the time of Ramadan, the month for prayer and fasting," but, though meant to be a "month of peace and happiness," it had turned "hard and bloody."[41] The most aggressive propaganda against Nazi Germany's enemies appeared in the final issue, published in the summer of 1944, when the division was engaged in heavy fighting. It featured articles condemning both the "enthusiast" Tito and the "Jews in Bosnia" as the fiercest enemies of the Muslims.[42] Furthermore, SS-Handžar reported about the celebrations of religious holidays. One issue was dedicated to the Ramadan Bairam festivities in Neuhammer and featured not only the speeches of Sauberzweig and the division imam but also many photographs of the event.[43] On the occasion of the Mawlid, SS-Handžar printed parts of a speech given by al-Husayni in Berlin.[44] Another issue covered the mufti's visit to Neuhammer.[45] Connecting notions of religiosity, masculinity, and militancy, al-Husayni was quoted addressing the recruits: "In my time with you, I discovered a life of manliness, fighting spirit, and willingness for sacrifice that Islam demands from everyone." The illustrated supplement featured many photos of the visit.[46] Visual propaganda was indeed a major characteristic of the SS-Handžar magazine. Well aware of the power of images, the SS printed more than a dozen photographs in each issue, depicting the life of the soldiers or their villages and, most frequently, mosques.[47] Perhaps more suprising was a photograph of a young woman in a bathing suit under the Mostar Bridge, printed next to a picture of a fully veiled woman, a combination that might have led to some incomprehension among pious readers.[48] In the summer of 1944 the SS finally stopped publishing SS-Handžar. Plans to publish two division papers, one in Bosnian, which was also to be distributed among the Muslim civil population, and another in German, never materialized.[49]

A paper of the Eastern Turkic SS Corps, Türk Birligi (Turkic Unity), appeared for only a very short time in late 1944.[50] Published in different Turkic languages, the paper was "to enhance militant impulses for the strengthening of the troops' morale," as Olzscha put it.[51] Its first issue, published on 25 November 1944, took the *Qurban Bairam* as its theme and featured articles on Islam and the battle against Bolshevism.[52] Al-Husayni also contributed a piece, calling on the faithful, in the name of Allah, to fight alongside Hitler's Germany. *Türk Birligi* was published under the censorship of Johannes Benzing and other German experts on Islam in the Soviet Union.

The propaganda papers circulated in the Wehrmacht's Eastern Legions lasted somewhat longer: *Ghazavat* (*Holy War*) for the North Caucasian Legion, *Idel-Ural* (*Volga-Ural*) for the Volga-Ural Legion, and *Azerbaijan* (*Azerbaijan*) for the Azerbaijani Legion. Information about the papers distributed in the fourth Muslim legion, Turkestan, is no longer available, but their content was most likely similar to that of the papers of the other three Muslim legions.[53] In addition, Niedermayer's headquarters (162nd Infantry Division) gave the paper *Svoboda* (*Freedom*) to all of its recruits. Most of the legions' magazines were published on a weekly or bimonthly basis. Normally they were eight pages long, later only six or four. Most of them were established between summer 1942 and spring 1943 and ceased publication in the winter of 1944–1945.[54] During the entire war, around one hundred issues of each paper were produced. The articles were written mostly by Muslim collaborators in Berlin and tightly controlled and censored by the East Ministry and the Wehrmacht's propaganda division, which compiled summaries of every issue.[55] These summaries provide the basis of the following analysis. As the early copies of these summaries from 1942 have not survived the war, this study concentrates on the issues that were published between 1943 and 1945.

The reason for the variety of newspapers was first and foremost the diversity of languages spoken by the Muslim recruits. Some papers, most importantly *Ghazavat*, were multilingual, and along with Russian articles contained texts in Chechen, Ingush, Karachai, Balkar, and other languages. The journals' contents were often similar and, in fact, resembled the typical field papers published for German soldiers. A number of reports were translations of articles that had appeared in German publications such as the *Völkischer Beobachter*, the *Deutsche Allgemeine Zeitung*, and *Das Reich*. The majority of the articles dealt with the military situation, while fewer touched upon political and ideological issues. Historians have either ignored the papers or dismissed them as politically and propagandistically irrelevant.[56] A careful reading of the papers, however, shows that the articles do give insight into the ways in which the Germans tried to influence their recruits.

Generally speaking, nationalism was a significant part of this propaganda, as is reflected in the papers' names. At the same time, religious themes were also pervasive. Indeed, the title *Ghazavat* had an explicit religious meaning, drawing on the North Caucasian tradition of Islamic resistance and jihad. The following pages address some of the key religious themes in the articles of *Ghazavat*, *Idel-Ural*, *Azerbaijan*, and *Svoboda* and assess their political functions.

A remarkable number of articles in these publications aimed to educate legionnaires about Islam and foster an Islamic identity among them. All of the papers repeatedly underlined the importance of religion as the defining element of national culture. "Religion is a keystone of our national morale," *Idel-Ural* proclaimed in early 1944.[57] A few months later *Azerbaijan* assured readers that the nation could be founded only on the pure teachings of the Prophet and the Qur'an.[58] "In the new Azerbaijan, religion is to play a leading role," the Azerbaijani journalist Ibrahim Oglu wrote. A few weeks earlier he had made it clear that the legionnaires' mission was, apart from the liberation of Azerbaijan, the preservation of religion.[59] In fact, *Azerbaijan* made no secret of its "efforts" to educate the legionnaires "in a religious way."[60] *Ghazavat* asserted in a headline that "the life of our Prophet should serve as an example for us."[61] Among the articles with an explicit educational purpose were texts about the teachings of Islam and Islamic history, often written by religious authorities. A certain mullah Filankias, for instance, gave "a retrospective of the development of Islam" for the readers of *Azerbaijan*, while the Azerbaijani major Abdul Fatalibey published a historical essay series on "The Prophet and Islam" in *Idel-Ural*.[62] A month earlier, Fatalibey had written two historical overviews about "the Prophet and his true Credo" in *Azerbaijan*.[63] A former Red Army officer, Fatalibey had impressed the Germans with his combat performance in the battle for the Caucasus and had soon become a recognized speaker for the Azerbaijani cause and a fervent promoter of pan-Islamic unity.[64] Other articles that appeared in *Idel-Ural* and *Azerbaijan* praised the glorious history of science in the Islamic world during the medieval period.[65] The papers also translated and republished articles about Islam that had been printed in

German newspapers. *Idel-Ural* and *Azerbaijan*, for instance, both published a lengthy article on al-Azhar that had first appeared in the *Deutsche Allgemeine Zeitung*.[66] It described how al-Azhar had expanded over the centuries into a complex of madrasas, soup kitchens, and dormitories and had become a global religious institution, illuminating "almost all corners of the Islamic world." The article also emphasized—and exaggerated—al-Azhar's political influence and power, and claimed that its leaders had confronted the British Empire and even consulted with King Faruq about a restoration of the caliphate based in Egypt. *Ghazavat* and *Azerbaijan* printed articles about Ibn Saud, Islam, and Wahhabism in Saudi Arabia that had first appeared in the *Völkische Beobachter*.[67] The mere fact that a German military publication was reporting on Islamic themes could have had a propagandistic impact. Many articles, however, went much further, explicitly portraying Germany as the liberator of Islam.

Most articles that dealt with religion portrayed the Third Reich as the friend of Islam. Some reports even conveyed the idea of a wider Muslim mobilization movement in support of the Axis. Both *Ghazavat* and *Idel-Ural* reported in detail on the Wehrmacht's Arab units.[68] *Azerbaijan* published articles about Muslim volunteers from the Balkans alongside pictures of Bosnian Muslims.[69] An additional set of images showed life in Muslim villages in Croatia. Muslim life under Axis protection was, in fact, a popular theme. *Idel-Ural* published a series of photos titled "Muslim Life in Serbia," remarking: "Under German protection Muslim life can develop freely."[70] Unsurprisingly, German support of Islam in the East was a key theme in all of the papers for the Eastern Legions. "The Muslims are convinced that with the German victory the freedom of religion will become a reality," the *Ghazavat* headline ran in autumn 1943.[71] Under Soviet rule, the paper wrote, the practice of religion had been completely banned. "But when the German troops came to the Caucasus, they immediately opened all churches and mosques and granted full religious freedom." Muslims now pinned all their hopes on a German victory, as only Germany would bring freedom to Islam. This claim was substantiated with numerous articles on Muslim life, most importantly religious celebrations taking place under German protection. Islamic holidays regularly made it into the headlines. The papers printed celebratory wishes for the end of Ramadan or for *Qurban Bairam*.[72] Reports covered religious celebrations not only in the legions but also those across the occupied territories. At the close of Ramadan in

1943 *Azerbaijan* reported on celebrations organized by the Germans in the Crimea.[73] Around the same time, *Idel-Ural* published a picture of Tatar migrants celebrating the feast under German protection in Finland.[74] To a certain extent, reports about these celebrations drew on the idea of a global Muslim community. This became most obvious in Amin al-Husayni's speeches, which were printed in all of the papers.[75] More important, however, was the use of religious holidays as a marker of difference between German and Stalinist rule. In 1943, for instance, *Azerbaijan* reported on "Mullah Suleiman," who was said to grow "happier from day to day" because of his new freedom to practice his religion without restriction, a freedom "that had been refused in the Soviet Union for 25 years."[76] At the same time, a Muslim legionnaire wrote in *Idel-Ural*: "Today the entire Muslim world celebrated the Uraza Bairam to end the fasting. And yet the 30 million Muslims who live in the Soviet Union are not able to celebrate this holiday with dignity. For 25 years they have lived under the oppression of the Bolsheviks, and only in secret can Muslims practice their religion."[77] In *Ghazavat*, Muslim legionnaire wrote about the occasion:

> The Ramadan feast binds together all Muslims for one month, wherever they might be. On the occasion of this celebration, which ended on 30 August [1943], we want to remember the Bolshevists, how they banned every free religious practice, arrested our mullahs and sent them to Siberia, terrorized and subjugated us. The German Wehrmacht has drawn the sword against Bolshevism, which represses all freedoms. Bolshevism lies in its own blood. It is grasping for its last breaths. May Allah protect the German Wehrmacht and help it as well as all people who unite against Bolshevism. We remember only how the Soviets rode roughshod over us and our clerics.[78]

In the same issue, another article promised that "the day is not far off" when also the Muslims in the Soviet territories would be able to celebrate again.[79]

Indeed, one purpose of many of the articles dealing with religion was to portray the Soviet Union as an atheist oppressor of Islam. "Everywhere in those countries which the Soviet Union attacks, Muslims can practice their faith freely," *Ghazavat* observed.[80] "Only in the Soviet Union, where the Supreme-Godless-Jew Yaroslavskii Gubelman has let all mosques be closed or destroyed, is this not the case. 40 million Muslims have to live without the opportunity for religious practice because the mullahs have been banished or murdered." Minei Israilevich Gubelman, better known as Emelian Mikhailovich Yaroslavskii, had been chairman of the "Society of the God-less" before Stalin abolished the organization in 1941.[81] The dissolution was, of course, ignored by German propaganda, which claimed that the situation was becoming worse than ever before. "Moscow is intensifying its battle against religion," *Idel-Ural* wrote.[82] Moscow had instructed all Soviet teachers anew to confront religious belief at the schools. The papers printed detailed, emotional stories about the suppression of Islam under Soviet rule. In the article "Bolshevism in the North Caucasus," *Ghazavat* described how Muslims had experienced the Soviets' takeover: "Their first 'deed' was to close all mosques and to arrest and deport the priests [*sic*]."[83]

Islam was often referred to as a bulwark against Russian and Soviet domination. *Idel-Ural* printed the story of Rizaeddin Fakhreddin, the famed Islamic theologian and last independent mufti of Ufa, who refused, when brought to Moscow in 1931, to sign a document affirming that Muslims of the USSR were living in freedom. "His answer was that he could not tell lies to the Islamic people," *Idel-Ural* (correctly) reported, praising him as a "custodian of the Islamic faith."[84] The slogan "For religion, for Islam" had accompanied the Caucasian uprisings, *Ghazavat* proclaimed in September 1943.[85] Remembering anti-Soviet uprisings in the Caucasus of the 1930s, it stated that they were nothing less than a "religious revolution against Bolshevism." The Bolshevists had tried to break all religious resistance. They had attempted to "poison" the youth, following their slogan that "religion is the opiate of the people." But they had failed, the paper assured its readers. The youth had maintained their beliefs and were now ready to fight alongside the Germans for the "freedom of their homeland and the continuance of our Muslim religion."[86]

Stories about the religious character of resistance also drew on historical narratives of Islamic opposition in the tsarist era. A historical tradition was constructed in which the German call to arms became self-explanatory and the war against Moscow an act of piety. Under Russian oppression, *Idel-Ural* wrote in October 1943, only Islam could be the driving force of resistance. Well aware that "the faith in Islam strengthened the spiritual power of our people," the tsarist empire had already attempted to weaken

Islam.[87] The paper remembered the "Russian missionaries" and the "persecution of Islamic leaders," "the forced baptism of Tatars and Bashkirs," and the "closing down of the mosques." These were constant topics. "Russian imperialism," *Idel-Ural* remembered, had made an "assassination attempt on our faith"; it had destroyed "mosques, which had been built over centuries," while, at the same time, the number of Russian churches on Islamic soil had grown "like trees in the forest."[88] The following year, both *Azerbaijan* and *Ghazavat* commemorated the tsarist capture of Imam Shamil eighty-five years earlier.[89] "Today, volunteers fight in the spirit of Shamil for the achievement of freedom, which will not be destroyed again."[90] In the next issue, *Ghazavat* printed another story about Shamil and also remembered other anti-tsarist Islamic movements in the northern Caucasus mountains.[91] The aim of Shamil's struggle and today's war against the Soviet Union, the paper explained, was the same—the only difference was that this time the peoples of the Caucasus could count on the support of the "great and indomitable German Wehrmacht."[92] *Ghazavat* announced: "We must help our people. And we will help. Germany is on our side. Allah is with us."[93] And in another issue, in February 1944, the paper proclaimed: "We hear today the call 'ghazawat.' Ghazawat—holy war, it is still waged far from home, but it will also lead us again to the mountains of our homeland."[94]

As the struggle for Muslim support accelerated, more and more articles directly confronted Stalin's campaign for Islamic mobilization. Reports about the Kremlin's attempts to court Islam were usually written in a tone of ridicule and malice and pointed out the inconsistencies of Soviet religious policies. "Now the Bolsheviks want to betray the people in the name of religion," *Idel-Ural* headlined in October 1943.[95] "The same Bolshevism, which battered religion for 25 years, today calls the people for a continuation of the war in the name of religion." Reports that "the Jew Gubelman Yaroslavskii" now advocated a more liberal stance on religion were dismissed as a "farce," but the paper warned readers about the "Soviet-Mufti" Rasulaev. "There have often been maneuvers of this kind in the Soviet Union—although never this false," wrote *Idel-Ural*, adding that the people would recognize the "swindle." "Our people will never forget the transgressions of the Bolsheviks against the believers." A month later, the paper again dismissed the new Soviet policy toward Islam as a "lie and fraud."[96] In early 1944 *Idel-Ural* denounced it as "Stalin's new betrayal."[97] "The believers, who have so far been against Stalin, are now supposed to thank Stalin for granting freedom of belief in the mosques." The paper made it clear that "Stalin's mullahs" were "nothing more than an instrument in the hands of the Kremlin," just as the whole campaign was "nothing more than a giant fraud." Similarly, *Ghazavat* denounced the "Soviet church swindle."[98] *Azerbaijan* pointed out the contradiction: "For twenty-five years Stalin bedeviled and persecuted the Muslim population and [he is responsible for] the murder of thousands. Now, suddenly, during the war he has discovered his heart for the Muslims," the paper scoffed, reminding the recruits that Stalin adhered to the Marxist slogan that "religion was the opiate of the people."[99] The soldiers were reminded that mosques had been closed and turned into "garages or theaters and clubs." The Soviet mufti Rasulaev was mocked by the paper as an "agent of the NKVD." "This red mufti will now be sitting next to Stalin and delivering speeches on the radio about the liberation of the Muslims. But nobody will be fooled, we are in the know." Moscow's "suddenly discovered love for religion" was a "villainous betrayal." The Muslims would not become henchmen of a "Comintern agent" who "likes to call himself 'mufti.'" A few months later the paper jeered that those who worked against religion had always been the most esteemed in the Soviet Union, only now these people had become "mullahs."[100] Another article in the same issue warned readers that "all the talk" about Muslims in the Soviet Union being free to attend mosques was "nothing more than a lie."[101] The few mosques that had been reopened would only serve the purpose of Bolshevist propaganda. A few months later the paper again asserted that mosques had been reopened only to propagate a "Bolshevist 'religion.'"[102] The Soviet Islam campaign, the papers warned readers, would threaten not just the Soviet Union but the entire Muslim world. In the summer of 1943 *Ghazavat* led with the headline "The Soviets Want to Create a Soviet Arabia."[103] And two issues later, an article, titled "Stalin Remembers the Qur'an," denounced Soviet propaganda in the Middle East.[104] Stalin had sent Mufti Rasulaev to Syria, Palestine, and Egypt with instructions to convince the Muslim populations there that "Communism was by no means incompatible with the Qur'an." *Azerbaijan*, too, warned that the "Bolshevist muftis" were crossing the borders into the Middle East.[105] *Idel-Ural* described the Muslim congress that Stalin had convened in Moscow (just like the pan-Slavic congress) as another expression of "Moscow's imperialist intentions."[106] Finally, the Soviet campaign for Islamic mobilization was also attacked by more general articles about an alleged ideological conflict between Communism and Islam. Under the headline "Communism and Islam Irreconcilable," both *Ghazavat* and *Azerbaijan* wrote in early 1944 that Moscow would follow the idea that religion was the opiate of the people.[107] "Communism," the papers warned its readers, meant the "downfall of Islam." Two months later *Ghazavat* explained that "Communism and Islam are eternal opposites," denouncing the Kremlin's attempts "to prove" that devout Muslims could also be devout Communists: "This will never come true because not only are Communism and Islam divided by an enormous abyss, but so too is Communism and any kind of religion in general."[108]

The Soviet Union was not the only power that was portrayed as an enemy of Islam. In early 1944 *Ghazavat* printed a series of articles on clashes between Anglo-American troops and the local Muslim population in French Morocco. In February the paper reported on riots that left twenty-four Muslims killed by "Senegal Negroes" of the Anglo-American army.[109] In the following months *Ghazavat* gave a more vivid picture of the massacre that took place in a mosque in Morocco—described as a "blood bath among the believers."[110] Although exaggerated by German propaganda, such clashes did indeed occur in wartime North Africa.

Among the Western Allies, however, it was Great Britain in particular that was portrayed as the oppressor of Muslims. Just before the beginning of the hajj in 1943, *Ghazavat* drew on a classic theme of anti-British Islam propaganda, headlining "The English prohibit travel to Mecca."[111] The following year, the paper wrote about discontent among Arab recruits in the British army, asserting that "the Muslims do not want to bleed for England."[112] Whereas the Soviets were portrayed as antireligious and as dishonest exploiters of religious sentiment, the British were blamed for fomenting religious conflict in India. In late 1944 *Svoboda* contrasted the Indian Legion of the Wehrmacht, which united Muslims, Sikhs, and Hindus, with the British policy of divide and rule.[113] Around the same time, *Idel-Ural*, too, agitated against the British "exploitation of religious tensions" in India.[114] "The Muslims Have No Trust in England," *Ghazavat* titled an article on India's Muslims, and *Azerbaijan* republished an article that had appeared in the *Völkische Beobachter* with an appeal to the Muslims of India to resist British rule.[115] Both *Ghazavat* and *Idel-Ural* also exploited British failures during the pan-Arabian congress that took place in Cairo in the summer of 1943. *Ghazavat* told its readers that the spectacle was a "power struggle waged on the back of the Islamic states," remarking that one of the most influential leaders of the "Islamic world," Ibn Saud, had refused to take part and was followed by Yemen's leader, Imam Yahya.[116] "Behind the scenes of the congress," the paper wrote, "stand the advocates of English interests," eager for power, "on the back of Islam." An article in the following issue of the paper denounced the "English efforts" to foster Muslim unity "under English-Jewish influence," an attempt that had even been criticized by al-Maraghi.[117]

Finally, the papers carried anti-Jewish propaganda. One of the most vicious anti-Jewish texts was printed by *Idel-Ural*. In the article series "The Jews: The Worst Enemies of the Muslims," anti-Jewish hatred was connected to the Qur'an and to the life of the Prophet.[118] In Muslim parts of the Soviet Union, readers were told, the Bolsheviks had deliberately given power to Jews so that they could rule over Muslims. Images of Jews as enemies of Islam were often combined with calls for Islamic solidarity with the Palestinians and denouncements of alleged British and US support of Zionism. In the summer of 1943, for instance, *Ghazavat* reported on Anglo-American plans to found a Jewish state in the Near East.[119] "The Arabs and the entire Muslim population are rising up against these intentions. Everywhere unrest is flaring up." A month later, the paper wrote about clashes between Muslims and Jews during the 1943 Ramadan celebrations, combining anti-Jewish agitation with an Islamic theme.[120] Indeed, reports about riots in Palestine, allegedly supported by London and Washington, were frequent, often exaggerated, and portrayed as part of a global conflict that involved the whole of the Muslim world.[121] *Idel-Ural* wrote about protests for Palestine organized by the Muslims in Berlin.[122] *Ghazavat* quoted Ibn Saud, saying that Palestine had never been a "Jewish home" but always the home of Muslims.[123] The agitations of Amin al-Husayni were also printed in detail. *Ghazavat* reported, for instance, on Berlin congress against the Balfour Declaration and the mufti's speech on the occasion.[124] The event had turned into an "enormous demonstration of numerous representatives of the Islamic world against the British-American-Jewish politics of suppression and exploitation of the Islamic countries," readers were told. *Idel-Ural* also reported on supportive announcements from representatives of Muslim countries during the congress, which was, in the words of the paper, a "demonstration of Islamic solidarity."[125]

This idea of global solidarity among Muslims was a recurring trope. Imagining the *umma*, authors regularly informed their readers about the wider Muslim world. Instead of focusing on the soldiers' place of origin, the papers reported on the al-Azhar mosque in Cairo or Ibn Saud in Saudi Arabia. Implying pan-Islamic mobilization in support of Germany, texts moreover dealt with the Arab units of the Wehrmacht or Muslim volunteers from the Balkans. They presented Germany as the protector of Islam not just in the Eastern territories but also in Muslim villages in the Balkans. They attacked Soviet Islam propaganda in the Middle East, British confessional policies in India, an alleged British ban on the hajj, and an Anglo-American massacre in a mosque in Morocco. They told their Eastern Turkic readers about the pan-Arab congress in Cairo and Yemenite and Saudi reactions to it and about Jewish migration to Palestine. In one article, *Azerbaijan* described how a Tatar legionnaire, strolling through the streets of German-occupied Paris, had stumbled upon the *Grande Mosquée de Paris*. Under the umbrella of Islamic solidarity and Axis protection, he was warmly welcomed by the Muslims there, "Indians, Persians, and Arabs."[126] The notion of *Weltislam* was omnipresent. The soldiers, *Azerbaijan* insinuated, were taking part in a global, pan-Islamic struggle. Furthermore, German propaganda made use of historical narratives and various forms of religious commemoration, most importantly by remembering figures like Imam Shamil.

Ultimately, articles were not only religious in content, but also in style. Those written by field imams and other religious figures in particular feature a distinct religious rhetoric, using expressions such as "in the name of Allah," "holy war," and "Allah is with us." As in the case of Nazi propaganda for the Middle East, the Balkans, and the Eastern territories, this language was not used to preach religious war in a narrow sense, with the intention of stirring up interreligious violence, but to promote holy war against profane ideologies and powers such as Communism or British imperialism.

In addition to proclamations and reports, German propaganda sometimes took the form of songs, such as the "Song of Imam Qasim Magama," printed by *Ghazavat* in the spring of 1944.[127] Even more popular was poetry written by volunteers. *Ghazavat* published poems such as "The Fast of the Bairam Feast,"[128] "The Mosque,"[129] "The Holy War Calls You,"[130] and "Ghazavat."[131] *Idel-Ural* printed the poems "Our Holy War,"[132] "The Mosque of Chan,"[133] and, on the occasion of Ramadan in 1943, "Solemn Evening."[134] Indeed, it was proclamations, songs, and poems that could most easily draw on religious sentiments and emotions. Finally, illustrations, especially photographs, played an important role. *Ghazavat*, *Idel-Ural*, and *Azerbaijan* all printed images of sacred places and global centers of Islam, photographs of al-Azhar ("The Spiritual Center of the Muslim"), Medina ("There lies the Tomb of the Prophet"), and Mecca ("The Holy City of Mecca").[135] The editor of *Idel-Ural*, Kiam Gliev, had a good sense for the propagandistic value of images of sacred places, printing depictions of famous mosques of the Eastern territories.[136] Gliev's colleague, Abdurrahman Avtorkhanov, a former Soviet journalist and now editor of *Ghazavat*, made similarly substantial use of pictures.[137] *Ghazavat* illustrated its articles on the tradition of religious resistance in the Caucasus with portraits of Imam Shamil.[138] Most prominent, however, were images that showed the religious practices of Muslim volunteers, portraying Germany as the protector of Islam. *Ghazavat* printed a photograph of a field imam speaking to his troops.[139] *Azerbaijan* published an image of "Chief Mullah Pashazade" at a military cemetery.[140] *Idel-Ural* printed pictures of the legionnaire in the Paris Mosque as well as of the ornately decorated hall of the Islamic school in Dresden.[141] Visual propaganda had the advantage that all soldiers, literate or not, could be addressed. Indeed, taking into account the high rates of illiteracy among the legionnaires, articles from the papers were frequently read aloud in the units. In the last months of the war, even the SS used the Wehrmacht's legion papers at the mullah school in Dresden.[142] Overall, the impact of the publications should not be underestimated. Ralph von Heygendorff was convinced that *Ghazavat* played a central role in the lives of the legionnaires.[143]

Discrimination and the Limits of Devotion

In the eyes of German officers, efforts to use Islam seemed destined to succeed in maintaining discipline and strengthening military morale. Yet, their work in the units encountered numerous obstacles, most importantly the potential lack of receptiveness of religious policies and propaganda and, more generally, religious beliefs, and the effects of discrimination, religious and racial, in the Wehrmacht and the SS.

Reports about the Muslims' piety were ambiguous. Religious policies in the units continued throughout the war, which suggests that the Germans had not found them a complete failure. After the war, Köstring and others emphasized that, compared to Christian Orthodox volunteers, the Muslims had been notably more religious.[144] Indeed, a number of reports from the field suggest that German efforts to employ Islam were not falling on deaf ears. Shortly after recruitment began in early 1942, a Wehrmacht instruction sheet insisted that the soldiers had joined the German ranks to seek both the "liberation of their home country from Bolshevism" and the "freedom of their faith."[145] This assessment may have derived from actual experience. A 1943 report on morale in a Muslim battalion explained that "the Mohammedan religion, as well as good rations," was an "essential pillar" of military morale and discipline.[146] From the Caucasus, Theodor Oberländer wrote to his wife about the enthusiastic reaction he had received from his Muslim soldiers when he had promised, in a public address to his unit, "complete religious freedom under German protection."[147] A newly recruited volunteer from the Caucasus, the forty-two-year-old Isa Musaiev, not only told his German interrogators that Bolshevism had erected a system of repression and economic exploitation but also complained that the "mosques were taken and used as storehouses, barns, and garages."[148] That this was more than empty rhetoric designed to pander to the Germans' expectations becomes clear from the field mail sent home by Muslim volunteers.

Letters written by Crimean Tatars in the months after their employment by the 11th Army reveal a striking intensity of religious sentiment.[149] Werner Otto von Hentig, who monitored some of these letters in spring 1942, stressed that they gave clear evidence not only of the Muslims' "deep gratitude" and "willingness to fight and work" but also of their "deeply rooted religiosity."[150] "Allah and Adolf Effendi," Hentig reported, were "inseparable terms" in the letters.[151] The soldier Majid Habilov, for instance, wrote to his family: "Thank Allah and Adolf Effendi! We are well! If Allah protects us, we will endure not one year, but ten years, of war." His comrade Ibrahim Said wished that: "Allah and Adolf Effendi may give the German army strength, so that we are victorious." Reading the letters,

Hentig also noted that many referred to prayers for Hitler.[152] "We pray to Allah day and night for the health of Adolf Effendi," asserted one soldier. Another told his family that he had attended a communal prayer in a mosque together with 120 of his comrades and officers, rejoicing: "From now on, we can go to the mosque together for every jumu'a." "Every Friday," the recruit Vasim Kurtamelov wrote, "we go to the mosque to perform our prayers," explaining: "I fight for the liberation of the Tatars and of the religion of Islam from the Bolshevist yoke." Numerous letters give a clear indication of a profound, religiously charged hatred for Moscow. "For 20 years we were prisoners of these godless Soviets, were starving and working day and night," the recruit Mambet Aliev declared. "God, the Almighty, will give us the strength to destroy the godless enemy quickly." In a more bitter tone, another volunteer exclaimed: "Thank Allah, now we will soon be liberated from the criminal Bolsheviks, whom we will chase out of our country like filthy dogs." The Muslim soldier Ibrahim Baqirov reassured a friend who also fought in a German unit: "Allah will protect us and the brave German soldiers, so that we will eradicate the accursed once and for all," while his comrade Rustam Asanov explained to his father: "I went to join the defense against the godless and to fight for their complete annihilation. May Allah help us to exterminate them. We will show these godless Communists whether God exists or not." The imminence of death shines through the lines of almost all of the letters. Explicitly referring to the prospect of martyrdom, the volunteer Bashid Cheldov wrote to his friend that "if I fall, so I will have fallen for Muhammad." Some of the letters monitored by the Germans reflect feelings of concern and discontent, most notably with respect to poor food provisions and retaliatory attacks by partisans against Muslim villages. "The freedom of the people means death for us. Now our luck is not worth much anymore," wrote one soldier. Most letters, though, show the high hopes the Crimean Tatar recruits had in the summer of 1942. Similarly, the mail the soldiers received from their friends and families was mostly optimistic. From a Tatar village, a Muslim woman wrote to the front that their lives had improved under German rule, wishing: "May Allah give you and the German army with the Führer Adolf Hitler health and success." "The mosque has been reopened and everybody goes to prayer," Majid Ablamit wrote to illustrate the perceived improvement of life in Muslim villages and quarters. In the end, the military situation had a considerable impact on the general tenor of the letters. Following the fall of Kerch in spring 1942, Hasan Ahmedov wrote home full of jubilation: "We have conquered Kerch and shattered the Red Russian Army, so that it can never recover," explaining the victory with reference to Islam: "The word of the victor is with us because we storm in the name of Allah, therefore victory is also with us. Allah has also given Adolf Effendi to us, therefore we will always remain winners." Enthused, Hentig reported that "Kerch has given them back self-confidence, has filled them with pride, so that they, with deep religious devotion, attach faith and reliance to the banner of the Führer."[53] The situation on the Sevastopol front was similar. An officer who monitored letters sent by the Muslim recruits who fought to bring down the fortress in the summer of 1942 reported that there was "no control day" which would disprove the men's "deep gratitude to the Führer." And he, too, noted the Muslims' considerable religiosity.[54] One legionnaire wrote from Sevastopol: "I do not know how I can thank the Führer of the German people and army, Adolf Hitler." His comrade, in a letter to his mother, reveled in the new freedom of religion. "Allah may therefore strengthen us, soon to be able to smash these atheists and satans." The Tatar Ahmed Ibrahimov sent home a photograph of Hitler. Shevket Kermov praised "our liberator Adolf Hitler" and his army. The Muslim Yahya Umarov wrote to his brother, who was also fighting in the Wehrmacht: "May Allah give you energy and a victory before Sevastopol." The soldier Baqir Osman wished that the "great Allah may give us and our friends a rapid victory over our enemies." German officers reading these letters were content, summarizing: "Thanks to the considerate support of their superiors and the friendly attitude of their comrades, all Tatar letters attest to physical and emotional well-being." Yet these Crimean field letters must be read with caution. There was certainly a degree of self-censorship among the Tatar soldiers who were used to police-state surveillance. Moreover, only a few field letters from Muslims have survived the war. Those discussed here were exclusively written by Crimean Tatar recruits during a period of military success. It is therefore impossible to make a balanced assessment of the soldiers' piety on the basis of these letters, let alone to extrapolate from these attitudes to those of all Muslims fighting in the German armies. Nevertheless, they do show that religion, at least for some of the Muslim recruits, played a significant role beyond empty everyday rhetoric.

In the case of the Eastern Muslim units of the SS, Harun al-Rashid also gave a positive assessment of the soldiers' piety. In one of his first reports to Berger, al-Rashid wrote that he had arrived at the Muslim regiment expecting that the Muslims, "as a consequence of Bolshevist anti-religious propaganda," would by no means be "convinced Mohammedans" any longer.[155] However, to his "delight," he had discovered that the opposite was true. The "Mohammedan idea" was strong and served as a good instrument "to powerfully exploit East Turkdom for German interests."[156] Antireligious ideas were promoted only by the East Ministry's nationalist exiles around Veli Kajum. Some recruits did indeed draw on their piety when communicating with al-Rashid. Strong piety came to the fore, for instance, in a letter written by a volunteer in the Eastern Turkic SS Corps to al-Rashid, bemoaning Soviet "atrocities and abolition of faith."[157] The letter echoed German propaganda, arguing that the Muslims of the Soviet Union had always been aware that Germany was a "friend of the Muslims." "You are Muslim like us. For us, you are not only commander but also father, in whom we have confidence with full heart," the soldier wrote. Similarly, a spokesman of the Azerbaijanis, who wrote to al-Rashid as a "brother in our holy faith," stressed his and his comrades' strong piety and emphasized, repeating German slogans, the ideals Islam and Nazism supposedly shared: "While the German people began their fight against Judaism in 1933, the Muslims were already against them 1,363 years ago." He added: "This is only one of many facts that connect us to the German people."[158] Al-Rashid, however, soon realized that the overall picture was more complex. A few months later he felt confident enough to classify different degrees of religiosity, which were in his eyes related to ethnicity and origin. The Turkestanis, "considerably influenced by the mullahs and especially by the chief mullah as well as by the German staff," had proven themselves to be pious and loyal soldiers. His assessment of the Azerbaijanis was similar. Only the Volga Tatars, he reported, were unreliable, and he did not yet have the confidence to assess the "Mohammedan-religious side" of the Crimean Tatars. "The general Islamic bond can yield good results among the Turkestanis, the Azerbaijanis, and, according to my impressions, also the Crimean Tatars, while I do not expect any success in this respect for a considerable part of the Volga Ural Tatars," he stated.[159] This view of the Volga Tatars was confirmed in a letter sent to the Islamic Central Institute in Berlin by a Muslim solider from the Idel-Ural Legion:

Until 1918 we were all religious and avouched our Islamic faith, but, as we have been under Soviet rule for 25 years, many of us are now godless. At the moment, we stand in the ranks of the German Wehrmacht. We would like to become religious again, which is also in the interests of our military leaders. Among us are many who know how to conduct prayers, but there is nobody who offers them with full authority because he does not know the theoretical tenets of the Islamic religion. My appeal is for someone to help us and to teach us the theoretical tenets of our religion and help us to enter deeper into the nature of the Islamic religion, especially those who are still aloof. We can write and speak Tatar and Russian. Arabic we can only read. From my standpoint, Islam would have to become an organizing power for our people and our nation.[160]

In its attempts to boycott the pan-Islamic line of the SS, the East Ministry did not miss the opportunity to exploit the Volga Tatars' apparent lack of religiosity. As late as early 1945, the head of the East Ministry's Tatar section, Count Leon Stamati, argued that only 20 to 30 percent of the Volga Tatars were religious: "The youths, especially the most active and intelligent, think little of religion."[161] The imams represented the past. The national identity was far more important than the religious. Also, "religious fanaticism" would not "suit" the Tatars, whom he characterized as a "somber peasant people," stressing that "pan-Islamism would not find the least resonance" with them. This assessment was exaggerated and part of the East Ministry's attempts to stop the SS's Islamic mobilization campaign in the last months of the war. In his report opposing the Islamic revolutionary policy of the SS in the Soviet Union, Mende had already alluded to the lack of religiosity among Eastern Muslims.[162] Furthermore, though Wehrmacht and SS reports gave a generally more positive assessment of their Muslim soldiers' religiosity, some Wehrmacht reports suggested that Muslims from the Soviet Union at times appeared less religious than the army command would have liked. Thus, although in July 1943 Heygendorff noted that the "reawakening of religion" was "considered by the legionnaires generally with gratitude," he remarked a few months later: "The religious life of the legionnaires demands special support as participation is very low. If attendance at a sermon were completely optional, only a few legionnaires would attend."[163] Similarly, the commander of the Azerbaijani

Legion reported that "not very many of the younger age groups attend the religious instruction classes."[164] Those who did would often be discriminated against by their comrades with the derogatory nickname "mullahs." The commander also advised dealing cautiously with religious questions, as German soldiers who engaged in religious discussions about Islam would be asked such questions as "Why are you not a Muslim then?" Indeed, Germans lacked authenticity when launching Islamic propaganda in the units. Richard Hartmann, Olzscha's Islam expert, warned that former Red Army soldiers who had been "well trained" by the Soviets would "quickly see through this theater."[165] At the SS these warnings fell on deaf ears. Only after the war did Olzscha acknowledge that his policies were based on the "erroneous assumption" that all soldiers were "devout Mohammedans."[166]

In the Balkans, assessments of the Muslim soldiers' religiosity varied as well. While Himmler and Berger repeatedly showed themselves convinced of the piety of Handžar's soldiers, reports from the field were mixed. There were signs indicating that the attendance at prayers by the Muslims of Handžar was not very high.[167] In April 1944, Karl-Gustav Sauberzweig reported from Bosnia that his men were "only too happy" to adopt "National Socialist teachings."[168] In many respects, National Socialism was proving stronger than Islam, he remarked, although hurriedly adding that religion still remained the core element of troop support: "We, however, want to preserve the foundation of Islam in our people, and I take care of that." This patronizing attitude could also easily turn into discrimination. Indeed, the biggest obstacle to the success of Germany's Islam policies and propaganda in the units, and indeed the whole military project, was discrimination.

From the outset, the recruitment of Muslims raised concerns in Berlin about racial and religious discrimination. On 6 August 1943, Himmler explicitly urged the German SS officers of Handžar to be tolerant toward their Muslim comrades.[169] "They have followed the call of the Islamic leadership and emerged through hatred of the common Jewish-English-Bolshevist enemy and through adoration of and loyalty to the universally admired Führer, Adolf Hitler," he declared. The Germans were therefore obliged to show them every kind of respect: "I do not want that, because of foolishness or narrow-minded bigotry, even just by one individual, a number rising to tens of thousands of brave volunteers and their families becomes discontented with and concerned about the rights that they have been granted." Also, the "joking and teasing common among comrades" was strictly forbidden around Muslim volunteers. "There is to be no discussion, and certainly not in the circle of comrades, about the special privileges granted to the Mohammedans."[170] Himmler's concerns were shared by the Wehrmacht leadership. After the war, Heygendorff stressed that he had always expected tactful behavior on the part of his officers toward Islam and the Muslims.[171] He had advised them not to be too curious, not to drink alcohol in the presence of Muslims, and not to indulge in rough talk about women. Heygendorff's statement was not just part of his postwar apologia. He had indeed given these kinds of orders during the war.[172] In a directive dated 22 March 1944 he exhorted the Germans in the legions to have "respect for the religious feelings of the volunteers," warning that any "mockery of unfamiliar religious performances," or "contemptuous remarks" about religious questions, were strictly forbidden.[173] Similar instructions had also been issued by Niedermayer's headquarters.[174] And in the summer of 1942, just after the units had been deployed, the Wehrmacht instructed the German personnel of the Muslim battalions "to respect and not to ridicule" the volunteers' religious customs "even though they seem strange."[175] In the end, however, these repeated instructions and appeals may suggest that religious and racial discrimination was indeed a problem.

Despite all efforts to instruct the German personnel on the need to respect Islam, a number of sources draw a vivid picture of religious discrimination in the Muslim units. Disregarding the religious authority and dignity of the chief imam of his battalion, one adjutant forced the mullah to do repeated "lie-down-stand-ups" to discipline him for arriving late to a parade.[176] A similar punishment was meted out to another imam by an army physician because the imam's act of prayer caused him to arrive late for medical service. Another mullah, who passed out for a short time while being treated by a dentist, had his beard shorn despite the significant religious and symbolic meaning that facial hair traditionally had for the authority of his position. Heygendorff punished all these offenses and removed the German officers from the battalions, warning that such "hostility toward religious attitudes" led to bitterness among the good elements in the units and strengthened the bad. In the SS, similar incidents occurred. Harun al-Rashid, for instance, complained about the conduct of a German officer who had beaten Muslims, thrown stones at them, and called them "swine"—the "worst insult for a Mohammedan," al-Rashid explained.[177] From the Balkans, Sauberzweig reported to Berger that he had to invest "a great deal of energy" every day "in order to instill in the German commanders a sense of the mission and the value of the imams."[178] "If anyone supported the imams and drew parallels between Islam and National Socialism, it was always me," he boasted.

In addition to insults of religious sentiments, racism, which had been promoted by the regime for a decade, became a problem in everyday interactions between volunteers and Germans. After the war, Mende remembered that the German staff in the Eastern Legions had often regarded the recruits from the Soviet Union as second-rate soldiers and had called them "blackamoors" (*Mohren*), "wogs" (*Kanaken*), and even "traitors" (*Landesverräter*).[179] Other insults were "Hottentots" (*Hottentotten*), "savages" (*Wilde*), "bushmen" (*Buschmänner*), "Mongols" (*Mongolen*), "Bolsheviks" (*Bolschewiken*), "partisan reserve" (*Partisanenersatz*), and "booty comrades" (*Beutekameraden*).[180] In Warsaw, Heygendorff was infuriated when he read the slogan "Poles, Jews, and Legionnaires, last wagon" daubed on a train car.[181] Muslims from the Soviet Union abstained from taking their furlough in the Reich simply to avoid personal insults and harassment by Germans. Heygendorff wrote about a Caucasian lieutenant who returned early to his unit from a visit to his sister, who worked in Austria. When asked for the reason, he answered that they had been thrown off a tram in Vienna. An SS man had told the tram conductor that he would not enter the wagon until the "beasts" (*Viehzeug*) had left it.[182] Indeed, these kinds of incidents became particularly significant in the final months of the war, when Muslim units of the Eastern Legions were employed in Western Europe and the Reich. "In the métro, the Parisians now gaze at Mongols in German uniforms," noted Ernst Jünger, Germany's notorious First World War veteran, in his diary in May 1944, recounting his experiences with Turkic legionnaires in France.[183] Fascinated with the Islamic character of the units, he even described the emblem on their badges: "A mosque with two minarets and the circumscription 'Biz Alla Bilen. Turkistan.'" Negative images of Muslims and the East lingered, however. Instructions and brochures distributed to German army personnel, designed to overcome existing stereotypes of the Asiatic subhuman (*Untermensch*), had little influence. German officers in the Balkans were often no less discriminatory in their attitudes to the Muslim recruits there. Bosnian Muslims who served in the Waffen-SS were sometimes derogatively called "Mujos" by their German comrades.[184] The commander of Skanderbeg complained about "primitive Albania," which had in his view remained "more Turkish" than Turkey itself, "beginning with the women's headscarf."[185] The alleged "valor of the Albanian" was nothing more than a myth, he sneered. "With a light grenade launcher you can virtually chase him around the entire globe. In attack he goes only so far with you until he finds something to steal and plunder." Ultimately, Berlin's attempt to exempt Muslims, whether Arabs, Bosniaks, Albanians, Turks, or Tatars, from the regime's conventional racism proved difficult to communicate to ordinary German soldiers in the field. Years of Nazi indoctrination and racist propaganda were not easily overcome.

Although the military command faced difficulties in controlling the everyday behavior of German soldiers, it proved easier to minimize the degree of institutionalized discrimination. In the early months of German recruitment, German officers stood higher in the military hierarchy than any legionnaire, no matter what his rank. Thus, German soldiers could only be disciplined by German superiors, not by non-German recruits, even if those recruits had a higher rank.[186] This changed. Eventually German soldiers even had to salute the Muslim recruit first if he held a higher rank. Moreover, legionnaires were soon, from May 1943 on, paid the same as German soldiers in the Wehrmacht.[187] Only one area seemed to be nonnegotiable, revealing the problems the regime still had when dealing with its foreign recruits: German authorities were most concerned to avoid any contact between Muslims from the Soviet Union and German women whom they met during their furlough in Germany. German women who became pregnant by Eastern volunteers were forced by the NSDAP Race Office to abort the child.[188] Even Muslim contact with Russian or Ukrainian "Eastern women workers" (*Ostarbeiterinnen*) in the Reich was disapproved of, although these "Eastern marriages" (*Ostehen*) were eventually tolerated in order to avoid relationships with German women.[189] These limitations derived from racial rather than religious motives. Despite some ideological pragmatism, race remained a firm obstacle in Germany's religious policies toward Muslims.

Defeat

On all fronts, Muslim soldiers kept fighting until the end. Only in the chaos of the last months of the war, when all hopes for a German victory were shattered, did it become difficult to maintain morale and discipline in the units. Both the Wehrmacht and the SS had to deal with an ever-rising number of desertions. In the Balkans, Handžar unmistakably began to fall to pieces in autumn 1944.[190] A number of Muslims deserted to fight in the green cadres.[191] Soldiers left individually and in groups or simply did not return from furlough.[192] Others engaged in acts of self-mutilation to enforce discharge.[193] By the end of September, around 2,000 Muslims had deserted; on 17 October a further 140 recruits refused to fight the Soviets; and on 21 October, near Zagreb, nearly 600 men ran away.[194] With a growing number of deserters, the SS was eventually compelled to demobilize the division. On 29 October 1944, Kasche reported that 2,000 men had been disarmed and moved to the west of Zagreb for labor service.[195] A further 10,000 were to be disarmed in the coming days.[196] In the end, Himmler gave the Muslim recruits the choice to either fight in SS and Ustaša units or to work in the labor service in the Reich.[197] The performance of Skanderbeg also did not meet the expectations of the SS.[198] As the military situation spun out of control, Albanian recruits deserted en masse, and the SS had to demobilize the division. Among the Muslim volunteers from the Soviet Union the number of desertions was lower.[199] Some, however, as Germany crumbled, hastily tried to change sides. Julian Amery, one of the British liaison officers with the Albanian partisans, was much struck by the desertions from Turkestani Wehrmacht units, which had been employed in the Balkans: when defecting to the partisans, a group of the Muslim soldiers brought with them not only their weapons but also the ears of their German officers, wrapped in a large green handkerchief.[200] In the *Osttürkischer Waffenverband* the only significant case of a mass desertion was the defection of Ghulam Alimov and his comrades to the Slovak partisans in late December 1944. The Azerbaijanis under Fatalibey immediately distanced themselves from Alimov and his men.[201] In the end, the majority of the recruits from the Soviet Union showed more discipline than one might have expected given the hopelessness of the military situation. It was this hopelessness, in fact, that drove them to continue fighting. There was no going back.

The Muslims in the German forces were well aware that defeat would mean retaliation and possibly death.

After the war was over, the fate of Germany's Muslim soldiers was grim. In the Balkans, they faced Tito's retribution.[202] The religious leaders of the SS units were the first to be punished. Halim Malkoč, the last division imam of Handžar, was executed in 1948.[203] The fate of his predecessor, Muhasilović, remains unclear. Imam Husein Džozo was sentenced to five years of imprisonment and forced labor and a five-year revocation of all political rights; he later adapted and became an influential functionary in Communist Yugoslavia.[204]

In the East, Moscow, having already deported the Muslims of the Caucasus and the Crimea, saw the collaboration of all those who had fought in German units as high treason. Muslim soldiers from the Soviet Union, now scattered in SS and Wehrmacht units across Western Europe, were not saved. At the Yalta Conference, the Big Three had agreed to repatriate all former Soviet citizens. Accordingly, the British and Americans disarmed all soldiers of the Eastern Legions and the Eastern Turkic SS Corps and detained them in special camps. Together with civilian refugees from the Caucasus and the Crimea who had followed the Wehrmacht, the Western Allies eventually turned legionnaires over to the Red Army.[205] The extradition began in the summer of 1945. The Muslim soldiers of the 162nd Turk Division, for instance, which had been detained in a large camp near Modena, Italy, were handed over to the Soviets in Taranto. Some had been able to escape the poorly guarded camp.[206] The extradition of the remainder was accompanied by dramatic scenes. Dozens jumped from moving trains. As they docked in Odessa, many others leaped from the deportation ships into the Black Sea; some committed suicide. One of the imams died in an act of self-immolation. In the Soviet Union many were massacred by Soviet cadres or deported to gulags. "All during 1945 and 1946 a big wave of genuine, at-long-last, enemies of the Soviet government flowed into the Archipelago," Alexander Solzhenitsyn later recalled in *The Gulag Archipelago*.[207] "These were the Vlasov men, the Krasnov Cossacks, and Moslems from the national units created under Hitler." Protests by the Red Cross made no impression on British and US authorities. The international press also showed little interest. Working as a war correspondent on the continent at the time, George Orwell was one of the few to publicly criticize these deportations. "These facts, known to many journalists on the spot, went almost unmentioned in the British Press," he noted in 1946, condemning the apparent public disinterest in the forced repatriations.[208] Only when it became indisputable that the extraditions ended with executions and slave labor did the Allies abandon their repatriation policy. Those Muslims who had remained in the camps or had escaped were granted the status of "displaced persons," and several thousand stayed in the West.

Conclusion

In the last months of the war, in the Berlin bunker, Hitler lamented that the Third Reich's efforts to mobilize the Muslim world had not been strong enough.[1] "All Islam vibrated at the news of our victories," and Muslims had been "ready to rise in revolt," he told Bormann.[2] "Just think what we could have done to help them, even to incite them, as would have been both our duty and our interest!" Instead, Germany had too long respected Italian interests in the Muslim world, which had hindered, as Hitler put it, a "splendid policy with regard to Islam." "For the Italians in these parts of the world are more bitterly hated, of course, than either the British or the French." The German-Italian alliance had "created a feeling of malaise among our Islamic friends, who inevitably saw us as accomplices, willing or unwilling, of their oppressors," he bemoaned. Unbound from Italy, Germany could have liberated the Muslims from Vichy and Italian rule in North Africa, which would then have found strong repercussions in Muslim lands under British rule. A movement could have been incited in North Africa that would have spilled over to the rest of the Muslim world. "Such a policy would have aroused the enthusiasm of the whole of Islam. It is a characteristic of the Moslem world, from the shores of the Atlantic to those of the Pacific, that what affects one, for good or for evil, affects all."[3] The German-Muslim alliance was, in fact, a recurring subject in the bunker during the final weeks of the regime.[4] Some days earlier, when reflecting on his visions of a European New Order, Hitler had insisted that his New Europe would have engaged in "a bold policy of friendship toward Islam."[5] In Hitler's view, Germany's Islam policy had not gone far enough.

These pages have, for the first time, comprehensively examined Germany's engagement with Islam during the Second World War. They have shown that Germany's attempts to employ Islam in its war effort were extensive, influencing policies in places like Sarajevo, Nalchik, Simferopol, Tunis, and even provincial Swabia. Instrumentalizing Islam in their policies and propaganda, German officials attempted to give legitimacy and authority to their war, to pacify the rear areas, to mobilize Muslims to fight on the side of the Third Reich, and to foment Muslim disobedience and incite religious violence in the enemies' hinterlands.

The first part of the book traced Germany's political involvement with Islam back to its colonial policies before 1914 and, more importantly, to its campaign to mobilize Muslims during the First World War. It explored debates during the Second World War, when, as the war reached Muslim lands in 1941, policy makers in Berlin again became interested in Islam. While diplomats in the Foreign Office were the first to discuss the employment of Islam, engaging in propaganda and employing Muslim collaborators, officials in the Wehrmacht and, to a lesser extent, the East Ministry soon joined in as well. It was the SS, however, which eventually took the lead in Germany's Islamic mobilization campaign, most importantly from 1943 on. In the end, almost all parts of the regime were involved.

The second part of the book addressed Germany's policies toward Muslims in the war zones, both in the occupied territories and behind the front lines. It showed that Germany granted Muslims religious concessions in these areas and launched religiously charged propaganda. It also demonstrated that the Germans encountered very different political and religious landscapes in the diverse war zones and that they adapted their policies and propaganda toward Muslims accordingly. Overall, Germany's religious policies and propaganda in the war zones had two functions— control and mobilization: they aimed to pacify and control the often unstable rear areas in a deteriorating war situation, and, at the same time, endeavored to instigate religious violence behind the enemy's front lines.

The third part addressed the recruitment and care of hundreds of thousands of Muslim soldiers by the Wehrmacht and the SS from 1941 on and examined the role that Islam played in the recruitment, treatment, and propagandistic indoctrination of these soldiers. The extent and intensity of this Muslim mobilization campaign can hardly be overestimated. From late 1943, the SS in particular focused on rallying Muslims and eventually went as far as to mobilize, or "activate," as it was put, all Muslims within its grasp, from East Africa to Bulgaria, though these plans were curtailed in the chaos of the final months of the war. Germany's religious policies and propaganda were intended to maintain military discipline in the Muslim units and enhance fighting morale. As with the policy in the war zones, here, too, control and mobilization were the main objectives.

German efforts to utilize Islam were remarkably consistent even when considered from a transregional perspective. Despite the chaos of the war and the often overlapping competencies of competing branches of the regime, German officials—from the traditional diplomat of the Foreign Office to the intellectual bureaucrat of the East Ministry to the ideological technocrat of the SS Head Office—routinely referred to the same notions of Islam and its role during the war. Overall, Muslims were not seen as threats or enemies but as powerful allies. In the war zones, German officials alluded to the general political significance of Islam when dealing with Muslims. The idea of Islamic unity, of *Weltislam* or *Weltmuselmanentum*, was omnipresent.

The reasons for Germany's efforts to promote an alliance with the Muslim world were closely connected to the course of the war, which reached Muslim territories in 1941–1942 and brought about a shift of German policy toward short-term planning and the mobilization of all available resources. Islam was, in this context, seen as a political force that could be employed against the Allies. Ideological considerations played only a marginal role. Although some Nazi ideologues, regime officials, and even members of the Nazi elite shared a positive ideological view of Islam, it was the military situation that led to Germany's campaign for Islamic mobilization.

Overall, these attempts failed. In North Africa and the Middle East, the reception was mixed. In areas like the Balkans or the Eastern territories, where Muslims often lived under terrible conditions, German courtship of Islam initially sparked some hope. In the end, many thousands of Muslims from these areas fought in the German armies. Religious policies and propaganda certainly sent the right messages. Still, it remains open to question whether religious policies and propaganda were the major reasons for this; in many cases other motivations were stronger. Ultimately, German propaganda failed to incite significant uprisings behind the front lines. Germany's policies in the Muslim world were less successful than officials in Berlin had hoped. They had been launched far too late and clashed too often with the violent realities of the war. Most importantly, they were founded upon too many misconceptions about Muslims and Islam.

A major obstacle to German efforts to employ Islam in its policies aimed at Muslims, be they under German rule, behind the front lines, or in German military units, was their lack of authenticity. It was all too obvious that the Germans wanted to instrumentalize Muslims for their interests and war necessities rather than for a truly religious cause. Berlin tried to solve the problem of authenticity by employing Muslim intermediaries, among them the numerous imams who worked in German units and major religious figures such as Amin al-Husayni, Jakub Szynkiewicz, and Muhamed Pandža. Trustworthy Muslim collaborators were to back the regime's directives and propaganda with their religious authority, while at the same time symbolizing German paternal care for Islam. The German authorities created Islamic hierarchies to administer and discipline Muslims in their military units as well as in the Muslim-populated regions of the occupied borderlands of the Soviet Union. But in other areas as well, they took care to involve the 'ulama. Yet, despite the use of intermediaries, Germany's claims that it protected the faithful lacked authenticity; often the practical, military motives were hard to hide. Another problem was that the Islamic world did not form a unified block. In seeing Muslims as a collective mass that could be manipulated if treated properly, German officials underestimated the religious, ethnic, linguistic, social, and political complexities and heterogeneities of the Muslim world. Put simply, the significance of pan-Islamic unity was overestimated. Islam was not organized according to hierarchical or ecclesiastical structures or led by a centralized authority that spoke for the faithful. Moreover, there was the question of religiosity. German efforts to employ Islam were based on the assumption that Muslims would follow a call to arms if it were legitimized by religion. To be sure, although Muslims' devotion to their faith had its limits, it should not be underestimated. Across the Balkans, the Eastern territories, North Africa, the Middle East, and beyond, religion played an important role in people's lives. Conflicts in the Balkans were often religiously charged. Resistance to Moscow frequently had a religious character. Since the nineteenth century, pan-Islamist and Islamic anti-imperialism had emerged across North Africa and the Middle East and experienced a revival after the First World War. On the other hand, one must ask whether other loyalties proved stronger than strictly religious ties. Tribal, ethnic, and national bonds mattered. After all, all Muslim populations between North Africa and Central Asia had strong national aspirations, which Berlin failed to recognize. And finally, Germany faced competition from all of the Allied powers in its courtship of Muslims and Islam. London and even Moscow could draw on age-old loyalties among their Muslim subjects. After all, hundreds of thousands of Muslims were fighting in the Red Army, the British forces, and the ranks of the Free French Forces.

The question of the wider appeal that this religious policy and propaganda had on Muslims across the world cannot be answered conclusively here, as the reception of German policies by Muslims has not been the focus of this study. A comprehensive examination of the reception of German policies and propaganda throughout the Muslim world is not feasible within the confines of a single book but must be undertaken through individual local, regional, and country studies in the future.[6]

Certainly the Germans found willing helpers among Islamic leaders such as Mufti Jakub Szynkiewicz in Vilnius, Imam Shakir Eriss in Riga, Mullah Alimseit Jamilov in Simferopol, Muhamed Pandža in Sarajevo, and the Berlin clerics Alimjan Idris, Taqi al-Din al-Hilali, and Amin al-Husayni. Yet this book has shown that the story was often much more complicated and that generalizations about the role of Muslims who became embroiled in Germany's war are almost impossible to make. Often it is not a clear-cut story of victims and perpetrators. Muslims could fall into either group or both. Some collaborated with military and occupation authorities. Thousands of Muslims fought in Hitler's armies and became involved in gruesome atrocities and massacres. Thousands fought against the German regime. In the war zones, the lines between Muslims and the victims of the Nazi policy of racial extermination could be thin—as seen in the cases of the Karaites and Krymchaks in the Crimea, the Judeo-Tats in the Caucasus, the Muslim Roma in the Balkans and Eastern territories, and Jewish converts to Islam—here, being Muslim or not could mean life or death. In the end, the Second World War and its immediate aftermath cost the lives of many thousands of Muslims.

Most of the key architects of Germany's policies toward Islam survived the war unharmed. Aged eighty-six, Max von Oppenheim died in 1946 in South Germany. In the final months of the war he had left Berlin for Dresden (here he had observed the founding of the SS mullah school though without getting involved) and later fled to Landshut.[7] His protégés, who had been so instrumental in Germany's policy toward Islam in the Second World War, mostly carried on. Fritz Grobba was arrested by the Soviets, spent ten years in prison, and afterward retired in West Germany. Otto Werner von Hentig remained at the Foreign Office and after his retirement worked as an advisor for the Saudi state. Curt Prüfer retired in Switzerland. Ernst Woermann was put on trial in Nuremberg, sentenced to five years in prison, and did not return to the Foreign Office. Oskar von Niedermayer's fate was bleaker. Having been imprisoned in 1944 after making some critical remarks about the regime, he survived the war but in 1945 was arrested by the Soviet authorities, sentenced to twenty-five years in prison, and eventually died in a prison near Moscow in 1948. The elderly Ernst-August Köstring was captured, interned as a US prisoner of war, and released in 1947. Otto Bräutigam, too, was held briefly in US custody but was soon set free and pursued a career in the German Foreign Office. Gerhard von Mende became head of the government-sponsored agency that dealt with non-German collaborators who had escaped repatriation; he also worked as director of a research institute of the Federal Ministry for Expellees, which was headed by none other than Theodor Oberländer, commander of one of the first Muslim Wehrmacht units. In contrast, the leading SS officials who had been involved in the campaign did not take up major postwar careers. Gottlob Berger was tried in Nuremberg and sentenced to twenty-five years in prison, though he was released in 1951 and took up work in German industry, keeping a casual interest in the Islamic world and visiting the Middle East in the 1950s. Reiner Olzscha was arrested by the Americans, then freed, but on returning to his family in the Soviet sector he was captured and brought to the Soviet Union, where he was executed in 1947. The aged Harun al-Rashid escaped imprisonment and worked as an author in West Germany. Karl-Gustav Sauberzweig was captured by the British and killed himself with cyanide in 1946 to avoid extradition to Yugoslavia.

The major Muslim collaborators escaped. As Germany sank into chaos in the final weeks of the war and Hitler lamented about Islam in his bunker, al-Husayni packed his suitcases.[8] Together with Werner Otto von Hentig, who had been ordered to bring him south, he went to Bad Gastein, where the two men parted.[9] On 7 May 1945, just hours before the capitulation, an unmarked Siebel Si 204 plane brought al-Husayni to an airport near Bern. Anxious to avoid trouble, the Swiss quickly handed him over to the French, who brought him to St.-Maur, near Paris, where he was provided with a villa.[10] In Paris, al-Husayni was warmly received by Si Kaddour Benghabrit, who on the occasion of the 1945 'Id al-Fitr hosted a grand dinner in honor of the mufti, attended by numerous Muslim diplomats.[11] The Allies received many petitions from across the Islamic world requesting al-Husayni's return to the Middle East—one of them came from Hasan al-Banna, who wrote to Miles Lampson on the matter.[12] Concerned that trying him as a war criminal would provoke Muslim uprisings, the Allies finally let him go. On 28 May 1946, a plane flew him from Paris to Cairo, where he was enthusiastically welcomed by some of his followers. Once back in the Middle East, al-Husayni supported efforts to bring some of the Muslim soldiers from the Soviet Union who had served in German ranks and escaped the forced repatriations to Middle Eastern countries.[13] Some did indeed settle in the Middle East. Even years after the war, the mufti marveled at Germany's former Muslim recruits, in his memoirs praising the "Arab, Bosnian, Azerbaijani, and other soldiers in the lands of the Axis" who had been "ready to combat the colonial states."[14] He also claimed that many of these recruits from the Eastern territories had "burned with zeal for jihad in the holy lands of Palestine," just like the soldiers from the Balkans had "longed for the jihad in Palestine."[15] In fact, some former Handžar soldiers fought in the 1948 war and were remembered in the mufti's memoirs as "martyrs" and "wounded heroes."[16] In 1947 Simon Wiesenthal and Maurice Pearlman published books revealing details of al-Husayni's Nazi collaboration.[17] In the Middle East the mufti never again rose to his prewar eminence; not only was he discredited because of his wartime activities but, more importantly, because he represented the past. In Germany, however, some still valued him as a partner. The December 1951 issue of *Zeitschrift für Geopolitik* published an interview with al-Husayni on German-Arab relations.[18] The Foreign Office also kept in contact with him. In the early 1950s it was none other than Hentig, then back in the diplomatic service, who again sought cooperation with the mufti.[19]

Among those who escaped was also Mufti Jakub Szynkiewicz of Vilnius, who had moved to Naumburg after the evacuation of the SS mullah school and eventually managed to leave for Cairo.[20] Alimjan Idris, who saw the end of the war in Bavaria, stayed in Munich.[21] Hitler had brought more Muslims to Germany than had ever lived there before, and some stayed on after the war. Many of the Muslim soldiers and refugees from the Soviet Union who escaped repatriation were interned in camps for foreign nationals in Limburg or in Mittenwald in South Germany. In Munich, these Muslims eventually formed the first Islamic community of postwar Germany.[22] It was, in fact, led by old wartime comrades around Alimjan Idris. In 1953 some of the

Munich Muslims founded the first Islamic organization of the Federal Republic, the so-called Islamic Religious Society (*Religiose Gemeinschaft Islam*) led by Ibrahim Gacaoglu, an ex-Wehrmacht imam. It was soon followed by the rival Ecclesiastical Administration of Muslim Refugees in the German Federal Republic (*Geistliche Verwaltung der Muslimflüchtlinge in der Bundesrepublik Deutschland*), headed by the former chief imam of the Eastern Muslim SS Division, Nurredin Namangani. Considered politically important, these groups received strong official support—while Namangani was funded by the West German state and supported by Mende's institute and Oberländer's refugee ministry, Gacaoglu's group was on the US payroll.

Indeed, US officials became increasingly interested in the Muslim veterans.[23] As in the early Cold War, Washington began to see Moscow's Muslim population as instruments to destabilize the Soviet Union, Germany's former Muslim helpers seemed to be ideal partners. Some of them were soon employed by US intelligence services, and many later worked for Radio Liberty in Munich, where they once again became involved in Islamic propaganda directed against Moscow. The Muslim employees of the US services included Said Shamil, Edige Kirimal, Abdul Fatalibey, who was eventually murdered by the KGB in a Munich apartment, and many others who had served the Germans in the war years.[24] Some were sent abroad on intelligence and propaganda missions. During the 1954 hajj, for instance, two of Germany's Muslim war veterans who were now in the service of Washington, Rusi Nasar and Hamid Rashid, were sent to Mecca, where they engaged in anti-Communist propaganda among Soviet and other pilgrims. A problem, however, US officials soon realized, was that all of these figures were tainted by their Nazi past and often lacked a proper religious education. US authorities therefore began to move away from them and to cooperate with more credible and more fundamentalist Muslims. The most prominent among them was the famous Said Ramadan, a disciple (and son-in-law) of al-Banna and leader of the Muslim Brotherhood in Western Europe, centered in Munich.

The US involvement with Germany's Muslim war veterans was of course part of a more general Cold War strategy. As the Cold War developed, officials in Washington began to see the Muslim corridor between North Africa and East Asia as a "green belt against Communism." During the Second World War, the legendary US intelligence officer Archibald Roosevelt Jr. had predicted: "In the post-war future, the Moslems as a whole will be a factor of increasing importance in world politics," stressing: "In the event of future wars, the United States as the recognized friend of the Moslems might find invaluable support in these strategically important regions."[25] In the global Cold War, Islam was soon considered crucial in the fight against Communism. Following the Indian partition, US diplomats leaned away from India and toward Pakistan because they viewed an Islamic state as more determined in the fight against Communism.[26] In the 1950s, the Eisenhower government made every effort to use Saudi Arabia as an explicitly religious counterweight to Nasser's nonaligned, secular, pan-Arab regime in Egypt.[27] Across the world, Washington began supporting Islamic political groups and propaganda. This engagement reached its peak in the 1980s with the support of the *mujahidin* against the Soviets in Afghanistan.[28] Here Washington distributed not only weapons but also propaganda with the call for jihad. In early 1980, just weeks after the Soviet invasion, Carter's National Security advisor, Zbigniew Brzezinski, personally exhorted Afghan *mujahidin* on the Afghan-Pakistani mountain border to confront the Soviet atheists: "That land over there is yours, you go back to it one day, because your fight will prevail and you have your homes and mosques back again. Because your cause is right and God is on your side."[29] Moscow had experienced Islam as its Achilles' heel ever since the Bolshevik seizure of power and increasingly began to implement its own religious policies toward Muslims in the Caucasus, Central Asia, and beyond.[30] Yet, in the end, the jihad supported by America in Afghanistan contributed considerably to the collapse of the Soviet Union and the Eastern Bloc. For the United States, Islam remained an instrument of foreign policy and warfare also after the Cold War.[31]

Throughout the modern period, from the age of imperialism to the Cold War and beyond, Islam played a significant role in the policies and strategies of the non-Muslim great powers. Whenever non-Muslim powers became involved in Muslim areas, their strategists, officers and policy makers perceived Islam to be of considerable relevance to their policies. They not only considered "Islamic sensibilities" but sought actively to employ Islam, whether to control and pacify Muslims or to mobilize them against enemies. These policies reflected a range of conceptions that informed (non-Muslim) politicians and strategists, military officers and administrative personnel. Religious affiliation was often a significant category of classification. Islam was understood to be an organized religion that could be studied and understood. Muslim communities seemed to be governed by a coherent system of rules, values, norms, and conventions. Islam seemed to offer a comprehensible religious code that non-Muslim authorities could decode and exploit for political aims. Moreover, Islamic imperatives, which Muslims seemed to follow and which were perceived to be intelligible, appeared to provide an ideal framework to legitimize authority. In fact, religious policy seemed to be the only way to control and mobilize Muslims since, in the eyes of non-Muslim officials, the devout Muslim recognized only one legitimate authority, namely, Islam.

German attempts to make use of Islam during the Second World War can be seen as an episode in the longer historical story of the strategic employment of Islam by the (non-Muslim) great powers in the modern age. Compared to other campaigns for Islamic mobilization, Germany's policy was both one of the shortest-lived and one of the most improvised. In geographic scope and intensity, however, it was one of the most vigorous attempts to politicize and instrumentalize Islam in modern history.

NOTE ON SOURCES

NOTES

ACKNOWLEDGMENTS

INDEX

NOTE ON SOURCES

This book is based on a wealth of archival sources, including policy papers and memoranda, military reports and manuals, propaganda pamphlets, broadcast monitoring records, speeches, field post letters and memoirs, Nuremberg interrogation transcripts, petitions, and numerous military orders. Given that it does not include a bibliography, readers may find it helpful to have a list of the archives consulted.

Most of the documents used in this work are stored in German archives, most importantly the German Federal Archives (*Bundesarchiv*), Berlin-Lichterfelde (BAB); the German Federal Archives (*Bundesarchiv*), Koblenz (BAK); the Political Archives of the German Foreign Office (*Politisches Archiv des Auswärtigen Amts*), Berlin (PA); the German Federal Military Archives (*Bundesarchiv, Militärarchiv*), Freiburg (BA–MA); and the Archives of the Federal Commissioner for the Stasi Documents (*Bundesbeauftragter für die Stasi-Unterlagen*), Berlin (BStU). Various smaller German archives were also consulted, including the German Broadcasting Archive (*Deutsches Rundfunkarchiv*), Frankfurt (DRA), and the Archive of the Institute of Contemporary History (*Archiv des Instituts für Zeitgeschichte*), Munich (IfZ); municipal archives, including the Berlin State Archive (*Landesarchiv Berlin*), Berlin (LArchB), and the Stuttgart General State Archive (*Hauptstaatsarchiv Stuttgart*), Stuttgart (LArchBWSt); and private archives, including the Oppenheim Bank Archive (*Hausarchiv Sal. Oppenheim*), Cologne (OA), and the Family Archive Oberländer (*Familienarchiv Oberländer*), Bonn (FAO).

Moreover, the work draws on sources stored in various non-German archives, including the British National Archives, Kew (NA); the Archive of the Imperial War Museum, London (IWM); the United States National Archives, Maryland (USNA); the Archives of the Center for Advanced Holocaust Studies, Washington, D.C. (USHMA); the Vienna City and State Archive (*Wiener Stadt- und Landesarchiv*), Vienna (WstLArch); the Czech Central Military Archives (*Vojenský Ústřední Archiv*), Prague (VÚA); the National Archives of the Czech Republic, Prague (*Národní Archiv České Republiky*) (NAČR) (accessed through ZMO); the Russian State Military Archive (*Rossiiskii Gosudarstvenni Voennyi Arkhiv*), Moscow (RGVA) (accessed through USHMA); the Latvian State Historical Archive (*Latvijas Valsts Vēstures Arhīvs*), Riga (LVVA) (accessed through USHMA); the State Archives of the Crimea (*Derzhavnyi Arkhiv v Avtonomnii Respublitsi Krym*), Simferopol (DAARK); the Albanian Central State Archive (*Arkivi Qendror Shtetëror*), Tirana (AQSH); and the Iranian National Archives (*Sazman-i Asnad-i Milli-yi Iran*), Tehran (SAMI).

Finally, some of the primary documents used are stored in the archival collections of libraries, notably the German National Library (*Deutsche Nationalbibliothek*), Leipzig (DNB); the Berlin State Library (*Staatsbibliothek zu Berlin*), Berlin (SBB); the Library of the Center for Modern Oriental Studies (*Zentrum Moderner Orient*), Berlin (ZMO); the National and University Library of Zagreb (*Nacionalna i Sveučilišna Knjižnica*), Zagreb (NSK); and the Gazi Husrev Beg Library (*Gazi Husrev-Begova Biblioteka*), Sarajevo (GHB).

Newspapers consulted include the *Völkischer Beobachter, Deutsche Allgemeine Zeitung, Frankfurter Zeitung, National-Zeitung, Illustrierter Beobachter, Deutsche Rundschau Leipzig, Berliner Illustrierte Nachtausgabe, Das 12 Uhr Blatt: Neue Berliner Zeitung, Westdeutsche Zeitung, Rheinisch-Westfälische Zeitung, Brünner Tagblatt, Brünner Abendblatt, Donau-Zeitung, Signal, Krakauer Zeitung, Deutsche Zeitung im Ostland, Wiener Illustrierte, Freie Innerschweiz, Daily Telegraph, New York Times, Christian Science Monitor, Le Temps, Le Petit Parisien, Le Petit Marseillais, La Gazette de Lausanne, La Bourse Egyptienne, Shanghai Times*, and *al-Manar*.

Finally, this work draws on countless other published primary sources, contemporary books and articles, and memoirs. Memoirs, rich as they are, were by their nature written some time after the events and were usually influenced by their authors' ambitions to give themselves a place in history, and, in some cases, to distance themselves from crimes committed during the war; they have therefore been treated with particular caution.

A similarly cautious approach was taken regarding the illustrations. Many of the photographs reprinted in the book were originally produced for propaganda purposes, and, for all the historical insights they may provide, have to be treated with this in mind. Illustrations used in this book are stored in the German Federal Archives; the Ullstein Picture Archive (*Ullstein Bild*) (Ullstein); the Prussian Heritage Image Archive (*Bildarchiv Preußischer Kulturbesitz*), Berlin (BPK); the Archive of the Mémorial de la Shoah (*Archives du Mémorial de la Shoah*), Paris (MS); the Polish National

Digital Archives (*Narodowe Archiwum Cyfrowe*), Warsaw (NAC); the Archive of the Croatian Historical Museum (*Hrvatski Povijesni Muzej*), Zagreb (HPM); the Gazi Husrev Beg Library; and the Archive of the Historical Museum of Bosnia and Herzegovina (*Historijski Muzej Bosne i Hercegovine*), Sarajevo (HMBH).

NOTES

INTRODUCTION

1 Mark Mazower, *Hitler's Empire: Nazi Rule in Occupied Europe* (London, 2008), esp. 454–460.

2 Paul Kluke, "Nationalsozialistische Europaideologie," *Vierteljahreshefte für Zeitgeschichte* 3, 3 (1955), 240–275, 270.

3 David Motadel, "Anticolonial Nationalists and Germany's War for a New World Order, 1941–1945," in Nikolaus Wachsmann and Jan Rüger (eds.), *Essays in German History* (London, forthcoming), examines Germany's anti-imperial campaign.

4 Apparent are the parallels to conceptions of other religions, which were equally seen as global, at times even political, such as "world Judaism" (*Weltjudentum*) or "world Catholicism" (*Weltkatholizismus*), each imbued with a specific set of meanings.

5 Clifford Geertz, *Islam Observed: Religious Development in Morocco and Indonesia* (New Haven, CT, 1968), famously illustrated cultural diversity within the Islamic world. Other discussions of the heterogeneity of Islam, globally and within Muslim majority societies, include Ernest Gellner, *Muslim Society* (Cambridge, 1981); Aziz Al-Azmeh, *Islams and Modernities* (London, 1993); and Dale Eikelman and James Piscatori, *Muslim Politics* (Oxford, 1996). On the emergence of modern conceptions of the "Islamic world" among Muslims and non-Muslims, see Cemil Aydin, "Globalizing the Intellectual History of the Idea of the 'Muslim World,'" in Samuel Moyn and Andrew Sartori (eds.), *Global Intellectual History* (New York, 2013), 159–186. This study follows a very basic definition of the "Muslim world" or "Islamic world" as referring to territories that were populated by Muslims, either as majorities or significant minorities, without implying homogeneity, unity, or any general characteristics.

6 Detailed references to the literature in these fields follow in the chapters of this book. Among the most notable studies on the Middle East are Bernd Philipp Schröder, *Deutschland und der Mittlere Osten im Zweiten Weltkrieg* (Göttingen, 1975); and, more narrowly on the Arab world, Heinz Tillmann, *Deutschlands Araberpolitik im Zweiten Weltkrieg* (East Berlin, 1965); Łukasz Hirszowicz, *The Third Reich and the Arab East* (London, 1966); and Jeffrey Herf, *Nazi Propaganda to the Arab World* (New Haven, CT, 2009); on the Balkans, Jozo Tomasevich, *War and Revolution in Yugoslavia, 1941–1945: Occupation and Collaboration* (Stanford, CA, 2001); Enver Redžić, *Bosnia and Herzegovina in the Second World War* (New York, 2005); Marko Attila Hoare, *Genocide and Resistance in Hitler's Bosnia: The Partisans and the Chetniks, 1941–1943* (Oxford, 2006); and Marko Attila Hoare, *The Bosnian Muslims in the Second World War: A History* (London, 2013); on the Soviet borderlands, Patrik von zur Mühlen, *Zwischen Hakenkreuz und Sowjetstern: Der Nationalismus der sowjetischen Orientvölker im Zweiten Weltkrieg* (Düsseldorf, 1971); Alex Alexiev, *Soviet Nationalities in German Wartime Strategy,*

1941–1945 (Santa Monica, CA, 1982); and Andrej Angrick, *Besatzungspolitik und Massenmord: Die Einsatzgruppe D in der Südlichen Sowjetunion 1941–1943* (Hamburg, 2003); and, more narrowly on the Crimea, Michel Luther, "Die Krim unter deutscher Besatzung im Zweiten Weltkrieg," *Forschungen zur osteuropäischen Geschichte* 3 (1956), 28–98; and Norbert Kunz, *Die Krim unter deutscher Herrschaft 1941–1944: Germanisierungsutopie und Besatzungsrealität* (Darmstadt, 2005); and on the Caucasus, Joachim Hoffmann, *Kaukasien 1942/43: Das deutsche Heer und Orientvoelker der Sowjetunion* (Freiburg, 1991); Joachim Hoffmann, *Die Ostlegionen 1941–1943: Turkotataren, Kaukasier und Wolgafinnen im deutschen Heer* (Freiburg, 1976).

7 Interest in the mufti's collaboration with National Socialism is as old as his involvement itself. The most notable studies are Joseph B. Schechtman, *The Mufti and the Fuehrer: The Rise and Fall of Haj Amin el-Husseini* (London, 1965); Jennie Lebel, *The Mufti of Jerusalem: Haj-Amin el-Husseini and National-Socialism* (Belgrade, 2007); and Klaus Gensicke, *The Mufti of Jerusalem and the Nazis: The Berlin Years, 1941–1945* (London, 2011). Anthony R. de Luca, "'Der Großmufti' in Berlin: The Politics of Collaboration," *International Journal of Middle East Studies* 10, 1 (1979), 125–138, provides a concise overview. For a comprehensive biography, see Zvi Elpeleg, *The Grand Mufti: Haj Amin al-Hussaini: Founder of the Palestinian National Movement* (London, 1993). Gerhard Höpp, "Der Gefangene im Dreieck: Zum Bild Amin al-Husseinis in Wissenschaft und Publizistik seit 1941: Ein Bio-Bibliographischer Abriß," in Rainer Zimmer-Winkel (ed.), *Eine umstrittene Figur: Hadj Amin al-Husseini, Mufti von Jerusalem* (Trier, 1999), 5–23, gives an overview of the vast literature on al-Husayni.

8 Gerhard Höpp, "Der Koran als 'Geheime Reichssache': Bruchstücke deutscher Islampolitik zwischen 1938 und 1945," in Holger Preißler and Hubert Seiwert (eds.), *Gnosisforschung und Religionsgeschichte: Festschrift für Kurt Rudolph zum 65. Geburtstag* (Marburg, 1994), 435–446, has alluded to facets of Germany's wartime engagement with Islam, as has the more detailed study by Volker Koop, *Hitler's Muslime: Die Geschichte einer unheiligen Allianz* (Berlin, 2012).

9 Overviews of Christian groups in the war zones and under German occupation are given by Xavier de Montclos, *Les chrétiens face au nazisme et au stalinisme: L'épreuve totalitaire 1939–1945* (Paris, 1983); and by contributions to part I of Karl-Joseph Hummel and Christoph Kösters (eds.), *Kirchen im Krieg: Europa 1939–1945* (Paderborn, 2007); and in Lieve Gevers and Jan Bank (eds.), *Religion under Siege*, vol. 1 (*The Roman Catholic Church in Occupied Europe [1939–1950]*), and vol. 2 (*Protestant, Orthodox and Muslim Communities in Occupied Europe [1939–1950]*) (Leuven, 2007), which contains one chapter on Muslims in the Croatian Ustaša state. The most comprehensive accounts of Germany's horrific policies toward Jews are Gerald Reitlinger, *The Final Solution: The Attempt to Exterminate the Jews of Europe, 1939–1945* (New York, 1953); Raul Hilberg, *The Destruction of the European Jews* (London, 1961); and Saul Friedländer, *Nazi Germany and the Jews*, vol. 1 (*The Years of Persecution*) and vol. 2 (*The Years of Extermination*) (New York, 1997–2007).

10 John L. Wright, "Mussolini, Libya, and the Sword of Islam," in Ruth Ben-Ghiat and Mia Fuller (eds.), *Italian Colonialism* (New York, 2005), 121–130, 123–125; and more generally, Manuela A. Williams, *Mussolini's Propaganda Abroad: Subversion in the Med-*

iterranean and the Middle East, 1935–1940 (London, 2006), esp. 205; and Nir Arielli, *Fascist Italy and the Middle East, 1933–40* (New York, 2010), esp. 1 and 97–98.

11 *Die Tagebücher von Joseph Goebbels*, ed. Elke Fröhlich et al, part I (9 vols.), part II (15 vols.), and part III (3 vols.) (Munich, 1993–2008), part I, vol. 4, 50–51 (14 March 1937), 50. Bernd Sösemann, "Propaganda—Macht—Geschichte: Eine Zwischenbilanz der Dokumentation der Niederschriften und Diktate von Joseph Goebbels," *Das Historische Buch* 50, 2 (2002), 117–125, provides an assessment of the value and problems of the Goebbels diaries as a historical source.

12 Harry J. Benda, *The Crescent and the Rising Sun: Indonesian Islam under the Japanese Occupation, 1942–1945* (The Hague, 1958), on the occupation of the Dutch East Indies; and Abu Talib Ahmad, *Malay-Muslims, Islam and the Rising Sun 1941–1945* (Selangor, 2003); as well as Abu Talib Ahmad, "Research on Islam and Malay-Muslims during the Japanese Occupation of Malaya, 1942–45," *Asian Research Trends* 9 (1999), 81–119, and Abu Talib Ahmad, "Japanese Policy towards Islam in Malaya during the Occupation: A Reassessment," *Journal of Southeast Asian Studies* 33, 1 (2002), 107–122; and, for a concise overview of the occupation of the Malaya peninsula, Yoji Akashi, "Japanese Military Administration in Malaya: Its Formation and Evolution with Reference to the Sultans, the Islamic Religion and Malay-Muslims, 1941–45," *Asian Studies* (*University of the Philippines*) 7, 1 (1969), 81–110. Yoichi Itagaki and Koichi Kishi, "Japanese Islamic Policy—Sumatra/Malaya," *Intisari* 2, 2 (1966), 11–23, give a more general account. Selçuk Esenbel, "Japan's Global Claim to Asia and the World of Islam: Transnational Nationalism and World Power, 1900–1945," *American Historical Review* 109, 4 (2004), 1140–1170, gives an account of the long-term origins of Japan's policy toward Islam.

13 Anonymous, "Japan Muslims Confident of Nippon Victory: 94-Year-Old Patriarch of Tokyo Mosque Visions Emancipation of Millions from Servitude," *Shanghai Times* (14 June 1942). On Abdurreshid Ibrahim, see Komatsu Hisao, "Muslim Intellectuals and Japan: A Pan-Islamist Mediator, Abdurreshid Ibrahim," in Stéphanie A. Dudoignon, Komatsu Hisao, and Kosugi Yasushi (eds.), *Intellectuals in the Modern Islamic World* (London, 2006), 273–288.

14 Winston S. Churchill, *The Story of the Malakand Field Force: An Episode of Frontier War* (London, 1898); and Winston S. Churchill, *The River War: A Historical Account of the Reconquest of the Soudan* (London, 1899).

15 Winston S. Churchill, *The Second World War*, 6 vols. (London, 1948–1954), vol. 4 (*The Hinge of Fate*), 185–186, quoting a letter from Churchill to Roosevelt of 4 March 1942.

16 Chapter 3 provides a closer examination of British policies toward Islam during the war.

17 Humayun Ansari, *The Infidel Within: Muslims in Britain since 1800* (London, 2004), 134 and 342 (East London Mosque), and 134 and 341 (London Central Mosque); and, more detailed on the London Central Mosque, A. L. Tibawi, "History of the London Central Mosque and the Islamic Cultural Centre 1910–1980," *Die Welt des Islams* 21, 1–4 (1981), 193–208.

18 R. H. Markham, "Islam: Pathway to Mastery of the Middle East," *Christian Science Monitor* (16 November 1940). A few months later, G. H. Archambault, "Moslem Influence Held with Britain: Islam's Opposition to Axis Is Seen as Vital Factor in

North African Events," *New York Times* (8 February 1941), assured its readers about "Islam's Opposition to Axis."

19 Chapter 3 provides a more detailed assessment of America's wartime policies toward Islam.

20 Chapter 4 provides a more detailed picture of Soviet wartime policies toward Islam.

21 Orlando Figes, *Crimea* (London, 2010), passim. On tsarist anxieties about Islam and their reactions, see Mara Kozelsky, "Casualties of Conflict: Crimean Tatars during the Crimean War," *Slavic Review* 67, 4 (2008), 862–891.

22 Major accounts of the Islamic campaign during the First World War are Herbert Landolin Müller, *Islam, Gihâd ("Heiliger Krieg") und Deutsches Reich: Ein Nachspiel zur wilhelminischen Weltpolitik im Maghreb 1914–1918* (Frankfurt, 1992); Peter Hopkirk, *On Secret Service East of Constantinople: The Plot to Bring Down the British Empire* (London, 1994); Donald M. McKale, *War by Revolution: Germany and Great Britain in the Middle East in the Era of World War I* (Kent, OH, 1998); Tilman Lüdke, *Jihad Made in Germany: Ottoman and German Propaganda and Intelligence Operations in the First World War* (Münster, 2005); Salvador Oberhaus, *"Zum wilden Aufstande entflammen:" Die deutsche Propagandastrategie für den Orient im Ersten Weltkrieg am Beispiel Ägypten* (Saarbrücken, 2007); and Sean McMeekin, *The Berlin-Baghdad Express: The Ottoman Empire and Germany's Bid for World Power, 1898–1918* (London, 2010).

23 Quoted in Fritz Fischer, *Germany's Aims in the First World War* (New York, 1967), 121.

24 William L. Cleveland, "The Role of Islam as Political Ideology in the First World War," in Edward Ingram (ed.), *National and International Politics in the Middle East: Essays in Honour of Elie Kedourie* (London, 1986), 84–101.

25 Dwight E. Lee, "The Origins of Pan-Islamism," *American Historical Review* 47, 2 (1942), 278–287, 286.

26 Matthew F. Jacobs, "The Perils and Promises of Islam: The United States and the Muslim Middle East in the Early Cold War," *Diplomatic History* 30, 4 (2006), 705–739; and, similarly, Matthew F. Jacobs, *Imagining the Middle East: The Building of an American Foreign Policy, 1918–1967* (Chapel Hill, NC, 2011), 55–94; and, on the late Cold War, Steve Coll, *Ghost Wars: The Secret History of the CIA, Afghanistan, and Bin Laden, from the Soviet Invasion to September 10, 2001* (London, 2004).

27 For the most significant accounts, see the literature in note 22.

28 Fischer, *Germany's Aims in the First World War*, 120–131; Hew Strachan, *The First World War* (London, 2003), 95–123; and David Stevenson, *1914–1918: The History of the First World War* (London, 2004), 115 and 125.

29 Jacob M. Landau, *The Politics of Pan-Islam: Ideology and Organization* (Oxford, 1990), 105–142; Martin S. Kramer, *Islam Assembled: The Advent of the Muslim Congresses* (New York, 1986), 55–68; Rudolph Peters, *Jihad in Classical and Modern Islam* (Princeton, NJ, 2005), 55–57; and Cemil Aydin, *The Politics of Anti-Westernism in Asia: Visions of World Order in Pan-Islamic and Pan-Asian Thought* (New York, 2007), 106–111.

30 Marshall G. S. Hodgson, *The Venture of Islam: Conscience and History in a World Civilization*, 3 vols. (Chicago, 1974), vol. 3, 414–415, is a notable exception.

31 Landau, *Politics of Pan-Islam*, 248. While Landau deals with Islamic mobilization during the First World War at length (73–142), the Second World War (245–247) is covered only in brief.

32 Eric D. Weitz, "From Vienna to the Paris System: International Politics and the Entangled Histories of Human Rights, Forced Deportations, and Civilizing Missions," *American Historical Review* 113, 5 (2008), 1313–1343, esp. 1314–1315.

33 Michael A. Reynolds, *Shattering Empires: The Clash and Collapse of the Ottoman and Russian Empires, 1908–1918* (Cambridge, 2011), provides an excellent case study of the geopolitics of ethnic populations in great power conflicts. Other notable studies on the subject are Seppo Zetterberg, *Die Liga der Fremdvölker Russlands 1916–1918: Ein Beitrag zu Deutschlands antirussischem Propagandakrieg unter den Fremdvölkern Russlands im Ersten Weltkrieg* (Helsinki, 1978); Reinhard R. Doerries, *Prelude to the Easter Rising: Sir Roger Casement in Imperial Germany* (London, 2000), 1–31; and the works on the Arab Revolt discussed in Chapter 1.

34 Notable studies of Jewish populations in great power politics are Egmont Zechlin, *Die deutsche Politik und die Juden im Ersten Weltkrieg* (Göttingen, 1969); Isaiah Friedman, *Germany, Turkey, and Zionism 1914–1918* (Oxford, 1977); Carole Fink, *Defending the Rights of Others: The Great Powers, the Jews, and International Minority Protection, 1878–1938* (Cambridge, 2004); and Abigail Green, "Intervening in the Jewish Question, 1840–1878," in Brendan Simms and D. J. B. Trim (eds.), *Humanitarian Intervention: A History* (Cambridge, 2011), 139–158.

1. ORIGINS

1 Oppenheim, Memorandum, 25 July 1940, Berlin, Political Archives of the German Foreign Office (*Politisches Archiv des Auswärtigen Amts*), Berlin (PA), Nachlass Hentig, vol. 84; sent attached to the letter by Oppenheim to Habicht, 25 July 1940, Berlin, PA, Nachlass Hentig, vol. 84. On Oppenheim's memorandum, see Wolfgang G. Schwanitz, "Max von Oppenheim und der Heilige Krieg: Zwei Denkschriften zur Revolutionierung islamischer Gebiete 1914 und 1940," *Sozial.Geschichte* 19 (2004), 79–102. Tragically, Oppenheim had a Jewish background. He belonged to the Salomon Oppenheim banking dynasty. His father, Albert, had converted to Catholicism, the faith of his mother, Paula. His connections helped him survive the war. The vast body of literature on Oppenheim includes Wilhelm Treue, "Max Freiherr von Oppenheim: Der Archäologe und die Politik," *Historische Zeitschrift* 209, 1 (1969), 37–74; Robert L. Melka, "Max Freiherr von Oppenheim: Sixty Years of Scholarship and Political Intrigue in the Middle East," *Middle Eastern Studies* 9, 1 (1973), 81–93; Donald M. McKale, "'The Kaiser's Spy': Max von Oppenheim and the Anglo-German Rivalry before and during the First World War," *European History Quarterly* 27, 2 (1997), 199–219; Johannes Baumgartner, "Max von Oppenheim—Lawrence of Arabia: Zwei Archäologen als politische Gegenspieler," *Antike Welt* 30 (1999), 411–415; Jan-Dirk Studt, "Max von Oppenheim und der Nahe Osten: Lebenstraum oder Politische Intrige?," *Asien, Afrika, Lateinamerika* 27 (1999), 137–157; Martin Kröger, "Max von Oppenheim: Mit Eifer ein Fremder im Auswärtigen Dienst," in Gabriele Teichmann and Gisela Völger (eds.), *Faszination Orient: Max von Oppenheim, Forscher, Sammler, Diplomat* (Cologne, 2001), 106–139; Gabriele Teichmann, "Fremder wider Willen: Max von Oppenheim in der wilhelminischen Epoche," in Eckart Conze, Ulrich Schlie, and Harald Seubert (eds.), *Geschichte zwischen Wissenschaft und Politik:*

Festschrift für Michael Stürmer zum 65. Geburtstag (Baden-Baden, 2003), 231–248; and Lionel Gossman, *The Passion of Max von Oppenheim: Archaeology and Intrigue in the Middle East from Wilhelm II to Hitler* (Cambridge, 2013).

2 Oppenheim published an account of his experiences in Max Freiherr von Oppenheim, *Vom Mittelmeer zum Persischen Golf durch den Hauran, die Syrische Wüste und Mesopotamien*, 2 vols. (Berlin, 1899–1900).

3 On Islam in Germany's West and East African colonies, see Holger Weiss, "German Images of Islam in West Africa," *Sudanic Africa* 11 (2000), 53–93; Michael Pesek, "Islam und Politik in Deutsch-Ostafrika," in Albert Wirz, Andreas Eckert, and Katrin Bromber (eds.), *Alles unter Kontrolle: Disziplinierungsverfahren im kolonialen Tanzania (1850–1960)* (Hamburg, 2003), 99–140; Michael Pesek, "Für Kaiser und Allah: Ostafrikas Muslime im Großen Krieg für die Zivilisation, 1914–1919," *Bulletin der Schweizerischen Gesellschaften Mittlerer Osten und Islamische Kulturen* 19 (2005), 9–18; and Rebekka Habermas, "Islam Debates around 1900: Colonies in Africa, Muslims in Berlin, and the Role of Missionaries and Orientalists," *Chloe: Beihefte zum Daphnis* 46 (2012), 123–154. Per Hassing, "Islam at the German Colonial Congresses," *Muslim World* 67, 3 (1977), 165–174, discusses the role of missionaries in German colonial debates about Islam. Holger Weiss, "European Images of Islam in the Northern Hinterlands of the Gold Coast through the Early Colonial Period," *Sudanic Africa*, 12 (2001), 83–110, compares German, British, and French colonial perceptions of Islam. More general studies on German colonial policies in Africa are, for the provinces of northern Cameroon, Monika Midel, *Fulbe und Deutsche in Adamaua (Nord-Kamerun) 1809–1916: Auswirkungen afrikanischer und kolonialer Eroberung* (Frankfurt, 1990); for Togo, Peter Sebald, *Togo 1884–1914: Eine Geschichte der deutschen "Musterkolonie" auf Grundlage amtlicher Quellen* (East Berlin, 1988), esp. 461–469; and, for German East Africa, Detlef Bald, *Deutsch-Ostafrika 1900–1914: Eine Studie über Verwaltung, Interessengruppen und wirtschaftliche Erschließung* (Munich, 1970); and Rainer Tetzlaff, *Koloniale Entwicklung und Ausbeutung: Wirtschafts- und Sozialgeschichte Dt.-Ostafrikas 1885–1914* (Berlin, 1970).

4 On Islamic resistance in the German colonies, see B. G. Martin, "Muslim Politics and Resistance to Colonial Rule: Shaykh Uways B. Muhammed Al-Barawi and the Qadiriya Brotherhood in East Africa," *Journal of African History* 10, 3 (1969), 471–486; Thea Büttner, "Die Mahdi-Erhebungen 1907 in Nordkamerun im Vergleich mit antikolonialen islamischen Bewegungen in anderen Regionen West- und Zentralafrikas," in Peter Heine and Ulrich van der Heyden (eds.), *Studien zur Geschichte des deutschen Kolonialismus in Afrika* (Pfaffenweiler, 1995), 147–159; and, more generally, the literature in note 3. The Mahdi uprising in Sudan had already captivated German popular imagination, most famously reflected in the novels of the eminent writer Karl May, who would publish his *Im Lande des Mahdi* in 1891–1892, see I. Hofmann and A. Vorbichler, *Das Islam-Bild bei Karl May und der islamochristliche Dialog* (Vienna, 1979), 210–241.

5 Ludmilla Hanisch, *Die Nachfolger der Exegeten: Deutschsprachige Erforschung des Vorderen Orients in der ersten Hälfte des 20. Jahrhunderts* (Wiesbaden, 2003), 1–85; Sabine Mangold, *Eine "weltbürgerliche Wissenschaft": Die deutsche Orientalistik im 19. Jahrhundert* (Stuttgart, 2004); Suzanne L. Marchand, *German Orientalism in the Age of Em-*

pire: Religion, Race, and Scholarship (Cambridge, 2009); and Ursula Wokoeck, *German Orientalism: The Study of the Middle East and Islam from 1800 to 1945* (London, 2009), 1–184, provide the wider story of German Oriental studies in the imperial age. On Islam in the nineteenth-century German imagination more generally, see Soegeng Hardiyanto, *Zwischen Phantasie und Wirklichkeit: Der Islam im Spiegel des deutschen Denkens im 19. Jahrhundert* (Frankfurt, 1992).

6 Becker never published his results, but some preliminary findings appeared in C. H. Becker, "Vorbericht über die islamkundlichen Ergebnisse der Innerafrika-Expedition des Herzogs Adolf Friedrich zu Mecklenburg," *Der Islam* 3, 3 (1912), 258–272; and, reprinted in C. H. Becker, *Islamstudien: Vom Werden und Wesen der Islamischen Welt*, vol. 2 (Leipzig, 1932), 127–148. A revised version of a questionnaire (1910) can be found in the appendix of the reprint, see ibid., 143–148. His first, less elaborate, version (1908) of his questionnaire was published in Weiss, "German Images of Islam in West Africa," 92–93.

7 Hartmann did not publish any results, either, but his questionnaire was printed in Martin Hartmann, "Zur Islamausbreitung in Afrika: Mit einem Frageblatt," *Mitteilungen des Seminar für orientalische Sprachen* 14 (1911), 159–162; and a progress report about the research project was given in Martin Hartmann, "Fragebogen über den Islam in Afrika," *Die Welt des Islams* 1, 1 (1913), 42–44.

8 Westermann's questionnaire was published in Diedrich Westermann, "Fragebogen," 44–47; and his results appeared in Diedrich Westermann, "Die Verbreitung des Islam in Togo und Kamerun: Ergebnisse einer Umfrage," *Die Welt des Islams* 2, 2/4 (1914), 188–276.

9 Becker was a highly prolific writer, publishing many articles on Islam and imperial rule in the German colonies, see, for instance, C. H. Becker, "Ist der Islam eine Gefahr für unsere Kolonien?," *Koloniale Rundschau* 1, 5 (1909), 266–293; C. H. Becker, "Der Islam und die Kolonisierung Afrikas," *Internationale Wochenschrift* 4 (1910), 227–252; C. H. Becker, "Materialien zur Kenntnis des Islam in Deutsch-Ostafrika," *Der Islam* 2, 1 (1911), 1–48; and C. H. Becker, "Islamisches und modernes Recht in der kolonialen Praxis," *Der Islam* 4, 1/2 (1913), 169–172. Becker famously opposed the anti-Islamic stance of missionaries at the German Colonial Congress of 1910, see C. H. Becker, "Staat und Mission in der Islampolitik," *Verhandlungen des deutschen Kolonialkongresses 1910* (Berlin, 1910), 638–651; and C. H. Becker, "Die Islamfrage auf dem Kolonialkongreß 1910," *Der Islam* 1, 1 (1910), 390–391. He later wrote the entry on Islam in the German colonial lexicon, see C. H. Becker, "Islam," in Heinrich Schnee (ed.), *Deutsches Kolonial-Lexikon*, 3 vols. (Leipzig, 1920), vol. 2, 106–114. Most of his works on Islam and colonialism were reprinted in C. H. Becker, *Islamstudien*, vol. 2.

10 Diedrich Westermann, "Die Edinburger Weltmissionskonferenz in ihrer Bedeutung für die Mission in den deutschen Kolonien," in Karl Schneider (ed.), *Jahrbuch über die deutschen Kolonien* 4 (Essen, 1911), 130–131; and, on his views of Islam in colonial Africa, see also Diedrich Westermann, "Der Islam in West- und Zentral-Sudan," *Die Welt des Islams* 1, 2 (1913), 85–108.

11 Martin Hartmann was one of the few experts who claimed that Islam was culturally, morally, and politically worthless, see Martin Hartmann, *Islam, Mission, Politik* (Leipzig, 1912); and he was also critical of the Islam proclamation of Wilhelm II in

1898, see Martin Hartmann, "Deutschland und der Islam," *Der Islam* 1, 1 (1910), 72–92, 74. Hartmann would later change his views and support the German-Ottoman jihad campaign during the First World War, see the literature in note 24.

12 For missionary statements on Islam in the German colonies and criticism of German colonial rule in Muslim areas, see, for instance, the proceedings of the first German Colonial Congress in 1902: P. W. Schmidt, "Die Behandlung der Polygamie in unseren Kolonien," in *Verhandlungen des deutschen Kolonialkongresses 1902* (Berlin, 1903), 467–479; the papers given at the second congress in 1905: Julius Richter, "Der Islam eine Gefahr für unsere afrikanischen Kolonien," in *Verhandlungen des deutschen Kolonialkongresses 1905* (Berlin, 1906), 510–527; and Jos. Froberger, "Welches ist der Kulturwert des Islam für koloniale Entwicklung?," in *Verhandlungen des deutschen Kolonialkongresses 1905*, 527–538; and the papers of the third congress in 1910: Hubert Hansen, "Welche Aufgaben stellt die Ausbreitung des Islam den Missionen und Ansiedlern in den deutschen Kolonien?," in *Verhandlungen des deutschen Kolonialkongresses 1910*, 652–673; Josef Froberger, "Die Polygamie und deren kulturelle Schäden," in *Verhandlungen des deutschen Kolonialkongresses 1910*, 717–732; and Karl Axenfeld, "Die Ausbreitung des Islam in Afrika und ihre Bedeutung für die deutschen Kolonien," in *Verhandlungen des deutschen Kolonialkongresses 1910*, 629–638; as well as Karl Axenfeld, "Geistige Kämpfe in der Eingeborenen-Bevölkerung an der Küste Ostafrikas," *Koloniale Rundschau* 4, 11 (1913), 647–673; Pater Amandus Acker, "Der Islam und die Kolonisierung Afrikas," *Jahrbuch der deutschen Kolonien* 4 (1911), 113–127; and F. O. Karstedt, "Zur Beurteilung des Islam in Deutsch-Ostafrika," *Koloniale Rundschau* 4, 4 (1913), 728–736; and the books by Carl Mirbt, *Mission und Kolonialpolitik in den deutschen Schutzgebieten* (Tübingen, 1910); Martin Klamroth, *Der Islam in Deutsch-Ostafrika* (Berlin, 1912); and Erich Schultze, *Soll Deutsch-Ostafrika christlich oder mohammedanisch werden?* (Berlin, 1913).

13 Insights into German debates about pan-Islam are given by J. T. von Eckardt, "Panislamismus und die islamitische Mission," *Deutsche Rundschau* 25, 4 (1899), 61–81; C. H. Becker, "Panislamismus," *Archiv für Religionswissenschaft* 7 (1904), 169–192, reprinted in C. H. Becker, *Islamstudien*, vol. 2, 231–251; in response, K. Vollers, "Ueber Panislamismus," *Preußische Jahrbücher* 117 (1904), 18–40; in A. Tavilet, "Über den Panislamismus," *Das freie Wort: Frankfurter Halbmonatsschrift für Fortschritt auf allen Gebieten des geistigen Lebens* 11, 6 (1911), 218–221; and Martin Hartmann, "Das Ultimatum des Panislamismus," *Das freie Wort: Frankfurter Halbmonatsschrift für Fortschritt auf allen Gebieten des geistigen Lebens* 11 (1911), 605–610.

14 On Wilhelm II's Ottoman tour of 1898, see Jan Stefan Richter, *Die Orientreise Kaiser Wilhelms II. 1898: Eine Studie zur deutschen Außenpolitik an der Wende zum 20. Jahrhundert* (Hamburg, 1997); see also articles published in Klaus Jaschinski and Julius Waldschmidt (eds.), *Des Kaisers Reise in den Orient 1898* (Berlin, 2002); particularly Günter Wirth, "Protestantischer Pilger und Protektor von Weltreligionen: Zu Zielen und Folgen der Orient-Reise von Kaiser Wilhelm II. in kirchengeschichtlicher Perspektive," in Jaschinski and Waldschmidt (eds.), *Des Kaisers Reise*, 133–153; and Friedrich Scherer, *Adler und Halbmond: Bismarck und der Orient, 1878–1890* (Paderborn, 2001), 319–332. A contemporary account is given by Adolf Meyer, *Ins Heilige Land: Reisebilder von der großen Festfahrt nach Jerusalem* (Berlin, 1899); a fascinating

eyewitness account and Muslim interpretation of the kaiser's visit to Jerusalem is presented by Rudolf Prietze, "Der Besuch des deutschen Kaisers 1898 in Jerusalem: Nach dem von einem Augenzeugen, dem Haussa-Pilger Achmed, aufgeschriebenen und erläuterten Bericht," *Mitteilungen des Seminars für orientalische Sprachen* 29 (1926), 99–134. Wilhelm's speech is printed in Johannes Penzler (ed.), *Die Reden Kaiser Wilhelms II.*, vol. 2 (*1896–1900*) (Leipzig, n.d.), 126–127; and in Michael A. Obst (ed.), *Die politischen Reden Kaiser Wilhelms II.* (Paderborn, 2011), 179. An analysis of the speech and its reception is given by Michael A. Obst, *"Einer nur ist Herr im Reiche": Kaiser Wilhelm II. als politischer Redner* (Paderborn, 2010), 216–223.

15 On pan-Islam, see Jacob Landau, *The Politics of Pan-Islam*; Nikki R. Keddie, "Pan-Islam as Proto-Nationalism," *Journal of Modern History* 41, 1 (1969), 17–28; Naimur Rahman Farooqi, "Pan-Islamism in the Nineteenth Century," *Islamic Culture* 57, 4 (1983), 283–296; and Adeeb Khalid, "Pan-Islamism in Practice: The Rhetoric of Muslim Unity and Its Uses," in Elisabeth Özdalga (ed.), *Late Ottoman Society: The Intellectual Legacy* (Abingdon, 2005), 201–224. The perceived pan-Islamic threat to the European empires and imperial policies toward pan-Islam are discussed by Azmi Özcan, *Pan-Islamism: Indian Muslims, the Ottomans and Britain (1877–1924)* (Leiden, 1997); and John Darwin, *The Empire Project: The Rise and Fall of the British World System 1830–1970* (Cambridge, 2009), 295–297.

16 Overviews of the various Islamic anticolonial movements are given by Rudolph Peters, *Islam and Colonialism: The Doctrine of Jihad in Modern History* (The Hague, 1979), 39–104; and Nikki R. Keddie, "The Revolt of Islam, 1700 to 1993: Comparative Considerations and Relations to Imperialism," *Comparative Studies in Society and History* 36, 3 (1994), 463–487, esp. 481–485.

17 The Ottoman text of the fatwas as well as a German translation appeared in Rudolf Tschudi, "Die Fetwas des Scheich-ül-Islâm über die Erklärung des Heiligen Krieges, nach dem Ṭanîn, Nummer 2119 vom 15. November 1914," *Der Islam* 5, 4 (1914), 391–393. A slightly different German translation of the fatwas was later printed in Martin Hartmann, "Kriegsurkunden," *Die Welt des Islams* 3, 1 (1915), 2–23, 2–3. For an English translation, see Geoffrey Lewis, "The Ottoman Proclamation of Jihād in 1914," *Islamic Quarterly: A Review of Islamic Culture* 19, 3–4 (1975), 157–163, 157–158, reprinted in *Arabic and Islamic Garland: Historical, Educational and Literary Papers presented to Abdul-Latif Tibawi* (London, 1977), 159–165, 159–160. A slightly different English translation is given in Peters, *Islam and Colonialism*, 90–91, and was reprinted in Peters, *Jihad in Classical and Modern Islam*, 56–57. On the proclamation of the fatwas in the provinces of the Ottoman Empire, see Martin Hartmann, "Verlesung der heiligen Fetwas in den Provinzen," *Die Welt des Islams* 3, 1 (1915), 31–65, 36.

18 A proclamation by reputed Ottoman 'ulama on the jihad was printed in German translation in Martin Hartmann, "Kriegsurkunden," *Die Welt des Islams* 3, 1 (1915), 2–23, 10–18; and, in English translation, in Lewis, "Ottoman Proclamation of Jihād in 1914," 159–163, reprinted in *Arabic and Islamic Garland*, 161–165; and, for an abstract of this proclamation in a slightly different English transliteration, Peters, *Islam and Colonialism*, 91–92. A declaration of the Ottoman 'ulama addressed to Arab soldiers in the sultan's army was published in German translation in Martin Hartmann, "Kriegsurkunden," *Die Welt des Islams* 3, 2 (1915), 121–133, 121–125. Fatwas of

the Shiʻa ʻulama in Najaf and Karbala were printed in Martin Hartmann, "Auszüge aus der Zeitschrift 'Chāwer,'" *Die Welt des Islams* 3, 1 (1915), 48–56, 51–56; in Martin Hartmann, "Kriegsurkunden," *Die Welt des Islams* 3, 2 (1915), 121–133, 131–133; in Martin Hartmann, "Kriegsurkunden," *Die Welt des Islams* 3, 3–4 (1916), 205–213; and in Helmut Ritter, "Kriegsurkunden," *Die Welt des Islams* 4, 3/4 (1917), 217–225. The Shiʻa fatwas have been examined by Werner Ende, "Iraq in World War I: The Turks, the Germans, and the Shiʻite Mujtahids' Call for Jihad," in Rudolph Peters (ed.), *Proceedings of the Ninth Congress of the Union Européenne des Arabisants et Islamisants* (Leiden, 1981), 57–71; Nasrollah Salehi, "Les fatwas des ulémas persans de Najaf et Kerbala," in Oliver Bast (ed.), *La Perse et la Grande Guerre* (Tehran, 2002), 157–176; and, for the wider context, Yitzhak Nakash, *The Shiʻis of Iraq* (Princeton, NJ, 1994), 55–61.

19 On the concept of "jihad," see, for instance, Peters, *Jihad in Classical and Modern Islam*; David Cook, *Understanding Jihad* (Berkeley, CA, 2005); David Cook, *Martyrdom in Islam* (Cambridge, 2007); Richard Bonney, *Jihād: From Qu'rān to Bin Laden* (New York, 2007); and Michael Bonner, *Jihad in Islamic History: Doctrines and Practice* (Princeton, NJ, 2008).

20 On the Ottoman sponsorship of pan-Islamism, see Hasan Kayalı, *Arabs and Young Turks: Ottomanism, Arabism, and Islamism in the Ottoman Empire, 1908–1918* (Berkeley, CA, 1997); Kemal H. Karpat, *The Politicization of Islam: Reconstructing Identity, State, Faith, and Community in the Late Ottoman State* (Oxford, 2001); and, more generally, Frederick F. Anscombe, "Islam and the Age of Ottoman Reform," *Past and Present* 208, 1 (2010), 159–189.

21 Fischer, *Germany's Aims in the First World War*, 120–131, and, for the statement of Wilhelm II, 121, and, for Moltke's formal endorsement, 126. Major accounts of the German sponsorship of the Islamic campaign during the First World War are Müller, *Islam, Gihâd ("Heiliger Krieg") und Deutsches Reich*; Hopkirk, *On Secret Service East of Constantinople*; McKale, *War by Revolution*; Lüdke, *Jihad Made in Germany*; Oberhaus, *"Zum wilden Aufstande entflammen"*; and McMeekin, *The Berlin-Baghdad Express*. Concise overviews are given by Stephen Casewit, "Background to the Holy War of 1914: Towards an Understanding," *Islamic Quarterly* 29, 4 (1985), 220–233; Martin Kröger, "Revolution als Programm: Ziele und Realität deutscher Orientpolitik im Ersten Weltkrieg," in Wolfgang Michalka (ed.), *Der Erste Weltkrieg: Wirkung, Wahrnehmung, Analyse* (Munich, 1994), 366–391; Wolfgang G. Schwanitz, "Djihad 'Made in Germany': Der Streit um den Heiligen Krieg (1914–1915)," *Sozial.Geschichte* 18, 2 (2003), 7–34; and Gottfried Hagen, "German Heralds of Holy War: Orientalists and Applied Oriental Studies," *Comparative Studies of South Asia, Africa and the Middle East* 24, 2 (2004), 145–162. A critical reassessment of the view that Germany was the driving force behind the jihad declaration is given by Mustafa Aksakal, "'Holy War Made in Germany'? Ottoman Origins of the 1914 Jihad," *War in History* 18, 2 (2011), 184–199. Jennifer Jenkins, "Fritz Fischer's 'Programme for Revolution:' Implications for a Global History of Germany in the First World War," *Journal of Contemporary History* 48, 2 (2013), 397–417, discusses the broader context.

22 Oppenheim, Memorandum ("Denkschrift betreffend die Revolutionierung der islamischen Gebiete unserer Feinde"), 1914, Berlin, PA, R 20938. The memorandum,

together with a comment, has also been printed in Tim Epkenhans, "Geld darf keine Rolle spielen," *Archivum Ottomanicum* 18 (2000), 247–250, and 19 (2001), 121–163.

23 These comments were made in the revised 1916 edition of Ernst Jäckh, *Der aufsteigende Halbmond: Auf dem Weg zum deutsch-türkischen Bündnis* (Stuttgart, 1916 [1909]), 237. For Jäckh's assessment of the jihad policy, see also Ernst Jäckh, *Die deutschtürkische Waffenbrüderschaft* (Stuttgart, 1915); and Ernst Jäckh, *Die Türkei und Deutschland* (Berlin, 1916). His memoirs, Ernst Jäckh, *Der goldene Pflug: Lebensernte eines Weltbürgers* (Stuttgart, 1954), do not discuss the jihad campaign of the First World War.

24 Martin Hartmann, "Islampolitik," *Koloniale Rundschau* 5, 11–12 (1914), 580–603; Martin Hartmann, "Deutschland und der Heilige Krieg," *Das neue Deutschland* (29 May 1915), 268–273; and Martin Hartmann, "Die weltwirtschaftlichen Wirkungen des Heiligen Krieges," *Weltwirtschaft* (January–February 1915), 255.

25 C. H. Becker, *Deutschland und der Islam* (Stuttgart, 1914).

26 Ibid., 19.

27 Ibid., 6.

28 C. Snouck Hurgronje, "Heilige Oorlog Made in Germany," *De Gids* 79, 1 (1915), 1–33; and, for the English translation, which appeared in the same year, C. Snouck Hurgronje, *The Holy War "Made in Germany"* (London, 1915).

29 C. H. Becker, "Deutschland und der Heilige Krieg," *Internationale Monatsschrift für Wissenschaft, Kunst und Technik* 9, 7 (1915), 631–662; and in response, C. Snouck Hurgronje, "Deutschland und der Heilige Krieg: Erwiderung," *Internationale Monatsschrift für Wissenschaft, Kunst und Technik* 9, 10 (1915), 1025–1034; and, again in response, C. H. Becker, "Deutschland und der Heilige Krieg: Schlußwort," *Internationale Monatsschrift für Wissenschaft, Kunst und Technik* 9, 10 (1915), 1033–1042. On the debate, see Peter Heine, "C. Snouck Hurgronje versus C. H. Becker: Ein Beitrag zur Geschichte der Angewandten Orientalistik," *Die Welt des Islams* 23/24 (1984), 378–387. Becker's further publications on Islam and politics in the war are C. H. Becker, "England und der Islam," *Das größere Deutschland: Wochenschrift für deutsche Welt- und Kolonialpolitik* 28 (1914), 841–848; C. H. Becker, "Die Türkei," in Otto Hintze, Friedrich Meinecke, Hermann Oncken, and Hermann Schumacher (eds.), *Deutschland und der Weltkrieg* (Leipzig, 1915), 285–309; C. H. Becker, "Islampolitik," *Die Welt des Islams* 3, 2 (1915), 101–120; and C. H. Becker, "Die Senussi," *Deutsche Kolonialzeitung* 32, 2 (1915), 25–26. With the exception of his article on the Sanusi, all of these texts by Becker were reprinted in C. H. Becker, *Islamstudien*, vol. 2.

30 Gottfried Simon, *Die Welt des Islam und die neue Zeit* (Wernigerode, 1925), 12, offers a vivid account of Islam mania during the First World War in Germany; see also the section "Zeitungsschau," in *Die Welt des Islams* during the war years. Examples from the flood of brochures and booklets on the subject are Hubert Grimme, *Islam und Weltkrieg* (Münster, 1914); Hugo Grothe, *Deutschland, die Türkei und der Islam: Ein Beitrag zu den Grundlinien der deutschen Weltpolitik im islamischen Orient* (Leipzig, 1914); Eugen Mittwoch, *Deutschland, die Türkei und der Heilige Krieg* (Berlin, 1914); Rudolf Tschudi, *Der Islam und der Krieg* (Hamburg, 1914); Joseph Froberger, *Weltkrieg und Islam* (Mönchen Gladbach, 1915); Gottfried Galli, *Dschihad: Der Heilige Krieg des Islams und seine Bedeutung im Weltkriege unter besonderer Berücksichtigung*

der Interessen Deutschlands (Freiburg, 1915); Richard Schäfer, *Islam und Weltkrieg* (Leipzig, 1915); and Kurt L. Walter van der Bleek (ed.), *Die Vernichtung der englischen Weltmacht und des russischen Zarismus durch den Dreibund und den Islam* (Berlin, 1915). Marchand, *German Orientalism in the Age of Empire*, 436–454, provides an account of the role of German writers and Orientalists during the jihad campaign.

31 Maren Bragulla, *Die Nachrichtenstelle für den Orient: Fallstudie einer Propagandainstitution im Ersten Weltkrieg* (Saarbrücken, 2007).

32 Schaich Salih Aschscharif Attunisi, *Ḥaqiqat Aldschihād: Die Wahrheit über den Glaubenskrieg*, translated by Karl E. Schabinger, introduced by Martin Hartmann (Berlin, 1915); and, for the French translation, Schaich Salih Aschscharif Attunisi, *La Vérité au Sujet de la Guerre Sainte* (Bern, 1916). On al-Tunisi's role in the war, see Peter Heine, "Ṣaliḥ ash-Sharif at-Tunisi: A North African Nationalist in Berlin during the First World War," *Revue de l'Occident Musulman et de la Méditerranée* 33 (1982), 89–95. A propaganda text of 'Abd al-'Aziz Shawish can be found in "1915 Ottoman Fatwa," in Andrew G. Bostom, *The Legacy of Jihad: Islamic Holy War and the Fate of Non-Muslims* (Amherst, NY, 2005), 221–225.

33 Gerhard Höpp, *Muslime in der Mark: Als Kriegsgefangene und Internierte in Wünsdorf und Zossen, 1914–1924* (Berlin, 1997); and, for concise overviews, Gerhard Höpp, "Muslime in Märkischer Heide: Die Wünsdorfer Moschee, 1915 bis 1924," *Moslemische Revue* 1 (1989), 21–28; Gerhard Höpp, "Die Wünsdorfer Moschee: Eine Episode islamischen Lebens in Deutschland, 1915–1930," *Die Welt des Islams* 36, 2 (1996), 204–218; Gerhard Höpp, "Die Privilegien der Verlierer: Über Status und Schicksal muslimischer Kriegsgefangener und Deserteure in Deutschland während des Ersten Weltkrieges und der Zwischenkriegszeit," in Gerhard Höpp (ed.), *Fremde Erfahrungen: Asiaten und Afrikaner in Deutschland, Österreich und in der Schweiz bis 1945* (Berlin, 1996), 185–210; and Margot Kahleyss, "Muslimische Kriegsgefangene in Deutschland im Ersten Weltkrieg: Ansichten und Absichten," in Gerhard Höpp and Brigitte Reinwald (eds.), *Fremdeinsätze: Afrikaner und Asiaten in Europäischen Kriegen 1914–1945* (Berlin, 2000), 79–117. A fascinating collection of photographs can be found in Margot Kahleyss, *Muslime in Brandenburg: Kriegsgefangene im 1. Weltkrieg: Ansichten und Absichten* (Berlin, 1998).

34 Peter Heine, "Al-Ǧihād: Eine deutsche Propagandazeitung im 1. Weltkrieg," *Die Welt des Islams* 20, 3–4 (1980), 197–199.

35 Idris, Curriculum Vitae, n.d. (post-1933), n.p. (Berlin), PA, R 60740. On Idris, see also Mühlen, *Zwischen Hakenkreuz und Sowjetstern*, 35, 39, 142, and 228; Höpp, *Muslime in der Mark*, passim; Gerhard Höpp, "Die Wünsdorfer Moschee," 9, 11, and 15–16; Gerhard Höpp, "Die Privilegien der Verlierer," 189; Iskander Gilyazov, "Die Wolgatataren und Deutschland im ersten Drittel des 20. Jahrhunderts," in Michael Kemper et al. (eds.), *Muslim Culture in Russia and Central Asia from the 18th to the Early 20th Centuries*, 2 vols. (Berlin, 1996–1998), vol. 2 (*Inter-Regional and Inter-Ethnic Relations*), 335–353, passim; Sebastian Cwiklinski, *Wolgatataren im Deutschland des Zweiten Weltkriegs: Deutsche Ostpolitik und tatarischer Nationalismus* (Berlin, 2002), 9–10, 33–34, 54–55, and 72; and, for an account from the perspective of the Muslim community in the Federal Republic, Ilyas Gabid Abdulla, *Islam in West Deutschland* (Munich, n.d. [1966]), 14, and, for a photograph of Idris, 12.

36 Armin T. Wegner, "Beiram der Verbannten," *Der Neue Orient* 4, 1 (1918), 41–43, 42.

37 Major overviews of these German missions are Müller, *Islam, Gihâd ("Heiliger Krieg") und Deutsches Reich*; Hopkirk, *On Secret Service East of Constantinople*; McKale, *War by Revolution*; Lüdke, *Jihad Made in Germany*; Oberhaus, *"Zum wilden Aufstande entflammen;"* and McMeekin, *The Berlin-Baghdad Express*. A fascinating collection of propaganda material spread by the German and Ottoman authorities across the Islamic world is provided by Gottfried Hagen, *Die Türkei im Ersten Weltkrieg: Flugblätter und Flugschriften in arabischen, persischer und osmanisch-türkischer Sprache aus einer Sammlung der Universitätsbibliothek Heidelberg eingeleitet, übersetzt und kommentiert* (Frankfurt, 1990). This paragraph is based on this literature. In cases where more specific regional studies exist, these are mentioned in separate references.

38 Peter Heine, "Leo Frobenius als politischer Agent: Ein Beitrag zu seiner Biographie," *Paideuma* 26 (1980), 1–5.

39 Donald M. McKale, *Curt Prüfer: German Diplomat from the Kaiser to Hitler* (Kent, OH, 1987), 25–56; and Hans Werner Neulen, *Feldgrau in Jerusalem: Das Levantekorps des kaiserlichen Deutschland* (Munich, 1991).

40 Russell McGuirk *The Sanusi's Little War: The Amazing Story of a Forgotten Conflict in the Western Desert, 1915–1917* (London, 2007); and, on the Sanusi more generally, E. E. Evans-Pritchard, *The Sanusi of Cyrenaica* (Oxford, 1949).

41 Edmund Burke, "Moroccan Resistance, Pan-Islam and German War Strategy, 1914–1918," *Francia* 3 (1975) 434–464; Jide Osuntokun, "Nigeria's Colonial Government and the Islamic Insurgency in French West Africa, 1914–1918," *Cahiers d'Études Africaines* 15, 57 (1975), 85–93; and, on British and French colonial Africa more generally, William Deakin, "Imperial Germany and the 'Holy War' in Africa, 1914–1918," *University of Leeds Review* 28 (1985), 75–95. A primary account of a German agent who was involved in Morocco is Albert Bartels, *Mein Krieg auf eigene Faust: Meine Erlebnisse vor und während des Weltkrieges in Marokko* (Leipzig, 1925), and, for the English translation, Albert Bartels, *Fighting the French in Morocco* (London, 1932).

42 Ende, "Iraq in World War I"; and, for memoirs of two participants of the mission, see Hans Lührs, *Gegenspieler des Obersten Lawrence* (Berlin, 1936); Edgar Stern-Rubarth, *Three Men Tried: Austin Chamberlain, Stresemann, Briand and their Fight for a New Europe* (London, 1939), 24–26; and Edgar Stern-Rubarth, *Aus zuverlässiger Quelle verlautet: Ein Leben für Presse und Politik* (Stuttgart, 1964), 66–83, who show that the German emissaries had problems navigating through the Shi'a hierarchies, mistaking 'Ali al-Mazandarani (Shaykh al-'Iraqain), a minor cleric and younger brother of the eminent *marja' al-taqlid* Muhammad Husayn al-Mazandarani, for one of the most important religious authorities of the Shi'a world.

43 Firoozeh Kashani-Sabet, *Frontier Fictions: Shaping the Iranian Nation, 1840–1946* (Princeton, NJ, 1999), 145–148; and, for a collection of Iranian fatwas issued by the Iranian 'ulama in support of the war against the Entente, Muhammad Hasan Kavusi 'Iraqi and Nasr Allah Salihi (eds.), *Jihadiyah: Fatava-yi jihadiyah-i 'ulama va maraji '-i 'izam dar jang-i jahani-yi avval (Jihadieh: The Holy War Fatwas of the Grand 'Ulama and Mujtaheds in World War I)* (Tehran, 1375/1996).

44 Christopher Sykes, *Wassmuss: The German Lawrence* (London, 1936); Dagobert von Mikusch, *Wassmuss, der deutsche Lawrence* (Leipzig, 1937); Ulrich Gehrke, *Persien in*

der deutschen Orientpolitik während des Ersten Weltkrieges, 2 vols. (Stuttgart, 1960); and Oliver Bast, *Les Allemands en Perse pendant la Première Guerre mondiale* (Paris, 1997). Fascinating insights are also provided by Pierre Oberling, *The Qashqā'i Nomads of Fars* (The Hague, 1974), 127–147.

45 Renate Vogel, *Die Persien- und Afghanistanexpeditionen von Oskar Ritter v. Niedermayers, 1915/1916* (Osnabrück, 1976); Hans-Ulrich Seidt, *Berlin, Kabul, Moskau: Oskar Ritter von Niedermayer und Deutschlands Geopolitik* (Munich, 2002), 43–119; and Thomas L. Hughes, "The German Mission to Afghanistan, 1915–1916," *German Studies Review* 25, 3 (2002), 447–476. In the last year of the war, Hentig published an account of his mission in German, see Werner Otto von Hentig, *Meine Diplomatenfahrt ins verschlossene Land* (Berlin, 1918). He also writes of his activities during both world wars in his memoirs, see Werner Otto von Hentig, *Mein Leben: Eine Dienstreise* (Göttingen, 1962). Also, Niedermayer published an account of the mission during the First World War, see Oskar von Niedermayer, *Afghanistan* (Leipzig, 1924), 1–10; and Oskar von Niedermayer, *Unter der Glutsonne Irans: Kriegserlebnisse der deutschen Expedition nach Persien und Afganistan* (Dachau, 1925), which was later reprinted as *Im Weltkrieg vor Indiens Toren: Der Wüstenzug der deutschen Expedition nach Persien und Afghanistan* (Hamburg, 1936); and, in a shortened version, as *Krieg in Irans Wüsten: Erlebnisse der deutschen Expedition nach Persien und Afghanistan* (Hamburg, 1940).

46 Winfried Baumgart, *Deutsche Ostpolitik 1918: Von Brest-Litowsk bis zum Ende des Ersten Weltkrieges* (Munich, 1966), 151–155 (Crimea) and 174–207 (Caucasus); Wolfdieter Bihl, *Die Kaukasus-Politik der Mittelmächte,* 2 vols. (Vienna, 1975–1992); and Hans-Ulrich Seidt, "From Palestine to the Caucasus: Oskar Niedermayer and Germany's Middle Eastern Strategy in 1918," *German Studies Review* 24, 1 (2001), 1–18.

47 The German missions fueled British popular fascination with and anxiety about the jihad campaign, reflected in a number of books and novels, most famously, of course, the adventure classic by John Buchan, *Greenmantle* (London, 1916); and the lesser-known nonfictional account by E. F. Benson, *Deutschland über Allah?* (London, 1917).

48 Quoted in Landau, *The Politics of Pan-Islam,* 102.

49 Jacques Frémeaux, *La France et l'Islam depuis 1789* (Paris, 1991), 139–157; Pascal Le Pautremat, *La politique musulmane de la France au XXe siècle: De l'hexagone aux terres d'Islam* (Paris, 2003), 75–87; Sadek Sellam, *La France et ses Musulmans: Un siècle de politique musulmane (1895–2005)* (Paris, 2006), 171–184; Belkacem Recham, "Les Musulmans dans l'armée française, 1900–1945," in Mohammed Arkoun (ed.), *Histoire de l'Islam et des Musulmans en France du Moyen Âge à nos jours* (Paris, 2006), 742–761, 744–747; and, focusing on Algeria, Charles-Robert Ageron, *Les Algériens musulmans et la France (1871–1919),* 2 vols. (Paris, 1968), vol. 2, 1139–1227. Driss Bensaid, "Les oulémas marocains et la Grande Guerre (1914–18)," in A. Bendaoud and M. Berriane (eds.), *Marocains et Allemands: La perception de l'autre* (Rabat, 1995), 37–57, provides insights into the reactions of the Moroccon 'ulama to the French war effort.

50 Cleveland, "The Role of Islam as Political Ideology in the First World War."

51 Eliezer Tauber, "Rashīd Riḍā's Political Attitudes during World War I," *Muslim World* 85, 1/2 (1995), 107–121; and, more generally, Umar Ryad, "Islamic Reformism and Great Britain: Rashid Rida's Image as reflected in the Journal Al-Manār in

Cairo," *Islam and Christian-Muslim Relations* 21, 3 (2010), 263–285; and, on the 'ulama of India, Özcan, *Pan-Islamism*, 179–183.

52 John Fisher, "British Responses to Mahdist and Other Unrest in North and West Africa, 1919–1930," *Australian Journal of Politics and History* 52, 3 (2006), 347–361, 351.

53 Robert D. Crews, *For Prophet and Tsar: Islam and Empire in Russia and Central Asia* (Cambridge, MA, 2006), 351–352.

54 There is a vast body of literature on the Sharifian revolt, see, for instance, Eliezer Tauber, *The Arab Movements in World War I* (London, 1993); Haifa Alangari, *The Struggle for Power in Arabia: Ibn Saud, Hussein and Great Britain, 1914–1924* (Reading, UK, 1998); Joshua Teitelbaum, *The Rise and Fall of the Hashimite Kingdom of Arabia* (London, 2001); James Barr, *Setting the Desert on Fire: T. E. Lawrence and Britain's Secret War in Arabia, 1916–1918* (New York, 2008); Polly A. Mohs, *Military Intelligence and the Arab Revolt: The First Modern Intelligence War* (London, 2008); and, for the wider story, David Fromkin, *A Peace to End All Peace: The Fall of the Ottoman Empire and the Creation of the Modern Middle East* (New York, 1989). On the role of Islam in the Sharifian revolt and the question of an Arab caliphate, see Cleveland, "Role of Islam as Political Ideology in the First World War;" Elie Kedourie, "Egypt and the Caliphate, 1915–52," in Elie Kedourie (ed.), *Chatham House Version and Other Middle Eastern Studies* (London, 1970), 177–207, 179–182; and Saad Omar Khan, "The 'Caliphate Question': British Views and Policy toward Pan-Islamic Politics and the End of the Ottoman Caliphate," *American Journal of Social Sciences* 24, 4 (2007), 1–25, 6–11.

55 T. E. Lawrence, *Seven Pillars of Wisdom* (Hertfordshire, 1997 [Oxford, 1922]), 35.

56 Albert Christiaan Niemeijer, *The Khilafat Movement in India, 1919–1924* (The Hague, 1972); Gail Minault, *The Khilafat Movement: Religious Symbolism and Political Mobilisation in India* (New York, 1982); Özcan, *Pan-Islamism*, 184–204; M. Naeem Qureshi, *Pan-Islam in British Indian Politics: A Study of the Khilafat Movement, 1918–1924* (Leiden, 1999); and, on London's engagement with the caliphate question more generally, Khan, "The 'Caliphate Question.' "

57 Gary Troeller, *The Birth of Saudi Arabia: Britain and the Rise of the House of Sa'ud* (London, 1976), 216–235; Haifa Alangari, *The Struggle for Power in Arabia: Ibn Saud, Hussein, and Great Britain, 1914–1924* (Reading, 1998), 191–246; and Timothy J. Paris, *Britain, the Hashemites, and Arab Rule, 1920–1925: The Sherifian Solution* (London, 2003), 341–362.

58 Bernard Lewis, *The Emergence of Modern Turkey* (London, 1961), 395–436; Ali M. Ansari, *Modern Iran since 1921: The Pahlavis and After* (London, 2003), 46–47; and Bernd J. Fischer, *King Zog and the Struggle for Stability in Albania* (Boulder, CO, 1984), 170 and 247–250.

59 Leon B. Poullada, *Reform and Rebellion in Afghanistan, 1919–1929: King Amanullah's Failure to Modernize a Tribal Society* (Ithaca, NY, 1973).

60 Richard P. Mitchell, *The Society of the Muslim Brothers* (London, 1969); Brynjar Lia, *The Society of the Muslim Brothers in Egypt: The Rise of an Islamic Mass Movement 1928–1942* (Reading, UK, 1998); Abd Al-Fattah Muhammad El-Awaisi, *The Muslim Brothers and the Palestine Question 1928–1947* (London, 1998); and, on al-Banna, Gudrun Krämer, *Hasan al-Banna* (New York, 2010).

61 Kramer, *Islam Assembled*.

62 Erez Manela, *The Wilsonian Moment: Self-Determination and the International Origins of Anticolonial Nationalism* (New York, 2007).

63 Martin Thomas, *Empires of Intelligence: Security Services and Colonial Disorder after 1914* (Berkeley, CA, 2008), esp. 73–90, gives an overview of imperial anxieties about Islam in the interwar period.

64 Johannes H. Voigt, "Hitler und Indien," *Vierteljahrshefte für Zeitgeschichte* 19 (1971), 33–63, 50; Milan Hauner, "Das Nationalsozialistische Deutschland und Indien," in Manfred Funke (ed.), *Hitler, Deutschland und die Mächte: Materialien zur Außenpolitik des dritten Reiches* (Düsseldorf, 1976), 430–453, 436; and Milan Hauner, *India in Axis Strategy: Germany, Japan, and Indian Nationalists in the Second World War* (Stuttgart, 1981), 33. The movie is based on a famous novel by the British Indian army officer Francis Yeats-Brown, *Lives of a Bengal Lancer* (London, 1930).

65 Islam and pan-Islamic movements were also carefully monitored by the German Foreign Office in the interwar period, see the files in PA, R 78240 (*Religions- und Kirchenwesen: Islam, 1924–1928*); PA, R 78241 (*Religions- und Kirchenwesen: Islam, 1928–1931*); PA, R 78242 (*Religions- und Kirchenwesen: Islam, 1932–1936*); and PA, R 104801 (*Religions- und Kirchenwesen: Islam, 1936–1939*).

66 On geopolitics, see Frank Ebeling, *Geopolitik: Karl Haushofer und seine Raumwissenschaft, 1919–1945* (Berlin, 1994); and, on Haushofer specifically, Hans-Adolf Jacobsen, *Karl Haushofer: Leben und Werk*, 2 vols. (Boppard, 1979); and Bruno Hipler, *Hitlers Lehrmeister: Karl Haushofer als Vater der NS-Ideologie* (St. Ottilien, 1996).

67 Karl Haushofer, "Historische Belege zur Religionsgeopolitik," *Zeitschrift für Geopolitik* 20, 8 (1943), 278–280. In the same issue, Heinrich Frick published his "georeligious considerations on the connection between soil and religion," see Heinrich Frick, "Regionale Religionskunde," *Zeitschrift für Geopolitik* 20, 8 (1943), 281–290. In his article, Haushofer refers to research on world politics and religion under the Nazi regime, linking it to research conducted in the nineteenth century. "Islam," Haushofer proclaimed, was the "Leitmotif"; for a special issue on the Middle East, see Karl Haushofer, "Der Nahe Osten im Vorschatten eurasischer Festlandpolitik," *Zeitschrift für Geopolitik* 16, 11 (1939), 781–783, 783.

68 Haushofer's major work on "pan" ideas is Karl Haushofer, *Geopolitik der Pan-Ideen* (Berlin, 1931); reference to Islam can be found on 8, 11, 15, 23, 37–39, 47, 63, and 81. Haushofer saw in pan-Islam an idea and a movement that impeded other "pan-creations" as it stretched over "Pan-Asia, Pan-Europe, and Pan-Africa" (ibid., 39, and, for a similar argument, 81). On "pan" ideas, see also Karl Haushofer, *Weltpolitik von Heute* (Berlin, 1934), particularly chapter 10 ("Übervölkische und überstaatliche Zusammenfassungsversuche: Kirchenstaaten; Panideen; Völkerbund"), in which he refers to the "area of Islam" (*Bereich des Islam*) (100), and chapter 28 ("Machtverlagerung seit 1914: Internationale Fronten der Panideen"), referring to the "dreams of pan-Islam" (*Panislamträume*), which he saw as challenging British interests (240); see also Karl Haushofer, *Der Kontinentalblock, Mitteleuropa, Eurasien, Japan* (Munich, 1941), in which he refers to the role of Islam in India (53). His "pan" ideas and the whole field of *Geopolitik* were influenced by anthropological theories on "cultural

circles" (*Kulturkreis*), the so-called *Kulturkreistheorie*; see also the entry by Karl Strupp, "Pan-Islamismus," *Wörterbuch des Völkerrechts*, vol. 6 (Berlin, 1929). In this compendium, Strupp also wrote various other articles on "pan" movements.

69 Hans Rabl, "Über das Kalifat," *Zeitschrift für Geopolitik* 15, 11 (1938), 848–857. Hans Rabel had proposed some of these ideas on the caliphate earlier in Hans Rabl, "Der Nahe Osten auf dem Weg zur Einigung," *Zeitschrift für Geopolitik* 13, 5 (1936), 293–302; and Hans Rabl, "Nah-Ost Nachtrag," *Zeitschrift für Geopolitik* 13, 6 (1936), 402–404.

70 Rabl, "Über das Kalifat," 854.

71 Ibid., 857.

72 Ibid., 849.

73 Hans Lindemann, "Der Islam im Aufbruch und Angriff," *Zeitschrift für Geopolitik* 16, 11 (1939), 784–789.

74 Ibid., 786.

75 Ibid., 787.

76 Ibid., 785.

77 Hans Lindemann, *Der Islam im Aufbruch, in Abwehr und Angriff* (Leipzig, 1941).

78 Ibid., 84.

79 Anonymous, "Die britische Islampolitik I," *Zeitschrift für Geopolitik* 19, 3 (1942), 133–143; and Anonymous, "Die britische Islampolitik II," *Zeitschrift für Geopolitik* 19, 4 (1942), 187–196.

80 Anonymous, "Die britische Islampolitik I," 133.

81 Ibid., 136.

82 Ibid., 143.

83 Anonymous, "Die britische Islampolitik II," 196.

84 Pandit K. A. Bhatta, "Innenpolitische Probleme Indiens," *Zeitschrift für Geopolitik* 16, 12 (1939), 837–850, esp. 837–838 and 843; and Pandit K. A. Bhatta, "Britische Wehrpolitik in Indien," *Zeitschrift für Geopolitik* 17, 4 (1940), 172–181. Another remarkable example is *Der Islam in Indien* of 1942, which examined Islam in India in the context of developments in the Middle East, Africa, and Asia and concluded with a chapter on contemporary "British Policy towards Islam," see Abid Hassan, *Der Islam in Indien: Indien im Weltislam* (Heidelberg, 1942), esp. 83–118; and, for a review of the book, Anonymous, "Weltreligionen als geopolitische Formkräfte," *Zeitschrift für Geopolitik* 19, 12 (1942), 561–562.

85 Herbert Hörhager, "Die Haltung der indo-afghanischen Grenzstämme zur indischen Krise," *Zeitschrift für Geopolitik* 17, 3 (1940), 119–124; and Habibur Rahman, "Die Stellung Afghanistans in Zentralasien," *Zeitschrift für Geopolitik* 17, 4 (1940), 182–184.

86 Walter Leifer, "Der Freiheitskampf der Araber," *Zeitschrift für Geopolitik* 17, 2 (1940), 65–70.

87 Ibid., 65.

88 H. A. Fakoussa, "Ägyptens auswärtige Politik," *Zeitschrift für Geopolitik* 17, 3 (1940), 125–127, 125.

89 Ibid., 125.

90 Rudolf Friedmann, "Frankreich und der Islam," *Zeitschrift für Geopolitik* 4, 1 (1927), 58–68, 58.

91 Djamal Udin, "Zur Kulturpolitik Indonesiens I," *Zeitschrift für Geopolitik* 5, 3 (1928), 258–264; and Djamal Udin, "Zur Kulturpolitik Indonesiens II," *Zeitschrift für Geopolitik* 5, 4 (1928), 317–325, quotation on 320.

92 Willmar Freischütz, "Die indisch-englische Auseinandersetzung," *Zeitschrift für Geopolitik* 7, 4 (1930), 308–318, 309.

93 Heinrich Eck, "Russisch-Asien am Scheidewege," *Zeitschrift für Geopolitik*, 13, 2 (1936), 76–86, 85. The author also includes the Crimea and the Caucasus when speaking of "Russian-Asia."

94 Ibid., 82.

95 Ibid., 85; and, on the role of pan-Islam, 85–86.

96 Not every book that referred to "Islam" in its title was really concerned with religion: *The Sword of Islam* (*Das Schwert des Islam*) by the Nazi publicist Othmar Krainz, for instance, does not deal with Islam but is an anti-Semitic tract, mainly concerned with the Middle East and particularly British policies and Jewish migration to Palestine, see Othmar Krainz, *Das Schwert des Islam* (Hersching, 1938).

97 Thomas Reichardt, *Der Islam vor den Toren* (Leipzig, 1939). After the involvement of German troops in North Africa and the invasion of the Soviet Union, Reichardt would underline his claims in Thomas Reichardt, "Der Islam: Totale Mohammedanische Lebensschau," *Krakauer Zeitung* (21 November 1941).

98 Reichardt, *Der Islam vor den Toren*, 318. Reichardt referred to the idea of the *Kulturkreis*, see ibid., 6 and passim.

99 Ibid., 322.

100 Ibid., 241–244, quotation on 241.

101 Ibid., 190–193, 254–245; on the caliphate question after the abolishment of the Ottoman caliphate, see 243.

102 Ibid., 245–317.

103 Ibid., 297–298.

104 Ibid., 299.

105 Ibid., 326.

106 Ibid., 277 and, on the idea that Islam was genuinely anti-Bolshevist, 9 and passim.

107 On Japan's employment of Islam in its bid for hegemony in Asia, see ibid., 272–276; about Italy's policy and Mussolini's claim to protect Islam, see ibid., 300–308.

108 Ibid., 328.

109 Zaki Ali, "Großdeutschland und der Islam," in Reichardt, *Der Islam vor den Toren*, 329–340. A year earlier, Zaki Ali had already published a pan-Islamic tract, see Zaki Ali, *Islam in the World* (Lahore, 1938), positively reviewed in the *Die Welt des Islams*, see W. Björkman, "Zaki Ali, Islam in the World" (Review), *Die Welt des Islams* 20 (1938), 137–139. Ali would also reaffirm his views after the outbreak of the war, publishing the article on the day France and Britain declared war on Germany, see Zaki Ali, "Großdeutschland und der Islam," *Rheinisch-Westfälische Zeitung* (3 September 1939). Ali had already played a leading role in the organization of the European Islamic congress in Geneva in 1935, see Kramer, *Islam Assembled*, 145.

110 Ali, "Großdeutschland und der Islam," 331–332.

111 Ibid., 330.

112 Paul Schmitz, *All-Islam! Weltmacht von morgen?* (Leipzig, 1937). The book also received international attention, see Robert Gale Woolbert, "Recent Books on International Relations," *Foreign Affairs* 16, 4 (1938), 728–744, 729, and was even translated into Japanese, see Paul Schmitz, *Kaikyô no Zenbô: Ashita no Sekai Seiryoku (All-Islam: World Power of Tomorrow)* (Tokyo, 1938). Paul Schmitz was a prolific writer of popular books. Apart from his most-cited *All-Islam* he wrote many books on the Arab world, see Paul Schmitz, *Politiker und Propheten am Roten Meer* (Leipzig, 1939); Paul Schmitz, *Neubau der arabischen Welt* (Leipzig, 1937); Paul Schmitz, *Die Arabische Revolution* (Leipzig, 1942); Paul Schmitz, *Ägyptens Weg zur Freiheit* (Leipzig, 1941); Paul Schmitz, *Englands Gewaltpolitik am Nil* (Berlin, 1940); Paul Schmitz, *Frankreich in Nord-Afrika* (Leipzig, 1938); and a more general book, Paul Schmitz, *Die britische Schwäche* (Leipzig, 1940). Schmitz's books had a clear anti-imperial tinge. Islam, Islamic anti-imperialism, and imperial engagement with Islam played a role in most. He referred to French attempts to emphasize differences between Berbers and Arabs to counter an "increasingly aggressive Islam" in North Africa (*Frankreich in Nordafrika*, 126; and also *Die arabische Revolution*, 182–207); the Druze rebellion against the French in Syria (*Die arabische Revolution*, 94–95); British brutality against Mahdi rebels in Sudan (*Englands Gewaltpolitik*, 24–45; *Ägyptens weg zur Freiheit*, 114–115; and *Politiker und Propheten am Roten Meer*, 118); Muslim opposition in British India (*Die britische Schwäche*, 165, although this book is more generally focused on anti-imperialism); Muslim confrontation with British and Jewish migrants in Palestine (*Die arabische Revolution*, 152–154); Italian confrontations with the Islamic Sanusi rebels in North Africa (*Neubau der arabischen Welt*, 106); and the jihad of the First World War (*Neubau der arabischen Welt*, 7 and 21; and *Die Arabische Revolution*, 5–6). Schmitz was accredited as correspondent for the *Völkischer Beobachter* in Cairo before being expelled by the Egyptian authorities under British pressure in 1939, see Schmitz to Bohle (Foreign Organization of the NSDAP), 21 May 1939, Oberursel, PA, R 29533; Bohle to Weizsäcker (Foreign Office), 26 May 1939, Berlin, PA, R 29533; and Mildenstein (Foreign Office), Report, n.d. (1939), n.p. (Berlin), German Federal Archives (*Bundesarchiv*), Berlin-Lichterfelde (BAB), R 58/783.

113 He referred to terms like "Lebensraum," "Raumbedeutung," or "Islamische Schicksalsgemeinschaft," see Schmitz, *All-Islam!*, passim.

114 Ibid., 131.

115 Ibid., 241 and passim; about Mecca, see ibid., 114.

116 Ibid., 219–220.

117 Richard Hartmann, "Paul Schmitz, All-Islam: Neubau der Arabischen Welt" (Review), *Der Islam* 26 (1942), 67–71.

118 Ibid., 67–68.

119 Richard Hartmann, *Die Religion des Islam: Eine Einführung* (Berlin, 1944); and, similarly, Richard Hartmann, "Nationalismus und Islam: Ein Vortrag von Prof. Dr. Hartmann," *Deutsche Zeitung in den Niederlanden* (29 July 1942). Hartmann had expressed similar views in the interwar years, see Richard Hartmann, *Die Welt des Islam Einst und Heute* (Leipzig, 1927); and Richard Hartmann, *Die Krisis des Islam* (Leipzig, 1928).

120 Thomas Duve, "Die Gründung der Zeitschrift für Politik: Symbol und Symptom für die Entstehung einer Politikwissenschaft um 1900?," *Zeitschrift für Politik* 45 (1998), 405–426; and, on the *Deutsche Hochschule für Politik*, Antonio Missiroli, *Die deutsche Hochschule für Politik* (St. Augustin, 1988); Steven D. Korenblat, "A School for the Republic? Cosmopolitans and Their Enemies at the Deutsche Hochschule für Politik, 1920–1933," *Central European History* 39, 3 (2006), 394–430; Gideon Botsch, *"Politische Wissenschaft" im Zweiten Weltkrieg: Die "Deutschen Auslandswissenschaften" im Einsatz 1940–1945* (Paderborn, 2006); and the contributions to Gerhard Göhler and Bodo Zeuner (eds.), *Kontinuitäten und Brüche in der deutschen Politikwissenschaft* (Baden-Baden, 1991).

121 Kurt Prüfer, "Arabien im Umbau," *Zeitschrift für Politik* 24, 6 (1934), 362–368. Notable examples for discussions of an Islamic awakening and Islam as a strong geopolitical force are Walter Schönfelder, "Politik und Religion im Osten," *Zeitschrift für Politik* 24, 10 (1934), 610–615; Walter Schönfelder, "Asien im Umbruch," *Zeitschrift für Politik* 27, 10 (1937), 469–473; Habibur Rahman, "Aufmarsch des Islams," *Zeitschrift für Politik* 26, 10 (1936), 570–577; and Habibur Rahman, "Die islamische Welt—eine ewige Grenze: Die Randprobleme des modernen islamischen Staatensystems," *Zeitschrift für Politik* 27, 3 (1937), 163–167.

122 Erich Müller, "Mekka: Der Kraftpol des Nahen Orients," *Zeitschrift für Politik* 28, 5 (1938), 312–315, 313.

123 Ibid., 312.

124 Walter Hagemann, "Das französische Kolonialreich in Afrika," *Zeitschrift für Politik* 17, 7 (1928), 612–633; Edgar Pröbster, "Die kolonialpolitische Literatur Frankreichs (Seit 1922)," *Zeitschrift für Politik* 17, 1 (1927), 64–76; Edgar Pröbster, "Die kolonialen Probleme Frankreichs auf Grund der neuesten kolonialpolitischen Literatur," *Zeitschrift für Politik* 18, 1 (1928), 52–57; Edgar Pröbster, "Die Entwicklung von Frankreichs Islampolitik 1830–1930," *Zeitschrift für Politik* 20, 7/8 (1930), 477–486; Edgar Pröbster, "Die Entislamisierung der marokkanischen Berbern und ihre Folgen," *Zeitschrift für Politik* 23, 3 (1933), 201–204; A. Grabowsky, "Niederländisch-Indien im weltpolitischen Rahmen: Vorbemerkung," *Zeitschrift für Politik* 23, 5 (1933), 307–309; and Karl Helbig, "Niederländisch-Indien gestern, heute und morgen," *Zeitschrift für Politik* 23, 5 (1933), 309–320; Habibur Rahman, " 'Dschihadistan': Die friedlose Nordwestgrenze Indiens," *Zeitschrift für Politik* 28, 2 (1938), 121–125.

125 Sophie Freifrau v. Wangenheim, "Auf verlorenem Posten," *Zeitschrift für Politik* 26, 8/9 (1936), 498–508; and Sophie Freifrau v. Wangenheim, "Oberst Lawrence und der Aufstand der Araber im Weltkrieg (Auf Grund der 'Seven Pillars of Wisdom')," *Zeitschrift für Politik* 27, 7/8 (1937), 417–437.

126 I. Jorda, "Die Westmächte und die Araber," *Zeitschrift für Politik* 31, 5 (1941), 294–302.

127 Richard Hartmann, "Der Mufti Amīn el-Ḥusainī," *Zeitschrift für Politik* 31, 7 (1941), 430–439; Ernst Klingmüller, "Hadj Emin el-Huseini: Großmufti von Jerusalem," *Zeitschrift für Politik* 33, 8/9 (1943), 413–417; and, for a prewar article on al-Husayni, Walther Björkman, "Der Mufti von Jerusalem," *Zeitschrift für Politik* 28, 5 (1938), 306–311. Another Muslim collaborator honored with an article in the *Zeitschrift für Politik* was the Syrian rebel Fawzi al-Qawuqji, see I. Jorda, "Fauzi el-Kawukschi—

der Held der Wüste: Das Leben eines arabischen Freiheitskämpfers," *Zeitschrift für Politik* 32, 4 (1942), 261–265.

128 Paschasius: "Europa und die islamische Welt des Nahen Ostens," *Militärwissenschaftliche Rundschau* 7, 2 (1942), 192–204, 197. This article was also reviewed by the Wehrmacht during the Second World War, see German Federal Military Archives (*Bundesarchiv, Militärarchiv*), Freiburg (BA–MA), RH 2/1764.

129 Johannes Benzing, "Bolschewismus, Turkvölker und Islam: Ein Beitrag zur Nationalitätenpolitik des Bolschewismus," *Osteuropa* 13, 3 (1937), 187–194. Benzing would also refer to the importance of Islam and "holy war" in Muslim resistance movements in Russia since the tsarist era in his historical article, Johannes Benzing, "Das turkestanische Volk im Kampf um seine Selbstständigkeit," *Die Welt des Islams* 19 (1937), 94–137, esp. 101–102, 105.

130 Benzing, "Bolschewismus, Turkvölker und Islam," 194.

131 Ibid., 194.

132 Ibid., 193.

133 Johannes Benzing, *Turkestan* (Berlin, 1943); and Johannes Benzing, "Die Türkvölker der Sowjetunion," in Hans Heinrich Schaeder (ed.), *Der Orient in deutscher Forschung* (Leipzig, 1944), 18–26, which was also read in the SS by those responsible for Islamic mobilization during the war, see the documents in BAB, NS 31/29.

134 Gerhard von Mende, *Der nationale Kampf der Russlandtürken: Ein Beitrag zur nationalen Frage in der Sowjetunion* (Berlin, 1936), on Islam and nationalism in the Soviet Union, see esp. 180–182. Mende reiterated his views three years later in Gerhard von Mende, *Die Völker der Sowjetunion* (Reichenau, 1939).

135 G. J., "Gerhard von Mende, Der nationale Kampf der Russlandtürken" (Review), *Die Welt des Islams* 18 (1936), 146–147.

136 Ibid., 146.

137 Ibid.

138 Gotthardt Jäschke, "Kommunismus und Islam im Türkischen Befreiungskriege," *Die Welt des Islams* 20 (1938), 110–117.

139 Ibid., 110.

140 Paul Schmitz, *Moskau und die islamische Welt* (Munich, 1938), quotation on 15.

141 Ibid., 21.

142 Ibid., 22.

143 Ibid., 58.

144 J. Benzing, "Paul Schmitz, Moskau und die islamische Welt" (Review), *Die Welt des Islams* 20 (1938), 151–152, 152.

145 Karl Krüger, "Der Islam als Wirtschaftsfaktor in Mittelasien," *Organ des Deutschen Orient Vereins* 2, 8 (1941), 48–53. For Krüger's early reflection on the "psyche" of the "Islamic man," see Karl Krüger, "Der neue Wirtschaftsgeist im Islamischen Orient," *Zeitschrift für Politik* (1923), 248–263.

146 Franz Ronneberger, "Der Islam im Antlitz Europas," *Völkischer Beobachter* (19 October 1942). Having written his doctoral dissertation on "Bismarck and the Southeast" (1938) and published a book on the contemporary politics of the Balkans (1940), Ronneberger was one of the regime's most ambitious and prolific experts on the Balkans, see Franz Ronneberger, *Einführung in die politischen Probleme Südosteuropas*

(Munich, 1940); Franz Ronneberger, *Bismarck und Südosteuropa* (Berlin, 1941); and the fifteen-page brochure, Franz Ronneberger, *Der nahe Osten* (Vienna, 1942). On Franz Ronneberger, see Peer Heinelt, *"PR-Päpste": Die kontinuierlichen Karrieren von Carl Hundhausen, Albert Oeckl und Franz Ronneberger* (Berlin, 2003), esp. 130–188; and Peer Heinelt, "Portrait eines Schreibtischtäters: Franz Ronneberger (1913–1999)," in Wolfgang Duchkowitsch, Fritz Hausjell, and Bernd Semrad (eds.), *Die Spirale des Schweigens: Zum Umgang mit der nationalsozialistischen Zeitungswissenschaft* (Münster, 2004), 198–201; Gerhard Seewann, "Das Südost-Institut 1930–1960," in Mathias Beer and Gerhard Seewann (eds.), *Südostforschung im Schatten des Dritten Reiches: Institutionen, Inhalte, Personen* (Munich, 2004), 49–92; and Carsten Klingemann, "Franz Ronneberger: Sozialwissenschaft, Publizistik, Nachrichtendienst: Zum Verhältnis von 'Intelligence' und Wissenschaft," in Christina Holtz-Bacha, Arnulf Kutsch, Wolfgang Langenbucher, and Klaus Schönbach (eds.), *Fünfzig Jahre Publizistik* (Wiesbaden, 2006), 144–175. A number of Ronneberger's intelligence reports about the Balkans and the Middle East can be found in PA, R 67569.

147 Anonymous, "Zum Mohammedanerproblem in Bosnien und der Herzegowina," *Volkstum im Südosten* 7 (1943), 103–112.

148 Interestingly, authors described Kemalist Turkey as an exception in the Muslim world or claimed that Islam still played a significant role in Turkey. Lindemann saw the case of Kemalist Turkey as an exception in the Muslim world, see Lindemann, "Der Islam im Aufbruch und Angriff," 788. Reichhardt even claimed that Kemalist laicism was opposed by most Muslims in Turkey as heresy, see Reichardt, *Der Islam vor den Toren*, 321–322. His view was shared by Schmitz, who asserted that a "closer look" at Turkey showed that religion could not be completely abolished; Schmitz, *All-Islam!*, 106. During the war the *Militärwissenschaftliche Rundschau* also explained that Kemalist Turkey had remained Muslim "after all," see W. Paschasius, "Europa und die islamische Welt," 197.

149 Perhaps the best example is Rolf Beckh, *Der Islam und die überstaatlichen Mächte* (Munich, 1937), who described Islam as a backward, antinational, and "Semitic religion," which he compared to Communism; also Beckh acknowledged that there was a revival of Islam. Others believed in a religious resurgence throughout the Muslim world but assessed it primarily as a threat, see, for instance, Meinulf Küster, "Bewegung im Islam," *Deutsche Rundschau Leipzig* (January 1938), 8–30. Küster remembered Islamic uprisings and Mahdism in the late nineteenth century and even the "Mecca letters" in German East Africa (30), describing Islam as "fanatical" and "longing for death" (30). Although rare in Germany, these perceptions were shared by some prominent non-German thinkers such as the American eugenicist and political scientist Lothrop Stoddard, who saw the rise of Islam as a threat to the "West," see Lothrop Stoddard, *The New World of Islam* (New York, 1921). Interestingly, Haushofer admitted to having derived "deep insights" about pan-Islamism from Stoddard's work, although he explicitly distanced himself from Stoddard's negative assessment of Islam, see Haushofer, *Geopolitik der Pan-Ideen*, 15 and 37–38. Naturally, missionary publicists like Gottfried Simon would also assess the perceived political revival of Islam after the First World War as a threat (against Christianity),

see Simon, *Die Welt des Islam und die neue Zeit*; and Gottfried Simon, *Islam und Bolschewismus* (Wernigerode, 1937).

150 Robert L. Baker, *Oil, Blood and Sand* (New York, 1942), 39. French publications also assessed Germany's policy toward the Muslim world, most significantly Bernard Vernier, *La politique islamique de l'Allemagne* (Paris, 1939). Vernier even connected Hitler's strategy to Germany's campaign for Islamic mobilization of the First World War (10).

151 Baker, *Oil, Blood and Sand*, 42–44.

152 Ibid., 42.

153 Ibid.

154 Ibid., 45.

155 Ibid., 44.

156 Ebeling, *Geopolitik*; on Haushofer and his impact on Hitler, see Jacobsen, *Karl Haushofer*; and Hipler, *Hitlers Lehrmeister*. Whereas Jacobsen argues that Haushofer's influence should not be overestimated, Hipler writes that his school of thought had a strong impact on Hitler.

157 On the literature on Islam read in the SS, see the documents in BAB, NS 31/30; for the East Ministry, see the documents in R 6/510, R 6/512, and R 6/555.

2. BERLIN'S MUSLIM MOMENT

1 Oppenheim, Memorandum, 25 July 1940, Berlin, PA, Nachlass Hentig, vol. 84.

2 Habicht to Oppenheim, 27 July 1940, Berlin, PA, Nachlass Hentig, vol. 84.

3 On Nazi Germany's prewar foreign policy schemes, see Hans-Adolf Jacobsen, *Nationalsozialistische Außenpolitik 1933–1938* (Frankfurt, 1968); Bernd-Jürgen Wendt, *Großdeutschland: Außenpolitik und Kriegsvorbereitung des Hitler-Regimes* (Munich, 1987); Marie-Luise Becker, *Die Aussenpolitik des Dritten Reiches* (Munich, 1990); Rainer F. Schmidt, *Die Aussenpolitik des Dritten Reiches 1933–1939* (Stuttgart, 2002); Lars Lüdicke, *Griff nach der Weltherrschaft: Die Aussenpolitik des Dritten Reiches 1933–1945* (Berlin, 2009), 1–130; Eckart Conze et al., *Das Amt und die Vergangenheit: Deutsche Diplomaten im Dritten Reich und in der Bundesrepublik* (Munich, 2010), 74–137; and the articles in Funke (ed.), *Hitler, Deutschland und die Mächte*; and, on the colonial world, Klaus Hildebrand, *Vom Reich zum Weltreich: Hitler, NSDAP und koloniale Frage, 1919–1945* (Munich, 1969), 441–624; and, on Hitler's foreign policy ideas, Axel Kuhn, *Hitlers außenpolitisches Programm: Entstehung und Entwicklung 1919–1939* (Stuttgart, 1970), which somewhat overstates the coherence of his foreign policy "program."

4 Stohrer, Internal Note, 18 November 1941, Berlin, PA, R 29533.

5 Ibid.

6 On Schrumpf-Pierron, see André-Paul Weber, *Conseiller du grand mufti: L'odyssée du Docteur Pierre Schrumpf-Pierron 1882–1952* (Paris, 2005).

7 Schrumpf-Pierron, Memorandum, 12 May 1941, Cairo, BA–MA, RH 2/1765.

8 Woermann, Internal Note ("Aufzeichnung zur arabischen Frage"), 7 March 1941, Berlin, PA, R 261123.

9 Woermann, Internal Note, 23 January 1942, Berlin, PA, R 27501.

10 Woermann, Internal Note, 11 February 1942, Berlin, PA, R 27501 (also in PA, R 60670).

11 Woermann to Weizsäcker, 3 March 1942, Berlin, PA, R 30005.

12 In these discussions the Muslims of India were considered a special case as Germany tried to avoid supporting Muslim separatism on the subcontinent. The major memoranda on Islam and politics in British India are Alsdorf (Foreign Office), Internal Note ("Die indischen Mohammedaner, der Pakistan-Plan und die deutsche Orientpolitik"), n.d. (1941), Berlin, PA, R 27501; and Keppler, Internal Note ("Propagandistische Erfassung der indischen Moslems"), 8 March 1943, Berlin, PA, R 67660; and, in accordance, Keppler, Internal Note ("Sprachregelung über das Problem der Moslem-Liga"), 3 April 1943, Berlin, PA, R 60677.

13 On the policies of the Foreign Office in North Africa and the Middle East, see Tillmann, *Deutschlands Araberpolitik im Zweiten Weltkrieg*; Hirszowicz, *The Third Reich and the Arab East*; and Schröder, *Deutschland und der Mittlere Osten im Zweiten Weltkrieg*.

14 On Grobba, see Francis R. Nicosia, "Fritz Grobba and the Middle East Policy of the Third Reich," in Edward Ingram (ed.), *National and International Politics in the Middle East: Essays in Honour of Elie Kedourie* (London, 1986), 206–228; Edgar Flacker, "Fritz Grobba and Nazi Germany's Middle Eastern Policy, 1933–1942" (PhD diss., University of London, 1998); and Wolfgang G. Schwanitz, "'The Jinnee and the Magic Bottle': Fritz Grobba and the German Middle Eastern Policy 1900–1945," in Wolfgang G. Schwanitz (ed.), *Germany and the Middle East 1871–1945* (Princeton, NJ, 2004), 86–117; and his memoirs, Fritz Grobba, *Männer und Mächte im Orient: 25 Jahre diplomatische Tätigkeit im Orient* (Göttingen, 1967). Grobba also wrote two books on the Middle East during and after the war, see Fritz Grobba, *Irak* (Berlin, 1941); and Fritz Grobba (alias Hans Ludwig Wegener), *Der britische Geheimdienst im Orient: Terror und Intrige als Mittel englischer Politik* (Berlin, 1942). For the quotation, see Albert Viton, "Britain and the Axis in the Near East," *Foreign Affairs* 2 (January 1941), 370–384, 380.

15 On Prüfer, see Paul Kahle, "Curt Prüfer," *Zeitschrift der deutschen Morgenländischen Gesellschaft* 111 (1961), 1–3; McKale, *Curt Prüfer*; and his (revised and unrevised) wartime diaries, Donald M. McKale (ed.), *Rewriting History: The Original and Revised World War II Diaries of Curt Prüfer, Nazi Diplomat* (Kent, OH, 1988).

16 Ilan Pappe, *The Rise and Fall of a Palestinian Dynasty: The Husaynis 1700–1948* (London, 2010).

17 Uri M. Kupferschmidt, *The Supreme Muslim Council: Islam under the British Mandate for Palestine* (Leiden, 1987), esp. 19–28.

18 On Amin al-Husayni in Berlin, see Schechtman, *The Mufti and the Fuehrer*; Lebel, *The Mufti of Jerusalem*; and Gensicke, *The Mufti of Jerusalem and the Nazis*; and, for a collection of German documents on al-Husayni's activities in Germany, Gerhard Höpp (ed.), *Mufti-Papiere: Briefe, Memoranden, Reden und Aufrufe Amin al-Husainis aus dem Exil, 1940–1945* (Berlin, 2002). A historiographical overview is given in Höpp, "Der Gefangene im Dreieck." The German press was following the mufti's journey to Berlin, see, for instance, Anonymous, "Der Mufti von Jerusalem in Italien," *Frankfurter Zeitung* (27 October 1941); and Anonymous, "Der Großmufti kommt nach Berlin," *Deutsche Allgemeine Zeitung* (6 November 1941).

19 On the meeting between Hitler and al-Husayni, see Schechtman, *The Mufti and the Fuehrer*, 122–124; Lebel, *The Mufti of Jerusalem*, 110–116; and Gensicke, *The Mufti of Jerusalem and the Nazis*, 66–69. The *Wochenschau* broadcast the visit, and, according to the SS, these reels were met with "great interest" by the German population, see Heinz Boberach (ed.), *Meldungen aus dem Reich, 1938–1945: Die geheimen Lageberichte des Sicherheitsdienstes der SS*, vol. 9 (Berlin, 1984), 3101–3119 (18 December 1941), 3106.

20 *Mudhakkirat al-Hajj Muhammad Amin al-Husayni* (*The Memoirs of Hajj Muhammad Amin al-Husayni*), ed. 'Abd al-Karim al-'Umar (Damascus, 1999), 108–112, and, for the quotation, 108. The memoirs are in part based on al-Husayni's diary and clearly reflect the mufti's anxious desire to portray himself as a great statesman.

21 Fritz Grobba and Hitler's official translator, Paul Schmidt, wrote reports about the meeting for the Foreign Office, giving a detailed account of the content of the discussion, see Schmidt, Internal Note ("Aufzeichnung über die Unterredung zwischen dem Führer und dem Grossmufti von Jerusalem in Anwesenheit des Reichsaussenminsiters u. des Gesandten Grobba in Berlin am 28. November 1941"), 30 November 1941, Berlin, PA, R 35475; and Grobba, Internal Note ("Empfang des Großmufti durch den Führer"), 1 December 1941, Berlin, PA, R 261123. Leonard Mosley, *The Cat and the Mice* (London, 1958), 26–29, provides another account of the encounter, allegedly based on a postwar testimony by Johannes Eppler, who also acted as a translator during the meeting. Mosley's claims that Hitler acted rather awkwardly when meeting al-Husayni and even refused to shake hands are explicitly contradicted in Eppler's memoirs, which also recount the meeting, see John Eppler, *Operation Condor: Rommel's Spy* (London, 1977), 193–197 and, on Mosley, 241–243; accounts of the meeting are not part of Eppler's German memoirs, see John W. Eppler, *"Rommel ruft Kairo": Aus dem Tagebuch eines Spions* (Gütersloh, 1959); and John W. Eppler, *Geheimagent im Zweiten Weltkrieg: Zwischen Berlin, Kabul und Kairo* (Preußisch Oldendorf, 1974).

22 Ettel (Foreign Office), Internal Note, 16 April 1943, Berlin, PA, R 27322.

23 The documentation of this conflict is extensive and runs through the documents in the Foreign Office files PA, R 27322–27328. On the rivalry, see Schechtman, *The Mufti and the Fuehrer*, passim; Lebel, *The Mufti of Jerusalem*, passim; and Gensicke, *The Mufti of Jerusalem and the Nazis*, passim. After the war, Wilhelm Melchers gave a good overview of the conflict, see Melchers, Nuremberg Interrogation Statement ("Die Politik des Mufti"), 6 August 1947, Nuremberg, Archives of the Center for Advanced Holocaust Studies, Washington, DC (USHMA), RG 71, Box 248.

24 On Ettel, see Frank Bajohr, "'Im übrigen handle ich so, wie mein Gewissen es mir als Nationalsozialist vorschreibt': Erwin Ettel—vom SS-Brigadeführer zum außenpolitischen Redakteur der ZEIT, in Jürgen Matthäus and Klaus-Michael Mallmann (eds.), *Deutsche, Juden, Völkermord: Der Holocaust als Geschichte und Gegenwart* (Darmstadt, 2006), 241–255.

25 Schechtman, *The Mufti and the Fuehrer*; Lebel, *The Mufti of Jerusalem*; and Gensicke, *The Mufti of Jerusalem and the Nazis*.

26 An overview is given in the literature in note 25; and by Gerhard Höpp, "'Nicht 'Alī zuliebe, sondern aus Hass gegen Mu'āwiya': Zum Ringen um die 'Arabien-Erklärung'

der Achsenmächte 1940–1942," *Asien, Afrika, Lateinamerika* 27 (1999), 569–587. The mufti repeatedly pushed for a declaration of Arab independence but faced the resistance of the Nazi elite, most importantly Hitler, who, in May 1942, complained about diplomats who pressured for a declaration of Arab independence during his table talks, see *Hitler's Table Talk 1941–1944*, ed. H. R. Trevor-Roper and transl. Norman Cameron and R. H. Stevens (London, 1953), 488 (16 May 1942, dinner).

27 On these interventions, see Hilberg, *The Destruction of the European Jews*, 504–505, and, in the revised edition, Raul Hilberg, *The Destruction of the European Jews*, 3 vols. (London, 1985), vol. 2, 789–790; Schechtman, *The Mufti and the Fuehrer*, 154–159; Lebel, *The Mufti of Jerusalem*, 246–255; and Gensicke, *The Mufti of Jerusalem and the Nazis*, 117–129.

28 On al-Husayni's salary, see Schechtman, *The Mufti and the Fuehrer*, 142–144; Lebel, *The Mufti of Jerusalem*, 136–138; and Gensicke, *The Mufti of Jerusalem and the Nazis*, 161–167. Detailed information about the payments the mufti received for his services was also provided by SS foreign intelligence chief Walter Schellenberg and diplomat Carl Rekowski during their interrogations at Nuremberg, conducted by Robert Kempner, see Robert M. W. Kempner, *Das Dritte Reich im Kreuzverhör: Aus den unveröffentlichten Vernehmungsprotokollen des Anklägers in den Nürnberger Prozessen* (Munich, 2005 [1969]), 301–305 (Schellenberg), esp. 303–305, and 305–306 (Rekowski).

29 The mufti's attempts to portray himself as an Arab nationalist after his arrival in Berlin, in 1941–1942, are obvious in all of his letters to the Foreign Office, see the documents in PA, R 27322–27328. In June 1942 he even told Ettel that he had not been properly educated in theology and that it would be wrong to see him just as a religious figure, though emphasizing that true Muslims would normally not distinguish between politics and religion, see Ettel, Internal Note, 26 June 1942, Berlin, PA, R 27324.

30 Grobba to Woermann, 19 October 1942, Berlin, PA, R 27322.

31 Ettel to Ribbentrop, 22 September 1942, Berlin, PA, R 27324.

32 Idris, Curriculum Vitae, n.d. (post-1933), n.p. (Berlin), PA, R 60740. On Idris, see also literature in Chapter 1, note 35.

33 Anonymous (Rashid Rida), "Fatawa al-Manar," *Al-Manar* 33 (5 September 1933), 347–351, which includes the letter from Alimjan Idris on 347. The issue of *al-Manar* is stored in the British Library.

34 On the history of the Islamic Central Institute from the perspective of the Muslim minority in Germany, see Gerhard Höpp, "Muslime unterm Hakenkreuz: Zur Entstehung des Islamischen Zentralinstituts zu Berlin e.V.," *Moslemische Revue* 1 (1994), 16–27; and Bernd Bauknecht, *Muslime in Deutschland von 1920 bis 1945* (Cologne, 2001), 107–117. The government files on the institute can be found in the Berlin State Archive (*Landesarchiv Berlin*), Berlin (LArchB), A Pr. Br. Rep 030-04 (*Polizeipräsidium Berlin, Vereine*), no. 2314 (*Islam-Institut, 1939–1940*); and LArchB, A Pr. Br. Rep. 030-04 (*Polizeipräsidium Berlin, Vereine*), no. 2840 (*Islamisches Zentral-Institut zu Berlin, 1942–1945*); and, on the inauguration ceremony of 1942, in PA, R 27322, R 27324, R 27327, and R 60601. The invitation to the inauguration has also survived the war, see Invitation Card ("Einladung zur Eröffnung des Islamischen Zentral-Instituts zu Berlin e.V."), n.d. (December 1943), Berlin, PA, R 27327.

35 Prüfer to Woermann, 13 December 1942, Berlin, PA, R 27327.

36 Al-Husayni, Speech, 18 December 1942, Berlin, PA, R 27327.

37 Ibid.

38 Ettel, Internal Note, 11 December 1942, Berlin, PA, R 27327, on the approval of the opening speech by Ribbentrop; and, on the organization of the broadcast transmission, see Prüfer, Internal Note, 10 December 1942, Berlin, PA, R 27327; Ettel, Internal Note, 11 December 1942, Berlin, PA, R 27327; and Ettel, Internal Note, 16 December 1942, Berlin, PA, R 27327. Before the idea of the inauguration of the institute came up, the Foreign Office had already planned a propaganda event on the 'Id al-Adha in the Berlin Mosque, which was to be broadcast to North Africa and the Middle East, see Grobba, Minutes ("38. Sitzung, Arabien-Komitee"), 3 December 1942, Berlin, PA, R 27327; and Ettel, Internal Note, 8 December 1942, Berlin, PA, R 27327.

39 Anonymous, "Dieser Krieg kann dem Islam die Freiheit bringen!," *Völkischer Beobachter* (19 December 1942); two months earlier, the paper had already reported on Islam in a similar way, see H. Höpfl'l, "Der Islam in der Prüfung," *Völkischer Beobachter* (6 October 1942); and it would continue to do so in the following months, see, for instance, Anonymous, "Aufruf des Großmuftis gegen die Todfeinde des Islams: Araber werden für ihre Freiheit an der Seite der Achse kämpfen," *Völkischer Beobachter* (20 March 1943).

40 Anonymous, "Der Großmufti über den Befreiungskampf des Islams: Eröffnung eines Islamischen Kulturinstitutes in Berlin," *Deutsche Allgemeine Zeitung* (19 December 1942). A day later, the paper printed a photograph of the event, see Anonymous, "Der Großmufti von Jerusalem sprach in Berlin," *Deutsche Allgemeine Zeitung* (20 December 1942).

41 Anonymous, "Der Sprecher von 400 Millionen klagt an," *Das 12 Uhr Blatt: Neue Berliner Zeitung* (19 December 1942); and, for the photographs, Anonymous, "Der Großmufti sprach," *Berliner Illustrierte Nachtausgabe* (19 December 1942); and Anonymous, "Islamische Freiwillige beim Großmufti," *Berliner Illustrierte Nachtausgabe* (19 December 1942).

42 On the reestablishing of the institute, see the literature in note 34; and, for concise overviews, Ettel, Internal Note, 11 December 1942, Berlin, PA, R 27327; and Ettel, Internal Note, 16 December 1942, Berlin, PA, R 27327.

43 On the Muslim minority in interwar Germany and the Berlin Mosque, see Gerhard Höpp, "Zwischen Moschee und Demonstration: Muslime in Berlin, 1920–1930," *Moslemische Revue* 3 (1990), 135–146; 4 (1990), 230–238; and 1 (1991), 13–19; Gerhard Höpp, "Die Wünsdorfer Moschee": Britta Richter, "Islam im Deutschland der Zwischenkriegsjahre," *Zeitschrift für Türkeistudien* 2 (1996), 257–266; and Bauknecht, *Muslime in Deutschland von 1920 bis 1945*.

44 Melchers to Woermann, 16 December 1942, Berlin, PA, R 27327; and Tismar to Ettel, 17 December 1942, Berlin, PA, R 27327.

45 Kurt Munzel, head of the Middle East section in the Broadcast Department of the Foreign Office, was responsible for all financial matters of the institute, see Minutes ("Protokoll der neuen Gründungsversammlung des Islamischen Zentral-Instituts"), October 1942, Berlin, LArchB, A Pr. Br. Rep. 030-04, no. 2840.

46 Ettel, Internal Note, 11 December 1942, Berlin, PA, R 27327.

47 Ettel, Internal Note, 26 February 1943, Berlin, PA, R 27322.

48 On the Foreign Office's policies in the Caucasus and Crimea, see Alexander Dallin, *German Rule in Russia, 1941–1945: A Study of Occupation Policies* (London, 1957), 235–240, 272, and 257–259; and Mühlen, *Zwischen Hakenkreuz und Sowjetstern*, 68–81.

49 On Hentig, see, with a focus on his time in the Crimea, Johannes Hürter, "'Nachrichten aus dem Zweiten Krimkrieg': Werner Otto v. Hentig als Vertreter des Auswärtigen Amts bei der 11. Armee," in Wolfgang Elz and Sönke Neitzel (eds.), *Internationale Beziehungen im 19. und 20. Jahrhundert: Festschrift für Winfried Baumgart zum 65. Geburtstag* (Paderborn, 2003), 361–387; and, for his memoirs, Hentig, *Mein Leben*. In the war years, Hentig published Werner Otto von Hentig, *Der Nahe Osten rückt näher* (Leipzig, 1940).

50 Hentig, Internal Note ("Turanismus"), n.d. (November 1941), Berlin, PA, R 28876 (also in PA, R 261179). His superiors in the Foreign Office were quite receptive to such schemes. Woermann summarized and commented on the report from Hentig in an internal note for Ribbentrop, see Woermann, Internal Note ("Aufzeichnung über Fragen des Vorderen Orients"), 6 November 1941, Berlin, PA, R 28876 (also in PA, R 261179). Ribbentrop then eagerly delivered a report to Hitler about the political importance of the Eastern Turks, based on the internal notes by Woermann and Hentig, emphasizing: "They are Mohammedan throughout and stand in opposition to the Russians," see Ribbentrop, Report ("Notiz für den Führer"), 13 November 1941, n.p., PA, R 28876. A few days later, Ribbentrop also sent Hitler a map to show where the Turkic peoples of the Soviet Union lived, see Ribbentrop, Report ("Notiz für den Führer"), 19 November 1941, n.p., PA, R 28876.

51 Hentig, Internal Note ("Stand der sog. Turanischen Frage"), 25 February 1942, Berlin, PA, R 60690 (also in PA, R 261175).

52 Ibid.

53 On the conflict between the Foreign Office and the East Ministry, see the literature in note 48.

54 On the East Ministry's policies in the Caucasus and Crimea and the national committees, see Dallin, *German Rule in Russia*, 228–231, 235–240, 253–257, and 264–270; Mühlen, *Zwischen Hakenkreuz und Sowjetstern*, 68–138; and, for the general context, Andreas Zellhuber, *"Unsere Verwaltung treibt einer Katastrophe zu . . .": Das Reichsministerium für die besetzten Ostgebiete und die deutsche Besatzungsherrschaft in der Sowjetunion 1941–1945* (Munich, 2006).

55 Mende to Dallin, 19 November 1953, n.p., quoted in Dallin, *German Rule in Russia*, 267.

56 Bräutigam, Internal Note ("Politische Richtlinien hinsichtlich Turkestan"), 25 November 1941, Berlin, BAB, R 6/247.

57 On the Wehrmacht's policies in the Caucasus and Crimea, see Dallin, *German Rule in Russia*, 238–249 and 259–264; and Mühlen, *Zwischen Hakenkreuz und Sowjetstern*, 57–68 and 183–195.

58 Schweitzer (Army), Internal Note ("Verbreitung des Islams unter den Kriegsgefangenen"), 18 November 1941, Berlin, United States National Archives, Maryland (USNA), RG 242, T454, Roll 92. The army was early confronted with Muslim prisoners of war, who offered to fight alongside the Wehrmacht against atheist Bolshevism, see, for instance, Uzbek Prisoners of War (signed by forty Muslims) to Hitler, n.d. (1941), n.p. (German translation from Uzbek, 7 September 1941, Vienna), PA,

R 29900, who thanked Hitler in the name of millions of Muslims for their liberation and assured him that Moscow had not succeeded in its attempts to destroy Islam and religious sentiment.

59 Schweitzer, Internal Note ("Verbreitung des Islams unter den Kriegsgefangenen"), 18 November 1941, Berlin, USNA, RG 242, T454, Roll 92.

60 Wehrmacht, Internal Note ("UdSSR und Islam"), 15 May 1942, Berlin, BA–MA, RH 2/1764; the report was sent to Reinhard Gehlen's Eastern section of the Wehrmacht intelligence, see Wehrmacht Foreign Intelligence (*Amt Ausland/Abwehr*) to Foreign Armies East (*Fremde Heere Ost*), 22 May 1942, Berlin, BA–MA, RH 2/1764.

61 Wehrmacht, Internal Note ("UdSSR und Islam"), 15 May 1942, Berlin, BA–MA, RH 2/1764.

62 On Niedermayer, see Franz W. Seidler, "Oskar Ritter von Niedermayer im Zweiten Weltkrieg: Ein Beitrag zur Geschichte der Ostlegionen," *Wehrwissenschaftliche Rundschau* 20, 3 (1970), 168–174 (Part 1) and 20, 4 (1970), 193–208 (Part 2); and Seidt, *Berlin, Kabul, Moskau.*

63 Niedermayer tirelessly promoted the expertise he had gained in the First World War. After the outbreak of the war, Niedermayer turned to the Foreign Office to propose stirring up revolts in the Arab world and India against the British, referring to his experience, see Niedermayer, Report ("Politik und Kriegsführung im Vorderen Orient: Eine wehrpolitisch-strategische Studie"), 3 November 1939, Berlin, PA, R 261179.

64 Grobba to Woermann, 19 October 1942, Berlin, PA, R 27322, emphasized that al-Husayni "was opposed by the High Command of the Wehrmacht as unreliable."

65 On Berger, see Gerhard Rempel, "Gottlob Berger and Waffen-SS Recruitment: 1939–1945," *Militärgeschichtliche Mitteilungen* 27, 1 (1980), 107–122, which focuses on his role in *Waffen-SS* recruitment; and, more generally, Gerhard Rempel, "Gottlob Berger: 'Ein Schwabengeneral der Tat,'" in Ronald Smelser and Enrico Syring (eds.), *Die SS: Elite unter dem Totenkopf: 30 Lebensläufe* (Paderborn, 2000), 45–59; Joachim Scholtyseck, "Der 'Schwabenherzog' Gottlob Berger, SS-Obergruppenführer," in Joachim Scholtyseck and Michael Kißener (eds.), *Die Führer der Provinz: NS-Biographien aus Baden und Württemberg* (Konstanz, 1997), 77–110; and Alfred Hoffmann, "Der 'maßlose Drang, eine Rolle zu spielen': Gottlob Berger," in Wolfgang Proske (ed.), *Täter, Helfer, Mitläufer: NS-Belastete von der Ostalb* (Münster, 2010), 21–51.

66 On German policies in the Balkans, see Tomasevich, *War and Revolution in Yugoslavia,* esp. 466–510; Redžić, *Bosnia and Herzegovina in the Second World War;* Hoare, *Genocide and Resistance in Hitler's Bosnia;* and Hoare, *The Bosnian Muslims in the Second World War.*

67 On the SS involvement with the Turkic peoples of the Soviet Union, see Dallin, *German Rule in Russia,* 168–181 and 587–612; Mühlen, *Zwischen Hakenkreuz und Sowjetstern,* 139–165; and Sebastian Cwiklinski, "Die Panturkismus-Politik der SS: Angehörige sowjetischer Turkvölker als Objekte und Subjekte der SS Politik," in Höpp and Reinwald (eds.), *Fremdeinsätze,* 149–166.

68 After the war Olzscha wrote a detailed report about his work in the SS Head Office and the Eastern Muslim formations of the Waffen-SS, see Olzscha, Report, 1945, n.p., Archives of the Federal Commissioner for the Stasi Documents (*Bundesbeauftragter für die Stasi-Unterlagen*), Berlin (BStU), MfS, HA IX/11, ZR 920, A. 54.

Based on Olzscha's report, see also Ministry of State Security of the German Democratic Republic, Information Card on Olzscha, n.d. (post-1945), n.p., BStU, MfS, HA IX/11, FV 2/72 PA, A. 7.

69 On the *Arbeitsgemeinschaft Turkestan* in Dresden, see Burchard Brentjes, "Die 'Arbeitsgemeinschaft Turkestan im Rahmen der DMG': Ein Beispiel des Mißbrauchs der Wissenschaften gegen die Völker Mittelasiens," in Burchard Brentjes (ed.), *60 Jahre Nationale Sowjetrepubliken in Mittelasien im Spiegel der Wissenschaften* (Halle an der Saale, 1985), 151–172; and Horst Kißmehl, "Mittelasien: Ziel- und Einsatzgebiet deutscher bürgerlicher Wissenschaften: Bemerkungen zu einigen Aspekten der Organisation und Kontinuität deutscher imperialistischer und faschistischer Mittelasienforschung, in Brentjes (ed.), *60 Jahre Nationale Sowjetrepubliken*, 127–150. Reiner Olzscha had also published on Central Asia, see Reiner Olzscha and Georg Cleinow, *Turkestan: Die politisch-historischen und wirtschaftlichen Probleme Zentralasiens* (Leipzig, 1942), which contained various passages on the political significance of Islam in the region, esp. on 336–408; and, for a sympathetic review that stressed the importance of the region as an arena for the Anglo-Russian "struggle for influence on the Mohammedan world," see Fritz Machatschek, "Die Probleme Turkestans," *Petermanns Geographische Mitteilungen* 88 (1942), 327–330, 327. His writings also appeared in the *Zeitschrift für Geopolitik*, see Reiner Olzscha, "Zur Wirtschaftsentwicklung Irans," *Zeitschrift für Geopolitik* 14, 2 (1937), 83–97.

70 Olzscha, Internal Note ("Schaffung einer turkotatarischen (osttürkischen) Dachorganisation in Deutschland"), 24 April 1944, Berlin, BAB, NS 31/42.

71 Olzscha, Internal Note ("Rücksprache mit SS-Standartenführer Spaarmann und SS-Hstuf. Ullrich"), 12 May 1944, Berlin, BAB, NS 31/42.

72 Olzscha, Internal Note ("Unterlagen über Fremdvölker in der Sowjet-Union"), 17 October 1944, Berlin, BAB, NS 31/28.

73 Olzscha, Report, 1945, n.p., BStU, MfS, HA IX/11, ZR 920, A. 54.

74 Melchers, Nuremberg Interrogation Statement ("Die Politik des Mufti"), 6 August 1947, Nuremberg, USHMA, RG 71, Box 248.

75 Olzscha, Report, 1945, n.p., BStU, MfS, HA IX/11, ZR 920, A. 54.

76 Hermann (SS Head Office), Internal Note ("Mobilisierung des Islam"), 28 February 1944, Berlin, BAB, NS 31/42 (also in BAB, NS 31/43).

77 Situated within Spaarmann's "Volunteer Section" (DI), Olzscha's office (DI/4k and DI/5k) was subordinated to both the subsection "Volunteer Section East" (DI/5) and the subsection "Volunteer Section Southeast" (DI/4). The office was initially in charge of only Caucasian and Turkestani formations but soon also became concerned with other non-European (mostly Islamic) units. Several structural plans for the office were worked out in 1944. Initially, it was known as the *Muselmanen-Abteilung*. The "Mohammedan areas of operation," as it was put, included Bosnia and Herzegovina, Eastern Turkic questions, Albania, Arab questions, and the mullah schools. It was later reorganized according to ethnic categories. In the end, it was known as the department "DI/4k and DI/5k" (DI/5k dealt with Turkestan and the Caucasus, and DI/4k with the Middle East and Asia, although it included a third section, "Research, Press and Propaganda," which was overarching and included an Islam office). Other structural plans emphasized a thematic organization of the office: "SS Volunteer For-

mations," "Political Affairs," and "Research, Press and Propaganda." Nevertheless, in all structures, Muslims from North Africa to Turkestan were dealt with in this one office. Offices with overarching responsibilities like the "Islam office" were also part of every structure plan. As late as October 1944, officials at the SS Head Office referred to Olzscha's department as *Muslim-Abteilungen*, see the documents and structure plans in BAB, NS 31/170.

78 The "Islam office" (also *Referat 11*) was apparently commanded by various officers over the course of 1944. One source indicates Officer Bethke, see Olzscha, Order ("Besetzung der Referate"), 5 November 1944, Berlin, BAB, NS 31/170; another one mentions Major Killinger, see Structure Plan ("Aufbau der Dienststelle DI/4k und DI/5k"), n.d., Berlin, BAB, NS 31/170; and according to another, the office was directed by Olzscha personally, see Structure Plan ("Organisationsplan Dienststelle DI/4k u. DI/5k"), n.d., Berlin, BAB, NS 31/170; and Olzscha, Internal Note ("Einstufung von Fachführern"), 14 December 1944, Berlin, BAB, NS 31/170.

79 Melchers, Nuremberg Interrogation Statement ("Die Politik des Mufti"), 6 August 1947, Nuremberg, USHMA, RG 71, Box 248.

80 A letter exchange between Oppenheim and Hentig between July 1940 and February 1942 reveals that they regularly discussed political affairs of the Islamic world and met frequently and that Oppenheim also had contact with other officials in the Foreign Office, see PA, Nachlass Hentig, vol. 84. Prüfer's unrevised diaries, which cover the years between November 1942 and September 1943, show that Prüfer also met frequently with his old friend Oppenheim and discussed political affairs of the Muslim world with him, see McKale (ed.), *Rewriting History*, 10–11 (entry of 21 November 1942), 21 (entry of 10 December 1942), 33 (entry of 12 January 1943), 41 (entry of 23 January 1943), 51 (entry of 16 February 1943), 57 (entry of 2 March 1943), 87 (entry of 16 May 1943), 107 (entry of 7 July 1943), 111 (entry of 14 July 1943), 116 (entry of 20 July 1943), and 119 (entry of 30 July 1943). In the revised diaries, not every Oppenheim meeting is recorded, but here Prüfer stressed Oppenheim's Jewish background to give the impression that he was opposed to anti-Semitism, see 150 (entry of 21 November 1942).

81 Oppenheim, Memoirs ("Leben im NS-Staat, 1933–1945"), n.d. (1945/1946), n.p. (Landshut), Oppenheim Bank Archive (*Hausarchiv Sal. Oppenheim*), Cologne (OA), Nachlass Max von Oppenheim no. 1/14.

82 Mark Mazower ranked continuities of ideas from the imperial period above those of personnel, see Mazower, *Hitler's Empire*, 584.

83 Adolf Hitler, *Mein Kampf* (Munich, 1942 [1925–1926]), 747.

84 Alfred Rosenberg, *Der Mythus des 20. Jahrhunderts: Eine Wertung der seelisch-geistigen Gestaltenkämpfe unserer Zeit* (Munich, 1937 [1930]), 662–666. Rosenberg was, in fact, the only leading Nazi who openly denounced the Islamic religion as culturally inferior, see ibid., 365–369.

85 Documents on the debate about the official racial categorization of Arabs, Turks, and Iranians are stored in two files, titled "Membership of Egyptians, Iraqis, Iranians, Persians and Turks to the Aryan Race" (*Zugehörigkeit der Ägypter, Iraker, Iraner, Perser und Türken zur arischen Rasse*) in PA, R 99173, and PA, R 99174, and, more generally, in the file "Repercussions of the German Race Policy to Relations with Foreign States" (*Rückwirkung der deutschen Rassenpolitik auf die Beziehungen zu fremden Staaten*) in PA,

R 99182, which also shows that Germans were equally pragmatic in the case of Latin American and East and South Asian countries. On this debate, see Herf, *Nazi Propaganda for the Arab World*, 17–24; and, regarding the role of Iranians, David Motadel, *Iran and the Aryan Myth*, in Ali M. Ansari (ed.), *Perceptions of Iran: History, Myths and Nationalism from Medieval Persia to the Islamic Republic* (London, 2013), 119–145, 125–135. On racial discrimination against Arabs in Germany, see Gerhard Höpp, "Der verdrängte Diskurs: Arabische Opfer des Nationalsozialismus," in Gerhard Höpp, Peter Wien, and René Wildangel (eds.), *Blind für die Geschichte? Arabische Begegnungen mit dem Nationalsozialismus* (Berlin, 2004), 215–268, 217–219; and Sophie Wagenhofer, *"Rassischer" Feind—politischer Freund? Inszenierung und Instrumentalisierung des Araberbildes im nationalsozialistischen Deutschland* (Berlin, 2010), 32–43. Dietmut Majer, *"Fremdvölkische" im Dritten Reich* (Boppard, 1981), provides the wider context.

86 Hinrichs (Foreign Office) to Interior Ministry, Propaganda Ministry, and NSDAP Race Office, 17 January 1936, Berlin, PA, R 99173; and for the prominent case of the discrimination of Johannes Ruppert, son of a German and a Turk, who, when forced to leave the Hitler Youth in 1935, threatened to complain to the Turkish embassy, Pilger (Foreign Office), Internal Note, 20 December 1935, Berlin, PA, R 99173.

87 Hinrichs to Interior Ministry, Propaganda Ministry, and NSDAP Race Office, February, 30 March 1936, Berlin, PA, R 99173, referring to a conference on 12 February 1935, when this decision was made. The decision was endorsed separately by Groß (NSDAP Race Office) to Foreign Office, 4 April 1936, Munich, PA, R 99173; Weyssenhoff (Propaganda Ministry) to Foreign Office, 8 April 1936, Berlin, PA, R 99173; and Pfundtner (Interior Ministry) to Foreign Office, 12 May 1946, Berlin, PA, R 99173; and circulated by the Foreign Office to all ministries, 30 April 1936, PA, R 99173 (also in PA, R 99182).

88 Anonymous, "Les Turcs promus 'aryens,'" *Le Temps* (14 June 1936).

89 Stohrer (German Embassy Egypt) to Foreign Office, 15 June 1936, Cairo, PA, R 99173 (also in PA, R 99174); and Keller (German Embassy Turkey) to Foreign Office, 19 June 1936, Tarabya, PA, R 99173. Although the Iraqi paper *Al-Istiqlal* on 17 June 1936 published a similar report, officials in Baghdad apparently showed little interest in the issue, see Grobba (German Embassy Iraq) to Foreign Office, 23 June 1936, Baghdad, PA, R 99173.

90 Foreign Office, Press Release ("Notiz für die Presse"), 16 June 1936, Berlin, PA, R 99173 (also in PA, R 99174).

91 Pilger, Internal Note, 16 June 1936, Berlin, PA, R 99173; and, informing the German embassies in Egypt, Iraq, and Iran of the press statement and the conversation with the Egyptian and Iranian ambassador in Berlin, see Bülow-Schwante to German embassies in Cairo, Baghdad, and Tehran, 18 June 1936, Berlin, PA, R 99173 (also in PA, R 99174).

92 Pilger, Internal Note, 16 June 1936, Berlin, PA, R 99173; and Egyptian Embassy Berlin to Foreign Office, 22 June 1936, Berlin PA, R 99173 (also in PA, R 99174).

93 Iranian Foreign Office, Memorandum for Iranian Consulates and Embassies Abroad (Document no. 41749), 3/10/1313 (1935), Tehran, Iranian National Archives (*Sazman-i Asnad-i Milli-yi Iran*), Tehran (SAMI), Film 22–240, 21/6/214 (Archive no. 297036473).

The memorandum was sent out along with a letter written by the Iranian foreign secretary on the issue, see Baqir Kazimi to Iranian Embassies Abroad (Document no. 41797), 4/10/1313 (1935), Tehran, SAMI, File 510006, Box 444 (Archive no. 297036473).

94 Hinrichs, Report ("Sitzung vom 1. Juli 1936 im Auswärtigen Amt zwecks Beantwortung der ägyptischen und iranischen Anfragen und Klärung des Begriffs 'artverwandt'"), 2 July 1936, Berlin, PA, R 99174; and, for the invitation, Bülow-Schwante (Foreign Office) to various German ministries, 26 June 1936, Berlin, PA, R 99173 (also in PA, R 99174).

95 Foreign Office to Egyptian Embassy Berlin, 4 July 1936, Berlin, PA, R 99173 (also in PA, R 99174); and, on the Egyptian response, Hinrichs to German Embassy Cairo, 14 July 1936, Berlin, PA, R 99174; and similarly, Hinrichs to various ministries, 15 July 1936, Berlin, PA, R 99174.

96 Hinrichs to German Embassy Tehran, 11 July 1936, Berlin, PA, R 99174; and on the Iranian response, Smend (German Embassy Tehran) to Foreign Office, 18 July 1936, Tehran, PA, R 99174.

97 Groß to Foreign Office, 28 April 1937, Berlin, PA, R 99182.

98 On the official abolition of the term "anti-Semitism" in Nazi Germany, see Cornelia Berning, Vom "Abstammungsnachweis" zur "Zuchtwart": Vokabular des Nationalsozialismus (Berlin, 1954), 13–14; Cornelia Schmitz-Berning, Vokabular des Nationalsozialismus (Berlin, 1998), 34–39; Thomas Nipperdey and Reinhard Rürup, "Antisemitismus," in Otto Brunner, Werner Conze, and Reinhart Koselleck (eds.), Geschichtliche Grundbegriffe: Historisches Lexikon zur politisch-sozialen Sprache in Deutschland, vol. 1 (Stuttgart, 1972), 129–153, 151–152; Moshe Zimmermann, "Aufkommen und Diskreditierung des Begriffs Antisemitismus," in Ursula Büttner (ed.), Das Unrechtsregime: Internationale Forschung über den Nationalsozialismus, vol. 1 (Hamburg, 1986), 59–77, 73–74; Moshe Zimmermann, "Mohammed als Vorbote der NS-Judenpolitik? Zur wechselseitigen Instrumentalisierung von Antisemitismus und Antizionismus," Tel Aviver Jahrbuch für deutsche Geschichte 33 (2005), 290–305, 292–294; Jeffrey Herf, The Jewish Enemy: Nazi Propaganda during World War II and the Holocaust (Cambridge MA, 2006), 159–160; and Lebel, The Mufti of Jerusalem, 237–241.

99 Directive of the Press Conference ("Anweisung der Pressekonferenz"), 22 August 1935, Berlin, German Federal Archives (Bundesarchiv), Koblenz (BAK), ZSg 101/6; and also in Hans Bohrmann (ed.), NS-Presseanweisungen der Vorkriegszeit: Edition und Dokumentation, vol. 3/II (Munich, 1987), 522.

100 Zimmermann, "Mohammed als Vorbote der NS-Judenpolitik?," 293; Herf, The Jewish Enemy, 159; and Lebel, The Mufti of Jerusalem, 238–239.

101 Propaganda Ministry, Instructions ("Die islamische Welt als Kulturfaktor"), Zeitschriften-Dienst, no. 7514 (11 September 1942); and, similarly, Propaganda Ministry, Instructions ("Die islamische Welt als Kulturfaktor"), Deutscher Wochendienst, no. 7514 (11 September 1942). The Zeitschriften-Dienst had also given out similar instructions on the eve of the war, see Propaganda Ministry, Instructions ("Antisemitismus"), Zeitschriften-Dienst, no. 222 (13 June 1939); and Propaganda Ministry, Instructions ("Antisemitismus"), Zeitschriften-Dienst, no. 372 (1 July 1939). The Zeitschriften-Dienst, which provided propaganda instructions for German magazine

editors, and the *Deutscher Wochendienst*, which functioned as a weekly supplement to the *Zeitschriften-Dienst*, can be found in the collection of the German National Library (*Deutsche Nationalbibliothek*), Leipzig (DNB), ZB 38957 and ZB 38957-Beil; and also in BAB, RD 32/1.

102 Hagemeyer (Amt Rosenberg), Internal Note ("Aktennotiz für Dr. Koeppen"), 17 May 1943, Berlin, in Leon Poliakov and Josef Wulf, *Das Dritte Reich und die Juden: Dokumente und Aufsätze* (Berlin, 1955), 369; Schleier (Foreign Office), Decree, 5 July 1944, Berlin, PA, Bern 2833; and Olzscha, Internal Note ("Antisemitismus"), 7 October 1944, Berlin, BAB, NS 31/170.

103 Groß to Al-Kilani, 17 October 1942, printed in "Antisemitismus oder Antijudaismus?," *Weltkampf: Die Judenfrage in Geschichte und Gegenwart* 3, 9–12 (1944), 168.

104 Ibid.

105 *The Trial of Adolf Eichmann: Record of Proceedings in the District Court of Jerusalem*, ed. State of Israel (Ministry of Justice), vol. IV (Jerusalem, 1993), 1805–1823 (Session no. 106, 21 July 1961), 1814–1815.

106 SS Head Office, Internal Note ("Geschichte und Entstehung der SS-Freiwilligen-b.h.-Geb. Division (13. SS-Division)"), 10 November 1943, Berlin, Archive of the Institute of Contemporary History (*Archiv des Instituts für Zeitgeschichte*), Munich (IfZ), NO-3577. Berger had already declared that the Muslims of the Balkans were racially part of the Germanic world, while being spiritually connected to the Orient, see Berger (Schulte), Decree ("Weltanschaulich geistige Erziehung der muselmanischen SS-Division"), 19 May 1943, Berlin, BAB, NS 19/2601. The decree was written by the SS officer Gerd Schulte in accordance with an oral order from Berger.

107 *Ein General im Zwielicht: Die Erinnerungen Edmund Glaises von Horstenau*, ed. Peter Broucek, vol. 3 (Vienna, 1988), 241 and 400.

108 On the question of the racial discrimination and categorization of the Eastern Turks, see Dallin, *German Rule in Russia*, 270–273; and Mühlen, *Zwischen Hakenkreuz und Sowjetstern*, 46–56.

109 East Ministry, Instructions ("Vorläufige Sprachregelung über Begriffe des Ostens"), 14 March 1942, Berlin, BAB, R 6/206; and, similarly, East Ministry, Instructions ("Erster Nachtrag zur Sprachregelung über Begriffe des Ostens vom 5. März 1942"), 31 March 1942, Berlin, PA, R 105165; and on the limits of these instructions, see Edige Kirimal, *Der nationale Kampf der Krimtürken* (Emsetten, 1952), 317–318.

110 Propaganda Ministry, Instructions ("Polemische Bemerkungen gegen Turkestaner"), *Zeitschriften-Dienst*, no. 7434 (21 August 1942); and again in Propaganda Ministry, Instructions ("Die Verfolgung der Mohammedaner durch die Sowjets"), *Zeitschriften-Dienst*, no. 8577 (26 March 1943); and, similarly, Propaganda Ministry, Instructions ("Die Verfolgung der Mohammedaner durch die Sowjets"), *Deutscher Wochendienst*, no. 8577 (26 March 1943).

111 Werner Otto v. Hentig, "Turan—Tatarei," *Zeitschrift für Politik* 32, 3 (1942), 185–188. Before publication, Hentig had given this article to Woermann, see Hentig, Internal Note, 17 January 1942, Berlin, PA, R 29900. Woermann forwarded it to Weizsäcker and Ribbentrop, see Woermann, Internal Note, 22 January 1942, Berlin, PA, R 29900; and endorsed it, see Woermann, Internal Note, 23 January 1942, Berlin, PA, R 29900.

112 "Die rassische Einheit unserer Stämme," *Gasavat* 32 (75) (1944), German translation, High Command of the Wehrmacht (*Oberkommando der Wehrmacht*), 4 August 1944, Berlin, BA–MA, MSG 2/18238.

113 "Die deutsche Rassenlehre nicht gegen andere Völker gerichtet," *Gasavat* 36 (1943), German translation, High Command of the Wehrmacht, 20 October 1943, Berlin, BA–MA, MSG 2/18238; also printed in *Idel-Ural* 30 (36) (1943), German translation, High Command of the Wehrmacht, 25 July 1943, Berlin, BA–MA, MSG 2/18231.

114 Heygendorff, Instructions ("Merkblatt für deutsche Offiziere über wehrgeistige Führung der Legionäre"), 1 July 1943, Radom, BA–MA, RH 58/62.

115 High Command of the Wehrmacht, Newsletter ("Mitteilungen für den deutschen Soldaten in Freiwilligen-Verbänden"), November 1944, n.p., BA–MA, MSG 2/18262.

116 Ernest Renan, "L'Islamisme et la Science," *Journal des Débats* (30 March 1883).

117 Peter Longerich, *Heinrich Himmler: A Life* (Oxford, 2011), 267 and 677.

118 *Ein General im Zwielicht*, ed. Broucek, vol. 3, 189–190 (February 1943), quotations on 189.

119 Ibid., 322 (November 1943).

120 Kersten wrote down his impressions in a diary during the war. After the war, he organized his remarks according to themes and published them. The first version came out in Swedish in 1947 and was translated into English in the same year, see *The Memoirs of Doctor Felix Kersten*, ed. Herma Briffault, transl. Ernst Morwitz, intr. Konrad Heiden (New York, 1947). In 1952 Kersten published a more comprehensive version in German, see Felix Kersten, *Totenkopf und Treue: Heinrich Himmler ohne Uniform* (Hamburg, 1952). This version was translated into English in 1956, see *The Kersten Memoirs 1940–1945*, transl. Constantine Fitzgibbon and James Oliver, intr. H. R. Trevor-Roper (London, 1956). The memoirs have to be read with some caution. While some of the parts, especially those about his role in the rescue of Jews and other victims of the regime, were manipulated by the author, others have proven to be accurate. The passages about Islam match other accounts of Himmler's views about Muslims and can be considered credible. On Kersten, see Hans-Heinrich Wilhelm and Louis de Jong, *Zwei Legenden aus dem Dritten Reich* (Stuttgart, 1974), 77–142; Raymond Palmer, "Felix Kersten and Count Bernadotte: A Question of Rescue," *Journal of Contemporary History* 29, 1 (1994), 39–51; John H. Waller, *The Devil's Doctor: Felix Kersten and the Secret Plot to Turn Himmler against Hitler* (New York, 2002); Werner Neuß, *Menschenfreund und Mörder: Himmlers Leibarzt Felix Kersten* (Halle, 2010); and Longerich, *Heinrich Himmler*, 381 and 724–731.

121 Kersten, *Totenkopf und Treue*, 203–208 (ch. 19, *Begeisterung für den Islam*). The English translation of the German version, which was published in 1956, has only scattered notes on Islam.

122 *The Memoirs of Doctor Felix Kersten*, 12.

123 Kersten, *Totenkopf und Treue*, 205 (2 December 1942).

124 Quoted in ibid., 203 (1 December 1942).

125 Quoted in ibid., 204 (1 December 1942).

126 Quoted in ibid., 205 (2 December 1942).

127 Quoted in ibid., 206–207 (7 December 1942).

128 *The Kersten Memoirs*, 149 (8 August 1942).

129 Ibid., 221 (8 September, 1944); this anecdote and Himmler's interest in books on Islam have been mentioned—with errors—by Roger Manvell and Heinrich Fraenkel, *Himmler, Kleinbürger und Massenmörder* (Munich, 1965), 100; and by Willi Frischauer, *Himmler: The Evil Genius of the Third Reich* (New York, 1953), 123; Manvell and Fraenkel claim that Kersten wrote that Himmler constantly carried the Qur'an with him, which also lay next to his bed. Frischauer asserts that Kersten wrote that the Qur'an was always at Himmler's bedside. Both statements are incorrect.

130 *The Memoirs of Doctor Felix Kersten*, 67.

131 *Mudhakkirat al-Hajj Muhammad Amin al-Husayni*, 123–126, on the meetings with Himmler.

132 Ibid., 125–126.

133 Ibid., 124.

134 Erich von dem Bach-Zelewski, Interrogation Interview, conducted by Mr. Petersen, n.d. (1945–1947), n.p. (Nuremberg), USHMA, RG 71, Box 237.

135 Hitler, *Mein Kampf*, 292–293; in the Berlin bunker, Hitler would make similar remarks in the last days of the regime: "Can anyone assert that colonization has increased the number of Christians in the world? Where are those conversions en masse which mark the success of Islam?," see *The Testament of Adolf Hitler: The Hitler-Bormann Documents, February–April 1945*, ed. François Genoud, transl. R. H. Stevens, intr. H. R. Trevor-Roper (London, 1961), 42–46 (7 February 1945), 45; for the German text, see *Hitlers politisches Testament: Die Bormann Diktate vom Februar und April 1945*, intr. H. R. Trevor-Roper, afterw. André François-Poncet (Hamburg, 1981), 54–59 (7 February 1945), 56.

136 Hitler, *Mein Kampf*, 747.

137 Ilse Braun made this comment in a conversation with Werner Maser in May 1971, see Werner Maser, *Adolf Hitler: Legende—Mythos—Wirklichkeit* (Cologne, 1971), 475. Although Maser's statements have to be treated with caution, in the context of Hitler's attitude toward Islam, this account seems plausible.

138 On Hitler's views on Christianity and on Catholicism in particular, see the classic by J. S. Conway, *The Nazi Persecution of the Churches 1933–45* (London, 1968), passim; and, for an alternative view, Richard Steigmann-Gall, *The Holy Reich: Nazi Conceptions of Christianity, 1919–1945* (Cambridge, 2003), passim.

139 *Hitler's Table Talk*, 60 (14 October 1941, midday, special guest: Himmler).

140 Ibid.

141 Ibid., 143 (13 December 1941, midnight; special guests: Ribbentrop, Rosenberg, Goebbels, Terboven, Bouhler); almost identical (although with reference to another time of the day) in *Hitlers Tischgespräche im Führerhauptquartier*, ed. Henry Picker (Stuttgart, 1976), 81 (13 December 1941, midday). The German version of Hitler's remark sounds even sharper: "Der Mohammedanismus könnte mich noch für den Himmel begeistern. Aber wenn ich mir den faden christlichen Himmel vorstelle!"

142 *Hitler's Table Talk*, 393 (4 April 1942, midday); almost identical in *Hitlers Tischgespräche im Führerhauptquartier*, 184 (4 April 1942, midday).

143 *Hitler's Table Talk*, 514 (5 June 1942, midday); almost identical in *Hitlers Tischgespräche im Führerhauptquartier*, 355 (5 June 1942, midday).

144 *Hitler's Table Talk*, 606 (1 August 1942, evening).

145 Ibid., 607 (1 August 1942, evening).

146 Albert Speer, *Inside the Third Reich* (New York, 1970), 96.

147 Quoted in ibid.

148 Nicolaus von Below, *Als Hitlers Adjutant* (Mainz, 1980), 45; the English translation of the book, which is considerably shorter than the original, omits these passages as, despite the title, it begins with the outbreak of the war in 1939, see Nicolaus von Below, *At Hitler's Side: The Memoirs of Hitler's Luftwaffe Adjutant, 1937–1945* (London, 2001). In his memoirs, the Aga Khan mentioned the meeting with Hitler only in passing, see Aga Khan, *The Memoirs of the Aga Khan: World Enough and Time* (London, 1954), 262.

149 Hentig, Internal Note ("Aufzeichnung über den Empfang des Sondergesandten von König Abdul Aziz Ibn Saud, des Königlichen Rats Khalid Al Hud al Gargani"), 20 June 1939, Berlin, PA, R 35504. In his memoirs, Hentig also gave an account of the meeting, although without mentioning the discussion about Islam, see Hentig, *Mein Leben*, 346–347.

150 Hermann Neubacher, *Sonderauftrag Südost 1940–1945: Bericht eines fliegenden Diplomaten*, (Göttingen, 1956), 33.

151 *Tischgespräche im Führerhauptquartier 1941–1942*, ed. Henry Picker and Gerhardt Ritter (Stuttgart, 1951), 16.

152 Johann von Leers, "Judentum und Islam als Gegensätze," *Die Judenfrage in Politik, Recht, Kultur und Wirtschaft* 6, 24 (1942), 275–278, 278; and, for the English translation, Johann von Leers, "Judaism and Islam as Opposites," in Andrew G. Bostom (ed.), *The Legacy of Islamic Antisemitism: From Sacred Texts to Solemn History* (New York, 2008), 619–625. On Leers, see Gregory Paul Wegner, "A Propagandist of Extermination: Johann von Leers and the Anti-Semitic Formation of Children in Nazi Germany," *Paedagogica Historica* 43, 3 (2007), 299–325, and, on his views of Islam, 305 and 318–320; Zimmermann, "Mohammed als Vorbote der NS-Judenpolitik?," 301; and Herf, *The Jewish Enemy*, 180–181. Leers had initially expressed anti-Islamic views, denouncing the Muslim faith as democratic and blind to racial differences, see Johann von Leers, "Mustafa Kemal Pascha," *Zeitschrift für Politik* 24, 1 (1934), 4–27. He was also the author of a geopolitical study, see Johann von Leers, *Brennpunkte der Weltpolitik* (Stuttgart, 1941).

153 Leers, "Judentum und Islam als Gegensätze," 276.

154 Ibid., 278.

155 Ibid.

156 Johann von Leers, "Islam und Judentum im Laufe der Jahrhunderte," *Der deutsche Erzieher: Reichszeitung des Nationalsozialistischen Lehrerbundes* 5 (1938), 427–429, quotes on 427 and 429.

157 Else Marquardsen-Kamphövener, "Der Islam und sein Begründer," *Wir und die Welt* 3, 4 (1941), 45–56. The article was republished in two parts in *Die Auslese*, part 1 (September 1941, 612–617) and part 2 (October 1941, 677–682). On the author, see Ilse Wilbrandt, *Elsa Sophia von Kamphoevener* (Unterwössen, 1969); Helga Moericke, *Die Märchenbaronin: Elsa Sophia von Kamphoevener* (Dortmund, 1995); and Helga Moericke, *Leben und Werk der Märchenerzählerin Elsa Sophia von Kamphoevener* (Aachen, 1996).

158 Marquardsen-Kamphövener, "Der Islam und sein Begründer," *Die Auslese*, part 2, 678.

159 Various articles on Islam that appeared in the German press during the Second World War are quoted in the chapters of this book.

160 Directive of the Press Conference ("Anweisung der Pressekonferenz"), 18 May 1938, Berlin, BAK, ZSg 102/10; and also in Hans Bohrmann and Gabriele Toepser-Ziegert (eds.), *NS-Presseanweisungen der Vorkriegszeit: Edition und Dokumentation*, vol. 6/II (Munich, 1999), 1427. Two years earlier the Propaganda Ministry had instructed the press to avoid reports about the "holy war" as Islam was too fragmented to consider such a war realistic, see Directive of the Press Conference ("Anweisung der Pressekonferenz"), 2 November 1935, Berlin, BAK, ZSg 102/1; and also in Bohrmann (ed.), *NS-Presseanweisungen der Vorkriegszeit*, vol. 3/II, 729.

161 Propaganda Ministry, Instructions ("Die islamische Welt als Kulturfaktor"), *Zeitschriften-Dienst*, no. 7514 (11 September 1942). These instructions were substantiated in great detail in Propaganda Ministry, Instructions ("Die islamische Welt als Kulturfaktor"), *Deutscher Wochendienst*, no. 7514 (11 September 1942).

162 Propaganda Ministry, Instructions ("Die USA als Feinde des Islam"), *Zeitschriften-Dienst*, no. 7976 (4 December 1942).

163 Propaganda Ministry, Instructions ("USA auch in Vorderasien"), *Zeitschriften-Dienst*, no. 8435 (26 February 1943).

164 Propaganda Ministry, Instructions ("Die Verfolgung der Mohammedaner durch die Sowjets"), *Zeitschriften-Dienst*, no. 8577 (26 March 1943). These instructions were further elaborated upon in Propaganda Ministry, Instructions ("Die Verfolgung der Mohammedaner durch die Sowjets"), *Deutscher Wochendienst*, no. 8577 (26 March 1943).

165 Olzscha to Dolezalek (SS Head Office), 14 December 1944, Berlin, BAB, NS 31/61, referring to Helmut Sündermann, "Wir klagen an: Krieg als Prinzip der Kremlpolitik," *Völkischer Beobachter* (29 November 1944).

166 Scholars of the history of German Oriental studies during the Third Reich have not yet systematically inquired into academic discussions about Islam. On Oriental studies in the Nazi period, see Ludmilla Hanisch, "Akzentverschiebung: Zur Geschichte der Semitistik und Islamwissenschaft während des 'Dritten Reichs,'" *Berichte zur Wissenschaftsgeschichte* 18 (1995), 217–226; Hanisch, *Die Nachfolger der Exegeten*, 114–173, esp. 159–166; Ekkehard Ellinger, *Deutsche Orientalistik zur Zeit des Nationalsozialismus 1933–1945* (Neckarhausen, 2006), esp. 319–322 and 362–367; Suzanne Marchand, "Nazism, Orientalism and Humanism," in Wolfgang Bialas and Anson Rabinbach (eds.), *Nazi Germany and the Humanities* (Oxford, 2007), 267–305, esp. 294–296; and Wokoeck, *German Orientalism*, 185–209, esp. 204.

167 Ernst Kühnel, "Islamische Kunst," in Hans Heinrich Schaeder (ed.), *Der Orient und Wir: Sechs Vorträge* (Berlin, 1935), 54–68. The address was part of a lecture series on "German Oriental Studies: Its Relevance in Current Affairs and Its Mission" (*Die deutsche Orientforschung: Ihre Gegenwartsbedeutung und ihre Gegenwartsaufgaben*), organized by the main research bodies in the field, including the Society for Islamic Studies; see also Ernst Kühnel, "Nordische und islamische Kunst," *Die Welt als Geschichte* 1 (1935), 203–217; and Ernst Kühnel, "Nordische und islamische Kunst," *Westdeutsche Zeitung* 10 (19 and 20 February 1935).

168 Kühnel, "Islamische Kunst," 67.

169 Hans Heinrich Schaeder, "Bemerkungen zum modernen Islam," *Süddeutsche Monatshefte* 33 (1936), 549–553.

170 Hans Heinrich Schaeder, "Muhammed," in Hans Heinrich Schaeder, Walther Björkman, Reinhard Hüber, et al. (eds.), *Arabische Führergestalten* (Heidelberg, 1944), 1–72; and Franz Taeschner, *Geschichte der arabischen Welt* (Heidelberg, 1944), 45–46.

171 Johann Fück, "Die Originalität des arabischen Propheten," *Zeitschrift der Deutschen Morgenländischen Gesellschaft* 90 (1936), 509–525, 525.

172 Felix Wiedemann, "Der doppelte Orient: Zur völkischen Orientromantik des Ludwig Ferdinand Clauß," *Zeitschrift für Religions- und Geistesgeschichte* 1 (2009), 1–24, esp. 16–17; and, on Clauß more generally, Peter Weingart, *Doppel-Leben: Ludwig Ferdinand Clauss: Zwischen Rassenforschung und Widerstand* (Frankfurt, 1995); and, on his work for the SS, Michael H. Kater, *Das "Ahnenerbe" der SS 1935–1945: Ein Beitrag zur Kulturpolitik des Dritten Reiches* (Stuttgart, 1974), 208–211.

173 Clauß, Report ("Erster Bericht über den Sonderauftrag Clauß 'Die Rassen im Kampf'"), 13 November 1944, Rüthnick, BAB, NS 31/171.

174 Clauß to Spaarmann, 26 February 1945, Rüthnick, BAB, NS 31/171.

175 Schmitz, *All-Islam*, 219.

176 Lindemann, *Islam im Aufbruch*, 3.

177 Ibid., 4.

178 Reichardt, *Der Islam vor den Toren*, 321.

179 Ibid., 328.

180 Ibid., 85–92.

181 Zaki Ali, "Großdeutschland und der Islam," 329–340.

182 Ibid., 340.

183 Mohamed Sabry, *Islam, Judentum, Bolschewismus* (Berlin, 1938). This book also influenced Johann von Leers's writings about Islam, see Leers, "Judentum und Islam als Gegensätze," 277; and it was recommended by the Propaganda Ministry, along with other books such as Lindemann's *Der Islam im Aufbruch in Abwehr und Angriff* and Reichardt's *Der Islam vor den Toren*, to magazine editors and journalists who wanted to report on Islam, see Propaganda Ministry, Instructions ("Die islamische Welt als Kulturfaktor"), *Deutscher Wochendienst*, no. 7514 (11 September 1942); and Propaganda Ministry, Instructions ("Die Verfolgung der Mohammedaner durch die Sowjets"), *Deutscher Wochendienst*, no. 8577 (26 March 1943).

184 On Islam and Bolshevism, see Sabry, *Islam, Judentum, Bolschewismus*, 5–21; quotation on 20.

185 On Islam and Judaism, see ibid., 22–32.

186 Ibid., 15.

187 On the history of the institution, see Chapter 1, note 120. One of the institute's lecturers was, in fact, Johann von Leers.

188 Saïda Savitri, *L'Islam devant le National Socialisme* (Paris, 1943).

189 On Kiram, see Umar Ryad, "From an Officer in the Ottoman Army to a Muslim Publicist and Armament Agent in Berlin: Zekî Hishmat Kirâm (1886–1946)," *Bibliotheca Orientalis* 63, 3–4 (2006), 235–268; and, on Kiram's connections with Rida, Umar Ryad, *Islamic Reformism and Christianity: A Critical Reading of the Works of*

Muhammad Rashid Rida and His Associates (Leiden, 2009), 14–15 and 49–53; and for a selection of documents on Kiram, Umar Ryad, *Watha'iq Tijarat al-Silah al-Almani fi al-Jazira al-Arabiyya: Qira'a fi Arsif Zaki Kiram (Documents on the German Arms Trade in the Arabian Peninsula: Readings in the Archive of Zeki Kiram)* (Cairo, 1432/2011). Kiram had already shown his admiration for the German state in his article "A Muslim about the New Germany," published in 1938 in the German-speaking Muslim journal *Moslemische Revue*, which was published in Berlin, see Zeki Kiram, "Ein Moslem über das Neue Deutschland: Hitler ist der berufene Mann," *Moslemische Revue* 14, 2 (1938), 59–60. For SS secret police (Gestapo) reports about Kiram, see the documents in PA, R 60618 and PA, R 60619.

190 Martini (Foreign Office), Internal Note, 2 August 1940, Berlin, PA, R 60619. At the same time, Kiram had also submitted a second manuscript, titled "The English-Jewish Policy in Arabia" (*Die englisch-jüdische Politik in Arabien*), which dealt with conflict in Palestine.

191 On the offer of the manuscript, see Paul Alfred Merbach to Boehm (*Ahnenerbe-Stiftung Verlag*), 10 July 1942, Berlin, BAB, NS 21/397; on the interest shown by the SS *Ahnenerbe*, see Boehm to Merbach, 15 July 1942, Berlin, BAB, NS 21/397; on the submission of the manuscript, see Merbach to Boehm, 18 July 1942, Berlin, BAB, NS 21/397; on the internal debate about the book, see Boehm to Sievers, n.d. (summer 1942), Berlin, BAB, NS 21/397; Schneider, Internal Note, 29 July 1942, Berlin, BAB, NS 21/397; Förster to Sievers, 13 August 1942, Berlin, BAB, NS 21/397; and Sievers to Förster, 13 August 1942, Berlin, BAB, NS 21/397; and on the rejection, see *Ahnenerbe-Stiftung Verlag* to Kiram, 7 September 1942, Berlin, BAB, NS 21/397.

192 Schneider, Internal Note, 29 July 1942, Berlin, BAB, NS 21/397; and Sievers to Förster, 13 August 1942, Berlin, BAB, NS 21/397.

193 Tismer (Foreign Office) to Ettel, 23 December 1942, Berlin, PA, R 27327.

194 Kurt Fischer-Weth, *Amin Al-Husseini: Großmufti von Palästina* (Berlin, 1943). A year later, a similar book, with biographical portrayals of the Prophet, Saad Zaghlul, the Hashemites, Ibn Saud, al-Husayni, and al-Kilani, was the mentioned volume by Schaeder, Björkman, Hüber, et al. (eds.), *Arabische Führergestalten*.

195 Fischer-Weth, *Amin Al-Husseini*, 8.

196 Bormann (NSDAP Party Chancellery), Circular Letter ("Zugehörigkeit von Parteigenossen zum Islam"), 2 September 1943, n.p., BAB, NS 6/342.

3. ISLAM AND THE WAR IN NORTH AFRICA AND THE MIDDLE EAST

1 John Darwin, "An Undeclared Empire: The British in the Middle East, 1918–39," *Journal of Imperial and Commonwealth History* 27, 2 (1999), 159–176.

2 Peters, *Islam and Colonialism*, 39–104; and Keddie, "The Revolt of Islam," 481–485, provide overviews.

3 Romain Rainero, "La capture: L'exécution d'Omar El-Muktar et la fin de la guérilla libyenne," *Cahiers de Tunisie* 28, 111–112 (1980), 59–74.

4 The best analysis is given by Francis R. Nicosia, *The Third Reich and the Palestine Question* (Austin, TX, 1985), 29–49; and, more generally, Francis R. Nicosia, "Arab Nationalism and National Socialist Germany, 1933–1939: Ideological and Strategic

Incompatibility," *International Journal of Middle East Studies* 12, 3 (1980), 351–372. Other notable studies are Werner Feilchenfeld, Dolf Michaelis, and Ludwig Pinner, *Haavara-Transfer nach Palästina und Einwanderung deutscher Juden 1933–1939* (Tübingen, 1972); David Yisraeli, "The Third Reich and the Transfer Agreement," *Journal of Contemporary History* 6, 2 (1972), 129–148; Łukaz Hirszowicz, "The Course of German Foreign Policy in the Middle East between the World Wars," *Jahrbuch des Instituts für Deutsche Geschichte, Beiheft* 1 (1975), 175–190; Alexander Schölch, "Das Dritte Reich, die Zionistische Bewegung und der Palästina-Konflikt," *Vierteljahreshefte für Zeitgeschichte* 30, 4 (1982), 646–674; Andreas Hillgruber, "The Third Reich and the Near and Middle East, 1933–1939," in Uriel Dann (ed.), *The Great Powers in the Middle East, 1919–1939* (New York, 1988), 274–282; Avraham Barkai, "German Interests in the Haavara-Transfer Agreement 1933–1939," *Yearbook of the Leo Baeck Institute* 35 (1990), 245–266; and Basheer M. Nafi, "The Arabs and the Axis: 1933–1940," *Arab Studies Quarterly* 19, 2 (1997), 1–24.

5　Broadcast Script "Deutsche Rundfunkerklärung vom 5. Dezember 1940," 7 February 1942, Berlin, PA, R 28876 (also in PA, R 261123 and R 261179). Höpp, "'Nicht 'Alī zuliebe, sondern aus Hass gegen Muʿāwiya,'" provides the context.

6　A comprehensive analysis of military events in North Africa is given by Martin Kitchen, *Rommel's Desert War: Waging World War II in North Africa, 1941–1943* (Cambridge, 2009). Other important studies are Vincent Jones, *Operation Torch* (New York, 1972); James Lucas, *Panzer Army Africa* (London, 1977); Volkmar Kühn, *Rommel in the Desert: Victories and Defeat of the Afrikakorps 1941–1943* (West Chester, PA, 1991); Christine Levisse-Touzé, *L'Afrique du Nord dans la guerre, 1939–1945* (Paris, 1998); and Rick Atkinson, *An Army at Dawn: The War in North Africa* (New York, 2002). An overview of the literature is provided by Colin F. Baxter, *The War in North Africa, 1940–1943: A Selected Bibliography* (Westport, CT, 1996).

7　On the wider Arab world and Middle East, see George Kirk, "The Middle East in the War" (Oxford, 1952); Mohamed-Kamal El Dessouki, "Hitler und der Nahe Osten" (PhD diss., Free University of Berlin, 1963); Tillmann, *Deutschlands Araberpolitik im zweiten Weltkrieg*; Hirszowicz, *The Third Reich and the Arab East*; Robert L. Melka, "The Axis and the Arab Middle East 1930–1945" (PhD diss., University of Minnesota, 1966); and, more generally, Schröder, *Deutschland und der Mittlere Osten im Zweiten Weltkrieg.* Concise overviews are given by Elias Cooper, "Nazi Policy in the Middle East, 1939–1945," *Midstream* 10 (1964), 61–75; H. M. Nahmad, "The Third Reich and the Arab East," *Wiener Library Bulletin* 21, 2 (1967), 26–29; Josef Schröder, "Die Beziehungen der Achsenmächte zur Arabischen Welt," *Zeitschrift für Politik* 18, 1 (1971), 80–95; and Haim Schamir, "The Middle East in the Nazi Conception," *Jahrbuch des Instituts für Deutsche Geschichte, Beiheft* 1 (1975), 167–174.

8　On German involvement in Iran, see Djalal Madani, *Iranische Politik und Drittes Reich* (Frankfurt, 1986); and, on secret missions after the Allied occupation of Iran, Burkhard Ganzer, "Virtuelle Kombattantenschaft und Cargo-Erwartung: Iranische Stämme und deutsche Agenten 1942–1944," in Höpp and Reinwald (eds.), *Fremdeinsätze*, 189–198; and the memoirs of Bernhardt Schulze-Holthus, *Frührot in Iran: Abenteuer im deutschen Geheimdienst* (Esslingen, 1952), on his involvement with religious authorities, see 306–307 (second edition: Bernhardt Schulze-Holthus,

Aufstand in Iran: Abenteuer im Dienste der deutschen Abwehr [Munich, 1980], 306–307); and, for the English translation, Bernhardt Schulze-Holthus, *Daybreak in Iran: A Story of the German Intelligence Service* (London, 1954), on religious authorities, 275–276; and Ata Taheri, *Deutsche Agenten bei iranischen Stämmen 1942–1944: Ein Augenzeugenbericht: Eingeleitet und übersetzt von Burkhard Ganzer* (Berlin, 2008). Oberling, *The Qashqā'i Nomads of Fars*, 169–182, provides fascinating insights into German activities in southern Iran.

9 On German involvement in Iraq, see Geoffrey Warner, *Iraq and Syria 1941* (London, 1974); Bernd Philipp Schröder, *Irak 1941* (Freiburg, 1980); and Majid Khadduri, *Independent Iraq 1932–1958: A Study in Iraqi Politics* (London, 1960), 212–243.

10 Al-Husayni's call for jihad against Britain, made on 9 May 1941, was printed in Italian translation in Al-Husseini, "Fetwà di Amin el-Huseini per la Guerra santa del maggio," *Oriente Moderno* 21 (1941), 552–553; and in English translation in Schechtman, *The Mufti and the Fuehrer*, 110–112.

11 On the Allied occupation of the Levant, see Warner, *Iraq and Syria 1941*; Anthony Mockler, *Our Enemies the French: Being an account of the war fought between the French and the British: Syria 1941* (London, 1976); and Aviel Roshwald, *Estranged Bedfellows: Britain and France in the Middle East during the Second World War* (New York, 1990); and, on Iran, see Miron Rezun, *The Iranian Crisis of 1941: The Actors, Britain, Germany and the Soviet Union* (Cologne, 1982); Richard A. Stewart, *Sunrise at Abadan: The British and Soviet Invasion of Iran, 1941* (New York, 1988); and Jana Forsmann, *Testfall für die "Großen Drei": Die Besetzung Irans durch Briten, Sowjets und Amerikaner 1941–1946* (Cologne, 2010).

12 The more general history of the European empires in the Second World War has been studied by Martin Thomas, *The French Empire at War, 1940–1945* (Manchester, 1998); and Chantal Metzger, *L'empire colonial français dans la stratégie du Troisième Reich (1936–1945)*, 2 vols. (New York, 2002), for France; and by R. D. Pearce, *The Turning Point: British Colonial Policy, 1938–48* (London, 1982); J. M. Lee and Martin Petter, *The Colonial Office: War and Development Policy: Organization and Planning of a Metropolitan Initiative, 1934–45* (London, 1982); Ashley Jackson, *The British Empire and the Second World War* (London, 2006); Christopher A. Bayly and Tim Harper, *Forgotten Armies: Britain's Asian Empire and the War with Japan* (London, 2004); and, for a concise overview, Keith Jeffery, "The Second World War," in Judith M. Brown and Roger Louis (eds.), *The Oxford History of the British Empire*, vol. 4 (*The Twentieth Century*) (Oxford, 1999), 306–328, for Britain. Rheinisches Journalistenbüro (ed.), *"Unsere Opfer zählen nicht": Die Dritte Welt im Zweiten Weltkrieg* (Hamburg, 2005), provides a good overview of the struggle for the non-European world during the Second World War.

13 *Die Tagebücher von Joseph Goebbels*, ed. Fröhlich et al., part II, vol. 5, 270–278 (8 August 1942), 274–275.

14 Viton, "Britain and the Axis in the Near East," 370–384, 376.

15 Pierre Crabitès, "Britain's Debt to King Farouk," *Foreign Affairs* 4 (July 1941), 852–860, 852.

16 Propaganda targeting Muslim soldiers in the French army and Muslims in French North Africa during the Battle of France has been examined by Charles-Robert

Ageron, "Contribution à l'étude de la propagande allemande au Maghreb pendant la Deuxième Guerre mondiale," *Revue d'Histoire Maghrébine* 7–8 (1977), 16–32, 21–22; and, almost identically, Charles-Robert Ageron, "Les populations du Maghreb face à la propagande allemande," *Revue d'Histoire de la Deuxième Guerre Mondiale* 29, 114 (1979), 1–39, 13–18; reprinted in Charles-Robert Ageron, *"L'Algérie algérienne" de Napoléon III à de Gaulle* (Paris, 1980), 167–216; Jamaâ Baida, "Le Maroc et la propagande du IIIème Reich," *Hespéris Tamuda*, 28 (1990), 91–106; and Wagenhofer, *"Rassischer" Feind—politischer Freund?*, 72–82.

17 Pamphlet "Musulmans" (star shaped), n.d. (1940), BA–MA, RH 45/28; and Pamphlet "Musulmans" (flag shaped), n.d. (1940), BA–MA, RH 45/28. Both pamphlets are printed in Klaus Kirchner, *Flugblätter aus Deutschland 1939/40* (Erlangen, 1982), 74–77, and, for information on their distribution, 276–277.

18 Richter (Liaison Officer of the Foreign Office at the Twelfth Army) to Tucher (Foreign Office), 31 December 1939, n.p., PA, R 60754.

19 Richter to Tucher, 13 January 1940, n.p., PA, R 60754. This letter and the response, Tucher to Richter, 28 February 1940, Berlin, PA, R 60754, also referred to a pamphlet shaped in the form of the "green flag of the Prophet," which may very well be the one referenced in note 17.

20 Raffael Scheck, "Nazi Propaganda toward French Muslim Prisoners of War," *Holocaust and Genocide Studies* 26, 3 (2012), 447–477, provides the most comprehensive account of Muslim prisoners of war from the French army and German propaganda and religious care in the camps. Other studies of the subject are Ageron, "Contribution à l'étude de la propagande allemande au Maghreb pendant la Deuxième Guerre mondiale," 23; and, almost identically, Ageron, "Les populations du Maghreb face à la propagande allemande," 19; Baida, "Le Maroc et la propagande du IIIème Reich," 103–105; Belkacem Recham, *Les Musulmans algériens dans l'armée française (1919–1945)* (Paris, 1996), 152–153 and 207–228, esp. 226–227; Recham, "Les Musulmans dans l'armée française," 748–750; Belkacem Recham, "Les indigènes nord-africains prisonniers de guerre (1940–1945)," *Guerres mondiales et conflits contemporains* 223, 3 (2006), 109–125; Höpp, "Der verdrängte Diskurs," 223–231; Wagenhofer, *"Rassischer" Feind—politischer Freund?*, 82–95; and, more generally, Martin Thomas, "The Vichy Government and French Colonial Prisoners of War, 1940–1944," *French Historical Studies* 25, 4 (2002), 657–692, esp. 670–675; and Armelle Mabon, *Prisonniers de guerre "indigènes": Visages oubliés* (Paris, 2010).

21 High Command of the Wehrmacht, Order ("Religionsausübung der Kriegsgefangenen"), 12 May 1941, Berlin, BA–MA, RH 49/51; and, similarly, for a case with special reference to Islam, Schierbrandt (Commander of Frontstalag 204), Instructions ("Merkblatt für die Bewachung franz. farbiger Kriegsgefangener"), 28 December 1942, Charleville, BA–MA, RH 49/67.

22 High Command of the Wehrmacht, Order ("Beerdigung verstorbener französischer Kriegsgefangener"), 30 January 1942, n.p., PA, R 67004.

23 Command of North-West France, Order ("Besondere Anordnungen für die Versorgung"), 18 September 1943, St. Germain, BA–MA, RH 49/67.

24 Regina Clausnitzer, "Eine Moschee in Großbeeren? Kein Hirngespinst: Es gab sie wirklich!," *Amtsblatt Großbeeren* 11 (10 November 1999), 12; and Regina Clausnitzer,

"Moschee in Großbeeren: Suche nach einer Fotoaufnahme nun doch noch erfolgreich," *Amtsblatt Großbeeren* 5 (12 April 2000). On the establishment of mosques and prayer rooms in prisoner of war camps in occupied France, see reports in PA, R 40769, R 40770, R 40988, and R 40989.

25 On the employment of imams and marabouts in various prisoner of war camps in France and Germany, see reports in PA, R 40769, R 40770, R 40988, R 40989, and R 67003.

26 Bran (Foreign Office), Internal Note ("Araberzeitung für Nordafrikanische Kriegsgefangene"), 6 May 1941, Berlin, PA, R 67003.

27 Insights into the miserable conditions in the camps and maltreatment are given in the literature quoted in note 20.

28 Raffael Scheck, *Hitler's African Victims: The German Army Massacres of Black French Soldiers in 1940* (Cambridge, 2006); and, for a summary, Raffael Scheck, "'They Are Just Savages': German Massacres of Black Soldiers from the French Army in 1940," *Journal of Modern History* 77, 2 (2005), 325–344.

29 On the Paris Mosque and Si Kaddour Benghabrit, see Alain Boyer, *L'institut musulman de la mosquée de Paris* (Paris, 1992), 19–33; Michel Renard, "Gratitude, contrôle, accompagnement: Le traitement du religieux islamique en métropole (1914–1950)," *Bulletin de l'Institut d'Histoire du Temps Présent* 83 (2004), 54–69; Michel Renard, "Les débuts de la présence musulmane en France et son encadrement," in Arkoun (ed.), *Histoire de l'Islam et des Musulmans en France du Moyen Age à nos jours*, 712–740, 718–730; as well as the general studies by Pautremat, *La politique musulmane de la France au XXe siècle*, 333–342; Sellam, *La France et ses Musulmans*, 171–184; and Naomi Davidson, *Only Muslim: Embodying Islam in Twentieth-Century France* (Ithaca, NY, 2012), 36–61. Biographical studies of Benghabrit are Jalila Sbaï, "Trajectoire d'un homme et d'une idée: Si Kaddour Ben Ghabrit et l'Islam de France, 1892–1926," *Hespéris Tamuda* 39, 1 (2001), 45–58; and, very sympathetic, Hamza Ben Driss Ottmani, *Kaddour Benghabrit: Un Maghrébin hors du commun* (Rabat, 2010).

30 Schleier (Embassy Paris) to Foreign Office, 8 February 1941, Paris, PA, R 40747.

31 Sethe (Foreign Office) to Embassy Paris, 6 March 1942, Berlin, PA, R 40747, first approved Benghabrit's proposal, though noting that it was not necessary to send imams to Germany since most Muslim prisoners of war were detained in camps in France. Benghabrit sent a more concrete proposal to Vichy officials, who approached the Wehrmacht about the issue see Scapini (Vichy's Diplomatic Service for Prisoners of War) to Rosenberg (Army), 19 February 1941, Paris, PA, R 40747. The Wehrmacht rejected this proposal, pointing out that most Muslim prisoners were detained in France, not in Germany, and that sending Benghabrit's imams to Germany would be a security risk, see Wehrmacht to Foreign Office, 7 March 1941, Berlin, PA, R 40747; and it was eventually officially rejected, see Sethe to Scapini, 15 March 1941, Berlin, PA, R 40747. Bürkner (Army), Internal Note ("Behandlung der Araberfragen und Vorschläge von arabischer Seite"), Berlin, 13 March 1942, BA–MA, RH 2/1765, which is based on Biyoud, Memorandum ("Denkschrift zur deutschen Nordafrikapropaganda, insbesondere in den Kriegsgefangenenlagern"), n.d. (March 1942), n.p., BA–MA, RH 2/1765, recalls that the Germans had not taken up Benghabrit's offer due to a lack of trust in his imams.

32 Strack (Foreign Office) to Rahn (Consulate Tunis), 12 December 1942, Berlin, PA, R 27767; and, in response, Rahn to Foreign Office, 13 December 1942, Tunis, PA, R 27766, regarding the preparation of the *'Id al-Adha*, give an example of the everyday cooperation between Benghabrit and the German authorities.

33 The debate about the role of the Paris Mosque in supporting Jews and members of the resistance began with an article by Albert Assouline, "Une vocation ignorée de la mosquée de Paris," *Almanach du Combattant* (1983), 123–124. Assouline's claim that 1,732 resistance fighters and Jews found refuge in the mosque has been proven incorrect. It is sure, however, according to oral testimonies, that Benghabrit and the mosque's senior imam, Si Muhammad Benzouaou, unsystematically helped some individual Jews of North African background by providing them with Islamic identity certificates. The only known primary document in this regard is a letter by Vichy authorities of 24 September 1940 on the German suspicion that such identity certificates were issued to Jews, but no definite archival evidence has yet appeared, see Robert Satloff, *Among the Righteous: Lost Stories from the Holocaust's Long Reach into Arab Lands* (New York, 2006), 139–158; and, offering a more complex picture of collaboration, resistance, and accommodation, Ethan Katz, "Did the Paris Mosque Save Jews? A Mystery and Its Memory," *Jewish Quarterly Review* 102, 2 (2012), 256–287, esp. 270–283. The most notable work among the popular accounts that portray the Paris Mosque as a shelter for Jews is Mohammed Aïssaoui, *L'étoile jaune et le croissant* (Paris, 2012).

34 Jost (SS Reich Security Head Office) to Altenburg (Foreign Office), 13 April 1940, Berlin, PA, R 60652, suggested pamphlet propaganda in French Morocco. The Foreign Office agreed and approached Eberhard von Stohrer, then ambassador in Madrid, to support the transport of the propaganda material to Morocco via Spain, see Altenburg to Stohrer, 23 April 1940, Berlin, PA, R 60652; and, in response, Stohrer to Foreign Office, 25 April 1940, Madrid, PA, R 60652.

35 Pamphlet "Die Gelegenheit, die nie wiederkommt!" (German translation), n.d. (1940), PA, R 60652; and, for the Arabic original, Pamphlet "Al-fursa, al-fursa, al-fursa allati la t'aud" ("The Opportunity, Opportunity, Opportunity that is not going to come back"), n.d. (1940), PA, R 60652.

36 Altenburg, Internal Note, 6 May 1940, Berlin, PA, R 60652; and, similarly, Simon (Foreign Office), Internal Note, 14 May 1940, Berlin, PA, R 60652, and, for the confirmation of completed production, Simon, Internal Note, 18 May 1940, Berlin, PA, R 60652, and, on the dispatch, Simon, Internal Note, 20 May 1940, Berlin, PA, R 60652.

37 Herf, *Nazi Propaganda for the Arab World*, includes an examination of some German propaganda pamphlets distributed in North Africa and the Middle East. Earlier important studies of German pamphlet propaganda in North Africa and the Middle East are Ageron, "Contribution à l'étude de la propagande allemande au Maghreb pendant la Deuxième Guerre mondiale," 21–32; and, almost identically, Ageron, "Les populations du Maghreb face à la propagande allemande," 13–39; and Baida, "Le Maroc et la propagande du IIIème Reich," 95–97. Peter Longerich, *Propagandisten im Krieg: Die Presseabteilung des Auswärtigen Amtes unter Ribbentrop* (Munich, 1987), 27–148, gives insights into the general context of the organization of this propaganda.

38 Schmid (Foreign Office), Internal Note, 18 August 1942, Berlin, PA, R 60748; the list included the *Zeitschrift für Geopolitik* and *Die Welt des Islams*.

39 Pamphlet "Krieg und Hungersnot" (Draft in German), n.d. (1941), PA, R 60747.

40 Pamphlet "O Ihr, die Ihr glaubt" (Draft in German), n.d. (1941), PA, R 60747. English translations of Qur'anic verses, here and throughout the book, follow the translation by Arthur J. Arberry, *The Koran Interpreted*, 2 vols. (London, 1955).

41 Neurath to Foreign Office, 17 November 1941, n.p., PA, R 60747, shows that both pamphlets were produced in the days before the beginning of the British counteroffensive of 18 November 1941.

42 Neurath to Foreign Office, 8 May 1942, n.p., PA, R 29533, referring to the army's request of 8 April 1942 and reminding the Foreign Office to act; and, in reaction to the reminder, Megerle (Foreign Office), Internal Note, 19 May 1942, n.p., PA, R 60649, internally asking, in the name of Ribbentrop, for suggestions for further propaganda pamphlets; and Schmieden (Foreign Office), Internal Note, 29 May 1942, Berlin, PA, R 29533, delivering the minister's formal order to intensify German propaganda directed toward Egypt. Kapp (Foreign Office), Internal Note, 20 May 1942, Berlin, PA, R 60649, reports the expansion of the production of pamphlets for Egypt. Apparently not informed about these activities, Neurath asked again a month later, now in the name of Rommel, for propaganda to Egypt, see Neurath to Foreign Office, 25 June 1942, n.p., PA, R 29537 (also in PA, R 60748).

43 Wüster (Foreign Office) to Neurath, 25 June 1942, Berlin, PA, R 60748.

44 Wüster to Neurath, 29 June 1942, Berlin, PA, R 60748.

45 Ibid.

46 Wüster to Neurath, 30 June 1942, Berlin, PA, R 60650.

47 Wüster, Internal Note, 2 July 1942, Berlin, PA, R 60651.

48 Wüster to Neurath, 13 July 1942, Berlin, PA, R 60748.

49 Wüster, Internal Note, 12 August 1942, Berlin, PA, R 60650.

50 Pamphlet "O Ägypten" (German translation), n.d. (1942), PA, R 60650; and, for the Arabic original, Pamphlet "Ya misr!" ("O Egypt!"), n.d. (1942), PA, R 60650.

51 Kapp, Internal Note, 28 August 1942, Berlin, PA, R 60678.

52 Ibid.

53 Kapp, Internal Note, 7 January 1943, Berlin, PA, R 27332.

54 Pamphlet "England und die Araber" (German translation), n.d., BA–MA, RH 21-5/27; and, for the Arabic original, Pamphlet "Inkiltara wa'l-'Arab" ("England and the Arabs"), n.d., BA–MA, RH 21-5/27.

55 Postcard "Gewiss wirst Du finden, . . ." (German translation), n.d., BA–MA, RH 21-5/26; and, for the Arabic original, Pamphlet "Tadhkira barid" ("A Postal Reminder"), n.d., BA–MA, RH 21-5/26. The number of this verse varies in different Qu'ran editions. It is verse 82 according to the verse enumeration of the official Cairo edition of the Qur'an (1925) and verse 85 according to the enumeration of the North African edition popularized among European scholars through Gustav Flügel (1834). Arthur J. Arberry's translation follows the enumeration of the Flügel edition. German officials in the Second World War also usually referred to the numbers of the Flügel Qur'an.

56 Schmitz, *All-Islam*, 219; and Sabry, *Islam, Judentum, Bolschewismus*, 16.

57 Luther (Foreign Office) to Rahn, 21 November 1942, Berlin, PA, R 27767.

58 Rahn to Wüster, 4 January 1943, Tunis, PA, R 27766.

59 Rahn to Wüster, 8 April 1943, Tunis, PA, R 27767.

60 J. M. Storch de Gracia, "Die Abwehr und das deutsche Generalkonsulat in Tanger," *Die Nachhut* 2 (1967), 7–15; and, on the occupation by Spain, Claire Spencer, "The Spanish Protectorate and the Occupation of Tangier in 1940," in George Joffé (ed.), *North Africa: Nation, State, and Region* (London, 1993), 91–107.

61 Pörzgen (Consulate Tangier), Report ("Tanger: Propagandazelle für Nordafrika"), n.d. (August 1942), Tangier, PA, R 60690.

62 Pamphlet "O moslemische Freunde!" (German translation), n.d. (1942), PA, R 60660; and, for the Arabic original, Pamphlet "'Id muburak sa'id" ("Happy blessed Eid!"), n.d. (1942), PA, R 60660. Rieth (Consulate Tangier) to Foreign Office, 19 December 1942, Tangier, PA, R 60660, provides further information about the pamphlet and its distribution.

63 Pamphlet "Aux croyants bénis du Maroc très Chéris" (French translation), PA, R 60649; and, for the Arabic original, Pamphlet "Ila a'izzana al-mu'minin al-mukhilisin min abna' al-maghrib!" ("To our Beloved, the righteous Believers from among the Sons of Morocco!"), n.d. (1942), PA, R 60649. Rieth to Foreign Office, 28 December 1942, Tangier, PA, R 60649, provides further information about the pamphlet and its distribution.

64 Pamphlet "A nos frères musulmans du Maroc très honorés!" (French translation), PA, R 60649; and, for the Arabic original, Pamphlet "Ila al-ikhwan al-muslimin!" ("To the Muslim Brothers!"), n.d. (1942), PA, R 60649. Rieth to Foreign Office, 28 December 1942, Tangier, PA, R 60649, provides further information about the pamphlet and its distribution.

65 Pamphlet "O marokkanische Brueder!" (German translation), n.d. (1943), PA, R 60649; and, for the Arabic original, Pamphlet "Ayyuha al-ikhwan al-mugharba!" ("O Moroccan brothers!"), n.d. (1943), PA, R 60649. Pörzgen to Foreign Office, 22 March 1943, Tangier, PA, R 60649, provides further information about the pamphlet and its distribution.

66 Doob (US Office of War Information), Internal Note, 17 April 1944, USNA, RG 208, Entry 374, Box 434.

67 Rantzau (Foreign Office) to Consulate Tangier, 3 February 1943, Berlin, PA, R 60650; and, identical, Rantzau to Rahn, 4 February 1943, Berlin, PA, R 27768.

68 Winkler (Foreign Office), Internal Note, 16 February 1943, Berlin, PA, R 102974; and, for the identical list of dispatched pamphlets, Langmann (Foreign Office), Internal Note ("Aufzeichnung über die Propaganda nach Nordafrika"), 18 February 1943, Berlin, PA, R 102974. On the dispatch of material on the mufti, see Rantzau to Consulate Tangier, 3 February 1943, Berlin, PA, R 60650; and, identical, Rantzau to Rahn, 4 February 1943, Berlin, PA, R 27768; and, on mufti brochures, Rantzau to Rahn, 5 February 1943, Berlin, PA, R 27768. In the summer of 1943, Arabic propaganda material, including a mufti speech given at the *Mawlid*, was sent to Turkey to be distributed in Arab countries, see Winkler, Internal Note, 14 July 1943, Berlin, PA, R 101400.

69 Winkler, Internal Note, 16 February 1943, Berlin, PA, R 102974; and, identically, Langmann, Internal Note ("Aufzeichnung über die Propaganda nach Nordafrika"), 18 February 1943, Berlin, PA, R 102974.

70 Langmann, Internal Note ("Aufzeichnung über die Besprechungen betreffend die Koordination der Propaganda nach Nordafrika"), 11 March 1943, Berlin, PA, R 102974.

71 Ibid.

72 Anonymous, "3 Reich plotters try to win Syria: Following gains in Iraq, Nazis seek support for Hitler as 'Protector of Islam,'" *New York Times* (7 April 1941), referring to a trip made by Otto von Hentig to Syria in 1941.

73 Pamphlet "Das neue Königreich" (German translation), n.d. (1942), PA, R 60650; and, for the Arabic original, Pamphlet "Hal t'arif haaha al-'alam ayyuha al-'arabi?" ("O Arab, do you know this Flag?"), n.d. (1942), PA, R 60650. Wüster, Internal Note, 12 August 1942, Berlin, PA, R 60650, provides further information about the pamphlet and its distribution.

74 Brochure, n.d. (1944), BAB, R 55/20712; and, for details on the production, see the documents in BAB, R 55/20712.

75 Eve Curie, *Journey among Warriors* (London, 1943), 79.

76 Landau, *The Politics of Pan-Islam*, 247.

77 The most comprehensive collection of *Barid al-Sharq* can be found in DNB, ZB 47105; further issues are stored in the Berlin State Library (*Staatsbibliothek zu Berlin*), Berlin (SBB), 4 Stabi 670; for general details, see Gerhard Höpp, *Arabische und islamische Periodika in Berlin und Brandenburg, 1915 bis 1945: Geschichtlicher Abriss und Bibliographie* (Berlin, 1994), 66; and Gerhard Höpp, *Texte aus der Fremde: Arabische politische Publizistik in Deutschland, 1896–1945: Eine Bibliographie* (Berlin, 2000), 43. A good assessment of the content is given in Munir Hamida, "Amīn al-Ḥusaynī in der deutschen Kriegspropaganda des Zweiten Weltkrieges: Eine Studie zur arabischsprachigen Zeitschrift 'Barīd aš-Šarq'" (MA thesis, Free University of Berlin, 2007); for details on distribution, finances, and organization, see 12–23; on writers and editors, see 35–42.

78 On the content of *Barid al-Sharq*, see Hamida, "Amīn al-Ḥusaynī in der deutschen Kriegspropaganda des Zweiten Weltkrieges," 23–33 and 35–42; on religious suppression in the Soviet Union (1941), see 26; on Anglo-American attitudes toward the Islamic world (1943), see 28; on the Islamic Central Institute (1943), see 37; on speeches of the Nazi elite, see 30–31; on the speech of Muhammad Mustafa al-Maraghi (1944), see 31; on the ten speeches by al-Husayni that were published in *Barid al-Sharq*, see 68–127; on the article by Abdurreshid Ibrahim (1941), see 40–41; on an article by Shakib Arslan (1942–1943), see 39–40; on the articles of von Leers (1942–1943), see 41–42.

79 Rahn to Foreign Office, 28 March 1943, Tunis, PA, R 27766; and, on the distribution of this special issue, see also documents in PA, R 27766, R 27767, and R 27768.

80 Nöhring (Consulate Tangier) to Foreign Office, 8 May 1942, Tangier, PA, R 60660; and, in response, Wüster to Consulate Tangier, 15 July 1942, Berlin, PA, R 60660. The brochures were probably destroyed by the Spanish authorities, see Rieth to Foreign Office, 24 July 1942, Tangier, PA, R 60660.

81 As the Spanish authorities repeatedly confiscated the paper, the Germans tried to bypass censorship by sending it unofficially via the embassy in Madrid. On the

distribution and confiscation of *Barid al-Sharq* in the Tangier zone, see the documents in PA, R 60660.

82 Stohrer, Internal Note, 18 November 1941, Berlin, PA, R 29533.

83 Himmler to Reich Security Head Office, 14 May 1943, n.p., BAB, NS 19/3544. On this episode, see also Höpp, "Der Koran als 'geheime Reichssache,'" 443–446; and Herf, *Nazi Propaganda for the Arab World*, 202–204.

84 Kaltenbrunner to Himmler, 3 September 1943, Berlin, BAB, NS 19/3544.

85 Kaltenbrunner to Himmler, 13 September 1943, Berlin, BAB, NS 19/3544.

86 The most comprehensive study of the Sudanese Mahdi rebellion is P. M. Holt, *Mahdist State in the Sudan, 1881–98: A Study of Its Origins, Development and Overthrow* (Oxford, 1972). Mahdism had also remained a force in anticolonial struggles in the interwar period, see, for instance, C. N. Ubah, "British Measures against Mahdism in Dumbulwa in Northern Nigeria, 1923: A Case of Colonial Overreaction," *Islamic Culture* 50, 3 (1976), 196–283; Asma'u G. Saeed, "The British Policy towards the Mahdiyya in Northern Nigeria: A Study of the Arrest, Detention and Deportation of Shaykh Sa'id b. Hayat, 1923–1959," *Kano Studies* 2, 3 (1982–1985), 95–119; and Fisher, "British Responses to Mahdist and Other Unrest in North and West Africa." On messianism in anticolonial struggles more generally, see Michael Adas, *Prophets of Rebellion: Millenarian Protest Movements against the European Colonial Order* (Chapel Hill, NC, 1979).

87 Brandt to Berger, 11 September 1943, n.p., BAB, NS 19/3544; and Brandt to Sievers (*SS Ahnenerbe*), 11 September 1943, n.p., BAB, NS 19/3544.

88 Berger to Brandt, 10 October 1943, Berlin, BAB, NS 19/3544, which had attached a list with some passages from the Qur'an that refer to war as well as some messianic passages from medieval Iranian Pahlavi scriptures.

89 Sievers to Wüst, 28 September 1943, Berlin, BAB, NS 19/3544; and, for the report, Wüst to Brandt, 31 January 1944, Munich, BAB, NS 19/3544; and, for an earlier progress report, Wüst to Brandt, 14 December 1943, Munich, BAB, NS 19/3544; and, for the response after the submission of the final report, Brandt to Wüst, 8 March 1944, n.p., BAB, NS 19/3544.

90 Kaltenbrunner to Himmler, 6 December 1943, Berlin, BAB, NS 19/3544, which had attached the report, written by Otto Rössler and Walter Lorch of the Research Section "Orient," and the propaganda pamphlet in Arabic and in German translation, produced by the Research Section "Orient" as well. The report and the pamphlets were also obtained by Walther Wüst, who later also submitted them along with his final report, see attachments of Wüst to Brandt, 31 January 1944, Munich, BAB, NS 19/3544.

91 Pamphlet (German translation), n.d. (1943), BAB, NS 19/3544; and, for the Arabic original, Pamphlet "Wa-innahu la-'ilm li'l-sa'a" ("Verily, it is the Knowledge of the Hour"), n.d. (1943), BAB, R 55/20712. The German translation is printed in Höpp, "Der Koran als 'geheime Reichssache,'" 445; and an alternative English translation in Herf, *Nazi Propaganda for the Arab World*, 204.

92 Brandt to Kaltenbrunner, 28 December 1943, n.p., BAB, NS 19/3544.

93 Zeischka (Propaganda Ministry), Internal Note ("Druck und Verbreitung von Flugblättern in arabischen Ländern"), 26 January 1944, Berlin, BAB, R 55/20712, for the print request from the SS; Zeischka, Internal Note ("Druck und Verbreitung von

Flugblättern in arabischen Ländern"), 17 March 1944, Berlin, BAB, R 55/20712, for Goebbel's approval and the endorsement to print 1 million copies; Schmidt-Dumont, Internal Note ("Antijüdisches Flugzettel für den arabischen Raum"), 6 April 1944, Berlin, for the endorsement of the Foreign Office; and documents in BAB, R 55/20712, for details on the production of 1 million copies of the pamphlet.

94 Hentig to Knothe (Propaganda Ministry), 28 March 1938, Berlin, PA, R 104800. On the discussions about translations of *Mein Kampf* into Arabic, see Stefan Wild, "National Socialism in the Arab Near East between 1933 and 1939," *Die Welt des Islams* 25, 1/4 (1985), 126–173, 147–170.

95 Quoted in Wild, "National Socialism in the Arab Near East between 1933 and 1939," 166–167; the article was published on 9 December 1939 in *L'Orient*.

96 Anonymous, "Faschistische Umtriebe in den Ländern des Islams," *Freie Innerschweiz* (14 April 1939); and Jean Vignaud, "L'esprit de l'empire français," *Le Petit Parisien* (8 May 1940). The latter article caused some debate in Whitehall, see the documents in British National Archives, Kew (NA), FO 395/650.

97 A first complete translation of *Mein Kampf* appeared as late as 1960 in Beirut; for a critical review, see Stefan Wild, "'Mein Kampf' in arabischer Übersetzung," *Die Welt des Islams* 9, 1–4 (1964), 207–211.

98 Wild, "National Socialism in the Arab Near East between 1933 and 1939," 147–170. Shakib Arslan had been in contact with the German authorities in the Foreign Office and would remain so throughout the war, trying to influence Berlin's policies toward the Islamic world; most of his correspondence went in fact via Arslan's old friend Max von Oppenheim, see the documents in PA, Nachlass Hentig, vol. 84, as well as in PA, R 104812 and R 104813; and, on SS plans for an official visit by Arslan to Germany in 1938, BAB, NS 19/391. On Arslan, see William L. Cleveland, *Islam against the West: Shakib Arslan and the Campaign for Islamic Nationalism* (Austin, TX, 1985); Raja Adal, "Constructing Transnational Islam: The East-West Network of Shakib Arslan," in Stéphanie A. Dudoignon, Komatsu Hisao, and Kosugi Yasushi (eds.), *Intellectuals in the Modern Islamic World* (London, 2006), 176–210; and Raja Adal, "Shakib Arslan's Imagining of Europe: The Coloniser, the Inquisitor, the Islamic, the Virtuous, and the Friend," in Nathalie Clayer and Eric Germain (eds.), *Islam in Inter-War Europe* (London, 2008), 156–182.

99 Pamphlet "Im Namen Gottes, des Allbarmherzigen! El Emir Ab del Kadirel Djezeiiri" (German translation), n.d. (1944/1945), BAB, NS 19/2637.

100 Pamphlet "Im Namen Gottes, des Barmherzigen! Hört zu, Ihr tapferen Krieger Nordafrikas!" (German translation), n.d. (1944/1945), BAB, NS 19/2637.

101 Pamphlet "Aufruf seiner Eminenz des Großmufti Il Sayid Mohammed Amin El Usseini [*sic*]" (German translation), n.d. (1944/1945), BAB, NS 19/2637.

102 Pamphlet "Arabische Soldaten!" (German translation), n.d. (1944/1945), BAB, NS 19/2637.

103 Callum A. MacDonald, "Radio Bari: Italian Wireless Propaganda in the Middle East and British Countermeasures 1934–38," *Middle Eastern Studies* 13, 2 (1977), 195–207; and, more generally on Italian policies and propaganda in prewar North Africa and the Middle East, including considerations of Islam, Wright, "Mussolini,

Libya, and the Sword of Islam"; Williams, *Mussolini's Propaganda Abroad*; and Arielli, *Fascist Italy and the Middle East*.

104 C. L. Sulzberger, "Axis Radio Blankets Islam: American Aid Needed to Fight Propaganda Aimed at Lands of the Middle East," *New York Times* (1 February 1942).

105 On Nazi Germany's foreign broadcast propaganda, see Werner Schwipps, "Wortschlacht im Äther," in Deutsche Welle (ed.), *Wortschlacht im Äther: Der deutsche Auslandsrundfunk im Zweiten Weltkrieg* (Berlin, 1971), 13–97, esp. 56–57 (Empire Zone) and 58–62 (Orient Zone); Willi A. Boelcke, *Die Macht des Radios: Weltpolitik und Auslandsrundfunk 1924–1976* (Frankfurt, 1977), 405–416 (Arab World) and 416–430 (Iran, Afghanistan, and India); and Horst J. P. Bergmeier and Rainer E. Lotz, *Hitler's Airwaves: The Inside Story of Nazi Radio Broadcasting and Propaganda Swing* (New Haven, CT, 1997), 42–43 and 222–223. Reimund Schnabel, *Mißbrauchte Mikrophone: Deutsche Rundfunkpropaganda im Zweiten Weltkrieg* (Vienna, 1967), provides a collection of documents on Berlin's foreign broadcast propaganda. A contemporary account of Zeesen is given by Herbert Schröder, *Ein Sender erobert die Welt: Das Buch vom deutschen Kurzwellenrundfunk* (Essen, 1940). Longerich, *Propagandisten im Krieg*, 27–148, provides the general context.

106 On the Orient office of Zeesen, see Schwipps, "Wortschlacht im Äther," 58–62; Boelcke, *Die Macht des Radios*, 405–430; Bergmeier and Lotz, *Hitler's Airwaves*, 42–43 and 222–223; and Bernd Trentow and Werner Kranhold, "Im Dienst imperialistischer Weltherrschaftspläne: Zum Orient-Einsatz des faschistischen Rundfunks im Zweiten Weltkrieg," *Beiträge zur Geschichte des Rundfunks* 7, 4 (1973), 22–51. Bofinger wrote a four-page report on the work of his "Orient Office" after the war, see Gustav Bofinger, Report ("Entstehung und Geschichte der Zone Orient KWS"), n.d. (post-1945), n.p., German Broadcasting Archive (*Deutsches Rundfunkarchiv*), Frankfurt (DRA), A18/1.

107 For an (incomplete) list of the staff from the year 1942, see Telephone Register ("Telefonverzeichnis der RRG"), 1942, DRA, RRG 2/002.

108 Kurt Georg Kiesinger, *Dunkle und helle Jahre: Erinnerungen 1904–1958* (Stuttgart, 1989), 213–264, provides Kiesinger's perspective of the broadcast department, claiming that he did everything to keep Nazi ideology out of the broadcast propaganda and generally downplaying the influence of the Foreign Office.

109 Bofinger, Report ("Entstehung und Geschichte der Zone Orient KWS"), n.d. (post-1945), n.p., DRA, A18/1.

110 On Yunus Bahri, see Lebel, *The Mufti of Jerusalem*, 138, 151–154 and 225. After the war Bahri fled to Lebanon and published his memoirs about his Berlin years in five volumes, which include numerous incorrect statements and need to be read with much caution, see Yunus Bahri, *Huna Birlin! Hayya al-'Arab!* (*This Is Berlin! Long Live the Arabs!*), 5 vols. (Beirut, n.d.).

111 Information Sheet on Yunis Bahri, n.d. (July 1939), sent by Lampson (Embassy Cairo) to Halifax (Foreign Office), 6 July 1939, Alexandria, NA, FO 395/664.

112 Oppenheim, Memoirs ("Leben im NS-Staat, 1933–1945"), n.d. (1945/1946), n.p. (Landshut), OA, Nachlass Max von Oppenheim, no. 1/14.

113 A photograph of Iraqi employees of the Arab broadcast service can be found in Anonymous, "Moslems als Deutschlands Gäste," *Signal* (February 1942, 1st issue), 16.

114 On Taqi al-Hilali, see Muhlis al-Sabti, *Al-salafiyya al-wahhabiyya bi-l-maghrib: Taqi al-Din al-Hilali ra'idan* (*Wahhabi Salafism in Morocco: The Leader Taqi al-Din al-Hilali*) (Casablanca, 1993); Henri Lauzière, "The Evolution of the Salafiyya in the Twentieth Century through the Life and Thought of Taqi al-Din al-Hilali" (PhD diss., Georgetown University, 2008); and Mehdi Sajid, "Säkularisierung durch Augenzeugenschaft kontern: Der Bericht von Taqī al-Dīn al-Hilālī (gest. 1987) aus Bonn über die Religiosität der Europäer," in Bekim Agai and Stephan Conermann (eds.), *"Wenn einer eine Reise tut, hat er was zu erzählen": Präfiguration, Konfiguration, Refiguration in muslimischen Reiseberichten* (Berlin, 2013), 191–228.

115 Mildenstein, Report, n.d. (1939), n.p. (Berlin), BAB, R 58/783.

116 Ibid.

117 Bahri, *Huna Birlin!*, vol. 2 (*Zu'ama al-naziyya ka ma 'araftuhum* [*The Nazi Leaders as I Knew Them*]) (Beirut, n.d.), 31; and, on Idris, Bahri, *Huna Birlin!*, vol. 3 (*Hitlir wa'l-shuyu'iyya* [*Hitler and Communism*]) (Beirut, n.d.), 78.

118 Broadcast scripts of Arabic programs sent between December 1940 and February 1941 can be found in BAB, R 901/73039. From 1942 onward, US diplomats in Cairo recorded Germany's Arabic-language propaganda broadcasts. They translated them into English and sent them to Washington. These scripts can be found in USNA, RG 84, Entry UD 2410, Box 77 (for 1942), and Box 93 (for 1943), and Box 112 (for 1944). Some scripts of German Arabic broadcasts of 1945 are stored in USNA, RG 208, Entry 373, Box 417. Further Arabic broadcast scripts and summaries of Axis broadcast programs can also be found in USNA, RG 262, Entry 3, Box 9; USNA, RG 208, Entry 362, Box 133; USNA, RG 208, Entry 373, Box 421; USNA, RG 208, Entry 374, Box 430; and USNA, RG 208, Entry 387, Box 622. For a six-page American evaluation of the broadcast programs before 1942, see US Coordinator of Information, Report ("Axis Propaganda in the Moslem World"), 23 December 1941, Washington, USNA, RG 165, Box 3061. An assessment of German propaganda to the Arab world in 1941 by the US intelligence officer Anne H. Fuller can be found in USNA, RG 208, Entry 373, Box 418. Similar reports are stored in USNA, RG 208, Entry UD 577, Box 4. The British also compiled monitoring scripts of Germany's Arabic services that were used by various ministries in London and are today stored in the BBC Archives in Reading. Some original records of the Arabic propaganda program have survived the war and are today stored in the DRA.

119 Herf, *Nazi Propaganda for the Arab World*, providing an overview of the content of German broadcast propaganda in Arabic with a focus on its anti-Jewish content; and Thomas J. Kehoe, "Fighting for Our Mutual Benefit: Understanding and Contextualizing the Intentions behind Nazi Propaganda for the Arabs during World War Two," *Journal of Genocide Research* 14, 2 (2012), 137–157, deemphasizing the primacy of anti-Jewish themes in this propaganda. Vera Henssler, "'Für die Propaganda nach dem Orient ist bei weitem die wirksamste Waffe der Rundfunk': NS-Auslandspropaganda in den Nahen Osten und Nordafrika," *Zeitschrift für Geschichtswissenschaft* 59, 11 (2011), 920–937, provides an overview based on German broadcast guidelines. Earlier important studies of German broadcast propaganda in North Africa and the Middle East are Ageron, "Contribution à l'étude de la propagande allemande au Maghreb pendant la Deuxième Guerre mondiale," 21–32; and,

almost identically, Ageron, "Les populations du Maghreb face à la propagande allemande," 13–39; and Baida, "Le Maroc et la propagande du IIIème Reich," 93–95.

120 Bofinger, Report ("Entstehung und Geschichte der Zone Orient KWS"), DRA, A18/1; and, similarly, Schwipps, "Wortschlacht im Äther," 60.

121 Rühle to Rahn, 13 March 1943, Berlin, PA, R 27768; and, in response, Rahn to Rühle, 4 April 1943, Tunis, PA, R 27766.

122 Broadcast Monitoring Script "Berlin in Arabic," 29 July 1942 (recorded), USNA, RG 84, Entry UD 2410, Box 77.

123 Broadcast Script "Der Freiheitsheld Jusuf Abu Durra" (German translation), 8 February 1941 (sent), BAB, R 901/73039.

124 Broadcast Monitoring Script "Voice of Free Arabism: Britain and Islam," 6 August 1942 (recorded), USNA, RG 84, Entry UD 2410, Box 77. In June 1943, the speaker in Berlin even read out an article from *Barid al-Sharq* about Muslims under British rule in India, see Broadcast Monitoring Script "Athens in Arabic," 7 June 1943 (recorded), USNA, RG 84, Entry UD 2410, Box 93.

125 Broadcast Monitoring Script "Voice of Free Arabism: Al Azhar University and the Moslem Cause," 3 September 1943 (recorded), USNA, RG 84, Entry UD 2410, Box 93.

126 Fuller (Office of War Information), Report ("Necessary Precautions in Broadcasting to the Arab World"), 6 October 1941, n.d., USNA, RG 208, Entry 373, Box 418.

127 Broadcast Monitoring Script "Berlin in Arabic," 1 July 1942 (recorded), USNA, RG 84, Entry UD 2410, Box 77; see also Broadcast Monitoring Script "Berlin in Arabic: The British Do Not Want to Declare Cairo an Open City," 27 June 1942 (recorded), USNA, RG 84, Entry UD 2410, Box 77.

128 On the caliphate, see Broadcast Monitoring Script "Voice of Free Arabism: The Mufti of Tripoli," 14 February 1943 (recorded), USNA, RG 84, Entry UD 2410, Box 93; on the Bairam celebration in Cairo, see Broadcast Monitoring Script "Athens in Arabic: Bairam and Our Policy," 30 September 1943 (recorded), USNA, RG 84, Entry UD 2410, Box 93.

129 On Egypt and India, see Broadcast Monitoring Script "The Arab Nation: The Pilgrimage," 4 December 1942 (recorded), USNA, RG 84, Entry UD 2410, Box 77; on India, see also Broadcast Monitoring Script "Berlin in Arabic: Pilgrims," 12 January 1943 (recorded), USNA, RG 84, Entry UD 2410, Box 93. The hajj as a wartime concern of British imperial officials is discussed later in this chapter.

130 Broadcast Monitoring Script "Berlin in Arabic: Pilgrimage," 8 December 1942 (recorded), USNA, RG 84, Entry UD 2410, Box 77.

131 Broadcast Monitoring Script "Voice of Free Arabism: The Pilgrimage," 14 December 1942 (recorded), USNA, RG 84, Entry UD 2410, Box 77; two days later Berlin's Arabic service sent greetings for the pilgrimage again, see Broadcast Monitoring Script "Athens in Arabic: The Pilgrimage," 17 December 1942 (recorded), USNA, RG 84, Entry UD 2410, Box 77.

132 Broadcast Monitoring Script "Voice of Free Arabism: British Obstacles for Arab Palestinian Pilgrims," 30 September 1943 (recorded), USNA, RG 84, Entry UD 2410, Box 93.

133 On Syria and India, see Broadcast Monitoring Script "Athens in Arabic: The Pilgrimage," 12 August 1943 (recorded), USNA, RG 84, Entry UD 2410, Box 93; on

India, see Broadcast Monitoring Script "Voice of Free Arabism: India," 12 August 1943 (recorded), USNA, RG 84, Entry UD 2410, Box 93; and Broadcast Monitoring Script "Athens in Arabic: Indian Pilgrims," 15 August 1943 (recorded), USNA, RG 84, Entry UD 2410, Box 93.

134 Broadcast Monitoring Script "Berlin in Arabic: News of the Arab Countries: The Moslems of the World," 27 October 1943 (recorded), USNA, RG 84, Entry UD 2410, Box 93.

135 Broadcast Monitoring Script "Voice of Free Arabism," 1 July 1942 (recorded), USNA, RG 84, Entry UD 2410, Box 77.

136 Broadcast Monitoring Script "Voice of Free Arabism: The London Mosque," 16 July 1942 (recorded), USNA, RG 84, Entry UD 2410, Box 77.

137 Broadcast Monitoring Script "Voice of Free Arabism: The Moslem Fraternity," 27 April 1943 (recorded), USNA, RG 84, Entry UD 2410, Box 93; see also Broadcast Monitoring Script "Berlin in Arabic: Palestine: Talk: Moslem Attention," 17 June 1944 (recorded), USNA, RG 84, Entry UD 2410, Box 112.

138 Broadcast Monitoring Script, "Voice of Free Arabism: The Jews Have Their Religion and the Moslems Have Theirs," 29 December 1943 (recorded), USNA, RG 84, Entry UD 2410, Box 112.

139 Broadcast Monitoring Script "Berlin in Arabic: Talk: Forgiveness in Islam," 12 January 1944 (recorded), USNA, RG 84, Entry UD 2410, Box 112.

140 Hirszowicz, *The Third Reich and the Arab East*, 311.

141 Broadcast Monitoring Script "Berlin in Arabic: America," 5 September 1942 (recorded), USNA, RG 84, Entry UD 2410, Box 77.

142 Broadcast Monitoring Script "Berlin in Arabic: An American Paradise," 4 June 1943 (recorded), USNA, RG 84, Entry UD 2410, Box 93.

143 Broadcast Monitoring Script "Voice of Free Arabism: Bolshevism and Islam," 7 September 1942 (recorded), USNA, RG 84, Entry UD 2410, Box 77.

144 Broadcast Monitoring Script "Voice of Free Arabism: The Russians and the Qoran," 6 April 1944 (recorded), USNA, RG 84, Entry UD 2410, Box 112; for similar reports, see Broadcast Monitoring Script "Berlin in Arabic: Bolshevik Attrocities [*sic*] against the Moslems," 2 February 1943 (recorded), USNA, RG 84, Entry UD 2410, Box 93; Broadcast Monitoring Script "Berlin in Arabic: Russia," 25 February 1943 (recorded), USNA, RG 84, Entry UD 2410, Box 93; and Broadcast Monitoring Script "Athens in Arabic: The Soviets and the Moslems," 23 October 1943 (recorded), USNA, RG 84, Entry UD 2410, Box 93; Berlin also reported on the general suppression of religion in the Soviet Union, see, for instance, Broadcast Monitoring Script "Berlin in Arabic: Bolshevik Propaganda and the Freedom of Religion in Russia," 12 January 1943 (recorded), USNA, RG 84, Entry UD 2410, Box 93.

145 Broadcast Monitoring Script "Berlin in Arabic: Communism and Islam," 12 April 1943 (recorded), USNA, RG 84, Entry UD 2410, Box 93.

146 Broadcast Monitoring Script "Independent Egypt: An Important Historical Document for the Egyptian Public," 15 July 1943 (recorded), USNA, RG 84, Entry UD 2410, Box 93.

147 Broadcast Monitoring Script "Berlin in Arabic: Stalin's Ambitions in the Near East and Arab Countries," 10 December 1943 (recorded), USNA, RG 84, Entry UD 2410, Box 112.

148 Broadcast Monitoring Script "Berlin in Arabic: Talk: Bolshevism and Its Dangers," 22 August 1944 (recorded), RG 84, Entry UD 2410, Box 112.

149 Broadcast Script "Zur Regierungserklärung für die Araber" (German translation), 12 December 1940 (sent), BAB, R 901/73039. This declaration was sent just days after the "Arab declaration," Broadcast Script "Deutsche Rundfunkerklärung vom 5. Dezember 1940," 7 February 1942, Berlin, PA, R 28876 (also in PA, R 261123 and R 261179).

150 Broadcast Monitoring Script "Berlin in Arabic: Islam and National-Socialism," 22 May 1943 (recorded), USNA, RG 84, Entry UD 2410, Box 93.

151 Broadcast Monitoring Script, "Berlin in Arabic: The Axis and the Moslems," 5 August 1942 (recorded), USNA, RG 84, Entry UD 2410, Box 77.

152 These reports began particularly with the German military involvement in Bosnia and Herzegovina in early 1943, see Broadcast Monitoring Script "Berlin in Arabic: The Mufti of Jerusalem," 1 May 1943 (recorded), USNA, RG 84, Entry UD 2410, Box 93; on British support of the Serbian Četniks, see Broadcast Monitoring Script "The Arab Nation: 'Have You Heard, Ye Moslems?,'" 26 May 1943 (recorded), USNA, RG 84, Entry UD 2410, Box 93; on Anglo-American support of the Communist partisans on the Balkans, see, for instance, Broadcast Monitoring Script "Berlin in Arabic: The Moslems in the Balkans," 31 July 1944 (recorded), USNA, RG 84, Entry UD 2410, Box 112; and "Berlin in Arabic: The Moslems of the Balkans," 4 August 1944 (recorded), USNA, RG 84, Entry UD 2410, Box 112.

153 Broadcast Monitoring Script "Berlin in Arabic: Moslem Women in Yugoslavia," 4 February 1944 (recorded), USNA, RG 84, Entry UD 2410, Box 112.

154 Broadcast Monitoring Script "Berlin in Arabic: Allied Terror in the Balkans," 27 June 1944 (recorded), USNA, RG 84, Entry UD 2410, Box 112.

155 Broadcast Monitoring Script "Berlin in Arabic: Moslem Thanksgivings for Hitler's Safety," 24 July 1944 (recorded), USNA, RG 84, Entry UD 2410, Box 112.

156 Ibid.

157 Broadcast Monitoring Script "Berlin in Arabic: Palestine," 13 October 1943 (recorded), USNA, RG 84, Entry UD 2410, Box 93.

158 On Muslims in the Allied armies, see Broadcast Monitoring Script "Berlin in Arabic: Talk: Moslem Soldiers Fight in Italy," 22 May 1944 (recorded), USNA, RG 84, Entry UD 2410, Box 112; on Muslims in the German armies, see Broadcast Monitoring Script "Berlin in Arabic: Moslem Soldiers Fight in the Balkans," 22 May 1944 (recorded), USNA, RG 84, Entry UD 2410, Box 112.

159 Rühle, Internal Note ("Aufzeichnung betr. die Rundfunkpropaganda in dem arabischen Raum"), 5 May 1941, Berlin, PA, R 67482.

160 Broadcast Script "Religiöser Wochentalk: Die Frömmigkeit" (German translation), 5 December 1940 (sent), BAB, R 901/73039; Broadcast Script "Religiöser Wochentalk: Die Wahrhaftigkeit" (German translation), 26 December 1940 (sent), BAB, R 901/73039; Broadcast Script "Talk: Die gute Behandlung des Dieners, Sklaven und

Tieres" (German translation), 23 January 1941 (sent), BAB, R 901/73039; Broadcast Script "Kultureller Talk: Die Wahrhaftigkeit und die Stärke des Glaubens" (German translation), 31 December 1940 (sent), BAB, R 901/73039; Broadcast Script "Religiöser Talk: Die Pilgerfahrt" (German translation), 2 January 1941 (sent), BAB, R 901/73039; and Broadcast Script "Religiöser Wochentalk" (German translation), 19 December 1940 (sent), BAB, R 901/73039.

161 Broadcast Script "Religiöser Wochentalk: Die Freigebigkeit" (German translation), 12 December 1940 (sent), BAB, R 901/73039.

162 Broadcast Script "Talk: Die Selbstsucht" (German translation), 16 January 1941 (sent), BAB, R 901/73039.

163 Broadcast Script "Talk: Wachet auf!" (German translation), 6 February 1941 (sent), BAB, R 901/73039.

164 Broadcast Script "Talk: Die Wissenschaft und der Unterricht" (German translation), 13 February 1941 (sent), BAB, R 901/73039.

165 Broadcast Script "Neuerungen und Aberglaube im Islam" (German translation), 20 February 1941 (sent), BAB, R 901/73039.

166 Office of War Information, Special Daily Propaganda Report, 11 March 1942, USNA, RG 208, Entry UD 577, Box 4.

167 Broadcast Script "Talk: Glückwünsche zum Beiram-Fest" (German translation), 8 January 1941 (sent), BAB, R 901/73039.

168 Broadcast Script "Talk: Festglückwünsche und Ausprache eines Mitgliedes der arabischen Kolonie über die Lebensverhältnisse in Deutschland" (German translation), 10 January 1941 (sent), BAB, R 901/73039.

169 Broadcast Script "Talk: Glückwünsche zum mohammedanischen Neujahrsfest" (German translation), 28 January 1941 (sent), BAB, R 901/73039.

170 Broadcast Script "Talk: Über das neue Hedschra-Jahr" (German translation), 30 January 1941 (sent), BAB, R 901/73039.

171 Broadcast Monitoring Script "Voice of Free Arabism: What Moslems Should Remember," 18 December 1942 (recorded), USNA, RG 84, Entry UD 2410, Box 93.

172 Al-Husayni, Speech (German translation), 19 March 1943, Berlin, BA–MA, RH 45/71; for the invitation card to the event, see Invitation ("Einladung Islamisches Zentral-Institut zu Berlin E.V.: Die Rede seiner Eminenz des Großmufti von Palästina anläßlich des Geburtstages des Gottesgesandten Muhameds"), n.d. (March 1943), Berlin, PA, R 27327.

173 Al-Husayni, Speech (German translation), 1 October 1943, Berlin, BAB, NS 19/2637.

174 Broadcast Monitoring Script "Voice of Free Arabism: Bairam," 19 September 1944 (recorded), USNA, RG 84, Entry UD 2410, Box 112.

175 Broadcast Monitoring Script "Berlin in Arabic: Celebration of This Holy Occasion in the Mosque in Berlin," 7 March 1944 (recorded), USNA, RG 84, Entry UD 2410, Box 112.

176 Schwipps, "Wortschlacht im Äther," 59; and, similarly, Boelcke, *Die Macht des Radios*, 405.

177 Schirmer (Foreign Office) to Embassy Paris, 1 January 1942, Berlin, PA, Paris 1116C, informed the Paris embassy of the suggestion, which had come from the German consulate in Tangier. Schleier to Foreign Office, 15 January 1943, Paris, PA, Paris

1116C, had welcomed the proposal. Vycichl (Embassy Paris), Internal Note ("Reportage in arabischen Arbeitslagern der Organisation Todt"), 21 January 1943, Paris, PA, Paris 1116C, assessed the documentary and confirmed that it had been sent on 17 January 1943.

178 On German involvement in Turkey, see Lothar Krecker, *Deutschland und die Türkei im Zweiten Weltkrieg* (Frankfurt, 1964); Johannes Glasneck and Inge Kircheisen, *Türkei und Afghanistan: Brennpunkte der Orientpolitik im Zweiten Weltkrieg* (Berlin, 1968); and, more generally, Zehra Önder, *Die türkische Außenpolitik im Zweiten Weltkrieg* (Munich, 1977); and Selim Deringil, *Turkish Foreign Policy during the Second World War: An "Active" Neutrality* (Cambridge, 2004); and, on ideological perceptions, Stefan Ihrig, "Nazi Perceptions of the New Turkey 1919–1945" (PhD diss., University of Cambridge, 2011).

179 Papen to Foreign Office, 26 April 1940, Ankara, PA, R 67484; and, similarly, Papen to Foreign Office, 3 May 1940, Ankara, PA, R 67484; both letters had press reports attached.

180 Papen to Foreign Office, 3 May 1940, Ankara, PA, R 67484.

181 Rühle, Internal Note ("Deutsche Sendungen in türkischer Sprache"), 18 April 1941, Berlin, PA, R 67483.

182 Foreign Office, Instructions ("Standardthesen für die Propaganda nach dem Iran"), n.d. (4 January 1942), n.p. (Berlin), PA, R 27329; and, identical, Foreign Office, Instructions ("Standardthesen für die Propaganda nach dem Iran"), 4 January 1942, printed in Foreign Office, Instructions ("Zusammenfassung der vom Herrn RAM angeordneten Standardthesen für die deutsche Auslandspropaganda in laufender Nummernfolge"), 1942, Berlin, PA, R 101400; and, similar, Foreign Office, Instructions ("Standardthesen für die Propaganda nach dem Iran"), 27 March 1942, printed in Foreign Office, Instructions ("Zusammenfassung der vom Herrn RAM angeordneten Standardthesen für die deutsche Auslandspropaganda in laufender Nummernfolge"), 1942, Berlin, PA, R 27330.

183 Ettel, Guidelines ("Richtlinien für die deutsche Propaganda nach dem Iran"), 24 August 1942, Berlin, PA, R 27329 (also in PA, R 27330). The file PA, R 27329 contains drafts of these guidelines, as well as Ribbentrop's endorsement of the final version, Sonnleithner, Internal Note, 29 August 1942, Feldmark, PA, R 27329. An earlier draft of the guidelines claimed that Hitler was revered widely in Iran as the Twelfth Imam, see Ettel, Guidelines ("Richtlinien für die Propaganda nach Iran"), 11 August 1942, Berlin, PA, R 27329.

184 Ettel, Internal Note ("Rundfunkpropaganda nach Iran"), 21 December 1942, Berlin, PA, R 27329. Only a few German broadcast transcripts for Iran have survived the war, and they give no evidence of the religious dimension of Germany's broadcasts to Iran. Scripts that survived the war deal with German Oriental studies (sent on 29 January 1941), the role of the Iranian national epic in German literature (sent on 11 February 1941), the propaganda film *Der Sieg im Westen* (sent on 14 February 1941), and the reception of Iranian poetry in Germany (sent on 18 February 1941), see scripts in BAB, R 901/73039.

185 Ettel to Foreign Office, 2 February 1941, Tehran, PA, R 60690.

186 Ibid.

187 Winkler, Internal Note ("Erfahrungen aus der deutschen Propagandaarbeit in Iran vom November 1939 bis September 1941"), 10 January 1942, Berlin, PA, R 60690. On Winkler, see Chapter 5.

188 George Lenczowski, *Russia and the West in Iran 1918–1948: A Study in Big-Power Rivalry* (Ithaca, NY, 1949), 159.

189 Sulzberger, "Axis Radio blankets Islam," and, similarly, C. L. Sulzberger, *A Long Row of Candles: Memoirs and Diaries, 1934–1954* (London, 1969), 191.

190 On German policies toward India, see Reimund Schnabel, *Tiger und Schakal: Deutsche Indienpolitik 1941–1943* (Vienna, 1968); Voigt, "Hitler und Indien;" Hauner, "Das Nationalsozialistische Deutschland und Indien;" Milan Hauner, *India in Axis Strategy: Germany, Japan, and Indian Nationalists in the Second World War* (Stuttgart, 1981); Milan Hauner, "The Professionals and the Amateurs in National Socialist Foreign Policy: Revolution and Subversion in the Islamic and Indian World," in Gerhard Hirschfeld and Lothar Kettenacker (eds.), *The "Führer State": Myth and Reality: Studies on the Structure and Politics of the Third Reich* (Stuttgart, 1981), 305–328; Eugene J. D'Souza, "Nazi Propaganda in India," *Social Scientist* 28, 5/6 (2000), 77–90; Hans-Bernd Zöllner, *"Der Feind meines Feindes ist mein Freund": Subhas Chandra Bose und das zeitgenössische Deutschland unter dem Nationalsozialismus 1933–1943* (Hamburg, 2000); and Jan Kuhlmann, *Netaji in Europe* (New Delhi, 2012). Johannes H. Voigt, *India in the Second World War* (New Delhi, 1987); and Manzoor Ahmad, *Indian Response to the Second World War: A Political Study* (New Delhi, 1987), provide the general context of India in the Second World War.

191 The speech was jointly organized by Germany and Italy and given during a sojourn by the mufti in Rome. On the organization of the speech and German involvement, see the documents in PA, R 27326 and PA, R 60675. The speech apparently received little attention in the Arab world (Schweinitz to Foreign Office, 27 August 1942, Alexandretta, PA, R 27326) and Central Asia (Pilger to Foreign Office, 28 August 1942, Kabul, PA, R 27322). There is no assessment of its reception in India, but German officials in Thailand noted that Indian exile movements there had reacted positively (Wendler to Foreign Office, 27 August 1942, Bangkok, PA, R 27322). The Germans also reported on the speech in Zeesen's Arabic service, see Broadcast Monitoring Script "Berlin in Arabic: The Grand Mufti Appeals to the Indians," 13 September 1942 (recorded), USNA, RG 84, Entry UD 2410, Box 77. On the speech, see also Schechtman, *The Mufti and the Fuehrer*, 134; Lebel, *The Mufti of Jerusalem*, 164–171; and Gensicke, *The Mufti of Jerusalem and the Nazis*, 104–106. Tokyo's suggestion to make al-Husayni also address the Muslims of East Asia through their shortwave stations in Japan and Indochina was not followed, see Ott (Tokyo) to Foreign Office, 3 January 1942, Tokyo, PA, R 60669.

192 Broadcast Department (Foreign Office), Monitoring Script, 25 August 1942, Berlin, PA, R 60675; and, similarly, German News Agency (Deutsches Nachrichtenbüro), Confidential Report ("DNB-Radioaufnahme"), 25 August 1942, Berlin, PA, R 27326.

193 Mackensen (Embassy Rome) to Foreign Office, 30 September 1942, Rome, PA, R 27326 (also in PA, R 60675 and in BA–MA, RH 2/1785); for the text of the speech, see "Mirza Ali Khan," Speech, 2 October 1942, PA, R 27326; the German press also

reported on the fakir's alleged statement, see, for instance, Anonymous, "Die Bolschewisierung Englands," *Deutsche Allgemeine Zeitung* (1 October 1942).

194 Mackensen to Foreign Office, 30 September 1942, Rome, PA, R 27326 (also in PA, R 60675 and in BA–MA, RH 2/1785).

195 Milan Hauner, "One Man against the Empire: The Faqir of Ipi and the British in Central Asia on the Eve of and during the Second World War," *Journal of Contemporary History* 16, 1 (1981), 183–212, gives a good overview of the Fakir of Ipi during the Second World War and of the support his insurgents received from the Germans and the Italians. More general accounts on the Northwest Frontier and the Fakir of Ipi in the interwar and war periods are Hauner, *India in Axis Strategy*, passim; J. G. Elliott, *The Frontier 1939–1947: The Story of the North-West Frontier of India* (London 1968), 242–281; Sayed Wiqar Ali Shah, *Ethnicity, Islam, and Nationalism: Muslim Politics in the North-West Frontier Province 1937–1947* (Karachi, 1999), 1–158; Alan Warren, *Waziristan, the Faqir of Ipi, and the Indian Army: The North West Frontier Revolt of 1936–37* (Oxford, 2000); and Christian Tripodi, *Edge of Empire: the British Political Officer and Tribal Administration on the North-West Frontier 1877–1947* (Farnham, VT, 2011), 109–221. Habibur Rahman, "Ali Naggar, the Fakir of Ipi," *Living Age* (June 1937), 330–331, is an early article on the Fakir of Ipi by a later Muslim member of the German propaganda service to India.

196 Lenz (Foreign Office), Internal Report ("Die Indische Nord-West-Grenzprovinz"), August 1941, Berlin, PA, R 27501.

197 Documents stored in the archives of the German Foreign Office give evidence of regular contacts between the Germans and Mirza Ali Khan and payments from early 1941, see PA, R 27326, R 27772, R 29534, and the India files R 60667–77 and R 67660.

198 Transfers of arms, ammunition, money, and messages from the German legation in Kabul are recorded in the weekly reports from General Headquarters India, Report ("Weekly Intelligence Summary of the North-West Frontier and Afghanistan of 1941 and 1942"), NA, WO 208/773. The "Monthly Intelligence Summary" reports of the headquarters of the British Indian Army give a similar account. When the Germans captured two of these reports in North Africa in 1942, they were delighted to read how their support for the Fakir of Ipi troubled the British authorities, see Trott (Foreign Office), Internal Note ("Zwei Geheimberichte des indischen Intelligence Service"), 5 August 1942, Berlin, PA, R 60674, with the attached intelligence reports General and Air Headquarters India, Monthly Intelligence Summary (4 March 1942) and General and Air Headquarters India, Monthly Intelligence Summary (4 April 1942). A summary gives Woermann to Legation Kabul, 5 August 1942, Berlin, PA, R 67660.

199 General Headquarters India, Report ("Weekly Intelligence Summary of the North-West Frontier and Afghanistan"), 15 July 1941, 29 July 1941, 13 February 1942, 6 March 1942, and 19 June 1942, NA, WO 208/773.

200 Pilger to Foreign Office, 10 September 1942, Kabul, PA, R 27326; and, for details of the content, Pilger to Foreign Office, 28 September 1942, Kabul, PA, R 27326; and, on the German internal reaction, see the documents in PA, R 27326.

201 Erhard Tewes, *Der Freiheitsheld von Waziristan: Von England gefürchtet, von Indien geliebt* (Aalen, 1940).

202 Stanley Wolpert, *Jinnah of Pakistan* (New York, 1984), 171–246.

203 H. H. the Nawab of Bhopal, "Islamic Support in the War," *Asiatic Review* 37, 130 (1941), 281–286, calling the war a "Battle of Islam," is an example.

204 Pilger to Foreign Office, 24 August 1942, Kabul, PA, R 27326, brought up the issue of contacting Kifayat Ullah and asks for opinion of al-Husayni on the issue; and Ettel to Embassy Rome, 1 September 1942, Berlin, PA, R 27326, turned to al-Husayni, then on visit in Rome, about the issue; and, in response, Mackensen to Foreign Office, 9 September 1942, Rome, PA, R 27326, explains that al-Husayni expressed full trust in Kifayat Ullah and described him as "uncompromisingly anti-English." Keppler, Internal Note, 3 September 1942, Berlin, PA, R 27326, expressed concerns about such contacts; though, Keppler to Legation Kabul, 5 September 1942, Berlin, PA, R 67660, asked about practical steps. Finally, Pilger to Foreign Office, 10 September 1942, Kabul, PA, R 27326, reports that Kifayat Ullah was imprisoned, thereby ending the discussion.

205 Fuller, Memorandum ("Memorandum on Radio Reception in the Near East and India"), 18 August 1941, n.p., USNA, RG 208, Entry 373, Box 418.

206 Neurath to Foreign Office, 3 April 1942, n.p., PA, R 60747.

207 Newton (Embassy Baghdad) to Foreign Office, 17 June 1939, Baghdad, NA, FO 395/664. This led to a discussion in the British Foreign Office about how the coffee shops could be prompted to play BBC Arabic service, see Foreign Office, Internal Discussion Sheet, 17 June–12 July 1939, London, NA, FO 395/664. On the effectiveness of Grobba's efforts, see Newton to Foreign Office, 5 July 1939, Baghdad, NA, FO 395/664; and Newton to Foreign Office, 21 July 1939, Baghdad, NA, FO 395/664.

208 Lampson to Halifax (Foreign Office), 6 July 1939, Alexandria, NA, FO 395/664.

209 Charles (Embassy Rome) to Cavendish-Bentinck (Foreign Office), 1 June 1939, Rome, NA, FO 395/664.

210 Mackereth (Legation Damascus) to Foreign Office, 10 May 1939, Damascus, NA, FO 395/663.

211 Galloway (Political Agency Kuwait) to Persian Gulf Residency Bushire, 23 June 1939, Kuwait, NA, FO 395/664; the letter was then forwarded to the India Office and the Foreign Office.

212 Knight (Consulate General Tunis) to Foreign Office, 14 June 1939, Tunis, NA, FO 395/664, provides an example of outrage with regard to the propagandistic exploitation of the Qur'an.

213 Gerhard Höpp, "Frontwechsel: Muslimische Deserteure im Ersten und Zweiten Weltkrieg und in der Zwischenkriegszeit," in Höpp and Reinwald (eds.), *Fremdeinsätze*, 129–141.

214 The reception of Nazism in the Arab world is an immensely researched subject. The following authors have shown that the popularity of Nazism in the Arab world in the 1930s and 1940s should not be overestimated: On Iraq, see Peter Wien, *Iraqi Arab Nationalism: Authoritarian, Totalitarian and Pro-Fascist Inclinations, 1932–1941* (London, 2006). On Palestine, see Nezam Al-Abbasi, "Die palästinensische Freiheitsbewegung im Spiegel ihrer Presse von 1929 bis 1945" (PhD diss., University of Freiburg,

1981); Hammad Hussein, "Die Palästinenser und der Nationalsozialismus: Ansichten in den dreissiger Jahren," *Asien, Afrika, Lateinamerika* 28 (1999), 589–600; and René Wildangel, *Zwischen Achse und Mandatsmacht: Palästina und der Nationalsozialismus* (Berlin, 2007). On Lebanon and Syria, see Götz Nordbruch, *Nazism in Syria and Lebanon: The Ambivalence of the German Option, 1933–1945* (London, 2009); Götz Nordbruch, "Bread, Freedom, Independence: Opposition to Nazi Germany in Lebanon and Syria and the Struggle for a Just Order," *Comparative Studies of South Asia, Africa and the Middle East* 28, 3 (2008), 416–427. On Egypt, see Shimon Shamir, "The Influence of German National-Socialism on Radical Movements in Egypt," *Jahrbuch des Instituts für Deutsche Geschichte, Beiheft* 1 (1975), 200–208; Ami Ayalon, "Egyptian Intellectuals versus Fascism and Nazism in the 1930s," in Dann (ed.), *Great Powers in the Middle East*, 391–404; Edmond Cao-Van-Hoa, *"Der Feind meines Feindes . . .": Darstellungen des nationalsozialistischen Deutschland in ägyptischen Schriften* (Frankfurt, 1990); Israel Gershoni, "Confronting Nazism in Egypt: Tawfiq al-Hakim's Anti-Totalitariansim 1938–1945," *Tel Aviver Jahrbuch für deutsche Geschichte* 26 (1997), 121–150; Israel Gershoni, "Egyptian Liberalism in an Age of 'Crisis of Orientation': Al-Risāla's Reaction to Fascism and Nazism, 1933–1939," *International Journal of Middle East Studies* 31, 4 (1999), 551–576; Israel Gershoni and James Jankowski, *Confronting Fascism and Egypt: Dictatorship versus Democracy in the 1930s* (Stanford, CA, 2010); and Israel Gershoni and Götz Nordbruch, *Sympathie und Schrecken: Begegnungen mit Faschismus und Nationalsozialismus in Ägypten, 1922–1937* (Berlin, 2011). On the Maghrib, see Mahfoud Kaddache, "L'opinion politique musulmane en Algérie et l'administration française (1939–1942)," *Revue D'histoire de la Deuxième Guerre mondiale* 29, 114 (1979), 95–115; Jamaâ Baida, "Die Wahrnehmung der Nazi-Periode in Marokko: Indizien für den Einfluß der deutschen Propaganda auf die Geisteshaltung der Marokkaner," in Herbert Popp (ed.), *Die Sicht des Anderen: Das Marokkobild der Deutschen, das Deutschlandbild der Marokkaner* (Passau, 1994), 193–196, reprinted in A. Bendaoud and M. Berriane (eds.), *Marocains et Allemands: La perception de l'autre* (Rabat, 1995), 13–19; Mokhtar El Harras, "Die Printmedien und das Deutschlandbild in der spanischen Protektoratszone von Nordmarokko (1934–1945)," in Popp (ed.), *Die Sicht des Anderen*, 197–207, reprinted in Bendaoud and Berriane (eds.), *Marocains et Allemands*, 21–36; and Satloff, *Among the Righteous*. For broader overviews of perceptions of German Nazism in the Arab world, see Fritz Steppart, "Das Jahr 1933 und seine Folgen für die arabischen Länder des Vorderen Orients," in Gerhard Schulz (ed.), *Die große Krise der dreißiger Jahre: Vom Niedergang der Weltwirtschaft zum Zweiten Weltkrieg* (Göttingen, 1985), 261–278; Wild, "National Socialism in the Arab Near East between 1933 and 1939"; Gerhard Höpp, "Araber im Zweiten Weltkrieg: Kollaboration oder Patriotismus?," in Wolfgang Schwanitz (ed.), *Jenseits der Legenden: Araber, Juden, Deutsche* (Berlin, 1994), 86–92; and Gilbert Achcar, *Arabs and the Holocaust* (London, 2010); as well as the contributions in Höpp, Wien and Wildangel (eds.), *Blind für die Geschichte*, and in the special issues of *Geschichte und Gesellschaft* 37, 3 (2011) and *Orient-Institut Studies* 1 (2012). Some authors have argued that German propaganda—particularly its anti-Jewish content—had a sustained influence in the Middle East, see Matthias Küntzel, *Jihad and Jew-Hatred: Islamism, Nazism and the Roots of 9/11* (New York,

2007); David Patterson, *A Genealogy of Evil: Anti-Semitism from Nazism to Islamic Jihad* (New York, 2011); and Barry Rubin and Wolfgang G. Schwanitz, *Nazis, Islamists, and the Making of the Modern Middle East* (New Haven, CT, 2014). Historiographical reviews of the literature on perceptions and influences of Nazism in the Arab world are given by Peter Wien, "Coming to Terms with the Past: German Academia and Historical Relations between the Arab Lands and Nazi Germans," *International Journal of Middle East Studies* 42, 2 (2010), 311–321; and Götz Nordbruch, "'Cultural Fusion' of Thought and Ambitions? Memory, Politics and the History of Arab-Nazi German Encounters," *Middle Eastern Studies* 47, 1 (2011), 183–194. The reception of Nazism in Iran and Turkey and among Muslims in British India and other parts of Asia remains widely neglected.

215 Amir Taheri, *The Spirit of Allah: Khomeini and the Islamic Revolution* (London, 1985), 97–100, makes this claim, though without providing any evidence.

216 Ruhullah Khomeini, *Kashf al-Asrar* (*The Revealing of Secrets*) (n.p., n.d. (1399/1979 [1361/1942]), 222 and, for further attacks on Hitler's Germany, 272 and 302; and, for the English translation of the passage, Ruhullah Khomeini, "A Warning to the Nation," in *Islam and Revolution: Writings and Declarations of Imam Khomeini (1941–1980)*, transl. and annot. Hamid Algar (Berkeley, CA, 1981), 169–173, 170. Baqer Moin, *Khomeini: Life of the Ayatollah* (London, 1999), 57–64, gives an account of Khomeini's activities during the Second World War, and Vanessa Martin, *Creating an Islamic State: Khomeini and the Making of a New Iran* (London, 2000), 103–112, provides a good analysis of *Kashf al-Asrar.* It should be noted that Khomeini's later *Islamic Government* was full of heavily anti-Jewish passages, see Ruhullah Khomeini, *Hokumat-i Islami (Islamic Government)* (Najaf, 1391/1971); and, for the English translation, Ruhullah Khomeini, "Islamic Government," in *Islam and Revolution*, transl. and annot. Algar, 25–166.

217 Yann Richard, "Ayatollah Kashani: Precursor of the Islamic Republic?," in Nikki R. Keddie (ed.), *Religion and Politics in Iran: Shi'ism from Quietism to Revolution* (New Haven, CT, 1983), 101–124, 107–108.

218 Shahrough Akhavi, *Religion and Politics in Contemporary Iran: Clergy-State Relations in the Pahlavi Period* (Albany, 1980), 60–90; Azar Tabari, "The Role of the Clergy in Modern Iranian Politics," in Keddie (ed.), *Religion and Politics in Iran*, 47–72, 59–64; and Majid Yazdi, "Patterns of Clerical Political Behavior in Postwar Iran, 1941–53," *Middle Eastern Studies* 26, 3 (1990), 281–307, 285–288.

219 Ali Davani, *Ayatollah Burujirdi* (Tehran, 1371/1992).

220 Nakash, *The Shi'is of Iraq*, 127 and 133.

221 Foreign Office, Report ("Activities of the Mufti"), 18 January 1940, London, NA, KV 2/2085.

222 Foreign Office, Report ("The Mufti's Activities"), 21 February 1940, London, NA, KV 2/2085.

223 Schwendemann (Embassy Paris) to Foreign Office, 27 April 1942, Paris, PA, R 29533.

224 Sultan bin Muhammad al-Qasimi, *My Early Life* (London, 2011), 10–11.

225 Nordbruch, *Nazism in Syria and Lebanon*, 120–122. Popular reformist groups like the Syrian Muslim Brotherhood tended to remain generally opposed to both Vichy and

Free French imperial rule, see Johannes Reissner, *Ideologie und Politik der Muslim-brüder Syriens* (Freiburg, 1980).

226 Anwar el-Sadat, *In Search of Identity* (London, 1978), 31 and 32, these passages were also reprinted in Anwar el-Sadat, "Rommel at El-Alamain: An Egyptian View (1942)," in Bernard Lewis (ed.), *A Middle East Mosaic: Fragments of Life, Letters and History* (New York, 2000), 314–316, 314, and 315.

227 Lampson to Foreign Office, 7 April 1941, Cairo, NA, FO 371/27429; and, similarly, Lampson to Foreign Office, 12 April 1941, Cairo, NA, FO 371/27429; and, a few months later, Lampson to Foreign Office, 7 July 1941, Cairo, NA, FO 371/27431.

228 Rühle, Internal Note ("Aufzeichnung betr. die Rundfunkpropaganda in dem arabischen Raum"), 5 May 1941, Berlin, PA, R 67482.

229 Charles D. Smith, "4 February 1942: Its Causes and Its Influence on Egyptian Politics and on the Future of Anglo-Egyptian Relations, 1937–45," *International Journal of Middle East Studies* 10, 4 (1979), 453–479, esp., on the pro-German protests, 468.

230 *The Killearn Diaries 1934–1946*, ed. Trefor E. Evans (London, 1972), 197–201 (1 February 1942) and 206–217 (4 February 1942), and, on the "Long live Rommel" slogan, 209. Lampson recalled these chants also months later in a government report, see Lampson to Foreign Office, 28 June 1942, Cairo, NA, FO 371/31573. Schwendemann to Foreign Office, 27 April 1942, Paris, PA, R 29533, reported "Heil Rommel" chants.

231 Lampson to Foreign Office, 28 June 1942, Cairo, NA, FO 371/31573.

232 Lampson to Foreign Office, 29 June 1942, Cairo, NA, FO 371/31573.

233 Lampson to Foreign Office, 4 July 1942, Cairo, NA, FO 371/31573.

234 Lampson to Foreign Office, 11 July 1942, Cairo, NA, FO 371/31573.

235 Lampson to Foreign Office, 1 February 1943, Cairo, NA, FO 371/35528.

236 Jakob Skovgaard-Petersen, *Defining Islam for the Egyptian State: Muftis and Fatwas of the Dār Al-Iftā* (Leiden, 1997), 159–170.

237 Francine Costet-Tardieu, *Un réformiste à l'Université al-Azhar: Œuvre et pensée de Mustafâ al-Marâghi (1881–1945)* (Paris, 2005), 169–175; and, for al-Maraghi's leadership of *al-Azhar*, Rainer Brunner, "Education, Politics, and the Struggle for Intellectual Leadership: Al-Azhar between 1927 and 1945," in Meir Hatina (ed.), *Guardians of Faith in Modern Times: "Ulama" in the Middle East* (Leiden, 2009), 109–140, 116–124, and 131–137.

238 List of Personalities in Egypt, 1941, Cairo, enclosed to Lampson to Eden (Foreign Office), 22 July 1941, Cairo, NA, FO 371/27431. A revised version of this report is List of Personalities in Egypt, 1943, Cairo, enclosed in Lampson to Eden, 5 January 1943, Cairo, NA, FO 371/35528.

239 Richard Capell, "Egypt Has Her Ambitions in the Post-War World," *Daily Telegraph* (3 February 1944).

240 The role of the Muslim Brotherhood in the Second World War is discussed by Mitchell, *The Society of the Muslim Brothers*, 19–34; Lia, *The Society of the Muslim Brothers in Egypt*, 256–269; and, on al-Banna specifically, Krämer, *Hasan al-Banna*, 61–65.

241 On German financial assistance to the Muslim Brotherhood before the war, see the British Military Intelligence's notes: Internal Note ("Note on Wilhelm Stell-bogen"), 23 October 1939, n.p., NA, WO 208/502; Internal Note ("Correspondence

and Notes of Mr. Wilhelm Stellbogen"), n.d. (1939), n.p., NA, WO 208/502; and Internal Note ("Found among Stellbogen's Papers"), n.d. (1939), n.p., NA, WO 208/502; and also GHQ Middle East Forces, Report ("The Ikhwan al Muslimin Reconsidered"), 10 December 1942, Cairo, NA, FO 141/838. This assistance is also mentioned in the literature, see Lia, *The Society of the Muslim Brothers in Egypt*, 179–180; and Krämer, *Hasan al-Banna*, 62–63.

242 Naldrett-Jays (Alexandria City Police), Intelligence Note ("Pro-Axis Propaganda"), 31 October 1942, Alexandria, NA, FO 141/838.

243 GHQ Middle East Forces, Report ("The Ikhwan al Muslimin Reconsidered"), 10 December 1942, Cairo, NA, FO 141/838.

244 Ibid.

245 Political Intelligence Centre, Middle East (PICME), Report ("The Ikhwan El Muslimeen"), 25 February 1944, Cairo, NA, WO 201/2647 (also in NA, FO 371/41329).

246 Neurath to Foreign Office, 1 June 1941, n.p., PA, R 60747; and, for the offensive in 1942, Neurath to Foreign Office, 3 April 1942, n.p., PA, R 60747, on the positive responses; but Neurath to Foreign Office, 14 October 1941, n.p., PA, R 60747; Hermann, Report ("Reiseeindruecke in Libyen Oktober 1941"), 14 October 1941, n.p., PA, R 60747; and, for the offensive in 1942, Neurath to Foreign Office, 21 March 1942, n.p., PA, R 60747, on mixed responses and hostility.

247 Claudio G. Segrè, *Fourth Shore: The Italian Colonization of Libya* (Chicago, 1974); and on Italian atrocities in wartime Libya, Patrick Bernhard, "Behind the Battle Lines: Italian Atrocities and the Persecution of Arabs, Berbers, and Jews in North Africa during World War II," *Holocaust and Genocide Studies* 26, 3 (2012), 425–446.

248 On British-Sanusi relations, see Saul Kelly, *War and Politics in the Desert: Britain and Libya during the Second World War* (London, 2010); and, with a focus on British debates about the role of Islam and politics, Todd M. Thompson, "Covert Operations, British Views of Islam and Anglo-Sanusi Relations in North Africa, 1940–45," *Journal of Imperial and Commonwealth History* 37, 2 (2009), 293–323.

249 Broadcast Monitoring Script, "Voice of Free Arabism: The Mufti of Tripoli," 14 February 1943 (recorded), USNA, RG 84, Entry UD 2410, Box 93.

250 Hayyim J. Cohen, "The Anti-Jewish Farhūd in Baghdad, 1941," *Middle Eastern Studies* 3, 1 (1996), 2–17.

251 Michel Abitbol, *The Jews of North Africa during the Second World War* (Detroit, 1989); Michael M. Laskier, *North African Jewry in the Twentieth Century: The Jews of Morocco, Tunisia and Algeria* (New York, 1994), 55–83; and Satloff, *Among the Righteous*, provide overviews of the fate of Jews in North Africa during the Second World War. Klaus-Michael Mallmann and Martin Cüppers, *Nazi Palestine: The Plans for the Extermination of the Jews in Palestine* (New York, 2010), gives insights into German plans for the murder of the Jews in North Africa and the Middle East.

252 Robert Assaraf, *Mohammed V et les Juifs du Maroc à l'époque de Vichy* (Paris, 1997).

253 Yves C. Aouate, "Les Algériens musulmans et les mesures antijuives du gouvernement de Vichy (1940–1942)," *Pardès* 16 (1992), 189–202, esp. 195–198; and, more generally, Henri Msellati, *Le Juifs d'Algérie sous le régime de Vichy* (Paris, 1999).

254 Jacques Sabille, *Les Juifs de Tunisie sous Vichy et l'occupation* (Paris, 1954); and Claude Nataf, "Les Juifs de Tunisie face à Vichy et aux persécutions allemandes," *Pardès* 16 (1992), 203–231.

255 Renzo de Felice, *Jews in an Arab Land: Libya, 1835–1970* (Austin, TX, 1985), 168–184; and Rachel Simon, "It Could Have Happened There: The Jews of Libya during the Second World War," *African Journal* 16 (1994), 391–422; and, with a focus on the riots of 1945, Harvey E. Goldberg, *Jewish Life in Muslim Libya: Rivals and Relatives* (Chicago, 1990), 97–122.

256 Gudrun Krämer, *The Jews in Modern Egypt, 1914–1952* (London, 1989), 154–166.

257 There is no comprehensive study on Muslims in the British army during the Second World War. On the British Indian Army, see Philip Mason, *A Matter of Honour: An Account of the Indian Army: Its Officers and Men* (London, 1974), 471–527; and the contributions in Alan Jeffreys and Patrick Rose (eds.), *The Indian Army, 1939–47: Experience and Development* (Farnham, VT, 2012). On the Arab Legion, see Godfrey Lias, *Glubb's Legion* (London, 1956); and, for accounts by a British officer of the unit, James Lunt, *Glubb Pasha: A Biography* (London, 1984); and James Lunt, *The Arab Legion* (London, 1999); and, for the memoirs of its commander, John Bagot Glubb, *The Story of the Arab Legion* (London, 1948); and John Bagot Glubb, *A Soldier with the Arabs* (London, 1959).

258 The history of Muslim soldiers in the French army during the Second World War is well researched, see Recham, "Les Musulmans dans l'armée française," 748–753, esp., on the Free French Forces, 750–751; and, focusing on Algerian soldiers, Recham, *Les Musulmans algériens dans l'armée française*, 175–274, esp., on the Free French Forces, 229–274; and, on Moroccan soldiers, Moshe Gershovich, "Scherifenstern und Hakenkreuz: Marokkanische Soldaten im Zweiten Weltkrieg," in Höpp, Wien, and Wildangel (eds.), *Blind für die Geschichte*, 335–364.

259 Crabitès, "Britain's Debt to King Farouk," 860.

260 Anonymous, "Die arabische Welt sammelt ihre Kräfte: Strömungen und Gegenströmungen im ersten Kriegsjahr," *Frankfurter Zeitung* (25 May 1941).

261 Leeper (Foreign Office), Minutes, 6 January 1939, London, NA, FO 395/650, on a first meeting of officials from the Foreign Office, Indian Office, Colonial Office, War Office, BBC, and British Council to discuss propaganda on the question "What Britain has done for Islam." One of the first general memoranda on the issue of Islamic propaganda, discussing key issues like British imperialism in Islamic territories, the Palestine question, the Christian missionary enterprise, and the caliphate question with regard to a future war, was drawn up in the Ministry of Information, see Gibb (Ministry of Information), Memorandum ("The General Principles of Publicity among Moslems"), 16 August 1939, London, NA, INF 1/407.

262 Nevill Barbour, "Broadcasting to the Arab World: Arabic Transmissions from the B.B.C. and other Non-Arab Stations," *Middle East Journal* 5, 1 (1951), 57–69. A comparative perspective on all the foreign propaganda broadcast stations that sent programs to the Middle East is provided by Seth Arsenian, "Wartime Propaganda in the Middle East," *Middle East Journal* 2, 4 (1948), 417–429.

263 Perowne (BBC) to Bigg (Colonial Office), 13 July 1939, London, NA, CO 323/1651/9.

264 Perowne to Bowen (Foreign Office), 16 May 1939, London, NA, FO 395/664. On the consultations between Whitehall and the embassy in Egypt about Qur'an readings, see the documents in NA, FO 395/663 and NA, FO 395/664.

265 Gary Leiser, "Bombs and Leaflets: Allied Propaganda and the Tunisians during the Winter Campaign of 1942–43," *Maghreb Review* 19, 3–4 (1994), 284–318, which includes a number of religiously charged pamphlets distributed by Anglo-American forces in Axis-occupied Tunisia, 295–314; and Richard Pennell, "Propaganda and its Target: The Venom Campaign in Tangier during World War II," in Driss Maghraoui (ed.), *Revisiting the Colonial Past in Morocco* (London, 2013), 157–183.

266 Pamphlet "By Order of Hitler the Khanzir Mosques Are Bombed" (English translation), n.d. (1941), NA, HS 6/945; and, for the Arabic original, Pamphlet "Hitlir al-khinzir a'ta al-aydin li-tiyarat mata'ahu bash al-wahu al-bumb 'ala al-juwama'" ("The Pig Hitler Ordered Planes to Drop Bombs on the Mosques"), n.d. (1941), NA, HS 6/945. The number of the referred verse varies in different Qu'ran editions. It is verse 114 according to the verse enumeration of the Cairo edition and verse 108 according to the enumeration of the Gustav Flügel edition.

267 Pamphlet "Truth" (English translation), n.d. (1941), NA, HS 6/945; and, for the Arabic original, Pamphlet "Al-haqq" ("Truth"), n.d. (1941), NA, HS 6/945; the file also contains documentation from 11 November 1941 that 4,000 copies of the pamphlets in Maghribi Arabic were sent to North Africa.

268 Pamphlet, "Lies, Lies, Nothing but Lies" (English translation), n.d. (1942), NA, FO 898/128; and, for the Arabic original, Pamphlet "Al-kdub, al-kdub u ma kayn ghayr al-kdub" ("Lies, Lies and Nothing but Lies"), n.d. (1942), NA, FO 898/128.

269 Abulafia (Political Warfare Executive), Internal Note, 25 August 1942, London, NA, FO 898/128.

270 Ibid.

271 Pamphlet "Ten of the Reasons Why Great Britain Will Win this War" (English translation), n.d. (1941), NA, HS 6/945; and, for the Arabic original, Pamphlet "Eshra al-hajat 'lash al-ingliz u-ashabu arjuhu al-harb" ("Ten Reasons why the English and their Friends are winning the War"), n.d. (1941), NA, HS 6/945; the file also contains documentation from 8 September 1941 and 16 October 1941 that 2000 copies of the pamphlet in Maghribi Arabic and 1,000 in Hebrew Arabic were sent to North Africa.

272 Brochure "Satwa quwwat britaniya al-musallaha" ("The Strength of Britain's Armed Forces"), n.d. (1942), NA, FO 898/128.

273 Postcard "Bi-l-munasaba d-l-khul d-shehr d-ramadhan" ("On the Occasion of the exalted, blessed, and happy Month of Ramadan"), n.d. (1941), NA, HS 6/945; the file also contains documentation from 8 September 1941, 11 September 1941, 15 September 1941, and 22 September 1941 that 3,000 copies in standard Arabic and 5,000 copies in Maghribi Arabic were sent to North Africa.

274 Pamphlet "On the occasion of the glorious month of Ramadan" (English translation), n.d. (1942), NA, FO 898/128; and, for the Arabic original, Pamphlet "Bi-l-munasaba d-shehr d-ramadhan" ("On the Occasion of the blessed and joyous Month of Ramadan"), n.d. (1942), NA, FO 898/128.

275 John P. Slight, "The British Empire and the Hajj, 1865–1956" (Ph.D. diss., University of Cambridge, 2011), 213–215.

276 Postcard "Friendship for the Arabs" (English translation), n.d. (1941), NA, HS 6/945; and, for the Arabic original, Propaganda Postcard "Quwwa Inglitir fi-l-bahr" ("The Power of England at Sea"), n.d. (1941), NA, HS 6/945; the file also contains documentation from 6 December 1941 about the shipment of 3,700 pilgrimage postcards to North Africa.

277 Pamphlet "London Mosque and Mecca" (English translation), n.d. (1942), NA, FO 898/128; and, for the Arabic original, Pamphlet "Al-bawabir ingliz hamlu al-muminin li-l-hajj" ("English Ships Carried the Believers to the Hajj"), n.d. (1942), NA, FO 898/128.

278 Hajj Souvenir Brochure, 1942, NA, CO 732/87/18; and, for information on the brochure, see Government of Palestine, Report ("Hajj Souvenir Brochure"), December 1942, Jerusalem, NA, CO 732/87/18.

279 Pamphlet "China" (English translation), n.d. (1942), NA, FO 898/128; and, for the Arabic original, Pamphlet "Bilad al-sin" ("China"), n.d. (1942), NA, FO 898/128.

280 Nöhring to Foreign Office, 6 May 1942, Tangier, PA, R 60660, which had attached a summary of *Akhbar al-'Usbua* 1 (1 May 1942); and, similarly, Nöhring to Foreign Office, 8 May 1942, Tangier, PA, R 60660.

281 Vycichl, Internal Note ("Die englische Druckschriftenpropaganda in den islamischen Ländern"), 3 October 1942, Paris, PA, Paris 1116C.

282 Vycichl, Internal Note ("Die englische Druckschriftenpropaganda in den islamischen Ländern"), 3 October 1942, Paris, PA, Paris 1116C, forwarding samples of these Arabic pamphlets, among them those mentioned in notes 272 and 277 and the quoted Pamphlet "Al-amir 'Abd Allah malik sharq al-'urdun" ("The Amir 'Abd Allah King of Transjordan"). The same materials had also been assessed on the ground by Pörzgen, Report ("Tanger: Propagandazelle für Nordafrika"), n.d. (August 1942), Tangier, PA, R 60690, and were later discussed more thoroughly in the Foreign Office by Winkler, Internal Note ("Feindliche Drucksachen-Propaganda in Nord-Afrika"), 23 February 1943, Berlin, R 60660.

283 MacMichael to Colonial Office, 28 January 1942, Palestine, NA, CO 733/439/12.

284 MacMichael to Colonial Office, 8 September 1942, Palestine, NA, CO 733/439/12.

285 MacMichael to Colonial Office, 1 October 1942, Palestine, NA, CO 733/439/12.

286 MacMichael to Colonial Office, 13 March 1942, Palestine, NA, CO 733/439/12.

287 Film "Courban Bairam Celebration in Benghazi," 19 November 1942, Archive of the Imperial War Museum, London (IWM), Reel AYY 286/5–1; it should be noted that the sequence, although catalogued, has been cut and is not on the reel anymore. Also, the month indicated in this source is incorrect—the '*Id al-Adha* was a month later.

288 US Intelligence (USAFIME) Report ("Annex no. 3 to Report no. 5"), 19 December 1942, New York, USNA, RG 84, Entry UD 2412, Box 5.

289 Peel (India Office) to Baggallay (Foreign Office), 26 July 1940, London, NA, FO 371/24549, on the suggestion and reservations within the India Office; and both Foreign Office, Internal Discussion Sheet, 30 June–1 July 1940, London, NA, FO 371/24549; and Baggallay to Peel, 1 August 1940, London, NA, FO 371/24549, on reservations within the Foreign Office that the conference would turn into an anti-British event.

290 The text is stored in the Donovan Operation Torch files, US Army War College, Fort Carlisle, Carlisle, PA, quoted in Anthony C. Brown, *Oil, God, and Gold: The Story of Aramco and the Saudi Kings* (Boston, 1999), 104–105.

291 Hudson (Office of War Information at Beirut Mission) to Office of War Information, 5 September 1943, Beirut, USNA, RG 208, Entry 362, Box 133.

292 Badeau (Office of War Information), Internal Note ("Comments on Lt. Siblini's proposed memo of September 28th"), 30 September 1943, Washington, USNA, RG 208, Entry 387, Box 614

293 Office of War Information, Internal Note ("Weekly Program near East Station for Arabic Broadcast from Sunday 6th February 1944 to Saturday 12th"), USNA, RG 208, Entry 387, Box 641.

294 On German racism as a theme in British and American propaganda, see, for instance, Winkler, Internal Note ("Erfahrungen aus der deutschen Propagandaarbeit in Iran vom November 1939 bis September 1941"), 10 January 1942, Berlin, PA, R 60690; for US propaganda in Arabic, which drew on both Nazi hostility toward religion and German racism, see, for instance, Index of Press and Pamphlet Material, prepared by the Office of the Press Attaché, British Legation, Beirut, November 1942, USNA, RG 208, Entry 387, Box 625; another good example is the US propaganda cartoon "The Giha Plan," n.d. (1942/3), USNA, RG 208, Entry 373, Box 426 (also in USNA, RG 208, Entry 387, Box 621); and George Britt, Memo (with attachment of anti-Axis propaganda cartoon poster), 12 August 1943, Beirut, USNA, RG 208, Entry 387, Box 622.

295 Driss Maghraoui, "'Den Marokkanern den Krieg verkaufen': Französische Anti-Nazi Propaganda während des Zweiten Weltkrieges," in Höpp, Wien, and Wildangel (eds.), *Blind für die Geschichte*, 191–213.

296 E. Rubin, *Le racisme et l'Islam* (Paris, 1939), which contains cartoons, including one of Hitler stepping with his boot on books titled "Islam" and "Qur'an." Its author also approached the British authorities about distribution in the wider Middle East, see Rubin to Vansittart (10 Downing Street), 27 July 1939, Paris, NA, FO 395/651; Rubin to Ridgeway (Colonial Office), 27 July 1939, Paris, NA, FO 395/651; and Rubin to British Foreign Office, 30 July 1939, Paris, NA, FO 395/651. The British Foreign Office was very interested and contacted the British embassy in Paris about the booklet, asking the officials there to consult the Quai d'Orsay or the French Ministry of the Colonies about the booklet and the possibility of having a copy in standard Arabic (rather than in North African Arabic), see Warner (Foreign Office) to Wright (Embassy Paris), 4 August 1939, London, NA, FO 395/651.

297 Maurice Muret, "Le monde musulman pour la France," *Gazette de Lausanne* (30 April 1940), which refers to a *Mawlid* celebration in Beirut attended by Maxime Weygand; and Anonymous, "Les grandioses fêtes du 'Mouloud' ont eu lieu à Fez malgré les assertions de la propaganda nazie," *Le Petit Marseillais* (5 May 1940), which includes photographs of *Mawlid* celebrations in French North Africa.

298 Charles de Gaulle, *Lettres, notes et carnets, Juillet 1941–Mai 1943* (Paris, 1982), 499–500.

299 Yaacov Ro'i, *Islam in the Soviet Union: From the Second World War to Gorbachev* (New York, 2000), 113–114, and, on the extensive Soviet efforts to win over Shi'a clerics in Iran, Lenczowski, *Russia and the West in Iran*, 213–215.

300 Broadcast Monitoring Script "Voice of Free Arabism: Kill the Jews before They Kill You," 7 July 1942 (recorded), USNA, RG 84, Entry UD 2410, Box 77.

301 Broadcast Monitoring Script "Berlin in Arabic: Talk: The B.B.C. and the Qoran," 5 August 1944 (recorded), USNA, RG 84, Entry UD 2410, Box 112.

302 Ibid.

303 The German occupation of Tunisia has been researched in depth. Among the most notable studies are Waldis Greiselis, *Das Ringen um den Brückenkopf Tunesien 1942/43: Strategie der "Achse" und Innenpolitik im Protektorat* (Bern, 1976), which provides the most comprehensive account. Other notable studies are Rachid Driss, "La Tunisie sous l'Occupation allemande Novembre 1942–Mai 1943," *Les Cahiers de Tunisie* 27, 109–110 (1979), 455–485; S. El Mechat, "La Tunisie pendant la Deuxième Guerre mondiale (1939–1944)," *Revue d'Histoire Maghrebine* 11, 33–34 (1984), 64–84; and Annie Rey-Goldzeiguer, "L'occupation germano-italienne de la Tunisie: Un tournant dans la vie politique tunisienne," in Charles-Robert Ageron, *Les chemins de la décolonisation de l'empire colonial français, 1936–1956* (Paris, 1986), 325–340.

304 *Der Islam*, Tornisterschrift des Oberkommandos der Wehrmacht (Ernst Rodenwaldt), Heft 52 (1941); the brochure is stored in BA–MA, RH 53–18/292. Olzscha, Report, 1945, n.p., BStU, MfS, HA IX/11, ZR 920, A. 54, also provides some information on the booklet. On the cultural training and ideological indoctrination of German Wehrmacht troops more generally, see Frank Vossler, *Propaganda in die eigene Truppe: Die Truppenbetreuung in der Wehrmacht 1939–1945* (Paderborn, 2005).

305 *Der Islam*, Tornisterschrift des Oberkommandos der Wehrmacht (Ernst Rodenwaldt), Heft 52 (1941), 5.

306 Ibid.

307 Ibid.

308 Ibid., 63–64.

309 Ibid., 6.

310 Ibid.

311 Ibid.

312 Ibid., 63 (point 3).

313 Ibid. (point 9).

314 Ibid.

315 Ibid., 45.

316 Ibid., 64 (point 10).

317 Ibid. (point 12).

318 For a contemporary assessment of the problem, see the essays in C. Christine Fair and Sumit Ganguly (eds.), *Treading on Hallowed Ground: Counterinsurgency Operations in Sacred Spaces* (Oxford, 2008).

319 *Der Islam*, Tornisterschrift des Oberkommandos der Wehrmacht (Ernst Rodenwaldt), Heft 52 (1941), 63 (point 5).

320 Ibid. (point 6).

321 Ibid., 64 (point 16).

322 Ibid., 63 (point 4).

323 Ibid., 52–54.

324 Ibid., 64 (point 19).

325 Ibid., 47.

326 Ibid., 51 and, on gender generally, 47–52.

327 Ibid., 64 (points 14 and 15).

328 Richard J. Evans, *The Third Reich at War* (London, 2008), 477–478 and 745; and, more detailed, Frank Snowden, "Latina Province 1944–1950," *Journal of Contemporary History* 43, 3 (2008), 509–526.

329 *Der Islam*, Tornisterschrift des Oberkommandos der Wehrmacht (Ernst Rodenwaldt), Heft 52 (1941), 65; the bibliography of five works included Martin Hartmann, *Der Islam* (Leipzig, 1909); Th. W. Juynboll, *Handbuch des islamischen Gesetzes* (Leipzig, 1910); C. Snouck Hurgronje, *Mekka* (The Hague, 1888–1889); Ignaz Goldziher, *Muhammedanische Studien* (Halle an der Saale, 1889–1890); and Traugott Mann, *Der Islam einst und jetzt* (Leipzig, 1914).

330 *Tunis*, ed. Deutschen Gesellschaft für Wehrpolitik und Wehrwissenschaften (Glahn), February 1939, BA–MA, RH 53–18/292.

331 Anonymous, "Muhammed und der Islam I" (15 July 1941), in *Handbuch der Wehrbetreuung*, ed. Luftfahrtführungsstab, 8 vols. (Stuttgart, 1939–1942), vol. 3a, 1–11; and Anonymous, "Muhammed und der Islam II" (15 August 1941), in *Handbuch der Wehrbetreuung*, ed. Luftfahrtführungsstab, vol. 3a, 13–33.

332 On the *Oase*, see Fischer (*Panzer-Propaganda-Kompanie*), Report ("Tätigkeitsbericht über die geistige Betreuung der Truppe durch die P. K. Afrika im Monat Mai 1942"), 19 September 1942, n.p., BA–MA, RH 19VIII/78; and Fischer, Report ("Tätigkeitsbericht über die geistige Betreuung der Truppe durch die Propaganda-Kompanie Afrika für den Monat April 1942"), 1 May 1942, n.p., BA–MA, RH 19VIII/78. On the *Karawane*, see Mähnert, Report, n.d. (December 1942), n.p. (Tunis), PA, R 60660. Examples for instruction leaflets, which demand respect of Islamic customs and conventions, are the Wehrmacht's Instructions ("Merkblatt über das Verhalten gegenüber der nordafrikanischen Bevölkerung"), n.d., BA–MA, RH 21-5/27; and, for Tunisia, the Wehrmacht's Instructions ("Merkblatt für die deutschen Soldaten in Französisch Nordafrika"), n.d., BA–MA, RH 21-5/26.

333 Cremeans (Joint Intelligence Collection Agency Algiers), Report ("Summary of General Conditions in Tunisia"), 27 December 1944, Algiers, USNA RG 226, Entry 16, Box 1258.

334 Grobba, Internal Note ("38. Sitzung, Arabien-Komitee"), 3 December 1942, Berlin, PA, R 27327.

335 Jodel, Instructions ("Richtlinien für die inhaltliche Gestaltung der Aktivpropaganda in die feindliche Truppe und in die Bevölkerung der besetzten Gebiete des französisch-nordafrikanischen Raumes"), n.d., n.p., PA, R 60660; these instructions were part of the general guidelines for the organization of propaganda in Tunis, see Jodel, Order ("Weisung für die Handhabung der Propaganda im französisch-nordafrikanischen Raum"), 20 November 1942, Berlin, PA, R 60660.

336 US Military Intelligence Division, Report ("North Africa"), 26 August 1943, Regional File of the US War Department/Military Intelligence Division (MID), 1918–1945, USNA, accessed through USHMA, RG 6, Reel 15.

337 *A Pocket Guide to North Africa*, ed. War and Navy Department (Washington, DC, 1942), quoted in Michael B. Oren, *Power, Faith and Fantasy: America in the Middle*

East: 1776 to the Present (New York, 2007), 446–447. Anonymous, "U.S. Troops Learn Moslem Manners," *Moslem World* 32, 2 (1943), 150–151, provides a contemporary press report on these measures.

338 Bassewitz (Army), Report ("Bericht über meine Reise zur Oase Siwa vom 9.–20.8.42"), 22 August 1942, n.p., PA, R 60748, gives examples of such contacts with local religious authorities.

339 Rahn to Foreign Office, 9 April 1943, Tunis, PA, R 27767.

340 The mufti offered his services to the Wehrmacht, see Canaris, Internal Note, 9 December 1942, Berlin, PA, R 27332; and to the Foreign Office, see Weizsäcker, Internal Notes, 10 December 1942, Berlin, PA, R 261124. Documents on the discussions about the proposal can be found in various files, most importantly in PA, R 27332, R 27766, and R 27767. At a meeting between Germans and Italians in Rome in early 1943 it was decided to postpone the mufti's tour until the military situation was stabilized, see Mackensen to Foreign Office, 2 January 1943, Rome, PA, R 27771.

341 Rahn, Report ("Besuch beim Bey von Tunis"), 19 December 1942, Tunis, BA–MA, RH 19VIII/359.

342 Rahn to Foreign Office, 22 December 1942, Tunis, PA, R 27766.

343 B. Wundshammer, "Empfang bei Seiner Kgl. Hoheit," *Signal* (March 1943, 2nd issue), 15, which includes photographs of the visit.

344 Wied (Embassy Stockholm) to Foreign Office, 11 September 1941, Stockholm, PA, R 29533. Apparently, at the same time, the Egyptian government sent out similar memoranda to the governments of Muslim countries, asking them to complain to the Germans, see Pilger to Foreign Office, 16 September 1941, Kabul, PA, R 29534.

345 Woermann, Internal Note, 18 September 1941, Berlin, PA, R 29533.

346 Woermann to Embassy Stockholm, 18 September 1941, Berlin, PA, R 29533.

347 Neurath to Foreign Office, 14 October 1941, n.p., PA, R 60747; and, for the second quotation, Hermann, Report ("Reiseeindruecke in Libyen Oktober 1941"), 14 October 1941, n.p., PA, R 60747.

348 Biyoud, Memorandum ("Denkschrift zur deutschen Nordafrikapropaganda, insbesondere in den Kriegsgefangenenlagern"), n.d. (March 1942), n.p., BA–MA, RH 2/1765.

349 Ibid.

350 Bürkner, Report ("Behandlung der Araberfragen und Vorschläge von arabischer Seite"), 13 March 1942, Berlin, BA–MA, RH 2/1765.

351 Christian Koller, *"Von Wilden aller Rassen niedergemetzelt": Die Diskussion um die Verwendung von Kolonialtruppen in Europa zwischen Rassismus, Kolonial- und Militärpolitik (1914–1930)* (Stuttgart, 2001); and Jean-Yves Le Naour, *La honte noir: L'Allemagne et les troupes coloniales françaises, 1914–1945* (Paris, 2003). Gisela Lebzelter, "Die 'Schwarze Schmach': Vorurteile, Propaganda, Mythos," *Geschichte und Gesellschaft* 11, 1 (1985), 37–58, provides a concise account.

352 Klaus Mann, *The Turning Point: Thirty-Five Years in This Century* (London, 1944), 58–59.

353 On negative stereotypes of North African colonial soldiers in German propaganda during the war against France in 1940, see Koller, *"Von Wilden aller Rassen niedergemetzelt,"* 350–361; Naour, *La honte noir,* 236–244; and Wagenhofer, *"Rassischer" Feind—politischer Freund?,* 21–24 and 43–61.

4. ISLAM AND THE WAR ON THE EASTERN FRONT

1   Recalled by Alexander Werth, *Russia at War, 1941–1945* (London, 1964), 573.

2   On tsarist policies toward Islam, see the general studies by Crews, *For Prophet and Tsar,* and the overviews by Muhammad M. A. Khan, "Islam under the Tsars and the October 1917 Revolution," *Journal of Muslim Minority Affairs* 12, 1 (1991), 23–40; Elena I. Campbell, "The Autocracy and the Muslim Clergy in the Russian Empire (1850s–1917)," *Russian Studies in History* 44, 2 (2005), 8–29; and Vladimir Bobrovnikov, "Islam in the Russian Empire," in Dominic Lieven (ed.), *The Cambridge History of Russia,* vol. 2 (*Imperial Russia, 1689–1917*) (Cambridge, 2006), 202–223; on the Caucasus, see Firouzeh Mostashari, *On the Religious Frontier: Tsarist Russia and Islam in the Caucasus* (London, 2006); and Austin Jersild, *Orientalism and Empire: North Caucasus Mountain Peoples and the Georgian Frontier, 1845–1917* (London, 2006); on the Crimea, see Kelly O'Neill, "Between Subversion and Submission: The Integration of the Crimean Khanate into the Russian Empire, 1783–1853" (PhD diss., Harvard University, 2006); and Kelly O'Neill, "Constructing Russian Identity in the Imperial Borderland: Architecture, Islam, and the Transformation of the Crimean Landscape," *Ab Imperio* 2 (2006), 163–192; and, on Central Asia, see Allen J. Frank, *Muslim Religious Institutions in Imperial Russia: The Islamic World of Novouzensk District and the Kazakh Inner Horde, 1780–1910* (Leiden, 2001); and A. S. Morrison, *Russian Rule in Samarkand 1868–1910: A Comparison with British India* (Oxford, 2008), esp. 51–87; see also the contributions in Kemper et al. (eds.), *Muslim Culture in Russia and Central Asia from the 18th to the Early 20th Centuries.*

3   On Muslim resistance to tsarist Russia in the Caucasus, see Moshe Gammer, *Muslim Resistance to the Tsar: Shamil and the Conquest of Chechnia and Daghestan* (London, 1994); Anna Zelkina, *In Quest of God and Freedom: Sufi Responses to the Russian Advance in the North Caucasus* (London, 2000); Michael Kemper, *Herrschaft, Recht und Islam in Daghestan: Von den Khanaten und Gemeindebünden zum ğihād-Staat* (Wiesbaden, 2005); and Clemens P. Sidorko, *Dschihad im Kaukasus: Antikolonialer Widerstand der Dagestaner und Tschetschenen gegen das Zarenreich (18. Jahrhundert bis 1859)* (Wiesbaden, 2007).

4   On Soviet policies toward Islam in the interwar period, see the overviews by Galina M. Yemelianova, *Russia and Islam: A Historical Survey* (New York, 2002), 99–120; and Alexandre Bennigsen and Chantal Lemercier-Quelquejay, *Islam in the Soviet Union* (London, 1967), 19–163; the general works on religion in the Soviet Union by Walter Kolarz, *Russia and Her Colonies* (London, 1952), 186–188; Walter Kolarz, *Religion in the Soviet Union* (London, 1961), 406–425; and Hans Bräker, *Kommunismus und Weltreligonen Asiens: Zur Religions- und Asienpolitik der Sowjetunion,* vol. 1 (*Kommunismus und Islam: Religionsdiskussion und Islam in der Sowjetunion*) (Tübingen, 1969), 91–121; and the more specific studies by Fanny Bryan, "Anti-Islamic Propaganda: Bezbozhnik, 1925–1935," *Central Asian Survey* 5, 2 (1986), 29–47; Michael Kemper, "The Soviet Discourse on the Origin and Class Character of Islam, 1923–1933," *Die Welt des Islams* 49, 1 (2009), 1–48; and the contributors to Kemper et al. (eds.), *Muslim Culture in Russia and Central Asia from the 18th to the Early 20th Centuries.* On the moderate period and attempts to create a "Soviet Islam," see Alexandre Bennigsen

and S. Enders Wimbush, *Muslim National Communism in the Soviet Union: A Revolutionary Strategy for the Colonial World* (Chicago, 1979); Alexandre Bennigsen and Chantal Lemercier-Quelquejay, *Sultan Galiev: Le père de la revolution Tier-Mondiste* (Paris, 1986); Sh. F. Mukhamedyarov and B. F. Sultanbekov, "Mirsaid Sultan-Galiev: His Character and Fate," *Central Asian Survey* 9, 2 (1990), 109–117; and Gabriele Bucher-Dinç, *Die mittlere Wolga im Widerstreit sowjetischer und nationaler Ideologien (1917–1920): Eine Untersuchung anhand autobiographischer und publizistischer Schriften des Wolgatataren Mirsaid Sultan-Galiev* (Wiesbaden, 1997). On Soviet interwar policies toward Islam in the Crimea, see Alan Fisher, *The Crimean Tatars* (Stanford, CA, 1978), 130–149; and Brian G. Williams, *The Crimean Tatars: The Diaspora Experience and the Forging of a Nation* (Leiden, 2001), 356 and 359–360. On Soviet interwar policies toward Islam in the Caucasus, see Robert Conquest, *The Great Terror: Stalin's Purge of the Thirties* (New York, 1968), 300; Robert Conquest, *The Nation Killers: The Soviet Deportation of Nationalities* (London, 1970), 38 and 98; Chantal Lemercier-Quelquejay, "Sufi Brotherhoods in the USSR: A Historical Survey," *Central Asian Survey* 2, 4 (1983), 1–35, 14–16; Alexandre Bennigsen, "Muslim Guerilla Warfare in the Caucasus (1918–1928)," *Central Asian Survey* 2, 1 (1983), 45–56; Alexandre Bennigsen, "The Qādirīyah (Kunta Hājjī) Tarīqah in North-East Caucasus: 1850–1987," *Islamic Culture* 62, 2–3 (1988), 69–71; Alexandre Bennigsen and S. Enders Wimbush, *Mystics and Commissars: Sufism in the Soviet Union* (London, 1985), 24–29; Abdurahman Avtorkhanov, "The Chechens and the Ingush during the Soviet Period and Its Antecedents," in Marie Bennigsen Broxup (ed.), *The North Caucasus Barrier: The Russian Advance towards the Muslim World* (London, 1992), 146–194, 152–179; Marie Bennigsen Broxup, "The Last Ghazawat: The 1920–21 Uprising," in Marie Bennigsen Broxup (ed.), *The North Caucasus Barrier*, 112–145; Jörg Baberowski, *Der Feind ist überall: Stalinismus im Kaukasus* (Munich, 2003), 420–442, 599–608, 633–662; Jörg Baberowski, "Stalinismus als imperiales Phänomen: Die islamischen Territorien der Sowjetunion 1920–1941," in Stefan Plaggenborg (ed.), *Stalinismus: Neue Forschungen und Konzepte* (Berlin, 1998), 113–150, esp. 127–137; Jörg Baberowski, "Stalinismus an der Peripherie: Das Beispiel Azerbajdzan 1920–1941," in Manfred Hildermeier (ed.), *Stalinismus vor dem Zweiten Weltkrieg: Neue Wege der Forschung* (Munich, 1998), 307–335, esp. 319–325; and Jörg Baberowski, "Verschleierte Feinde: Die kulturellen Ursprünge des Stalinismus im sowjetischen Orient," *Geschichte und Gesellschaft* 30 (2004), 10–36, esp. 24–36. On Soviet interwar policies toward Islam in Central Asia, see the general works by Shoshana Keller, *To Moscow, Not Mecca: The Soviet Campaign against Islam in Central Asia, 1917–1941* (Westport, CT, 2001); Shoshana Keller, "Islam in Soviet Central Asia, 1917–1930: Soviet Policy and the Struggle for Control," *Central Asian Survey* 11, 1 (1992), 25–50; and the more specific studies by G. J. Massel, *The Surrogate Proletariat: Moslem Women and Revolutionary Strategies in Soviet Central Asia, 1919–1929* (Princeton, NJ, 1974); Douglas Northrop, *Veiled Empire: Gender and Power in Stalinist Central Asia* (Ithaca, NY, 2004); and Marianne Kamp, *The New Woman in Uzbekistan: Islam, Modernity, and Unveiling under Communism* (Seattle, WA, 2006). Some of the quoted literature on Islam in the Soviet Union produced during the Cold War needs to be read with some caution, although it provides valuable factual material. On a critique of these studies' conceptual and analytical angle, see Devin DeWeese, "Islam and the Legacy of Sovietology: A Review Essay on Ya'acov Ro'i's *Islam in the Soviet Union*," *Journal of Islamic Studies* 13, 3 (2002), 298–330.

5 Religious leaders were accused of being agents of Turkey and Britain and, later, Japan and Germany, see Conquest, *The Great Terror*, 300; Bennigsen, "Qādirīyah (Kunta Hājjī) Tarīqah in North-East Caucasus," 70–71; and Bennigsen and Wimbush, *Mystics and Commissars*, 28–29.

6 On Soviet attacks against mosques, see Yemelianova, *Russia and Islam*, 114; Baberowski, "Stalinismus als imperiales Phänomen," 128; Baberowski, "Stalinismus an der Peripherie," 319–320; Baberowski, "Verschleierte Feinde," 24–25; and, on the numbers, Ro'i, *Islam in the Soviet Union*, 58.

7 The limits of Soviet religious suppression in the interwar period are discussed by the literature in note 4. On the survival of the shari'a courts and religious education, see in particular Kolarz, *Russia and Her Colonies*, 186–188; and Conquest, *The Nation Killers*, 38 and 98. On the failure of the veiling campaign, see in particular Kolarz, *Religion in the Soviet Union*, 416–419; Baberowski, *Der Feind ist überall*, 442–478; Baberowski, "Stalinismus als imperiales Phänomen," 128–134; Baberowski, "Stalinismus in der Peripherie," 320–323; and Baberowski, "Verschleierte Feinde," 17 and 27–36. On the confrontations during Ashura processions, see Baberowski, *Der Feind ist überall*, 427–435; Baberowski, "Stalinismus an der Peripherie," 319; and Baberowski, "Verschleierte Feinde," 17–18 and 25–27. And on the conflict at the Chechen pig-breeding farm, see Avtorkhanov, "Chechens and the Ingush during the Soviet Period and Its Antecedents," 166.

8 On revolts in the Caucasus in the interwar period, see Kolarz, *Russia and Her Colonies*, 186–188; Kolarz, *Religion in the Soviet Union*, 414–416; Conquest, *The Nation Killers*, 38, 45–46, and 96; Lemercier-Quelquejay, "Sufi Brotherhoods in the USSR," 12–16; Bennigsen, "Muslim Guerilla Warfare in the Caucasus"; Bennigsen, "The Qādirīyah (Kunta Hājjī) Tarīqah in North-East Caucasus," 69–71; Bennigsen and Wimbush, *Mystics and Commissars*, 24–29; Avtorkhanov, "The Chechens and the Ingush during the Soviet Period and Its Antecedents," 152–179; and Broxup, "The Last Ghazawat."

9 On revolts in the Caucasus in the Second World War, see Conquest, *The Nation Killers*, 98; Lemercier-Quelquejay, "Sufi Brotherhoods in the USSR," 16; Bennigsen, "The Qādirīyah (Kunta Hājjī) Tarīqah in North-East Caucasus," 71; Bennigsen and Wimbush, *Mystics and Commissars*, 29; Avtorkhanov, "Chechens and the Ingush during the Soviet Period and Its Antecedents," 181–184; J. Otto Pohl, *Ethnic Cleansing in the USSR, 1937–1949* (Westport, CT, 1999), 73, 75–76, 79, 81–83, and 89; Norman M. Naimark, *Fires of Hatred: Ethnic Cleansing in Twentieth-Century Europe* (Cambridge, MA, 2001), 94–96; Alexander Statiev, "The Nature of Anti-Soviet Armed Resistance, 1942–1944: The North Caucasus, the Kalmyk Autonomous Republic, and Crimea," *Kritika: Explorations in Russian and Eurasian History* 6, 2 (2005), 281–314, 284–299; and Jeffrey Burds, "The Soviet War against 'Fifth Columnists': The Case of Chechnya, 1942–4," *Journal of Contemporary History* 42, 2 (2007), 267–314. In a special mission, called "Operation Shamil," a Wehrmacht special unit was parachuted behind the front lines to incite and unite the rebels of Chechnya but, in the

end, failed, see Julius Mader, *Hitlers Spionagegenerale sagen aus: Ein Dokmentarbericht über Aufbau, Struktur und Operationen des OKW-Geheimdienstamtes Ausland/Abwehr mit einer Chronologie seiner Einsätze von 1944 bis 1944* (East Berlin, 1970), 191–192; and Günther W. Gellermann, *Tief im Hinterland des Gegners: Ausgewählte Unternehmen deutscher Geheimdienste im Zweiten Weltkrieg* (Bonn, 1999), 107–127; and, for the mission reports, see the documents in BA–MA, RW 49/143.

10 Erich v. Manstein, *Verlorene Siege* (Bonn, 1955), 233; the passage was omitted from the English translation, see Erich von Manstein, *Lost Victories* (London, 1958).

11 R. Konrad, *Kampf um den Kaukasus* (Munich, 1954), 22–23; and Helmut Blume to his parents, 28 October 1942, n.p., in Helmut Blume, *Zum Kaukasus 1941–1942: Aus Tagebuch und Briefen eines jungen Artilleristen* (Tübingen, 1993), 138–139, 139, are examples.

12 Sipo and SD Command, Report ("Meldungen aus den besetzten Ostgebieten"), 6 November 1942, Berlin, BAB, R 58/699; similar assessments were given in most reports from the field.

13 Fears about the Caucasus were also shared by Moscow's Western Allies, see Simpson (Mid-Asiatic Bureau, General Headquarters, Middle East Forces), Report ("Separatism in the Caucasus"), 23 August 1942, Cairo, NA, FO 371/32931; and Simpson, Report ("The Caucasus: Probable Consequences of a German Occupation"), 6 October 1942, Cairo, NA, WO 208/1814.

14 Engelbert Graf, "Die Freiheitskämpfe der Kaukasusvölker," *Deutsche Allgemeine Zeitung* (1 November 1942). On glorifications of the history of the *ghazawat* in the German press, see also Hans Rempel, "Die Völker des Kaukasus," *Völkischer Beobachter* (27 August 1942); Anonymous, "Der Kaukasus: 'Berg der Sprachen,'" *National-Zeitung* (18 August 1942); Wilhelm Ren, "Verfolgung im Kaukasus," *Frankfurter Zeitung* (31 August 1942); and Karl Wenig, "Schamyl lebt in jedem Legionär: Vom Freiheitskampf der Nordkaukasier gegen ihre Unterdrücker," *Deutsche Zeitung im Ostland* (30 May 1944), among others. This popular fascination had roots in the interwar years, see Karl von Seeger, *Imam Schamil: Prophet und Feldherr* (Leipzig, 1937).

15 On German warfare and occupation policy in the Caucasus and the Crimea, see the general works by Dallin, *German Rule in Russia*, 226–252 (Caucasus) and 253–275 (Crimea); Gerald Reitlinger, *The House Built on Sand: The Conflicts of German Policy in Russia, 1939–1945* (New York, 1960), 287–308 (Caucasus) and 185–187 (Crimea); Mühlen, *Zwischen Hakenkreuz und Sowjetstern*, 189–193 (Caucasus) and 183–187 (Crimea); Aleksandr M. Nekrich, *The Punished Peoples: The Deportation and Fate of Soviet Minorities at the end of the Second World War* (New York, 1978), 36–65 (Caucasus) and 13–35 (Crimea); Alexiev, *Soviet Nationalities in German Wartime Strategy*, 20–25 (Caucasus) and 32 (Crimea); Timothy Patrick Mulligan, *The Politics of Illusion and Empire: German Occupation Policy in the Soviet Union, 1942–1943* (New York, 1988), 127–130 (Caucasus) and 130–131 (Crimea); Angrick, *Besatzungspolitik und Massenmord*, 545–715 (Caucasus) and 323–361 and 452–544 (Crimea); and Manfred Oldenburg, *Ideologie und militärisches Kalkül: Die Besatzungspolitik der Wehrmacht in der Sowjetunion 1942* (Cologne, 2004), 259–306 (Caucasus) and 57–224 (Crimea). On the Caucasus in particular, see Hoffmann, *Kaukasien*; Manfred Zeidler, "Das 'kaukasische Experiment': Gab es eine Weisung Hitlers zur deutschen Besatzungspolitik im Kaukasus?," *Vierteljahreshefte für Zeitgeschichte* 53 (2005), 475–500; Dieter Pohl,

Die Herrschaft der Wehrmacht: Deutsche Militärbesatzung und einheimische Bevölkerung in der Sowjetunion 1941–1944 (Munich, 2008), 299–304; and Hermann Frank Meyer, *Blutiges Edelweiß: Die 1. Gebirgs-Division im Zweiten Weltkrieg* (Berlin, 2008), 82–111. On the Crimea in particular, see Luther, "Die Krim unter deutscher Besatzung im Zweiten Weltkrieg"; Kunz, *Die Krim unter deutscher Herrschaft*; and O. V. Roman'ko, *Krym pod piatoi Gitlera: Nemetskaia okkupatsionnaia politika v Krymu 1941–1944* (*The Crimea under Hitler's Heel: German Occupation Policy in the Crimea 1941–1944*) (Moscow, 2011); and the more general accounts by Fisher, *The Crimean Tatars*, 150–164; and Williams, *The Crimean Tatars*, 376–382. With the notable exception is Iskander Giljazov, "Die Muslime Rußlands in Deutschland während der Weltkriege als Subjekte und Objekte der Großmachtpolitik," in Höpp and Reinwald (eds.), *Fremdeinsätze*, 143–148, scholarship on Germany's religious policies on the Eastern Front during the Second World War has so far focused on the Orthodox Church, while ignoring Islam, see Friedrich Heyer, *Die orthodoxe Kirche in der Ukraine von 1917 bis 1945* (Cologne, 1953), 170–227; Harvey Fireside, *Icon and Swastika: The Russian Orthodox Church under Nazi and Soviet Control* (Cambridge, 1971); Wassilij Alexeev and Theofanis G. Stavrou, *The Great Revival: The Russian Church under German Occupation* (Minneapolis, 1976); Hans-Heinrich Wilhelm, "Der SD und die Kirchen in den besetzten Ostgebieten 1941/42," *Militaergeschichtliche Mitteilungen* 29 (1981), 55–99; Michail Škarovskij, "Deutsche Kirchenpolitik auf dem besetzten Territorium der USSR, 1941–1944," in Gabriele Gorzka and Knut Stang (eds.), *Der Vernichtungskrieg im Osten: Verbrechen der Wehrmacht in der Sowjetunion aus Sicht russischer Historiker* (Kassel, 1999), 69–85; and Michail Škarovskij, *Natsistskaia Germaniia i Pravoslavnaia Tserkov: Natsistskaia politika v otnoshenii Pravoslavnoi Tserkvi i religioznoe vozrozhdenie na okkupirovannoi territorii SSSR* (*Nazi Germany and the Orthodox Church: Nazi Policy toward the Orthodox Church and Religious Revival in the Occupied Territories of the USSR*) (Moscow, 2002).

16 Schulenburg to Ribbentrop, 15 May 1942, Berlin, BAB, R 6/22. Said Shamil had received some fame in the Islamic international during the interwar period and was celebrated at the Muslim congress in Jerusalem in 1931, see Kramer, *Islam Assembled*, 132. Based in Turkey, he had offered his services to the Germans just after Barbarossa, see Papen to Ribbentrop, 25 July 1941, Therapia, PA, R 29900; and, soon after, in early 1942, came to Germany, see the documents in PA, R 261175.

17 On the "pragmatic" approach of the Wehrmacht in the Caucasus and the Crimea, see the literature in note 15.

18 On the Turkic population as allies, see ibid.

19 On concessions, see ibid.

20 Kunz, *Die Krim unter deutscher Herrschaft*, 213–217.

21 On the history of the battle for the Caucasus, see the literature in note 15.

22 Otto Bräutigam, *So hat es sich zugetragen: Ein Leben als Soldat und Diplomat* (Würzburg, 1968), 510. Although it gives insights into policies, the book is notorious in that he tries to obscure his role in the Nazi genocides, see H. D. Heilmann, "Aus dem Kriegstagebuch des Diplomaten Otto Bräutigam," in H. D. Heilmann et al. (eds.), *Biedermann und Schreibtischtäter: Materialien zur deutschen Täter-Biographie* (Berlin, 1987), 123–187.

23 Theodor Oberländer, "Dritte Denkschrift," autumn 1942, printed in Theodor Oberländer, *Der Osten und die deutsche Wehrmacht: Sechs Denkschriften aus den Jahren 1941–1943 gegen die NS-Kolonialthese* (Sendorf, 1987), 67–84, 69. In his first memorandum, he had already emphasized that Islam was a strong and important element of the North Caucasus, reminding Wehrmacht officers of the Soviet suppression of Islam, and assuring them of a religious reawakening throughout the Muslim world, see Theodor Oberländer, "Erste Denkschrift," October 1941, printed in ibid., 15–50, 28–31, and 38–39. In his fourth memorandum, he even urged the Wehrmacht command to make a general "declaration for the active support of Islam," see Theodor Oberländer, "Vierte Denkschrift," 9 November 1942, printed in ibid., 85–101, 100. Oberländer also wrote an instruction sheet for the Axis troops deployed in the Caucasus, see Wehrmacht Instruction Sheet ("Merkblatt an alle im Kaukasus eingesetzten Truppen"), n.d. (August 1942), Private Family Archive Oberländer (*Familienarchiv Oberländer*), Bonn (FAO). It seems to have served as a model for a Wehrmacht instruction sheet that was distributed in September (note 25), see Philipp-Christian Wachs, *Der Fall Theodor Oberländer (1905–1998): Ein Lehrstück deutscher Geschichte* (Frankfurt, 2000), 125–126; and Hoffmann, *Kaukasus*, 126–127. On the significance of the assumption of pan-Islamic unity, see also Angrick, *Besatzungspolitik und Massenmord*, 591.

24 List, Order ("Befehl an alle im Kaukasus eingesetzten Truppen [Bekanntzugeben bis zu den Kompanien]"), n.d. (summer 1942), n.p., BAB, R 6/65.

25 Wehrmacht Instruction Sheet ("Merkblatt für das Verhalten gegenüber kaukasischen Völkern"), n.d. (11 August 1942), BA–MA, RW 41/7 (also in BA–MA, RH 22/211a).

26 Kleist, Speech, according to Report ("Schlussbemerkungen des Herrn Oberbefehlshabers, Generaloberst v. Kleist, im Anschluss an den Vortrag des Stabsoffiziers für Propagandaeinsatz"), 15 December 1942, BAB, R 6/65.

27 East Ministry, Conference Report ("Grundsätzliche Gedanken aus der Aussprache des Reichsministers für die besetzten Ostgebiete mit den Befehlshabern der Heeresgebiete im Osten"), 22 December 1942, n.d. (Berlin), BAB, R 58/225.

28 East Ministry, Guidelines ("Richtlinien für die Behandlung der Völker Kaukasiens"), 26 August 1942, Berlin, BAB, R 6/143.

29 East Ministry, Order ("Anweisung für den Bevollmächtigten des Reichsministers für die besetzten Ostgebiete beim Oberkommando der Heeresgruppe A"), October 1942, Berlin, BAB, R 6/66.

30 Mende, Guidelines ("Richtlinien für die Behandlung der Ostvölker: Kaukasien"), 11 December 1942, Berlin, BAB, R 6/66.

31 Sipo and SD Command, Report ("Meldungen aus den besetzten Ostgebieten"), 6 November 1942, Berlin, BAB, R 58/699.

32 Wehrmacht Instruction Sheet ("Merkblatt für das Verhalten gegenüber kaukasischen Völkern"), n.d. (11 August 1942), BA–MA, RW 41/7 (also in BA–MA, RH 22/211a). The reopening of houses of worship had also been instructed in List's earlier order, see List, Order ("Befehl an alle im Kaukasus eingesetzten Truppen"), n.d. (September 1942), n.p., BAB, R 6/65.

33 Town Command I/920, Report ("Monatsmeldung über die politische und wirtschaftliche Lage sowie Stand der Propaganda"), 27 November 1942, Cherkessk, BA–MA, RH

20-17/709; and, similarly, Field Command 538, Report ("Lagebericht für die Zeit vom 16.10. bis 15.11.1942"), 16 November 1942, Maikop, BA–MA, RH 20-17/709.

34 Field Command 538, Report ("Lagebericht für die Zeit vom 16.10. bis 15.11.1942"), 16 November 1942, Maikop, BA–MA, RH 20-17/709.

35 Schütte to Bräutigam, 13 October 1942, n.p., BAB, R 6/65.

36 Field Command 538, Report ("Lagebericht für die Zeit vom 16.10. bis 15.11.1942"), 16 November 1942, Maikop, BA–MA, RH 20-17/709.

37 Merk (Headquarters of Army Group A), Report ("Schulwesen im Bereich der Heeresgruppe A"), 21 October 1942, n.p., BAB, R 6/65.

38 Field Command 538, Report ("Lagebericht für die Zeit vom 16.11. bis 15.12.1942"), 16 December 1942, Maikop, BA–MA, RH 20-17/709.

39 Himpel (East Ministry), Guidelines ("Richtlinien für die Behandlung der Völker"), 26 August 1942, Berlin, BAB, R 6/66.

40 Sipo and SD Command, Report ("Meldungen aus den besetzten Ostgebieten"), 18 December 1942, Berlin, BAB, R 58/699.

41 Images: "Ueberreichung des Koran" and "Efendi Mullah spricht zu den Legionären," *Ghazavat* 29 (1943), German translation, High Command of the Wehrmacht, 1 September 1943, Berlin, BA–MA, MSG 2/18238.

42 The East Ministry early on decided to avoid references to the future political order of the Caucasus and instead to put emphasis on religious and especially Islamic propaganda, see Conradi (Foreign Office), Internal Note ("Sondersprachregelung Osten"), 5 November 1941, Berlin, PA, R 105165 (also in PA, R 60737); Großkopf (Foreign Office), Internal Note, 5 November 1941, Berlin, PA, R 105165; and Baum (Foreign Office), Internal Note, 19 November 1941, Berlin, PA, R 105165. For the East Ministry's general propaganda guidelines, see East Ministry, Guidelines ("Richtlinien des RM f. d. besetzen Ostgebiete für die Propaganda im Kaukasus"), 5 December 1941, Berlin, PA, R 105165 (also in PA, R 261174); East Ministry, Guidelines ("Richtlinien für die Propaganda unter den Kaukasischen Völkern"), 19 February 1942, BA–MA, RH 19 III/481; East Ministry, Guidelines ("Richtlinien für die Propaganda unter den Kaukasischen Völkern"), 20 April 1942, Berlin, PA, R 105165 (also in PA, R 105171); and East Ministry, Guidelines ("Richtlinien für die Propaganda im Kaukasus"), n.d., BAB, R 6/66. On German propaganda in the Caucasus in general, see Ortwin Buchbender, *Das tönende Erz: Deutsche Propaganda gegen die Rote Armee im zweiten Weltkrieg* (Stuttgart, 1978), 191–198.

43 Pamphlet "Völker Kaukasiens!" (German translation), n.d. (1942), BAB, R 6/36 (also in BAB, R 6/66 and R 6/277).

44 Pamphlet "An die Völker des Ostens!" (German translation), 4 August 1942, BAB, R 6/36.

45 Pamphlet "Aufruf an die Völker Kaukasiens!" (German translation), n.d. (1942), BAB, R 6/36.

46 Pamphlet "Völker des Kaukasus!" (German translation), 16 April 1942, BAB, R 6/36.

47 Ibid.

48 Town Command I/920, Report ("Monatsmeldung über die politische und wirtschaftliche Lage sowie Stand der Propaganda"), 27 November 1942, Cherkessk, BA–MA, RH

20-17/709; and, similarly, Field Command 538, Report ("Lagebericht für die Zeit vom 16.10. bis 15.11.1942"), 16 November 1942, Maikop, BA–MA, RH 20-17/709.

49 Town Command I/920, Report ("Monatsmeldung über die politische und wirtschaftliche Lage sowie Stand der Propaganda"), 27 November 1942, Cherkessk, BA–MA, RH 20-17/709.

50 Field Command 538, Report ("Lagebericht für die Zeit vom 16.10. bis 15.11.1942"), 16 November 1942, Maikop, BA–MA, RH 20-17/709.

51 Schütte to Bräutigam, 13 October 1942, n.p., BAB, R 6/65.

52 Sipo and SD Command, Report ("Meldungen aus den besetzten Ostgebieten"), 18 December 1942, Berlin, BAB, R 58/699.

53 The celebrations are mentioned by Dallin, *German Rule in Russia*, 246–247; Mühlen, *Zwischen Hakenkreuz und Sowjetstern*, 191; Nekrich, *The Punished Peoples*, 61–62; Alexiev, *Soviet Nationalities in German Wartime Strategy*, 23; Angrick, *Besatzungspolitik und Massenmord*, 634; Hoffmann, *Kaukasien*, 443–444; and Wachs, *Der Fall Theodor Oberländer*, 117–118.

54 Schiller, Report ("Besuch des Uraza Bairam Festes in Kislowodsk"), 11 October 1942, n.p., BAB, R 6/65. The following description of the celebration is based on this report unless otherwise indicated.

55 Sipo and SD Command, Report ("Meldungen aus den besetzten Ostgebieten"), 18 December 1942, Berlin, BAB, R 58/699.

56 Schiller, Report ("Besuch des Uraza Bairam Festes in Kislowodsk"), 11 October 1942, n.p., BAB, R 6/65.

57 Figure 4.1; also described by Schiller, Report ("Besuch des Uraza Bairam Festes in Kislowodsk"), 11 October 1942, n.p., BAB, R 6/65.

58 On the Soviet language reforms, see Guy Imart, "Le movement de 'latinisation' en URSS," *Cahirs du Monde Russe et Soviétique* 8 (1967), 223–239; and Ingeborg Baldauf, *Schriftreform und Schriftwechsel bei den muslimischen Russland- und Sowjettürken (1850–1937): Ein Symptom ideengeschichtlicher und kulturpolitischer Entwicklungen* (Budapest, 1993). On the burning of books with Arabic script, see Keller, "Islam in Soviet Central Asia," 45; and on the opposition of the mullahs, see Conquest, *The Nation Killers*, 38.

59 Heinz Grothe, "Tagebuchnotizen aus dem Kaukasus," *Donau-Zeitung* (15 November 1942). The prayer also impressed his colleague, who also wrote a detailed description, see Horst v. Kobilinski, "Urasa Bayram 1942: Das mohammedanische Fest der Karatschaier," *Brünner Abendblatt* (23 November 1942).

60 Schiller, Report ("Besuch des Uraza Bairam Festes in Kislowodsk"), 11 October 1942, n.p., BAB, R 6/65.

61 Köstring, Report ("Berater für die das Operationsgebiet der Heeresgruppe A betreffenden Fragen"), n.d. (post-1945), n.p., IfZ, ZS 85.

62 Hans von Herwarth, *Zwischen Hitler und Stalin: Erlebte Zeitgeschichte 1931 bis 1945* (Frankfurt, 1982), 270; and, similar, in the English translation, Hans von Herwarth, *Against Two Evils* (London, 1981), 234.

63 Bräutigam wrote two reports about the celebration, see Bräutigam, Short Report ("Über das mohammedanische Kurmanfest in Naltschik 1942"), 22 December 1942, n.p., BAB, R 6/65; and Bräutigam, Long Report ("Über das mohammedanische Kurmanfest in Naltschik 1942"), 22 December 1942, Stavropol, BAB, R 6/65; see also

the official program of the celebration: Program ("Befreigungsfeier von Kabardino-Balkarien am Kurman-Fest: 18.–20. Dezember 42"), 1942, BAB, R 6/65. Bräutigam also wrote on the Nalchik celebration at length in his memoirs, see Bräutigam, *So hat es sich zugetragen*, 537–541; and Bräutigam, Report ("Als Bevollmächtigter des Ostministeriums bei der Heeresgruppe Süd"), n.d. (post-1945), n.p., IfZ, ZS 400. The following description of the celebration is based on Bräutigam's reports unless otherwise indicated.

64 Nekrich, *The Punished Peoples*, 61 and 63.

65 Bräutigam, *So hat es sich zugetragen*, 539.

66 Oberländer to Erika Oberländer, 20 December 1942, n.p., FAO; see also Theodor Oberländer, Diary (Entries of 17 and 18 December 1942), FAO.

67 On the celebration in Gundelen, see Bräutigam, Long Report ("Über das moham-medanische Kurmanfest in Naltschik 1942"), 22 December 1942, Stavropol, BAB, R 6/65; and Bräutigam, *So hat es sich zugetragen*, 543–544.

68 Grothe, "Tagebuchnotizen aus dem Kaukasus."

69 Kobilinski, "Urasa Bayram 1942."

70 Grimm-Kastein, "Hirten und Krieger im Kaukasus," *Illustrierter Beobachter* (29 October 1942); and Kaiser, "Kaukasische Miliz," *Illustrierter Beobachter* (10 December 1942). These photographs of the Karachais and German soldiers were most likely taken during the celebration.

71 Bräutigam, *So hat es sich zugetragen*, 523. Bräutigam himself did not attend the celebrations of Kislovodsk as he was still in Berlin when the event took place.

72 On the history of the occupation of the Crimea, see the literature in note 15.

73 Nekrich, *The Punished Peoples*, 13–14; and Mühlen, *Zwischen Hakenkreuz und Sowjet-stern*, 184, on the percentages.

74 Manstein, Order, 20 November 1941, reprinted in *Der Prozeß gegen die Hauptkriegsver-brecher vor dem Internationalen Militärgerichtshof*, 42 vols. (Nuremberg, 1947–1949), vol. 34, 129–132, 130 (on "Jewish-Bolshevist system") and 131 (on Tatars); and in Gerd R. Ueberschär and Wolfram Wette (eds.), *"Unernehmen Barbarossa": Der deutsche Überfall auf die Sowjetunion 1941* (Paderborn, 1984), 343–344, 344. For the English translation, see *Trial of the Major War Criminals before the International Military Tribunal*, 42 vols. (Nuremberg, 1947–1949), vol. 20, 641–643, 642 (on "Jewish-Bolshevist system") and 643 (on Tatars). On the order, see also Oliver von Wrochem, *Erich von Manstein: Vernichtungskrieg und Geschichtspolitik* (Paderborn, 2006), 58–63; and Mungo Melvin, *Manstein* (London, 2010), 240–245. Unsurprisingly, Manstein did not mention the order or indeed anything about the extermination of the Jewish population in his memoirs, Manstein, *Verlorene Siege*; Manstein, *Lost Victories*.

75 High Command 11th Army, Instructions ("Merkblatt für die Behandlung der Ta-taren"), 9 January 1942, n.p., BA–MA, WF-03/10433.

76 Hürter, "'Nachrichten aus dem Zweiten Krimkrieg,'" esp. 375–377, 381, and 386; see also his own memoirs, Hentig, *Mein Leben*, 349–357.

77 Hentig to Oppenheim, 11 October 1941, n.p., PA, Nachlass Hentig, vol. 84; and, in response, Oppenheim to Hentig, 31 October 1941, Berlin, PA, Nachlass Hentig, vol. 84.

78 Hentig, Report ("Tataren auf der Krim"), 10 April 1942, n.p. (Simferopol), PA, R 60739 (also in PA, R 261175). In fact, Hentig repeatedly stressed the impact of German policies toward the Crimean Tatars on Muslims beyond the peninsula, see Hentig, Internal Note ("Turanismus"), n.d. (November 1941), Berlin, PA, R 28876 (also in PA, R 261179); and, similarly, Hentig, Internal Note ("Stand der sog. Turanischen Frage"), 25 February 1942, Berlin, PA, R 60690 (also in PA, R 261175).

79 W. K., "Beim Sieger von Sewastopol," *National-Zeitung* (20 August 1942). He expressed the same view in his memoirs, see Manstein, *Verlorene Siege*, 233, 247; the passages were omitted from the English translation, see Manstein, *Lost Victories*.

80 Hufnagel (Army), Report ("Verwaltungsbericht für Monat Februar 1943"), 6 March 1943, n.p., BA–MA, RH 24-42/225.

81 Siefers (Army), Report ("Aufstellung von Tataren- und Kaukasierformationen im Bereich des A.O.K. 11"), 20 March 1942, n.p., BA–MA, RH 19V/108 (also in PA, R 60739); this assessment was based on High Command 11th Army, Instructions ("Merkblatt für die Behandlung der Tataren"), 9 January 1942, n.p., BA–MA, WF-03/10433.

82 SS and Police Command Crimea, Report ("Lagebericht der SS- und Polizeiführer auf der Krim"), n.d. (August 1943), BA–MA, RH 19V/113.

83 Military Command Crimea to Town Command Sevastopol, 15 February 1943, n.p., BA–MA, RH 20-17/713; and Town Command Sevastopol to Military Command Crimea, 23 February 1943, Sevastopol, BA–MA, RH 20-17/713, give evidence of such a case. The issue was subsequently discussed more generally between the military and the economic agencies, see Military Command Crimea to Economic Command Crimea, 15 February 1943, n.p., BA–MA, RH 20-17/713; and Economic Command Crimea to Military Command Crimea, 24 February 1943, n.p., BA–MA, RH 20-17/713. Initially, it was decided that Sunday should remain the day of rest on the entire peninsula, see Military Command Crimea to Town Command Crimea, 28 February 1943, n.p., BA–MA, RH 20-17/713.

84 Military Command Crimea to Town and Field Commands Crimea, 30 March 1943, n.p., BA–MA, RH 20-17/713.

85 Headquarters of Army Group A, Report ("Verwaltungsbericht für den Monat Juli 1943"), 14 August 1943, n.p., BA–MA, RH 20-17/710.

86 "Ramadsan und Erntefest," *Azerbaijan* 44 (72) (1943), German translation, High Command of the Wehrmacht, 31 October 1943, Berlin, BA–MA, MSG 2/18239; see also Image: "Nationale Tänze in Simferopol anläßlich des Ramadsan- und Erntedankfestes," *Azerbaijan* 44 (72) (1943), German translation, High Command of the Wehrmacht, 31 October 1943, Berlin, BA–MA, MSG 2/18239.

87 *Einsatzgruppe D*, Report ("Die Rekrutierung der Krimtataren"), 15 February 1942, n.p., BA–MA, RH 20-11/433 (also in BA–MA, WF-03/10435); and Zinkler (Town Command Karasubazar [Bilohirsk]), Report ("Bericht über die Zeit v. 22.–27.4.4"), 28 April 1942, Seitler, BA–MA, RH 23/90, provide examples.

88 Buchholz (Field Command 751), Report ("Lagebericht für die Zeit vom 15.5.–31.5.1942"), 31 May 1942, n.p., BA–MA, RH 23/90.

89 Command of Army Rear Area 553, Report ("Tatarenspenden"), 7 May 1942, n.p., BA–MA, RH 23/95.

90 See, for instance, Simferopol Central Muslim Committee, Report ("Die Frage der mohammedanischen Religion in der Krim"), n.d. (1943), Simferopol, BA–MA, RH 20-17/713.

91 Herwarth, *Zwischen Hitler und Stalin*, 275; and, slightly varied, in the English version, Herwarth, *Against Two Evils*, 239–240.

92 *Die Tagebücher von Joseph Goebbels*, ed. Fröhlich et al., part II, vol. 3, 214–223 (30 January 1942), 214.

93 Kirimal, *Der nationale Kampf der Krimtürken*, 303–322 and 307.

94 Simferopol Central Muslim Committee, Report ("Die Frage der mohammedanischen Religion in der Krim"), n.d. (1943), Simferopol, BA–MA, RH 20-17/713.

95 Ibid.

96 Simferopol Central Muslim Committee, Report ("Historische Denkmäler, Museen und Archive der Krim"), n.d., Simferopol, BA–MA, RH 20-17/713.

97 On the Muslim committees, see Dallin, *German Rule in Russia*, 261; Mühlen, *Zwischen Hakenkreuz und Sowjetstern*, 185; Nekrich, *The Punished Peoples*, 19–21; Mulligan, *Politics of Illusion and Empire*, 130–131; Angrick, *Besatzungspolitik und Massenmord*, 469–471 and 473; Oldenburg, *Ideologie und militärisches Kalkül*, 120 and 125; Luther, "Die Krim unter deutscher Besatzung im Zweiten Weltkrieg," 51, 62, 65, 74, and 77–78; Kunz, *Die Krim unter deutscher Herrschaft*, 214; Roman'ko, *Krym pod piatoi Gitlera*, 137–149 and 195–205; Fisher, *The Crimean Tatars*, 157–158; and Williams, *The Crimean Tatars*, 379.

98 Nekrich, *The Punished Peoples*, 19.

99 Statutes of the Simferopol Central Committee ("Statuten des Tatarischen Komitees Simferepol"), n.d. (1942), Simferopol, BA–MA, RH 20-17/713. On the inaugural ceremony, see Siefers, Report ("Aufstellung von Tataren- und Kaukasierformationen im Bereich des A.O.K. 11"), 20 March 1942, n.p., BA–MA, RH 19V/108 (also in PA, R 60739). According to Kirimal, the committee was founded in November 1941, see Kirimal, *Der nationale Kampf der Krimtürken*, 307.

100 Kirimal to Kurkchi, 19 December 1943, n.p., BA–MA, RH 19V/96.

101 Zapp (SS and Police Command Crimea) to Military Command Crimea, 31 March 1943, n.p., BA–MA, RH 20-17/713. The letter contains a summary of the guidelines of the religious board of the Simferopol central committee.

102 Temporary Statutes for the Muslim Religious Communities ("Zeitweise Statuten für muselmanische Religionsgemeinden"), n.d. (1942), Simferopol, BA–MA, RH 20-17/713.

103 Zapp to Military Command Crimea, 31 March 1943, n.p., BA–MA, RH 20-17/713.

104 Crews, *For Prophet and Tsar*, 31–91.

105 Statutes of the Simferopol Central Committee ("Statuten des Tatarischen Komitees Simferepol"), n.d. (1942), Simferopol, BA–MA, RH 20-17/713.

106 Hentig, Report ("Tataren auf der Krim"), 10 April 1942, n.p. (Simferopol), PA, R 60739 (also in PA, R 261175).

107 Statutes of the Simferopol Central Committee ("Statuten des Tatarischen Komitees Simferepol"), n.d. (1942), Simferopol, BA–MA, RH 20-17/713.

108 Zapp to Military Command Crimea, 31 March 1943, n.p., BA–MA, RH 20-17/713.

109 On these conflicts between German authorities and Tatar nationalists, see Dallin, *German Rule in Russia*, 261–262; Mühlen, *Zwischen Hakenkreuz und Sowjetstern*, 185–187; Nekrich, *The Punished Peoples*, 21; Luther, "Die Krim unter deutscher Besatzung im Zweiten Weltkrieg," 77–78 and 81; and Roman'ko, *Krym pod piatoi Gitlera*, 140–148.

110 Statutes of the Simferopol Central Committee ("Statuten des Tatarischen Komitees Simferepol"), n.d. (1942), Simferopol, BA–MA, RH 20-17/713.

111 Siefers, Report ("Aufstellung von Tataren- und Kaukasierformationen im Bereich des A.O.K. 11"), 20 March 1942, n.p., BA–MA, RH 19V/108 (also in PA, R 60739).

112 Simferopol Central Muslim Committee, Report ("Die Frage der mohammedanischen Religion in der Krim"), n.d. (1943), Simferopol, BA–MA, RH 20-17/713.

113 Ibid.

114 On *Azat Kirim*, see Dallin, *German Rule in Russia*, 261; Mühlen, *Zwischen Hakenkreuz und Sowjetstern*, 184, Luther, "Die Krim unter deutscher Besatzung im Zweiten Weltkrieg," 51; Roman'ko, *Krym pod piatoi Gitlera*, 196–197; Fisher, *The Crimean Tatars*, 158; Mikhail Tyaglyy, "The Role of Antisemitic Doctrine in German Propaganda in the Crimea, 1941–1944," *Holocaust and Genocide Studies* 18, 3 (2004), 421–459, 439–440; and Mikhail Tyaglyy, "Antisemitic Doctrine in Crimean Tatar Newspaper 'Azat Kirim' (1942–1944)," *Dapim: Studies on the Holocaust* 25, 1 (2011), 161–182.

115 Simferopol Central Muslim Committee, Report ("Die Partisanen und die mohammedanischen Freiwilligenformationen der Krim"), n.d. (1943), Simferopol, BA–MA, RH 20-17/713.

116 Kurtiev to Military Command Crimea, 3 January 1943, Simferopol, in Simferopol Central Muslim Committee, Report ("Die Partisanen und die mohammedanischen Freiwilligenformationen der Krim"), n.d. (1943), Simferopol, BA–MA, RH 20-17/713.

117 Ibid.

118 Anonymous, "Yeşil cami" ("The Green Mosque"), *Azat Kirim* (22 March 1943). Copies of the paper are stored in the State Archives of the Crimea (*Derzhavnyi Arkhiv v Avtonomnii Respublitsi Krym*), Simferopol (DAARK).

119 M. Q., "Din ve medeniyet yolunda vazifelerimiz" ("Our Obligations on the Path of Religion and Civilization"), *Azat Kirim* (17 November 1942).

120 A. Zeni, "Bayramdan maqsadımız" ("What Are the Goals of the Bairam?"), *Azat Kirim* (18 December 1942).

121 Haberci, "Kefede qurban bayramı" ("Qurban Bairam in Kefe"), *Azat Kirim* (19 January 1943).

122 Abdulla (oca), "Bayram künlerinde" ("On the Days of Bairam"), *Azat Kirim* (22 December 1942).

123 Anonymous, "Musulmanlar azatlıq oğrında küreşeler" ("Muslims Are Fighting for Liberty"), *Azat Kirim* (29 December 1942).

124 Anonymous, "Şarknin kurtuluşu" ("The Liberation of the East"), *Azat Kirim* (16 January 1943).

125 Sandıqçı, "Qurban bayramı nasıl olmalı?" ("How the Qurban Bairam Should Be?"), *Azat Kirim* (12 December 1942).

126 Sudaqlı, "Kendi asradığıñ yüzümden şarap yapmaq arammı?" ("Is It Religiously Forbidden to Make Wine from the Grapes One Grows?"), *Azat Kirim* (27 August 1943).

127 Qrım merkezi diniye idaresi (The Central Religious Administration of the Crimea), "Cami cemaat (malle) şuraları için muvaqqat nizamname" ("Temporary Regulations for Congregation [Mosque, DM] Councils"), *Azat Kirim* (25 June 1943), is an example of such a proclamation.

128 Anonymous, "Qrım merkezi diniye idaresinde" ("At the Central Religious Administration of the Crimea"), *Azat Kirim* (25 July 1942); and, on charitable activities, Ziya (Efendi), "Müsülman Komitesi ve onıñ vazifesi" ("The Muslim Committee and Its Duties"), *Azat Kirim* (17 April 1942).

129 Anonymous, "Xuddamlarnin vazifeleri" ("The Duties of the Religious Functionaries"), *Azat Kirim* (29 September 1942); and, similarly, Qrımlı, "Bizge medeni, zemane huddamları kerek" ("We Need Modern Religious Functionaries"), *Azat Kirim* (16 October 1942).

130 Simferopol Central Muslim Committee, Report ("Die Partisanen und die mohammedanischen Freiwilligenformationen der Krim"), n.d. (1943), Simferopol, BA–MA, RH 20-17/713.

131 East Ministry, Guidelines ("Vorläufige Richtlinien für die Propaganda unter den Tataren"), (22) November 1941, Berlin, PA, R 105165. The text was also circulated within the Foreign Office, see Conradi, Internal Note, 22 November 1941, Berlin, PA, R 105165; and Baum, Internal Note, 29 November 1941, Berlin, PA, R 105165. The following month, these propaganda guidelines were extended to all Muslims of the Eastern territories, see East Ministry, Guidelines ("Richtlinien für die Propaganda unter den Turkvölkern"), 5 December 1941, Berlin, PA, R 105165 (also in PA, R 261174).

132 SS and Police Command Crimea, Report ("Lagebericht der SS- und Polizeiführer auf der Krim"), n.d. (August 1943), BA–MA, RH 19V/113.

133 Ibid.

134 Simferopol Central Muslim Committee, Report ("Die Frage der mohammedanischen Religion in der Krim"), n.d. (1943), Simferopol, BA–MA, RH 20-17/713.

135 Ibid.

136 Ibid.

137 Simferopol Central Muslim Committee, Report ("Die Partisanen und die mohammedanischen Freiwilligenformationen der Krim"), n.d. (1943), Simferopol, BA–MA, RH 20-17/713.

138 Simferopol Central Muslim Committee, Report ("Die Frage der mohammedanischen Religion in der Krim"), n.d. (1943), Simferopol, BA–MA, RH 20-17/713; and, similarly, Simferopol Central Muslim Committee, Report ("Die Partisanen und die mohammedanischen Freiwilligenformationen der Krim"), n.d. (1943), Simferopol, BA–MA, RH 20-17/713; and Simferopol Central Muslim Committee, Report ("Bedürfnisse und Gesuche der Mohammedaner-Komitees"), n.d. (1943), Simferopol, BA–MA, RH 20-17/713.

139 Simferopol Central Muslim Committee, Report ("Die Frage der mohammedanischen Religion in der Krim"), n.d. (1943), Simferopol, BA–MA, RH 20-17/713.

140 Ibid.; and, similarly, Simferopol Central Muslim Committee, Report ("Die Partisanen und die mohammedanischen Freiwilligenformationen der Krim"), n.d. (1943), Simferopol, BA–MA, RH 20-17/713.

141 Simferopol Central Muslim Committee, Report ("Die Frage der mohammedanischen Religion in der Krim"), n.d. (1943), Simferopol, BA–MA, RH 20-17/713.

142 Ibid.

143 On waqf foundations, see Murat Çizakça, *A History of Philanthropic Foundations: The Islamic World from the Seventh Century to the Present* (Istanbul, 2000); Shaik Abdul Kader, *The Law of Wakfs: An Analytical and Critical Study* (Calcutta, 1999); Jan-Peter Hartung, "Die fromme Stiftung (waqf): Eine islamische Analogie zur Körperschaft?," in Hans Gerhard Kippenberg and Gunnar Folke Schuppert (eds.), *Die verrechtlichte Religion: Der Öffentlichkeitsstatus von Religionsgemeinschaften* (Tübingen, 2005), 287–313; and R. Peters et al., "Wakf," in *The Encyclopaedia of Islam*, vol. 11, ed. P. J. Bearman, Th. Bianquis, C. E. Bosworth, E. van Donzel, and W. P. Heinrichs (Leiden, 2002), 59–99.

144 Jamilov, Memorandum ("Memorandum der religiösen Abteilung der Krim des Mohamedanerkomitees der Stadt Simferopol über die Wakufe und das Muftiat in der Krim"), 13 December 1942, Simferopol, in Simferopol Central Muslim Committee, Report ("Die Frage der mohammedanischen Religion in der Krim"), n.d. (1943), Simferopol, BA–MA, RH 20-17/713.

145 Simferopol Central Muslim Committee, Report ("Die Frage der mohammedanischen Religion in der Krim"), n.d. (1943), Simferopol, BA–MA, RH 20-17/713.

146 Temporary Statutes for the Muslim Religious Communities ("Zeitweise Statuten für muselmanische Religionsgemeinden"), n.d. (1942), Simferopol, BA–MA, RH 20-17/713.

147 Zapp to Military Command Crimea, 31 March 1943, n.p., BA–MA, RH 20-17/713.

148 Riecke (Head of Economic Staff East), Order, 22 May 1942, Berlin, PA, R 27358.

149 Jamilov, Memorandum ("Memorandum der religiösen Abteilung der Krim des Mohamedanerkomitees der Stadt Simferopol über die Wakufe und das Muftiat in der Krim"), 13 December 1942, Simferopol, in Simferopol Central Muslim Committee, Report ("Die Frage der mohammedanischen Religion in der Krim"), n.d. (1943), Simferopol, BA–MA, RH 20-17/713.

150 Simferopol Central Muslim Committee, Report ("Die Frage der mohammedanischen Religion in der Krim"), n.d. (1943), Simferopol, BA–MA, RH 20-17/713.

151 SS and Police Command Crimea, Report ("Lagebericht der SS- und Polizeiführer auf der Krim"), n.d. (August 1943), BA–MA, RH 19V/113.

152 On the Crimean muftiate, see Dallin, *German Rule in Russia*, 267–270; Mühlen, *Zwischen Hakenkreuz und Sowjetstern*, 186; Luther, "Die Krim unter deutscher Besatzung im Zweiten Weltkrieg," 91–93; Roman'ko, *Krym pod piatoi Gitlera*, 149–153; and Fisher, *The Crimean Tatars*, 162.

153 Kornelsen, Internal Note ("Einberufung eines Kongresses der von der Sowjetunion unterdrückten mohammedanischen Völker nach Berlin"), 11 November 1943, Berlin, IfZ, NO-3112.

154 Ibid.; Berger's note was dated 17 November 1943.

155 Kornelsen to Dreysing (Headquarters of High Command of the Army [Oberkommando des Heeres]), December 1943, Berlin, IfZ, NO-3113. Copies of the letter were

sent to the representative of the East Ministry in Crimea, to the head of the Sipo and SD, and to Party Chancellery in Munich.

156 Adamovich, Report ("Agenturbericht [sic] über den moralisch-politischen Stand der Krimtataren in Rumänien"), 30 June 1944, Berlin, BAB, NS 31/32, gives information on the background of Ozenbashli. On his conflicts with the Germans and his escape from the Crimea, see Dallin, German Rule in Russia, 261–262 and 269–270; Mühlen, Zwischen Hakenkreuz und Sowjetstern, 127–128 and 185–187; Luther, "Die Krim unter deutscher Besatzung im Zweiten Weltkrieg," 78 and 81; Roman'ko, Krym pod piatoi Gitlera, 143–145, 151–153, and 420–421; and Fisher, The Crimean Tatars, 162.

157 Headquarters of High Command of the Army to East Ministry, 28 February 1944, Berlin, IfZ, NO-3114.

158 On this issue the High Command of the Army contacted the Headquarters of Army Group A, which then consulted the Wehrmacht's Commissioner of Simferopol, see Dellingshausen (Headquarters of Army Group A) to Schumann (Military Commissioner of Simferopol), 27 February 1944, n.p., BA–MA, RH 19V/96. Schumann responded only after the Wehrmacht had officially rejected the East Ministry's proposal, see Schumann to Dellingshausen, 7 March 1944, Simferopol, BA–MA, RH 19V/96; and Dellingshausen to Jani (Headquarters of High Command of the Army), 12 March 1944, n.p., BA–MA, RH 19V/96.

159 Dellingshausen to Schumann, 27 February 1944, n.p., BA–MA, RH 19V/96.

160 SS and Police Command Crimea to SS and Police Command Crimea "Black Sea," 2 February 1944, n.p., BA–MA, RH 19V/96.

161 Schumann to Dellingshausen, 7 March 1944, Simferopol, BA–MA, RH 19V/96; and Dellingshausen to Jani, 12 March 1944, n.p., BA–MA, RH 19V/96.

162 Olzscha, Report ("Errichtung eines Muftiats für die Osttürken"), 6 November 1944, Berlin, BAB, NS 31/28.

163 Mende, Internal Note ("Gespräch mit dem Großmufti von Jerusalem"), 28 July 1944, Berlin, IfZ, PS-1111.

164 Adamovich, Report ("Agenturbericht [sic] über den moralisch-politischen Stand der Krimtataren in Rumänien"), 30 June 1944, Berlin, BAB, NS 31/32; and the literature in note 156.

165 Trampedach (East Ministry) to Mende, 14 October 1944, Berlin, BAB, R 6/179.

166 East Ministry, Newsletter ("Mitteilungen zur Ostpolitik"), 15 November 1944, Berlin, BAB, R 6/65.

167 Stamati (East Ministry), Report ("Religiöse Einstellung der Wolgatataren"), 22 March 1945, Berlin, BAB, NS 31/56 (also in BAB, NS 31/60).

168 Idris, Report ("Die Frage des Muftiats für die Russlandtürken"), 25 March 1945, Berlin, BAB, NS 31/60.

169 SS and Police Command Crimea to SS and Police Command Crimea "Black Sea," 2 February 1944, n.p., BA–MA, RH 19V/96.

170 On the history of Muslim populations in northeastern Europe, see Harry Norris, Islam in the Baltic: Europe's Early Muslim Community (London, 2009); Piotr Borawski, "Religious Tolerance and the Tatar Population in the Grand Duchy of Lithuania: 16th to 18th Century," Journal of Muslim Minority Affairs 9, 1 (1988), 119–133; Ta-

mara Bairašauskaitė, "Politische Integration und religiöse Eigenständigkeit der litauischen Tataren im 19. Jahrhundert," in Kemper et al. (eds.), *Muslim Culture in Russia and Central Asia from the 18th to the early 20th Centuries*, vol. 2 (*Inter-Regional and Inter-Ethnic Relations*), 313–333; Lucyna Antonowicz-Bauer, "The Tatars in Poland," *Journal of Muslim Minority Affairs* 5, 2 (1984), 345–359; György Lederer, "Islam in Lithuania," *Central Asian Survey* 14, 3 (1995), 425–448, esp. 429–438; György Lederer and Ibolya Takacs, "Among the Muslims of Poland," *Central Asian Survey* 9, 2 (1990), 119–131, esp. 119–125; Maciej Konopacki, "Les Musulmans en Pologne," *Revue des Études islamiques* 36 (1968), 115–130; Agata S. Nalborczyk, "Islam in Poland: The Past and the Present," *Islamochristiana* 32 (2006), 225–238, esp. 225–230; Shirin Akiner, *Religious Language of a Belarusian Tatar Kitab: A Cultural Monument of Islam in Europe* (Wiesbaden, 2009), 13–80; and Sebastian Cwiklinski, "Between National and Religious Solidarities: The Tatars in Germany and Poland in the Inter-War Period," in Clayer and Germain (eds.), *Islam in Inter-War Europe*, 64–88, 72–84. Fascinating contemporary overviews are given by L. Sternbach, "The Muhammedans in Poland," *Islamic Culture* 16, 4 (1942), 371–379; C. Bohdanowicz, "The Muslims in Poland," *Asiatic Review* 37, 131 (1941), 646–656; Arsalan Bohdanowicz, "Cultural Movements of Muslims in Poland," *Islamic Review* 31 (November 1942), 372–381; Leon Bohdanowicz, "Muslims in Poland," *Islamic Review* 23 (March 1935), 94–105; (April 1935), 125–131; (May 1935), 164–170; Leon Bohdanowicz, "The Muslims in Poland: Their Origin, History, and Cultural Life," *Journal of the Royal Asiatic Society of Great Britain and Ireland* 3 (1942), 163–180; and Leon Bohdanowicz, "The Polish Tatars," *Man* 44 (1944), 116–121.

171 Sternbach, "The Muhammedans in Poland," 379; C. Bohdanowicz, "The Muslims in Poland," 656; A. Bohdanowicz, "Cultural Movements of Muslims in Poland," 379–381; and L. Bohdanowicz, "The Polish Tatars," 120.

172 In fact, it was the only Muslim Tatar area in the East for which the East Ministry was responsible, see, for instance, Hentig, Report ("Stand der sog. Turanischen Frage"), 25 February 1942, Berlin, PA, R 60690 (also in PA, R 261175). On the general context, see Hans-Dieter Handrack, *Das Reichskommissariat Ostland: Die Kulturpolitik der deutschen Verwaltung zwischen Autonomie und Gleichschaltung 1941–1944* (Scheden, 1979).

173 Rosenberg to Lohse (Ostland) and Koch (Ukraine), 13 May 1942, Berlin, BAB, R 6/206 (also in BAB, R 6/22 and R 6/18).

174 Rosenberg, Decree ("Erlaß des Reichsministers für die besetzten Ostgebiete über die mohammedanischen Feiertage im Jahre 1943"), in SD Newsletter ("SD-Mitteilungsblatt no. 20"), 18 August 1943, Berlin, BAB, R 58/225.

175 Hentig, Report ("Stand der sog. Turanischen Frage"), 25 February 1942, Berlin, PA, R 60690 (also in PA, R 261175).

176 Kirimal, Report ("Bericht über die vom 28.1. bis 8.2.1942 nach dem Ostland (Litauen) gemachte Reise"), 16 February 1942, Berlin, PA, R 261175 (also in BStU, MfS, HA IX/11, RHE 28/88/SU, A. 3).

177 Eriss to Kapp (Reich Commissariat Ostland), n.d. (summer 1943), Riga, Latvian State Historical Archive (*Latvijas Valsts Vēstures Arhīvs*), Riga (LVVA), accessed through USHMA, RG 18, Reel 1; on Eriss, see Norris, *Islam in the Baltic*, 112–113.

178 Kapp, Internal Note, 12 October 1943, Riga, LVVA, accessed through USHMA, RG 18, Reel 1.

179 Eriss to Kapp, n.d. (summer 1943), Riga, LVVA, accessed through USHMA, RG 18, Reel 1.

180 Ibid.

181 Szynkiewicz to Idris, 21 January 1942, Vilnius, PA, R 261175.

182 Ibid.

183 Ibid.

184 Reitenbach (East Ministry), Internal Note ("Die 'Nationale Partei' der Krimtataren 'Milli Firka' und die Krimtataren Akcar, Bekir Bey, Yakub, Suleyman Schinke-witsch, Balic Halim Soysal Abdullah und Ortay Selim"), 14 March 1942, Berlin, BAB, R 6/18.

185 On Szynkiewicz, see Norris, *Islam in the Baltic*, 78–80; Antonowicz-Bauer, "The Tatars in Poland," 351, 356; Lederer, "Islam in Lithuania," 433–434; Lederer and Takacs, "Among the Muslims of Poland," 123–125; Konopacki, "Les Musulmans en Pologne," 119, 122; Nalborczyk, "Islam in Poland," 228–229; Akiner, *Religious Language*, 62–63; Cwiklinski, "Between National and Religious Solidarities," 76–84; Kramer, *Islam Assembled*, 148 and 223; Anonymous, "Der muslimische Kongreß von Europa, Genf September 1935," *Die Welt des Islams* 17, 3/4 (1935), 99–104, 100, and 102–104; Stern-bach, "The Muhammedans in Poland," 377–378; C. Bohdanowicz, "The Muslims in Poland," 653–655; A. Bohdanowicz, "Cultural Movements of Muslims in Poland," 375–376 and 380–381; L. Bohdanowicz, "The Muslims in Poland," 175–176; L. Bohda-nowicz, "Muslims in Poland," 166–170; and L. Bohdanowicz, "The Polish Tatars," 118.

186 Kirimal to Kurkchi, 19 December 1943, n.p., BA–MA, RH 19V/96. On the relationship between Edige and Jakub Szynkiewicz, see also Cwiklinski, "Between National and Religious Solidarities," 84.

187 SS and Police Command Crimea to SS and Police Command Crimea "Black Sea," 2 February 1944, n.p., BA–MA, RH 19V/96.

188 Ibid.

189 Kornelsen to Mende, 11 November 1943, Berlin, USNA, RG 242, T454/Roll 109.

190 Reitenbach (East Ministry), Report ("Die 'Nationale Partei' der Krimtataren 'Milli Firka' und die Krimtataren Akcar, Bekir Bey, Yakub, Suleyman Schinkewitsch, Balic Halim Soysal Abdullah und Ortay Selim"), 14 March 1942, Berlin, BAB, R 6/18. On Islam in the General Government, see Lederer and Takacs, "Among the Muslims of Poland," 124–125; Akiner, *Religious Language of a Belarussian Tatar Kitab*, 63–65; Sternbach, "The Muhammedans in Poland," 379; A. Bohdanowicz, "Cultural Movements of Muslims in Poland," 379–381; L. Bohdanowicz, "The Polish Ta-tars," 120; and Jan Tyszkiewicz, "Imam Ali Ismail Woronowicz w Warszawie i Klecku: 1937–1941" ("Imam Ali Ismail Woronowicz in Warsaw and Kletsk, 1937–1941"), *Rocznik Tatarów Polskich* 3 (1995), 7–17.

191 Wehrmacht Intelligence (Abwehr), Report ("Syrien: Volk und Staat"), 7 July 1942, n.p., BA–MA, RH 2/1790.

192 On these executions and the internal discussion about them, see Hilberg, *The De-struction of the European Jews*, 222–223; and, in the revised edition, Hilberg, *The Destruction of the European Jews*, vol. 1, 338–339; Hans-Adolf Jacobsen, "The Kom-

missarbefehl and Mass Executions of Soviet Russian Prisoners of War," in Martin Broszat et al. (eds.), *Anatomy of the SS State* (London, 1968), 505–535, 529–530; Christian Streit, *Keine Kameraden: Die Wehrmacht und die sowjetischen Kriegsgefangenen 1941–1945* (Stuttgart, 1978), 98; and the memoirs of Bräutigam, *So hat es sich zugetragen*, 390–393; and Herwarth, *Zwischen Hitler und Stalin*, 233; and for the English version, Herwarth, *Against Two Evils*, 205.

193 Quoted in Streit, *Keine Kameraden*, 98.

194 East Ministry, Decree ("Erlass betr. Bestimmung des Begriffs 'Jude' in den besetzten Ostgebieten"), May 1942, Berlin, BAB, R 6/634.

195 On these groups, see Mühlen, *Zwischen Hakenkreuz und Sowjetstern*, 49–51; and Angrick, *Besatzungspolitik und Massenmord*, 326–331 and 612; and, on the Karaites and Krymchaks in particular, Kunz, *Die Krim unter deutscher Herrschaft*, 187–194; and Kiril Feferman, "Nazi Germany and the Karaites in 1938–1944: Between Racial Theory and Realpolitik," *Nationalities Papers* 39, 2 (2011), 277–294; and on the Judeo-Tats in particular, Dallin, *German Rule in Russia*, 247; Hoffmann, *Kaukasien*, 439; Wachs, *Der Fall Theodor Oberländer*, 119–121; and Rudolf Loewenthal, "The Judeo-Tats in the Caucasus," *Historia Judaica* 14 (1952), 61–82, 79.

196 Donner and Seifert, Report ("Bericht über die Erkundung der Siedlungsmöglichkeiten in der Nogaischen Steppe (Taurien) und der Halbinsel Krim"), 10 March 1942, Berlin, BA–MA, MFB 4/44423.

197 Klopfer (NSDAP Party Chancellery) to Brandt, 27 September 1944, Munich, BAB, NS 31/33.

198 Ibid.

199 Bräutigam to East Ministry, 26 December 1942, n.p., BAB, R 6/65; and Bräutigam, Report ("Als Bevollmächtigter des Ostministeriums bei der Heeresgruppe Süd"), n.d. (post-1945), n.p., IfZ, ZS 400.

200 Ibid.

201 Martin Holler, *Der nationalsozialistische Völkermord an den Roma in der besetzten Sowjetunion (1941–1944)* (Heidelberg, 2009), 78–101 (Crimea) and 101–107 (North Caucasus); and Mikhail Tyaglyy, "Were the 'Chingené' Victims of the Holocaust? Nazi Policy toward the Crimean Roma, 1941–1944," *Holocaust and Genocide Studies* 23, 1 (2009), 26–53.

202 Holler, *Der nationalsozialistische Völkermord an den Roma in der besetzten Sowjetunion*, 91–101; and Tyaglyy, "Were the 'Chingené' Victims of the Holocaust?," 37–39, 41, and 43–44, provide overviews of the history of Muslim Roma in the Crimea and the role of the Tatar population during their persecution.

203 Quoted in Holler, *Der nationalsozialistische Völkermord an den Roma in der besetzten Sowjetunion*, 92; and, in a slightly different translation, in Tyaglyy, "Were the 'Chingené' Victims of the Holocaust?," 37.

204 Quoted in Holler, *Der nationalsozialistische Völkermord an den Roma in der besetzten Sowjetunion*, 92.

205 Ohlendorf Testimony ("Extracts from the Testimony of Defendant Ohlendorf"), in *Trials of War Criminals before the Nuernberg Military Tribunals under Control Council Law no. 10*, 15 vols. (Washington, DC, 1949–1953), vol. 4 (*The Einsatzgruppen Case*), 223–312, 290.

206 Bergmann Battalion, Report ("Bericht vom 25.8.–17.9.42"), 17 September 1942, n.p., BAB, R 6/65.

207 Wagner (Headquarters of High Command of the Army), Internal Note ("Notiz für Führer-Vortrag"), 23 September 1942, Berlin, PA, R 27358.

208 Hufnagel (Army), Report ("Verwaltungsbericht für die Zeit vom 21.9.1942 bis zum 20.11.1942"), 23 October 1942, n.p., BA–MA, RH 23/101.

209 On violence in the Crimea, see Dallin, *German Rule in Russia*, 259–264; Nekrich, *The Punished Peoples*, 23–24; Angrick, *Besatzungspolitik und Massenmord*, 323–361 and 452–544; Andrej Angrick, "Die Einsatzgruppe D," in Peter Klein (ed.), *Die Einsatzgruppen in der besetzten Sowjetunion 1941/42: Die Tätigkeits- und Lageberichte des Chefs der Sicherheitspolizei und des SD* (Berlin, 1997), 88–110, 101–102; Oldenburg, *Ideologie und militärisches Kalkül*, 57–224; Luther, "Die Krim unter deutscher Besatzung im Zweiten Weltkrieg," 45–46 and 90; Kunz, *Die Krim unter deutscher Herrschaft*, 109–178 and 210–211; Fisher, *The Crimean Tatars*, 150–164; and Williams, *The Crimean Tatars*, 380–382.

210 Kirimal, *Der nationale Kampf der Krimtürken*, 316; and Nekrich, *The Punished Peoples*, 23–24.

211 On violence in the Caucasus, see Dallin, *German Rule in Russia*, 248–249; Nekrich, *The Punished Peoples*, 41–42 and 62; Angrick, *Besatzungspolitik und Massenmord*, 545–715, esp. 601–602; Angrick, "Die Einsatzgruppe D," 88–110, 102–103; Oldenburg, *Ideologie und militärisches Kalkül*, 259–306; Pohl, *Die Herrschaft der Wehrmacht*, 301–304; and Dieter Pohl, "Deutsche Militärverwaltung: Die bessere Besatzung? Das Beispiel Kaukasus 1942/43," *Mitteilungen der Gemeinsamen Kommission für die Erforschung der jüngeren Geschichte der deutsch-russischen Beziehungen* 2 (2005), 51–59.

212 According to Nekrich, more than 9,000 civilians were killed in the Karachai-Circassia and 500 in the Balkar area during German occupation, see Nekrich, *The Punished Peoples*, 41–42. Compared to other areas of the East, partisan activities in the Caucasus seem to have been rather marginal, see Alexander Dallin, "The North Caucasus," in Paul A. Armstrong (ed.), *Soviet Partisans in World War II* (Madison, WI, 1964), 557–632, esp. 628.

213 Blume to his parents, 6 February 1943, n.p., in Blume, *Zum Kaukasus*, 154–155.

214 Moscow's new policy toward Islam during the war was part of a general shift in Soviet religious policies. On the Soviet campaign for Islamic mobilization, see Yemelianova, *Russia and Islam*, 120–124; Bennigsen and Lemercier-Quelquejay, *Islam in the Soviet Union*, 165–174; Kolarz, *Religion in the Soviet Union*, 425–428; Bräker, *Kommunismus und Weltreligonen Asiens*, vol. 1, 121–135; Ro'i, *Islam in the Soviet Union*, 100–107, 113–114, 167, 171–172, and 574; Mühlen, *Zwischen Hakenkreuz und Sowjetstern*, 220–221; and Lenczowski, *Russia and the West in Iran 1918–1948*, 213–215. Three early German reports are provided by Bertold Spuler, *Idel-Ural: Völker und Staaten zwischen Wolga und Ural* (Berlin, 1942), 96–97; Bertold Spuler, "Die Wolga-Tataren und Baschkiren unter russischer Herrschaft," *Der Islam* 29, 2 (1949), 142–216, 185–192; and Bertold Spuler, "Die Lage der Muslime in Rußland seit 1942," *Der Islam* 29, 3 (1950), 296–300.

215 Pohl, *Ethnic Cleansing in the USSR*, 75 and 82 (North Caucasians in Red Army) and 113 (Crimean Tatars in the Red Army). Only in the case of the Chechens did Moscow decide, in spring 1942, to temporarily stop recruiting, see Avtorkhanov,

"Chechens and the Ingush during the Soviet Period and Its Antecedents," 179–180; Nekrich, *The Punished Peoples*, 56–57; and Naimark, *Fires of Hatred*, 94; and, more generally, articles in Alexander R. Alexiev and S. Enders Wimbush (eds.), *Ethnic Minorities in the Red Army: Asset or Liability* (Boulder, CO, 1988).

216 Rasulaev (Central Muslim Spiritual Directorate), Appeal, 18 July 1941, printed in Stanley Evans, *The Churches of the USSR* (London, 1943), 158.

217 Rasulaev, Appeal, 7 August 1941, printed in ibid., 159.

218 Rasulaev, Appeal, 2 September 1941, printed in ibid., 158–159.

219 Mikhail Dolgopolov, "Soviet Mufti exposes Hitler Mufti," *Soviet War News* (24 October 1942).

220 On 27 October 1943, the Soviet broadcast service in Arabic also reported on a conference in Tashkent, see Broadcast Monitoring Script "Moscow in Arabic: Internal News," 27 October 1943 (recorded), USNA, RG 84, Entry UD 2410, Box 93; see also Anonymous, "Soviet Moslem Congress Elects Administration," *Soviet War News* (28 October 1943); and Mikhail Dolgopolov, "Interview with Moslem Leader of Tashkent," *Soviet War News* (24 May 1943).

221 Y. Gik, "Interview with Sheikh ul Islam of Transcaucasia," *Soviet War News* (11 October 1944), reprinted in *Soviet War News Weekly* (12 October 1944); and Anonymous, "Mohammedans Greet Marshall Stalin," *Soviet War News* (31 May 1944).

222 Jean Richard Bloch, "Interview with Soviet Mufti," *Soviet War News* (20 May 1942), reprinted in *Soviet War News Weekly* (28 May 1942). The Soviet translation from sura 9 (*al-Tawba*) varies from the more accurate one provided by Arberry: "slay the idolaters wherever you find them" (9:5).

223 Quoted in Werth, *Russia at War*, 575.

224 Conquest, *The Nation Killers*, 85–86; and, on changing perceptions of Shamil in the Soviet Union in general, ibid., 84–94 and 164–178; and Bülent Gökay, "The Longstanding Russian and Soviet Debate over Sheikh Shamil: Anti-Imperialist Hero or Counter-Revolutionary Cleric?," in Ben Fowkes (ed.), *Russia and Chechnia: The Permanent Crisis: Essays on Russo-Chechen Relations* (London, 1998), 25–64.

225 Quoted in Bräker, *Kommunismus und Weltreligonen Asiens*, vol. 1, 127–128.

226 Kornelsen, Internal Note ("Evakuierung der Krimtataren") 11 November 1943, Berlin, BAB, R 6/143.

227 Office of Strategic Services, Report ("German activity in connection with Caucasian groups"), 3 November 1943, Washington, DC, USNA, accessed through USHMA, RG 6, Reel 15.

228 Wolfgang Koerber, "Der Zug der Hunderttausend," *Völkischer Beobachter* (20 October 1943).

229 Kirimal, Abdullah, and Loysal to Berger, 29 October 1943, Berlin, BAB, NS 31/32; and Schulte (SS Head Office), Internal Note ("Zurücknahme der Krimtataren bei Aufgabe der Krim durch die deutsche Wehrmacht"), 30 October 1943, BAB, NS 31/32, on appeals to the SS; and Kornelsen, Internal Note ("Evakuierung der Krimtataren"), 11 November 1943, Berlin, BAB, R 6/143, on appeals to the Wehrmacht and the East Ministry and the request to evacuate at least the most important Muslim leaders. Andreas Hillgruber, *Die Räumung der Krim 1944* (Berlin, 1959), gives an account of the chaotic situation during the evacuation of the Crimea.

230 Kirimal, Abdullah, and Loysal to Al-Husayni, 30 September 1943, Berlin, BAB, NS 31/32; and Schulte, Internal Note ("Zukünftiges Schicksal der Krim-Mohammedaner"), 2 October 1943, Berlin, BAB, NS 31/32.

231 Kirimal to Kurkchi, 19 December 1943, n.p., BA–MA, RH 19V/96.

232 Al-Husayni to Berger, 20 October 1944, Oybin, BAB, NS 31/32. Apparently, in the last months of the war, they managed to move 1,000 Crimean Tatar civilians to Styria, see Olzscha to Spaarmann, 4 November 1944, Berlin, BAB, NS 31/32.

233 On the deportations in the Caucasus and Crimea, see Nekrich, *The Punished Peoples*, 36–65 (Caucasus) and 13–35 (Crimea); Pohl, *Ethnic Cleansing in the USSR*, 73–77 (Karachais), 87–92 (Balkars), 79–86 (Chechens and Ingush), and 109–118 (Crimean Tatars); and Naimark, *Fires of Hatred*, 85–107, esp. 92–99 (Caucasus) and 99–104 (Crimea); and, on the broader context, the classic by Conquest, *The Nation Killers*; and Vera Tolz, "New Information about the Deportation of Ethnic Groups in the USSR during World War 2," in Carol Garrard and John Garrard (eds.), *World War 2 and the Soviet People* (London, 1993), 161–179; and, on the Caucasus in particular, Alf Grannes, "The Soviet Deportation in 1943 of the Karachays: A Turkic Muslim People of North Caucasus," *Journal of Muslim Minority Affairs* 12, 1 (1991), 55–68; William Flemming, "The Deportation of the Chechen and Ingush Peoples: A Critical Examination," in Fowkes (ed.), *Russia and Chechnia*, 65–86; Daniel Bohse, "Ahndung einer 'zweiten Front' im Kaukasus? Die Deportation der Tschetschenen und Inguschen in den Jahren 1942–1945 und die Mär von der kollektiven Kollaboration mit dem deutschen Aggressor," *Hallische Beiträge zur Zeitgeschichte* 9 (2001), 37–55; and, on the Crimea in particular, Fisher, *The Crimean Tatars*, 162–179; Williams, *The Crimean Tatars*, 382–90; Brian G. Williams, "The Hidden Ethnic Cleansing of Muslims in the Soviet Union: The Exile and Repatriation of the Crimean Tatars," *Journal of Contemporary History* 37, 3 (2002), 323–347; and Brian G. Williams, "Hidden Ethnocide in the Soviet Muslim Borderlands: The Ethnic Cleansing of the Crimean Tatars," *Journal of Genocide Research* 4, 3 (2002), 357–373.

234 Nekrich, *The Punished Peoples*, 61–62.

235 Quoted (though incorrectly translated) in ibid., 58.

5 · ISLAM AND THE BATTLE FOR THE BALKANS

1 Fedrigotti to Foreign Office, 27 April 1941, Belgrade, PA, R 60681.

2 Fedrigotti to Foreign Office, 21 April 1941, Sarajevo, PA, R 60681 (also in PA, R 27363).

3 Fedrigotti to Foreign Office, 19 April 1941, Ključ, PA, R 60681 (also in PA, R 27363); and Fedrigotti to Foreign Office, 27 April 1941, Belgrade, PA, R 60681.

4 On Islam in the Ottoman Balkans, see Peter F. Sugar, *Southeastern Europe under Ottoman Rule, 1354–1804* (Seattle, WA, 1977); and, for the later phase, Fikret Karčić, *The Bosniaks and the Challenge of Modernity: Late Ottoman and Hapsburg Times* (Sarajevo, 1999), which also provides a good overview of Islam under Habsburg rule. On Islam in the Habsburg era, see Robert J. Donia, *Islam under the Double Eagle: The Muslims of Bosnia and Hercegovina, 1878–1914* (New York, 1981); Ferdinand Hauptmann, "Die Mohammedaner in Bosnien-Hercegovina," in Adam Wandruszka and Peter Urbanitsch (eds.), *Die Habsburgermonarchie 1848–1918*, vol. 4 (*Die Konfessionen*)

(Vienna, 1985), 670–701; Muhamed Mufaku al-Arnaut, "Islam and Muslims in Bosnia 1878–1918: Two Hijras and Two Fatwās," *Journal of Islamic Studies* 5, 2 (1994), 242–253; Rupert Klieber, *Jüdische–Christliche–Muslimische Lebenswelten der Donaumonarchie, 1848–1918* (Vienna, 2010), 157–168; Zlatko Hasanbegović, *Muslimani u Zagrebu, 1878–1945* (*Muslims in Zagreb, 1878–1945*) (Zagreb, 2007), 29–51; and Alexandre Popovic, *L'Islam balkanique: Les Musulmans du Sud-Est européen dans la période post-ottomane* (Berlin, 1986), 269–310. And on Islam in interwar Yugoslavia, see Sabina Ferhadbegović, "Fes oder Hut? Der Islam in Bosnien zwischen den Weltkriegen," *Wiener Zeitschrift zur Geschichte der Neuzeit* 5, 2 (2005), 69–85; Xavier Bougarel, "Farewell to the Ottoman Legacy? Islamic Reformism and Revivalism in Inter-War Bosnia-Herzegovina," in Clayer and Germain (eds.), *Islam in Inter-War Europe*, 313–343; Muhammed Aruçi, "The Muslim Minority in Macedonia and Its Educational Institutions during the Inter-War Period," in Clayer and Germain (eds.), *Islam in Inter-War Europe*, 344–361; Fikret Karčić, "The Reform of Shari'a Courts and Islamic Law in Bosnia and Herzegovina, 1918–1941," in Clayer and Germain (eds.), *Islam in Inter-War Europe*, 253–270; Fikret Karčić, *Šeriatski Sudovi u Jugoslaviji 1918–1941* (*Shari'a Courts in Yugoslavia 1918–1941*) (Sarajevo, 1986); Atif Purivatra, *Jugoslovenska Muslimanska Organizacija u Političkom Životu Kraljevine Srba, Hrvata i Slovenaca* (*The Yugoslav Muslim Organization in the Political Life of the Kingdom of Serbs, Croats and Slovenes*) (Sarajevo, 1974); Musnija Kamberović, *Mehmed Spaho (1883–1939): Politička Biografija* (*Mehmed Spaho [1883–1939]: A Political Biography*) (Sarajevo, 2009); Hasanbegović, *Muslimani u Zagrebu*, 53–166; and Popovic, *L'Islam balkanique*, 310–336. An insightful German contemporary account is Ingomar Heyer, *Beiträge zur Kenntnis des Islam in Bosnien und der Hercegovina* (Tübingen, 1940).

5 Scholarship on Germany's war in the territories of the former Yugoslav kingdom has considered the Muslim population, though without systematically inquiring into German policy toward Islam. The most comprehensive work remains Tomasevich, *War and Revolution in Yugoslavia*, esp. 466–510. On Bosnia in particular, see Redžić, *Bosnia and Herzegovina in the Second World War*, esp. 4–62 and 164–196; Enver Redžić, *Muslimansko Autonomaštvo i 13. SS Divizija: Autonomija Bosne i Hercegovine i Hitlerov Treći Rajh* (*The Muslim Autonomist Movement and the 13th SS Division: Bosnia Herzegovina's Autonomy and Hitler's Third Reich*) (Sarajevo, 1987), esp. 81–90 and 149–153; Hoare, *Genocide and Resistance in Hitler's Bosnia*; Hoare, *The Bosnian Muslims in the Second World War*; and Emily Greble, *Sarajevo, 1941–1945: Muslims, Christians, and Jews in Hitler's Europe* (Ithaca, NY, 2011). Significant general studies on Germany's war in the region include Martin Broszat and Ladislaus Hory, *Der Kroatische Ustascha-Staat 1941–1945* (Stuttgart, 1965); Gert Fricke, *Kroatien 1941–1944: Der "Unabhängige Staat" in der Sicht des deutschen Bevollmächtigten Generals in Agram Glaise v. Horstenau* (Freiburg, 1972); Paul N. Hehn, *The German Struggle against Yugoslav Guerrillas in World War II* (New York, 1979); Klaus Schmider, *Partisanenkrieg in Jugoslawien 1941–1945* (Hamburg, 2002); Meyer, *Blutiges Edelweiß*; Stevan K. Pavlowitch, *Hitler's New Disorder: The Second World War in Yugoslavia* (New York, 2008); and Ben Shepherd, *Terror in the Balkans: German Armies and Partisan Warfare* (Cambridge, MA, 2012).

6 On Islam in the Ustaša state, see Tomasevich, *War and Revolution in Yugoslavia*, 488–494; Redžić, *Bosnia and Herzegovina in the Second World War*, 68, 85–87, 166–169 and 172; Redžić, *Muslimansko Autonomaštvo i 13. SS Divizija*, 9–20; Hoare, *The Bosnian Muslims in the Second World War*; Greble, *Sarajevo*, esp. 58, 76–81, 84–85, 120–129, 192–195, 213–217, and 253; Hasanbegović, *Muslimani u Zagrebu*, 167–386; and Popović, *L'Islam balkanique*, 336–342.

7 On the Muslim population in the civil war, see the literature in note 5, esp. Tomasevich, *War and Revolution in Yugoslavia*, 491–494; Redžić, *Bosnia and Herzegovina in the Second World War*, 63–118 and 169–177; Redžić, *Muslimansko Autonomaštvo i 13. SS Divizija*, 29–62; and Hoare, *The Bosnian Muslims in the Second World War*, as well as Edmond Paris, *Genocide in Satellite Croatia, 1941–1945: A Record of Racial and Religious Persecutions and Massacres* (Chicago, 1961), 119–126; Yeshayahu Jelinek, "Nationalities and Minorities in the Independent State of Croatia," *Nationalities Papers* 8, 2 (1980), 195–210, esp. 200–203; Yeshayahu Jelinek, "Bosnia-Herzegovina at War: Relations between Moslems and Non-Moslems," *Holocaust and Genocide Studies* 5, 3 (1990), 275–292; Tomislav Dulić, "Mass Killing in the Independent State of Croatia, 1941–45: A Case for Comparative Research," *Journal of Genocide Research* 8, 3 (2006), 255–281, esp. 265–270; Damir Mirković, "Victims and Perpetrators in the Yugoslav Genocide, 1941–1945: Some Preliminary Observations," *Holocaust and Genocide Studies* 7, 3 (1993), 317–332, esp. 321–322; Valeria Heuberger, "Islam and Muslims in Bosnia-Herzegovina during World War II: A Survey," in Lieve Gevers and Jan Bank (eds.), *Religion under Siege*, vol. 2 (Leuven, 2007), 175–193, esp. 183–188; and Alexander Korb, *Im Schatten des Weltkriegs: Massengewalt der Ustaša gegen Serben, Juden und Roma in Kroatien 1941–1945* (Hamburg, 2013), passim. For excellent overviews of the Muslims in the civil war in Bosnia, see Noel Malcolm, *Bosnia: A Short History* (London, 1994), 174–192; Marko Attila Hoare, *The History of Bosnia: From the Middle Ages to the Present Day* (London, 2007), 197–308; and Robert J. Donia, *Sarajevo: A Biography* (London, 2006), 168–203. Vladimir Dedijer and Antun Miletić (eds.), *Genocid nad Muslimanima, 1941–1945: Zbornik Dokumenata i Svedočenja* (*Genocide against the Muslims, 1941–1945: A Collection of Documents and Testimonies*) (Sarajevo, 1990), provide a selection of primary documents on the civil war and Četnik violence against Muslims.

8 On 18 February 1942, Siegfried Kasche, the German envoy in Zagreb, forwarded a number of appeals from local Muslim groups to (Muslim) Ustaša authorities, complaining about their religious persecution, to Berlin, see Kasche to Foreign Office, 18 February 1942, Zagreb, PA, R 60608, and, attached, Memorandum ("Beschwerde der muselmanischen Bezirksbeauftragten von Prijedor an einige angesehene Muselmanen"), 23 September 1941, Prijedor, PA, R 60608; and Memorandum ("Denkschrift des Sarajevo Ulema-Verein 'El Hidaja'"), 12 October 1941, PA, R 60608; and Memorandum ("Denkschrift der muselmanischen Vertreter aus Banja Luka"), 12 November 1941, Banja Luka, PA, R 60608.

9 People's Committee ("Volkskomitee"), Memorandum, 1 November 1942, Sarajevo, PA, R 261144. The twenty-page memorandum was first assessed by army officials and then forwarded to Hitler at the end of 1942, see Wehrmacht Intelligence to Reich Chancellery, 28 December 1942, Berlin, PA, R 261144; the Reich Chancellery consulted the Foreign Office about the memorandum, see Stutterheim (Reich

Chancellery) to Heimburg (Foreign Office), 4 January 1943, Berlin, PA, R 261144; and this led to a discussion about it in the Foreign Office, see the documents in PA, R 261144. On the memorandum and Muslim appeals to the Germans and Italians, see Tomasevich, *War and Revolution in Yugoslavia*, 489 and 494–496; Redžić, *Bosnia and Herzegovina in the Second World War*, 19, 168, and 177–180; Redžić, *Muslimansko Autonomaštvo i 13. SS Divizija*, 71–79; Greble, *Sarajevo*, 163–166; and, for a Croatian translation of the complete memorandum, Dedijer and Miletić (eds.), *Genocid nad Muslimanima*, 249–264. Some pro-German Muslim leaders had already sent similar petitions to the Germans after the invasion in 1941, see Kuna to Hitler, 20 April 1941, Sarajevo, PA, R 60681; and Bosnian Representatives (signed by seventeen Muslims) to Command of the 132nd Division, 22 April 1941, Bosanska Krupa, PA, R 60681. In the following months, Muslim autonomists had repeatedly turned to the Germans. In autumn 1941 the *Reis-ul-Ulema*, Fehim Spaho, contacted the German consulate in Sarajevo to seek help, and in early 1942 a Muslim representative from Bosnia and Herzegovina sent a memorandum, addressed to the mufti of Jerusalem, to the German consulate in Zagreb, asking for Muslim autonomy under German protection, see Kasche to Foreign Office, 18 February 1942, Zagreb, PA, R 60608; and, attached, Salihagić (Head of the Waqf Committee for Bosnia and Hercegovina) to Al-Husayni, n.d. (January 1942), Banja Luka, PA, R 60608.

10 People's Committee ("Volkskomitee"), Memorandum, 1 November 1942, Sarajevo, PA, R 261144.

11 Ibid.

12 Kasche to Foreign Office, 18 February 1942, Zagreb, PA, R 60608; Kasche to Foreign Office, 22 April 1942, Zagreb, PA, R 60607; and Kasche, Report ("Politische Gesichtspunkte für Propagandaarbeit in Kroatien"), n.d. (1943), Zagreb, PA, R 27795, provide insights into Kasche's political notion of Islam and the Islamic world.

13 On the intensified German involvement in the Balkans in 1942–1943, see the literature in note 5.

14 Lüters, Report ("Aufstandsbewegung der Cetniks"), 5 May 1943, n.p., BA–MA, RS 3–7/16.

15 Wurianek (Army), Report ("Bericht über Bosnien"), 10 July 1943, Graz, BA–MA, RH 31III/5; and Wurianek, Speech ("Vortrag vor der Mannschaft der Kampftruppe Ost- und West-Bosnien"), 10 July 1943, Graz, BA–MA, RH 31III/5.

16 SS Reich Security Head Office, Intelligence Report ("Muselmanenproblem") n.d., n.p., BAB, R 58/92; and for views of other observers on the ground, NSDAP Organization Croatia, Report ("Monatsbericht"), 31 December 1942, Sarajevo, BA–MA, RH 31III/5, which was forwarded by the *NSDAP Landesgruppenleiter* Rudolf Empting to Horstenau, 13 January 1943, Zagreb, BA–MA, RH 31III/5; and Hille (*Einsatzstab Reichsleiter Rosenberg*), Report, 19 August 1942, Zagreb, Russian State Military Archive (*Rossiiskii Gosudarstvennyi Voennyi Arkhiv*), Moscow (RGVA), Special Collection (*Osobyi Archive*), accessed through USHMA, RG 11/Reel 131.

17 Meyer, *Blutiges Edelweiß*, 119. Also, representatives of the SS and the Foreign Office agreed on the exploitation of the Muslims for the pacification of the Sandžak, see Gredler (Foreign Office), Internal Note ("Bericht des Ustascha-Kommissars Murat Bayrović über die Lage im Sandschak"), 12 April 1943, Berlin, PA, R 100998. In his

memoirs, Karl Wilhelm Thilo, "Der Einsatz auf dem Balkan," in Hubert Lanz (ed.), *Gebirgsjäger: Die 1. Gebirgsdivision 1935–1945* (Bad Nauheim, 1954), 242–277, esp. 253 and 245–246, describes the cooperation with Muslims on the ground.

18 On Albania under German control, see Bernd J. Fischer, *Albania at War 1939–1945* (London, 1999), 157–256; Bernd J. Fischer, "German Political Policy in Albania, 1943–1944," in Richard B. Spence and Linda Nelson (eds.), *Scholar, Patriot, Mentor: Historical Essays in Honor of Dimitrije Djordjević* (Boulder, CO, 1992), 219–233; Hubert Neuwirth, *Widerstand und Kollaboration in Albanien 1939–1944* (Wiesbaden, 2008); Christoph Stamm, "Zur deutschen Besetzung Albaniens 1943–1944," *Militärgeschichtliche Mitteilungen* 30, 2 (1981), 99–120; Noel Malcolm, *Kosovo: A Short History* (London, 1998), 304–313; and, on religion in wartime Albania, Popovic, *L'Islam balkanique*, 36–42; and Roberto Morozzo della Rocca, *Nazione e religione in Albania (1920–1944)* (Bologna, 1990), 167–246, which points to German noninterference in the country's Islamic institutions and the work of the 'ulama.

19 On the Muslims of the Epirus area, see Mark Mazower, "Three Forms of Political Justice: Greece, 1944–1945," in Mark Mazower (ed.), *After the War Was over: Reconstructing the Family, Nation and State in Greece, 1943–1960* (Princeton, NJ, 2000), 24–41, 24–26; Meyer, *Blutiges Edelweiß*, 151–152, 204, 463–476, 539, and 620–621; and Fischer, *Albania at War*, 70–76, 85, and 168–169; and, for an account from the perspective of the Chams, Beqir Meta, *The Cham Tragedy* (Tirana, 2007), 59–105; and the documents in Robert Elsie and Bejtullah D. Destani (eds.), *The Cham Albanians of Greece: A Documentary History* (London, 2013), 335–394. Germany's policy toward the Muslims of Greece is not addressed in this chapter. It seems that Islam played only a marginal role in the occupation policies in Greece, although, in the Aegean, army officials tried to co-opt religious figures like the mufti of Rhodes, Seyh Suleyman Kaslioglu, to stabilize the late German occupation regime, see Headquarters of Commander East-Aegean, Report ("Stimmungsbericht"), 17 November 1944, n.p., BA–MA, RH 19XI/38. Kaslioglu hid some invaluable Torah scrolls in the pulpit of the island's Murat Reis Mosque during the war, see Isaac Benatar, *Rhodes and the Holocaust: The Story of the Jewish Community from the Mediterranean Island of Rhodes* (Bloomington, IN, 2010), 22–23 and 84. The German military authorities estimated that c. 130,000 Muslims lived in occupied Greece, see Headquarters of High Command Army Group E to Headquarters of Commander Southeast, n.d. (March 1944), n.p., BA–MA, RH 19XI/10b.

20 Neubacher, *Sonderauftrag Südost*, 32–33 and, similarly, 160.

21 Ibid., 32.

22 On the intersection of religion and politics in the Muslim areas of the Balkans, see Marco Dogo, "The Balkan Nation-States and the Muslim Question," in Marco Dogo and Stefano Bianchini (eds.), *Balkans: National Identities in a Historical Perspective* (Ravenna, 1998), 61–74; Pedro Ramet, "Religion and Nationalism in Yugoslavia," in Pedro Ramet (ed.), *Religion and Nationalism in Soviet and East European Politics* (Durham, NC, 1984), 149–169, 156–158; Ivo Banac, *The National Question in Yugoslavia: Origins, History, Politics* (Ithaca, NY, 1984), 359–378; and, more specifically, Ivo Banac, "Bosnian Muslims: From Religious Community to Socialist Nationhood and Post-Communist Statehood, 1918–1992," in Mark Pinson (ed.),

The Muslims of Bosnia and Herzegovina: Their Historical Development from the Middle Ages to the Dissolution of Yugoslavia (Cambridge, MA, 1994), 129–153; and Mitja Velikonja, *Religious Separation and Political Intolerance in Bosnia-Herzegovina* (College Station, TX, 2003). Mark Mazower, *The Balkans: A Short History* (London, 2000), provides a brilliant account of the Balkan communities before and after the nation-state.

23 On the Balkan tour of the mufti, see Schechtman, *The Mufti and the Fuehrer,* 139; Lebel, *The Mufti of Jerusalem,* 181–189; Gensicke, *The Mufti of Jerusalem and the Nazis,* 132–135; Tomasevich, *War and Revolution in Yugoslavia,* 498; Redžić, *Bosnia and Herzegovina in the Second World War,* 34, 39, and 182; Tomasevich, *Muslimansko Autonomaštvo i 13. SS Divizija,* 91–102; Greble, *Sarajevo,* 170–171; Hasanbegović, *Muslimani u Zagrebu,* 192–195, 208, 411, and, for an Ustaša security report on the visit, 506–507.

24 Berger to Himmler, 27 March 1943, Berlin, BAB, R 19/2255.

25 Al-Husayni to Foreign Office, 30 April 1943, Berlin, PA, R 27322 (also in PA, R 100998). Muslim attempts to send a delegation to the mufti in Berlin failed. A petition to this effect, which was sent to Kasche in late 1941, remained unanswered, see Salihagić (Head of the Waqf Committee of Bosnia and Hercevoina) to Kasche, 18 December 1941, Banja Luka, PA, R 60608. A memorandum for the mufti, with the same request, of early 1942 was probably never forwarded to al-Husayni, see Salihagić to Al-Husayni (via German envoy in Croatia), n.d., Banja Luka, PA, R 60608. On Kasche's assessment of these requests, see Kasche to Foreign Office, 18 February 1942, Zagreb, PA, R 60608; and, on the objections of diplomats in Berlin, Heinburg (Foreign Office), Internal Note, 22 May 1942, Berlin, PA, R 60608. In his memoirs, al-Husayni claims that he had received telegraphs from the Balkans asking for a reception in Berlin but that the Foreign Office had not given permission, see *Mudhakkirat al-Hajj Muhammad Amin al-Husayni,* ed. al-'Umar, 137–138. On the delegation's visit to Rome, see also Tomasevich, *War and Revolution in Yugoslavia,* 494–495; Redžić, *Bosnia and Herzegovina in the Second World War,* 175–176; and Redžić, *Muslimansko Autonomaštvo i 13. SS Divizija,* 64–67.

26 Kramer, *Islam Assembled,* 132 and 162; and, on the mufti's own assessment of the relevance of these ties during the war, *Mudhakkirat al-Hajj Muhammad Amin al-Husayni,* ed. al-'Umar, 137.

27 Kasche to Foreign Office, 13 August 1942, Zagreb, PA, R 27327.

28 Quoted in ibid.

29 Anonymous, "Der Großmufti von Jerusalem," *Völkischer Beobachter* (27 November 1942).

30 Berger to Himmler, 27 March 1943, Berlin, BAB, R 19/2255.

31 Ibid.

32 Berger to Himmler, 19 April 1943, Berlin, BAB, R 19/2255.

33 For a schedule of the tour, see ibid.

34 Ibid.; and, on his meetings, also Kasche to Foreign Office, 12 April 1943, Zagreb, PA, R 27322; Ettel, Internal Note, 16 April 1943, Berlin, R 27322; and on al-Husayni's own account of his tour and his meetings with religious dignitaries, *Mudhakkirat al-Hajj Muhammad Amin al-Husayni,* ed. al-'Umar, 138–140 and 143.

35 *Mudhakkirat al-Hajj Muhammad Amin al-Husayni*, ed. al-'Umar, 143.

36 Winkler, Report ("Die politische Lage der Mohammedaner Bosniens"), 4 May 1943, Berlin, PA, R 67675 (also in PA, R 261144).

37 German News Agency, Confidential Report ("Vertrauliches Rohmaterial"), 16 April 1943, Zagreb, PA, R 27327.

38 Winkler, Report ("Die politische Lage der Mohammedaner Bosniens"), 4 May 1943, Berlin, PA, R 67675 (also in PA, R 261144).

39 German News Agency, Confidential Report ("Vertrauliches Rohmaterial"), 16 April 1943, Zagreb, PA, R 27327.

40 German News Agency, Confidential Report ("Vertrauliches Rohmaterial"), 21 April 1943, Zagreb, PA, R 27327.

41 US Intelligence (FBIS), Report, 22 April 1943, n.p., USNA, accessed through USHMA, RG 6, Reel 22.

42 Al-Husayni to Foreign Office, 30 April 1943, Berlin, PA, R 27322.

43 Berger to Himmler, 19 April 1943, Berlin, BAB, R 19/2255; and similarly, ten days later, Berger to Himmler, 29 April 1943, Berlin, BAB, NS 19/2601.

44 Berger to Himmler, 19 April 1943, Berlin, BAB, R 19/2255.

45 Lüters, Report ("Aufstandsbewegung der Cetniks"), 5 May 1943, n.p., BA–MA, RS 3–7/16.

46 *Mudhakkirat al-Hajj Muhammad Amin al-Husayni*, ed. al-'Umar, 139. After his return to Berlin he also made the same complaint to Ettel, see Internal Note, 16 April 1943, Berlin, PA, R 27322.

47 Woermann, Internal Note, 29 April 1943, Berlin, USHMA, RG 71, Box 91.

48 Berger to Himmler, 19 April 1943, Berlin, BAB, R 19/2255.

49 Ibid.

50 Phleps (Commander of the Seventh Volunteer SS Mountain Division "Prinz Eugen") to Jüttner (Chief of the SS Leadership Head Office), 19 April 1943, n.p., BAB, NS 19/2601; this report was forwarded by Jüttner to Himmler, 27 April 1943, Berlin, BAB, NS 19/2601.

51 Anonymous, "Der Großmufti in Agram," *Deutsche Allgemeine Zeitung* (3 April 1943).

52 Berger to Himmler, 19 April 1943, Berlin, BAB, R 19/2255. Kasche explained that he did not receive the mufti because he believed that the trip was of an entirely "private character"; Kasche to Foreign Office, 12 April 1943, Zagreb, PA, R 27322; and Woermann complained that "neither the Foreign Office nor the Italian embassy was informed about the trip in advance," see Woermann, Internal Note, 31 March 1943, Berlin, PA, R 27322 (also in PA, R 100999). Prüfer also noted in his diary that al-Husayni visited Croatia without the knowledge of the Foreign Office and the Italians, see McKale (ed.), *Rewriting History*, 67–68 (3 April 1943). In fact, Ribbentrop had known about the tour and assigned the diplomat and SS veteran Erwin Ettel to deal with the issue. Ettel wrote a number of reports about the planning and realization of the visit for Ribbentrop, see Ettel, Internal Note, 19 March 1943, Berlin, PA, R 27322; Ettel, Internal Note ("Aufstellung einer bosnischen Division"), Berlin, 22 March 1943, PA, R 27322; Ettel, Internal Note, Berlin, 25 March 1943, PA, R 27322; Ettel, Internal Note ("Werbung für die Aufstellung einer mohammedanischen Division in Kroatien"), 26 March 1943, Berlin, PA, R 27322; and, based on a discussion

with al-Husayni after the tour, Ettel, Internal Note, Berlin, 16 April 1943, PA, R 27322.

53 Kasche to Foreign Office, 28 April 1943, Zagreb, PA, R 100998.

54 Winkler, Report ("Die politische Lage der Mohammedaner Bosniens"), 4 May 1943, Berlin, PA, R 67675 (also in PA, R 261144). On Winkler's stay in Sarajevo and Zagreb between 14 and 22 April 1943, see Kasche to Foreign Office, 28 April 1943, Zagreb, PA, R 100998; and, attached, German Legation in Zagreb, Report ("Unterredungen in Sarajevo"), n.d. (28 April 1943), Zagreb, PA, R 100998. Another critical assessment of the mufti's visit was given by Veesenmayer (Foreign Office), Internal Note ("Bericht über Kroatien"), 3 April 1943, Berlin, PA, R 261144.

55 Winkler, Report ("Die politische Lage der Mohammedaner Bosniens"), 4 May 1943, Berlin, PA, R 67675 (also in PA, R 261144).

56 Ibid.

57 On Winkler, see Horst Junginger, "Ein Kapitel Religionswissenschaft während der NS-Zeit: Hans Alexander Winkler (1900–1945)," Zeitschrift für Religionswissenschaft 3 (1995), 137–161; and Horst Junginger, "Das tragische Leben von Hans Alexander Winkler (1900–1945) und seiner armenischen Frau Hayastan (1901–1937)," Bausteine zur Tübinger Universitätsgeschichte 7 (1995), 83–110.

58 On al-Husayni's visit to Vienna, see Berger to Himmler, 19 April 1943, Berlin, BAB, R 19/2255; and Ettel, Internal Note, 16 April 1943, Berlin, PA, R 27322.

59 On the relations between German authorities and the Muslims of Vienna, and the institutionalization of the city's Muslim community during the war, see the documents in Vienna City and State Archive (Wiener Stadt- und Landesarchiv), Vienna (WstLArch), M. Abt. 119, A 32, 196/1943, as well as in PA, R 269669.

60 On the Muslim community of the Protectorate of Bohemia and Moravia during the war, see the documents stored in the National Archives of the Czech Republic (Národní Archiv České Republiky), Prague (NAČR), accessed through Center for Modern Oriental Studies (Zentrum Moderner Orient), Berlin (ZMO), Höpp Papers, Box 1.20.

61 Harrison to Hull (Secretary of State), 13 April 1943, Bern, USNA, accessed through USHMA, RG 6, Reel 22.

62 Ibid.

63 Propaganda Division South-East, Report ("Lage- und Tätigkeitsbericht für den Monat August 1942"), 4 September 1942, Belgrade, BA–MA, RW 4/232.

64 Propaganda Brochure "Život Muslimana u Njemačkoj" ("The Life of the Muslims in Germany"), n.d. (February 1943), BA–MA, RH 45/73.

65 Data Sheet on "Islam i Židovstvo" ("Islam and Judaism"), n.d. (February 1943), BA–MA, RH 45/76; and, on the content, Thomas Casagrande, Die volksdeutsche SS-Division "Prinz Eugen": Die Banater Schwaben und die nationalsozialistischen Kriegsverbrechen (Frankfurt, 2003), 333; and Lebel, The Mufti of Jerusalem, 311–319, which includes the full translation of the booklet.

66 Pamphlet "Muslimani!" ("Muslims!"), n.d., BA–MA, RH 45/51; and, for the German translation, see Pamphlet "Muselmanen!" (German translation), June 1943, BA–MA, RH 45/51; for details about the pamphlet and its distribution, see Data Sheet on "Muslimani!," June 1943, BA–MA, RH 45/51.

67 Pamphlet "Kämpfer des NOV!" (German translation), n.d., BA–MA, RH 45/49.

68 Pamphlet "Braćo muslimani!" ("Muslim Brothers!"), n.d., BA–MA, RH 45/51.

69 Pamphlet "Muslimani Bosne i Hercegovine!" ("Muslims of Bosnia and Herzegovina!"), n.d., BA–MA, RH 45/59.

70 Pamphlet "Treba li Staljinov plan da bude stvarnost?" ("Must Stalin's Plan Become a Reality?"), n.d., BA–MA, RH 45/53.

71 Pamphlet "Borci bosanskih i muslimanskih brigada!" ("Fighters of the Bosnian and Muslim Brigades"), n.d., BA–MA, RH 45/61.

72 Pamphlet "353 ubijenih Muslimana obtužuju Titu u području Vlasenice" ("353 Murdered Muslims Accuse Tito in the Vlasenica Area"), n.d., BA–MA, RH 45/53.

73 Pamphlet "Pucaj sa topom u džamiju!" ("Fire at the Mosque with the Cannon!"), n.d., BA–MA, RH 45/59.

74 Pamphlet "Borci Muslimani" ("Muslim Fighters"), n.d., BA–MA, RH 45/59.

75 Pamphlet "Braćo Muslimani!" ("Muslim Brothers!"), n.d., BA–MA, RH 45/59.

76 Poster, n.d., BA–MA, RH 45/54; the poster was printed 8,000 times on 7 February 1944 and put up on 9 February 1944 in Sarajevo, Banja Luka, Dubrovnik, and other towns, see Data Sheet in BA–MA, RH 45/54; and, for the poster depicting Roosevelt, see Poster, n.d., BA–MA, RH 45/54; on 1 March 1944, 10,000 copies of this poster were printed and put up on 8 March 1944 in Sarajevo, Banja Luka, Dubrovnik, and other towns, see Data Sheet in BA–MA, RH 45/54.

77 Pamphlet "Muslimani, Katolici i Pravoslavci Bosne" ("Muslims, Catholics and Orthodox of Bosnia"), n.d., BA–MA, RH 45/48; and, for the German translation, see Pamphlet "Muselmanen, Katholiken, Pravoslaven Bosniens" (German translation), n.d., BA–MA, RH 45/48; Pamphlet "Kroaten und Serben: Muselmanen, Katholiken und Pravoslaven" (German translation), n.d. (October 1943), BA–MA, RH 37/6853; and Pamphlet "Poštenim Hrvatima, Muslimanima i Pravoslavcima u partizanskim redovima!" ("Honest Croats, Muslims and Orthodox in the Ranks of the Partisans!"), n.d., BA–MA, RH 45/59.

78 Pamphlet "Muslimani, Katolici i Pravoslavci" ("Muslims, Catholics and Orthodox"), n.d., BA–MA, RH 45/48; and, for the German translation, see Pamphlet "Muselmanen, Katholiken und Pravoslaven" (German translation), n.d., BA–MA, RH 45/48.

79 Headquarters of Army Group F, Report ("Aktennotiz über Besprechung mit dem Sonderbevollmächtigten des Auswärtigen Amtes, Minister Neubacher, am 30.7.1944"), 31 July 1944, n.d., BA–MA, RH 19XI/29.

80 Office for Political and Ideological Education of the 13th SS Division, Structure Plan, 2 March 1944, n.p., BAB, NS 19/2601.

81 Wangemann (Chief of the Office for Political and Ideological Education of the 13th SS Waffen Mountain Division "Handžar"), Report ("Tätigkeitsbericht der Abt. VI"), 4 April 1944, n.p., BAB, NS 19/2601.

82 Ibid.

83 Ibid; and Wangemann to Sauberzweig (Commander of the 13th SS Waffen Mountain Division "Handžar"), 10 April 1944, n.p., BAB, NS 19/2601.

84 Propaganda Division (*Waffen-SS Standarte "Kurt Eggers"*) to Brandt, Berlin, 8 November 1943, BAB, NS 19/2601.

85 Wangemann, Report ("Tätigkeitsbericht der Abt. VI"), 4 April 1944, n.p., BAB, NS 19/2601.

86 Sauberzweig, Propaganda Letter "Moji dragi momci!" ("My dear lads!"), 28 February 1944, n.p., BAB, NS 19/2601; and, for the German translation, see Sauberzweig, Propaganda Letter "Meine lieben Männer" (German translation), 25 February 1944, n.p., BAB, NS 19/2601.

87 Pamphlet (Draft) "An alle Flüchtlinge!" (German translation), n.d., BAB, NS 19/2601.

88 Pamphlet "Bosniaken und Bosniakinen!" (German translation), n.d., BAB, NS 19/2601.

89 On Kulenović and Hadžić, see the literature in note 6. After the war, Kulenović migrated to Damascus and published a book on Serbian atrocities against Muslims in the Balkans, see Anonymous (Džafer Kulenović), *A Message of Croat-Moslems to Their Religious Brethren in the World* (Chicago, 1949).

90 Requard (German Legation in Zagreb), Report ("Bericht über Dienstreise nach Sarajevo"), 2 June 1943, Zagreb, PA, R 261144 (also in USHMA, RG 71, Box 237). Requard based his assessment on consultations with Islamic leaders, especially Ali Aganović.

91 Katschinka (German Legation in Zagreb), Report ("Muselmanen"), 27 March 1943, Zagreb, PA, R 261144 (also in USHMA, RG 71, Box 237).

92 On the history of the Islamic institutions, see Donia, *Islam under the Double Eagle*, 19–22; Hauptmann, "Die Mohammedaner in Bosnien-Hercegovina," 685–690; Al-Arnaut, "Islam and Muslims in Bosnia 1878–1918," 250–251; Klieber, *Jüdische–Christliche–Muslimische Lebenswelten der Donaumonarchie*, 159–63; Karčić, *Bosniaks and the Challenge of Modernity*, 124–139; Fikret Karčić, "The Office of Ra'īs al-'Ulamā' among the Bosniaks (Bosnian Muslims)," *Intellectual Discourse* 5, 2 (1997), 109–120; Karčić, *Šeriatski Sudovi u Jugoslaviji 1918–1941*; Karčić, "The Reform of Shari'a Courts and Islamic Law"; Bougarel, "Farewell to the Ottoman Legacy?," 317; Popovic, *L'Islam balkanique*, 273–278, 316–319, and 339; and, for an overview, Ferhat Šeta, *Reis-ul-Uleme u Bosni i Hercegovini i Jugoslaviji od 1882 do 1991 Godine* (*The Reis-ul-Ulema in Bosnia and Herzegovina and Yugoslavia from 1882 to 1991*) (Sarajevo, 1991).

93 On Spaho, see Tomasevich, *War and Revolution in Yugoslavia*, 467 and 490; Redžić, *Bosnia and Herzegovina in the Second World War*, 78 and 86–87; Bougarel, "Farewell to the Ottoman Legacy?," passim; Greble, *Sarajevo*, esp. 30–37, 64–65, 76–81, 85, 96, 99, 101, 112–113, 115, 124, 126, and 166; Hasanbegović, *Muslimani u Zagrebu*, passim; and Popovic, *L'Islam balkanique*, 339.

94 On Bašić, see Redžić, *Bosnia and Herzegovina in the Second World War*, 174; Redžić, *Muslimansko Autonomaštvo i 13. SS Divizija*, 91; Greble, *Sarajevo*, 161–162 and 217; Hasanbegović, *Muslimani u Zagrebu*, 293; and Popovic, *L'Islam balkanique*, 339.

95 Greble, *Sarajevo*, 32 and 166; and note 9.

96 On Handžić, see Redžić, *Bosnia and Herzegovina in the Second World War*, 189; Bougarel, "Farewell to the Ottoman Legacy?," passim; Greble, *Sarajevo*, 34, 78, 126, and 214; and Hasanbegović, *Muslimani u Zagrebu*, 119, 205–207, 210, and 261.

97 On El-Hidaje and the Young Muslims, see Redžić, *Bosnia and Herzegovina in the Second World War*, 103, 105, and 169; Redžić, *Muslimansko Autonomaštvo i 13. SS Divizija*, 16, 123, 142–143, and 205–206; Karčić, "Reform of Shari'a Courts and Islamic Law," 268; Bougarel, "Farewell to the Ottoman Legacy?," passim; Fikret Karčić, "From

Young Muslims to Party of Democratic Action: The Emergence of a Pan-Islamist Trend in Bosnia-Herzegovina," *Islamic Studies* 36, 2/3 (1997), 533–549; Greble, *Sarajevo*, esp. 33–34, 78, 160–163, 175–176, 184–185, 200–201, 214, 217, and 235; Hasanbegović, *Muslimani u Zagrebu*, passim; Popovic, *L'Islam balkanique*, 321, 328, and 340; and, on Izetbegović, Malcolm, *Bosnia*, 208.

98 Mehmed Handžić, "Palestinski veliki muftija u Sarajevu" ("The Palestinian Grand Mufti in Sarajevo"), *El-Hidaje* 6, 9 (5 May 1943), 250–252; the article includes the text of the speech given by al-Husayni after the Friday prayer in the Gazi Husrev Beg Mosque of Sarajevo (251); and a portrait photo of the mufti was printed on the front page of the issue. *El-Hidaje* is stored in the Gazi Husrev Beg Library (*Gazi Husrev-Begova Biblioteka*), Sarajevo (GHB).

99 German Legation in Zagreb, Report ("Unterredungen in Sarajevo"), n.d. (28 April 1943), Zagreb, PA, R 100998.

100 On Aganović, see Tomasevich, *War and Revolution in Yugoslavia*, 491; Greble, *Sarajevo*, 128; and Hasanbegović, *Muslimani u Zagrebu*, 293, 341, and, for his speech given at the opening of the Zagreb mosque, 519–520.

101 Requard, Report ("Bericht über Dienstreise nach Sarajevo"), 2 June 1943, Zagreb, PA, R 261144 (also in USHMA, RG 71, Box 237).

102 German Legation in Zagreb, Report ("Unterredungen in Sarajevo"), n.d. (28 April 1943), Zagreb, PA, R 100998.

103 British Security Service, Monitoring Intelligence Sheet, 19 December 1942, London, NA, KV 2/2085.

104 On Pandža, see Tomasevich, *War and Revolution in Yugoslavia*, 411, 495, and 503–504; Redžić, *Bosnia and Herzegovina in the Second World War*, 103, 174, 184–185, and 224; Redžić, *Muslimansko Autonomaštvo i 13. SS Divizija*, 22–23, 139–143, and 147; Bougarel, "Farewell to the Ottoman Legacy?," 324–325; Greble, *Sarajevo*, 173–174, 184–186, 192, and 237; and Hasanbegović, *Muslimani u Zagrebu*, 79–81, 205–210 and 345–346. A detailed report on Pandža is provided by an imam of the Handžar division, Hasan Bajraktarević, see Bajraktarević to Phleps, 15 November 1943, Mostar, BAB, NS 19/2601.

105 On Merhamet, see Tomasevich, *War and Revolution in Yugoslavia*, 409, 411, and 495; Redžić, *Bosnia and Herzegovina in the Second World War*, 174; Redžić, *Muslimansko Autonomaštvo i 13. SS Divizija*, 123 and 142–143; Greble, *Sarajevo*, esp. 34, 106, 139–141, 173–176, 213–217, 235, and 245–246; Popovic, *L'Islam balkanique*, 285, 287, 321, and 340; and, for a historical overview published by the organization itself, Uzeir Bavčić, *"Merhamet" (1913–2003)* (Sarajevo, 2003).

106 Greble, *Sarajevo*, 174.

107 Langenberger (Headquarters of the 369th Infantry Division), Report ("Niederschrift über eine Besprechung am 17.9.43 mit dem 2. Sekretär der 'Muslimansko Dobrotvorno Društvo: Merhamet Sarajevo' namens Mechmed Tokitsch"), 17 September 1943, n.p., BAB, NS 19/3893 (also in BA–MA, N 756/183b).

108 Berger to Himmler, n.d. (January 1944), Berlin, BAB, NS 19/319; and similarly, Berger to Himmler, 12 January 1944, Berlin, BAB, NS 19/2601.

109 Meine (Himmler's Staff) to Berger, n.d. (January 1944), n.p., BAB, NS 19/319.

110 Langenberger, Report ("Niederschrift über eine Besprechung am 17.9.43 mit dem 2. Sekretär der 'Muslimansko Dobrotvorno Društvo: Merhamet Sarajevo' namens Mechmed Tokitsch"), 17 September 1943, n.p., BAB, NS 19/3893 (also in BA–MA, N 756/183b); this report was forwarded by Phleps (Commander of the V SS Mountain Corps) to Himmler, 5 November 1943, n.p., BAB, NS 19/3893.

111 Schulte to Brandt, 11 January 1944, Berlin, BAB, NS 19/3893 (also in BA–MA, N 756/183b).

112 On the Muslim Liberation Movement, see Tomasevich, *War and Revolution in Yugoslavia*, 503–504; Redžić, *Bosnia and Herzegovina in the Second World War*, 103, 184–185, and 224; Redžić, *Muslimansko Autonomaštvo i 13. SS Divizija*, 139–143; Greble, *Sarajevo*, 184–186 and 192; and Hasanbegović, *Muslimani u Zagrebu*, 208–210.

113 Pandža, Pamphlet (German translation), n.d. (10 January 1944), BA–MA, RH 19XI/10a (also in BAB, NS 19/2601).

114 Headquarters of the 2nd Panzer Army to Headquarters of Army Group F, 8 January 1944, n.p., BA–MA, RH 19XI/10a; and, for a similar assessment, Bajraktarević to Phleps, 15 November 1943, Mostar, BAB, NS 19/2601.

115 Kasche, Internal Note ("Unterhaltung mit dem Führer am 29.10.1943 im Hauptquartier"), 11 November 1943, Zagreb, PA, Nachlass Kasche, vol. 23.

116 Posch (Waffen-SS), Report ("Abschlussbericht über die Tätigkeit als F.O. in Kroatien vom 10.3.1943–1.1.1944"), 30 December 1943, Zagreb, BAB, NS 19/319.

117 Anonymous, "Les Musulmans de Bosnie et d'Herzégovine meurent de faim: Nahas Pacha accorde 20.000 livres pour leur venir en aide," *La Bourse Egyptienne* (20 June 1944). The Egyptian Foreign Office would even contact the British embassy in Cairo about the issue, but the British responded coolly, alluding to Muslim provocations and collaboration with the Germans, see letter exchange in NA, FO 141/946. The Turkish government had already contacted the British in the spring of 1943 about Četnik atrocities against Muslims, particularly in the Sandžak, but, after the issue was discussed between the British Foreign Office, the Yugoslav government in exile, and Mihailović, London officially rejected the accusations and instead alluded to the massacres of Orthodox Serbs committed by Muslim militias and the German mobilization of Muslims, see the documents in NA, FO 536/7. On the British role in the Balkans during the war, see Walter R. Roberts, *Tito, Mihailović and the Allies, 1941–1945* (New Brunswick, NJ, 1973); Michael McConville, *A Small War in the Balkans: British Military Involvement in Wartime Yugoslavia, 1941–1945* (London, 1986); M. Deroc, *British Special Operations Explored: Yugoslavia in Turmoil, 1941–1943, and the British Response* (Boulder, CO, 1988); and Simon Trew, *Britain, Mihailović, and the Chetniks, 1941–1942* (New York, 1998).

118 Kammerhofer to Himmler, 11 January 1944, Zagreb, BAB, NS 19/319.

119 Sauberzweig to Berger, 5 November 1943, n.p., BAB, NS 19/2601; and, on the second collection, Himmler to Berger and Jüttner, 16 November 1943, n.p., BAB, NS 19/2601.

120 Berger to Himmler, 12 January 1944, Berlin, BAB, NS 19/2601.

121 Brandt to Berger, 31 January 1944, n.p., BAB, NS 19/2601; and on the actual transfer, documents in BAB, NS 19/2601.

122 Berger to Himmler, n.d. (January 1944), Berlin, BAB, NS 19/319.

123 Wangemann, Report ("Tätigkeitsbericht der Abt. VI"), 4 April 1944, n.p., BAB, NS 19/2601.

124 Krempler to Neubacher and Behrends (Higher SS and Police Leader Serbia), 20 April 1944, n.p., BAB, NS 19/3630.

125 Muslim Representatives of the Sandžak (*Landesausschuss der Muselmanischen Volksvereinigung Sandschak*) to Hitler (German translation), n.d. (spring 1944), n.p., BAB, NS 19/3630. The letter was forwarded by Krempler to Neubacher and Behrends, 20 April 1944, n.p., BAB, NS 19/3630; and then forwarded by Behrends to Brandt, 24 April 1944, Belgrade, BAB, NS 19/3630; Brandt to Behrends, 15 June 1944, n.p., BAB, NS 19/3630; and Himmler ordered it to be forwarded to Hitler with a request for an answer, see Brandt to Fegelein (Hitler's Staff), 13 June 1944, n.p., BAB, NS 19/3630.

126 Brandt to Behrends, 7 July 1944, n.p., BAB, NS 19/3630.

127 Behrends to Himmler, 31 July 1944, Belgrade, BAB, NS 19/3630.

128 Brandt to Behrends, 18 September 1944, n.p., BAB, NS 19/3630; and Venn (Himmler's Staff) to Propaganda Division (*Waffen-SS Standarte "Kurt Eggers"*), 18 September 1944, n.p., BAB, NS 19/3630.

129 Sauberzweig, Guidelines ("Richtlinien für die Sicherung des Landfriedens in Bosnien"), 9 March 1944, n.p., BAB, NS 19/2145 (also in PA, R 100998). On the guidelines, see also Tomasevich, *War and Revolution in Yugoslavia*, 499; Redžić, *Bosnia and Herzegovina in the Second World War*, 45–46; and Redžić, *Muslimansko Autonomaštvo i 13. SS Divizija*, 166–167.

130 *Die Tagebücher von Joseph Goebbels*, ed. Fröhlich et al., part II, vol. 12, 184–191 (26 April 1944), 188.

131 Brandt to Phleps, 20 November 1943, n.p., BAB, NS 19/3893. Himmler made this statement in response to Phleps's letter of 5 November 1943 about Tokić and the autonomists, see note 110.

132 Neubacher to Foreign Office, 9 April 1944, Belgrade, PA, R 101101.

133 Winkelbrandt (Headquarters of the 373rd Infantry Division), Report ("Feindnachrichtenblatt Nr. 7"), 16 July 1944, n.p., BA–MA, RH 37/6931.

134 On Muslim self-defense groups and the green cadres, see Tomasevich, *War and Revolution in Yugoslavia*, 504; Redžić, *Bosnia and Herzegovina in the Second World War*, esp. 105–110 and 183–191; and Redžić, *Muslimansko Autonomaštvo i 13. SS Divizija*, esp. 120–123, 147–149, 185–186, and 207.

135 Winkelbrandt, Report ("Feindnachrichtenblatt Nr. 6"), 17 June 1944, n.p., BA–MA, RH 37/6931; and, for a general military assessment of the Muslim militias, see all reports by Winkelbrandt in BA–MA, RH 37/6931.

136 On Četnik recruitment of Muslims, see Tomasevich, *War and Revolution in Yugoslavia*, 494 and 501; Jozo Tomasevich, *The Chetniks* (Stanford, CA, 1975), 105 and 240; Redžić, *Bosnia and Herzegovina in the Second World War*, esp. 97–98, 143–146, and 174; and Redžić, *Muslimansko Autonomaštvo i 13. SS Divizija*, esp. 105–108, 168–169, and 207–211.

137 *Ein General im Zwielicht*, ed. Broucek, vol. 3, 294 (October 1943).

138 Quoted in Vladimir Dedijer, *The War Diaries of Vladimir Dedijer*, vol. 3 (*From September 11, 1943, to November 7, 1944*) (Ann Arbor, MI, 1990), 131 (6 November 1943).

139 On Tito's recruitment of Muslims, see Tomasevich, *War and Revolution in Yugoslavia*, 502–504 and 506–510; Redžić, *Bosnia and Herzegovina in the Second World War*, esp. 170, 183–191 and 206–209; and Redžić, *Muslimansko Autonomaštvo i 13. SS Divizija*, esp. 108–110, 127–128, 157–159, and 211–212; and, on the propaganda brochure, Popovic, *L'Islam balkanique*, 341–342.

140 On German massacres of Muslims and attacks on Islamic institutions, see Tomasevich, *War and Revolution in Yugoslavia*, 503–504; Redžić, *Bosnia and Herzegovina in the Second World War*, 35 and 188; and Greble, *Sarajevo*, 183 and 213–214.

141 Quoted in Klaus Latzel, "Tourismus und Gewalt: Kriegswahrnehmung in Feldpostbriefen," in Hannes Heer and Klaus Naumann (eds.), *Vernichtungskrieg: Verbrechen der Wehrmacht, 1941–1944* (Hamburg, 1995), 447–459, 450.

142 On Jewish conversions to Islam, see Tomasevich, *War and Revolution in Yugoslavia*, 543–544; Redžić, *Bosnia and Herzegovina in the Second World War*, 78 and 172; Redžić, *Muslimansko Autonomaštvo i 13. SS Divizija*, 20; Jelinek, "Nationalities and Minorities," 201; Jelinek, "Bosnia-Herzegovina at War," 284 and 286–287; Greble, *Sarajevo*, esp. 17, 93–97, 112–113, 115, 117–118, 120–121, 124–125, and 243; Donia, *Sarajevo*, 174 and 176–179; and, more generally on the politics of conversion in the Ustaša state, Mark Biondich, "Religion and Nation in Wartime Croatia: Reflections on the Ustaša Policy of Forced Religious Conversions, 1941–1942," *Slavonic and East European Review* 83, 1 (2005), 71–116.

143 Donia, *Sarajevo*, 178–179.

144 Fedrigotti to Foreign Office, 21 April 1941, Sarajevo, PA, R 60681 (also in PA, R 27363).

145 Greble, *Sarajevo*, 106 and 140–141.

146 Martin Gilbert, *The Righteous: The Unsung Heroes of the Holocaust* (London, 2002), 204–205; Greble, *Sarajevo*, 37–38 and 132; and, on the scripture, Cecil Roth (ed.), *The Sarajevo Haggadah* (London, 1963).

147 Gilbert, *The Righteous*, 208–209; and Norman Gershman, *Besa: Muslims Who Saved Jews in World War II* (Syracuse, NY, 2008).

148 On Muslim Roma in the Ustaša state, see Tomasevich, *War and Revolution in Yugoslavia*, 609; Narcis Lengel-Krizman, "Prilog proucavanju terora u tzv. NDH: Sudbina Roma 1941–1945" ("A Contribution to the Study of the Terror in the So-Called Independent State of Croatia: The Fate of the Roma 1941–1945"), *Casopis za suvremenu povijest* 1 (1986), 29–42, 33–34; Michael Zimmermann, *Rassenutopie und Genozid: Die nationalsozialistische "Lösung der Zigeunerfrage"* (Hamburg, 1996), 285; Karola Fings, Cordula Lissner, and Frank Sparing, ". . . einziges Land, in dem Judenfrage und Zigeunerfrage gelöst": Die Verfolgung der Roma im faschistisch besetzten Jugoslawien 1941–1945* (Cologne, 1992), 20; Donald Kenrick and Grattan Puxon, *Gypsies under the Swastika* (Hatfield, 2009), 99 and 101; Mark Biondich, "Persecution of Roma-Sinti in Croatia, 1941–1945," in Paul A. Shapiro and Robert M. Ehrenreich (eds.), *Roma and Sinti: Under-Studied Victims of Nazism* (Washington, DC, 2002), 33–47, 37–38; Jelinek, "Nationalities and Minorities," 200; Jelinek, "Bosnia-Herzegovina at War," 286 and 289; and Greble, *Sarajevo*, 17, 90–93, 95, 117–118, 121, and 125; and, on German views of the "white gypsies," Sevasti Trubeta, "'Gypsiness,' Racial Discourse and Persecution: Balkan Roma during the Second World War," *Nationalities Papers* 31, 4 (2003), 495–514, 505–506.

149 On Muslim Roma in Serbia, see Zimmermann, *Rassenutopie und Genozid*, 249; and Fings, Lissner, and Sparing, ". . . *einziges Land, in dem Judenfrage und Zigeunerfrage gelöst*," 46 and 116–117 (documents).

150 On Muslim Roma in Albania and Macedonia, see Fings, Lissner, and Sparing, ". . . *einziges Land, in dem Judenfrage und Zigeunerfrage gelöst*," 43–46; Donald Kenrick and Grattan Puxon, *The Destiny of Europe's Gypsies* (London, 1972), 119–123; and Kenrick and Puxon, *Gypsies under the Swastika*, 74–77 and 97.

151 On Muslims in wartime Macedonia, see Fings, Lissner, and Sparing, ". . . *einziges Land, in dem Judenfrage und Zigeunerfrage gelöst*," 46 and 114–115 (documents); and, more generally on Sofia's wartime policy toward Bulgarian Muslims, see Mary C. Neuburger, *The Orient Within: Muslim Minorities and the Negotiation of Nationhood in Modern Bulgaria* (Ithaca, NY, 2004), 48–54 and 183–184. Bulgarian troops also ruled over the Muslims of Western Thrace in occupied Greece, see Kevin Featherstone, Dimitris Papadimitriou, Argyris Mamarelis, and Georgios Niarchos, *The Last Ottomans: The Muslim Minority of Greece, 1940–1949* (London, 2011), esp. 91–157.

152 On Islam in Tito's Yugoslavia, see Banac, "Bosnian Muslims," 144–146; Popovic, *L'Islam balkanique*, 343–365; Greble, *Sarajevo*, 234–235, 237, and 244; Donia, *Sarajevo*, 215–221; Zachary T. Irwin, "The Fate of Islam in the Balkans: A Comparison of Four State Policies," in Ramet (ed.), *Religion and Nationalism in Soviet and East European Politics*, 207–225, 216; Smail Balić, "Der bosnisch-herzegowinische Islam," *Der Islam* 44, 1 (1968), 115–137, esp. 121–122; and, on the arrests of Islamic dignitaries for wartime collaboration, Isma'il Balić, "The Present Position of the Muslims of Bosnia and Herzegovina," *Islamic Review* 37 (July 1949), 22–25, 24. Max Bergholz, "The Strange Silence: Explaining the Absence of Monuments for Muslim Civilians Killed in Bosnia during the Second World War," *East European Politics and Societies* 24, 3 (2010), 408–434, provides an account of the place of Muslims in the commemoration of the Second World War in Tito's Yugoslavia.

153 On Islam in Hoxha's Albania, see James S. O'Donnell, *A Coming of Age: Albania under Enver Hoxha* (Boulder, CO, 1999), 137–144; Raymond Zickel and Walter R. Iwaskiw (eds.), *Albania: A Country Study* (Washington, DC, 1992), 85–87; Popovic, *L'Islam balkanique*, 42–65; and, on the arrests or executions of the muftis of Tirana, Durrës, and Shkodër and others for wartime collaboration, Irwin, "The Fate of Islam in the Balkans," 212; and Peter Prifti, "Albania: Towards an Atheist Society," in Bohdan R. Bociurkiw and John W. Strong (eds.), *Religion and Atheism in the USSR and Eastern Europe* (Toronto, 1975), 388–404, 391.

154 On the expulsion of the Albanian Muslim Cham minority, see Mazower, "Three Forms of Political Justice," 24–26; Meyer, *Blutiges Edelweiß*, 620–621; and, from a Cham perspective, Meta, *The Cham Tragedy*, esp. 59–105; and the documents in Elsie and Destani (eds.), *The Cham Albanians of Greece*, 335–394.

6. MOBILIZING MUSLIMS

1 Himmler, Speech ("Rede des Reichsführers-SS Heinrich Himmler vor den Führern der 13. SS-Freiw. b.h. Gebirgs-Division (Kroatien) im Führerheim Westlager, Trup-

penübungsplatz Neuhammer am 11. Januar 1944"), 11 January 1944, Neuhammer, BAB, NS 19/4012 (also in BA–MA, SF-01/16263).

2 The most comprehensive general account is Hans Werner Neulen, *An deutscher Seite: Internationale Freiwillige von Wehrmacht und Waffen-SS* (Munich, 1992 [1985]). Concise overviews are given by Burkhart Müller-Hildebrand, *Das Heer 1933–1945,* vol. 3 (*Der Zweifrontenkrieg: Das Heer vom Beginn des Feldzuges gegen die Sowjetunion bis zum Kriegsende*) (Frankfurt, 1969), 68–71, 114–115, 140–142 and 183–184; and Mazower, *Hitler's Empire,* 454–470. On non-Germans in the Wehrmacht, see Rolf-Dieter Müller, *An der Seite der Wehrmacht: Hitlers ausländische Helfer beim "Kreuzzug gegen den Bolschewismus" 1941–1945* (Berlin, 2007). On non-Germans in the Waffen-SS, see Gerald Reitlinger, *The SS: Alibi of a Nation, 1922–1945* (London, 1956), 147–166 and 196–206; and George H. Stein, *The Waffen-SS: Hitler's Elite Guard at War, 1939–1945* (Ithaca, NY, 1966), 137–196. Muslims were recruited from the East, the Balkans, and the Arab world. On recruits from the East, see Hoffmann, *Die Ostlegionen;* Hoffman, *Kaukasien,* 42–58 and 82–429; Dallin, *German Rule in Russia,* 258 and 533–612; Mühlen, *Zwischen Hakenkreuz und Sowjetstern,* 57–68; Alexiev, *Soviet Nationalities in German Wartime Strategy,* 26–33; and Mulligan, *The Politics of Illusion and Empire,* 146–161. On recruits from the Balkans, see George Lepre, *Himmler's Bosnian Division: The Waffen-SS Handschar Division 1943–1944* (Atglen, PA, 1997); Redžić, *Muslimansko Autonomaštvo i 13. SS Divizija;* Zija Sulejmanpašić, *13. SS Divizija "Handžar": Istine i Laži* (*The 13th SS Division "Handžar": Truth and Lies*) (Zagreb, 2000); and Laurent Latruwe and Gordana Kostic, *La division Skanderbeg: Histoire des Waffen-SS albanais des origines idéologiques aux débuts de la Guerre Froide* (Paris, 2004). On Arab recruits, see Carlos Caballero Jurado, *La espada del Islam: Voluntarios árabes en elejército alemán 1941–1945* (Madrid, 1990); Tillmann, *Deutschlands Araberpolitik im Zweiten Weltkrieg,* 353–446; Hirszowicz, *The Third Reich and the Arab East,* 250–259 and 298–300; and Schröder, *Deutschland und der Mittlere Osten im Zweiten Weltkrieg,* 215–231. Good overviews are given by Mallmann and Cüppers, *Nazi Palestine,* 185–197; Christopher Hale, *Hitler's Foreign Executioners: Europe's Dirty Secret* (Stroud, 2011), 262–292; and O. V. Roman'ko, *Musulmanskie Legiony vo Vtoroi Mirovoi Voine* (*Muslim Legions during the Second World War*) (Moscow, 2004). The following pages do not discuss the Wehrmacht's Indian formation although it comprised a significant number of Muslims.

3 Franz Halder, *Kriegstagebuch: Tägliche Aufzeichnungen des Chefs des Generalstabes des Heeres 1939–1942,* 3 vols. (Stuttgart, 1964), vol. 3, 318. No numbers of losses are given in the English translation of the diaries, see *The Halder War Diaries, 1939–1942,* ed. Charles Burdick and Hans-Adolf Jacobsen (London, 1988), 570. According to Overmans, German losses were even higher than those registered by the German command, see Rüdiger Overmans, *Deutsche militärische Verluste im Zweiten Weltkrieg* (Munich, 1999), 276–284, esp. 283; see also Bernhard R. Kroener, "The Manpower Resources of the Third Reich in the Area of Conflict between Wehrmacht, Bureaucracy, and War Economy, 1939–1942," in Bernhard R. Kroener, Rolf-Dieter Müller, and Hans Umbreit (eds.), *Germany and the Second World War,* vol. 5/1 (*Organization*

and Mobilization of the German Sphere of Power: Wartime Administration, Economy, and Manpower Resources, 1939–1941) (Oxford, 2000), 787–1154, esp. 1009–1023.

4 On non-Germans in the Wehrmacht, see the literature in note 2.

5 On the numbers of the Eastern Troops, see Müller-Hildebrand, *Das Heer*, vol. 3, 70, 114, and 141; Müller, *An der Seite der Wehrmacht*, 155; Dallin, *German Rule in Russia*, 536; and Mühlen, *Zwischen Hakenkreuz und Sowjetstern*, 60.

6 On non-Germans in the Waffen-SS, see the literature in note 2.

7 On the numbers of non-Germans in the SS, see the literature in note 2.

8 In the winter of 1941/1942, conditions in the camps for Red Army prisoners were especially severe, see Streit, *Keine Kameraden*, 128–190.

9 "Mittagslage vom 12. Dezember 1942," in *Hitlers Lagebesprechungen: Die Protokollfragmente seiner militärischen Konferenzen 1942–1945*, ed. Helmut Heiber (Stuttgart, 1962), 73–74; for the English translation, see "Midday Situation Conference, December 12, 1942, in the Wolfsschanze," in *Hitler and His Generals: Military Conferences 1942–1945*, ed. Helmut Heiber and David M. Glantz (London, 2002), 20.

10 Ibid.

11 Sodenstern (High Command of Army Group South), Instructions ("Aufstellung von Verbänden aus Angehörigen der Turkvölker"), 19 May 1942, BA–MA, RH 19V/108. The words used were partly taken up in later orders and instructions by Halder (2 June 1942) and Niedermayer (4 July 1942), see notes 12 and 14.

12 Halder to High Command of Army Group South, 2 June 1942, n.p., BA–MA, RH 19V/108.

13 High Command of the Army, Instructions ("Merkblatt für das deutsche Personal der Turk-Stammlager und Turk-Btlne"), 2 June 1942, n.p., BA–MA, RH 19V/109.

14 Niedermayer, Order ("Grundlegender Befehl über die Aufstellung von Turk-Btlnen"), 4 July 1942, n.p., BA–MA, RH 19V/79 (also in BA–MA, RH 26-162/16).

15 Niedermayer, Order ("Grundlegender Befehl über die Aufstellung von Turk-Btlnen"), Annexe 8 ("Die Turk-Völker und ihre Behandlung"), 4 July 1942, n.p., BA–MA, RH 19V/79 (also in BA–MA, RH 26-162/16); and, similarly on the trustworthiness of the Muslims, Niedermayer, Order ("Grundlegender Befehl über die geistige Betreuung der 162. [Turk] Inf. Div."), 15 June 1943, n.p., BA–MA, RH 26-162/20.

16 "Besprechung des Führers mit Feldmarschall Keitel und General Zeitzler am 8. Juni 1943 auf dem Berghof," in *Hitlers Lagebesprechungen*, 263; see also "Meeting of the Führer with Field Marshall Keitel and General Zeitzler, June 8, 1943, in the Berghof," in *Hitler and His Generals*, ed. Heiber and Glantz, 162.

17 On these early units and their commanders, see the overviews in Neulen, *An deutscher Seite*, 323–324; and Müller, *An der Seite der Wehrmacht*, 230–232; the comprehensive account by Hoffmann, *Die Ostlegionen*, 25–30; and the more general studies by Hoffmann, *Kaukasien*, 50, 102–159; Dallin, *German Rule in Russia*, 533–538; Mühlen, *Zwischen Hakenkreuz und Sowjetstern*, 58; Alexiev, *Soviet Nationalities in German Wartime Strategy*, 32; and Mulligan, *The Politics of Illusion and Empire*, 148. On the *Sonderverband Bergmann*, see Wachs, *Der Fall Theodor Oberländer*, 96–135; and for reports written by German officers of the unit after the war, Albert Jeloschek et al., *Freiwillige vom Kaukasus: Georgier und Tschetschenen auf deutscher Seite: Der Sonderverband Bergmann und sein Gründer Theodor Oberländer* (Graz, 2004).

18 On Mayer-Mader, see Neulen, *An deutscher Seite*, 323–324; Müller, *An der Seite der Wehrmacht*, 232; Hoffmann, *Die Ostlegionen*, 27; Hoffmann, *Kaukasien*, 139; Mühlen, *Zwischen Hakenkreuz und Sowjetstern*, 58; and the account by Heygendorff, Report ("Die Entstehung des Kommandos der Ostlegionen"), n.d. (post-1945), n.p., IfZ, ZS 407.

19 On the Eastern Legions, see the overviews in Neulen, *An deutscher Seite*, 322–334; and Müller, *An der Seite der Wehrmacht*, 227–241; the comprehensive account by Hoffmann, *Die Ostlegionen*; and the more general studies by Hoffmann, *Kaukasien*, 42–58 and 82–429; Dallin, *German Rule in Russia*, 538–541; Mühlen, *Zwischen Hakenkreuz und Sowjetstern*, 57–68; Alexiev, *Soviet Nationalities in German Wartime Strategy*, 31–33; and Mulligan, *The Politics of Illusion and Empire*, 148 and 151–152. On specific units, see Eva-Maria Auch, "Aserbeidschaner in den Reihen der deutschen Wehrmacht," in Höpp and Reinwald (eds.), *Fremdeinsätze*, 167–180, esp. 170–177; Cwiklinski, *Wolgatataren im Deutschland des Zweiten Weltkriegs*, 21–24, 41–42, 44–54, and 70–74; Iskander Gilyazov, *Legion "Idel'-Ural": Predstaviteli narodov Povolzh'ia i Priuralia pod znamenami "Tretego Reikha"* (*The "Idel-Ural" Legion: Representatives of the Peoples of the Volga-Ural Regions under the Banner of the "Third Reich"*) (Kazan, 2005); and, on the 162nd Turkestani Infantry Division, Franz W. Seidler, "Zur Führung der Osttruppen in der deutschen Wehrmacht im Zweiten Weltkrieg," *Wehrwissenschaftliche Rundschau* 20, 12 (1970), 683–702; Seidler, "Oskar Ritter von Niedermayer im Zweiten Weltkrieg;" and Seidt, *Berlin, Kabul, Moskau*, 329–363. Camilla Dawletschin-Linder, "Die turko-tatarischen sowjetischen Kriegsgefangenen im Zweiten Weltkrieg im Dreiecksverhältnis zwischen deutscher Politik, turanistischen Aspirationen und türkischer Außenpolitik," *Der Islam* 80, 1 (2003), 1–29, 18–23, gives an account of the recruitment for the legions in the prisoner of war camps.

20 The Azerbaijani Legion comprised Azerbaijanis; the North Caucasian Legion comprised Caucasian Muslim volunteers such as Dargins, Chechens, Ingush, Kumyks, Circassians, Kabards, Balkars, Karachais, Lezghins, and Ossetians. The Turkestani Legion consisted of Muslim recruits from Central Asia, such as Karakalpaks, Kazakhs, Kirghiz, Tajiks, Turkomans, and Uzbeks. The Volga Tatar Legion was made up of Ufa- and Kazan-Tatars, Bashkirs, Maris, Mordvins, and Tatar-speaking Chuvashs and Udmurts. On the ethnic composition of the legions, see, for instance, Niedermayer, Order ("Grundlegender Befehl über die Aufstellung von Turk-Btlnen"), Attachment to Annexe 8 of 30 June 1942 ("Zusammensetzung der Legionäre nach Volksstämmen"), 4 July 1942, n.p., BA–MA, RH 19V/79 (also in BA–MA, RH 26-162/16); and Heygendorff, Instructions ("Merkblatt über Personalangelegenheiten der Legionäre"), 1 November 1943, n.p., BA–MA, RH 58/62. On the religious composition of the legions, see Niedermayer, Order ("Grundlegender Befehl über die Aufstellung von Turk-Btlnen"), Annexe 8 ("Die Turk-Völker und ihre Behandlung"), 4 July 1942, n.p., BA–MA, RH 19V/79 (also in BA–MA, RH 26-162/16).

21 Hoffmann, *Kaukasien*, 51–52, 55–56; and Hoffmann, *Die Ostlegionen*, 39, 76, 171–172.

22 On the numbers of the Eastern Legions, see Neulen, *An deutscher Seite*, 342; Müller, *An der Seite der Wehrmacht*, 237; Hoffmann, *Die Ostlegionen*, 172; Hoffmann, *Kaukasien*, 56–57, 136–137, 191, 220, 264, 323; Mühlen, *Zwischen Hakenkreuz und Sowjetstern*, 60; Alexiev, *Soviet Nationalities in German Wartime Strategy*, 32–33; and Gerhard von

Mende, "Erfahrungen mit Ostfreiwilligen in der deutschen Wehrmacht während des Zweiten Weltkrieges," *Vielvölkerheere und Koalitionskriege* 1 (1952), 24–33, 25. Although the numbers provided by these authors are identical or show very little variation, they have to be treated with caution.

23 The losses of all six legions are estimated to have been 100,000 men, see Neulen, *An deutscher Seite*, 333; Müller, *An der Seite der Wehrmacht*, 241; and Mühlen, *Zwischen Hakenkreuz und Sowjetstern*, 68. On the losses in the four Caucasian legions, see also Mende, "Erfahrungen mit Ostfreiwilligen in der deutschen Wehrmacht während des Zweiten Weltkrieges," 32.

24 On the Muslim labor units, see Hoffmann, *Die Ostlegionen*, 39 and 76; and Hoffmann, *Kaukasien*, 51–52 and 56.

25 On the units of Crimean Tatars, see the overviews in Neulen, *An deutscher Seite*, 325; and Müller, *An der Seite der Wehrmacht*, 237; the more general studies by Hoffmann, *Die Ostlegionen*, 39–50; Hoffmann, *Kaukasien*, 56; Dallin, *German Rule in Russia*, 258; Mühlen, *Zwischen Hakenkreuz und Sowjetstern*, 60 and 184; Alexiev, *Soviet Nationalities in German Wartime Strategy*, 33; Mulligan, *The Politics of Illusion and Empire*, 130 and 153; Angrick, *Besatzungspolitik und Massenmord*, 466–477 and 482–485; and Oldenburg, *Ideologie und militärisches Kalkül*, 121–123; and the accounts on the Crimea by Luther, "Die Krim unter deutscher Besatzung im Zweiten Weltkrieg," 60–62; Kunz, *Die Krim unter Deutscher Herrschaft*, 207–210; Roman'ko, *Krym pod piatoi Gitlera*, 165–239; Fisher, *The Crimean Tatars*, 155; and Williams, *The Crimean Tatars*, 378–379.

26 Ablajef to Hitler (German translation), n.d. (December 1941), Simferopol, PA, R 60738 (also in PA, R 261174). This letter was sent to Berlin by Hentig, Report ("Einstellung der Krimtataren"), 20 December 1941, n.p. (Simferopol), PA, R 60738 (also in PA, R 261174). The Wehrmacht had apparently received a number of similar offers from Crimean Tatars, see ibid.

27 Keitel to Bräutigam, 6 January 1942, n.p., PA, R 261174.

28 On the numbers, see the literature in note 25; and also Siefers, Report ("Aufstellung von Tataren- und Kaukasierformationen im Bereich des A.O.K. 11"), 20 March 1942, n.p., BA–MA, RH 19V/108 (also in PA, R 60739).

29 Siefers, Report ("Aufstellung von Tataren- und Kaukasierformationen im Bereich des A.O.K. 11"), 20 March 1942, n.p., BA–MA, RH 19V/108 (also in PA, R 60739); and, similarly, Command of the 11th Army, Report ("Bericht für die Zeit vom 1.3. bis 31.3.1942"), 31 March 1942, n.p., BA–MA, RH 21–11/415. A similar assessment was given by Hentig, Report ("Erfahrungen mit Tatarischen Kompanien"), 25 April 1942, n.p. (Simferopol), PA, R 60740; and Hentig, Report, 27 April 1942, n.p. (Simferopol), PA, R 60740.

30 On the *Sonderstab F* and the *Deutsch-Arabische Lehrabteilung*, see the overview in Neulen, *An deutscher Seite*, 365–367 and 370–374; the comprehensive account by Jurado, *La espada del Islam*; and the more general studies by Tillmann, *Deutschlands Araberpolitik im Zweiten Weltkrieg*, 353–446; Hirszowicz, *The Third Reich and the Arab East*, 250–259 and 298–300; Schröder, *Deutschland und der Mittlere Osten im Zweiten Weltkrieg*, 215–231; and Greiselis, *Das Ringen um den Brückenkopf Tunesien*, 148–153.

31 Command of Sonderstab Felmy to Army Ration Supply Office of the 12th Army, 8 July 1941, n.d., BA–MA, RH 24–68/2.

32 Grobba, Internal Note ("Die politische Vorbereitung des deutschen Vormarsches nach den arabischen Ländern"), 30 May 1942, PA, R 27332 (also in PA, R 261124). This number only grew marginally over the next months; by August 1942, 243 volunteers had been recruited, forming one company of 24 Iraqis, 112 Syrians and Palestinians, and 107 soldiers from North Africa, see Felmy, Report ("Stellungnahme"), n.d. (summer 1942), n.p., PA, R 261124.

33 Felmy, Report ("Zusammenfassender Bericht über die Tätigkeit des Sonderstabes F in der arabischen Frage"), 15 August 1942, n.p., PA, R 27325 (also in PA, R 261124).

34 *Mudhakkirat al-Hajj Muhammad Amin al-Husayni*, ed. al-'Umar, 121–122 and 145.

35 Felmy, Report ("Zusammenfassender Bericht über die Tätigkeit des Sonderstabes F in der arabischen Frage"), 15 August 1942, n.p., PA, R 27325.

36 Schnurre (Foreign Office), Internal Note ("Aufzeichnung betreffend deutsch-arabische Lehrabteilung"), 20 November 1942, Berlin, PA, R 27827 (also in PA, R 261125).

37 Ibid.

38 Al-Husayni had complained about the deployment of Arabs in the Caucasus and asked for their employment in North Africa, see Al-Husayni, Memorandum ("Denkschrift über die Verlegung des Lagers Sunion"), 29 August 1942, Rome, PA, R 27325 (also in PA, R 27827 and R 27828), sent by Al-Husayni to Keitel, 30 August 1942, Rome, PA, R 27325 (also in PA, R 27827 and R 27828).

39 Grote (Foreign Office) to Rahn, 12 December 1942, Berlin, PA, R 27767; and Ritter (Foreign Office), Internal Note, 14 December 1942, PA, R 27827, give a comprehensive overview of this merging. Arnim, Order ("Arabereinsatz"), 9 January 1943, n.p., PA, R 27770, provides insights into the recruitment of Arabs for labor and military service and the merging with the *Sonderstab Felmy*.

40 Rahn, Report ("Aufzeichnung über die politischen Vorgänge in Tunesien vom 21. November 1942 bis zum 10. Februar 1943"), 10 February 1943, Tunis, BA–MA, RH 19VIII/358.

41 On the *Phalange Africaine*, see Neulen, *An deutscher Seite*, 368–370; Jurado, *La espada del Islam*, 177–178; Hirszowicz, *The Third Reich and the Arab East*, 300; and Satloff, *Among the Righteous*, 86.

42 On the units in North Africa, see Neulen, *An deutscher Seite*, 365–367 and 373; Jurado, *La espada del Islam*, 171–182; Hirszowicz, *The Third Reich and the Arab East*, 298–300; and Greiselis, *Das Ringen um den Brückenkopf Tunesien*, 148–153.

43 Schnurre (Foreign Office), Internal Note ("Aufzeichnung betreffend arabischer Lehrabteilung"), 26 June 1943, Salzburg, PA, R 27332, provides a very critical assessment of the Arabs' performance. Even before their employment in North Africa, Rahn had predicted: "Arabs without combat value," see Rahn to Foreign Office, 21 November 1942, Tunis, BA–MA, RW 5/488.

44 Horstenau to Löhr (Commander-in-Chief South East), 2 March 1943, n.p., BA–MA, RW 4/515. Also in his memoirs, General Edmund Glaise von Horstenau recalled that Himmler was "obsessed" with the foundation of Handžar and that he had enthusiastically approved the idea to take "religious considerations" into account when employing the division. Horstenau also remarked in his notes that Himmler had somewhere seen a picture of Bosniaks in Habsburg Vienna and believed

that those wearing the fez had all been Muslims, see *Ein General im Zwielicht*, ed. Broucek, vol. 3, 189–190 (February 1943), quotations on 189, and, on Hitler's and Himmler's misconception that the old Habsburg regiments were exclusively Muslim, also 308 (November 1943). Kasche, too, noted these misconceptions about the Bosnian Habsburg regiments when consulting with Hitler, see Kasche, Internal Note ("Unterhaltung mit dem Führer am 29.10.1943 im Hauptquartier"), Zagreb, 11 November 1943, PA, Nachlass Kasche, vol. 23. On the Bosnian units in the Habsburg army, see Richard B. Spence, "Die Bosniaken kommen! The Bosnian-Hercegovinian Formations of the Austro-Hungarian Army, 1914–1918," in Spence and Nelson (eds.), *Scholar, Patriot, Mentor,* 299–314.

45 Quoted in *The Kersten Memoirs,* 263 (19 March 1945); see also Kersten, *Totenkopf und Treue,* 328 (19 March 1945).

46 Berger to Kasche, 24 July 1943, Berlin, PA, R 100999. Berger again alluded to the propagandistic value of the unit a few months later, when emphasizing the "enormous political importance" of the division and its "effects on the entire Mohammedan world," see Berger to Himmler, Berlin, 25 September 1943, BAB, NS 19/2601.

47 SS Head Office, Internal Note ("Geschichte und Entstehung der SS-Freiwilligen-b.h.-Geb. Division (13. SS-Division)"), 10 November 1943, Berlin, IfZ, NO-3577; and, similarly, Franje, Interrogation Statement ("Vernehmungsprotokoll"), 6 August 1947, Belgrade, IfZ, NO-4951.

48 On Handžar, see the overviews in Neulen, *An deutscher Seite,* 215–218; Reitlinger, *The SS,* 199–200; and Stein, *The Waffen-SS,* 179–184; the comprehensive accounts by Lepre, *Himmler's Bosnian Division;* Redžić, *Muslimansko Autonomaštvo i 13. SS Divizija;* and Sulejmanpašić. *13. SS Divizija "Handžar";* and the more general studies by Redžić, *Bosnia and Herzegovina in the Second World War,* esp. 34–35, 46–50, and 180–184; Tomasevich, *War and Revolution in Yugoslavia,* 496–501; Broszat and Hory, *Der kroatische Ustascha-Staat,* 155–161 and 171; Casagrande, *Die volksdeutsche SS-Division "Prinz Eugen,"* 331–335; and Holm Sundhaussen, "Zur Geschichte der Waffen-SS in Kroatien 1941–1945," *Südostforschungen* 30 (1971), 176–196, 192–196. On the name "Handžar," see Hitler, Order, 15 May 1944, n.p., BAB, NS 19/2601; and Himmler, Order, 15 May 1944, n.p., BAB, NS 19/2601.

49 People's Committee ("Volkskomitee"), Memorandum, 1 November 1942, Sarajevo, PA, R 261144.

50 Berger to Himmler, 19 April 1943, Berlin, BAB, R 19/2255.

51 By 14 April 1943, 8,000 men (including 6,000 of the Hadžiefendić militia) had been recruited, see Berger to Himmler, 19 April 1943, Berlin, BAB, R 19/2255. By 25 April 1943, 12,000 Bosnians had undergone medical examinations (8,000 to 9,000 of them were deemed suitable); moreover, 8,000 West Bosniaks and 8,000 to 10,000 Muslims from the Sandžak had been recruited, see Berger to Himmler, 29 April 1943, Berlin, BAB, NS 19/2601. On 19 April 1943, Phleps had reported that 20,000 to 25,000 volunteers had been recruited, see Phleps to Jüttner, 19 April 1943, n.p., BAB, NS 19/2601; this report was forwarded by Jüttner to Himmler, 27 April 1943, Berlin, BAB, NS 19/2601. Angry about the SS involvement in the Balkans, envoy Kasche continuously tried to portray SS recruitment as a failure, claiming in the summer of 1943 that only 8,500 men had been enlisted, see Kasche to Foreign Office, 21 June

1943, Zagreb, PA, R 100998; and, speaking of 8,000 to 9,000 a month later, see Kasche to Foreign Office, 8 July 1943, Zagreb, PA, R 100997 (also in PA, R 100998).

52 Hanns Aderle, "Kämpfer gegen Bolschewismus und Judentum," *Deutsche Zeitung in Kroatien* (15 May 1943).

53 On the wish of the Ustaša government to use "Ustaša" in the name of the division, see Kasche to Foreign Office, 18 February 1943, Zagreb, PA, R 27795 (also in PA, R 100998); Phleps to Himmler, 19 February 1943, n.p., BAB, NS 19/3523; Himmler to Phleps, n.d. (20 February 1943), n.p., BAB, NS 19/3523; and Himmler to Ribbentrop, 20 February 1943, n.p., BAB, NS 19/3523 (also in PA, R 27795 and R 100998). Horstenau and Himmler were against the use of "Ustaša" in the name, see Horstenau to Himmler, 25 February 1943, n.p., BAB, NS 19/3523; and Himmler to Horstenau, 3 March 1943, n.p., BAB, NS 19/3523.

54 Berger to Himmler, 25 September 1943, Berlin, BAB, NS 19/2601, states that, in the end, around 2,800 Catholics had been recruited.

55 Winkler, Report ("Die politische Lage der Mohammedaner Bosniens"), 4 May 1943, Berlin, PA, R 67675 (also in PA, R 261144). Winkler based this assessment on an Ustaša complaint about the Muslim nature of the division, see German Legation in Zagreb, Report ("Unterredungen in Sarajevo"), n.d. (28 April 1943), Zagreb, PA, R 100998. The SS isolated the small Christian contingent in order to create a "purely Mohammedan" division, see Phleps to Jüttner, 19 April 1943, BAB, NS 19/2601; this report was forwarded by Jüttner to Himmler, 27 April 1943, Berlin, BAB, NS 19/2601.

56 Phleps to Jüttner, 19 April 1943, n.p., BAB, NS 19/2601; this report was forwarded by Jüttner to Himmler, 27 April 1943, Berlin, BAB, NS 19/2601. On Kasche's complaints about the sidelining of Šuljak, see Kasche to Foreign Office, 28 April 1943, Zagreb, PA, R 100998; and on his reports about the initial appointment of Šuljak, see Kasche to Foreign Office, 23 March 1943, Zagreb, PA, R 27322 (also in PA, R 100998); and Kasche to Foreign Office, 2 April 1943, Zagreb, PA, R 100998.

57 Phleps to Jüttner, 19 April 1943, n.p., BAB, NS 19/2601 (this letter was forwarded by Jüttner to Himmler, 27 April 1943, Berlin, BAB, NS 19/2601).

58 Kaltenbrunner to Himmler, 24 April 1943, Berlin, BAB, NS 19/2601.

59 Himmler to Kammerhofer, 1 July 1943, n.p., BAB, NS 19/3523. A week earlier the SS had informed the Foreign Office of arrests of Muslim recruits by the Ustaša regime, see Riedweg (SS Head Office) to Reichel (Foreign Office), 25 June 1943, Berlin, PA, R 100998. Unsurprisingly, the Ustaša authorities rejected these reports, see Kasche to Ribbentrop, 8 July 1943, Zagreb, PA, R 100997 (also in PA, R 100998). In another case, in the autumn of 1943, a local Muslim functionary informed the Germans of Ustaša arrests of 500 Muslims who had deserted from the Croatian army to enlist in the SS, see Langenberger, Report ("Niederschrift über eine Besprechung am 17.9.43 mit dem 2. Sekretär der 'Muslimansko Dobrotvorno Društvo: Merhamet Sarajevo' namens Mechmed Tokitsch"), 17 September 1943, n.p., BAB, NS 19/3893 (also in BA–MA, N 756/183b); this report was forwarded by Phleps to Himmler, 5 November 1943, n.p., BAB, NS 19/3893. Himmler gave the order to free the 500 Muslims at once, see Brandt to Phleps, 20 November 1943, n.p., BAB, NS 19/3893. After further investigation, however, SS officers on the ground concluded the story was false, see Kumm (Chief of Staff of the V SS Mountain Corps) to Himmler, 31 December 1943, BAB, NS 19/3893.

60 Mirko D. Grmek and Louise L. Lambrichs, *Les révoltés de Villefranche: Mutinerie d'un bataillon de Waffen-SS à Villefranche-de-Rouergue, Septembre 1943* (Paris, 1998); and the literature in note 48. For a report on the revolt written by the mayor of Villefranche, Louis Fontages, see Fontages, Report ("SS et Croates à Villefranche de Rouergue, Aout 1943–Septembre 1943"), n.d., Villefranche, BA–MA, RS 3–13/5.

61 Berger to Himmler, 25 September 1943, Berlin, BAB, NS 19/2601; and similarly, Berger to Reichel, 11 October 1943, Berlin, PA, R 100998.

62 Kasche, Internal Note ("Unterhaltung mit dem Führer am 29.10.1943 im Hauptquartier"), Zagreb, 11 November 1943, PA, Nachlass Kasche, vol. 23.

63 Anonymous, "Der Großmufti von Jerusalem bei den bosnischen Freiwilligen der Waffen-SS," *Wiener Illustrierte* 63, 2 (12 January 1944).

64 Pamphlet (Draft) "Die große Stunde is gekommen!" (German translation), n.d. (February 1944), BAB, NS 19/2601.

65 Pamphlet (Draft) "Väter und Mütter! Brüder und Schwestern! Und Ihr, unsere lieben Kinder, Männer und Frauen aus Bosnien und der Herzegowina!" (German translation), n.d. (February 1944), BAB, NS 19/2601.

66 Himmler to Sauberzweig, 11 February 1944, n.p., BAB, NS 19/2601, on Himmler's approval; and SS Head Office, Internal Note, 5 March 1944, n.p., BAB, NS 19/2601, on Hitler's approval.

67 A collection of documents from the field of this period, including lists of personnel, disciplinary case files, and organizational and march orders of Handžar can be found in the Czech Central Military Archives (*Vojenský Ústřední Archiv*), Prague (VÚA), Box: N 13. SS-Fr. Geb. Div. "H." 1.

68 Wilson, Report ("General Report on Situation in Area of 3 Corps between Jan and Sep 1944"), n.d. (September 1944), n.p., NA, WO 202/298.

69 Franje, Interrogation Statement ("Vernehmungsprotokoll") (English translation), 6 August 1947, Belgrade, IfZ, NO-4951

70 "Mittagslage vom 6. April 1944," in *Hitlers Lagebesprechungen*, ed. Heiber, 560; see also "Midday Situation Report, April 6, 1944," in *Hitler and His Generals*, ed. Heiber and Glantz, 427.

71 Wehrmacht Report ("Reisenotizen von der Reise des Chefs Generalstab O.B. Südost vom 12.8.–17.8.44 im Bereich 2. Panzer-Armee und nach Skopije"), n.d. (August 1944), n.p., BA–MA, RH 19XI/17.

72 Quoted in *The Kersten Memoires*, 260 (25 February 1944); see also the German translation, Kersten, *Totenkopf und Treue*, 324 (25 February 1944).

73 Ibid.

74 On Skanderbeg and Kama, see the brief overviews in Neulen, *An deutscher Seite*, 217–218 and 239–240; Reitlinger, *The SS*, 199; and Stein, *The Waffen-SS*, 184–185; the comprehensive account about Skanderbeg by Latruwe and Kostic, *La division Skanderbeg*; the more general studies by Tomasevich, *War and Revolution in Yugoslavia*, 154 and 500; Broszat and Hory, *Der kroatische Ustascha-Staat*, 162; Casagrande, *Die volksdeutsche SS-Division "Prinz Eugen,"* 336–337; and Sundhaussen, "Waffen-SS," 193; and the accounts of Albania by Fischer, *Albania at War*, 185–187; Fischer, "German Political Policy in Albania, 1943–1944," 227–228; Neuwirth, *Widerstand und Kollaboration in Albanien*, 125–128 and 134; and Stamm, "Zur deutschen Be-

setzung Albaniens 1943–1944," 111. For a report on the formation and employment of the Albanian division Skanderbeg given by its commander, August Schmidhuber, see Schmidhuber, Report ("Zusammenfassender Bericht über die Aufstellung und den Zustand der 21. Waffen-Gebirgsdivision der SS 'Skanderbeg'"), 2 October 1944, n.p., BA–MA, RS 3–21/1.

75 Documents on the recruitment of Albanian civilians for the Skanderbeg Division can be found in the Albanian Central State Archive (*Arkivi Qendror Shtetëror*), Tirana (AQSH), in the files F. 158, V. 1944, D. 32; and F. 195, V. 1944, D. 34.

76 Keitel, Order ("Freilassung albanischer Kriegsgefangener für die Waffen-SS"), 12 February 1944, n.p., PA, R 100984; and, informing Neubacher of the order, Ritter to Neubacher, 17 February 1944, n.p., PA, R 100984.

77 Berger to Reichel (Foreign Office), 5 February 1944, PA, R 100984. This letter was prompted by a request by Neubacher, who had tried since autumn 1943 to get the Albanians of Handžar back to Albania, see the documents in PA, R 100984 and R 100998.

78 Wagner to Ribbentrop, 14 April 1944, Salzburg, PA, R 100679.

79 Martin Maller, *Die Fahrt gegen das Ende: Erlebnisse aus den Partisanenkämpfen im Balkan*, vol. 2 (Bonn, 1962), 221.

80 Ibid., 216.

81 Schmidhuber, Report ("Lagebericht"), 7 July 1944, n.p., BAB, NS 19/2071.

82 Ibid.

83 On Kama, see the literature in note 74.

84 On the Crimean Tatar units of the SS, see the literature in note 25.

85 *Einsatzgruppe D*, Report ("Die Rekrutierung der Krimtataren"), 15 February 1942, n.p., BA–MA, RH 20–11/433 (also in BA–MA, WF-03/10435).

86 Seibert to Army High Command 11, 16 April 1942, n.p., BA–MA, RH 20–11/488.

87 Hermann (SS Head Office), Internal Note ("Turkmuselmanen-Division"), 14 December 1943, Berlin, BA–MA, RS 3–39/1 (also in BAB, NS 31/44).

88 Schellenberg to Berger, 14 October 1943, Berlin, BAB, NS 31/43.

89 Schellenberg, Report ("Aufstellung einer mohammedanischen Legion der Waffen-SS aus Angehörigen der Fremdvölker der Sowjetunion"), 14 October 1943, Berlin, BAB, NS 31/43, enclosed to Schellenberg to Berger, 14 October 1943, Berlin, BAB, NS 31/43.

90 Berger to Himmler, 15 October 1943, Berlin, BAB, NS 31/43.

91 On the Eastern Muslim SS Division, see the overviews in Neulen, *An deutscher Seite*, 332–323; and Stein, *The Waffen-SS*, 188; and the general studies by Hoffmann, *Kaukasien*, 146–155; Dallin, *German Rule in Russia*, 600–602; Mühlen, *Zwischen Hakenkreuz und Sowjetstern*, 147–157; and Alexiev, *Soviet Nationalities in German Wartime Strategy*, 32. The name of the division was repeatedly changed: Ostmuselmanische SS-Division (17 November 1943), Turkmuselmanische SS-Division (11 December 1943), Turkmuselmanen-Division (14 December 1943), Turk-Division (3 January 1944), Muselmanische SS-Division Neu Turkestan (4 January 1944), Ost-Mohamedanische SS- und Polizei-Division (12 January 1944), see Anonymous, Report ("Ostmuselmanische SS- und Polizei-Division"), n.d. (post-1945), n.p., BA–MA, N 756/242b. In the following it is referred to as the "Eastern Muslim SS Division."

92 On the integration of the Wehrmacht battalions, see SS Head Office, Report ("Niederschrift über Absprechung der Aufstellung einer muselmanischen SS-Division Neu-Turkestan"), 4 January 1944, Berlin, BA–MA, RS 3–39/1; Schellenberg had already suggested the transfer of the unit in his initial memorandum, see Schellenberg, Report ("Aufstellung einer mohammedanischen Legion der Waffen-SS aus Angehörigen der Fremdvölker der Sowjetunion"), 14 October 1943, Berlin, BAB, NS 31/43.

93 Berger, Order ("Aufstellung der muselmanischen SS-Division 'Neu Turkestan'"), 14 January 1944, Berlin, BAB, NS 31/44. On the recruitment of Major Mayer-Mader, see also documents in BAB, NS 31/43, NS 31/45, NS 31/297, and BA–MA, RS 3–39/1.

94 On Mayer-Mader's plans to convert to Islam, see Mühlen, *Zwischen Hakenkreuz und Sowjetstern*, 148.

95 Anonymous, Report ("1. Ostmuselmanisches SS-Regiment"), n.d. (post-1945), n.p., BA–MA, N 756/242b.

96 On SS screening and recruiting of Muslim Eastern workers throughout the Reich in 1944 and early 1945, see the documents in BAB, NS 31/27 and NS 31/58. For the screening and recruiting order, see Trimm (Office of the General Plenipotentiary for Labour Deployment) to all Presidents of the Gau Labor Offices and Reich Trustees of Labor, 8 May 1944, Berlin, BAB, NS 31/27 (also in BAB, R 6/143). This order was confirmed in autumn 1944, see Sauckel to all Presidents of the Gau Labor Offices and Reich Trustees of Labor, 16 September 1944, Berlin, BAB, NS 31/27. Schellenberg had already suggested negotiating with Sauckel about the transfer of Muslim workers in his initial memorandum, see Schellenberg, Report ("Aufstellung einer mohammedanischen Legion der Waffen-SS aus Angehörigen der Fremdvölker der Sowjetunion"), 14 October 1943, Berlin, BAB, NS 31/43.

97 On SS screening and recruiting of Muslim Red Army prisoners of war, see the documents in BAB, NS 31/57. Schellenberg had already suggested transferring Muslim Red Army prisoners of war in his initial memorandum, see Schellenberg, Report ("Aufstellung einer mohammedanischen Legion der Waffen-SS aus Angehörigen der Fremdvölker der Sowjetunion"), 14 October 1943, Berlin, BAB, NS 31/43.

98 Berger to Keitel, 17 March 1944, Berlin, BAB, NS 31/57; and, on Terboven's cooperation, Berger to Terboven, 27 March 1944, Berlin, BAB, NS 31/57.

99 On the increasing conflict between the Wehrmacht and the SS about the recruitment of Eastern Muslims, see Fürst, Report ("Zersetzung der Wehrkraft durch unzulässige Werbung von Turk-Legionären durch SS Sturmbannführer Mayer-Mader"), 25 June 1944, Berlin, BAB, NS 31/44. For an example of these conflicts in the field, see Command of the Turk-Inf. Btl. 790 to Command Eastern Legions, 11 December 1943, Radzyn, BA–MA, RS 3–39/1; and High Command of the Army to Himmler, 4 January 1944, Berlin, BA–MA, RS 3–39/1. In the autumn of 1944, the SS appealed to the Wehrmacht to avoid persecution of the soldiers who had been illegally recruited from the Wehrmacht, see Olzscha, Internal Note ("Strafsache gegen Aserbeidshaner Babajew"), 15 October 1944, Berlin, BAB, NS 31/51; and Berger to Köstring, 15 October 1944, Berlin, BAB, NS 31/51.

100 On the revolt against Mayer-Mader, see the three very different assessments by Mayer-Mader, Report, 21 February 1944, Berlin, BAB, NS 31/45; Hermann, Report

("Meuterei im Ostmuselmanischen SS-Rgt."), 24 March 1944, Berlin, BAB, NS 31/43; and Fürst, Report ("Vorgänge beim 1. Ostmuselmanischen Regiment"), 11 May 1944, Berlin, BAB, NS 31/43. On Billig's sadistic command, see Hermann, Internal Note ("1. Ostm. SS-Rgt."), 26 April 1944, Berlin, BAB, NS 31/45; Fürst, Report ("Vorgänge beim 1. Ostmuselmanischen Regiment"), 11 May 1944, Berlin, BAB, NS 31/43; and Brucker (1st Eastern Muslim SS Regiment), Report ("Beleumdung des Hauptmann Billig"), 14 December 1944, n.p., BAB, NS 31/45.

101 The propaganda paper of the Azerbaijani Legion reported this in detail, see "Tapfere Freiwillige aus dem Osten," *Idel-Ural* 40 (97) (1943), German translation, High Command of the Wehrmacht, 7 October 1944, Berlin, BA–MA, MSG 2/18231.

102 On 2 May 1944, Himmler ordered that the already deployed Eastern Muslim SS Regiment be used as a basis for the formation of the Eastern Muslim Division over the course of the year, see Himmler, Order, 2 May 1944, n.p., BAB, NS 31/44, and similarly, Berger, Order, 24 September 1944, BAB, NS 31/27. On the deployment of an Eastern Muslim SS Corps, see Klumm (SS Head Office), Internal Note, 20 July 1944, Berlin, BAB, NS 31/44; and the deployment order by Himmler, Order, 20 October 1944, n.p., BAB, NS 31/44.

103 Fürst, Internal Note ("Osttürkisches SS-Korps"), 12 May 1944, Berlin, BAB, NS 31/44.

104 Berger to Himmler, 14 July 1944, Berlin, BAB, NS 31/44, based on Olzscha, Internal Note ("Osttürkisches (muselmanisches) Korps"), 13 July 1944, Berlin, BAB, NS 31/44. Al-Rashid was first suggested by Olzscha, Internal Note ("Politische Zusammenfassung der mohammedanischen Turkstämmigen aus der Sowjetunion. Aufstellung eines Osttürksichen Korps im Rahmen der SS"), 7 June 1944, Berlin, BAB, NS 31/29 (also in BAB, NS 31/43); and again by Olzscha, Internal Note ("Osttürkisches Korps"), 23 June 1944, Berlin, BAB, NS 31/44. On Himmler's decision to employ al-Rashid, see Klumm, Internal Note, 20 July 1944, BAB, NS 31/44.

105 Al-Rashid, Curriculum Vitae, 7 June 1944, Fürstenberg, BAB, NS 31/45; see also Harun El-Rashid Bey, *Aus Orient und Occident: Ein Mosaik aus buntem Erleben* (Bielefeld, 1954).

106 After the First World War, al-Rashid wrote a hagiographical book about the "Lion of Gallipoli," see H.e.R., *Marschall Liman von Sanders und sein Werk* (Berlin, 1932).

107 Al-Rashid, Curriculum Vitae, 7 June 1944, Fürstenberg, BAB, NS 31/45. Al-Rashid also wrote a book about his experiences in Africa, see Harun El-Rashid Bey, *Schwarz oder Weiß? Roman nach eigenem Erleben im Afrikanischen Kriege* (Berlin, 1940). A short account of al-Rashid's work in Ethiopia, based on his curriculum vitae, is given by Burchard Brentjes, "Der faschistische Agent 'Harun al-Raschid' im äthiopisch-italienischen Krieg," *Zeitschrift für Geschichtswissenschaft* 18, 5 (1970), 660–661.

108 Al-Rashid, Curriculum Vitae, 7 June 1944, Fürstenberg, BAB, NS 31/45.

109 Ibid.

110 Berger to Himmler, 14 July 1944, BAB, NS 19/2838.

111 Olzscha to Al-Rashid, 18 May 1944, Berlin, BAB, NS 31/44.

112 Olzscha, Internal Note ("Einziehung von ehemaligen Offizieren zur SS für das aufzustellende 'Osttürkische Korps'"), 13 July 1944, Berlin, BAB, NS 31/45.

113 On Himmler's order to form the Eastern Turkic SS Corps as a reservoir of all Eastern Muslim SS units, see Klumm, Internal Note, Berlin, 20 July 1944, BAB, NS 31/44; and Himmler, Order, 20 October 1944, n.p., BAB, NS 31/44.

114 Mansur Daoud had suggested his own employment, see Al-Rashid to Olzscha, 5 June 1944, Fürstenberg, BAB, NS 31/44; and on Daoud's recruitment, Berger to Himmler, 14 July 1944, Berlin, BAB, NS 31/44, based on Olzscha, Internal Note ("Osttürkisches (muselmanisches) Korps"), 13 July 1944, Berlin, BAB, NS 31/44; Olzscha, Internal Note ("Osttürkisches Korps"), 23 June 1944, Berlin, BAB, NS 31/44; and Olzscha, Internal Note ("Politische Zusammenfassung der mohammedanischen Turkstämmigen aus der Sowjetunion. Aufstellung eines Osttürksichen Korps im Rahmen der SS"), 7 June 1944, Berlin, BAB, NS 31/29 (also in BAB, NS 31/43). On Daoud's escape from Cairo via Istanbul to Berlin in 1942, see the documents in PA, R 29533.

115 Al-Rashid to Berger, 27 January 1945, n.p., BAB, NS 31/45. In reality, Daoud tried desperately to avoid military service, citing health issues for which he was seeking treatment in a private clinic in Saxony and making appeals to be granted leave, see the documents in BAB, NS 31/45.

116 On the numbers of the Eastern Muslim SS Corps, see the literature in note 92.

117 On the Tatar Waffen-Gebirgs-Brigade, see Anonymous, Report ("58. Waffen-Gebirgs-Brigade der SS (tatarische Nr. 1)"), n.d. (post-1945), n.p., BA–MA, N 756/242b. On 12 December, al-Rashid reported that the Crimean Tatars of the Waffen-Gebirgs-Brigade were about to be integrated into his Eastern Turkic SS Corps, see Al-Rashid to Spaarmann, 12 December 1944, n.p., BAB, NS 31/34. The idea to recruit the Crimean Tatars into the new Eastern Muslim formation of the SS had in fact already been brought up in late 1943, see Hermann, Internal Note ("Krimtataren"), 14 December 1943, Berlin, BAB, NS 31/32; and similarly, Hermann, Internal Note ("Krimtataren"), 16 December 1943, Berlin, BAB, NS 31/32. The plan was also supported by the East Ministry, see Kornelsen, Internal Note ("Gründung einer krimtatarischen Kavallerieformation im Verbande der Muselmanischen SS-Division"), 21 March 1944, Berlin, BAB, NS 31/32.

118 Pilot (SS Head Office) to Szynkiewicz, 21 March 1944, Berlin, BAB, NS 31/43.

119 SS Police Chief Danzig to SS Head Office, 21 November 1944, Danzig, BAB, NS 31/45; and, on presumably the same two Muslims, Kirimal to Olzscha, 30 November 1944, Frankfurt an der Oder, BAB, NS 31/45.

120 Himmler, Order, 11 December 1944, n.p., BAB, NS 31/50 (also in BAB, NS 31/53 and NS 31/327). The SS also consulted Oberländer about the formation of the Caucasian unit, see Arlt (SS Head Office) to Oberländer, 20 January 1945, Berlin, BAB, NS 31/37. On the early organization of the formation, see the documents in BAB, NS 31/34, NS 31/37, NS 31/50, and NS 31/53.

121 Alekberli to Al-Rashid, 9 November 1944, n.p., BAB, NS 31/34. On the decision to leave the Azerbaijanis in the Eastern Turkic SS Corps, see Arlt, Internal Note, 1 February 1945, Berlin, BAB, NS 31/51.

122 On the Alimov revolt, see Al-Rashid, Report ("Überlauf des Kommandeurs des Waffen-Rgts. der SS Turkistan Nr. 1, Waffen-Obersturmführer Gulam Alimow, mit etwa 500 Männern seines Regiments zu den Partisanen"), 26 December 1944, BAB, NS 31/29 (also in BAB, NS 31/44); and Al-Rashid, Report ("Bericht über die

Entwicklung des Osttürkischen Waffen-Verbandes der SS von Warschau bis Über-lauf Alimow und über die aus dieser sich ergebenden Folgerungen"), n.d. (December 1944), BAB, NS 31/29 (also in BAB, NS 31/44). A very detailed picture of the revolt is given in the interrogation reports, see Interrogation Report of Kuliev, n.d. (December 1944), BA–MA, RS 3–39/2; Interrogation Report of Abugatirov, 1 January 1945, n.p., BAB, NS 31/29 (also in BAB, NS 31/44); Interrogation Report of Abredinov, 5 January 1945, n.p., BAB, NS 31/29; Interrogation Report of Rachmanov and Islmailov, 8 January 1945, n.p., BAB, NS 31/29; Interrogation Report of Chasanov, 10 January 1945, n.p., BAB, NS 31/29 (also in BAB, NS 31/44); Interrogation Report of Atabaev, 10 January 1945, n.p., BAB, NS 31/29; Interrogation Report of Namangani (Chief Mullah), 10 January 1945, n.p., BAB, NS 31/29 (also in BAB, NS 31/44). On the Slovak partisans, see Ladislaus Hory, "Der slowakische Partisanenkampf 1944/45," *Osteuropa* 9, 12 (1959), 779–784; and Rudolf Urban, "Der slowakische Partisanen-kampf 1944/45: Eine Ergänzug," *Osteuropa* 10, 2/3 (1960), 153–154.

123 Olzscha, Report, 1945, n.p., BStU, MfS, HA IX/11, ZR 920, A. 54.

124 Hermann, Internal Note ("Turkmuselmanen-Division"), 14 December 1943, Berlin, BA–MA, RS 3–39/1 (also in BAB, NS 31/44).

125 Ibid. At the same time, Hermann also alluded to the "good attitude and deep religios-ity" of the Crimean Tatars, see Hermann, Internal Note ("Krimtataren"), 14 Decem-ber 1943, Berlin, BAB, NS 31/32.

126 Schulte, Report ("Turkmuselmanische SS-Division"), 11 December 1943, Berlin, BA–MA, RS 3–39/1.

127 Mayer-Mader, Report, 15 December 1943, Berlin, BAB, NS 31/43.

128 SS Head Office, Report ("Absprechung der Aufstellung einer muselmanischen SS-Division Neu-Turkestan"), 4 January 1944, Berlin, BA–MA, RS 3–39/1.

129 Olzscha, Internal Note ("Schaffung einer turkotatarischen (osttürkischen) Dachor-ganisation in Deutschland"), 24 April 1944, Berlin, BAB, NS 31/42. On this memo-randum and its context, see chapter 2.

130 Olzscha, Internal Note ("Politische Zusammenfassung der mohammedanischen Turkstämmigen aus der Sowjetunion. Aufstellung eines Osttürksichen Korps im Rahmen der SS"), 7 June 1944, Berlin, BAB, NS 31/29 (also in BAB, NS 31/43), and, similarly, Olzsch, Internal Note ("Politische Führung der Turkstämmigen. Abstim-mung zwischen SS und OKW"), 1 June 1944, Berlin, BAB, NS 31/29. Both notes were sent by Olzscha to Klumm, 7 June 1944, Berlin, BAB, NS 31/29; and Klumm forwarded both to Himmler, see Klumm to Grothmann (Himmler's Staff), 17 June 1944, n.p., BAB, NS 31/29.

131 Olzscha, Internal Note ("Osttürkisches Korps"), 23 June 1944, Berlin, BAB, NS 31/44.

132 Olzscha, Internal Note ("Osttürkisches (muselmanisches) Korps"), 13 July 1944, n.p., BAB, NS 31/44.

133 Berger to Himmler, 14 July 1944, Berlin, BAB, NS 31/44, based on Olzscha, Internal Note ("Osttürkisches (muselmanisches) Korps"), 13 July 1944, Berlin, BAB, NS 31/44.

134 Berger to Himmler, 17 August 1944, Berlin, BAB, NS 31/44.

135 Berger, Order ("Aufstellung des 'Osttürkischen Korps'"), n.d. (August 1944), Ber-lin, BAB, NS 31/27 (also in BAB, NS 31/44).

136 Ulrich, Internal Note ("Osttürkisches Korps"), 7 August 1944, Berlin, BAB, NS 31/44.

137 Al-Rashid, Report ("Grundsätzliches"), n.d., (1944), n.p., BAB, NS 31/44.

138 Al-Rashid to Olzscha, 24 July 1944, Fürstenberg, BAB, NS 31/45.

139 Al-Rashid, Report ("Bericht über die Entwicklung des Osttürkischen Waffen-Verbandes der SS von Warschau bis Überlauf Alimow und über die aus dieser sich ergebenden Folgerungen"), n.d. (December 1944), n.p., BAB, NS 31/29 (also in BAB, NS 31/44).

140 Al-Rashid to Olzscha, 5 June 1944, Fürstenberg, BAB, NS 31/44.

141 Al-Rashid to Olzscha, 31 July 1944, n.p., BAB, NS 31/45.

142 Olzscha, Internal Note ("1. National-Turkestanischen Kongress Wien"), 23 May 1944, Berlin, BAB, NS 31/44.

143 Ibid.; and, similarly, Olzscha, Internal Note ("Rücksprache mit SS-Standartenführer Spaarmann und SS-Hstuf. Ullrich"), 12 May 1944, Berlin, BAB, NS 31/42; and SS Head Office, Internal Note ("Besprechung im Auswärtigen Amt mit Sachbearbeiter Idris am 14.11."), 15 November 1944, Berlin, BAB, NS 31/30.

144 Mende, Internal Note ("Politische Richtlinien für die Turkverbände und die Ost-muselmanische SS-Division"), 12 February 1944, Berlin, BAB, NS 31/42.

145 Ibid.

146 Ibid.

147 Mende, Internal Note ("Turkestanischer Kongress in Wien"), 1 June 1944, Berlin, BAB, R 6/143; and, in response, Berger to Mende, n.d. (2 June 1944), Berlin, BAB, R 6/143, based on a draft letter written by Olzscha.

148 Mende, Internal Note ("Besprechung mit Dr. Olzscha vom SS Hauptamt am 13.9.1944"), 18 September 1944, Berlin, BAB, R 6/143; and, similarly, Olzscha, Internal Note ("Besprechung zwischen Professor v. Mende, Dr. Arlt und Dr. Olzscha"), 29 September 1944, Berlin, BAB, NS 31/27.

149 Hermann, Internal Note ("Mobilisierung des Islam"), 28 February 1944, Berlin, BAB, NS 31/42 (also in BAB, NS 31/43).

150 Ibid.

151 Berger to Himmler, 13 November 1943, Berlin, BAB, NS 19/2601.

152 Ibid.

153 Berger to Himmler, 4 December 1943, Berlin, BAB, NS 19/1896.

154 On the Brigade Nord-Africaine, see Neulen, An deutscher Seite, 374–375; Jurado, La espada del Islam, 183–188; Satloff, Among the Righteous, 86–87; Pascal Ory, Les Collaborateurs 1940–1945 (Paris, 1976), 258–259; and Marcel Hasquenoph, La Gestapo en France (Paris, 1987 [1975]), 351–359.

155 Brandt to Wagner (Foreign Office), 18 October 1944, n.p., BAB, NS 19/2637.

156 Brandt to Wagner, 23 October 1944, n.p., BAB, NS 19/2637.

157 Berger to Himmler, 13 April 1944, Berlin, BAB, NS 19/3560.

158 On SS screening and recruiting of Muslim concentration camp inmates in 1944, see the documents in BAB, NS 31/59.

159 Brandt to Berger, 31 May 1944, n.p., BAB, NS 31/59.

160 SS Economic and Administrative Head Office, List ("Aufstellung über Häftlinge islamitischen Glaubens"), 1944, BAB, NS 31/59.

161 Gerhard Höpp, "'Gefährdungen der Erinnerung': Arabische Häftlinge in nationalsozialistischen Konzentrationslagern," *Asien, Afrika, Lateinamerika* 30 (2002), 373–386; almost identically, Gerhard Höpp, "In the Shadow of the Moon: Arab Inmates in Nazi Concentration Camps," in Schwanitz (ed.), *Germany and the Middle East*, 216–240; and, in a more general context, Höpp, "Der verdrängte Diskurs," 246–252.

162 Olzscha, Internal Note ("Häftlinge islamischen Glaubens"), 16 November 1944, Berlin, BAB, NS 31/59.

163 Berger to Himmler, 10 December 1944, Berlin, BAB, NS 31/59, based on a draft letter written by Olzscha, BAB, NS 31/59.

7. ISLAM AND POLITICS IN THE UNITS

1 Himmler, Speech ("Rede des Reichsführers SS Reichsinnenminister Himmler auf der Tagung der RPA-Leiter am 28. Januar 1944"), 28 January 1944, n.p., BAB, NS 19/4012 (also in BA–MA, SF-01/16263). Himmler had made similar remarks in one of his Posen speeches, see Himmler, Speech ("Rede vor den Reichs- und Gauleitern in Posen am 6.10.1943"), in Bradley F. Smith and Agnes F. Peterson (eds.), *Heinrich Himmler: Geheimreden 1933 bis 1945 und andere Ansprachen* (Frankfurt, 1974), 162–183, 181.

2 On the accommodation of indigenous religions and cultures in the British Indian Army, see David Omissi, *The Sepoy and the Raj: The Indian Army, 1860–1940* (London, 1994), 76–112; John A. Lynn, *Battle: A History of Combat and Culture* (Oxford, 2003), 145–177; Tarak Barkawi, "Culture and Combat in the Colonies: The Indian Army in the Second World War," *Journal of Contemporary History* 41, 2 (2006), 325–355; and, on Islam in particular, Nile Green, *Islam and the Army in Colonial India: Sepoy Religion in the Service of Empire* (Cambridge, 2009).

3 The literature on religious life in Christian military units in modern history is vast. Notable studies include, on the Second World War, Donald F. Grosby, *Battlefield Chaplains: Catholic Priests in World War II* (Lawrence, KA, 1994); and Alan Robinson, *Chaplains at War: The Role of Clergymen during World War II* (London, 2008); and, on the First World War, Aleksandr Senin, "Russian Army Chaplains during World War I," *Russian Studies in History* 32, 2 (1993), 43–52; Duff Crerar, *Padres in No Man's Land: Canadian Chaplains and the Great War* (Montreal, 1995); and Richard Schweitzer, *The Cross and the Trenches: Religious Faith and Doubt among British and American Great War Soldiers* (Westport, CT, 2003); and, on the American Civil War, Sidney J. Romero, *Religion in the Rebel Ranks* (London, 1983); Gardiner H. Shattuck, *A Shield and Hiding Place: The Religious Life of the Civil War Armies* (Macon, GA, 1987); and Drew Gilpin Faust, "Christian Soldiers: The Meaning of Revivalism in the Confederate Army," *Journal of Southern History* 53, 1 (1987), 63–90; and, more generally, the articles in Doris L. Bergen (ed.), *Sword of the Lord: Military Chaplains from the First to the Twenty-First Century* (Notre Dame, IN, 2004).

4 On religious life and the political role of the army chaplaincy in Christian Wehrmacht units, see Manfred Messerschmidt, *Aspekte der Militärseelsorgepolitik in nationalsozialistischer Zeit (Sonderdruck aus Militärgeschichtliche Mitteilungen)* (Freiburg, 1969); Georg May, *Interkonfessionalismus in der deutschen Militärseelsorge von 1933 bis 1945*

(Amsterdam, 1978); Heinrich Missalla, *Für Volk und Vaterland: Die kirchliche Kriegshilfe im Zweiten Weltkrieg* (Königstein im Taunus, 1978); Heinrich Missalla, *Für Gott, Führer und Vaterland: Die Verstrickung der katholischen Seelsorge in Hitlers Krieg* (Munich, 1999); Johannes Güsgen, *Die katholische Militärseelsorge in Deutschland zwischen 1920 und 1945: Ihre Praxis und Entwicklung in der Reichswehr der Weimarer Republik und der Wehrmacht Nazi Deutschlands unter Berücksichtigung ihrer Rolle bei der Reichskonkordatsverhandlungen* (Cologne, 1989); Hans Jürgen Brandt, "Die katholische Militärseelsorge und Kleriker als Sanitätssoldaten in der großdeutschen Wehrmacht 1939 bis 1945," in Alfred Egid Hierold and Ernst Josef Nagel (eds.), *Kirchlicher Auftrag und politische Friedensgestaltung: Festschrift für Ernst Niermann* (Stuttgart, 1995), 178–193; Doris L. Bergen, " 'Germany Is Our Mission—Christ Is Our Strength': The Wehrmacht Chaplaincy and the 'German Christian' Movement," *Church History* 66, 3 (1997), 522–536; Doris L. Bergen, "Between God and Hitler: German Military Chaplains and the Crimes of the Third Reich," in Omer Bartov and Phyllis Mack (eds.), *In God's Name: Genocide and Religion in the Twentieth Century* (New York, 2001), 123–138; Doris L. Bergen, "German Military Chaplains in the Second World War and the Dilemmas of Legitimacy," in Bergen, *Sword of the Lord*, 165–186; and Dagmar Pöpping, "Die Wehrmachtseelsorge im Zweiten Weltkrieg: Rolle und Selbstverständnis von Kriegs- und Wehrmachtpfarrern im Ostkrieg 1941–1945," in Manfred Gailus and Armin Nolzen (eds.), *Zerstrittene "Volksgemeinschaft": Glaube, Konfession und Religion im Nationalsozialismus* (Göttingen, 2011), 257–286.

5 On the different religions in the Eastern Legions, see Hoffmann, *Die Ostlegionen*, 144–146.

6 *Einsatzgruppe D*, Report ("Die Rekrutierung der Krimtataren"), 15 February 1942, n.p., BA–MA, RH 20–11/433 (also in BA–MA, WF–03/10435); and, almost identically, Siefers, Report ("Aufstellung von Tataren- und Kaukasierformationen im Bereich des A.O.K. 11"), 20 March 1942, n.p., BA–MA, RH 19V/108 (also in PA, R 60739). On the meeting, see also Hoffmann, *Die Ostlegionen*, 43–44; Mühlen, *Zwischen Hakenkreuz und Sowjetstern*, 184; Angrick, *Besatzungspolitik und Massenmord*, 469–471; and Roman'ko, *Krym pod piatoi Gitlera*, 173 and 200–201.

7 *Einsatzgruppe D*, Report ("Die Rekrutierung der Krimtataren"), 15 February 1942, n.p., BA–MA, RH 20–11/433 (also in BA–MA, WF–03/10435); and, almost identically, Siefers, Report ("Aufstellung von Tataren- und Kaukasierformationen im Bereich des A.O.K. 11"), 20 March 1942, n.p., BA–MA, RH 19V/108 (also in PA, R 60739).

8 Siefers, Report ("Aufstellung von Tataren- und Kaukasierformationen im Bereich des A.O.K. 11"), 20 March 1942, n.p., BA–MA, RH 19V/108 (also in PA, R 60739).

9 Pamphlet "Hrvati Herceg-Bosne!" ("Croates of Herzeg-Bosna!"), n.d. (1943), PA, R 67675 (also in PA, R 100998); and, for the German translation, Pamphlet "Kroaten Herzeg-Bosnas!" (German translation), n.d. (1943), PA, R 67675 (also in PA, R 100998).

10 Winkler, Report ("Die politische Lage der Mohammedaner Bosniens"), 4 May 1943, Berlin, PA, R 67675 (also in PA, R 261144). Winkler based this assessment on an Ustaša complaint about the role of the imams in the recruitment campaign, see Ger-

man Legation in Zagreb, Report ("Unterredungen in Sarajevo"), n.d. (28 April 1943), Zagreb, PA, R 100998.

11 On Pandža's role in the recruitment, see Kasche to Foreign Office, 28 April 1943, Zagreb, PA, R 100998; and Bajraktarević to Phleps, 15 November 1943, Mostar, BAB, NS 19/2601.

12 Bajraktarević to Phleps, 15 November 1943, Mostar, BAB, NS 19/2601.

13 Ibid.

14 Quoted in *The Kersten Memoires*, 259 (25 February 1944); see also Kersten, *Totenkopf und Treue*, 324 (25 February 1944).

15 Sauberzweig to Berger, 30 September 1943, n.p., BAB, NS 19/2601.

16 Bajraktarević to Phleps, 15 November 1943, Mostar, BAB, NS 19/2601.

17 Ibid.

18 SS Head Office, Internal Note ("Geschichte und Entstehung der SS-Freiwilligen-b.h.-Geb. Division (13. SS-Division)"), 10 November 1943, Berlin, IfZ, NO-3577.

19 Kasche to Foreign Office, 2 April 1943, Zagreb, PA, R 100998; moreover, also the green flag, the flag of the Prophet, was used to attract recruits, see *Ein General im Zwielicht*, ed. Broucek, vol. 3, 241 (July/August 1943).

20 Anonymous, "Turkmenen werden deutsche Soldaten," *Brünner Tageblatt* (12 January 1944).

21 Idris to Schulenburg, 8 June 1942, Berlin, PA, R 261175.

22 Bräutigam to Schulenburg, 18 March 1942, Berlin, PA, R 261175.

23 Berger to Himmler, 19 April 1943, Berlin, BAB, R 19/2255.

24 Al-Husayni to Berger, 15 December 1943, Berlin, BAB, NS 31/43.

25 Hermann, Internal Note ("Besuch bei seiner Eminenz dem Großmufti"), 15 December 1943, Berlin, BAB, NS 31/44.

26 Berger to Himmler, 16 December 1943, Berlin, BA–MA, RS 3–39/1.

27 Pamphlet "Muselmannen" (German translation), n.d. (1944), BA–MA, RS 3–39/1.

28 Niedermayer, Report ("Auswertungsergebnis der Fragebogen für Legionäre"), 21 November 1942, n.p., BA–MA, RH 26-162/20.

29 Heygendorff, Instructions ("Merkblatt für deutsches Rahmenpersonal in ost-völkischen Einheiten über Behandlung der Legionäre"), 1 July 1943, Radom, BA–MA, RH 58/62.

30 Kunz, *Die Krim unter Deutscher Herrschaft*, 213.

31 Salihbegovic (Division Imam), Report ("Bericht zur Lage"), 25 September 1943, n.p., BAB, NS 19/2601.

32 Chapter 3 provides an account of these concessions for Muslim prisoners of war from the French army.

33 High Command of the Army, Instructions ("Richtlinien für die inneren Verhält-nisse in den Ostlegionen"), 24 April 1942, n.p., BA–MA, RH 19V/108. Earlier that year, it had already been ordered to respect the religious beliefs of the Tatar volunteers who were recruited separately in the Crimea, see 11th Army, Instructions ("Merkblatt für die Behandlung der Tataren"), 9 January 1942, n.p., BA–MA, WF–03/10433.

34 High Command of the Army, Instructions ("Merkblatt für das deutsche Personal der Turk-Stammlager und Turk-Btlne."), 2 June 1942, n.p., BA–MA, RH 19V/109.

35 Niedermayer, Instructions ("Vereinbarung über islamisch-religiöse Fragen"), 27 August 1942, Mirgorod (Myrhorod), BAB, R 6/247 (also in MA, BA–RH 26-162/16).

36 Niedermayer, Order ("Grundlegender Befehl über die Aufstellung von Turk-Btlnen"), 4 July 1942, n.p., BA–MA, RH 19V/79 (also in BA–MA, RH 26-162/16); and, on the respect for religious customs, Niedermayer, Order ("Grundlegender Befehl über die Aufstellung von Turk-Btlnen"), Annexe 8 ("Die Turk-Völker und ihre Behandlung"), 4 July 1942, n.p., BA–MA, RH 19V/79 (also in BA–MA, RH 26-162/16); and, similarly a year later, Niedermayer, Order ("Grundlegender Befehl über die geistige Betreuung der 162. (Turk) Inf. Div."), 15 June 1943, n.p., BA–MA, RH 26-162/20.

37 Heygendorff, Instructions ("Merkblatt für deutsches Rahmenpersonal in ostvölkischen Einheiten über Behandlung der Legionäre"), 1 July 1943, Radom, BA–MA, RH 58/62.

38 Heygendorff, Instructions ("Merkblatt für deutsche Offiziere über wehrgeistige Führung der Legionäre"), 1 July 1943, Radom, BA–MA, RH 58/62.

39 High Command of the Wehrmacht, Newsletter ("Mitteilungen für den deutschen Soldaten in Freiwilligen-Verbänden"), November 1944, BA–MA, MSG 2/18262.

40 Hoffmann (Army), Report ("Tätigkeitsbericht der Abteilung Ic/A.O. der 162. Inf. Division: 1. Oktober 1942 bis 31. März 1943"), 20 April 1943, n.p., BA–MA, RH 26-162/19; and also Niedermayer, Order ("Grundlegender Befehl über die geistige Betreuung der 162. (Turk) Inf. Div."), 15 June 1943, n.p., BA–MA, RH 26-162/20.

41 Himmler to Phleps, 13 February 1943, BAB, NS 19/2601; and Brandt to Jüttner, 16 February 1943, n.p., BAB, NS 19/2601. In the following, references to the Habsburg rights for Muslim Bosnian soldiers recur in documents on the employment of Handžar, see particularly documents in PA, R 27795 and R 100998.

42 Schellenberg, Memorandum ("Aufstellung einer mohammedanischen Legion der Waffen-SS aus Angehörigen der Fremdvölker der Sowjetunion"), 14 October 1943, Berlin, BAB, NS 31/43, enclosed to Schellenberg to Berger, 14 October 1943, Berlin, BAB, NS 31/43, had already stressed the role of Islam in the Eastern Muslim SS units and the need to employ military imams. The officers of the Eastern Muslim SS formation requested that they receive the same religious support as the soldiers of Handžar, see Al-Husayni to Berger, 15 December 1943, Berlin, BAB, NS 31/43.

43 Olzscha, Report, n.p., 1945, BStU, MfS, HA IX/11, ZR 920, A. 54.

44 Niedermayer, Instructions ("Vereinbarung über islamisch-religiöse Fragen"), 27 August 1942, Mirgorod, BAB, R 6/247 (also in BA–MA, RH 26-62/16).

45 Heygendorff, Instructions ("Merkblatt für deutsches Rahmenpersonal in ostvölkischen Einheiten über Behandlung der Legionäre"), 1 July 1943, Radom, BA–MA, RH 58/62.

46 Heygendorff, Report ("Wie es zu meiner Ernennung zum Kommandeur der Ostlegionen kam"), n.d. (post-1945), n.p., IfZ, ZS 407.

47 Niedermayer, Instructions ("Vereinbarung über islamisch-religiöse Fragen"), 27 August 1942, Mirgorod, BAB, R 6/247 (also in BA–MA, RH 26-62/16).

48 "Die Urasa-Feier im Erholungsheim," Idel-Ural 42 (48) (1943), German translation, High Command of the Wehrmacht, 17 October 1943, Berlin, BA–MA, MSG 2/18231.

49 "Der Festtag Bairam," *Ghazavat* 36 (1943), German translation, High Command of the Wehrmacht, 20 October 1943, Berlin, BA–MA, MSG 2/18238; see also an article a month earlier: "Ramasan," *Ghazavat* 29 (1943), German translation, High Command of the Wehrmacht, 1 September 1943, Berlin, BA–MA, MSG 2/18238.

50 "Die Freude des Mullah Suleiman," *Azerbaijan* 45 (73) (1943), German translation, High Command of the Wehrmacht, 7 November 1943, Berlin, BA–MA, MSG 2/18239.

51 "Die Fastenzeit zum Bajramfest," *Azerbaijan* 38 (117) (1944), German translation, High Command of the Wehrmacht, 25 September 1944, Berlin, BA–MA, MSG 2/18239.

52 "Kurban-Bajram," *Idel-Ural* 49 (106) (1944), German translation, High Command of the Wehrmacht, 9 December 1944, Berlin, BA–MA, MSG 2/18231. A German commander of a Tatar unit wrote celebratory wishes, urging the soldiers to believe in a "common victory," see "Kurban-Bajram," *Idel-Ural* 49 (106) (1944), German translation, High Command of the Wehrmacht, 9 December 1944, Berlin, BA–MA, MSG 2/18231.

53 On the celebrations in Carlsbad, see "Asarytürkische Einheit im Ort 'T,'" *Azerbaijan* 51 (130) (1944), German translation, High Command of the Wehrmacht, 25 December 1944, Berlin, BA–MA, MSG 2/18239; on the celebrations in Berlin, see "Kurban-Bajram in Berlin," *Azerbaijan* 49 (128) (1944), German translation, High Command of the Wehrmacht, 11 December 1944, Berlin, BA–MA, MSG 2/18239; for another article on the Azerbaijani *Qurban Bairam* feast of 1944, see "Kurban-Bajram wurde feierlich begangen," *Azerbaijan* 49 (128) (1944), German translation, High Command of the Wehrmacht, 11 December 1944, Berlin, BA–MA, MSG 2/18239.

54 Office for Political and Ideological Education of the 13th SS Division, Instruction ("Dienstanweisung für Imame der 13. SS-Freiwilligen b.h. Geb. Div. [Kroatien]"), 15 March 1944, n.p., BAB, NS 19/2601. These instructions are discussed later in more detail.

55 Bruce M. Borthwick, "The Islamic Sermon as a Channel of Political Communication," *Middle East Journal* 21, 3 (1967), 299–313; Asghar Fathi, "The Islamic Pulpit as a Medium of Political Communication," *Journal for the Scientific Study of Religion* 20, 2 (1981), 163–172; and, more generally, A. J. Wensinck, "Khutba," in *The Encyclopaedia of Islam*, vol. 5, ed. C. E. Bosworth, E. van Donzel, B. Lewis, and Ch. Pellat (Leiden, 1986), 74–75.

56 The division's propaganda magazine printed a number of photographs of the event, titled "SS-Brigadeführer und Generalmajor der Waffen-SS Sauberzweig spricht gelegentlich des Bajramfestes zu seinen Männern" ("SS-Brigadeühfer i Generalmajor SS-Oružja Sauberzweig govori prilikom bajramskog blagdana svojim vojnicima"), *SS-Handžar* 7 (n.d. [1943]); and "Die feierlichen Tage des Bajramfestes der Division" ("Svečani bajramski dani u diviziji"), *SS-Handžar* 7 (n.d. [1943]). On the *SS-Handžar* propaganda magazine, see chapter 8.

57 M. N., "Eine Gemeinschaft auf Gedeih und Verderb: Ansprachen des Kommandeurs und des Divisionsimams zum Bajramfest" ("Zakleta zajednica: Govor zapoviednika i divizijskog imama prilikom bajramske svečanosti"), *SS-Handžar* 7 (n.d. [1943]).

58 Zvonimir Bernwald, *Muslime in der Waffen-SS: Erinnerungen an die bosnische Division Handžar (1943–1945)* (Graz, 2012), 64, and, on his memories of the celebrations in Neuhammer more generally, see 62–64 and 175–177.

59 Sauberzweig, Order ("Feier des Geburtstages Mohammeds"), 4 March 1944, n.p., BAB, NS 19/2601.

60 Office for Political and Ideological Education of the 13th SS Division, Instruction ("Dienstanweisung für Imame der 13. SS-Freiwilligen b.h. Geb. Div. [Kroatien]"), 15 March 1944, n.p., BAB, NS 19/2601.

61 Ibid.

62 Al-Rashid, Report ("Behandlung der Ostmuselmanen"), 20 September 1944, Warsaw, BAB, NS 31/44, attached to Al-Rashid to Spaarmann, 22 September 1944, Berlin, BAB, NS 31/44; and, on the report, Olzscha, Internal Note ("Bericht des SS-Standartenführers Harun el Raschid über seinen Besuch beim 1. Ostmuselmanischen Regiment"), 24 September 1944, Berlin, BAB, NS 31/44.

63 Niedermayer, Instructions ("Vereinbarung über islamisch-religiöse Fragen"), 27 August 1942, Mirgorod, BAB, R 6/247 (also in BA-MA, RH 26-162/16).

64 Arnim, Order ("Arabereinsatz"), 9 January 1943, n.p., PA, R 27770.

65 Himmler to Berger, 22 July 1943, n.p., BAB, NS 19/2601; a copy of this inquiry was sent to Oswald Pohl, head of the Main SS Economic and Administrative Department.

66 Berger to Himmler, 26 July 1943, Berlin, BAB, NS 19/2601.

67 Himmler, Order, 6 August 1943, n.p., BAB, NS 19/3285.

68 Himmler to Berger, 22 July 1943, n.p., BAB, NS 19/2601.

69 Propaganda Division (*Waffen-SS Standarte "Kurt Eggers"*) to Brandt, 8 November 1943, Berlin, BAB, NS 19/2601.

70 Ibid.

71 Maller, *Die Fahrt gegen das Ende*, vol. 2, 216.

72 Boria Sax, *Animals in the Third Reich: Pets, Scapegoats, and the Holocaust* (New York, 2000), 139–150, and for the English translation of the law, see 175–179; Martin F. Brumme, "'Mit dem Blutkult der Juden ist endgültig in Deutschland Schluß zu machen': Anmerkungen zur Entwicklung der Anti-Schächt-Bewegung," in Michael Hubenstorf et al. (eds.), *Medizingeschichte und Gesellschaftskritik: Festschrift für Gerhard Baader* (Husum, 1997), 378–397; and Shai Lavi, "Unequal Rites: Jews, Muslims and the History of Ritual Slaughter in Germany," *Tel Aviv Yearbook for German History* 37 (2009), 164–184, 173.

73 Anonymous, "Gefangene, in Frankreich gemacht," *Signal* (15 July 1940), 9–10.

74 Heygendorff, Instructions ("Merkblatt für deutsches Rahmenpersonal in ostvölkischen Einheiten über Behandlung der Legionäre"), 1 July 1943, Radom, BA–MA, RH 58/62.

75 Buttlar (High Command of the Wehrmacht) to Köstring, 6 February 1944, n.p., BAB, NS 31/29.

76 Command Staff of Himmler to High Command of the Wehrmacht, 2 February 1944, n.p., BAB, NS 31/29.

77 Ibid.

78 Schnittker (Office of Higher SS and Police Leader East) to SS Head Office, 14 January 1944, Cracow, BA–MA, RS 3–39/1.

79 Schulte to Schnittker, 19 January 1944, Berlin, BA–MA, RS 3–39/1.

80 Office for Political and Ideological Education of the 13th SS Division, Instruction ("Dienstanweisung für Imame der 13. SS-Freiwilligen b.h. Geb. Div. [Kroatien]"), 15 March 1944, n.p., BAB, NS 19/2601.

81 Text printed in 2. *Land.Schütz.Btl.411* to *Fü.Arb.Kdo. No. 7902* (Allmendingen), 28 June 1944, Laupheim, Stuttgart General State Archive (*Hauptstaatsarchiv Stuttgart*), Stuttgart (LArchBWSt), E 151/11 Bü55.

82 Ibid.

83 The entire process is described by the *Landrat* of Ehingen, Albert Bothner, see Bothner to interior minister of Württemberg (Stuttgart), 20 Juli 1944, Ehingen, LArchBWSt, E 151/11 Bü55; an officer of the labor unit had sent Bothner the letter of request, see 2. *Land.Schütz.Btl.411* to *Fü.Arb.Kdo. Nr. 7902* (Allmendingen), 28 June 1944, Laupheim, LArchBWSt, E 151/11 Bü55.

84 Schwarz (Reich Interior Ministry) to Interior Ministry of Württemberg, 1 September 1944, Berlin, LArchBWSt, E 151/11 Bü55.

85 For the insignia of the Eastern Legions, see Hoffmann, *Die Ostlegionen*, 35–36.

86 N. B. Nemtseva, "Istoki kompozitsii i etapy formirovaniya ansamblya Shakhi-zinda" ("The Origins and Architectural Development of the Shah-i Zinda"), *Iran: Journal of the British Institute of Persian Studies* 15 (1977), 51–73.

87 On the naming, see Hitler, Order, 15 May 1944, n.p., BAB, NS 19/2601.

88 Hermann, Internal Note ("Ostmuselmanische SS-Division"), 13 November 1944, Berlin, BA–MA, RS 3–39/1; and, similarly, Mayer-Mader to Schulte, 9 January 1944, n.p., BA–MA, RS 3–39/1.

89 "Legionäre!," *Azerbaijan* 16 (95) (1944), German translation, High Command of the Wehrmacht, 24 April 1944, Berlin, BA–MA, MSG 2/18239.

90 On the armbands of the Eastern Turkic SS Corps, see SS Head Office, Internal Note ("Abzeichen für den osttürkischen Waffenverband"), 12 October 1944, Berlin, BAB, NS 31/42; and SS Head Office, Internal Note ("Abzeichen für 'osttürkischen Waffen-Verband der SS'"), 12 October 1944, Berlin, BAB, NS 31/42; on the insignias of the Eastern Turkic SS Corps, see drawings in BAB, NS 31/42; and Al-Rashid, Report ("Behandlung der Ostmuselmanen"), 20 September 1944, Warsaw, BAB, NS 31/44; on the flag of the Eastern Turkic SS Corps, see Hermann, Internal Note ("Turkmuselmanische Division"), 15 December 1943, n.p., BA–MA, RS 3–39/1 (also in BA–MA. SF-01/14701 and BAB, NS 31/43); and for drawings of the flag, see BA–MA, RS 3–39/1 and BAB, NS 31/44.

91 Jüttner, Internal Note ("Aufstellung der Kroatische SS-Freiwilligen-Division"), 30 April 1943, Berlin, BAB, NS 19/3523.

92 On the fez, see Houchang Chehabi, "Dress Codes for Men in Turkey and Iran," in Touraj Atabaki and Erik J. Züricher (eds.), *Men of Order: Authoritarian Modernization under Atatürk and Reza Shah* (London, 2004), 209–237, 210–211; Margrit Pernau, *Bürger mit Turban: Muslime in Delhi im 19. Jahrhundert* (Göttingen, 2008), 349–355; and, on the meaning of the fez in the Balkans, Ferhadbegović, "Fes oder Hut?"; and Bougarel, "Farewell to the Ottoman Legacy?," 338–339.

93 Himmler to Pohl, 26 November 1943, n.p., BAB, NS 19/2601.

94 Niedermayer, Instructions ("Vereinbarung über islamisch-religiöse Fragen"), 27 August 1942, Mirgorod, BAB, R 6/247 (also in BA–MA, RH 26-162/16).

95 Heygendorff, Instructions ("Merkblatt für den deutschen Truppenarzt in ost-völkischen Einheiten"), 1 September 1943, Radom, BA–MA, RH 58/62.

96 Jüttner, Order ("Beerdigung von gefallenen oder verstorbenen sowjetischen Kriegs-gefangenen"), 28 January 1943, Berlin, VÚA, Box: SS-Rekruten Depot Debica 3, on the adoption of this Wehrmacht order by the SS. On the burial of French prisoners of war, see Chapter 3.

97 Office for Political and Ideological Education of the 13th SS Division, Instruction ("Dienstanweisung für Imame der 13. SS-Freiwilligen b.h. Geb. Div. [Kroatien]"), 15 March 1944, n.p., BAB, NS 19/2601.

98 Wangemann, Report ("Tätigkeitsbericht der Abt. VI"), 4 April 1944, n.p., BAB, NS 19/2601.

99 Niedermayer, Instructions ("Vereinbarung über islamisch-religiöse Fragen"), 27 August 1942, Mirgorod, BAB, R 6/247 (also in BA–MA, RH 26-162/16). On the military ranks, see Hoffmann, Report ("Tätigkeitsbericht der Abteilung Ic/A.O. der 162. Inf. Division: 15. Mai 1942 bis 1. Oktober 1942"), 20 October 1942, n.p., BA–MA, RH 26-162/19; and, on the later abolishment of the post of division mullah, Hoff-mann, Report ("Tätigkeitsbericht der Abt. Ic/A.O. für die Zeit vom 1. April bis 31. Mai 1943"), 5 June 1943, n.p., BA–MA, RH 26-162/19.

100 Jüttner to Himmler, 10 May 1943, Berlin, BAB, NS 19/2601; and Brandt to Jüttner, 13 May 1943, n.p., BAB, NS 19/2601. On the imams of Handžar, see Redžić, *Musli-mansko Autonomaštvo i 13. SS Divizija*, 119–120; and, mostly based on interviews with contemporaries, Lepre, *Himmler's Bosnian Division*, 71–80.

101 Brandt to Wagner (Foreign Office), 13 May 1943, n.p., BAB, NS 19/2601 (also in PA, R 100998); and, for the answer from the Foreign Office, Wagner to Brandt, 31 May 1943, Salzburg, BAB, NS 19/2601 (also in PA, R 100998). This answer was forwarded to Jüttner, see Brandt to Jüttner, 5 June 1943, n.p., BAB, NS 19/2601. In the Foreign Office, Prüfer had immediately objected to the plan, see Reichel (Foreign Office), Internal Note, 21 May 1943, Berlin, PA, R 100998. Moreover, the embassy in Zagreb had also raised objections, see Wagner to Kasche, 15 May 1943, Berlin, PA, R 100998; and Schubert (Embassy Zagreb) to Foreign Office, 23 May 1943, Zagreb, PA, R 100998. Prüfer's internal suggestion—to give out green armbands to the imams and to equip them with a turban wrapped around a fez—was also not put forward to the SS, see Reichel to Wagner, 3 June 1943, Berlin, PA, R 100998. In 1944 Berger, how-ever, decided to give field imams of his Eastern Muslim formation armbands with a green crescent and a star—without previously consulting the Foreign Office, see Dolezalek, Internal Note ("Abzeichen für 'osttürkischen Waffen-Verband der SS'"), 12 October 1944, Berlin, BAB, NS 31/42.

102 On the restructuring, see Wangemann, Report ("Tätigkeitsbericht der Abt. VI"), 4 April 1944, n.p., BAB, NS 19/2601.

103 Office for Political and Ideological Education of the 13th SS Division, Instruction ("Dienstanweisung für Imame der 13. SS-Freiwilligen b.h. Geb. Div. [Kroatien]"), 15 March 1944, n.p., BAB, NS 19/2601; on the earlier instructions, see Wangemann, Report ("Tätigkeitsbericht der Abt. VI"), 4 April 1944, n.p., BAB, NS 19/2601.

104 Sauberzweig, Order ("Stellung der Imame innerhalb der Division"), 8 March 1944, n.p., BAB, NS 19/2601.

105 Office for Political and Ideological Education of the 13th SS Division, Instruction ("Dienstanweisung für Imame der 13. SS-Freiwilligen b.h. Geb. Div. [Kroatien]"), 15 March 1944, n.p., BAB, NS 19/2601.

106 On Muhasilović, see Lepre, *Himmler's Bosnian Division*, 71–72, 120–123, 184, and 266–267.

107 On Džozo, see ibid., 72, 77–79, 124, and 185–186; and Bougarel, "From Young Muslims to Party of Democratic Action," 541–542.

108 On Malkoč, see Redžić, *Muslimansko Autonomaštvo i 13. SS Divizija*, 119–120; and Lepre, *Himmler's Bosnian Division*, 72, 85–90, and 267.

109 *Mudhakkirat al-Hajj Muhammad Amin al-Husayni*, ed. al-'Umar, 149.

110 SS Head Office, Structure Plan ("Gliederung des Stabes einer Waffengruppe, osttürkischer Waffenverband"), n.d., n.p., BAB, NS 31/44; and SS Head Office, Service Instruction ("Dienstanweisung für den Stab des osttürkischen Verbandes"), n.d. (1944), BAB, NS 31/44.

111 Eastern Muslim SS Regiment to SS Head Office, 4 June 1944, n.p., BA–MA, RS 3–39/1.

112 Al-Rashid to Olzscha, 7 August 1944, Fürstenberg, BAB, NS 31/45.

113 Ibid.; and Olzscha, Internal Note ("Rücksprache mit Abdul-Gani-Osman"), 15 August 1944, Berlin, BAB, NS 31/31. In 1944 Osman wrote about the meaning of the *Qurban Bairam* celebration, see "Die Kurban-Bairam-Feier," *Idel-Ural* 47 (104) (1944), German translation, High Command of the Wehrmacht, 14 October 1944, Berlin, BA–MA, MSG 2/18231.

114 Al-Rashid to Olzscha, 21 October 1944, n.p., BAB, NS 31/44.

115 Interrogation Report of Namangani, 10 January 1945, n.p., BAB, NS 31/29 (also in BAB, NS 31/44), identifies Namangani (though using his middle name as his surname) as "chief-imam."

116 SS Identification Card of Osman, n.d. (1 November 1944), BAB, NS 31/31; and Unglaube, Internal Note ("Ausweis für Herrn Osman von der Tatarischen Leitstelle"), 27 October 1944, Berlin, BAB, NS 31/31.

117 Al-Rashid to Olzscha, 31 July 1944, Fürstenberg, BAB, NS 31/45.

118 Al-Rashid, Report ("Bericht über die Entwicklung des osttürkischen Waffen-Verbandes der SS von Warschau bis Überlauf Alimow und über die aus dieser sich ergebenden Folgerungen"), n.d. (December 1944), BAB, NS 31/44 (also in BAB, NS 31/29).

119 Heygendorff, Instructions ("Strafrechtsfälle"), 15 May 1943, Radom, BA–MA, RH 58/62.

120 Heygendorff, Report ("Turkvölkische und kaukasische Verbände im Kampf an Deutschlands Seite im Zweiten Weltkriege"), October 1949, Uelzen, IfZ, ZS 407.

121 Heygendorff, Instructions ("Behandlung der Legionäre"), 15 August 1943, Radom, BA–MA, RH 58/62.

122 Heygendorff, Instructions ("Behandlung der Legionäre"), 15 July 1943, Radom, BA–MA, RH 58/62.

123 Fürst, Report ("Osttürkisches SS-Korps"), 12 May 1944, Berlin, BAB, NS 31/44.

124 Sauberzweig, Order ("Stellung der Imame innerhalb der Division"), 8 March 1944, n.p., BAB, NS 19/2601.

125 Lepre, *Himmler's Bosnian Division*, 86–94; and Grmek and Lambrichs, *Les Révoltés de Villefranche*, 177–195.

126 Interrogation Report of Namangani, 10 January 1945, n.p., BAB, NS 31/29 (also in BAB, NS 31/44).

127 Al-Rashid, Report ("Bericht über die Entwicklung des osttürkischen Waffen-Verbandes der SS von Warschau bis Überlauf Alimow und über die aus dieser sich ergebenden Folgerungen"), n.d. (December 1944), BAB, NS 31/44 (also in BAB, NS 31/29).

128 See, for example, a report of the division imam from September 1943, which came with two letters the imam had received from Bosnian civilians: Sauberzweig to Berger, 30 September 1943, n.p., BAB, NS 19/2601; Salihbegovic, Report ("Bericht zur Lage"), 25 September 1943, n.p., BAB, NS 19/2601; and the two forwarded letters from Muslim civilians, Anonymous to Muhasilović, n.d. (autumn 1943), n.p., BAB, NS 19/2601; and Anonymous to Kadia, n.d. (autumn 1943), n.p., BAB, NS 19/2601.

129 Masic (imam) to Muhasilović, 20 May 1944, Ilijaš, BA–MA, RS 3–7/16; and Masic to Muhasilović, 16 June 1944, Ilijaš, BA–MA, RS 3–7/16.

130 Office for Political and Ideological Education of the 13th SS Division, Instruction ("Dienstanweisung für Imame der 13. SS-Freiwilligen b.h. Geb. Div. [Kroatien]"), 15 March 1944, n.p., BAB, NS 19/2601; see also Office for Political and Ideological Education of the 13th SS Division, Structure Plan, 2 March 1944, n.p., BAB, NS 19/2601; and Wangemann, Report ("Auszüge aus den Div.-Tagesbefehlen"), 1 April 1944, n.p., BAB, NS 19/2601.

131 Heygendorff, Instructions ("Behandlung der Legionäre"), 15 July 1943, Radom, BA–MA, RH 58/62; and, similarly, Heygendorff, Instructions ("Merkblatt für deutsche Offiziere über wehrgeistige Führung der Legionäre"), 1 July 1943, Radom, BA–MA, RH 58/62.

132 Rosenberg to Hitler, 26 May 1943, Berlin, BAB, R 6/634.

133 Jumabaev, Instructions ("An die Legions- und Bataillonsmullahs"), 5 May 1943, n.p., BA–MA, RH 26-162/19.

134 Berger (Schulte), Decree ("Weltanschaulich geistige Erziehung der muselmanischen SS-Division"), 19 May 1943, Berlin, BAB, NS 19/2601.

135 Ibid.

136 Office for Political and Ideological Education of the 13th SS Division, Structure Plan, 2 March 1944, n.p., BAB, NS 19/2601.

137 Sauberzweig, Order, 4 April 1944, n.p., BAB, NS 19/2601.

138 Wangemann, Speech ("Dienstbesprechung der Kommandeure und Imame am 8.4.1944 in Brčko"), 8 April 1944, Brčko, BAB, NS 19/2601.

139 Office for Political and Ideological Education of the 13th SS Division, Instruction ("Dienstanweisung für Imame der 13. SS-Freiwilligen b.h. Geb. Div. [Kroatien]"), 15 March 1944, n.p., BAB, NS 19/2601.

140 Office for Political and Ideological Education of the 13th SS Division, Structure Plan, 2 March 1944, n.p., BAB, NS 19/2601; and Office for Political and Ideological Education of the 13th SS Division, Instruction ("Dienstanweisung für Imame der 13. SS-Freiwilligen b.h. Geb. Div. [Kroatien]"), 15 March 1944, n.p., BAB, NS 19/2601.

141 Office for Political and Ideological Education of the 13th SS Division, Instruction ("Dienstanweisung für Imame der 13. SS-Freiwilligen b.h. Geb. Div. [Kroatien]"), 15 March 1944, n.p., BAB, NS 19/2601.

142 Office for Political and Ideological Education of the 13th SS Division, Structure Plan, 2 March 1944, n.p., BAB, NS 19/2601; Sauberzweig, Order ("Stellung der Imame innerhalb der Division"), 8 March 1944, n.p., BAB, NS 19/2601; and Office for Political and Ideological Education of the 13th SS Division, Instruction ("Dienstanweisung für Imame der 13. SS-Freiwilligen b.h. Geb. Div. [Kroatien]"), 15 March 1944, n.p., BAB, NS 19/2601.

143 M. N., "Eine Gemeinschaft auf Gedeih und Verderb."

144 Ibid.

145 Heygendorff, Instructions ("Merkblatt für deutsche Offiziere über wehrgeistige Führung der Legionäre"), 1 July 1943, Radom, BA–MA, RH 58/62; and, at the same time, similarly, Niedermayer, Order ("Grundlegender Befehl über die Aufstellung von Turk-Btlnen"), Annexe 8 ("Die Turk-Völker und ihre Behandlung"), 4 July 1942, n.p., BA–MA, RH 19V/79 (also in BA–MA, RH 26-162/16); and Niedermayer, Order ("Grundlegender Befehl über die geistige Betreuung der 162. (Turk) Inf. Div."), 15 June 1943, n.p., MA, RH 26-162/20.

146 Heygendorff, Instructions ("Behandlung der Legionäre"), 15 September 1943, n.d., BA–MA, RH 58/62.

147 Wehrmacht Report ("Beurteilung des Nordkaukasus Batl. 801"), 13 November 1942, n.p., BA–MA, RH 19V/110.

148 Wangemann, Report ("Tätigkeitsbericht der Abt. VI"), 4 April 1944, n.p., BAB, NS 19/2601.

149 Lepre, *Himmler's Bosnian Division*, 266–267.

150 Seraphim, Report ("Kaukasische und turkvölkische Freiwillige im deutschen Heer"), 1948, Nuremberg, MA, MSG 2/18298.

151 Hoffmann, Report ("Tätigkeitsbericht der Abteilung Ic/A.O. der 162. Inf. Division: 15. Mai 1942 bis 1. Oktober 1942"), 20 October 1942, n.p., BA–MA, RH 26-162/19; and, similarly, Hoffmann, Report ("Tätigkeitsbericht der Abteilung Ic/A.O. der 162. Inf. Division: 1. Oktober 1942 bis 31. März 1943"), 20 April 1943, n.p., BA–MA, RH 26-162/19.

152 Heygendorff, Instructions ("Merkblatt für deutsche Offiziere über wehrgeistige Führung der Legionäre"), 1 July 1943, Radom, BA–MA, RH 58/62.

153 On Wehrmacht courses in Göttingen, see Hoffmann, *Die Ostlegionen*, 139–142; Peter Heine, "Die Imam-Kurse der deutschen Wehrmacht im Jahre 1944," in Höpp (ed.), *Fremde Erfahrungen*, 229–238; and Hanisch, *Exegeten*, 162–163. On SS courses in Babelsberg and Guben, see Peter Heine, "Die Mullah-Kurse der Waffen-SS," in Höpp and Reinwald (eds.), *Fremdeinsätze*, 181–188; and Lepre, *Himmler's Bosnian Division*, 71–77 and 185–186. On SS courses in Dresden, see Brentjes, "Die 'Arbeitsgemeinschaft Turkestan im Rahmen der DMG,'" 157–158; Heine, "Mullah-Kurse"; and Pieter Sjoerd van Koningsveld, "The Training of Imams by the Third Reich," in Willem B. Drees and Pieter Sjoerd van Koningsveld (eds.), *The Study of Religion and the Training of Muslim Clergy in Europe: Academic and Religious Freedom in the 21st Century* (Leiden, 2008), 333–347.

154 Bräutigam, Internal Note ("Politische Richtlinien hinsichtlich Turkestan"), 25 November 1941, Berlin, BAB, R 6/247.

155 On Spuler, see Heribert Busse, "Bertold Spuler (1911–1990)," *Der Islam* 67, 2 (1990), 199–205; Werner Ende, "Bertold Spuler," in Hans Günter Hockerts (ed.), *Neue deutsche Biographie*, vol. 24 (Berlin, 2010), 769–770; Werner Ende, Bert Fragner, and Dagmar Riedel, "Spuler, Bertold," in *Encyclopaedia Iranica* (2010), online; and Ellinger, *Deutsche Orientalistik*, passim, esp. 37, 254–256, and 531. During the war Spuler published *Idel-Ural*, "Die Wolga-Tataren und Baschkiren unter russischer Herrschaft," and "Die Lage der Muslime in Rußland seit 1942," which consider not only the political role of Islam in the region's history but also contemporary Soviet policies toward Islam; before the war, he wrote, perhaps in response to Schmitz's *All-Islam*, "Statt 'All-Islam': Volkstumsgedanken im arabischen Orient," *Orient-Nachrichten* 5 (1939), 193–195.

156 The German Orientalist Richard Hartmann, who was involved in the founding of the SS mullah school in Dresden, criticized that the courses in Göttingen were taught by a non-Muslim teacher, see Olzscha, Report, 1945, n.p., BStU, MfS, HA IX/11, ZR 920, A. 54. Part of the report is printed in Drees and Koningsveld, *Study of Religion*, 348–368. Spuler reacted to this criticism in the report on his fifth course, see Spuler, Report ("5. Mulla-Lehrgang"), 21 November 1944, Göttingen, BA–MA, MSG 2/18298.

157 Spuler, Report ("Die Freiwilligen-Einheiten"), n.d. (post-1945), n.p. (Göttingen), BA–MA, MSG 2/18284; and Spuler, "Muslime in Rußland," 298.

158 Szynkiewicz's dissertation was published in German, see Jakob Schinkewitsch, "Rabγūzis Syntax," in *Mitteilungen des Seminars für orientalitsche Sprachen zu Berlin* 29 (1926), 130–172; 30 (1927), 1–57. It became a "Turkological classic," according to Robert Dankoff, "Rabghuzi's Stories of the Prophets" (review article), *Journal of the American Oriental Society* 117, 1 (1997), 115–126, 115.

159 A. Bohdanowicz, "Cultural Movements of Muslims in Poland," 375–376; L. Bohdanowicz, "The Muslims in Poland," 175; Norris, *Islam in the Baltic*, 79; and Cwiklinski, "Between National and Religious Solidarities," 77.

160 Spuler had initially recommended that the courses run "not under four weeks," see Spuler, Report ("Mullakurse"), 11 April 1944, Göttingen, BA–MA, MSG 2/18298. The first course took only two weeks, and Spuler again requested an extension of three or four weeks, see Spuler, Report ("1. Mulla-Lehrgang"), 19 June 1944, Göttingen, BA–MA, MSG 2/18298. It seems that the army command never granted the extension, though.

161 Spuler, Report ("Mullakurse"), 11 April 1944, Göttingen BA–MA, MSG 2/18298.

162 Spuler, Report ("1. Mulla-Lehrgang"), 19 June 1944, Göttingen, BA–MA, MSG 2/18298; and Spuler, Report ("2. Mulla-Lehrgang"), 5 August 1944, Göttingen, BA–MA, MSG 2/18298.

163 Spuler, Report ("3. Mulla-Lehrgang"), 4 September 1944, Göttingen, BA–MA, MSG 2/18298.

164 Spuler, Report ("2. Mulla-Lehrgang"), 5 August 1944, Göttingen, BA–MA, MSG 2/18298. Also in the fifth course, Spuler noted that some of the students had studied at madrasas or had been taught the Qur'an in private, see Spuler, Report ("5. Mulla-Lehrgang"), 21 November 1944, Göttingen, BA–MA, MSG 2/18298.

165 Spuler, Report ("Mullakurse"), 11 April 1944, Göttingen, BA–MA, MSG 2/18298; and Spuler, Report ("1. Mulla-Lehrgang"), 19 June 1944, Göttingen, BA–MA, MSG 2/18298.

166 Spuler, Report ("Mullakurse"), 11 April 1944, Göttingen, BA–MA, MSG 2/18298.

167 Ibid.

168 Ibid.

169 Spuler, Report ("1. Mulla-Lehrgang"), 19 June 1944, Göttingen, BA–MA, MSG 2/18298.

170 Spuler, Report ("3. Mulla-Lehrgang"), 4 September 1944, Göttingen, BA–MA, MSG 2/18298; this assessment was repeated in the fourth and fifth courses, see Spuler, Report ("4. Mulla-Lehrgang"), 21 October 1944, Göttingen, BA–MA, MSG 2/18298; and Spuler, Report ("5. Mulla-Lehrgang"), 21 November 1944, Göttingen, BA–MA, MSG 2/18298.

171 Spuler, Report ("2. Mulla-Lehrgang"), 5 August 1944, Göttingen, BA–MA, MSG 2/18298. Spuler had planned to organize guest lectures of "trustworthy Muslims," see Spuler, Report ("Mullakurse"), 11 April 1944, Göttingen, BA–MA, MSG 2/18298. In the end, Inoyatev's speech remained the only guest lecture.

172 Spuler, Report ("1. Mulla-Lehrgang"), 19 June 1944, Göttingen, BA–MA, MSG 2/18298.

173 For the questions, see Spuler, Report ("2. Mulla-Lehrgang"), 5 August 1944, Göttingen, BA–MA, MSG 2/18298; Spuler, Report ("3. Mulla-Lehrgang"), 4 September 1944, Göttingen, BA–MA, MSG 2/18298; Spuler, Report ("4. Mulla-Lehrgang"), 21 October 1944, Göttingen, BA–MA, MSG 2/18298; Spuler, Report ("5. Mulla-Lehrgang"), 21 November 1944, Göttingen, BA–MA, MSG 2/18298. In the third course, two students who were illiterate, both Azerbaijanis, were tested orally.

174 Spuler, Report ("2. Mulla-Lehrgang"), 5 August 1944, Göttingen, BA–MA, MSG 2/18298.

175 Spuler, Report ("Mullakurse"), 11 April 1944, Göttingen, BA–MA, MSG 2/18298.

176 Ibid.

177 Spuler, Report ("1. Mulla-Lehrgang"), 19 June 1944, Göttingen, BA–MA, MSG 2/18298; Spuler, Report ("2. Mulla-Lehrgang"), 5 August 1944, Göttingen, BA–MA, MSG 2/18298; Spuler, Report ("5. Mulla-Lehrgang"), 21 November 1944, Göttingen, BA–MA, MSG 2/18298; and Spuler, Report ("6. Mulla-Lehrgang"), 20 December 1944, Göttingen, BA–MA, MSG 2/18298.

178 Spuler, Report ("5. Mulla-Lehrgang"), 21 November 1944, Göttingen, BA–MA, MSG 2/18298.

179 Spuler, Report ("Mullakurse"), 11 April 1944, Göttingen, BA–MA, MSG 2/18298; and Spuler, Report ("2. Mulla-Lehrgang"), 5 August 1944, Göttingen, BA–MA, MSG 2/18298. Spuler also used the library of the University of Göttingen, see Spuler, Report ("1. Mulla-Lehrgang"), 19 June 1944, Göttingen, BA–MA, MSG 2/18298.

180 Spuler, Report ("2. Mulla-Lehrgang"), 5 August 1944, Göttingen, BA–MA, MSG 2/18298.

181 Spuler, Report ("1. Mulla-Lehrgang"), 19 June 1944, Göttingen, BA–MA, MSG 2/18298.

182 Ibid.

183 Ibid.

184 Spuler, Report ("3. Mulla-Lehrgang"), 4 September 1944, Göttingen, BA–MA, MSG 2/18298.

185 Spuler, Report ("Mullakurse"), 11 April 1944, Göttingen, BA–MA, MSG 2/18298.

186 Spuler, Report ("3. Mulla-Lehrgang"), 4 September 1944, Göttingen, BA–MA, MSG 2/18298.

187 Bernwald, *Muslime in der Waffen-SS*, 47, and, on the Babelsberg course more generally, see 46–54 and 71–84.

188 Ibid., 73–84, provides brief biographical sketches of the course participants.

189 Al-Husayni, Speech (German translation), n.d. (July 1943), n.p. (Berlin), PA, R 27327.

190 Ibid.

191 Bernwald, *Muslime in der Waffen-SS*, 50–52.

192 Himmler to Berger, 24 November 1943, n.p., BAB, NS 19/2601.

193 Berger to Himmler, 22 April 1944, Berlin, BAB, NS 19/2637.

194 Al-Husayni, Speech (German translation), 21 April 1944, Guben, BAB, NS 19/2637.

195 Džozo, Speech (German translation), 21 April 1944, Guben, BAB, NS 19/2637; on Džozo's role in Guben, see Lepre, *Himmler's Bosnian Division*, 185–186.

196 Džozo, Speech (German translation), 21 April 1944, Guben, BAB, NS 19/2637.

197 Olzscha, Report, 1945, n.p., BStU, MfS, HA IX/11, ZR 920, A. 54; and, more detailed, *Mudhakkirat al-Hajj Muhammad Amin al-Husayni*, ed. al-'Umar, 142 and 149.

198 *Mudhakkirat al-Hajj Muhammad Amin al-Husayni*, ed. al-'Umar, 142.

199 Ibid., 142 and 149.

200 Hentig, Internal Note, 4 October 1944, Berlin, PA, R 100998; and Thadden (Foreign Office), Internal Note ("Reise des Grossmufti nach Budapest"), 5 October 1944, Berlin, PA, R 100998; on the preparations for al-Husayni's visit by Edmund Veesenmayer, the Reich plenipotentiary in Hungary, see Veesenmayer to Foreign Office, 5 October 1944, Budapest, PA, R 100998, and Wagner to Veesenmayer, 6 October 1944, Berlin, PA, R 100998.

201 Schellenberg, Speech (Draft) ("Entwurf für Ansprache zur Eröffnung der ost-türkischen Mullah-Schule in Dresden am 26. November 1944"), 26 November 1944, BAB, NS 31/60. A summary of Schellenberg's speech can be found in SS Head Office, Internal Note ("Zusammenfassung der Ansprache von SS-Brigadeführer Schellenberg"), 29 November 1944, Berlin, BAB, NS 31/60.

202 Victor Klemperer, *Ich will Zeugnis ablegen bis zum letzten: Tagebücher 1941–1945*, ed. Walter Nowojski (Berlin, 1995), 610 (12 November 1944), about the house, see also 230, 354, and 406; see also *To the Bitter End: The Diaries of Victor Klemperer 1942–1945*, ed. Martin Chalmers (London, 1999), 358, and about the house, 130, 206, and 234. On the acquisition of the villa by the SS, see the documents in BAB, R 58/305. The SS had some trouble getting one of the last tenants out of the building and even contacted Ludolf von Alvensleben, Higher SS and Police Leader in Dresden, for help, see Olzscha, Leo, and Krallert, Internal Note ("Mullah-Schule in Dresden"), 18 July 1944, Berlin, BAB, R 58/305; and East Ministry, Internal Note, n.d. (July 1944), Berlin, BAB, R 58/305.

203 Olzscha, Report, 1945, n.p., BStU, MfS, HA IX/11, ZR 920, A. 54.

204 Ibid.

205 East Ministry, Newsletter ("Mittelungen zur Ostpolitik"), 15 November 1944, Berlin, BAB, R 6/65.

206 SS Head Office, Report ("Bericht über Besprechung im Auswärtigen Amt mit Sachbearbeiter Idris am 14.11."), 15 November 1944, Berlin, BAB, NS 31/30.

207 Naumann (State Secretary Propaganda Ministry) to Berger, 9 January 1945, Berlin, BAB, NS 31/40. On the negotiations between the Propaganda Ministry and the SS, see also Olzscha, Internal Note ("Prof. Idris und Prof. Steuerwald"), 24 January 1945, Berlin, BAB, NS 31/40; Berger to Naumann, 24 January 1943, Berlin, BAB, NS 31/40; and Naumann to Berger, 21 February 1945, Berlin, BAB, NS 31/40.

208 Naumann to Berger, Berlin, 21 February 1945, BAB, NS 31/40.

209 Olzscha, Report, 1945, n.p., BStU, MfS, HA IX/11, ZR 920, A. 54.

210 Ibid. It is unknown how long Ildar Idris stayed in Dresden. Although the report of Olzscha suggests a longer period, a document from the SS Head Office mentions a short stay of a few days in late November for the *Qurban Bairam* celebration at the school, see SS Head Office, Internal Note, 24 November 1944, Berlin, BAB, NS 31/45.

211 Olzscha, Report, 1945, n.p., BStU, MfS, HA IX/11, ZR 920, A. 54.

212 Ibid.

213 On the employment of Stambuli, see SS Head Office, Information Sheet about Stambuli, n.d. (1944), n.p., NS 31/40; and Schloms (*Arbeitsgemeinschaft Turkestan*) to Olzscha, 26 September 1944, Dresden, BAB, NS 31/40. On the recruitment of Mehmet Resulzade, see Olzscha, Internal Note ("Rücksprache mit Professor von Mende"), 12 October 1944, Berlin, BAB, NS 31/62. Resulzade apparently rejected the offer from Olzscha with reference to his advanced age, see Olzscha, Report, 1945, n.p., BStU, MfS, HA IX/11, ZR 920, A. 54.

214 Idris to Schyia, 6 March 1945, Berlin, BAB, NS 31/40; and Schyia to Idris, 13 March 1945, Berlin, BAB, NS 31/40.

215 Ibid.

216 Class List of the First Course, n.d. (1945), Dresden, BAB, NS 31/60; Class List of the Second Course, n.d. (1945), Dresden, BAB, NS 31/60; and Class List of the Third Course, n.d. (1945), Dresden, BAB, NS 31/60; see also Degree Certificate of the SS Mullah School (Drafts), 1945, Dresden, BAB, NS 31/40. After the war, Olzscha claimed that only one class of forty Muslims from the East, which ended in December 1944, graduated, see Olzscha, Report, 1945, n.p., BStU, MfS, HA IX/11, ZR 920, A. 54.

217 Idris to Michel (High Command of the Army), 19 January 1945, Berlin, BAB, NS 31/40.

218 SS Head Office, Report ("Bericht über Besprechung im Auswärtigen Amt mit Sachbearbeiter Idris am 14.11."), 15 November 1944, Berlin, BAB, NS 31/30.

219 Idris to Michel, 19 January 1945, Berlin, BAB, NS 31/40.

220 Olzscha, Report, 1945, n.p., BStU, MfS, HA IX/11, ZR 920, A. 54.

221 Ibid. In this case, even the East Ministry supported the antisectarian line of the SS, see Olzscha, Internal Note ("Besprechung zwischen Professor v. Mende, Dr. Arlt und Dr. Olzscha"), 29 September 1944, Berlin, BAB, NS 31/27. After the war Bräutigam argued that "disputes between Sunnis and Shi'ites did not exist" and that this problem had been merely created by the "overeager German head of the Mullah School

in Göttingen," see Bräutigam, Report ("Richtigstellung zu den Ausführungen des General Koestring"), n.d. (post-1945), n.p., IfZ, ZS 400. He was responding to a post-war report by Köstring, who had drawn attention to the "friction between Sunnis and Shi'ites" at the imam training courses, see Köstring, Report ("Erfahrung mit den Freiwilligen aus dem russischen Raum im Kampf mit dem Bolschewismus, 1941–1945"), n.d. (post-1945), n.p., IfZ, ZS 85.

222 Olzscha, Report, 1945, n.p., BStU, MfS, HA IX/11, ZR 920, A. 54.

223 Idris to Michel, 19 January 1945, Berlin, BAB, NS 31/40.

224 Olzscha to Al-Rashid, 1 December 1944, Berlin, BAB, NS 31/45; Schyia, Internal Note ("Sachbearbeiter bei DI/5k für islamreligiöse Betreuung den muselmanischen Verbänden"), 23 December 1944, Berlin, BAB, NS 31/40; and Olzscha, Report, 1945, n.p., BStU, MfS, HA IX/11, ZR 920, A. 54.

225 Köstring to Olzscha, 13 September 1944, n.p., BAB, NS 31/31; Olzscha to Köstring, 22 September 1944, Berlin, BAB, NS 31/31; and Olzscha, Report, 1945, n.p., BStU, MfS, HA IX/11, ZR 920, A. 54.

226 Olzscha, Internal Note ("Rücksprache mit Herrn Müller"), 26 September 1944, Berlin, BAB, NS 31/32; Olzscha, Internal Note ("Rücksprache mit Professor von Mende"), 12 October 1944, Berlin, BAB, NS 31/62; Olzscha, Report, 1945, n.p., BStU, MfS, HA IX/11, ZR 920, A. 54; and Spuler, "Muslime in Rußland seit 1942," 298.

227 Mende, Internal Note ("Gespräch mit dem Großmufti von Jerusalem"), 28 July 1944, Berlin, IfZ, PS-1111.

228 Olzscha had informed the mufti of the plans and had asked him for his opinion of the teachers. Internally, he made it clear that the mufti's involvement had to be avoided, see Olzscha, Internal Note ("Rücksprache mit SS-Standartenführer Spaarmann und SS-Hstuf. Ullrich"), 12 May 1944, Berlin, BAB, NS 31/42. After the war, Olzscha recalled that Idris was also not eager to work with al-Husayni and that Richard Hartmann had explicitly advised against an employment of the mufti in Dresden, see Olzscha, Report, 1945, n.p., BStU, MfS, HA IX/11, ZR 920, A. 54. In his memoirs, al-Husayni thus mentions the Dresden seminary only in passing, see *Mudhakkirat al-Hajj Muhammad Amin al-Husayni*, ed. al-'Umar, 142.

229 Al-Husayni to Himmler, 27 November 1944, Dresden, BAB, NS 19/2637.

230 Himmler to al-Husayni, 30 November 1944, n.p., BAB, NS 19/2637.

231 Olzscha, Report, 1945, n.p., BStU, MfS, HA IX/11, ZR 920, A. 54; and, similarly, Forschungsgruppe des Dokumentationszentrums des Ministeriums des Inneren der DDR, Report ("Arbeitsgemeinschaft Turkestan and Mullahschule in Dresden"), 1 August 1968, Berlin, BStU, MfS, HA IX, No. 21976.

232 Schyia to Army Command Weissenfels, 23 February 1945, Berlin, BAB, NS 31/40.

233 Army Command Weissenfels to Olzscha, 28 February 1945, Weissenfels, BAB, NS 31/40.

234 Schyia to Army Command Weissenfels, 1 March 1945, Berlin, BAB, NS 31/40.

235 SS Head Office, Report ("Bericht über Besprechung im Auswärtigen Amt mit Sachbearbeiter Idris am 14.11."), 15 November 1944, Berlin, BAB, NS 31/30.

236 Heygendorff, Report ("Führung fremden Volkstumes"), n.d. (post-1945), n.p., IfZ, ZS 407.

237 Ibid.

8. ISLAM AND MILITARY PROPAGANDA

1 Niedermayer, Guidelines ("Anhaltspunkte für den politischen Unterricht in turkvölkischen Einheiten"), 15 January 1943, n.p., BA–MA, RH 26-162/19; and, on the guidelines, Niedermayer, Internal Note ("Anhaltspunkte für den politischen Unterricht in turkvölkischen Einheiten"), 15 January 1943, n.p., BA–MA, N 122/3.

2 Berger (Schulte), Decree ("Weltanschaulich geistige Erziehung der muselmanischen SS-Division"), 19 May 1943, Berlin, BAB, NS 19/2601.

3 On the political officers in the German army, see Jürgen Förster, "Ideological Warfare in Germany, 1919 to 1945," in Ralf Blank, Jörg Echternkamp, Karola Fings et al. (eds.), *Germany and the Second World War*, vol. 9/1 (*German Wartime Society 1939–1945: Politicization, Disintegration, and the Struggle for Survival*) (Oxford, 2008), 485–669, esp. 563–569 and 614–626; Vossler, *Propaganda in die eigene Truppe*, 154–190; and Omer Bartov, *The Eastern Front, 1941–1945: German Troops and the Barbarisation of Warfare* (London, 1985), 75–76.

4 "Für den heiligen Krieg!," *Gasavat* 37 (80) (1944), German translation, High Command of the Wehrmacht, 8 September 1944, Berlin, BA–MA, MSG 2/18238.

5 The Propaganda Division of the High Command of the Wehrmacht organized the short courses for Turkic legionnaires in Berlin and Potsdam. For the programs and reports of some of these courses, see High Command of the Wehrmacht (Propaganda Division), Program ("Programm für den 5. Lehrgang der Ostlegionäre, 10. August 1942–19. August 1942"), 6 August 1942, Berlin, BA–MA, RW 4v/237; High Command of the Wehrmacht (Propaganda Division), Program ("Programm für den 6. Lehrgang der Ostlegionäre, 24. August 1942–3. September 1942"), n.d. (August 1942), Berlin, BA–MA, RW 4v/237; and High Command of the Wehrmacht (Propaganda Division), Program ("Programm für den 7. Lehrgang der Ostlegionäre, 7. September 1942–16. September 1942"), 1 September 1942, Berlin, BA–MA, RW 4v/237; and, for the reports on the three courses, High Command of the Wehrmacht (Propaganda Division), Report ("Lehrgang von 60 Ostlegionären in Berlin und Potsdam, 10. August 1942–19. August 1942"), n.d. (August 1942), Berlin, BA–MA, RW 4v/237; High Command of the Wehrmacht (Propaganda Division), Report ("Lehrgang von 60 Ostlegionären in Berlin und Potsdam, 24. August 1942–3. September 1942"), 3 September 1942, Berlin, BA–MA, RW 4v/237; and High Command of the Wehrmacht (Propaganda Division), Report ("Lehrgang von 60 Ostlegionären in Berlin und Potsdam, 7. September 1942–16. September 1942"), 18 September 1942, Berlin, BA–MA, RW 4v/237; see also High Command of the Army to High Command of the Wehrmacht (Propaganda Division), 12 September 1942, Berlin, BA–MA, RW 4v/237; and High Command of the Wehrmacht, Report ("Lehrgang von 60 Ostlegionären in Berlin und Potsdam"), 29 September 1942, Berlin, BA–MA, RW 4v/237; on these trips more generally, see Mühlen, *Zwischen Hakenkreuz und Sowjetstern*, 101; and Hoffmann, *Die Ostlegionen*, 123.

6 High Command of the Wehrmacht (Propaganda Division), Report ("Lehrgang von 60 Ostlegionären in Berlin und Potsdam, 24. August 1942–3. September 1942"), 3 September 1942, Berlin, BA–MA, RW 4v/237; and High Command of the Wehrmacht (Propaganda Division), Report ("Lehrgang von 60 Ostlegionären in Berlin und

Potsdam, 7. September 16. September 1942"), 18 September 1942, Berlin, BA–MA, RW 4v/237.

7 High Command of the Army, Instructions ("Merkblatt für das deutsche Personal der Turk-Stammlager und Turk-Btlne."), 2 June 1942, n.p., BA–MA, RH 19V/109.

8 High Command of the Wehrmacht, Newsletter ("Mitteilungen für den deutschen Soldaten in Freiwilligen-Verbänden"), February 1944, n.p., BA–MA, MSg MSG 2/18262.

9 Siefers, Report ("Aufstellung von Tataren- und Kaukasierformationen im Bereich des A.O.K. 11"), 20 March 1942, n.p., BA–MA, RH 19V/108 (also in PA, R 60739).

10 Anonymous (Local Propagandist), Report ("Bericht über Beobachtungen und Erfahrungen über den Lehrgängen für Propagandisten unter den freiwilligen Tataren, Kaukasiern und Kriegsgefangenen, Russen und Ukrainern"), enclosed to Hentig, Report, 6 May 1942, n.p. (Simferopol), PA, R 60740. On the courses, see also Worms (Army), Report ("Propagandistische Schulung der freiwilligen Tataren"), 18 February 1942, n.p., BA–MA, WF–03/10435; and Hentig, Report ("Tataren auf der Krim"), 10 April 1942, n.p. (Simferopol), PA, R 60739 (also in PA, R 261175).

11 On the political officers in the Waffen-SS, see Förster, "Ideological Warfare," 485–669, esp. 568–569.

12 Handžar, Syllabus ("Lehrplan für den Kurzlehrgang der Einsatzredner"), 5 March 1944, n.p., BAB, NS 19/2601.

13 Handžar, Service Schedule ("Dienstplan für den Pol.-Kurslehrgang vom 29.3-1.4.44"), 29 March 1944, n.p., BAB, NS 19/2601.

14 Handžar, Exam Questions ("Schriftliche Arbeit des 6. We-Kurzlehrgangs vom 29.3.-1.4.44"), 1 April 1944, n.p., BAB, NS 19/2601.

15 Windisch, Exam ("Schriftliche Arbeit, 6. We-Kurzlehrgang"), 1 April 1944, n.p., BAB, NS 19/2601.

16 Ibid.

17 Vukelić, Exam ("Schriftliche Arbeit, 6. We-Kurzlehrgang") (German translation), 5 April 1944, n.p., BAB, NS 19/2601.

18 Ibid.

19 Wangemann, Report ("Tätigkeitsbericht der Abt. VI"), 4 April 1944, n.p., BAB, NS 19/2601; and, on the obligatory participation in these courses, see also Sauberzweig, Order, 9 March 1944, n.p., BAB, NS 19/2601.

20 Fürst to Olzscha, 27 September 1944, Berlin, BAB, NS 31/44.

21 Olzscha to Fürst, 28 September 1944, Berlin, BAB, NS 31/44.

22 Ibid.

23 On the brochure, see Chapter 5.

24 Berger (Schulte), Decree ("Weltanschaulich geistige Erziehung der muselmanischen SS-Division"), 19 May 1943, Berlin, BAB, NS 19/2601.

25 Wangemann, Report ("Auszüge aus den Div.-Tagesbefehlen"), 1 April 1944, n.p., BAB, NS 19/2601; for examples, see Sauberzweig, Propaganda Letter "Moji dragi momci!" ("My dear lads!"), 28 February 1944, n.p., BAB, NS 19/2601; and, for the German translation, Sauberzweig, Propaganda Letter "Meine lieben Männer" (German translation), 25 February 1944, n.p., BAB, NS 19/2601; as well as Sauberzweig, Propaganda Letter "Moji dragi momci!" ("My dear lads!"), 27 March 1944, n.p., BAB, NS 19/2601; and the German translation, Sauberzweig, Propaganda Let-

ter "Meine lieben Männer" (German translation), 27 March 1944, n.p., BAB, NS 19/2601.

26 Pamphlet "An meine muslimischen Brüder!" (German translation), n.d. (1944), BAB, NS 31/44.

27 Ibid.

28 Bräutigam to East Ministry, 3 December 1942, n.p., BAB, R 6/65.

29 Herwarth, *Zwischen Hitler und Stalin*, 310; and, in the English version, Herwarth, *Against two Evils*, 266.

30 Arlt, Report ("Fürsorge für die Ostverbände bzw. deren Angehörigen"), n.d. (post-1945), n.p., IfZ, ZS 399.

31 On Qur'anic talismans, see Kathleen Malone O'Connor, "Popular and Talismanic Uses of the Qur'ān," in *Encyclopaedia of the Qur'ān*, ed. Jane Dammen McAuliffe, vol. 4 (Leiden, 2004), 163–182; Kathleen Malone O'Connor, "Amulets," in ibid., vol. 1 (Leiden, 2001), 77–79; Robert Hoyland and Venetia Porter, "Epigraphy," in ibid., vol. 2 (Leiden, 2002), 25–43, esp. 35–39; Gabriel Mandel Khān, "Magic," in ibid., vol. 3 (Leiden, 2003), 245–252, esp. 248–249; Priscilla P. Soucek, "Material Culture and the Qur'ān," in ibid., 296–330; Venetia Porter, "Talismans and Talismanic Objects," in *Medieval Islamic Civilization: An Encyclopaedia*, ed. Josef W. Meri (London, 2006), 794–796; Constant Hamès, "Le Coran talismanique," in A. de Surgy (ed.), *Religion et pratiques de puissance* (Paris, 1997), 129–160; and J. Ruska, B. Carra de Vaux, and C. E. Bosworth, "Tilsam," in *The Encyclopaedia of Islam*, vol. 10, ed. P. J. Bearman et al. (Leiden, 2000), 500–502.

32 Spuler, Report ("Mullakurse"), 11 April 1944, Göttingen, BA–MA, MSG 2/18298.

33 East Ministry, Report ("Besuch von General von Heygendorff beim Aserbeidscha-nischen Verbindungsstab"), 29 February 1944, Berlin, BAB, R 6/165.

34 The copies of the *SS-Handžar* magazine are stored in the National and University Library of Zagreb (*Nacionalna i Sveučilišna Knjižnica*), Zagreb (NSK). A number of issues have been printed in Bernwald, *Muslime in der Waffen-SS*, 329–412.

35 Pero Blašković, "Bosnien und die Herzegowina im Weltkrieg" ("Bosna i Hercegovina u Svjetskom ratu"), part 1, *SS-Handžar* 1 (15 July 1943); part 2, *SS-Handžar* 2 (1 August 1943); part 3, *SS-Handžar* 3 (n.d. [1943]); and part 4, *SS-Handžar* 4 (n.d. [1943]); Pero Blašković, "Osman" ("Osman"), *SS-Handžar* 5 (n.d. [1943]), providing an extract from Blašković's book *Sa Bosnjacima u svjetskom ratu* (*With the Bosniaks in the World War*) (Belgrade, 1939); and Sa.-Be., "Vereidigung" ("Prisega"), *SS-Handžar* 2 (1 August 1943).

36 Sauberzweig, "Soldaten der SS-Freiwilligen Bosnisch-Hercegow. Gebirgs-Division!" ("Vojnici dobrovoljne Bosansko-hercegovačke brdske SS divizije!"), *SS-Handžar* 6 (n.d. [1943]).

37 On quotations from Hitler, see "Führerworte" ("Rieči Vodje"), *SS-Handžar* 2 (1 August 1943); "Worte des Führers" ("Führero ve rieči"), *SS-Handžar* 3 (n.d. [1943]); "Adolf Hitler" ("Adolf Hitler"), *SS-Handžar* 7 (n.d. [1943]); "Der Führer" ("Der Führer"), *SS-Handžar* 8 (n.d. [1943]); "Adolf Hitler" ("Adolf Hitler"), *SS-Handžar* 9 (n.d. [1943]); and some more quotations from Hitler with references to religion, in A. B. (Albert Bauer), "Der Sieg wird unser sein" ("Pobjeda će nama pripasti"), *SS-Handžar* 9 (n.d. [1943]). On quotations from the Prophet and the Qur'an, see "Worte

Muhammeds" ("Rieči Muhameda"), *SS-Handžar* 1 (15 July 1943); "Worte Muhammeds" ("Rieči Muhameda"), *SS-Handžar* 1 (15 July 1943); and "Ku'ran" ("Quran"), *SS-Handžar* 11 (n.d. [1944]).

38 Office for Political and Ideological Education of the 13th SS Division, Instruction ("Dienstanweisung für Imame der 13. SS-Freiwilligen b. h. Geb. Div. (Kroatien)"), 15 March 1944, n.p., BAB, NS 19/2601, explicitly directs the imams to contribute to *SS-Handžar*.

39 Husejin Djozo, "Über die Aufgaben des SS-Mannes" ("Zadaća SS-vojnika"), *SS-Handžar* 7 (n.d. [1943]).

40 Omer Zukić, "Bosnien, du unser Leben" ("Moja Bosno, moje živovanje"), *SS-Handžar* 6 (n.d. [1943]).

41 Omer Zuhrić, "Das Bataillon Begić greift an" ("Bojna Begić stiže"), *SS-Handžar* 10 (n.d. [1943]).

42 Anonymous, "Bosna plaća hirove jednog zanešenjaka" ("Bosnia pays for the vagaries of an enthusiast"), *SS-Handžar* 11 (n.d. [1944]); and Anonymous, "Židovi u Bosni" ("Jews in Bosnia"), *SS-Handžar* 11 (n.d. [1944]).

43 M. N., "Eine Gemeinschaft auf Gedeih und Verderb."

44 Amin al-Husayni, "Aus der Rede seiner Eminenz des Großmufti von Palästina anläßlich des Geburtstags Muhammeds" ("Iz govora Njegove Preuzvišenosti Velikog Palestinskog Muftije Emin El Husseinia povodom dana rodjenja Božijeg Poslanika Muhameda"), *SS-Handžar* 4 (n.d. [1943]).

45 Horst Mauersberger, "Der Grossmufti bei der Division" ("Veliki Muftija posjećuje diviziju"), *SS-Handžar* 8 (n.d. [1943]); Omer Zuhrić, "Meine erste Begegnung mit dem Grossmufti" ("Moj prvi susret sa Velikim Muftijom"), *SS-Handžar* 8 (n.d. [1943]); Himmler, "Telegramm des Reichsministers des Inneren und Reichsführers-SS Heinrich Himmler an den Grossmufti Amin El-Husseini" ("Brozojavka državnog ministra nutarnjih poslova i Reichsführera-SS Heinricha Himmlera"), *SS-Handžar* 8 (n.d. [1943]); and Amin al-Husayni, "Der Großmufti an die Division: Männer der SS-Frw. b. h. Geb. Division (Kroatien)!" ("Rieči Velikog Muftije diviziji: Vojnici SS-Drag. b. h. gorske divizije (Hrvatska)!"), *SS-Handžar* 8 (n.d. [1943]).

46 Image: "Der Grossmufti schreitete die Front der Ehrenkompanie ab" ("Veliki Muftija obilazi počastnu satniju"), *SS-Handžar* 8 (n.d. [1943]); and Images: "Drei festliche Tage" ("Tri svečana dana"), *SS-Handžar* 8 (n.d. [1943]).

47 Image: "Der harte Kampf der Männer ermöglicht der Heimat ein friedliches Weiterleben" ("Odlučna borbenost čovjeka omogućuje domovini daljnji obstanak u miru"), *SS-Handžar* 1 (15 July 1943); Image (Mosque) in Images: "Aus der Heimat" ("Iz zaviča"), *SS-Handžar* 5 (n.d. [1943]); Image (Mosque) in Images: "Aus der Heimat" ("Iz domovine"), *SS-Handžar* 8 (n.d. [1943]); Image (Mosque) in Abdulah, "Nekad spokojstvo i sreća, a danas palež i umorstvo" ("Once serenity and happiness, and today murder and arson"), *SS-Handžar* 11 (n.d. [1944]); and, on the Poglavnik mosque, Image: "Auf einem der schönsten Plätze Agrams liess der Poglavnik eine moderne Moschee zum Zeichen der Verbundenheit aller kroatischen Volksteile errichten" ("Na jednom od najljepših trgova Zagreba dao je Poglavnik sagraditi modernu džamiju kao znak povezanos i svih dielova Hrvatskog naroda"), *SS-Handžar* 3 (n.d.

[1943]); and Image (Poglavnik Mosque) in Anonymous, "Mošeja zapada" ("Mosque of the West"), *SS-Handžar* 11 (n.d. [1944]).

48 Images: "Bosnische Heimat" ("Bosanski zavičaj"), *SS-Handžar* 1 (15 July 1943); this observation was made by Greble, *Sarajevo*, 173.

49 Wangemann, Report ("Tätigkeitsbericht der Abt. VI"), 4 April 1944, n.p., BAB, NS 19/2601.

50 On *Tyrk Birligi*, see Mühlen, *Zwischen Hakenkreuz und Sowjetstern*, 103; Cwiklinski, "Panturkismus-Politik," 154–158; and Cwiklinski, *Wolgatataren im Deutschland des Zweiten Weltkriegs*, 31–32 and 65–67. The documents on *Tyrk Birligi* are stored in BAB, NS 31/47, NS 31/61, and NS 31/62. A summary of its history is also given in Olzscha, Report, 1945, n.p., BStU, MfS, HA IX/11, ZR 920, A. 54. For a list of the editorial staff of *Türk Birligi*, see BAB, NS 31/61.

51 Olzscha, Internal Note ("Herausgabe einer Zeitung für den 'Osttürkischen Verband'"), 1 September 1944, Berlin, BAB, NS 31/62.

52 Olzscha, Internal Note ("Zeitung für den osttürkischen Waffenverband der SS"), 2 December 1944, BAB, NS 31/62. An article about Schellenberg's speech at the mullah school in Dresden was also prepared, although it is unclear whether it was ever printed, see Anonymous, Article for *Türk Birligi*, n.d. (December 1944), BAB, NS 31/62. In their editorial offices in Berlin, the twenty-five staff writers of *Türk Birligi* celebrated both the Islamic feast of sacrifice and the publication of the first issue of their paper, requesting from the SS alcohol and cigarettes, see Wynand (German Staff of *Türk Birligi*) to Olzscha, 21 November 1944, BAB, NS 31/62; and SS Head Office, Internal Note ("Tabak- und Spirituosen-Sonderzuteilung für die Redaktion der osttürkischen Zeitung"), 13 December 1944, BAB, NS 31/62.

53 The papers of the Turkestan Legion "The National Turkestan" (*Milli Turkistan*), published by the East Ministry, and "The New Turkestan" (*Yeni Turkistan*), published by the Wehrmacht propaganda division, are therefore not examined in this book.

54 The Azerbaijani paper *Azerbaijan* was founded in the summer of 1942, see *Azerbaijan* 22 (101) (1944), German translation, High Command of the Wehrmacht, 5 June 1944, Berlin, BA–MA, MSG 2/18239. *Ghazavat* was founded in March 1943, and the one-year celebration took place on 4 March 1944, see *Ghazavat* 11/12 (54/55) (1944), German translation, High Command of the Wehrmacht, 15 March 1944, Berlin, BA–MA, MSG 2/18238. *Idel-Ural* was founded on 15 November 1942, and the one-hundredth issue was published in October 1944, *Idel-Ural* 43 (100) (1943), German translation, High Command of the Wehrmacht, 28 October 1944, Berlin, BA–MA, MSG 2/18231.

55 On the papers of the legions, see Hoffmann, *Die Ostlegionen*, 128–130; Mühlen, *Zwischen Hakenkreuz und Sowjetstern*, 59–60, 78–79, 95–96, 98, 125–126; Cwiklinski, "Panturkismus-Politik," 151, 158; and Cwiklinski, *Wolgatataren im Deutschland des Zweiten Weltkriegs*, 78–104.

56 Mühlen, *Zwischen Hakenkreuz und Sowjetstern*, 59–60.

57 "Die Religion ist ein Grundpfeiler unserer nationalen Moral: Rede des Herrn Gabdullan," *Idel-Ural* 10/11 (67/68) (1943), German translation, High Command of the Wehrmacht, 19 March 1944, Berlin, BA–MA, MSG 2/18231.

58 "Das Volk muß seine religiöse Ueberzeugung behalten," *Azerbaijan* 27 (106) (1944), German translation, High Command of the Wehrmacht, 10 July 1944, Berlin, BA–MA, MSG 2/18239.

59 "Wir werden unserem Volk die Religion erhalten," *Azerbaijan* 24 (103) (1944), German translation, High Command of the Wehrmacht, 19 June 1944, Berlin, BA–MA, MSG 2/18239.

60 "Auf dem Weg zu neuem kulturellen Leben," *Azerbaijan* 38 (117) (1944), German translation, High Command of the Wehrmacht, 25 September 1944, Berlin, BA–MA, MSG 2/18239. The paper also reported on an Azerbaijani conference in Berlin, at which the foundations of a future religious education of the people had been discussed. "Vom aserbeidschanischen Verbindungsstab," *Azerbaijan* 36 (115) (1944), German translation, High Command of the Wehrmacht, 11 September 1944, Berlin, BA–MA, MSG 2/18239.

61 "Das Leben unseres Propheten diene uns als Beispiel," *Ghazavat* 39 (82) (1944), German translation, High Command of the Wehrmacht, 22 September 1944, Berlin, BA–MA, MSG 2/18238.

62 "Ueber unsere Religion," *Azerbaijan* 34 (113) (1944), German translation, High Command of the Wehrmacht, 28 August 1944, Berlin, BA–MA, MSG 2/18239; "Der Prophet und der Islam" (part 1), *Idel-Ural* 40 (97) (1943), German translation, High Command of the Wehrmacht, 7 October 1944, Berlin, BA–MA, MSG 2/18231; and "Der Prophet und der Islam" (part 2), *Idel-Ural* 41 (98) (1943), German translation, High Command of the Wehrmacht, 14 October 1944, Berlin, BA–MA, MSG 2/18231.

63 "Der Prophet und sein richtiges Glaubensbekenntnis" (part 1), *Azerbaijan* 35 (114) (1944), German translation, High Command of the Wehrmacht, 4 September 1944, Berlin, BA–MA, MSG 2/18239, and "Der Prophet und sein richtiges Glaubensbekenntnis" (part 2), *Azerbaijan* 36 (115) (1944), German translation, High Command of the Wehrmacht, 11 September 1944, Berlin, BA–MA, MSG 2/18239.

64 On Fatalibey, see Hoffmann, *Kaukasien*, 215–221, 227, 252, and 320; and Hoffman, *Die Ostlegionen*, 142.

65 "Wissenschaft im Osten," *Azerbaijan* 48 (127) (1944), German translation, High Command of the Wehrmacht, 4 September 1944, Berlin, BA–MA, MSG 2/18239; see also "Der Platz der Völker des Ostens im Lichte der Wissenschaft," *Idel-Ural* 30 (87) (1943), German translation, High Command of the Wehrmacht, 29 July 1944, Berlin, BA–MA, MSG 2/18231.

66 "Al-Azhar, tausendjährige Universität," *Idel-Ural* 13 (70) (1943), German translation, High Command of the Wehrmacht, 1 April 1944, Berlin, BA–MA, MSG 2/18231; and "Al-Azhar, tausendjährige Universität," *Azerbaijan* 8 (87) (1944), German translation, High Command of the Wehrmacht, 29 February 1944, Berlin, BA–MA, MSG 2/18239.

67 "Porträt Ibn Sauds," *Ghazavat* 19 (62) (1944), German translation, High Command of the Wehrmacht, 5 May 1944, Berlin, BA–MA, MSG 2/18238; and "Porträt Ibn Sauds," *Azerbaijan* 18 (97) (1944), German translation, High Command of the Wehrmacht, 8 May 1944, Berlin, BA–MA, MSG 2/18239.

68 "Kampfgruppe 'Freies Arabien,'" *Ghazavat* 35 (78) (1944), German translation, High Command of the Wehrmacht, 25 August 1944, Berlin, BA–MA, MSG 2/18238; and "Kampfgruppe 'Freies Arabien,'" *Idel-Ural* 34 (91) (1943), German translation, High Command of the Wehrmacht, 26 August 1944, Berlin, BA–MA, MSG 2/18231.

69 "Unter kroatischen Muselmanen," *Azerbaijan* 33 (112) (1944), German translation, High Command of the Wehrmacht, 21 August 1944, Berlin, BA–MA, MSG 2/18239.

70 Images: "Muselmanisches Leben in Serbien," *Idel-Ural* 33 (39) (1943), German translation, High Command of the Wehrmacht, 15 August 1943, Berlin, BA–MA, MSG 2/18231.

71 "Die Muselmanen sind überzeugt, daß im Sieg Deutschlands die Religionsfreiheit wahr wird," *Ghazavat* 37 (1943), German translation, High Command of the Wehrmacht, 27 October 1943, Berlin, BA–MA, MSG 2/18238.

72 See, for instance, "Wir grüßen unsere Legionäre zum Festtag Urasa," *Idel-Ural* 40 (46) (1943), German translation, High Command of the Wehrmacht, 3 October 1943, Berlin, BA–MA, MSG 2/18231; "Der Monat Ramadsan," *Idel-Ural* 33 (90) (1944), German translation, High Command of the Wehrmacht, 19 August 1944, Berlin, BA–MA, MSG 2/18231; Image: "Glückwunsch zum großen Feiertag Ramadsan-Bairam," *Azerbaijan* 40 (68) (1943), German translation, High Command of the Wehrmacht, 3 October 1943, Berlin, BA–MA, MSG 2/18239; "Aserbaidschanische Legionäre!," *Azerbaijan* 40 (68) (1943), German translation, High Command of the Wehrmacht, 3 October 1943, Berlin, BA–MA, MSG 2/18239; "Glückwunsch zum Ramadsan-Bairam-Fest an die nordkaukasische Legion von Fatalibaile," *Azerbaijan* 40 (68) (1943), German translation, High Command of the Wehrmacht, 3 October 1943, Berlin, BA–MA, MSG 2/18239; "Glückwunsch des nordkaukasischen Nationalen Komitees an die aserbaidschanische Legion anläßlich des Festes Ramadsan-Bairam," *Azerbaijan* 40 (68) (1943), German translation, High Command of the Wehrmacht, 3 October 1943, Berlin, BA–MA, MSG 2/18239; Kurban-Bajram," *Azerbaijan* 47 (126) (1944), German translation, High Command of the Wehrmacht, 27 November 1944, Berlin, BA–MA, MSG 2/18239; see also articles about the celebrations in the units discussed in Chapter 7.

73 "Ramadsan und Erntefest," *Azerbaijan* 44 (72) (1943), German translation, High Command of the Wehrmacht, 31 October 1943, Berlin, BA–MA, MSG 2/18239; and Image: "Nationale Tänze in Simferopol anläßlich des Ramadsan- und Erntedank-festes," *Azerbaijan* 44 (72) (1943), German translation, High Command of the Wehrmacht, 31 October 1943, Berlin, BA–MA, MSG 2/18239.

74 Image: "Tatarische Emigranten in Finnland feiern das Urasa-Fest," *Idel-Ural* 40 (46) (1943), German translation, High Command of the Wehrmacht, 3 October 1943, Berlin, BA–MA, MSG 2/18231.

75 In autumn 1943, for instance, *Idel-Ural* printed the transcription of a broadcast speech given by the mufti at the end of Ramadan, see "Die Rede des Großmufti," *Idel-Ural* 42 (48) (1943), German translation, High Command of the Wehrmacht, 17 October 1943, Berlin, BA–MA, MSG 2/18231. A year later, in September 1944, the paper would again print the Ramadan proclamation of the mufti, see "Ein Radioaufruf des Großmufti von Arabien," *Idel-Ural* 38 (95) (1944), German translation,

High Command of the Wehrmacht, 23 September 1944, Berlin, BA–MA, MSG 2/18231. And only a few months later, *Ghazavat* printed the transcription of a broadcast speech given by the mufti on the *Qurban Bairam*, see "Die Rede des Großmufti anläßlich der Kurban-Bajram-Feier," *Ghazavat* 50 (93) (1944), German translation, High Command of the Wehrmacht, 8 December 1944, Berlin, BA–MA, MSG 2/18238. *Idel-Ural* and *Azerbaijan* documented the mufti's involvement with a picture of him among Muslim recruits at a *Qurban Bairam* celebration, see Image: "Der Großmufti beim Kurban-Bajram unter muselmanischen Freiwilligen," *Idel-Ural* 49 (106) (1944), German translation, High Command of the Wehrmacht, 9 December 1944, Berlin, BA–MA, MSG 2/18231; and Image: "Der Großmufti und Major Fatal-ibejli bei einer Freiwilligen-Feier des Kurban-Bajram," *Azerbaijan* 49 (128) (1944), German translation, High Command of the Wehrmacht, 11 December 1944, Berlin, BA–MA, MSG 2/18239.

76 "Die Freude des Mullah Suleiman," *Azerbaijan* 45 (73) (1943), German translation, High Command of the Wehrmacht, 7 November 1943, Berlin, BA–MA, MSG 2/18239.

77 "Das Urasa-Fest verlief schön," *Idel-Ural* 40 (46) (1943), German translation, High Command of the Wehrmacht, 3 October 1943, Berlin, BA–MA, MSG 2/18231.

78 "Ramasan-Monat," *Ghazavat* 29 (1943), German translation, High Command of the Wehrmacht, 1 September 1943, Berlin, BA–MA, MSG 2/18238.

79 "Muselmanische Festtage," *Ghazavat* 29 (1943), German translation, High Command of the Wehrmacht, 1 September 1943, Berlin, BA–MA, MSG 2/18238.

80 Ibid.

81 Yemelianova, *Russia and Islam*, 114.

82 "Moskau verschärft den Kampf gegen die Religion," *Idel-Ural* 47 (104) (1943), German translation, High Command of the Wehrmacht, 14 October 1944, Berlin, BA–MA, MSG 2/18231.

83 "Der Bolschewismus im Nordkaukasus," *Ghazavat* 15 (58) (1944), German translation, High Command of the Wehrmacht, 7 April 1944, Berlin, BA–MA, MSG 2/18238.

84 "Mufti Risaetdin bin Fachretdin," *Idel-Ural* 16 (73) (1943), German translation, High Command of the Wehrmacht, 22 April 1944, Berlin, BA–MA, MSG 2/18231. On Fakhreddin, see Mahmud Tahir, "Rizaeddin Fahreddin," *Central Asian Survey* 8, 1 (1989), 111–115; A. Battal-Taymas, *Rizaeddin Fahreddinoğlu* (Istanbul, 1958); Ro'i, *Islam in the Soviet Union*, 101–102 and 172; and Bennigsen and Wimbush, *Mystics and Commissars*, 38–39, though the last publication incorrectly states that Fakhreddin died in a Soviet prison. In 1936 Bertold Spuler had written about Fakhreddin's death in Bertold Spuler, "Zum Tode des obersten Geistlichen der Mohammedaner in der UdSSR," *Osteuropa* 11, 11/12 (1935/6), 782–783.

85 "Brüder Legionäre!," *Ghazavat* 29 (1943), German translation, High Command of the Wehrmacht, 1 September 1943, Berlin, BA–MA, MSG 2/18238.

86 Ibid.

87 "Wodurch kennzeichnet sich der Beginn der russischen Herrschaft in unserem Lande?," *Idel-Ural* 42 (48) (1943), German translation, High Command of the Wehrmacht, 17 October 1943, Berlin, BA–MA, MSG 2/18231.

88 "Offener Brief an die Legionäre," *Idel-Ural* 35 (41) (1943), German translation, High Command of the Wehrmacht, 29 August 1943, Berlin, BA–MA, MSG 2/18231.

89 "Vor 85 Jahren fiel Imam Schamil in Gefangenschaft," *Azerbaijan* 36 (115) (1944), German translation, High Command of the Wehrmacht, 11 September 1944, Berlin, BA–MA, MSG 2/18239; and "Vor 85 Jahren geriet Iman Schamil in Gefangenschaft," *Ghazavat* 36 (79) (1944), German translation, High Command of the Wehrmacht, 1 September 1944, Berlin, BA–MA, MSG 2/18238.

90 Ibid.

91 "Die Jugend Schamils," *Ghazavat* 37 (80) (1944), German translation, High Command of the Wehrmacht, 8 September 1944, Berlin, BA–MA, MSG 2/18238; and "Die Tarichat-Lehre im Nordkaukasus," *Ghazavat* 37 (1943), German translation, High Command of the Wehrmacht, 27 October 1943, Berlin, BA–MA, MSG 2/18238.

92 "Die Tarichat-Lehre im Nordkaukasus," *Ghazavat* 37 (1943), German translation, High Command of the Wehrmacht, 27 October 1943, Berlin, BA–MA, MSG 2/18238.

93 Images, *Ghazavat* 31 (1943), German translation, High Command of the Wehrmacht, 15 September 1943, Berlin, BA–MA, MSG 2/18238.

94 "Unsere heutige Aufgabe," *Ghazavat* 7 (51) (1944), German translation, High Command of the Wehrmacht, 16 February 1944, Berlin, BA–MA, MSG 2/18238.

95 "Nun wollen die Bolschewiken das Volk im Namen der Religion betrügen," *Idel-Ural* 40 (46) (1943), German translation, High Command of the Wehrmacht, 3 October 1943, Berlin, BA–MA, MSG 2/18231.

96 "Krieg und Politik," *Idel-Ural* 44 (50) (1943), German translation, High Command of the Wehrmacht, 31 October 1943, Berlin, BA–MA, MSG 2/18231.

97 "Der alte Betrug," *Idel-Ural* 7 (64) (1944), German translation, High Command of the Wehrmacht, 20 February 1944, Berlin, BA–MA, MSG 2/18231.

98 "Jenseits der Front," *Ghazavat* 36 (1943), German translation, High Command of the Wehrmacht, 20 October 1943, Berlin, BA–MA, MSG 2/18238.

99 "Die bolschewistischen Winkelzüge werden sich nicht erfüllen," *Azerbaijan* 44 (72) (1943), German translation, High Command of the Wehrmacht, 31 October 1943, Berlin, BA–MA, MSG 2/18239.

100 "Das englische Blut und der bolschewistische Mullah," *Azerbaijan* 12 (91) (1944), German translation, High Command of the Wehrmacht, 27 March 1944, Berlin, BA–MA, MSG 2/18239.

101 "Sind in Aserbaidschan Moscheen eröffnet worden?," *Azerbaijan* 12 (91) (1944), German translation, High Command of the Wehrmacht, 27 March 1944, Berlin, BA–MA, MSG 2/18239.

102 "Wie ist es in der Heimat?," *Azerbaijan* 28 (107) (1944), German translation, High Command of the Wehrmacht, 17 July 1944, Berlin, BA–MA, MSG 2/18239.

103 "Die Sowjets möchten ein Sowjetarabien schaffen," *Ghazavat* 28 (1943), German translation, High Command of the Wehrmacht, 25 August 1943, Berlin, BA–MA, MSG 2/18238.

104 "Stalin entsinnt sich des Koran," *Ghazavat* 30 (1943), German translation, High Command of the Wehrmacht, 8 September 1943, Berlin, BA–MA, MSG 2/18238; and similarly, "Das englische Blut und der bolschewistische Mullah," *Azerbaijan* 12

(91) (1944), German translation, High Command of the Wehrmacht, 27 March 1944, Berlin, BA–MA, MSG 2/18239.

105 "Der rote Imperialismus und der Nahe Osten," *Azerbaijan* 48 (127) (1944), German translation, High Command of the Wehrmacht, 4 September 1944, Berlin, BA–MA, MSG 2/18239.

106 "Der rote Imperialismus," *Idel-Ural* 44 (50) (1943), German translation, High Command of the Wehrmacht, 31 October 1943, Berlin, BA–MA, MSG 2/18231; on the congress, see also "Das englische Blut und der bolschewistische Mullah," *Azerbaijan* 12 (91) (1944), German translation, High Command of the Wehrmacht, 27 March 1944, Berlin, BA–MA, MSG 2/18239.

107 "Kommunismus und Islam unvereinbar," *Ghazavat* 9 (52) (1944), German translation, High Command of the Wehrmacht, 23 February 1944, Berlin, BA–MA, MSG 2/18238; and "Kommunismus und Islam unvereinbar," *Azerbaijan* 7 (86) (1944), German translation, High Command of the Wehrmacht, 19 February 1944, Berlin, BA–MA, MSG 2/18239.

108 "Kommunismus und Islam sind ewige Gegensätze," *Ghazavat* 15 (58) (1944), German translation, High Command of the Wehrmacht, 7 April 1944, Berlin, BA–MA, MSG 2/18238.

109 "Es gärt in Französisch-Marokko," *Ghazavat* 9 (52) (1944), German translation, High Command of the Wehrmacht, 23 February 1944, Berlin, BA–MA, MSG 2/18238.

110 "Blutige Zwischenfälle in einer Moschee," *Ghazavat* 11/12 (54/55) (1944), German translation, High Command of the Wehrmacht, 15 March 1944, Berlin, BA–MA, MSG 2/18238. A similar report followed in April, see "Zusammenstöße zwischen Polizei und Mohammedanern in Marokko," *Ghazavat* 16 (59) (1944), German translation, High Command of the Wehrmacht, 14 April 1944, Berlin, BA–MA, MSG 2/18238.

111 "Engländer verbieten Reise nach Mekka," *Ghazavat* 28 (1943), German translation, High Command of the Wehrmacht, 25 August 1943, Berlin, BA–MA, MSG 2/18238; see also Chapter 3.

112 "Die Araber wollen nicht Kanonenfutter werden: Die Muselmanen wollen nicht für England bluten," *Ghazavat* 13 (56) (1944), German translation, High Command of the Wehrmacht, 22 March 1944, Berlin, BA–MA, MSG 2/18238.

113 "Moslems, Sikhs und Hindus—gute Kameraden," *Svoboda* 9 (1944), German translation, High Command of the Wehrmacht, 1 November 1944, Berlin, BA–MA, MSG 2/18235.

114 "Treffen zwischen Gandhi und Jinnah," *Idel-Ural* 39 (96) (1944), German translation, High Command of the Wehrmacht, 30 September 1944, Berlin, BA–MA, MSG 2/18231.

115 "Die Mohammedaner haben kein Vertrauen zu England," *Ghazavat* 15 (58) (1944), German translation, High Command of the Wehrmacht, 7 April 1944, Berlin, BA–MA, MSG 2/18238; and "Aufruf Sahids an die Muselmanen in Indien," *Azerbaijan* 18 (97) (1944), German translation, High Command of the Wehrmacht, 8 May 1944, Berlin, BA–MA, MSG 2/18239.

116 "Machtkampf auf dem Rücken der islamischen Staaten," *Ghazavat* 30 (1943), German translation, High Command of the Wehrmacht, 8 September 1943, Berlin, BA–MA, MSG 2/18238.

117 "Aufruf zur Einigung der Muselmanen," *Ghazavat* 31 (1943), German translation, High Command of the Wehrmacht, 15 September 1943, Berlin, BA–MA, MSG 2/18238. *Ghazavat* and *Idel-Ural* continued reporting on the conference until 1944, see "Nachwirkungen der Panarabischen Konferenz," *Idel-Ural* 43 (100) (1944), German translation, High Command of the Wehrmacht, 28 October 1944, Berlin, BA–MA, MSG 2/18231; and "Schwierigkeiten bei den panarabischen Verhandlungen," *Ghazavat* 39 (82) (1944), German translation, High Command of the Wehrmacht, 22 September 1944, Berlin, BA–MA, MSG 2/18238.

118 Cwiklinski, *Wolgatataren im Deutschland des Zweiten Weltkriegs*, 99–100, referring to an article that was published in three parts in *Idel-Ural* 50 (56) (1943); 1 (58) (1944); and 8 (65) (1944); it was not summarized in the Wehrmacht monitoring reports, see BA–MA, MSG 2/18231.

119 "Unruhen im Nahen Osten," *Ghazavat* 26 (1943), German translation, High Command of the Wehrmacht, 11 August 1943, Berlin, BA–MA, MSG 2/18238.

120 "Chronik: Zusammenstöße in Palästina zwischen Arabern und Juden während des Ramadsan-Fastens," *Ghazavat* 31 (1943), German translation, High Command of the Wehrmacht, 15 September 1943, Berlin, BA–MA, MSG 2/18238.

121 "USA und arabische Länder," *Ghazavat* 13 (56) (1944), German translation, High Command of the Wehrmacht, 22 March 1944, Berlin, BA–MA, MSG 2/18238; "Zwischenfälle zwischen Arabern und Juden," *Ghazavat* 39 (1943), German translation, High Command of the Wehrmacht, 10 November 1943, Berlin, BA–MA, MSG 2/18238; "Der Kampf um Palästina," *Ghazavat* 11/12 (54/55) (1944), German translation, High Command of the Wehrmacht, 15 March 1944, Berlin, BA–MA, MSG 2/18238; "Jüdische Emigrantenregierung in Amerika," *Ghazavat* 28 (1943), German translation, High Command of the Wehrmacht, 25 August 1943, Berlin, BA–MA, MSG 2/18238; "Zusammenarbeit zwischen den US-Amerikanischen Imperialisten und den Juden," *Ghazavat* 36 (1943), German translation, High Command of the Wehrmacht, 20 October 1943, Berlin, BA–MA, MSG 2/18238; "Attentat auf den Hohen Kommissar von Palästina," *Idel-Ural* 33 (90) (1944), German translation, High Command of the Wehrmacht, 19 August 1944, Berlin, BA–MA, MSG 2/18231.

122 "Demonstrativer Protest der Muselmanen in Berlin," *Idel-Ural* 46 (52) (1943), German translation, High Command of the Wehrmacht, 14 November 1943, Berlin, BA–MA, MSG 2/18231.

123 "Ibn Saud zur Judenfrage," *Ghazavat* 25 (1943), German translation, High Command of the Wehrmacht, 4 August 1943, Berlin, BA–MA, MSG 2/18238.

124 "Die Rede des Mufti gegen die Balfour-Erklärung," *Ghazavat* 39 (1943), German translation, High Command of the Wehrmacht, 10 November 1943, Berlin, BA–MA, MSG 2/18238.

125 "Die Rede des Mufti," *Idel-Ural* 46 (52) (1943), German translation, High Command of the Wehrmacht, 14 November 1943, Berlin, BA–MA, MSG 2/18231; and "Die Rede des Mufti gegen die Balfour-Erklärung," *Ghazavat* 39 (1943), German translation, High Command of the Wehrmacht, 10 November 1943, Berlin, BA–MA, MSG 2/18238; and Image: "Großmufti von Jerusalem," *Ghazavat* 39 (1943), German translation, High Command of the Wehrmacht, 10 November 1943, Berlin, BA–MA, MSG 2/18238. All of the papers informed their Muslim readers of speeches given by the

Palestinian mufti: "Die Muselmanen zerstören die amerikanischen Pläne gegen die Araber: Aus der Rede des Großmufti in der Palästinafrage," *Ghazavat* 11/12 (54/55) (1944), German translation, High Command of the Wehrmacht, 15 March 1944, Berlin, BA–MA, MSG 2/18238. On Ramadan 1944, *Idel-Ural* reported the mufti's broadcast speech on its front page, see "Ein Radioaufruf des Großmufti von Arabien," *Idel-Ural* 38 (95) (1944), German translation, High Command of the Wehrmacht, 23 September 1944, Berlin, BA–MA, MSG 2/18231. In October 1944 both *Ghazavat* and *Azerbaijan* finally reported on the mufti's broadcast speech on the British formation of a Jewish army in Palestine, see "Rundfunkansprache des Großmufti," *Ghazavat* 41 (84) (1944), German translation, High Command of the Wehrmacht, 6 October 1944, Berlin, BA–MA, MSG 2/18238; and "Rundfunkansprache des Großmufti," *Azerbaijan* 40 (119) (1944), German translation, High Command of the Wehrmacht, 9 October 1940 [*sic*; correct: 1944]), Berlin, BA–MA, MSG 2/18239.

126 "Die Moschee in Paris," *Azerbaijan* 10 (89) (1944), German translation, High Command of the Wehrmacht, 13 March 1944, Berlin, BA–MA, MSG 2/18239, and Image: "Teilansicht der Moschee in Paris," *Azerbaijan* 10 (89) (1944), German translation, High Command of the Wehrmacht, 13 March 1944, Berlin, BA–MA, MSG 2/18239.

127 "Lied von Imam Gasimmagama," *Ghazavat* 16 (59) (1944), German translation, High Command of the Wehrmacht, 14 April 1944, Berlin, BA–MA, MSG 2/18238.

128 "Die Fastenzeit zum Bajramfest," *Ghazavat* 39 (82) (1944), German translation, High Command of the Wehrmacht, 22 September 1944, Berlin, BA–MA, MSG 2/18238.

129 "Die Moschee," *Ghazavat* 53 (96) (1944), German translation, High Command of the Wehrmacht, 29 December 1944, Berlin, BA–MA, MSG 2/18238.

130 "Euch ruft der heilige Krieg," *Ghazavat* 36 (79) (1944), German translation, High Command of the Wehrmacht, 1 September 1944, Berlin, BA–MA, MSG 2/18238.

131 "Ghazavat (Der Heilige Krieg)," *Ghazavat* 19 (62) (1944), German translation, High Command of the Wehrmacht, 5 May 1944, Berlin, BA–MA, MSG 2/18238.

132 "Unser heiliger Krieg," *Idel-Ural* 32 (38) (1943), German translation, High Command of the Wehrmacht, 8 August 1943, Berlin, BA–MA, MSG 2/18231.

133 "Die Moschee des Chan," *Idel-Ural* 43 (100) (1943), German translation, High Command of the Wehrmacht, 28 October 1944, Berlin, BA–MA, MSG 2/18231.

134 "Festlicher Abend," *Idel-Ural* 40 (46) (1943), German translation, High Command of the Wehrmacht, 3 October 1943, Berlin, BA–MA, MSG 2/18231.

135 Image: "Al-Azhar-Universität in Kairo," *Ghazavat* 29 (1943), German translation, High Command of the Wehrmacht, 1 September 1943, Berlin, BA–MA, MSG 2/18238; Illustrations: "Al-Azhar, tausendjährige Universität," *Idel-Ural* 13 (70) (1943), German translation, High Command of the Wehrmacht, 1 April 1944, Berlin, BA–MA, MSG 2/18231; and "Al-Azhar, tausendjährige Universität," *Azerbaijan* 8 (87) (1944), German translation, High Command of the Wehrmacht, 29 February 1944, Berlin, BA–MA, MSG 2/18239; Image: "Medina," *Ghazavat* 29 (1943), German translation, High Command of the Wehrmacht, 1 September 1943, Berlin, BA–MA, MSG 2/18238; Image: "Die heilige Stadt Mekka," *Idel-Ural* 40 (97) (1943), German translation, High Command of the Wehrmacht, 7 October 1944, Berlin, BA–MA, MSG 2/18231.

136 Image: "Die Moschee in Charbin," *Idel-Ural* 40 (46) (1943), German translation, High Command of the Wehrmacht, 3 October 1943, Berlin, BA–MA, MSG 2/18231; Image: "Moschee in der Stadt Kasan," *Idel-Ural* 16 (73) (1943), German translation, High Command of the Wehrmacht, 22 April 1944, Berlin, BA–MA, MSG 2/18231; Three Images: "Moscheen in Schiita, Rasan und im Dorf Uraslake," *Idel-Ural* 33 (90) (1943), German translation, High Command of the Wehrmacht, 19 August 1944, Berlin, BA–MA, MSG 2/18231; Image: "Moschee im Dorf Mantschalli," *Idel-Ural* 7 (64) (1943), German translation, High Command of the Wehrmacht, 20 February 1944, Berlin, BA–MA, MSG 2/18231; Image: "Blick in das Innere der Moschee in Irkutzk," *Idel-Ural* 41 (98) (1943), German translation, High Command of the Wehrmacht, 14 October 1944, Berlin, BA–MA, MSG 2/18231; Image: "Die Moschee in Kargalle," *Idel-Ural* 10/11 (67/68) (1943), German translation, High Command of the Wehrmacht, 19 March 1944, Berlin, BA–MA, MSG 2/18231; Image: "Moschee," *Idel-Ural* 47 (104) (1943), German translation, High Command of the Wehrmacht, 14 October 1944, Berlin, BA–MA, MSG 2/18231. On the editor, see *Idel-Ural* 7 (64) (1943), German translation, High Command of the Wehrmacht, 20 February 1944, Berlin, BA–MA, MSG 2/18231.

137 On Aftorchanov, see Mühlen, *Zwischen Hakenkreuz und Sowjetstern*, 126, 228–229, and 231.

138 See, for instance, Images of the articles "Die Jugend Schamils," *Ghazavat* 37 (80) (1944), German translation, High Command of the Wehrmacht, 8 September 1944, Berlin, BA–MA, MSG 2/18238; and "Vor 85 Jahren geriet Iman Schamil in Gefangenschaft," *Ghazavat* 36 (79) (1944), German translation, High Command of the Wehrmacht, 1 September 1944, Berlin, BA–MA, MSG 2/18238.

139 Images: "Ueberreichung des Koran" and "Efendi Mullah spricht zu den Legionären," *Ghazavat* 29 (1943), German translation, High Command of the Wehrmacht, 1 September 1943, Berlin, BA–MA, MSG 2/18238.

140 Image: "Obermullah Paschasade auf einem Heldenfriedhof," *Azerbaijan* 44 (123) (1944), German translation, High Command of the Wehrmacht, 6 November 1944, Berlin, BA–MA, MSG 2/18239.

141 Image: "Wolgatatarische Legionäre in der Pariser Moschee," *Idel-Ural* 9 (66) (1943), German translation, High Command of the Wehrmacht, 5 March 1944, Berlin, BA–MA, MSG 2/18231. Also *Azerbaijan* had published an image of the mosque with its article on the visiting Tatar legionnaire, see Image: "Teilansicht der Moschee in Paris," *Azerbaijan* 10 (89) (1944), German translation, High Command of the Wehrmacht, 13 March 1944, Berlin, BA–MA, MSG 2/18239, and Image: "Blick in die Halle des islamischen Instituts in Dresden," *Idel-Ural* 49 (106) (1943), German translation, High Command of the Wehrmacht, 9 December 1944, Berlin, BA–MA, MSG 2/18231.

142 Schloms to Olzscha, 20 November 1944, Dresden, BAB, NS 31/64; and Olzscha to Grothe (High Command of the Wehrmacht), 23 November 1944, Dresden, BAB, NS 31/64.

143 See *Ghazavat* 11/12 (54/55) (1944), German translation, High Command of the Wehrmacht, 15 March 1944, Berlin, BA–MA, MSG 2/18238.

144 Köstring, Report ("Erfahrung mit den Freiwilligen aus dem russischen Raum im Kampf mit dem Bolschewismus, 1941–1945"), n.d. (post-1945), n.p., IfZ, ZS 85; and,

similarly, Spuler, Report ("Die Freiwilligen-Einheiten"), n.d. (post-1945), n.p. (Göttingen), MA, MSG 2/18284.

145 High Command of the Army, Instructions ("Richtlinien für die inneren Verhältnisse in den Ostlegionen"), 24 April 1942, n.p., BA–MA, RH 19V/108.

146 Field Command 372, Report ("Bericht über Leistung und Verhalten der Turk. Inf. Batl. 782 und 790 für die Zeit vom 16.10. bis 15.11.43"), attachment of Field Command 372, Report ("Monatsbericht für die Zeit vom 16.10. bis 15.11.1943"), 21 November 1943, Lublin, BA–MA, RH 53–23/43.

147 Oberländer to Erika Oberländer, 20 December 1942, FAO; see also Theodor Oberländer, Diary (entries of 17 and 18 December 1942), FAO.

148 High Command of the Army, Report ("Aussagen eines neu hinzugekommenen Legionärs"), n.d. (2 July 1942), n.p., BA–MA, RH 19V/109.

149 Army Postal Service of the 11th Army (Censorship Department), Report ("Tataren: Briefe aus den Monatsberichten der F.P.P."), 24 July 1942, n.p., PA, R 60741. All examples of field letters given in this paragraph up to note 170 can be found in this report.

150 Hentig, Report ("Tatarische Freiwillige"), 22 May 1942, n.p. (Simferopol), PA, R 60740. Hentig based this report on field mail abstracts that are included in Army Postal Service of the 11th Army (Censorship Department), Report ("Tataren: Briefe aus den Monatsberichten der F.P.P."), 24 July 1942, n.p., PA, R 60741.

151 Ibid.

152 Ibid.

153 Hentig, Report ("Auszüge aus der Tatarenpost"), 21 July 1942, n.p. (Simferopol), PA, R 60741. Hentig based this report on field mail abstracts, which are included in Army Postal Service of the 11th Army (Censorship Department), Report ("Tataren: Briefe aus den Monatsberichten der F.P.P."), 24 July 1942, n.p., PA, R 60741.

154 Army Postal Service of the 11th Army (Censorship Department), Report ("Auszug aus dem Tätigkeitsbericht der Feldpostprüfstelle beim A.O.K. 11: Tatarische Soldaten im deutschen Heer"), July 1942, n.p., BA–MA, RW 4v/237. This monitoring report was forwarded to the Propaganda Section of the High Command of the Wehrmacht, see High Command of the Army to Ellenbeck (Propaganda Section of the High Command of the Wehrmacht), 16 August 1942, n.p., BA–MA, RW 4v/237. The file contains some examples of letters sent home by Muslims.

155 Al-Rashid, Report ("Behandlung der Ostmuselmanen"), 20 September 1944, Warsaw, BAB, NS 31/44, attached to Al-Rashid to Spaarmann, 22 September 1944, Berlin, BAB, NS 31/44; and, on the report, Olzscha, Internal Note ("Bericht des SS-Standartenführers Harun el Raschid über seinen Besuch beim 1. Ostmuselmanischen Regiment"), 24 September 1944, Berlin, BAB, NS 31/44.

156 Al-Rashid, Report ("Behandlung der Ostmuselmanen"), 20 September 1944, Warsaw, BAB, NS 31/44.

157 Nasarow (Nazarov) to Al-Rashid, n.d. (early 1945), n.p., BAB, NS 31/44.

158 Alekberli to Al-Rashid, 9 November 1944, n.p., BAB, NS 31/34.

159 Al-Rashid, Report ("Bericht über die Entwicklung des osttürkischen Waffen-Verbandes der SS von Warschau bis Überlauf Alimow und über die aus dieser sich ergebenden Folgerungen"), n.d. (December 1944), n.p., BAB, NS 31/29 (also in BAB, NS 31/44).

160 Gabdullan to Islamic Central Institute (German translation), 22 February 1944, n.p., BAB, NS 31/44.

161 Stamati, Report ("Religiöse Einstellung der Wolgatataren"), 22 March 1945, Berlin, BAB, NS 31/56 (also in BAB, NS 31/60).

162 Mende, Internal Note ("Politische Richtlinien für die Turkverbände und die Ostmuselmanische SS-Division"), 12 February 1944, Berlin, BAB, NS 31/42.

163 Heygendorff, Instructions ("Merkblatt für deutsche Offiziere über wehrgeistige Führung der Legionäre"), 1 July 1943, Radom, BA–MA, RH 58/62; and, for the second quotation, Heygendorff, Instructions ("Behandlung der Legionäre"), 15 September 1943, n.p., BA–MA, RH 58/62.

164 Böhme, Report ("Psychologische Erfahrungen in der Legion, Nr. 2"), 7 December 1943, n.p., BA–MA, RH 58/62.

165 Olzscha, Report, 1945, n.p., BStU, MfS, HA IX/11, ZR 920, A. 54.

166 Ibid.

167 Wangemann, Speech ("Dienstbesprechung der Kommandeure und Imame am 8.4.1944 in Brčko"), 8 April 1944, Brčko, BAB, NS 19/2601.

168 Sauberzweig to Berger, 16 April 1944, n.p., BAB, NS 19/2601.

169 Himmler, Order, 6 August 1943, n.p., BAB, NS 19/3285.

170 Ibid.

171 Heygendorff, Report ("Der Kampf gegen Windmühlenflügel"), n.d. (post-1945), n.p., IfZ, ZS 407.

172 On Heygendorff's decrees for religious toleration, see Chapter 7.

173 Heygendorff, Newsletter ("Mitteilungen für die Kommandeure der Osttruppen z.b.V. und Stabsoffiziere für landeseigene Hilfskräfte"), 22 May 1944, n.p., BA–MA, RH 19XI/86.

174 On Niedermayer's decrees for religious toleration, see Chapter 7.

175 High Command of the Army, Instructions ("Merkblatt für das deutsche Personal der Turk-Stammlager und Turk-Btlne."), 2 June 1942, n.p., BA–MA, RH 19V/109.

176 Heygendorff, Instructions ("Behandlung der Legionäre"), 15 July 1943, Radom, BA–MA, RH 58/62.

177 Al-Rashid, Report ("Behandlung der Ostmuselmanen"), 20 September 1944, Warsaw, BAB, NS 31/44, attached to Al-Rashid to Spaarmann, 22 September 1944, Berlin, BAB, NS 31/44; and, on the report, Olzscha, Internal Note ("Bericht des SS-Standartenführers Harun el Raschid über seinen Besuch beim 1. Ostmuselmanischen Regiment"), 24 September 1944, Berlin, BAB, NS 31/44.

178 Sauberzweig to Berger, 16 April 1944, n.p., BAB, NS 19/2601.

179 Mende, "Erfahrungen mit Ostfreiwilligen in der deutschen Wehrmacht während des Zweiten Weltkrieges," 27 and 30.

180 Anonymous, "Erfahrungen eines Betreuungsoffiziers für Freiwillige aus den Völkern der Sowjetunion in der deutschen Wehrmacht," *Vielvölkerheere und Koalitionskriege* (1952), 34–39, 35.

181 Heygendorff, Report ("Der Kampf gegen Windmühlenflügel"), n.d. (post-1945), n.p., IfZ, ZS 407.

182 Ibid.

183 Ernst Jünger, *Das zweite Pariser Tagebuch*, Werke, Tagebücher, vol. 3 (*Strahlungen, Zweiter Teil*) (Stuttgart, 1962 [1949]), 272 (12 May 1944).

184 Paul Hausser, *Waffen-SS im Einsatz* (Göttingen, 1953), 106–107.

185 Schmidhuber, Report ("Zusammenfassender Bericht über die Aufstellung und den Zustand der 21. Waffen-Gebirgsdivision der SS 'Skanderbeg'"), 2 October 1944, n.p., BA–MA, RS 3–21/1.

186 Hoffmann, *Die Ostlegionen*, 37.

187 Ibid., 57–58.

188 On contacts and marriages with German women, see the documents in BAB, NS 31/28; and on the problem of race, see also Chapter 2. On the forced abortions, see Horstmann (SS Head Office), Internal Note ("Verbindungen zwischen deutschen Mädchen und fremdstämmigen SS-Angehörigen"), 18 November 1944, Berlin, BAB, NS 31/28. Official instructions to avoid contacts between German women and volunteers were given frequently, see, for instance, Heygendorff, Instructions ("Merkblatt für deutsche Offiziere über wehrgeistige Führung der Legionäre"), 1 July 1943, Radom, BA–MA, RH 58/62; and High Command of the Wehrmacht, Newsletter ("Mitteilungen für den deutschen Soldaten in Freiwilligen-Verbänden"), November 1944, BA–MA, MSG 2/18262.

189 On marriages with Eastern workers, see the documents in BAB, R 6/129.

190 On Handžar's last days, see the literature in Chapter 6, note 48.

191 Finck (German Staff of Handžar), Interrogation Report of Abdullah Memisevic, 21 August 1944, n.p, VÚA, Box: N 13. SS-Fr. Geb. Div. H. 1; and Finck, Report, 22 August 1944, n.p., VÚA, Box: N 13. SS-Fr. Geb. Div. H. 1.

192 Various individual reports about desertions can be found in VÚA, Box: N 13. SS-Fr. Geb. Div. H. 1.

193 SS Medical Report of Omećević Muhamed, 9 August 1944, n.p., VÚA, Box: N 13. SS-Fr. Geb. Div. H. 1.

194 Kasche to Foreign Office, 28 October 1944, Zagreb, PA, R 27796 (also in PA, R 100998).

195 Kasche to Foreign Office, 29 October 1944, PA, R 27796.

196 Ibid.

197 Wagner to Kasche, 14 December 1944, Berlin, PA, R 100998.

198 On the last days of Skanderbeg, see the literature in Chapter 6, note 74.

199 On the low number of desertions among Muslim volunteers from the East, see Neulen, *An deutscher Seite*, 329–334; and, on the military discipline in general, Hoffmann, *Die Ostlegionen*, 146–162, esp. 157.

200 Julian Amery, *Sons of the Eagle: A Study in Guerilla War* (London, 1948), 139–142 and 271–329, esp. 274; and similarly, Julian Amery, *Approach March: A Venture in Autobiography* (London, 1973), 376–383, esp. 382.

201 Al-Rashid, Report ("Überlauf des Kommandeurs des Waffen-Rgts. der SS Turkistan Nr. 1, Waffen-Obersturmführer Gulam Alimow, mit etwa 500 Männern seines Regiments zu den Partisanen"), 26 December 1944, n.p., BAB, NS 31/29 (also in BAB, NS 31/44).

202 Nikolai Tolstoy, "The Klagenfurt Conspiracy: War Crimes and Diplomatic Secrets," *Encounter* 60, 5 (1983), 24–37, on Tito's retaliation more generally.

203 Srećko M. Džaja, *Die politische Realität des Jugoslawismus 1918–1991: Mit besonderer Berücksichtigung Bosnien-Herzegowinas* (Munich, 2002), 228.

204 Ibid., 229.

205 On the forced repatriation, see Neulen, *An deutscher Seite*, 333–334; Mühlen, *Zwischen Hakenkreuz und Sowjetstern*, 226–229; Jürgen Thorwald, *Wen sie verderben wollen: Bericht des großen Verrats* (Stuttgart, 1952), esp. 572–574; and, with a focus on the repatriation of the Cossacks, Peter J. Huxley-Blythe, *The East Came West* (Caldwell, ID, 1964); and Nicholas Bethell, *The Last Secret: Forcible Repatriation to Russia 1944–7* (London, 1974); on the British role, see Nikolai Tolstoy, *The Victims of Yalta* (London, 1977), esp. 381–386; and, more controversially and with a focus on the Cossacks, Nikolai Tolstoy, *The Minister and the Massacres* (London, 1986); on the US role, see Julius Epstein, *Operation Keelhaul: The Story of Forced Repatriation from 1944 to the Present* (Old Greenwich, CT, 1973); Julius Epstein, "Die Zwangsrepatriierung von antikommunistischen Kriegsgefangenen in die Sowjetunion," *Politische Studien* 196 (1971), 149–156; and Mark R. Elliott, *Pawns of Yalta: Soviet Refugees and America's Role in Their Repatriation* (Urbana, IL, 1982); a vivid tale of these events, focusing on the Cossacks, was offered by the Polish novelist Josef Mackiewicz, *Tragödie an der Drau: Die verratene Freiheit* (Munich, 1957).

206 Heygendorff, Report ("Das Schicksal der 162. (Turk.) Inf. Div."), n.d. (post-1945), n.p., IfZ, ZS 407.

207 Alexander Solzhenitsyn, *The Gulag Archipelago, 1918–1945*, 3 vols. (London, 1974–1978), vol. 1, 85. Solzhenitsyn criticized the forced repatriation, particularly of civilians, denouncing the "act of betrayal" as "the last secret, or one of the last, of the Second World War," see ibid., note 45.

208 George Orwell, "The Prevention of Literature," *Polemic* 2 (January 1946), 4–14, 6.

CONCLUSION

1 In the last weeks of the war, Hitler dictated to Bormann his final views on world politics, ideology, and the war. These dictates became known as *The Testament of Adolf Hitler* (see Chapter 2, note 135). Islam was a recurring theme and is even listed in the book's index. The German version was not published until 1981, see *Hitlers politisches Testament*.

2 *The Testament of Adolf Hitler*, 69–75 (17 February 1945), 70–71; for the German text see *Hitlers politisches Testament*, 84–90 (17 February 1945), 85–86.

3 Ibid.

4 *The Testament of Adolf Hitler*, 29–37 (4 February 1945), 33–34; and 42–46 (7 February 1945), 45; and 69–75 (17 February 1945), 70–71; and 103–109 (2 April 1945), 107, all of which discuss Islam; for the German text, see *Hitlers politisches Testament*, 42–49 (4 February 1945), 46; and 54–59 (7 February 1945), 56; and 84–90 (17 February 1945), 85–86; and 120–127 (2 April 1945), 123.

5 *The Testament of Adolf Hitler*, 29–37 (4 February 1945), 33–34; for the German text, see *Hitlers politisches Testament*, 42–49 (4 February 1945), 46; for this passage, see also Joachim C. Fest, *Hitler: Eine Biographie* (Berlin, 1973), 1013; the English translation of Fest's biography does not translate Hitler's words correctly as it claims that France

and Italy would have engaged in "a bold policy of friendship with Islam," see Fest, *Hitler* (London, 1974), 741.

6 Most research in this respect has been carried out in the field of Arab history, see Chapter 3.

7 Oppenheim, Memoirs ("Leben im NS-Staat, 1933–1945"), n.d. (1945/1946), n.p. (Landshut), OA, Nachlass Max von Oppenheim No. 1/14.

8 On the escape of al-Husayni from Germany, see Schechtman, *The Mufti and the Fuehrer*, 164–190; Lebel, *The Mufti of Jerusalem Haj-Amin el-Husseini and National-Socialism*, 268–276 and 277–310; and Gensicke, *The Mufti of Jerusalem and the Nazis*, 181–204.

9 Hentig, Report ("Eidesstattliche Erklärung"), 6 August 1947, PA, Nachlass Hentig 84; and, on the report, Hentig, Report ("Aufzeichnung über meine Vernehmung durch Dr. Robert Kempner"), n.d. (1947), PA, Nachlass Hentig 84.

10 Tsilla Hershco, "Le grand mufti de Jérusalem en France: Histoire d'une évasion," *Controverses: Revue d'idées* 1 (2006), 244–273.

11 Young (Legation Beirut) to Foreign Office, 25 September 1945, Beirut, NA, FO 226/300, which is based on the letter by the Lebanese diplomat Daouk (Legation Paris) to Solh (prime minister of Lebanon) (English translation), 13 September 1945, Paris, NA, FO 226/300.

12 Al-Banna to Lampson, 3 April 1946, Cairo, NA, KV 2/2087.

13 Anonymous, "Arabs Seek to Aid Soviet Deserters: British-U.S. Captors Said to Agree to Settlement of Caucasian Soldiers," *New York Times* (15 December 1946).

14 *Mudhakkirat al-Hajj Muhammad Amin al-Husayni*, ed. al-'Umar, 142–143.

15 Ibid., 144 for the first quotation and 142 for the second quotation.

16 Ibid., 144. On these soldiers in the 1948 War, see Seth J. Frantzman and Jovan Ćulibrk, "Strange Bedfellows: The Bosnians and Yugoslav Volunteers in the 1948 War in Israel/Palestine," *Istorija 20. Veka* 1 (2009), 189–200.

17 Simon Wiesenthal, *Großmufti: Großagent der Achse* (Vienna, 1947); and Maurice Pearlman, *Mufti of Jerusalem: The Story of Haj Amin El Husseini* (London, 1947). During the war, an early booklet on al-Husayni had already appeared in Britain, see M. P. Waters, *Mufti over the Middle East* (London, 1942).

18 Anonymous, "Gespräch mit dem Großmufti von Jerusalem," *Zeitschrift für Geopolitik* 22, 12 (1951), 761.

19 Conze et al., *Das Amt und die Vergangenheit*, 548.

20 Spuler, "Muslime in Rußland," 298; and, similarly, Olzscha, Report, 1945, n.p., BStU, MfS, HA IX/11, ZR 920, A. 54. He soon began publishing on the situation of Muslims in Poland, see Jakub C. Szynkiewicz, "The Religious Situations of Muslims in Poland," *Moslem World* 37, 3 (1947), 240–242.

21 Olzscha, Report, 1945, n.p., BStU, MfS, HA IX/11, ZR 920, A. 54.

22 Mohammad Aman Hobohm, "Neuanfänge muslimischen Gemeindelebens in Berlin nach 1945," *Moslemische Revue* 1 (1994), 28–40.

23 Mühlen, *Zwischen Hakenkreuz und Sowjetstern*, 226–233; Ian Johnson, *A Mosque in Munich: Nazis, the CIA, and the Rise of the Muslim Brotherhood in the West* (Boston, 2010); and Stefan Meining, *Eine Moschee in Deutschland: Nazis, Geheimdienste und der Aufstieg*

des politischen Islam im Westen (Munich, 2011), provide in-depth accounts of the employment of Germany's Muslim war veterans in the Cold War.

24 John Barron, *KGB: The Secret Work of the Soviet Secret Agents* (London, 1974), 312.

25 Roosevelt Jr., Report ("Arab Situation in Morocco"), 29 April 1943, n.p., NA, WO 204/6235.

26 Harold R. Isaacs, *Scratches on Our Minds: American Views of China and India* (New York, 1980 [1958]), 274–279; the book was appraised by Andrew J. Rotter, "In Retrospect: Harold A. Isaac's Scratches on Our Minds," *Reviews in American History* 24 (1996), 177–188, and particularly 187–188; and, similarly, Isaacs, "Christians, Muslims, and Hindus: Religion and US–South Asia Relations, 1947–1954," *Diplomatic History* 24, 4 (2000), 593–613.

27 Jacobs, "The Perils and Promises of Islam"; and, similarly, Jacobs, *Imagining the Middle East*, 55–94, on US engagement with Islam in the Middle East in the early Cold War.

28 Olivier Roy, *Islam and Resistance in Afghanistan* (Cambridge, 1986); A. Z. Hilali, *US-Pakistan Relationship: Soviet Invasion of Afghanistan* (Burlington, VT, 2005); Ahmed Rashid, *Taliban, Militant Islam, Oil and Fundamentalism in Central Asia* (New Haven, CT, 2000); Coll, *Ghost Wars*; and R. Kim Cragin, "Early History of Al-Qa'ida," *Historical Journal* 51, 4 (2008), 1047–1067.

29 Quoted in Patrick Vaughan, "Zbigniew Brzezinski and Afghanistan," in Anna Kasten Nelson (ed.), *The Policy Makers: Shaping American Foreign Policy from 1947 to the Present* (Lanham, MD, 2009), 107–130, 109–110.

30 Ro'i, *Islam in the Soviet Union*; and Yemelianova, *Russia and Islam*. Bennigsen and Lemercier-Quelquejay, *Islam in the Soviet Union*; Michael Rywkin, *Moscow's Muslim Challenge: Soviet Central Asia* (London, 1982); Karen Dawisha and Hélène Carrere D'Encausse, "Islam in the Foreign Policy of the Soviet Union: A Double-Edged Sword?," in Adeed Dawisha (ed.), *Islam in Foreign Policy* (Cambridge, 1983), 160–177; Alexandre Bennigsen and Marie Broxup, *The Islamic Threat to the Soviet State* (London, 1983); and the contributions in Alexandre Bennigsen et al. (eds.), *Soviet Strategy and Islam* (London, 1989), are Cold War studies on the subject. On developments after the Cold War, see Ahmed Rashid, *Jihad: The Rise of Militant Islam in Central Asia* (New Haven, CT, 2002); and Adeeb Khalid, *Islam after Communism: Religion and Politics in Central Asia* (Berkeley, CA, 2007).

31 David Motadel, "Uneasy Engagement," *The World Today* 67, 1 (2011), 27–29.

ACKNOWLEDGMENTS

This book developed over the course of nearly a decade, and during that time I have benefited from countless people who offered me guidance and assistance. I owe particular thanks to Sir Richard J. Evans, whose unfailing support, advice, and encouragement were critical in shaping this book. He was an endless fount of knowledge, not only on the Nazi regime and the Second World War, but also on the craft of history in general. I am also profoundly grateful to Houchang E. Chehabi, who read the manuscript with his characteristically sharp eye for detail and his immense historical knowledge of the lands of Islam and was a constant source of inspiration. Moreover, I would like to express my gratitude to Cemil Aydin, Ivo Banac, John Casey, Robert D. Crews, Tim Harper, Sir Noel Malcolm, Alexander Morrison, Michael A. Reynolds, and Nicholas Stargardt, all of whom took the time to read manuscript drafts, either in whole or in part, and offered their insightful comments.

Over the years of writing this book I had the privilege of working in the intellectual community of Cambridge—first at Pembroke College, where I was a student, and later, as a research fellow, at Gonville and Caius College. Cambridge provided a unique environment to read, think, and write, and I benefited greatly from conversations and exchanges with outstanding scholars, including David Abulafia, Andrew Arsan, Christopher Clark, Michael Frisch, Bianca Gaudenzi, Stefan Ihrig, Hubertus Jahn, Alois Maderspacher, Toby Matthiesen, Tom Neuhaus, Lisa Niemeyer, Jacob Norris, Valentina Pugliano, James L. W. Roslington, Christopher N. B. Ross, Hugo Service, Toby Simpson, Murat Siviloglu, John Slight, Astrid Swenson, and Mehmet Yercil. The comments of the participants of the Cambridge modern German history workshop were particularly helpful.

Throughout the years of my research I passed through many places, and everywhere I went I met people who offered me support. My first ideas for this project emerged during my time at the University of Freiburg, where I had the good fortune to study with two outstanding scholars, Ulrich Herbert and Willi Oberkrome, and I am thankful to them both for their encouragement and sustained interest in my work. During my time as a visiting fellow at the History Department at Harvard I benefited from the guidance, time, and support of David Blackbourn, Niall Ferguson, and Emma Rothschild. At Yale, where I spent a wonderful year as a research fellow, Abbas Amanat, John Lewis Gaddis, and Paul Kennedy made my time there enjoyable and productive. In Berlin I enjoyed the hospitality and support of Ulrike Freitag and Gudrun Krämer. Finally, I would like to thank the following colleagues for advice they gave me at different stages of my research: Nir Arielli, Paul Betts, Xavier Bougarel, Moritz Deutschmann, Detlev Hellfaier, Bastian Herbst, Daniel Jütte, Alexandre Kazerouni, Anna Olejnik, Stefan Petke, Oleksiy Popov, Dagmar Riedel, Bing Rong, and Umar Ryad. There are many more who influenced and improved this book, and I extend a warm thank you to all whom I have not directly named.

The book draws on materials in many languages, and I would not have been able to write it without some assistance with the translations. I thank Rozaliya Garipova, Vesna Novakovic, Revi Panidha, and Harith Bin Ramli for their help with the translations from Tatar, Bosnian, Albanian, and Arabic, respectively. Moreover, thanks go to Philip Stickler, who prepared the map.

My research was facilitated by numerous archivists and librarians across the globe. I am particularly grateful to Sandra Burkhardt, Suela Çuçi, Jenny Gohr, Snježana Gregić, Martin Kröger, Alma Leka, Sonja Martinović, Lutz Möser, Erwin Oberländer, Fatimah Qaziha, Thomas Ripper, Gabriele Teichmann, Jan Warßischek, and Alison Zammer for helping me to find documents, articles, and books. The Cambridge University Library, Widener Library, Sterling Memorial Library, and the Berlin State Library have been rich treasures, and I thank the staff of these institutions in particular.

Work on this book was made possible by generous grants from the Cambridge Gates Trust, the Arts and Humanities Research Council, the Smith Richardson Foundation, the Sir John Plumb Trust, the Royal Historical Society, the German History Society, the German Historical Institute Washington, the Cambridge Center for History and Economics, the Cambridge History Faculty, Pembroke College, Cambridge, and Gonville and Caius College, Cambridge.

Parts of Chapters 4 and 5 appeared previously in articles published in the *Journal of Contemporary History* 48, 4 (2013), 784–820, and the *Historical Journal* 56, 4 (2013), 1007–1039, and I thank the publishers for granting me permission to use the material in this book.

ACKNOWLEDGMENTS

Finally, I would also like to thank the anonymous referees from Harvard University Press for their support; my editor, Ian Malcolm, who was enthusiastic about the book from the outset and read the manuscript with incredible care; and Joy Deng, John Donohue, and Carol Hoke, who ensured the smooth production and copyediting of the book. I am also grateful to the team of the Wylie Agency, who have been enormously helpful in realizing this book. Jeremy Lowe proofread the entire manuscript and saved me from countless errors.

The greatest thanks I owe to my family: Rachel G. Hoffman, a brilliant scholar, read the manuscript more than once and supported me with her love, humor, and care; my parents, Sabine and Iradj Motadel, who, with their love and boundless belief in my work, have done more for me than I can put into words; and my grandmother, Dorothea Dorn, whose wisdom and wit kept up my spirits. I dedicate this book to them.

INDEX